THE MAKING OF THE MODERN WORLD

CONNECTED HISTORIES, DIVERGENT PATHS
1500 TO THE PRESENT

SECOND EDITION

THE MAKING OF THE MODERN WORLD

CONNECTED HISTORIES, DIVERGENT PATHS
1500 TO THE PRESENT

SECOND EDITION

SENIOR AUTHOR

Robert W. Strayer
State University of New York, College at Brockport

CONTRIBUTING AUTHORS

Robert J. Smith
State University of New York, College at Brockport

Robert B. Marks
Whittier College

Sandria B. Freitag

Donald C. Holsinger
Seattle Pacific University

Lynn H. Parsons
State University of New York, College at Brockport

James J. Horn
State University of New York, College at Brockport

Joe B. Moore
University of Victoria, British Columbia

ST. MARTIN'S PRESS
NEW YORK

Editor: Louise H. Waller
Managing editor: Patricia Mansfield Phelan
Project editor: Amy Horowitz/Erica Appel
Production manager: Patricia Ollague
Art director: Sheree Goodman
Text design: Caryl Silvers
Photo research: Gene Crofts
Maps: Maryland Cartographics
Cover design: Sheree Goodman
Cover art: Rejoicings on the birth of Salim, son of Akbar and the Mariam
Uz-Zamani Begum, at Fatephur Sikri, from the 'Akbar-nama', Mughal,
c. 1590, Victoria & Albert Museum, London/Bridgeman Art Library, London.

Library of Congress Catalog Card Number: 92-62723

Manufactured in the United States of America.

9 8 7 6 5
f e d c b a

For information, write:
St. Martin's Press, Inc.
175 Fifth Avenue
New York, NY 10010

ISBN: 0-312-05017-8

ACKNOWLEDGMENTS

The second edition of *The Making of the Modern World,* like the first, has been a team effort, an exercise in collaboration, often at a distance.

Senior author Robert Strayer has served as overall editor of the book. He wrote the Preface, Prologue, Introduction, Chapters 1, 6, 9, and 21–24, Conclusion, and the Comparative Essays.

Contributing authors assumed primary responsibility for particular chapters:

ROBERT SMITH: Chapters 2–5
LYNN PARSONS: Chapter 7
JAMES HORN: Chapter 8
DONALD HOLSINGER: Chapters 10–12
SANDRIA FREITAG: Chapters 13–15
ROBERT MARKS: Chapters 16–19
JOE MOORE: Chapter 20

The genesis of this book lies in the work of Professor Arden Bucholz, who came to SUNY—Brockport in 1970 from graduate training with William McNeil at the University of Chicago, full of contagious enthusiasm for the idea of world history. The overall approach and structure embodied in this text evolved through many years of teaching world history under his leadership at Brockport. But virtually everything we have ever read, taught, or written; every trip we have taken; and every intellectual encounter we have had are grist for the mill of world history. The list of appropriate acknowledgments would be staggering; hence, we forgo the attempt.

We are grateful for the encouragement and support of Louise Waller, the St. Martin's editor with whom we have been privileged to work, and the many reviewers who have commented on the book, either in whole or in part: Nathan M. Brooks, New Mexico State University; Richard Bulliet, Middle East Institute; Barbara Evans Clements, University of Akron; David M. Fahey, Miami University; Sheldon Garon, Princeton University; Dina Khoury, George Washington University; David Kopf, University of Minnesota; David McComb, Colorado State University; Kermit McKenzie, Emory University; Tong Chin Rhee, University of Dayton; Richard G. Robbins, University of New Mexico; and Kathryn Weathersby, The Florida State University. We hereby thank them for all the errors from which we have been saved and absolve them from responsibility for those that doubtless remain.

Robert W. Strayer
Robert J. Smith
Robert B. Marks
Sandria B. Freitag
Donald C. Holsinger
Lynn H. Parsons
James J. Horn
Joe B. Moore

PREFACE FOR INSTRUCTORS

Teaching world history confronts us with a central pedagogical and intellectual problem that is familiar in its general contours but unique in its scale. It is the question of selectivity or, put another way, the tension between coverage and coherence. The common problems of any kind of learning—what should be included and how the parts fit together—are particularly apparent in the case of global history. Since nothing is automatically excluded from its domain and no criteria for emphasis have achieved general acceptance, questions frequently arise as to how the subject can be taught in a term or two when even Western civilization or U.S. history cannot be adequately covered in such a relatively short period.

A teachable world history, in our view, embodies two major principles. First, global history is a history of encounters, intersections, and connections—not primarily the separate stories of particular nations, regions, or civilizations, even if those stories are globally inclusive. Such history in the premodern era puts the spotlight, for example, on the connections between ancient Egypt and Mesopotamia, on the creation of a China-centered world system in East Asia, on the world of Indian Ocean commerce, and on the multiple Afro-Eurasian relationships spawned by the spread of Islam.[1]

Over the past five centuries the most significant of these intersections or encounters has been between an expansive Western civilization and everyone else. The emergence of modern science and the explosion of technological innovation during the past five hundred years, together with Europe's growing political and economic domination of the globe, mark a distinctive era in human history, though one that built on earlier patterns of transcultural connection. The impact of those changes in Europe has touched and shaped virtually every society on the planet in some fashion, thus deepening and extending the network of global linkages and giving rise to connected histories to an unprecedented extent.

Here is a theme of long-term and global significance capable of bringing some coherence to the study of world history over this long period of time. Asians, Arabs, and Africans have had in common the need to make their way in the world in the face of growing European domination. Therefore, the first five chapters of *The Making of the Modern World* examine the European roots of this profound disturbance in human affairs. Chapter 6 then traces the global dimensions of Europe's expansion and subsequent contraction over the past five hundred years. The balance of the book explores the encounter of the world's major civilizations with Europe's expanding empires, cultures, and economic networks during those centuries.

Such an approach runs several risks. It may tend to reinforce a Eurocentric view of human history by overemphasizing the external sources of historical change in the experience of non-European peoples. We attempt to counteract this danger in several ways. While frankly acknowledging the Eurocentric character of modern world history, we repeatedly note the historical novelty of this situation and contrast it with earlier periods of Islamic or Chinese expansion. And we present each of the regions subsequently incorporated into the European world system in terms of its unique cultural values, social structure, political traditions, and historical dynamics. These factors shaped their respective encounters with an aggressive Europe and contributed much to the making of their own modern histories. One could, in fact, read the book as an extended discussion of the relative importance of and relationship between internal and external factors in the making of modern societies.

In doing this, we treat each major world region in its entirety before going on to the next. This has the advantage of recognizing there is no overall periodization of modern history that makes equal sense for all areas. Colonial conquest, for example, was a sixteenth-century phenomenon in Latin America, but a late nineteenth-century process in Africa. Our approach risks fragmentation—teaching world history as an abbreviated and unrelated sequence of regional histories. To counteract this possibility, however, we incorporate another major principle of global history: extensive use of comparison.

Whatever else it may be, world history is comparative history. Throughout the book, therefore, we raise a number of comparative questions: Why did parts of Europe, rather than China or the Middle East, emerge as the first modern societies? In what different ways did the various world regions experience European imperialism? How did their processes of modern development differ from those of Europe? What was the difference between the Capitalist road to development, such as that pursued in Europe and the United States, and the Socialist path taken by the Soviet Union and China in the twentieth century? How did the Russian and Chinese revolutions and their subsequent Communist regimes differ from one another? How did Chinese and Ottoman efforts at conservative modernization compare?

The comparative approach to world history finds expression here in a number of ways. The Introduction raises some of the most important issues about convergence and divergence in modern world history, while frequent comparative references punctuate the discussion of particular areas. Some entire chapters have a comparative focus. Chapter 7 on the United States, for example, is organized around a comparison of the American experience with that of heartland Europe. Chapter 8 on Latin America highlights its distinctive modern trajectory in contrast to that of North America. Chapter 20 compares Japan's modern experience with that of China, which is treated in the immediately preceding chapters. Furthermore, a series of Comparative Essays explores particular topics—revolution, industrialization, development, nationalism—in a global and comparative fashion. The first such essay, entitled "Paths to the Modern World: Patterns, Themes, and Questions," follows Chapter 6 and serves to introduce a set of issues and questions that are repeatedly encountered in the regional case studies that follow. The comparative emphasis of the text thus serves as an antidote to fragmentation and as a means of encouraging students to develop skills of comparative analysis.

The world historical picture is necessarily painted in very broad strokes with a focus on "big structures, large processes, and huge comparisons" (to cite the title of a book by Charles Tilly). Particular voices of individual people all too easily get lost in such a setting. Thus, we incorporate a series of brief, first-person extracts keyed to the major themes and culture areas treated in the book. This will enable students to hear some authentic and individual voices as well as note our necessarily more abstract reconstruction of their historical experience.

A final feature of the book involves a balance between narrative and analysis. We seek to tell in broad outline the story of modern world history, both at the global level and in terms of the particular societies whose history we explore. But we also want to raise some of the "big issues" about why things turned out the way they did, and why they did not turn out otherwise. To foster an understanding of history as an unfinished discussion about a series of intellectual problems, we frame much of the book in terms of questions. We try to convey some of the rich debate that informs historical inquiry into large controversial issues, but without getting bogged down in detailed discussions about which historians have said what.

Thus, we raise questions about the optimistic implications of the modernization paradigm as a framework for understanding world history. We introduce the world system concept as a means of explaining the continuation of sharp differences in levels of economic development. As a counterpoint to that approach, we also emphasize the explanatory significance of internal factors such as class relations, cultural values, and the strength and policy choices of state authorities. To convey some sense of the contingency of the historical record, we ask on occasion "what if" questions. We attempt to show that contemporary definitions of community—whether expressed in terms of national, tribal, or religious identity—are themselves the product of the historical process.

However, not everything is spelled out, and definitive answers to major questions are not always provided. Indeed, they frequently do not exist. We think this is a book that can be used, taught, discussed, and disagreed with, as well as assigned for background. We hope it can be an effective tool for engaging students, both with the world beyond their own cultural tradition and with that marvelous and continuing discourse about human affairs which is historical inquiry.

Note

1. See, for example, Jerry H. Bentley, *Old World Encounters* (New York: Oxford University Press, 1993).

PROLOGUE:
A NOTE TO
STUDENT READERS

People who write world history books obviously believe that a genuinely global approach to the human past is among the very best, if not the only, means of getting a handle on the world and locating ourselves in the larger scheme of things. *The Making of the Modern World* is an effort to convince you of the usefulness of that way of thinking.

Our justification for this approach is really quite simple: we need it! We need it to provide some perspective on the flow of events that cascade daily into our consciousness. The disintegration of the Soviet Union; the revival of democracy in Africa and Latin America; the expression of Islamic fundamentalism in the Middle East and of Hindu fundamentalism in India; the end of apartheid in South Africa; the growth of free-market economies in Communist China and elsewhere—such events remind us daily of the many ways we are connected to distant parts of the world. Human societies and cultures, our own very much included, are far from self-contained. If we want to understand the interconnected world of our times, we obviously need to know something of the origin, evolution, and impact of those connections. This is the central theme of world history.

Furthermore, we need world history because the most profound questions of the late twentieth century are increasingly global in scope. The proliferation of nuclear weapons, terrorism, tensions between rich and poor nations, population growth, the explosive power of ethnic hostility, and the multiple environmental dilemmas of our times are all world problems. Historians and other social scientists have turned increasingly to a global view of the past on the grounds that it is no longer possible to understand the processes of modern social change or the roots of our deepest current concerns in any other fashion.

And then there is, at least in the United States, the currently popular concern with cultural diversity, triggered not only by the cultural conflicts within America but also by the powerful forces of cultural assertion that have destroyed the Soviet Union, Somalia, and Yugoslavia; brought bitter conflict to the Islamic world; and sharpened Hindu-Muslim rivalry in India. Each of these conflicts, and many others, has a history. Viewing those histories in some comparative and global framework can only help us in understanding who we are as individuals, as members of particular communities, and as participants in the global village.

World history—indeed, any kind of history—can be useful not only for those who want to understand the past, but for those who seek to change the world in even modest ways as well. Because history has already "happened," it is easy to think, looking back, that it was inevitable, that it had to occur as it did. We believe, however, that at least to some extent, history has been "made" by the conscious choices of men and women who might have decided otherwise. Reflecting on those choices suggests that we can still "make" history and shape our societies anew. We want to be realistic about the possibilities for dramatic change in the world today, but also, quite frankly, to be encouraging to those who would seek actively to make a better world—one more free, more just, more secure, more equal, and more peaceful.

The study of history is a passionate affair. It touches on people's cultural identities; it exposes their fears of one another; it embodies their hopes for the future; it is used to justify both the status quo and radical change. For whatever purpose, each of us seeks a "usable past." Thus, the questions we ask of the past are often shaped by the needs of the present. Does this mean that we have given up an effort to be objective, fair, and balanced? Certainly not! The answers we give to those questions must be as rigorous, careful, and informed by the available evidence as we can make them. Professional historians and students alike can and should make every attempt to answer those questions without regard to preconceived ideas and cultural or political values. Only then can we find patterns, meaning, and significance in the past that can genuinely assist us in making our way through the complexities and confusions of the present.

BRIEF CONTENTS

INTRODUCTION The Shape of the
Modern World 1

Part I The First Modern Societies:
Europe since 1500 18

CHAPTER 1 Why Europe? 20
CHAPTER 2 "The Heavens and the Earth":
Europe's Scientific Revolution 38
CHAPTER 3 The "Hidden Hand":
Capitalism and the
Transformation of Europe 52
CHAPTER 4 "The Great Acceleration":
Industrialization and Social
Change in Europe 69
CHAPTER 5 Collapse and Reconstruction:
Europe in the Twentieth
Century 87

Suggestions for Further Reading: Europe 107

Part II Intersections and Encounters:
Global Connections
since 1500 108

CHAPTER 6 Europe and the World: Forms and
Phases of Global Expansion 110

Comparative Essay: Paths to the Modern
World: Patterns, Themes,
and Questions 130
Suggestions for Further Reading: Europe and
the World 135

Part III Europe's Extensions: Variations
on a Modern Theme 136

CHAPTER 7 European Offshoot or Unique
Experiment? The United States
in World History 138
CHAPTER 8 Social Inequality and Dependent
Development: The Latin
American Difference 159
CHAPTER 9 The Soviet Alternative:
The Rise and Fall of a
Communist Experiment 179

Comparative Essay: The Development
Debate 201
Suggestions for Further Reading: Europe's
Extensions 204

Part IV From the Middle Lands to the
Middle East: Islam and the
Challenge of the West 206

CHAPTER 10 Religion, Empire, and
Hemispheric Civilization:
The Making of the
Islamic World 208
CHAPTER 11 Reversal of Roles:
The Middle East and the West,
1500–1900 222
CHAPTER 12 Nationalism, Modernity, and
Islam: The Middle East in the
Twentieth Century 241

*Comparative Essay : Industrialization in the
            Developing World 262*
*Suggestions for Further Reading:
            The Middle East 265*

Part V Communities and States: India in Modern History 266

CHAPTER 13 Experiments in Diversity: States
            and Societies in Early Modern
            South Asia 268
CHAPTER 14 India and the British Raj 287
CHAPTER 15 Democracy, Development,
            and Cultural Pluralism: India
            since Independence 306

*Comparative Essay: Nationalisms in Modern
            World History 321*
Suggestions for Further Reading: India 324

Part VI East Asia and the Modern World: Comparing China and Japan 326

CHAPTER 16 The Middle Kingdom:
            The Making of the
            Chinese Empire 328
CHAPTER 17 "Foreign Devils": China and
            Western Imperialism,
            1500–1900 343
CHAPTER 18 Nationalists and Communists:
            The Chinese Revolution
            1900–1949 358
CHAPTER 19 Socialism, Development, and
            Politics: The People's Republic
            of China 374

CHAPTER 20 Japan: The Authoritarian Road
            to Capitalism 392

*Comparative Essay: Comparing Revolutions and
            Communist Regimes: Russia
            and China 415*
*Suggestions for Further Reading: China
            and Japan 417*

Part VII Colonialism, Nationalism, and Development: Africa in the Modern World 420

CHAPTER 21 Old Africa and New
            Pressures 422
CHAPTER 22 Modernization or Distorted
            Development? The Colonial
            Experience in Africa 439
CHAPTER 23 Toward Independence: Shaping
            New Societies in Africa 455
CHAPTER 24 Development or Deterioration?
            Beyond Independence
            in Africa 470

Suggestions for Further Reading: Africa 486

CONCLUSION East and West, North and
            South: Problems and
            Prospects in the Global
            Village 487

*Suggestions for Further Reading: The Global
            Village 503*

INDEX 505

CONTENTS

ACKNOWLEDGMENTS v

PREFACE FOR INSTRUCTORS vii

PROLOGUE: A Note to Student Readers xi

INTRODUCTION The Shape of the Modern World 1

1500: Before and After 1
Before 1500: Civilizations and Their Connections 1
Europe and the World 6
Europe's Modern Transformation 9
Invitations to Misunderstanding 11
Exaggerated Polarities 11
Ethnocentric Judgments 12
Becoming Like Us? Convergence and Divergence in Modern History 13

Suggestions for Further Reading 16

Part I The First Modern Societies: Europe since 1500 18

CHAPTER 1 Why Europe? 20
The Rise and Fall of the "Old" West: 500 B.C.E.–1000 C.E. 20
Starting Over: The Making of "New" Europe, 1000–1300 22
Sources of Growth: The Roots of Modern Europe 25
The Advantages of Backwardness: Europe as a Late Bloomer 25
Working Women and Late Marriages 27
"Countless Things Can Be Constructed": Europe's Technological Tradition 28
Christianity, Technology, and Science 30

The "Failure" of Empire: Europe's Political Framework 32
Free Cities and Urban Culture 33
Crisis, Renewal, and Overseas Expansion: 1350–1500 35
Europe's Religious Revolution: The Protestant Reformation 35
Conclusion 37

CHAPTER 2 "The Heavens and the Earth": Europe's Scientific Revolution 38
The Breakthrough of the Seventeenth Century 38
The World According to Aristotle and Ptolemy 39
From Copernicus to Newton: The Search for a New Model 40
Bacon and Descartes: The Search for a New Method 42
Science and Religion: Confrontation and Adjustment 42
The Implications of Science: The Enlightenment of the Eighteenth Century 43
The Science of Politics 43
Popularizing Scientific Attitudes 45
Voices: A Vision of Human Progress 46
Science and Progress 47
Beyond the Enlightenment: Science in the Nineteenth and Twentieth Centuries 47
Darwin and Evolution 47
Marx and History 48
Freud and Human Behavior 49
Einstein and the New Physics 50
Conclusion 50

CHAPTER 3   The "Hidden Hand":
             Capitalism and the
             Transformation of Europe 52

Capitalism in World History 52
   Markets and Morals, Commerce
      and Capital 53
Markets in the Middle Ages 55
*The Growth of Market Economies:
      1400–1800 56*
   Trade on a Global Scale 56
   Land, Labor, and the Market 56
Societies, States, and the Growth of Capitalism 58
   Early Leaders: Italy, Portugal, and Spain 60
   Protestants and Capitalists: Germany and
      the Netherlands 61
   Capitalism and the English Revolution 61
   France: The Old Regime, the Revolution, and
      Capitalism 63
      Voices: Revolutionary Dreams in Song 63
Toward a Capitalist Society and Culture 66

CHAPTER 4   "The Great Acceleration":
             Industrialization and Social
             Change in Europe 69

*Machines and Steam: Perspectives on the Industrial
      Revolution 69*
   Industrialization and Modern History 70
Preconditions for Industrialization 71
   Population and Technology 71
   Empire and Industry 72
   The State and the Economy 73
Separate Paths to Industrialization 73
   Great Britain: The Classic Case 74
      *Voices: The Life of an English
      Factory Girl, 1841 76*
   France: The Persistence of a
      Dual Economy 77
   Germany: Old Bottles and New Wine 79
   Industrial Comparisons and
      Commonalities 80
Social Change, Politics, and Culture 80
   Ideology and Class: Conservatism
      versus Liberalism 80
   Ideology and Class: Socialism 81
   Politics and Social Change 82
   Daily Lives: Men, Women, and Children 83
      Voices: "Only a Weaver" 84
Conclusion 86

CHAPTER 5   Collapse and Reconstruction:
             Europe in the Twentieth
             Century 87

Europe in 1914 87
   Politics and the Rise of the Masses 88
   The Coming of the Great War 89
The Collapse of Europe 91
   The First World War 92
   A Temporary and Uncertain Peace 93
Fascism and Modern Europe 94
   The Italian Precursor 96
   Hitler and the Nazis 96
   The Second World War: The End of
      European Hegemony 98
Europe Divided and Reconstructed 99
   Cold War: The Political Context of
      Postwar Europe 101
   The Common Market and West European
      Revival 103
   Eastern Europe: From Subjection to
      Liberation 104
Conclusion 105

Suggestions for Further Reading: Europe 107

*Part II Intersections and
          Encounters: Global
          Connections since 1500   108*

CHAPTER 6   Europe and the World: Forms and
             Phases of Global Expansion 110

*The World System in Transition:
      1200–1500 110*
*Remaking the World System: Europe's
      Early Empires, 1500–1800 111*
   Empires of Commerce in Asia 114
   Empires of Commerce in Africa 115
   Empires of Settlement in the Americas 118
      *Voices: Columbus from a Different
      Perspective 119*
*Empires of the Industrial Age:
      The Nineteenth Century 121*
   Industrialization and Imperialism 121
   From Informal to Territorial Empires 123
*Europe's World System under Attack:
      The Twentieth Century 124*
   The World System and the Collapse
      of Europe 125

"Standing Up": The Revolt of
the Colonies 126
Toward the World System of the
Twenty-first Century 127

*Comparative Essay: Paths to the Modern World:
Patterns, Themes, and
Questions 130*
Confronting the European Challenge 130
Revolutions from Below and Above 131
*Getting Out from Under: Anticolonial
Movements 132*
The Challenge of Development 132
Culture and Community 133

*Suggestions for Further Reading: Europe and
the World 135*

Part III Europe's Extensions: Variations on a Modern Theme 136

CHAPTER 7 European Offshoot or Unique
Experiment? The United States
in World History 138
Colonial Beginnings 139
Slavery in the Land of the Free 140
Puritanism and Religious Freedom 140
Europe and America 141
*The American Revolution: The
First Watershed 142*
The Case for American Exceptionalism 144
Born Equal? 144
Open Spaces and Free Security 145
"A House Divided": The Second Watershed 146
Industrial America 147
Reform without Socialism: The
Great Evasion? 148
Imperial America 149
American Prosperity and the
Great Depression 150
*Depression and World War: The
Third Watershed 151*
The American Century? 152
Cold War and Containment 153
America in Turmoil 154
*Conclusion: The Cold War's End Brings Victory
and Uncertainty 156*

CHAPTER 8 Social Inequality and
Dependent Development: The
Latin American Difference 159
*Aztecs and Incas: Latin America before
the Spanish 159*
*The Colonial Epoch in Latin America:
1500–1800 160*
Peons and Slaves: Patterns of
Labor Exploitation 161
Colonial Society in Latin America 164
Mercantilism and Dependency 165
Church, State, and Schools 166
Toward Independence 168
*After Independence: The Persistence
of Colonialism 169*
English Economic Imperialism 169
Yankee Imperialism 170
*Reform, Revolution, and Repression in the
Twentieth Century 171*
Mexico 171
Brazil 173
Cuba 174
Voices: Land Reform in Song 175
Reform in Perspective 175
Social Dimensions of Underdevelopment 176
Conclusion 177

CHAPTER 9 The Soviet Alternative:
The Rise and Fall of a
Communist Experiment 179
Mother Russia 180
*Reformers and Revolutionaries: Old Russia and
the West, 1700–1900 182*
Peter the Great: A Revolution
from Above 182
Serfs and Industry 183
Revolutionaries before the
Revolution 184
The Coming of the Revolution 185
1917: From March to November 186
Toward the Bolshevik Revolution 186
The Legacy of 1917 188
*From Lenin to Stalin: Building Socialism
in the Soviet Union 188*
Civil War: 1918–1921 189
"Liberal" Communism in the
Making? 189

Stalin and Stalinism 190
    Rural Revolution from Above 190
    Soviet-style Industrialization 191
    The Modernization of Autocracy 192
      Voices: Stalin's Victim 193
    Assessing Stalin's Revolution 194
From Gulag to Glasnost 195
    The Second Russian Revolution 197
    Explaining the Soviet Collapse 199

*Comparative Essay: The Development
      Debate 201*

*Suggestions for Further Reading:
      Europe's Extensions 204*

Part IV From the Middle Lands to the Middle East: Islam and the Challenge of the West 206

CHAPTER 10 Religion, Empire, and
      Hemispheric Civilization:
      The Making of the
      Islamic World 208
Lands, Peoples, and Historical Change 209
    Geography of the Middle East 209
The Birth of a World Religion 210
    Muhammad: Revelation and
      Revolution 210
    Islamic Belief and Practice 212
    Crisis and Expansion: The Early State 212
From Arab Empire to World Civilization 212
    The Formation of Islamic Civilization 213
    Patterns of Islamic Culture 214
*Political Disintegration and Cultural
      Expansion: The Middle Period
      of Islam, 950–1500 216*
    Turks, Mongols, and Christians: The Middle
      East and Its Invaders 217
    An Islamic World System 218
    The World of Ibn Battuta 220
Conclusion: The Islamic World in 1500 220

CHAPTER 11 Reversal of Roles:
      The Middle East and the West,
      1500–1900 222
The Rise of the Ottoman Empire 222
The Safavid Empire of Persia 225

The "Decline" of the Ottoman Empire 226
The Balance Shifts 227
*The Impulse to Return: Islamic Revival
      and Reform 229*
The Ottoman Empire in Crisis 230
    Ottoman Reforms 231
    The Problem of Cultural Identity 232
*Egypt: From Independent Development to
      Colonial Rule 233*
      *Voices: An Encounter with
      European Science 234*
    An Experiment in Independent
      Development 234
    The Suez Canal and Egyptian
      Debt 235
    Islam and Egyptian Reform 236
*Algeria: Settler Colonization and
      Muslim Resistance 238*
Conclusion 239

CHAPTER 12 Nationalism, Modernity, and
      Islam: The Middle East in the
      Twentieth Century 241
Arab Nationalism and the Arab Revolt 242
The Rise of the Turkish Nation 244
*The Second World War and the Crumbling
      of Imperialism 246*
*Arab Socialism and Nasser's Egyptian
      Revolution 247*
The Middle East on the Global Stage 249
    Competing Nationalisms: The Palestinian-
      Israeli Conflict 249
    The Question of Oil 252
The Islamic Resurgence 254
    Roots of Islamic Revival 254
    An Islamic Revolution in Iran 256
      *Contrasting Voices: Islam, Modernity, and
      Relations with the West 258*
    "Revolutionary Traditionalism": Iran in
      Comparative Perspective 259
Conclusion 260

*Comparative Essay: Industrialization in the
      Developing World 262*

*Suggestions for Further Reading:
      The Middle East 265*

Part V Communities and States: India in Modern History 266

CHAPTER 13 Experiments in Diversity: States and Societies in Early Modern South Asia 268

Indian Beginnings 268
Cultural Foundations of Indian Civilization 270

The Classical Indian Pattern 270
The Making of an All-Indian Tradition 270
Patterns of Society: Caste and Class 271
Patterns of Political Authority: Indian Empires and Local States 273

South Asia and the Wider World 273
India in 1500 274

State and Kingship in South India 276
The Vijayanagara Experiment 276
Politics and Ritual in Vijayanagara 276
Community and State 278

The North Indian Model: The Mughal Empire 279
Community and State 281
The Beginnings of Mughal Decline 283

The Eighteenth Century: Decline or Creativity? 283
Changing Society in the Eighteenth Century 284
European Traders in a Changing South Asia 285

CHAPTER 14 India and the British Raj 287

The Establishment of the Raj 287
Domesticating India 288
India in Rebellion 290

The Captive Jewel 291
Understanding and Misunderstanding India 291
Governing India 292
Indian Experiments under the Raj 294
The Imperial State and Indian Culture 295
The Economics of Empire 297

Community and Nation in the Struggle for Independence 299
Mahatma Gandhi 301
Hindus and Muslims 302
The End of the Raj 304

Conclusion 305

CHAPTER 15 Democracy, Development, and Cultural Pluralism: India since Independence 306

Launching a Republic 307
Creating a New Economy 308
Agriculture and Inequality 310
Voices: "The Young Men Speak" 311
Women and the New India 313

Civil Society and Competing Identities 315
Language and Identity: The Redrawing of Regional Boundaries 315
Ethnicity, Class, and Identity: The Case of Ex-Untouchables 316
Religious Nationalism 317

Conclusion: India in the 1990s 319

Comparative Essay: Nationalisms in Modern World History 321

Suggestions for Further Reading: India 324

Part VI East Asia and the Modern World: Comparing China and Japan 326

CHAPTER 16 The Middle Kingdom: The Making of the Chinese Empire 328

The Dynamics of Empire 328
The Imperial Chinese State 330
Examinations and Bureaucracy: The Civil Service System 332
China's Economic Revolution: 700s–1200s 332

Forces of Fragmentation 333
Voices: A Peasant's Story 334
The Dynastic Cycle 335

The Late Empire 335
State and Society in Late Imperial China 336
Chinese Women in the Late Empire 337
Voices: A Woman's Story 338
Why Not Capitalism? 339
The Decline of the Qing Dynasty 341

Conclusion 342

CHAPTER 17 "Foreign Devils": China and
Western Imperialism,
1500–1900 343

*From Trade to Imperialism: China and
the West 343*
The World According to the Chinese 344
Dealing with the West on China's Terms:
1500–1800 344
*Voices: The Chinese Emperor and
King George III 346*
Opium Wars and Unequal Treaties 346
The Imperialist Penetration of China:
1860–1895 349
The Significance of Imperialism in Chinese
History 349
The Taiping Revolution: 1850–1865 351
The Background of the Taipings 351
The Taiping Movement 352
A Revolution in the Making? 352
The Historical Significance of the
Taiping Revolution 354
*The Failure of Conservative Modernization:
1860–1895 354*
The Self-Strengthening Movement 354
Choosing the Past: The Failure of Self-
Strengthening 355
*Conclusion: Comparing China and the
Ottoman Empire 356*

CHAPTER 18 Nationalists and Communists:
The Chinese Revolution,
1900–1949 358

The End of Imperial China: 1895–1912 358
Reform and Reaction 358
Reform from Above 359
China's Political Revolution: 1911 359
The 1911 Revolution in Perspective 360
*China's First Cultural Revolution
1915–1923 361*
The New Culture Movement 361
The May Fourth Movement
of 1919 362
Marxism in China 362
The National Revolution: 1923–1927 363
*The Nanjing Decade (1927–1937):
The Second Failure of Conservative
Modernization 365*

*The Chinese Communists and Peasant Revolution:
1928–1949 367*
Communists and Peasants 367
The Jiangxi Soviet 368
The Long March: 1935 368
*Japanese Imperialism and the
Chinese Revolution 369*
The Japanese Invasion of China 369
The Yanan Way in Revolutionary China 370
The United Front and Its Breakdown 370
Voices: Revolution in Long Bow Village 371
People's War and Communist Victory 372
Conclusion 373

CHAPTER 19 Socialism, Development, and
Politics: The People's Republic
of China 374

*Starting Points: Comparing China and the Soviet
Union 374*
Backwardness, Development, and Socialism 375
*The New Chinese State and Economic Recovery:
1949–1953 375*
The Land Revolution 376
The 1950 Marriage Law and
Family Reform 377
Urban Recovery 377
The Korean War 377
*The Stalinist Model and the Transition
to Socialism 378*
The First Five-Year Plan 378
Agricultural Collectivization 379
Consequences of the Stalinist Model 379
*The Maoist Model of Socialist Development:
1958–1976 380*
The Great Leap and People's Communes 380
The Sino-Soviet Split 381
Retrenchment: The Origins of Market
Socialism 382
"To Rebel Is Justified": The Cultural
Revolution 383
Building a Maoist Society 383
The Maoist Era in Retrospect 385
*The Market Socialism Model: 1978 to
the Present 385*
Dismantling the Communes 386
Markets, Industry, and Bureaucrats 386
The 1989 Tiananmen Massacre 387
Voices: The Next Revolution 388

Population Policy 389
Did Socialism Liberate Women? 390
Conclusion 391

CHAPTER 20 Japan: An Authoritarian Road
                to Capitalism 392
Preview: Japan's Modern History 393
The Historical Setting 393
    Samurai and Shogun: Japanese
        Political Life 395
    Japanese Society 396
The Meiji Revolution from Above 398
    Contrasting China and Japan 398
    Consolidating Power and
        Building Industry 399
    Popular Protest and State Power 401
    Joining the Imperialist Club 402
    The Social Cost of Industrialization 403
*Imperial Japan in the Era of the
        World Wars 404*
    Japan's Dual Economy 404
    Democracy Denied: The Defection of
        the Parties 405
    The Drift toward World War II 406
*Postwar Japan: Peace, Managed Democracy, and
        the Economy 409*
    The Occupation: Democracy and
        Economic Efficiency 410
    Political Compromise and
        Economic Growth 411
    Japan at the End of the
        Twentieth Century 412
Conclusion 414

*Comparative Essay: Comparing Revolutions and
                Communist Regimes: Russia
                and China 415*

*Suggestions for Further Reading: China
                and Japan 417*

**Part VII Colonialism, Nationalism, and
        Development: Africa in the
        Modern World 420**
CHAPTER 21 Old Africa and
                New Pressures 422
Economic Foundations of African History 422
The Evolution of African Societies 424

    Kinship and Political Order:
        Lineage-based Societies 424
    Gold, Empire, and Islam in
        West Africa 427
    Variations on a Theme 430
    History and Myth in Africa 431
Africa and the West 432
    The Slave Trade: Patterns
        and Consequences 432
        Voices: Inside the Slave Trade 434
    Creeping Imperialism in the
        Nineteenth Century 435
    Conquest and Resistance 437

CHAPTER 22 Modernization or Distorted
                Development? The Colonial
                Experience in Africa 439
*States, Governors, and Chiefs: The Political
        Framework of Colonial Rule 439*
The Economics of Colonialism 441
    Capitalism and the Colonial State 442
    Forced Labor and Crude Exploitation 442
    Peasant Agriculture and the
        World Economy 443
    Land, Labor, and Settlers 443
    Mines and Profits 444
    Women and the Colonial Economy 445
*Race, Class, and Tribe: Cultural Identity and
        Social Structure in Colonial Africa 446*
    Colonial Racism 446
    The New Elite 447
    The Urban Poor 449
    Classes in the Countryside 450
    Colonial "Tribalism" 450
*Conclusion: The Limits of
        Colonial Development 452*

CHAPTER 23 Toward Independence: Shaping
                New Societies in Africa 455
*Before Nationalism: Rebellions, Churches,
        and Intellectuals 456*
    Rural Rebellion: The Case of Maji Maji 456
    The Africanization of Christianity 457
    The Protest of the Intellectuals 459
    Politics and the New Elite 460
The Nationalisms of Colonial Africa 461
    Nationalist Origins 461
    Achieving the Political Kingdom: The Way
        of Negotiated Settlements 464

Achieving the Political Kingdom: Wars of
National Liberation 465
Achieving the Political Kingdom:
South Africa 467
Conclusion: "All These Other Things . . ." 469

CHAPTER 24 Development or Deterioration?
Beyond Independence in
Africa 470
Changing the Political Framework 470
The Decline of Imported Democracy 471
Economic Failure and Political
Legitimacy 472
Social Inequality and Class Resentment 473
Tribes and Politics 474
New Directions 476
*The Dilemma of Development: Identifying
the Obstacles 477*
Nature, Tradition, and Famine:
The Environment and African
Development 477
Voices: Left Behind in Morocco 478
Africa and the World Economy: External
Obstacles to Development 479
Closer to Home: Internal Obstacles to
Development 480
*The Dilemma of Development: Searching
for Strategies 482*
Capitalism in an African Setting 482
African-Style Socialism 484

Conclusion: Time and Perspective 485

Suggestions for Further Reading: Africa 486

CONCLUSION East and West, North and
South: Problems and Prospects
in the Global Village 487
*The East and the West: The Cold War in
World History 487*
Hot Wars, the Cold War, and the
Long Peace 488
The End of the Cold War 490
*The North and the South: Global
Inequality and the Search for a
New Order 491*
The Demands of the South 492
The Response of the North 493
Prospects for Catching Up 494
*All of Us: Sustainability and the Limits
to Modernity 495*
"Borrowing from Our Children":
The Environmental Dilemma 495
Toward Sustainable Societies 498
*Conclusion: Rethinking Basic Assumptions of the
Modern Era 500*

*Suggestions for Further Reading:
The Global Village 503*

INDEX 505

THE MAKING OF THE MODERN WORLD

CONNECTED HISTORIES,
DIVERGENT PATHS
1500 TO THE PRESENT

SECOND EDITION

Introduction
The Shape of the Modern World

Making sense of what is called the *modern world,* defined by many historians as the years roughly since 1500, is no easy matter, for the events of the past five centuries encompass great contradictions and amazing diversities. We are often told, for example, that the world has become more "interdependent," and in an economic sense this is true. Yet the twentieth century bears painful witness to the hostilities and conflicts of our interdependent world: two world wars, a forty-year Cold War accompanied by an arms race in nuclear weapons, recurrent and deepening ethnic hostilities within many countries. Some parts of this interdependent world have become wealthy beyond the imaginations of people living in 1500, whereas other parts of the world have been impoverished and degraded. How are we to understand "interdependence" amid such enormous conflicts?

Furthermore, historians have highlighted the dramatic changes of recent centuries by identifying a series of revolutions; for example, the scientific revolution; the Industrial Revolution; the French, Russian, and Chinese revolutions; the sexual revolution. Yet the continuities are equally striking. "Caste" still structures elements of social life in modern India. Millions repeat daily the ancient Muslim creed: "There is no God but Allah and Muhammad is his prophet." Accusations of witchcraft continue to reflect social tension in Africa. And women in most of the world remain subordinate to men. All of this—continuity and change, cooperation and conflict—is the raw material of history.

No wonder, then, that historians disagree, sometimes bitterly, both in their efforts to describe the making of the modern world and to explain why things turned out as they did. We will not pretend that there is some grand consensus about modern world history. Nor will we shrink from stating our

own views on matters of controversy. In doing so, we hope to convey the sense that studying history is not a simple matter of "telling it like it was," but rather a human enterprise, full of conflict and disagreement and subject to all the limitations and uncertainties of life.

1500: Before and After

What is unique about the world of the past several hundred years? Why do history texts and history courses frequently identify the centuries since 1500 C.E. as marking a new era in human affairs? We believe the answer lies in two major and related changes—one in the relationship among the world's many societies, and the other in the emergence, first within Europe, of a new kind of society.

Before 1500: Civilizations and Their Connections

Most of the civilizations and cultures that have persisted into modern times took shape in the two millennia between 500 B.C.E. and 1500 C.E. On the huge Eurasian landmass, which accounted for the vast majority of the world's population, four distinctive centers of civilization had developed. The far-eastern extension of that landmass gave rise to Chinese civilization, with its unique written language and its centuries-long tradition of centralized and bureaucratic government. Indian civilization, occupying the large south Asian peninsula, developed a complex social institution known to us as "caste" as well as the tolerant and inclusive religious tradition of Hinduism, both of which served to accommodate an extremely diverse population within a common framework. In the area now known as the Middle East, home to the earliest human civilizations in Mesopotamia and Egypt, the civilization of Islam arose and flourished in the centuries after 600 C.E. Farther west, the Greeks provided the intellectual foundations of Western civilization with their freethinking rationality and secularism, while the Romans spread these ideas in an empire that encompassed the Mediterranean basin. And beyond the borders of such settled "civilized" societies lay the lands of Germans, Turks, Mongols, and others. Often nomadic, frequently militaristic, and sometimes called "barbarians" by their civilized neighbors, such peoples interacted continuously with the great civilizations of Eurasia, and through their migrations, invasions, technological ingenuity, and political skills shaped much of the history of this vast region.

On the African continent south of the Sahara, sophisticated kingdoms and empires developed in the grassland or savanna regions, while elsewhere smaller communities adapted to local conditions on the foundation of an agricultural and ironworking technology. Almost wholly isolated from the interacting world of Afro-Eurasia were the cultures and civilizations of the Americas, where the impressive achievements of the Aztecs, Mayas, and Incas derived largely from their own efforts and inspiration.

Each of these civilizations developed a unique "style," reflected in differing religions, social structures, political systems, and cultural values. But their isolation from one another was gradually eroded by commerce, migration, cultural contact, and conquest. And so alongside these separate civilizations there arose extensive networks of economic exchange, cultural borrowing, and sometimes political control that historians on occasion refer to as a "world system." These patterns of trans-regional contact had their own ups and downs—periods of growth and times of contraction. Much of the story of world history deals with these connections and with the fluctuating relationships between particular civilizations or regions and the larger world system with which they interacted.

Because the most extensive interactions occurred among the civilizations of Eurasia and parts of Africa, some historians have labeled this area the "intercommunicating zone" (see Map I.1). There the "Silk Road" connected ancient China with the Roman Empire in a land-based trading pattern across the length of Eurasia, and in the Indian Ocean basin well-established patterns of trade linked East Africa, Arabia, India, and China in a complex and freely operating commercial system. Extensive trade routes across the Sahara in the C.E. centuries connected the wealthy kingdoms of west Africa with the world of Mediterranean commerce.

Along these trade routes passed numerous items of material culture such as technological innovations, plants, and domesticated animals. Bananas and coconut palms spread from Southeast Asia to Africa, and chickens, sugarcane, and cotton were domesticated first in India and diffused from there to both the east and the west. China contributed block and movable-type printing, gunpowder, the magnetic compass, the manufacturing of paper, and many other innovations to the other peoples of Eurasia in a pattern of technological transfer that moved generally from east to west.

The longest-lasting consequences of these early contacts among very different civilizations were cultural and religious. The conquests of Alexander the Great spread Greek ideas and artistic styles throughout the Middle East and into India in the late B.C.E. centuries. Buddhism, a religion of Indian origin, diffused widely in East and Southeast Asia during the early C.E. centuries, while Christianity, a religion of Middle Eastern origin, was widely accepted in northern Africa and Ethiopia and became the state religion of the Roman Empire by 400 C.E. Most dramatic of all was the rise of Islam, which erupted out of Arabian trading cities after 632 C.E. and within several centuries had millions of adherents in places as far afield as western Africa, Spain, Persia, and India. More than any other creed, Islam served as a cultural bridge among the diverse peoples of the Afro-Eurasian world.

Associated with the rise of Islam was the creation of an Arab Empire that was far larger than the earlier regional empires such as the Roman and the Chinese. It extended from Spain and Morocco in the west, across northern Africa and the Middle East to India. In subsequent centuries, Muslim rulers came to control India and large parts of central Asia, southern Europe, and western Africa. Though the political unity of this huge empire fragmented well before 1000 C.E., the Arabic language and the Islamic religion created an unprecedented degree of cultural unity across large areas of Afro-Eurasia (as illustrated in Map I.2).

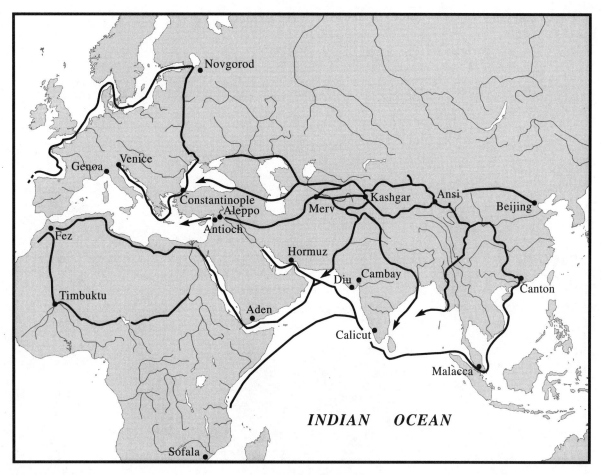

MAP I.1 The Intercommunicating Zone: Afro-Eurasian Trading Connections in 1400

In the centuries following 1000 C.E., first the central Asian Turks and then the Mongols likewise created large trans-regional empires. Even more than the Arab Empire, the conquests of the Mongols, led by Genghis Khan and his successors, brought unity to the Eurasian landmass for a brief period in the thirteenth century by incorporating China, central Asia, Persia, Russia, and parts of eastern Europe into a huge military confederacy (see Map I.3.) But an empire of that size could not be sustained for long. By 1300, it was well along the way toward disintegration, and its warrior elite was soon assimilated into the more advanced civilizations that it had conquered less than a century before.

The Arab, Turkish, and Mongol empires facilitated communication, travel, and trade among the peoples of the Old World. The Italian Marco Polo and the North African Ibn-Batuta were only the most famous of those travelers who made their way from one end of Eurasia to the other under the protection of Islamic or Mongol governments. But unlike the Arabs, who had changed both cultural and economic patterns of Afro-Eurasia, the Mongols left little lasting imprint on the world they had briefly and harshly governed.

By 1500, these super-empires had come apart, and the political landscape of Afro-Eurasia was once again characterized by a series of regional empires, including the Chinese Empire; the Mughal Empire in India; the Safavid Empire in Persia (today Iran); the Ottoman Empire in Turkey, the Balkans, and northern Africa; and the Songhai Empire in western Africa (see Map I.4.) That four of these large states were governed by rulers giving allegiance to Islam makes it all the more surprising that the further development of global connections would be spurred by the

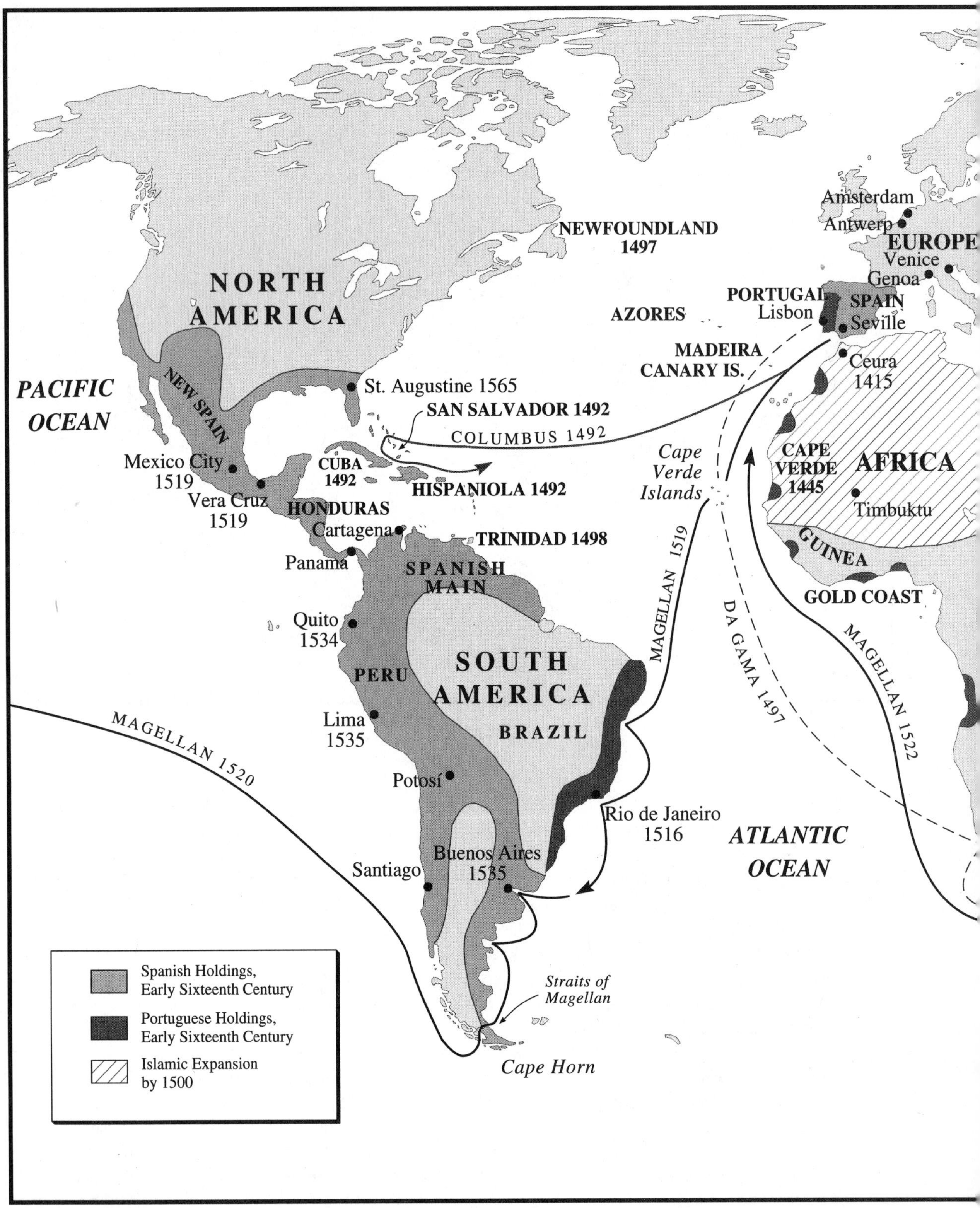

NORTH AMERICA

NEW SPAIN

PACIFIC OCEAN

Mexico City 1519

Vera Cruz 1519

HONDURAS

Cartagena

Panama

Quito 1534

PERU

Lima 1535

Potosí

Santiago

Buenos Aires 1535

SOUTH AMERICA

SPANISH MAIN

BRAZIL

Rio de Janeiro 1516

Straits of Magellan

Cape Horn

MAGELLAN 1520

St. Augustine 1565

SAN SALVADOR 1492

COLUMBUS 1492

CUBA 1492

HISPANIOLA 1492

TRINIDAD 1498

NEWFOUNDLAND 1497

AZORES

MADEIRA
CANARY IS.

Cape Verde Islands

MAGELLAN 1519

DA GAMA 1497

Amsterdam
Antwerp

EUROPE
Venice
Genoa

PORTUGAL
Lisbon

SPAIN
Seville

Ceura 1415

CAPE VERDE 1445

AFRICA

Timbuktu

GUINEA

GOLD COAST

MAGELLAN 1522

ATLANTIC OCEAN

Spanish Holdings, Early Sixteenth Century

Portuguese Holdings, Early Sixteenth Century

Islamic Expansion by 1500

MAP I.2 Islamic and European Expansion by the Sixteenth Century

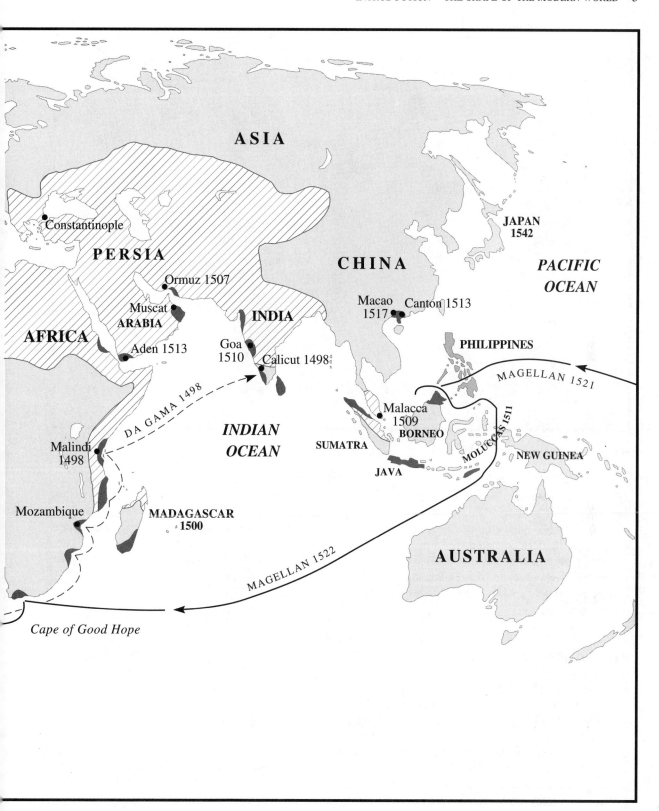

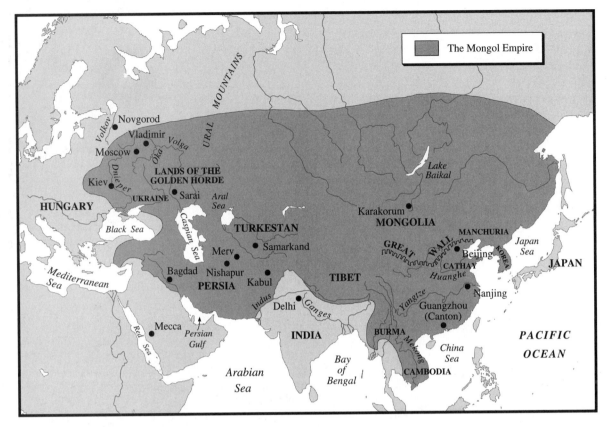

MAP I.3 The Mongol Empire, c. 1300

new, small, and squabbling states of Christian Europe rather than by some more established center of civilization. While Europeans made the decisive contribution to the interconnected world of the modern era, they built on a foundation of extensive linkages among the diverse peoples of Afro-Eurasia that were already in existence when Columbus launched his tiny fleet in 1492.

Europe and the World

Between 1500 and 1900, the intercommunicating zone expanded to encompass the entire world, and the global balance of power changed decisively. Intercultural connections began to occur on a far larger geographical scale, as the New World was brutally incorporated into the sphere of Afro-Eurasian interaction and as the world system assumed genuinely global dimensions. And these encounters came to have a more decisive impact on established cultures than ever before. In these enormously significant historical processes the peoples of Europe played the leading role.

Voyages of discovery undertaken by Christopher Columbus, Ferdinand Magellan, Vasco da Gama, and their successors gave Europeans a basic geographical knowledge of the entire world by 1800 (see Map I. 2.) By the mid-twentieth century, the revolution in communication technology provided global access to information about the wider world and, at least for some people, blurred the boundaries between civilizations and cultures. Today's scientists, for example, frequently relate to one another as members of a worldwide community whatever their national origins; businesses increasingly ignore national boundaries in the organization of production; and the notion of a global citizenship transcending loyalty to a particular state or civilization is a new element in human thought.

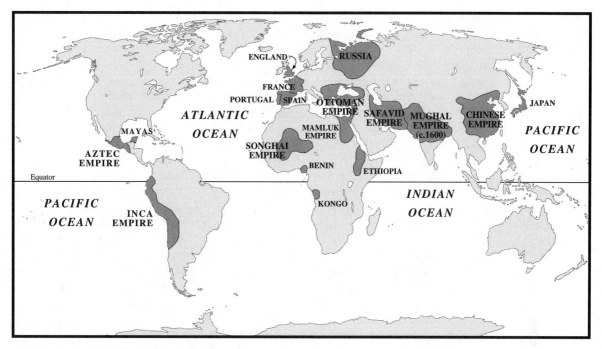

MAP I.4 Major States and Empires, c. 1500

Europe's outward thrust led not only to an increased awareness of other peoples but also to a growing trade with them. Much of that trade initially tapped into the vast network of Afro-Eurasian commerce that had arisen under Muslim auspices. But soon Europeans came to control and extend that trade, and by the early twentieth century, scarcely any part of the world lay entirely outside this gigantic network of global exchange. The world had become for the first time a single economic unit, with Europe at its hub and with a division of labor that operated on a global scale. Early in the process, gold and silver, looted from the "Indian" empires of the New World, were offered in exchange for passionately sought-after spices from Asia. The infamous triangular trade linked Africa, Europe, and the Americas in a pattern of exchange involving slaves, guns, rum, cloth, cotton, tobacco, and sugar. By the mid-twentieth century, African peasants living in Senegal, a French colony in West Africa, were devoting so much of their land and labor to producing peanuts for sale in Europe that they had to import rice grown in Southeast Asia. The threads of global commerce, of which these are but a few examples, were the strongest and most enduring of the ties that created the interdependent but highly unequal world system of the late twentieth century.

Accompanying the proliferation of trade routes was the spread of the techniques and ideas of a rapidly changing Europe. The methods and concepts of the natural sciences as well as the modern technologies of production, communication, and transportation were all widely adopted throughout the world. Since 1949, the leaders of China's one billion people, some 20 percent of the world's population, have claimed allegiance to a set of ideas first spelled out by the nineteenth-century German, Karl Marx. Furthermore, human migration on a massive scale, both voluntary and in chains, populated the New World with Europeans and Africans from the Old World. The global exchange of other life forms, such as plants, animals, and germs, provides further evidence of the connectedness of the world in the past several hundred years.

International conflict likewise came to operate on a global scale. The Spanish and Portuguese, the French and British, the Germans and Japanese, and most recently the Americans and Soviets have all played out their struggles for power and influence on a world stage. The major wars of the eighteenth century as well as those of the twentieth—both "hot" and "cold"—have been world wars.

The political dimension of these many connections is found in Europe's global empires, often the product of bloody wars of conquest. Perhaps most impressive about these European empires was their scope, for by the early twentieth century Europeans (or people of European origin) had come to dominate virtually the entire world (see Map I.5). The Americas, India, Africa, and Southeast Asia had been at some point formally incorporated into one or another European empire, and China and large areas of the Middle East were subjected to heavy economic and political influence amounting to what some historians have called an "informal empire." The Spanish and Portuguese, the British, French, and Dutch, and the Germans and Italians competed ferociously for the real and imagined benefits of global power. In addition to this overseas expansion, the Russians pushed eastward across Siberia to the Pacific, while in a similar process, transplanted Europeans conquered and

settled two continents in the New World and another in Australia. Driven at various times by religious fervor, personal greed, the perceived needs of dominant classes, national pride and paranoia, and almost always by a sense of intense competition with rivals, Europe's global dominion was without precedent in human history.

Equally impressive was the impact of Europe's expansion on the peoples it touched. The empires of Europe became vehicles for the spread of Europe's traditional culture (its languages and religion, for example) as well as its secular ideologies (such as the "rights of man," nationalism, and socialism). But, of far greater importance, the world became aware, often painfully, of Europe's revolutionary mastery of nature as reflected in modern science and its technological products: the steam engine, electricity, industrial production, the machine gun. These products of Europe's economic modernization cemented its domination of the globe during the nineteenth century and introduced the possibility of a radically different way of life to the subordinated peoples of the world by the twentieth.

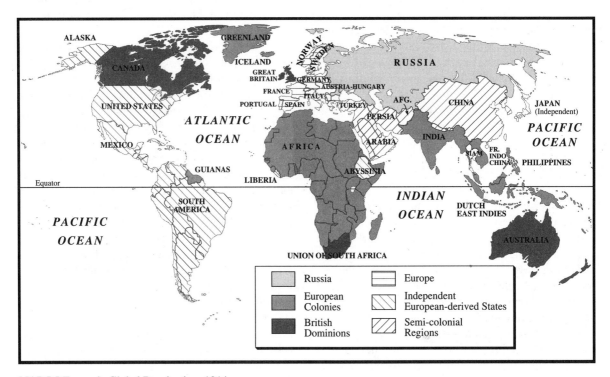

MAP I.5 Europe's Global Domination, 1914

Europe's Modern Transformation

Between 600 and 1000 C.E., the Islamic Middle East was the most dynamic and expansive part of the emerging world system. From 1000 to 1500, China's startling technological and commercial revolutions shifted the center of innovation and growth to the eastern end of Eurasia. It was only after 1500 that dramatic changes within western Europe came to have a decisive impact on the entire planet. In the perspective of world history, then, Europe's modern development is the most recent in a series of major breakthroughs that have shaped the world system as a whole.[1]

Some historians have described these enormous changes within Europe as modernization; others have spoken of development or of the "great transformation." Whatever the process is called, not since the agricultural revolution, which began some eight to ten thousand years ago, have human ways of life been so fundamentally altered as in the past four or five centuries.

Like the agricultural revolution, Europe's modern transformation has been rooted in enormous increases in the understanding of the world and in the ability to manipulate nature for human purposes. The breakthrough in understanding came with the scientific revolution of seventeenth-century Europe. There, Copernicus, Galileo, Isaac Newton, and others formulated a new picture of the universe and created a new method of inquiry that has since been applied to virtually every area of human interest. The ability to manipulate natural processes took a great leap forward in the Industrial Revolution, which began in England about 1780. By applying new sources of energy (first steam and later electricity and gasoline) to ingenious machines, the forgers of the Industrial Revolution produced a tremendous increase in human productivity and introduced the possibility of a material abundance of which men and women had only dreamed before. Soon the scientific and Industrial revolutions became linked and advances in knowledge were translated into new products—the smallpox vaccine, internal-combustion engines, and nuclear weapons, for example. Science and industry, or knowledge and technology, lay at the very heart of Europe's modern transformation.

But what made that process so dynamic was Europe's emerging capitalist economy. It was a system, unique in human history, in which more and more items (grain, cloth, tools, land, even human labor) were bought and sold on the market. Those who controlled commerce or production sought to make a profit and to accumulate wealth in the form of money rather than land. Growing numbers of men and women worked for wages to produce goods for sale in distant markets rather than for the use of the immediate community. Though the transition to capitalism was painful and disruptive, the system proved enormously productive in Europe and North America, for it motivated investment, technological innovation, and hard work and gave rise to the world's wealthiest economies.

Capitalism also fostered a new attitude toward economic and social life: the notion that it was possible to increase vastly the total wealth in a society and that doing so was the primary avenue to a good life. In premodern Europe and almost everywhere else, most people believed that the amount of wealth was essentially fixed and that whatever made for a good life, it was certainly not the single-minded pursuit of more money. Modern capitalist societies abandoned such notions, as they came to see consumption and production alike as almost unlimited. The possibility of continual economic growth provided the material foundation for the modern and revolutionary belief in "progress," the conviction that the future can be better than the past or present, and should be!

The social implications of these developments were profound and far-reaching. A sharp decline in the death rate during the nineteenth century produced a rapid growth in population. Most people found themselves living in cities rather than in rural areas, and millions migrated to the New World. Older groups or classes, such as the landowning nobility and artisans, found their sources of wealth and power threatened by the growing importance and numbers of the capitalist bourgeoisie, or middle class, which was in turn sharply challenged by the factory- working class later in the century. Particularly in the twentieth century, the continued development of sophisticated technologies gave rise to many highly specialized professions (chemists, engineers, academics, bureaucrats, all divided into numerous subspecialties) and to an increasingly complex society. And as the workplace was withdrawn from the home and farm into factories and offices, many women, particularly those of the middle class, lost their role as direct producers and became instead managers of consumption within the family. New attitudes and practices regarding leisure, aging, education, and child-rearing were likewise among the social changes associated with the modernizing process in Europe and the United States.

Europe's modern economic and social transformation also stimulated new political and cultural loyalties, as millions of people were uprooted from more familiar forms of community life. Many involved themselves actively in political affairs and came to reject the idea that rulers were established by God or that governments were beyond the reach of ordinary people. This political awakening of the masses took a variety of forms. In the seventeenth and eighteenth centuries, England, France, and the United States experienced revolutions based on ideas of human equality, individual rights, and civil liberties, which gave rise to democratic societies with mass participation in elections and political parties. During the nineteenth century, loyalty to the nation became the major substitute for older commitments to the village, region, or religious community. While these national identities were in many ways new and deliberate creations, they drew upon older traditions of language and custom and so provided for millions of people a reassuring sense of continuity amid the vast upheavals of modern life.

Finally, the modernizing process in the West had a profound impact at the psychological level, for it presented people with a growing range of options in areas of life that had previously been fixed by tradition. Whom to marry; where to live; what work to do; which religion to follow; what rulers to select—in none of these matters would most Europeans of 1500 have been confronted with a choice or even have been able to conceive of one. The extent of personal freedom in modern Western societies was wholly unprecedented in world history, though perceived in contradictory ways. Many found in this situation a sense of liberation from older forms of social restriction and gloried in their individuality. Others experienced it as rootlessness, insecurity, uncertainty, and anxiety; they sought, in Erich Fromm's provocative

Industrial production has become a central symbol of the modern era. *Visual Studies Workshop*

phrase, to "escape from freedom," or to create new forms of community.

Such, then, are the general contours of the unique type of society that emerged gradually in Europe after 1500. Much of the story of modern world history involves the impact of Europe's modern transformation on the rest of the world. And many controversial questions of our time derive from our efforts to understand and evaluate that process. What was gained and what was lost for humankind in Europe's modern transformation? Did Europe's dynamic growth stimulate new energies and foster modern development in the more slowly changing societies of Asia, Africa, and elsewhere? Or did it exploit, impoverish, and distort the development of those societies? To what extent were other peoples free to select which elements of Europe's modern legacy they would adopt? Was it possible to be "modern" without being European? And how could an increasingly connected world cope with the tensions and hostilities that accompanied a more intense experience of cultural diversity and Western domination? These are some of the larger questions to which we shall return in the chapters that follow.

Invitations to Misunderstanding

Europe's modern transformation and its global reach clearly lie at the center of the world's history during the past five centuries. But, particularly for people living in the West, and perhaps especially for Americans, that very fact invites distortion and misunderstanding. We may overemphasize our uniqueness; we may exaggerate the moral virtues (or failings) of modern societies; and we may assume that everyone else is, or ought to be, following in our historical footsteps. It will be useful, therefore, to highlight some of these potential misunderstandings and be alert to them as we proceed.

Exaggerated Polarities

The very idea of the "modern era" and the distinction between "modern" and "traditional" societies are useful concepts only because they highlight a major

turning point in the broad sweep of human history. But they also vastly oversimplify historical reality by grouping together very different societies. Did "traditional" African societies and "traditional" South Asian societies, for example, really have very much in common apart from the fact that neither was "modern"? It was, in fact, unlikely that a European villager and a Chinese peasant, meeting, say, in 1200 C.E., would have felt themselves to be living in similar societies. On his famous visits to China in the late thirteenth century, the Italian merchant Marco Polo was far more impressed by the differences than by the similarities. Concerned with the unique histories of particular peoples and cultures, historians are rightly suspicious of such broad categories as traditional and modern.

Furthermore, the notion of traditional societies too often implies that they have been stagnant and essentially changeless until stimulated by the dynamic and modernizing West. But India, the Middle East, China, and Africa, no less than Europe, have had their own long-established patterns of historical change. The evolution of local and long-distance trading networks; the formation and disintegration of states; the development of unique cultural traditions and the assimilation of foreign ideas; changing relationships among governing officials, landowning elites, merchant communities, peasants, serfs, and slaves—this and much more has been the stuff of history for the peoples of the premodern world.

In addition, the concept of modernization sometimes seems to suggest that old and new ways of life have been fundamentally incompatible and that as modern elements such as scientific outlooks, railroads, and factories proliferated, everything traditional receded and was eventually overwhelmed or replaced. This seems hardly an accurate portrayal of the way change has occurred over the past several centuries, in Europe or anywhere else. Representative political bodies such as the English Parliament began in feudal times as assemblies of landed nobles but have adapted in many ways to changing circumstances and have become modern democratic institutions. Nor have traditional religions inevitably declined as modernization took place, as evidenced by the resurgence of Islam in Iran and elsewhere. In fact, some elements of the modern technology of communication and transportation may in fact foster older religious values. In India the printing press has made possible far wider distribution of the Hindu scriptures than ever before, the train has carried far more people to the holy places, and television has allowed millions to enjoy filmed versions of traditional religious epics. Many scholars have suggested that the authoritarianism of the former Soviet political system was in fact a continuation into modern times of qualities associated with tsarist Russia. Thus, traditional features may survive, though not unchanged, and even be strengthened as they come into contact with modern forces and take on new functions. The emphasis on modern change must not blind us to the reality of historical continuities or to the subtle blendings of old and new.

Finally, we might question the extent to which 1500 represents the beginning of a distinctively modern era in world history. In marking the fateful encounter of the Eastern and Western hemispheres, previously isolated from one another, 1500 is surely a date of world historical importance. But widespread connections among the great civilizations of the Afro-Eurasian world began well before that date, forged by Arabs, Turks, Mongols, and Chinese. And the real distinctiveness of Europe—its Industrial Revolution—took shape well after 1500 in the late eighteenth century.

Thus the sharp distinctions reflected in the terms *traditional* and *modern,* and symbolized by the date 1500, may distort our view of the past. At the very least, we need to use these terms and this date with great care, recognizing that the organizing concepts we employ can mislead as well as inform.

Ethnocentric Judgments

Since North Americans are among the most modern of peoples, we tend to assume that what is modern is "good" because it represents "progress," and that obstacles to progress are "bad." But the Nazi death camps were just as modern as the Volkswagen, and both were products of Germany in the 1930s. Nuclear weapons of mass destruction are no less rooted in modern science and technology than is the polio vaccine or space exploration. Rather than viewing the process of modern development itself as good or bad, we may see it as providing human societies with certain capacities that can be used in a variety of ways.

Even the positive outcomes of the modernizing process were frequently bought at a fearful cost. The industrialization that ultimately raised the material standard of life for most Europeans and North Americans was associated, especially at the beginning, with sweatshops, child labor, sprawling urban slums, and other social abuses. Those who are tempted to see the modern transformation as a smooth road to progress need only reflect on the history of Europe, in which the slave trade, bitter class conflict, violent revolution, colonial exploitation, genocide, and world war have figured prominently. And as we are discovering so vividly in the late twentieth century, the standard of living that modern industrial societies make possible also generates global warming, ozone depletion, species extinction, and massive deforestation.

But for people who are disenchanted with modern life, there is the opposite danger of romanticizing the past, of praising the traditional world as a means of damning the modern. Those who see the modern world as rootless, materialistic, disrespectful of nature, and riven with conflict may portray earlier societies as harmonious, spiritual, village-based communities on which modern ways were imposed from outside. Clearly, however, life in medieval Europe, old India, or early China was hardly idyllic, even if most people were unable to imagine alternatives. Poverty, disease, early death, oppression, and great inequalities were part and parcel of most premodern societies. It is not surprising that many people saw wonderful new opportunities in modern life. Thus neither romanticism about what is traditional nor an easy optimism about what is modern is helpful in sorting out the moral complexities of history during the past several hundred years. These ambiguities, in fact, provide much of the basis for historical argument and debate.

Becoming Like Us? Convergence and Divergence in Modern History

Western thinking about its modern transformation has often assumed that all of the world's societies were moving in the same direction and becoming "more like us." A well-known book by W. W. Ros-

The jarring discontinuities and contrasts of modern life are reflected in this scene from India in 1934. *Visual Studies Workshop*

tow, *The Stages of Economic Growth* (1960), suggests that the whole world has been moving toward an industrial economy with high mass consumption, although not all societies are at the same stage of this modernizing process.[2] Certainly the desire for economic growth is almost universal and governments everywhere stake their popularity on their ability to promote it. The economic success of East Asian societies such as Japan, South Korea, and Taiwan point to the possibilities of substantial economic development outside of the Western world, as do the growing industrial sectors of Brazil, India, and China. Many of these developing countries have substantial middle classes in which secular and materialistic values play a prominent role. The collapse of communism and the corresponding acceptance of free-market economics and democratic politics in many countries provide further support for the idea that human societies are converging toward a model first developed in Europe and North America. Furthermore, the spread of European languages, religion, educational systems, and ideologies (to say nothing of American movies, Coca-Cola, and blue jeans) has persuaded some that the world is becoming culturally westernized as well as economically modernized.

But there is another side to the story. Critics of this "convergence" approach point to the enormous economic gap that has opened up in recent centuries between the rich countries of the North and the impoverished countries of the South. They argue that, at least in economic terms, the world has become more divided and unequal than ever before. To explain this "global rift" or North-South divide, some scholars have come to see the historical circumstances of Third World development as being very different from those that accompanied the European and American experience.

In western Europe, an increasingly productive capitalist agriculture provided generally ample food supplies for most of its growing population, and the New World offered a promising outlet for millions who were frustrated or impoverished. The factories of the Industrial Revolution supplied employment for the rapidly increasing number of urban dwellers and a gradually improved standard of living for the great majority of people. An increasingly democratic political system in the nineteenth century allowed the lower classes to use political means to gain some share of Europe's rapidly growing wealth. None of this occurred easily, and it was accompanied by considerable social conflict, violence, and suffering. But new societies emerged to replace the old order that had been eroded during the transformation of the preceding four centuries.

By contrast, in many Afro-Asian-Latin American countries of the mid- to late twentieth century, modern medicine had sharply reduced the death rate and pushed the population growth rate far higher than any Europe had ever known, but without the social or agricultural changes necessary to feed the people adequately. Urbanization has proceeded rapidly, but without the modern industry needed to provide jobs for millions of migrants to the city. Nor were there empty lands or sparsely settled continents open to their migration. Thus, massive poverty, hunger, malnutrition, and unemployment now characterize many of these countries. It appears that many of them have acquired the secondary characteristics of modern societies (urbanization, literacy, population growth, and mass participation in national politics) but have not acquired its one primary feature—the capacity to improve the basic material conditions of their people through the application of modern science and technology. Even where substantial economic growth has occurred, it has often made little difference in the living standards of the poor majority. These conditions are described by such terms as *lopsided* or *unbalanced development, truncated modernization,* and *underdevelopment.* Whether they represent the permanent condition of developing countries or the early stages of a long process of modern development is a major question of our time.

Furthermore, development in these countries has occurred in a very different global context than that of Europe. The West, in short, modernized in a world it increasingly dominated. Thus it had the "advantages" of cheap labor, especially in the form of slaves; ready access to raw materials; secure markets for its goods; and outlets for its surplus population. African, Asian, and Middle Eastern societies, however, generally began their modern history under the external pressure of European imperialism. Until the mid-twentieth century, many of these societies were directly controlled by European colonizers and thus were not free to chart their own course to development. Moreover, the world economy with which they were increasingly involved operated to their disadvantage by limiting them to the export of a few primary products, opening them to exploitative foreign investment, and generally shaping their economies to the needs of the more developed countries of Europe and North America.

So important has the global framework seemed to some scholars that a school of thought known as *world system theory* has recently emerged. This approach, most clearly developed by the American sociologist Immanuel Wallerstein, seeks to explain the extent and type of development (or lack of it) in various countries largely in terms of their position in the world system of interconnected but unequal societies.[3] It suggests that the story line of modern history is not the progressive modernization of successive segments of humanity but the gradual growth of an international division of labor, or a capitalist world economy, the product of Europe's global expansion. That system funneled surpluses from peripheral societies to those at the core and thus operated to produce the development of some societies, primarily in Europe and North America. At the same time, the system generated underdevelopment and impoverishment in other societies, largely in Asia, Africa, and Latin America. This view highlights and seeks to explain the growing divergence among human societies in the modern world.

A variety of more recent developments also casts doubt on the assumptions of the convergence theory. The rise of Islamic fundamentalism in the Middle East and of Hindu fundamentalism in India represents in part a rejection of Western culture and an assertion of the continued relevance of specifically religious values. The bitter ethnic rivalries that have accompanied the collapse of communism in the former Soviet Union, Yugoslavia, and Czechoslovakia reflect both ancient historical differences and modern economic inequalities and point away from interdependence and convergence. A well-known American political scientist has recently argued that world politics are entering a new phase in which culturally based conflicts among nations representing different civilizations will become more significant than economic or ideological hostilities.[4] Finally, the growing awareness of ecological concerns has raised questions about the limits to growth imposed by the world's resource base and its environmental support systems. It appears unlikely that planet Earth could sustain on a universal basis the standard of living that most North Americans and Europeans enjoy.

All of this is grist for the mill of historical argument about the general direction or trajectory of modern world history. Whether we have been growing together or growing apart is an issue of considerable debate and controversy. In the chapters that follow we will trace the shared journeys of the world's many peoples over the past five hundred years, as well as the conflicted relationships and divergent paths that have accompanied their historical evolution.

Notes

1. William H. McNeill, *"The Rise of the West* after Twenty-Five Years," *Journal of World History* 1:1 (Spring 1990): 1–21.

2. W. W. Rostow, *The Stages of Economic Growth* (Cambridge: Cambridge University Press, 1960).

3. Immanuel Wallerstein, *The Modern World System,* 3 vols, (New York: Academic Press, 1974–).

4. Samuel P. Huntington, "The Clash of Civilizations," *Foreign Affairs* (Summer 1993): 22–49.

SUGGESTIONS FOR FURTHER READING

Abu-Lughod, Janet. *Before European Hegemony.* 1989. (Argues that the world system began well before 1500.)

Adas, Michael. *Islamic and European Expansion.* 1993. (A series of provocative essays that link and compare the expansion of Islamic and European civilizations.)

Bentley, Jerry H. *Old World Encounters.* 1993. (An account of cross-cultural contacts in the premodern world.)

Chirot, Daniel. *Social Change in the Modern Era.* 1986. (A sociologist's view of modern world history.)

Curtin, Philip. *Cross-Cultural Trade in World History.* 1984. (Discusses the problems of commerce without political control in a variety of historical settings.)

Huntington, Samuel et al. *The Clash of Civilizations? The Debate.* 1993. (A discussion about the growing importance of cultural conflict in global politics, set in a historical context.)

McNeill, William H. *The Rise of the West.* 1963. (A pioneering effort to encompass the entire world's history in a single volume by the acknowledged American leader of the world history movement.)

Stavrianos, L. S. *Global Rift.* 1981. (A sweeping effort to link the origins of contemporary Third World poverty to the expansion of a capitalist world economy.)

————. *Lifelines from Our Past.* 1992. (A "big picture" survey of all human history in 250 pages.)

Wolf, Eric R. *Europe and the People without History.* 1982. (An anthropologist's argument that no society can be studied without considering the impact of Europe's capitalist expansion.)

PART I

THE FIRST MODERN SOCIETIES: EUROPE SINCE 1500

Chapter 1: *Why Europe?*

Chapter 2: *"The Heavens and the Earth": Europe's Scientific Revolution*

Chapter 3: *The "Hidden Hand": Capitalism and the Transformation of Europe*

Chapter 4: *"The Great Acceleration": Industrialization and Social Change in Europe*

Chapter 5: *Collapse and Reconstruction: Europe in the Twentieth Century*

Suggestions for Further Reading: *Europe*

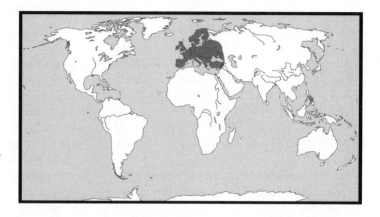

Unlike the development of agriculture, which probably occurred independently in several widely scattered parts of the world, the modern transformation began in one culture area, Europe, and spread so rapidly as to preclude its independent creation elsewhere. This is a basic fact of modern world history. Europe gained its significance as the most recent center of innovation and expansion in world history, one that produced an enormous global disturbance, upsetting established patterns of life and relationships among human societies.

Chapters 1–5 recount the essential features of this story. We begin with the obvious question in Chapter 1, "Why Europe?" What was it about the societies that developed on the far-western tip of the Eurasian landmass that allowed them to make the innovations that have proved so fateful for the entire human community in recent centuries?

Chapters 2–4 examine the revolutionary break-throughs that together constituted Europe's modern transformation: the rise of a scientific understanding of the world; the growth of a capitalist economic system and an increasingly democratic political system; and the development of an enormously productive industrial technology. But despite its remarkable successes, Europe's modern social order was fragile, vulnerable, and riven with conflict. Chapter 5 details its collapse in the twentieth century amid economic depression and thirty years of war (or preparation for it), as well as Europe's subsequent reconstruction and fundamentally altered position in the world community.

Chapter 1
Why Europe?

The sea which stretches beyond the country of the Slavs . . . is not frequented by any ship or boat and no products are exported from it. Likewise, the Western Ocean, where the Fortunate Islands are situated, has not been explored by any navigators and does not supply any objects for consumption.[1]

Written by a ninth-century Persian geographer living in the heart of the Muslim world, this unflattering description of the British Isles, France, and Germany indicates that Western Europe, not yet discovered by civilized people, produced nothing of interest to them. The geographer's assessment was not far off the mark, for Europe before 1000 C.E. possessed little if anything resembling organized states, had almost no large towns or cities, participated only infrequently in long-distance trading networks, and had few literate people. It lacked, in short, most of the characteristics usually associated with those complex societies called civilizations.

Yet by the sixteenth century this relatively unknown and backward part of the world made even the proud and ancient Chinese Empire take notice. In 1517, one Chinese official remarked with surprise, upon first encountering European ships and weapons, "The westerns are extremely dangerous because of their artillery. No weapon ever made since memorable antiquity is superior to their cannon."[2]

Europe's transformation from obscurity, isolation, and backwardness to wealth, power, and global dominance is surely one of the great surprises of world history. A survey of the world in the centuries immediately following 1000 C.E. would have suggested the Islamic Middle East as a more likely candidate for world leadership. Islam, after all, had expanded rapidly from its birthplace in seventh-century Arabia to conquer the ancient civilizations of the Middle East, and from there it spread to India, Africa, and southern Europe. In 1529 the Muslim Turks were laying siege to Vienna, in the very heart of Europe.

And China too would certainly have seemed a better prospect than Europe for global dominance. Its apparent advantages included a large and highly centralized state and, from the tenth to the fourteenth centuries, such impressive scientific and technological progress that it appeared to be on the threshold of an industrial revolution. The Chinese economy was highly commercialized, and both state-run and private industry developed large-scale production in salt, pottery, ironware, brewing, and cotton textiles. By 1160, the armaments industry, using techniques of standardized mass production, was producing more than three million weapons annually for an army of more than a million. In the fifteenth century, China launched a series of maritime expeditions in the Indian Ocean that made contemporary Portuguese voyages in the Atlantic look puny by comparison. Elsewhere, in India, the Middle East, and parts of Africa, there were prosperous merchant communities, extensive patterns of long-distance trade, and surges of economic growth. The impulses toward growth, development, and expansion were certainly not confined to Europe.

But nowhere else did these impulses lead to the kind of economic, scientific, and technological transformations that took place in Europe after 1500. From what sources and historical circumstances did Europe's extraordinary dynamism derive?

The Rise and Fall of the "Old" West: 500 B.C.E.–1000 C.E.

Modern Europeans and Americans have traditionally sought their deepest roots in the classical Greco-Roman and Christian world of ancient Western civilization, which flourished for nearly a millennium, from roughly 500 B.C.E. to 500 C.E., in the Mediterranean basin. There the early Greeks celebrated the powers of the human mind and spirit, sought to understand the world without reference to the gods, and developed the classical ideals of moderation, balance, order, and dignity of the individual. But if the Greeks achieved cultural magnificence, their inability to overcome the incessant conflicts among their staunchly independent city-states ultimately made them vulnerable to incorporation in Rome's emerging empire. The Romans imposed centralized political authority on the lands surrounding the Mediterranean Sea and developed the arts of law, administration, and military organization necessary for governing the diverse peoples of the empire (see Map 1.1). The rise and spread of Christianity within the Roman Empire provided a new vehicle for spiritual exploration in the idea of a God who loved, suffered, and actively

cared for his children. It also injected the notion of human equality, at least at the spiritual level, into a highly stratified Roman world and developed an organization, the Catholic church, that lasted far longer than the empire itself.

The Roman Empire, like many empires before it, fell or, perhaps more accurately, disintegrated, under the twin pressures of economic stagnation and repeated invasion. The conventional date marking its collapse is 476 C.E., when Emperor Romulus Augustulus was deposed by a barbarian war leader, one of many who had been invading the empire for centuries. In fact, it was only the western half of the empire that fell; the eastern half, later known as the Byzantine Empire, lasted another thousand years until conquered by the Turks in 1453.

But in the West the disintegration of Roman authority after 500 C.E. brought dramatic changes. Pop-

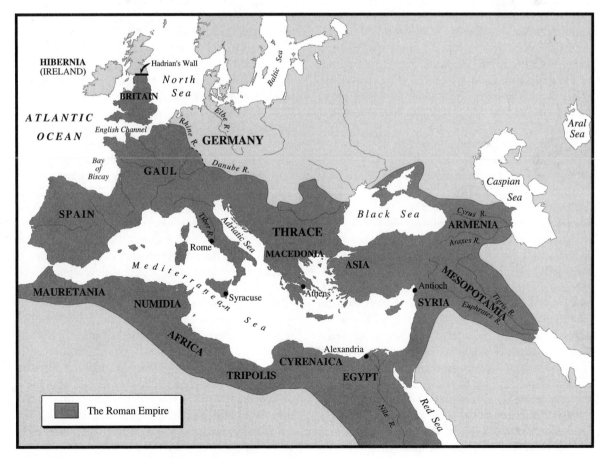

MAP 1.1 The Roman Empire, 100 C. E.

ulation declined sharply; urban life virtually disappeared; trade dried up; land under cultivation contracted while forest, marshland, and wasteland expanded; literacy expired, except within the church; and Europe's connection with the larger world system sharply contracted. What historians refer to as the European Middle Ages (500–1500 C.E.) began with the disappearance of much that had characterized civilized life under Roman rule. Only in southern cities, in surviving monuments, and in the Catholic church were there visible reminders of the cultural and organizational achievements of the classical age.

What was remarkable, however, was not so much that the Roman Empire fell but that it was never reconstructed. Here the contrast with the Chinese Empire is instructive. The Han Dynasty, which governed China during much of the Roman era, was itself subject to barbarian invasions, internal conflict, and the collapse of centralized government. But after some 250 years of chaos and disunity, the Sui Dynasty in the late sixth century reestablished imperial authority and political unity. Not so in the West. Despite the temporary success of the great warrior-emperor Charlemagne around 800 C.E., Europe has never since approached the degree of unity imposed by the Roman Empire. This failure, however, broke the hold of the past and forced the creation of new ways of life.

What replaced Roman authority in Europe was a social and political system called *feudalism*. Feudal society was highly fragmented and decentralized, consisting of thousands of independent, self-sufficient, and largely isolated landed estates or manors in which power—political, economic, and social—was exercised by a warrior elite of land-owning lords. In the constant competition of the early Middle Ages, lesser lords and knights swore allegiance to greater lords, thus becoming their "vassals," and frequently received lands and booty in return for military service. Such reciprocal ties between the superior and subordinate were also apparent at the bottom of the social hierarchy. Serfs, bound to their masters' estates as peasant laborers, owed various payments and services to the lord of the manor in return for a small family farm and such protection as the lord could provide. In a violent and insecure world adjusting to the absence of Roman authority, the only security available to many indi-

viduals or families lay in those communities where the ties of kin, manor, and church constituted the primary human loyalties.

Starting Over: The Making of "New" Europe, 1000–1300

Only after 1000 C.E. did the institutions of civilized society—cities, a more complex division of labor, long-distance trade, and centralized political authority—begin to reappear in Europe. When they did, leadership was often in the hands of Germanic peoples, recently converted to Christianity but otherwise touched only lightly if at all by Roman civilization. This new civilization extended well beyond the Mediterranean basin that had housed the Roman Empire; it incorporated the lands of northern and western Europe, which the Romans had seen as the remote and inhospitable territory of the barbarians.

It is difficult to say exactly what triggered the growth of this new civilization after 1000 C.E. For the preceding three hundred years, Europe had been subject to repeated invasions from most every direction: Muslim raids from the south, Magyar invasions from the east, and devastating Viking incursions from the north. But by the year 1000 these invasions had largely ceased, and it may be that the greater security and stability that came with relative peace opened the way to reestablishing a European civilization. The climate also seemed to cooperate. Studies of Alpine glaciers reveal a generally warming trend after 750 C.E., reaching its peak in the eleventh and twelfth centuries. This favorable climatic change opened new areas to agricultural development and temporarily permitted, for example, the cultivation of grapevines as far north as England.

Whatever may have launched the growth of Europe, the signs of expansion and new life were evident everywhere after roughly 1000. The population of Europe grew from perhaps 30 to 35 million in 1000 C.E. to about 80 million in 1340 C.E. With more people, many new lands had to be opened for cultivation. Great lords and religious orders such as the Cistercians organized new villages on what had recently been only forest or wasteland.

The increased production associated with agricultural expansion stimulated a renewal of long-distance trade. One center of commercial activity lay in northern Europe, from England to the Baltic coast, and involved the exchange of wood, beeswax, furs, rye, wheat, salt, cloth, and wine. Another major trading network centered on northern Italian towns, including Florence, Genoa, and Venice. Their trading partners were the more advanced civilizations of Islam and Byzantium, and the primary objects of the trade included the silks, drugs, precious stones, and spices of Asia. At great trading fairs, particularly those held in the Champagne area of France, near Paris, merchants from northern and southern Europe met to exchange the products of their respective areas, such as northern woolens for Mediterranean spices. Thus the self-sufficient communities of the Dark Ages began to forge commercial bonds among themselves.

At the same time, the newly emerging European civilization began to reintegrate itself with the intercommunicating zone or world system that connected the peoples of the Afro-Eurasian world, from the Mediterranean Sea to the Pacific Ocean. Europe gained a great deal from these renewed contacts—intellectual stimulation from Arab universities, techno-logical innovations from China, commercial opportunities in the Middle East and beyond. It is no accident that Europe's revival as a center of civilized life and its reconnection with the larger world system occurred simultaneously.

Associated with these developments was the growth of towns, which sprang up at trading crossroads, fortifications, and cathedral sites all over Europe. Some had only a few hundred people, but others grew much larger. In the early 1300s, London had about 40,000 people and Paris approximately 80,000; Venice, by the end of the century, could boast perhaps 150,000. These towns gave rise to and attracted new groups of people, particularly merchants, bankers, artisans, and university-trained professionals such as lawyers, doctors, and scholars. Many of these groups, including university professors and students, organized themselves into guilds to regulate their respective professions. In doing so, they introduced a new and more productive division of labor into European society.

A final sign of Europe's emerging civilization lay in the growth of territorial states with effective institutions of government commanding the loyalty, or at least the obedience, of their subjects. Since the disintegration of the Roman Empire, the loyalties of Europeans had focused on the family, the manor, or the religious community but seldom on the state. Great lords may have been recognized as kings, but their authority was extremely limited and was exercised through a complex network of feudal relationships including earls, counts, barons, and knights, who often felt little obligation to do the king's bidding. But in the twelfth and thirteenth centuries, the nominal monarchs of Europe gradually and painfully began to consolidate their authority, and the outlines of French, English, Spanish, and other lesser states began to appear (see Map 1.2.) In Italy, city-states predominated as urban areas grew wealthy and powerful, whereas the Germans remained loyal to a large number of small principalities within the Holy Roman Empire. Royal courts and state bureaucracies were established, and groups of professional administrators appeared. Within many of these new states representative assemblies, variously called parliament, *cortes,* diet, or estates-general, provided the great nobles, church leaders, and wealthy merchants an opportunity to influence the new monarchs and to limit

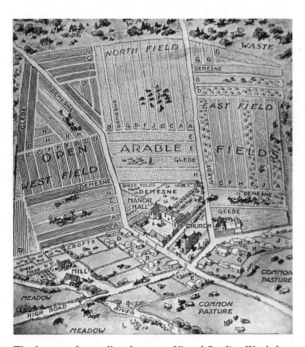

The layout of a medieval manor. *Visual Studies Workshop*

MAP 1.2 The Major States of Europe, c. 1360

their power, largely by giving or withholding financial support. These were certainly no democracies, but the principle of wider participation in political affairs—"what touches all should be approved by all"—represented a unique and important dimension of medieval government. It created a closer connection between rulers and at least some of the ruled than existed in many other societies.

Thus, the three centuries between 1000 and 1300 gave rise to the new institutions and culture of modern Europe. Yet civilization had emerged many times before—in ancient Egypt and Mesopotamia, in China and India, in Greece and Rome, in parts of Africa and the Western Hemisphere. What, then, was unique about the process in Europe after 1000 C.E.? Why were the barriers to innovation and economic growth apparently lower there than in other major civilizations? How did Europe develop the momentum of growth that allowed it to recover from sharp setbacks in the fourteenth century? Certainly no one feature of Europe's new civilization was unique. But the combination of features was, and it is this unique combination that best explains Europe's dramatic growth after 1500.

Sources of Growth: The Roots of Modern Europe

From a geographical perspective, there developed two Europes. The Mediterranean area, consisting of Spain, southern France, Italy, Greece, and the Balkans, was the heartland of classical Greco-Roman civilization. North of the Pyrenees, Alps, and Balkan mountains lay the lands of the emerging European civilization. Here the vast, fan-shaped plain stretching from southern France across central Europe and on into Russia was crossed by several easily navigable rivers, including the Loire, Seine, Rhine, Elbe, Vistula, Danube, and Dnieper. Together with a heavily indented coastline, these rivers ensured that most areas of Europe had ready access to the sea and potential for internal transportation and communication. The Rhine–Danube system, for example, offered an almost unbroken corridor between the North Sea and the Black Sea. Settlement patterns that separated small and clustered communities by large areas of forest and wasteland set the stage for a civilization with many economic links but little overall political integration.

The north–south distinction in Europe was visible in several ways (see Map 1.3). The rich, heavy, moist, and often virgin soils of the north contrasted sharply with the thin, light, and frequently exhausted soils of Italy and Greece, which had been heavily worked for centuries. When technological breakthroughs made it possible to drain and cultivate these rich northern lands, they were far more productive than the farming areas of the south. Furthermore, rainfall in the north was both plentiful and regular in contrast to the much greater seasonal variations in the south. Thus, rivers in the north ran deep the year round, making it possible to rely on them to power water mills, whereas the scarcity of such streams in the south limited the development of this important technology. And since northern Europe did not need to depend on irrigation, it was not vulnerable to natural or human destruction of its waterworks.

The new civilization of northwestern Europe after 1000 C.E. was the northern-most in world history. Its harsh winters killed many of the infectious microorganisms that so infested Asian populations and limited their labor productivity. Cooler weather and winter snow cover likewise slowed the disintegration of humus, or decayed vegetable matter, thereby providing nutrients for plants and producing richer, heavier, and far more durable soils.

One other environmental factor may have distinguished Europe from Asia: the former's more limited exposure to natural disasters such as earthquakes, volcanic eruptions, violent storms, floods, droughts, disease, and fires. Though all premodern societies were largely at the mercy of nature and life was everywhere precarious, one study notes that "Europe's overall losses seem[ed] markedly less serious than those of Asia."[3] In these environmental features lay the roots of Europe's greater accumulation of wealth as compared to the older but less productive centers of civilization in Asia.

The Advantages of Backwardness: Europe as a Late Bloomer

Despite its environmental advantages, Europe was late in making use of them. The newest of the world's civilizations did not emerge until after 1000 C.E. By contrast, Chinese and Indian civilizations originated well before 1000 B.C.E., and the tradition of urban and civilized life in the Middle East and Egypt was even more ancient. But unlike the older civilizations, whose patterns of life had long since hardened into established tradition, Europe was a frontier area, and its new settlers proved remarkably flexible and adaptable. They were open to ideas and techniques from other, more advanced parts of the world. "In our time," wrote a twelfth-century European scholar, "it is in Toledo [a Spanish city] that the teaching of the Arabs . . . is offered to the crowds. I hastened there to listen to the teaching of the wisest philosophers of this world."[4] Few Chinese scholars until the late nineteenth century would have been so receptive to ideas coming from outside China.

Despite Europeans' belief in Christianity as the one true religion, they eagerly embraced scientific treatises from the Arabs, philosophical and artistic ideas from the pagan Greeks, mathematical concepts from India, and the compass, gunpowder, and printing from China. They recognized the older civilizations of the East as superior to their own and sought

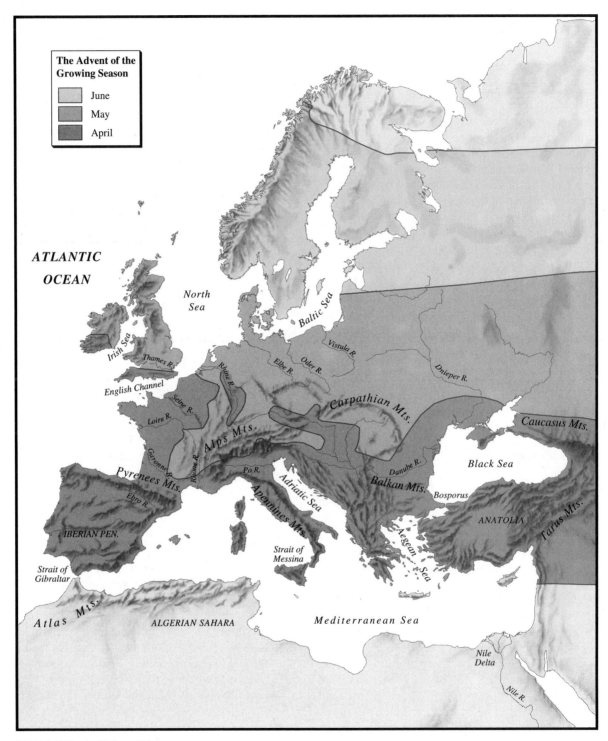

The Advent of the Growing Season

June

May

April

ATLANTIC OCEAN

North Sea

Baltic Sea

Irish Sea

Thames R.

English Channel

Seine R.

Loire R.

Rhine R.

Elbe R.

Oder R.

Vistula R.

Dnieper R.

Carpathian Mts.

Caucasus Mts.

Garonne R.

Pyrenees Mts.

Rhone R.

Alps Mts.

Po R.

Danube R.

Balkan Mts.

Black Sea

Bosporus

Ebro R.

Adriatic Sea

Apennines Mts.

ANATOLIA

Tarus Mts.

IBERIAN PEN.

Strait of Messina

Aegean Sea

Strait of Gibraltar

Atlas Mts.

ALGERIAN SAHARA

Mediterranean Sea

Nile Delta

Nile R.

MAP 1.3 Physical Map of Europe

out their wealth and wisdom. Being a latecomer thus had its advantages.

Working Women and Late Marriages

The flexibility of a European civilization not yet fully formed was evident in the place it accorded women, for although they nowhere approached equality with men, medieval women were "far more visible, vocal, and powerful than their sisters in antiquity."[5] This was particularly true regarding patterns of work. A less rigid sexual division of labor probably allowed an emerging Europe to tap the energy and skill of its women more fully than other established civilizations of the time.

Although most peasant women managed the household economy and worked in the fields, a substantial number of women among the rural nobility appear in the records of the ninth through the twelfth centuries as landowners in their own right. Approximately 10 percent to 12 percent of the land donated to the Catholic church by pious Christians seems to have come from women. Furthermore, the frequent absence of men for war or for opening up new lands meant that the woman of the manor exercised considerable administrative authority. The social prominence that women gained from these achievements was reflected in the frequency with which men, particularly in the eleventh century, identified themselves in legal papers by their maternal rather than paternal names.

Similarly, in the new towns of medieval Europe, the absence of rigid distinctions between male and female work allowed women a wider range of contribution to economic life than would later be the case. In twelfth-century Paris, for example, a list of one hundred occupations identified eighty-six as involving women workers, of which six were exclusively female. In England, women worked as silk weavers, hatmakers, tailors, brewers, and leather processers and were entitled to train female apprentices in some of these trades. In Frankfurt during the fourteenth century, about one-third of the crafts and trades were entirely female, another 40 percent were dominated by men, and the rest were open to both.

There were, of course, restrictions. Women were generally paid less than men for the same work on the grounds that they had fewer needs, and they were excluded from certain guilds. Fewer opportunities were available for women in trading than in craft production, but many women were active in small-scale local trade in food and clothing. Widows of great merchants sometimes continued their husbands' businesses, and one of them, Rose Burford, lent a large sum of money to the king of England to finance a war against Scotland in 1318.

But as the institutions of the new European civilization became more firmly established, restrictions on women increased. An early sign involved the practice of dowry. Among many European peoples, men had traditionally presented their brides with "morning gifts," which became the property of the women and were under their control. But by the mid-twelfth century in northern Italy, the flow of wealth was reversed, and women's families were expected to provide substantial gifts to the groom. These dowries, which grew larger over time, became a means of transferring capital among the great trading families of the growing commercial towns of Italy and restricted the wealth controlled by women. In addition, by the twelfth century fewer women landowners appeared in the legal documents, and by the fourteenth century more restrictions and bans on women in certain guilds and trades had become apparent. Women were being directed increasingly into domestic roles and away from more active participation in the public arena. The earlier centuries, when the new Europe was just taking shape, had presented the most opportunities for enterprising women, and their contributions may well have provided a crucial boost to a rapidly reviving Western civilization.

Yet the families to which women were increasingly restricted had certain qualities that may also have contributed to Europe's dynamic growth. One of these was an apparent preference for nuclear family units in which a newly married couple established their own home rather than living in an extended family with one or another set of parents and other relatives, as was common in most Asian societies. Some scholars suggest that this pattern may have extended back into the pre-Christian centuries. It has been clearly documented in western and central Europe long before the Industrial Revolution created modern pressures in that direction.

Also unique in European family life, at least north of the Alps and before the thirteenth century, were a much later age of marriage for both men and women and a much higher proportion of people who never married at all. In later centuries, girls began to marry in their mid- to late teens, but males continued to delay marriage until their mid-to-late twenties. Furthermore, a considerable number of people, perhaps as many as 15 percent to 20 percent, never married at all, partly, perhaps, because of the value placed on celibacy in European Christianity. In India, by contrast, teenage marriage was almost universal.

What impact did this have on the larger development of European civilization? Some have suggested that the pattern of marriage held down the European birthrate and thus ensured a higher per-capita income. This meant that Europeans, on the average, enjoyed a somewhat higher standard of living than their Asian counterparts and that more capital was available for investment. Although European travelers were impressed with the magnificence of Asian palaces, temples, and cities, they also noticed that ordinary people were less well fed, housed, and clothed than many of their own people. It seems likely, then, that the gap in wealth between Europeans and the rest of the world began to widen well before the Industrial Revolution and that European marriage patterns may have had a role in creating it.

Marriage patterns may also have been important in mobilizing European wealth for productive purposes. Late marriages meant a longer period of productive work without the responsibility of children and thus made saving easier, and savings stimulated demand for consumer goods as people prepared for marriage. In addition, the nuclear family may have fostered self-reliance and independence as couples made their own way in the world. Though these assumptions are difficult to prove, it seems likely that Europe's ability to mobilize the labor of its women together with its unique marriage and family patterns stimulated its economic growth.

"Countless Things Can Be Constructed": Europe's Technological Tradition

Europe's modern transformation was closely associated with its technological creativity, especially in the dramatic epoch of the Industrial Revolution in the eighteenth and nineteenth centuries. But the

This drawing from a twelfth-century German manuscript illustrates the rewards accruing to three kinds of women. Virgins, depicted in the top frame, reap the largest reward, whereas married women, in the bottom frame, reap the least. Widows, shown in the middle, are in between. *Reinisches Landsmuseum*

steam engine, the power loom, and the railroad were only the latest products of a technological tradition deeply embedded in European culture and representing one of the unique features of the new Europe. Plows, watermills, and elaborate mechanical clocks were just as characteristic of the Middle Ages as were churches and castles, which were themselves major technological feats.

By 1500, Europe's technological dynamism had revolutionized agriculture, industry, war, and sailing and had pushed Europe to the forefront of global technological development. This did not involve great bursts of technical inventiveness but a slow, unsystematic, yet steady accumulation of improved techniques, most of them developed by anonymous craftspeople and artisans. In fact, much of this growth was not, strictly speaking, invention at all but the adaptation of techniques first developed in Chinese, Indian, and Islamic societies. The new civilization of medieval Europe, remarkably curious and receptive to ideas from afar, was a great borrower.

Despite creativity in many fields, the Greeks and the Romans had shown little interest in mechanical technology; it was not until classical civilization had collapsed that European technological genius began to emerge. It first became apparent in agriculture as Europeans adapted to the very different environmental conditions north of the Alps in the several centuries following 500 C.E. They developed a heavy-wheeled plow, which could handle the dense soils of northern Europe far better than the light or "scratch" plow used in Mediterranean agriculture. To pull the plow, Europeans began to rely increasingly on horses rather than oxen and to use iron horseshoes and a more efficient collar, which probably originated in China or central Asia and could support much heavier loads. In addition, Europeans developed a new three-field system of crop rotation, which allowed considerably more land to be planted at any one time. Here were the technological foundations of an agricultural revolution that could support the growing population of a new European civilization, and especially its urban centers, far more securely than ever before.

Europeans also began to tap nonanimal sources of energy in a major way. The windmill, invented in Persia, was widely used in Europe by the twelfth and thirteenth centuries. The water-driven mill was even

more important. Though the Romans had used both largely to grind grain, their further development was limited because few streams flowed all year and many slaves were available to do the work. By the ninth century, however, watermills were rapidly becoming more evident in Europe. In 1086, England could boast 5,624 such mills, and in the early fourteenth century, a concentration of 68 mills dotted a one-mile stretch of the Seine near Paris. The monasteries of Europe, especially those associated with the Cistercian order, played a major role in pioneering the use of water power, for it freed the monks for prayer and meditation and contributed to monastic self-sufficiency.

In addition to grinding grain, the mills provided power for sieving flour, tanning hides, fulling cloth, making beer, sawing wood, and manufacturing iron. The making of paper, a Chinese invention that came to Europe via Islamic civilization, was mechanized by use of water power as soon as it reached the West in the thirteenth century. Devices such as cranks, flywheels, camshafts, and complex gearing mechanisms, when combined with water or wind power, enabled medieval Europeans to revolutionize production in several industries and to break with the ancient tradition of depending almost wholly on animal or human muscle as sources of energy. So intense was the interest of European artisans and engineers in tapping mechanical sources of energy that a number of them experimented with perpetual-motion machines, an idea borrowed from Indian philosophers.

The use of a "heavy" plow. Note the presence of both a man and a woman in the field. *Picture Collection, The Branch Libraries, The New York Public Library*

Technological borrowing was also evident in the arts of war. Gunpowder was invented in China around 1000 C.E., and its military applications were pioneered and spread by the Mongols. But Europeans by the fourteenth century proved able to build bigger and better guns than their Asian counterparts. By 1500, they had the most advanced arsenals in the world. Furthermore, advances in shipbuilding and navigational techniques, including the magnetic compass, sternpost rudder, and adaptations of the Arab lateen sail, which enabled vessels to sail against the wind, provided the foundation for European mastery of the seas.

The fifteenth-century development of printing with movable type, a practice of Chinese origin, combined with the mechanized production of paper and the invention of eyeglasses to enlarge the audience for printed materials. Prior to these discoveries, books had been so expensive that only a few very wealthy people could afford them. The significance of more widespread literacy for accumulating and spreading knowledge can hardly be overestimated.

Europe's passion for technology was reflected in its culture and ideas as well as in its machines. About 1260, the English scholar and Franciscan friar Roger Bacon wrote of the possibilities he foresaw and in doing so expressed the confident spirit of the age:

> Machines of navigation can be constructed, without rowers . . . which are borne under the guidance of one man at a greater speed than if they were full of men. Also a chariot can be constructed, that will move with incalculable speed without any draught animal. . . . Also flying machines may be constructed so that a man may sit in the midst of the machine turning a certain instrument by means of which wings artificially constructed would beat the air after the manner of a bird flying . . . and there are countless other things that can be constructed.[6]

The great Renaissance artist Leonardo da Vinci was obsessed with machinery and made numerous drawings of mechanical objects. During these centuries, intricate mechanical clocks were created and installed in churches and public buildings, signifying a new, unnatural view of time divided into artificially equal units of hours and minutes. Soon European philosophers began to think of the world as an intricate mechanism, of the human body as a machine, and of God as a "divine clockmaker." The increasingly mechanical outlook of the Middle Ages provided the background for the scientific revolution of the seventeenth century and later.

Describing Europe's technological creativity is easier than explaining it. Some scholars have pointed to the absence of slavery, the shortage of labor, and the frontier conditions of an emerging civilization to account for Europe's extraordinary interest in technical labor-saving innovations. Others have suggested that the key lies more in the attitudes toward nature fostered by the Christian culture of Europe.

Christianity, Technology, and Science

Was there something about the Christian culture of medieval Europe that better stimulated technological and scientific development than the Hinduism or Buddhism of Asia or the polytheism of classical Mediterranean civilization? With its roots in Judaism, Christianity had an understanding of time, of matter, and of human life that in some respects focused attention on the material world more sharply than many other religious traditions. The idea of a distinct creation, marking the beginning of history, and of a final judgment, marking its end, suggests that history moves not in endlessly repetitive cycles, as in Hinduism, but toward a destination that God has planned. In this linear view of time lies the intellectual foundation of the idea of progress that has been so important in the modern Western world.

Creation also implies that the world of nature and matter is real; Hinduism and Buddhism, on the other hand, perceive it as an illusion, a distraction from spiritual reality. In the creation story of the Judeo-Christian scriptures, "God saw everything he had made, and behold, it was very good." Here was a religious affirmation of the importance of the material world. Furthermore, to Christians, nature was a separate and distinct reality created by a single God who existed apart from it. Unlike the pagan animism of the ancient world, nature was not a mother-goddess; nor was it necessary to placate gods and spirits linked to streams, mountains, and trees. This dualistic view of the world (God and nature as distinct realities) meant that nature was open to human investigation and manipulation. "By destroying pagan animism," writes Lynn White, a historian of technology,

"Christianity made it possible to exploit nature in a mood of indifference to the feelings of natural objects."[7] And since the natural order had been designed and constructed by a divine artisan, it could be understood by people who were, they believed, made in his image.

Beyond the possibility of understanding nature, the Christian tradition justified human domination over nature. In the biblical creation story, God commands Adam to "fill the earth and subdue it and have dominion . . . over every living thing." The impressive achievements of old China and the Islamic world show clearly that other cultural traditions could likewise nurture technological and scientific development. But in terms of Europe, it is worth considering White's argument that Christianity created a cultural climate that encouraged an aggressive and manipulative attitude toward nature and thus fostered technological development.

Can the same be said for science—the effort to understand rather than manipulate the world of nature? From the fall of Rome to about 1000 C.E., it would be difficult to find much real attention to the physical world within teachings of the Christian church, which directed people's attention to matters of sin, salvation, and the comforts of life after death. It was enough for most people to know that God had revealed religious truth in the Bible and that it was made available through the rituals, texts, and practices of the church.

In the late eleventh century, however, the intellectual life of Christian Europe slowly began to change, particularly among the small group of literate clerics. An early sign of this change occurred when the students of a monastic school in France asked their teacher, Anselm, to provide them a proof for the existence of God based solely on reason, without using the Bible or other sources of divine revelation. Over the next several centuries a renewed interest in rational inquiry became widespread among the learned elite of the church. Stimulating this intellectual awakening more than anything else was the translation into Latin of the writings of the ancient Greek thinkers, such as Ptolemy, Euclid, and, especially, Aristotle. After the collapse of the Roman Empire, many of their works had been preserved by the new Islamic civilization and, together with the ideas of Indian and Persian thinkers, had stimulated among Arab intellectuals re-

markable work in astronomy, geography, medicine, mathematics, and chemistry. Much of this Arab science was likewise translated into Latin and provided an enormous boost to Europe's dawning intellectual life.

The assimilation of Greek and Arab learning took place largely in the new universities of twelfth- and thirteenth-century Europe, which were often situated in bustling commercial cities. It was an exciting time of argument, new ideas, and a belief that great progress was possible. To an English monk named Bartholomew, Paris of the thirteenth century was the Athens of Europe, "the mother of the liberal arts and of letters, the nurse of philosophers and all manner of science."[8]

A new interest in rational thought was applied first and foremost to theology, the "queen of the sciences" to medieval thinkers. Anselm, the great eleventh-century philosopher, theologian, and archbishop of Canterbury, argued, "We must strive to understand what we believe." Earlier thinkers had been content to know what they believed. The general problem that faced these theologians was that of reconciling the ideas of pagan Greek philosophy with those of Christianity, a task that involved many highly contentious questions. Although they often disagreed about the answers, these Christian thinkers were united in believing that human reason could illuminate theological issues without contradicting the revealed truth of their religion. William of Conches lashed out at those who opposed the use of reason: "You poor fools. God can make a cow out of a tree, but has he ever done so? Therefore show some reason why a thing is so or cease to hold that it is so."[9]

The early European intellectuals also applied their newly discovered confidence in human reason to the world of nature. By the mid-twelfth century, a number of Christian scholars in the new universities of Europe had come to see the natural order as operating largely by itself, without God's direct intervention. To investigate this domain, Robert Grosseteste, chancellor of Oxford University, developed a method of inquiry surprisingly similar to that of modern science. It included the framing of a hypothesis, the use of mathematical analysis and experiment, and the investigation of strictly limited problems. On this basis, serious work was accomplished in the field of optics (especially in the problem of the rainbow), in the study of motion, and in understanding magnetism.

However, there was opposition by those who held that rational inquiry represented a threat to the faith. A movement to reform the monasteries of Christian Europe, led by Bernard of Clairvaux, focused attention on personal spiritual experience and campaigned against an overemphasis on reason to penetrate divine mysteries. In 1277, the bishop of Paris issued a condemnation of 219 "execrable errors," many of which derived from Greek and Arab sources and were regarded by the bishop as incompatible with Christian orthodoxy. Despite the resistance of the official church, the intellectual developments of the Middle Ages made it clear that some thinkers found human rationality an aid rather than a threat to the faith and were ready to apply it to an understanding of nature. It was on this medieval foundation that

Copernicus, Galileo, and Newton would build the momentum for the scientific revolution of the seventeenth century.

The "Failure" of Empire: Europe's Political Framework

Another clue to Europe's modern transformation lies in its political system. Unlike the great cultures of the Middle East and Asia, Europe never developed into a single, centralized empire. Rather, the extreme political fragmentation of feudalism gave way to a system of competing states (including France, Spain, England, Sweden, Prussia, the Netherlands, and Poland, among others). This was very different from the more unified political structures of the Ottoman Empire in the Middle East, the Mughal Empire of India, and the Ming and Qing dynasties of imperial China. Europe's political consolidation went just so far and then stopped. Of course, there were those who tried to re-create something of the ancient unity of the Roman Empire: Charlemagne in the ninth century; the Habsburg ruler Charles V in the sixteenth; Louis XIV of France in the late seventeenth; Napoleon in the early nineteenth; and Hitler in the twentieth. But none succeeded. Geographical barriers, ethnic and linguistic diversity, and the shifting balances of power among its many states prevented the emergence of a single empire in Europe.

As a result, no single authority could prevent change or impose disastrous policies. A Chinese emperor of the fifteenth century could (and did) effectively stop large-scale maritime voyages into the Pacific and Indian oceans, but there was no one in Europe with similar authority. Once started, European expansion was relentlessly driven by political competition. In its economic and technological development as well, Europe's competing states provided "an insurance against . . . stagnation"[10] as innovations spread rapidly from one state to another. The agents of such diffusion were often skilled refugees such as Huguenots or Jews who, oppressed in or expelled from their own countries, could find refuge in a rival state.

Such a system clearly had its drawbacks. The Hundred Years' War between France and England

Europe's fascination with technology and the religious motivation for investigating the world are apparent in this medieval portrayal of God as an engineer, measuring out the world with a huge compass. *The Granger Collection*

(1337–1453); the religious wars of the sixteenth and seventeenth centuries; and the nationalist wars of the twentieth century represent the economic waste and human cost of endemic rivalry. Yet Europe's sharp political divisions never stopped, at least not for long, its economic progress. Capital, labor, and goods found their way around political barriers, and Europe became from the Middle Ages on an increasingly unified market area. Furthermore, the common assumptions of Christian culture and the use of Latin and, later, French by the literate elite fostered communication across political borders. Europe's multi-state system thus provided enough competition to be stimulating but also sufficient order and unity to allow economic endeavors to prosper.

The evolution of particular states within that system also served to minimize barriers to economic progress, at least in comparison to the great empires of Asia, and in some cases to promote it actively. In all of the great Asian empires, wealthy merchant groups had developed on the basis of an active commercial economy. But they operated in political systems that restricted their activity and provided little security for their property. In China, a powerful state favored the landowners over merchants, monopolized the salt and iron industries, and actively controlled and limited merchant activity. In the Muslim empires of India, Persia, and Turkey, despotic governments frequently confiscated merchant property and so encouraged wealthy traders to hide their wealth rather than display it by investing in expanding enterprises. In none of these empires did merchant groups have much political influence or social status. Thus, surplus production wrung from the peasantry was squandered in the creation of elaborate bureaucratic and military establishments and in the extravagant luxuries of the elite rather than in productive enterprises.

In the emerging states of Europe from the twelfth to the eighteenth centuries, a quite different situation prevailed, and it was rooted in the initial weakness of the state in relation to major social groups. Kings had to contend with a powerful nobility that was reluctant to pay taxes, and with an assertive church that frequently refused to recognize their authority. In this three-way struggle for power, urban-based merchants had a degree of political leverage almost completely missing in Asian empires. In their efforts to curb the power and independence of the feudal nobil-

ity, the monarchs of medieval Europe came to depend on the resources of the merchant communities in the new commercial cities. Wealthy merchants were a ready source of cash, eager to pay or lend money in return for royal favors promoting their trade. It soon became apparent that taxing merchant wealth was more profitable than confiscating it. For their part, the merchant communities welcomed the greater peace, security of property, and regularized legal system that came with the growth of the state.

By the seventeenth and eighteenth centuries, these states were providing a variety of valuable services, including the introduction of new industries and tariffs to protect them from foreign competition, the opening of new lands to settlement, the establishment of quarantine policies to deal with epidemics, and other measures to manage natural disasters. The uneasy alliance of merchant and monarch served to diminish chaos and unpredictability, the traditional enemies of the trader, and to provide for regular state revenues, the greatest need of the new kings. Nowhere else in Eurasia did such an arrangement prevail.

Free Cities and Urban Culture

Something quite remarkable was happening in the new states of medieval and early modern Europe: the economy was becoming partially independent of political authority, and its most dynamic element—the merchant class—was gaining a degree of economic freedom unknown in the rest of the world. The most dramatic expression of this lay in the new towns and cities that sprang up in Europe after the year 1000. In itself, the growth of towns was hardly unique, for urban centers had been a part of every major civilization. Thirteenth-century China, for example, was the most urbanized society in the world, with perhaps 10 percent of its population living in cities. But Chinese cities were simply a part of the empire. They had no special standing, and their inhabitants had no special rights or privileges. Like everyone else, they were subjects of the emperor.

In medieval Europe, however, the weakness and fragmentation of political authority allowed the emerging towns to demand, and to get, substantial "liberties" and to break free of certain feudal ties.

Many towns won the right to make and enforce their own local laws, to appoint their own officials, to hold regular markets, and to raise their own militias. Written charters, granted reluctantly by local lords or bishops, defined the legal rights of these new and largely independent towns. Some even secured the provision that serfs who remained in a town for "a year and a day" would be regarded as free of all feudal obligations.

Life was different in the towns. People regarded themselves as citizens rather than subjects and, in response to the hostility of the outside world, developed a sense of urban patriotism. Culture and values were likewise different. These urban dwellers or *bourgeoisie* were much more competitive and future-oriented than their rural counterparts; were concerned about the efficient use of time; and assumed a calculating, rational, and risk-taking attitude toward money.

Taking advantage of their freedom from oppressive political control, the merchants of medieval towns developed a unique set of business practices, including bills of exchange, checks, insurance, and various forms of partnership that served to transform accumulated wealth or savings into productive investment. Thus the autonomous towns of the Middle Ages nurtured the beginnings of European capitalism. Although the towns were later incorporated more fully into growing national states, the capitalist economy to which they had given birth came to dominate European society and to propel its modern transformation.

Nowhere were these trends more highly developed than in the energetic and wealthy cities of northern Italy, such as Venice, Florence, Milan, and Genoa. The economic basis of their prosperity lay in the international trade in luxury goods conducted with the older civilizations of Byzantium and Islam. To carry on its profitable role as a link in this trading network, Venice by 1400 C.E. had hundreds of large ships, thousands of smaller ones, and some twenty-eight thousand sailors. The great merchant families who controlled this trade invested some of their substantial profits in manufacturing industries, especially cloth and leather. By 1350, Florence employed some thirty thousand people, close to one-third of its population, in the manufacture of woolen cloth. The need to find profitable investment opportunities led these merchants into banking and moneylending as well. For several hundred years, northern Italy was the banker for all of Europe and, until the sixteenth century, was its most highly developed area.

Far more than the towns of northern Europe, Italian cities dominated the surrounding countryside. So prosperous, attractive, and powerful were these cities that feudalism was almost completely destroyed in northern Italy by the thirteenth century, and not until much later did centralized states emerge. With no real competition from feudal or state power, urban centers became fiercely independent city-states, small in area but very wealthy, largely dominated by great merchant families, and full of class conflict, careful financial calculation, wars with neighbors, and political intrigue.

Between 1350 and 1500 these cities also gave rise to the remarkable urban culture we know as the *Renaissance*. The term itself means "rebirth," and it reflected the belief of the wealthy elite that they were living in a wholly new era, far removed from the confined religious world of feudal Europe. Citizens of these cities sought inspiration in the literature of ancient Greece and Rome, not primarily to reconcile these writings with the ideas of Christianity, as the scholars of medieval universities had done, but to enjoy both the style and the content of these works on their own terms. The elite patronized great Renaissance artists such as Leonardo da Vinci, Michelangelo, and Raphael, whose paintings and sculptures were far more naturalistic, particularly in portraying the human body, than those of their medieval counterparts.

The themes of the Renaissance artists were no longer entirely religious but now included portraits and busts of well-known contemporary figures as well as scenes from ancient mythology. Heavily influenced by classical models, the artists were more interested in capturing the unique qualities of particular individuals and an accurate image of the physical world than in portraying symbols of eternal religious principles, even when their subject matter was explicitly religious. In its focus on the affairs of this world, Renaissance culture reflected the urban bustle and commercial preoccupations of the Italian cities. In its secularism, it represented a challenge to the otherworldliness of Christian culture. And in its individualism, it signaled the decline of a feudal society and the dawning of a capitalist economy.

Crisis, Renewal, and Overseas Expansion: 1350–1500

Although the major features of Europe's modern transformation—capitalism, science, technology, and the nation-state—had their roots in the centuries between 1000 and 1300, Europe's rise to global dominance did not occur on a single line of unbroken progress. The fourteenth century, in particular, was a time of severe crisis and social disaster. The most prominent feature of this troubled century—the plague or Black Death—was a result of Europe's growing integration with the world system. Carried by rats, the plague appeared in Europe from its Asian habitat in 1348, and within two years killed about twenty-five million people out of a population of eighty million. Between one-third and one-half of Europe's population was wiped out in the fourteenth century; not until the sixteenth century did it recover to the level of 1300. "[A] dead man," wrote Italian author Giovanni Boccaccio, "was then of no more account than a dead goat." It was not until the early eighteenth century that the plague completely disappeared from Europe.

Although the crisis of the fourteenth century produced tremendous social dislocations and suffering on an epic scale, it served to relieve Europe's overpopulation quickly and to increase its per-capita wealth. The plague had, after all, destroyed people, not goods or money. Since labor was scarce, peasants and the urban lower classes could demand higher wages and thus improve their position. The landowning nobility, dependent on fixed feudal payments, were hurt economically and looking for ways to regain their previous level of income. The higher cost of labor encouraged employers to use their workers more efficiently and to invest in labor-saving technology, such as larger and better-designed sailing ships. By the end of the fifteenth century, Europe's population started to climb again, and economic recovery had begun.

The events of the fourteenth century persuaded many Europeans to look farther afield for economic opportunities and resources, and the growth of their maritime technology made such expansion possible. Thus, Europe responded to crisis and economic decline by beginning that extraordinary pattern of overseas expansion that would become a central element in modern world history. The Portuguese led the way, and in a series of state-supported voyages after 1415, they pushed their way down the western coast of Africa. By the end of the fifteenth century, Vasco da Gama had rounded the southern tip of Africa and found his way to India. About this time, the Spanish sponsored the westward voyages of the Genoan navigator Christopher Columbus, who inadvertently came upon the New World. Europe's journey to global dominance had begun.

Europe's Religious Revolution: The Protestant Reformation

Both the Portuguese voyages of exploration and the Italian Renaissance are generally seen as marking Europe's transition from medieval to modern times. So too is the Protestant Reformation of the sixteenth century. It is fair to regard the Reformation as revolutionary, for it shattered the unity of the Christian church, which had for the previous one thousand years provided the cultural and organizational foundation of Western civilization. Furthermore, the faith the church proclaimed had provided answers to the most fundamental questions of life for impoverished peasants, wealthy nobles, and everyone in between. These answers were now called into question.

The Reformation began in 1517 when a German priest named Martin Luther publicly protested certain abuses of the Roman Catholic church. In itself, this was nothing new, for many people were critical of the luxurious life of the popes, the corruption and immorality of the clergy, the selling of indulgences said to remove the penalties for sin, and other aspects of church life and practice. What made Luther's protest potentially revolutionary, however, was its theological basis. A troubled and brooding man, anxious about his relationship with God, Luther had recently come to a new understanding of salvation: that it came through "faith alone." Neither the good works of the sinner nor the sacraments of the church had any bearing on the eternal destiny of the soul, for faith was a free gift of God, graciously granted to needy sinners. To Luther the source of these beliefs, and of religious authority in general, was not the teaching of the church but the Bible, interpreted according to the individual's conscience. All of this served to undermine the authority of the Catholic church generally and called into question the special position of the clerical hierarchy and of the pope in particular. In sixteenth-century Europe, this was the stuff of revolution.

Although Luther never intended it, his ideas ultimately provoked a massive schism within the Roman Catholic church, for they came to express a variety of political, economic, and social tensions. Kings and princes, many of whom had long disputed the political authority of the pope, found in these ideas a justification for their own independence and an opportunity to gain the lands and taxes previously held by

the church. In the Protestant idea that all vocations were of equal merit, middle-class urban dwellers found a new religious legitimacy for their growing role in society, since the Roman Catholic church was associated in their eyes with the rural and feudal world of aristocratic privilege. And for common people, offended by the corruption and luxurious living of bishops, abbots, and popes, the new religious ideas served to express their opposition to the entire social order, particularly in a series of German peasant revolts in the 1520s. Out of this social and religious upheaval sprang a variety of competing Protestant churches—Lutheran, Calvinist, Anglican, Anabaptist—all of them different but none giving allegiance to Rome or to the pope (see Map 1.4.)

In its profoundly religious attitude toward all of life, the Reformation continued the general outlook of the Middle Ages. Neither Catholic nor Protestant in the sixteenth century could imagine a society of

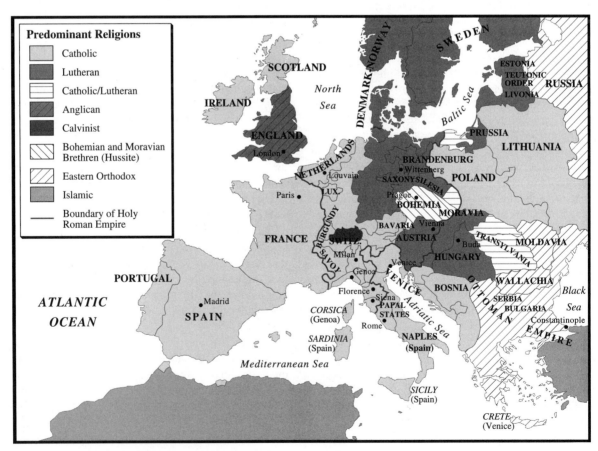

MAP 1.4 Reformation Europe, Sixteenth Century

religious diversity and freedom. It is difficult for late twentieth-century Americans to comprehend a view of the world in which different opinions on infant baptism, the way to salvation, and the number of sacraments were regarded as threats to the entire social order. That difficulty is perhaps a measure of how far removed we are from the world of the Middle Ages, of which the Reformation was a final stage.

But in other respects, the Reformers looked toward the modern world. Most important, the schism in the church strengthened many of the new states of Europe. Protestant rulers gained access to the economic resources of the church; kings everywhere could now justify taxation in terms of defending the faith; and some rulers had achieved control over the religious life of their nations. Religious conflict among the many states, cities, and principalities of Germany, for example, was initially resolved by an agreement in 1555 to allow each ruler to choose the religion for his own territory. Furthermore, the Reformation encouraged a skeptical attitude toward authority and tradition, for it had successfully challenged the immense prestige and power of the pope and the established church. In addition, the Reformers fostered religious individualism. People were now encouraged to read and interpret the scriptures themselves and to seek salvation without the mediation of the church. Thus, despite its intense religious fervor, the Reformation opened the way to secularism.

| Conclusion

The Reformation produced in Europe a cultural and religious variety to match its political and ethnic diversity. Protestants and Catholics alike regarded this as a failure, and each group would gladly have imposed its version of Christianity on everyone, had it only been possible. Tolerance became a necessity; it was not a virtue.

But it was precisely Europe's "failure" to achieve consensus and uniformity, in religious practices as well as in political life, that lowered the barriers to innovation and growth and set Europe, and Europe alone, on the path toward capitalist modernization and global domination.

Notes

1. Quoted in Robert Lopez and Irving W. Raymond, *Medieval Trade in the Mediterranean World* (New York: Columbia University Press, 1955), p. 31.

2. Quoted in Carlo Cipolla, *Before the Industrial Revolution* (New York: Norton, 1976), p. 207.

3. E. L. Jones, *The European Miracle* (Cambridge, Engl.: Cambridge University Press, 1981), p. 38.

4. Quoted in Jean Gimpel, *The Medieval Machine* (New York: Holt, 1976), p. 178.

5. Suzanne F. Wemple, *Women in Frankish Society* (Philadelphia: University of Pennsylvania Press, 1981), p. 189.

6. Quoted in S. Lilley, *Men, Machines, and History* (New York: International Publishers, 1965), p. 62.

7. Lynn White, "The Historical Roots of Our Ecological Crisis," *Science,* 10 Mar. 1967, 1205.

8. Quoted in Robert S. Lopez, *The Birth of Europe* (London: Dent, 1971), p. 324.

9. Quoted in L. Thorndike, *A History of Magic and Experimental Science,* vol. 2 (New York: Columbia University Press, 1923), p. 58.

10. Jones, *European Miracle,* p. 119.

Chapter 2
"The Heavens and the Earth": Europe's Scientific Revolution

At the center of Europe's modern transformation has been the development of a scientific view of the world, referred to as the *scientific revolution*. From the seventeenth century to the present, Europeans have accumulated a staggering amount of knowledge and have continually refined their techniques of observation and analysis. In the process, Europe gained one of its most distinctively modern qualities, and its people came to an understanding of the world vastly different from that of their medieval ancestors. No longer would they rely on the external authority of divinely revealed scripture, the speculations of ancient philosophers, or the received wisdom of cultural tradition. Rather, a combination of careful observations, controlled experiments, and the formulation of general "laws," expressed in mathematical terms, became the standard means of obtaining knowledge and understanding in every domain of life.

Although the modern scientific enterprise had its origins in Europe, it has become practically universal. Many of the world's peoples decisively rejected Europe's religious traditions, found little of interest in its classical Greco-Roman heritage, and have been unimpressed with its liberal and democratic political philosophy. But almost without exception, other societies have eagerly joined Europe's scientific quest. In the process, science has become the dominant global symbol of modernity and has largely lost its association with European culture.

Other cultures had already subjected the physical universe to careful investigation, with impressive results. From the Islamic world, for example, came major advances in algebra, geometry, and trigonometry; important discoveries in chemistry; widely used astronomical tables and maps of the stars; and much progress in medical and pharmaceutical knowledge. Between 1000 and 1400, China moved toward "a systematic experimental investigation of nature, and created the world's earliest mechanized industry."[1] Had Europe's burst of scientific creativity not intervened or spread so rapidly, similar intellectual and technological breakthroughs might have occurred elsewhere. But, as it happened, such an event occurred first in Europe, in the minds of a handful of individuals in the sixteenth and seventeenth centuries.

How did the scientific revolution occur? How did it spread from astronomy to virtually every other domain of human thought? What impact did it have on how Europeans regarded their relationship to the cosmos? What was gained and what was lost as the culture of science spread in Europe? These are some of the questions this chapter will explore.

The Breakthrough of the Seventeenth Century

Well-educated Europeans living in 1727, when Isaac Newton died, understood the world far differently from those living in 1543, the year Copernicus died. An intellectual revolution had occurred in the intervening years.

The intellectual and cultural changes that the scientific revolution represented did not appear abruptly. Before the Renaissance, in fact, the most important science in Europe was theology, not physics. For most scholars it was far more important to find divine grace and to understand the Holy Trinity than to explain motion, the tides, or the position of the planets and stars. But beneath the surface there were a number of factors that fostered intellectual inquiry and created the conditions in which modern science emerged. As described in Chapter 1, these included the stimulus of Islamic learning, the rediscovery of scientific texts from ancient Greece, and the growth of universities teaching mathematics, astronomy, and physics. Ever so slowly the study of the natural order began to diverge from that of philosophy or theology and to gain a separate, although very subordinate, identity.

Trends in the larger society reinforced this development. The secularism of the Renaissance, the increasing worldliness of the towns and cities, the demands of war, the prospects of commercial gain, the navigational needs of the early overseas explorers and the startling discoveries they made—all of these factors contributed to the ferment of ideas we call the scientific revolution. During this period, many traditional explanations for natural phenomena were called into question and overturned. Most dramatic was the succession of observations and theories that undermined the hierarchical and closed universe of the Middle Ages. It led to the idea of a complex, orderly, and infinite cosmos of Sir Isaac Newton.

The World According to Aristotle and Ptolemy

The view of the physical world held by educated Europeans in the late Middle Ages derived from Aristotle, perhaps the greatest of the ancient Greek philosophers, and from Ptolemy, a Greco-Egyptian mathematician and astronomer who lived in Alexandria during the second century. The intellectual leaders of the late medieval church sought to blend these ancient ideas with their own Christian claims concerning human origins, purpose, and destiny.

According to both Aristotle and Ptolemy, the earth was stationary and at the center of the universe, and around it revolved the sun, moon, and stars embedded in ten spheres of transparent crystal. Whereas Aristotle believed that the planets themselves revolved in circular orbits around the earth, Ptolemy claimed that the bodies beyond the earth described smaller circles, the centers of which

followed perfect circles around the earth. For years, these epicycles of the revolving bodies accounted for the irregularity of observed planetary motion in a universe that was assumed to be geometrically perfect—that is, constructed of concentric spheres. Thus, Ptolemy saved appearances for Aristotle's theory that the perfect shape, and hence the universe itself, was a sphere.

At the center of the Ptolemaic system was the motionless earth, and beyond the revolving spheres were fixed stars and a motionless heaven. Like Aristotle, Ptolemy believed in the logical necessity of an "unmoved mover," God, who watched over the whole system. The logic of the Greek conception coincided well with the religious purpose of the medieval church; the attention of the entire universe was centered on the earth, where the human drama of salvation took place. It was not a dead universe, for divine spirits according to their rank guided the hierarchically arranged spheres along their way. Bril-

A king, representing Atlas, holds the medieval universe with the earth at its center and the other heavenly bodies in spheres around it. *The Folger Library*

liantly evoked by the Italian poet Dante (1265–1321) in *The Divine Comedy,* this view of the cosmos was widely accepted by the literate public until the seventeenth century.

Two weaknesses of the Ptolemaic system caused its eventual collapse. First, Ptolemy had drawn attention to irregular and noncircular motion precisely by trying to account for it with a more subtle theory based on epicycles. To those still faithful to the Aristotelian principle of circularity, Ptolemy had strayed from the truth, for his planets did not describe perfect circles. Second, Ptolemaic charts and tables of the heavens proved to be inaccurate. Some scholars doubted that the Almighty would construct a universe as disorderly and unpredictable as the one described by Ptolemy, and so they sought a theory that would confirm their assumptions of a geometrically harmonious and orderly cosmos.

From Copernicus to Newton: The Search for a New Model

In the year of his death, the Polish mathematician and astronomer Nicolaus Copernicus (1473–1543) published a treatise that pointed the way to a correct description of the solar system and the heavens. The essential statement of *On the Revolutions of the Heavenly Spheres* was that the sun, not the earth, was the motionless center around which other bodies revolved. Like the other planets, the earth revolved around the sun in an eccentric circular orbit; the eccentric orbits accounted for the yearly variations in the distance to the sun. This arrangement of the planets made theory more closely correspond to observed phenomena without the special movements assumed by Ptolemy. Probably because of the work's radical claims and its technical complexity, it did not become influential for about fifty years.

Tycho Brahe (1546–1601), a Danish astronomer, intended to defend a modified version of the traditional view of the universe, but his argument that the planets revolved around the sun while everything revolved around the stationary earth proved to be a dead end in the search for a new conception of the universe. In his sophisticated observatory, however, he accumulated a mass of highly accurate observations of the planets throughout their orbits and made a detailed star map. His German student Johannes

Kepler (1571–1630) used this data in his search for mathematical formulas corresponding to the observed paths of the planets. Kepler sought to discover a celestial order reducible to mathematics. This he found, but it was not based on spheres at all: the planets followed elliptical, rather than circular, orbits around the sun, and their orbital speed varied depending on their proximity to the sun. These discoveries shattered the traditional idea that the planets were carried around the heavens by crystalline spheres. The doctrine of circularity was dead, but no new and coherent conception of the universe was yet available to replace it.

Meanwhile, Galileo Galilei (1564–1642), a brilliant Italian scholar, contributed a series of discoveries in physics. In his lectures at the universities of Padua and Pisa, Galileo forcefully supported the Copernican view of the solar system as he attacked the entire Aristotelian view of science. His method would guide modern science: one should prefer proven knowledge about small questions to hazy speculations about the universe as a whole. A practical inventor as well as a theorist, Galileo developed a telescope that permitted him to observe the moons of Jupiter and sunspots. Obviously the sun was not immaculate, as the Aristotelians had claimed. His experiments with falling objects yielded the correct mathematical expression of the relationship among distance, time, and acceleration: the formula $s = 1/2at^2$. Like Kepler, with whom he corresponded, Galileo found mathematical harmony in celestial and terrestrial motion; there was no need to invoke supernatural forces. Truth about the physical universe would come to the scholar who reasoned carefully from observations and experiments.

Building on this rich inheritance of ideas, the English mathematician and physicist Sir Isaac Newton (1642–1727) formulated the modern laws of motion and mechanics, scarcely modified until the twentieth century, and in doing so created a new and coherent view of the universe. Central to Newton's thinking was the concept of universal gravitation. Borrowing from the work of British physicist William Gilbert (1540–1603) on magnetism, Newton claimed that attraction between bodies was a property of the bodies themselves. Although calling gravitation universal did not explain it, Newton found that this force could be measured and expressed mathematically:

I began to think of Gravity extending to ye orb of the Moon, and (having found out how to estimate the force with which a globe revolving within a sphere presses the surface of the sphere), from Kepler's rule . . . I deduced that the forces which keep the Planets in their Orbs must be reciprocally as the squares of their distances from the centers about which they revolve.[2]

Likewise, Newton thought of the problem of motion in a new way. He could not explain scientifically why planets began to move in the first place, but he claimed that their continued motion was due to inertia: nothing held them back. They remained in their orbits because of a balance of forces: gravity pulled them toward the sun while their velocity created a centrifugal force that pulled them away. Thus Newton formulated his famous law of motion, which stated that objects in motion tend to remain in motion and those at rest tend to remain at rest. Newton had created a grand synthesis of Kepler's description of the heavens and Galileo's explanation of the behavior of falling objects on earth. The radical implication of this view was that the heavens and the earth, long regarded as separate and distinct spheres, were not so different after all.

Through the debates and research of more than a century, from the work of Copernicus to that of Newton, the view of the universe held by educated people had fundamentally changed. The physical universe was no longer thought to be propelled by angels and spirits but to function on its own according to timeless principles and mathematical formulas. It was no longer considered closed and surrounded by heaven and the Christian God but infinite in space, if not in time. Nor did the earth and its human inhabitants lie at the center; as if by mere chance, they occupied an orbit around the sun as did other planets.

Like the physical universe, the human organism also lost some of its mystery as scholars experimented and drew conclusions. The Flemish anatomist Andreas Vesalius (1514–1564) made careful dissections of cadavers and was able to describe the human body with the kind of accuracy shown in the accompanying illustration. His treatise *The Structure of the Human Body* appeared in 1543, the same year as Copernicus's masterpiece. But most brilliant in this field was William Harvey (1578–1657), who, after taking a degree at Cambridge, studied at the University of Padua, where Galileo taught. His patient research, including human dissection and animal vivisection, led to the correct description of the circulation of the blood and the function of the heart. Harvey demonstrated that the heart pumped out an enormous quantity of blood each hour, so much that it must flow in a closed circuit. But his study *On the Movement of the Heart and Blood* (1628) could not prove conclusively that the blood that left the heart through the arteries returned through the veins, for Harvey did not have the equipment to detect the capillaries. With a microscope, however, Marcello Malpighi (1628–1694) discovered the capillaries in 1661: the small vessels that Harvey had presupposed did exist. Thus the heart was no longer viewed as the mysterious center of the body's heat and the seat of its passions; it was instead a complex muscle that functioned as a pump.

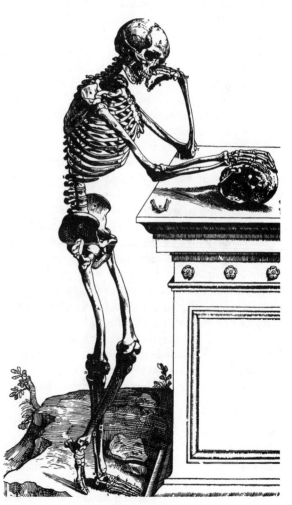

This drawing by Flemish anatomist Andreas Vesalius suggests a rational and philosophical approach to the human predicament even as it presents the human skeleton with great realism.

Bacon and Descartes: The Search for a New Method

In their methods of investigation as well as by their conclusions, scholars of the sixteenth and seventeenth centuries were revolutionary. Although they seldom completely ignored traditional wisdom, they relied far more than in the past on direct observation of the phenomena they wished to explain. Francis Bacon (1561–1626), a British lawyer, government official, essayist, and popularizer of science, helped to foster this empirical tradition. For Bacon, broad theories should always be provisional, contingent on further experiment, verification, and refinement. The scientist should be humble, start with the particular, and patiently build certainty upon certainty to attain more general truths. Bacon's prescription for science quickly became the most heeded in Europe.

Another philosopher of scientific method also had great influence. Whereas Bacon stressed experimentation and empirical inquiry, René Descartes (1596–1650) placed greater emphasis on rational deduction and mathematics. A superb mathematician and the father of analytic geometry, Descartes considered the physical universe a vast machine that obeyed laws of mathematics. At the beginning of time, God created matter and natural law, gave the system its original impetus, and thereafter watched without intervening. We might not understand God or our own feelings, but through systematic doubt of received opinions and careful deduction from undeniable assumptions, such as the existence of God the First Cause, Descartes believed that one could understand the physical world. In his classic *Discourse on Method* of 1637, he shared Bacon's skepticism of traditional theories. Yet he was more confident than Bacon in human powers to recognize true ideas without elaborate experimental proof and, furthermore, to deduce correct conclusions from such ideas. Whereas Bacon sought to grasp the physical universe by compiling data and observations, Descartes believed that the way to understanding was through clear insight concerning general principles followed by logical deduction and mathematical calculation.

Both Descartes and Bacon helped to change the way scholars went about scientific investigations. The Cartesian system was dogmatic, but it also helped to organize physical science through mathematics.

Baconian empiricism was more cautious, experimental, and open to new formulations as new evidence turned up. By the mid-eighteenth century, scientists made increasing use of mathematics, but, as Bacon wished, they built general theory from concrete observations and experiments.

Science and Religion: Confrontation and Adjustment

Both the new scientific method of systematic skepticism concerning traditional theories and the discoveries themselves challenged the authority of the Roman Catholic church. Although the church originally ignored Copernicus's work, it became obvious by the end of the sixteenth century that in placing the earth among the other planets, he had rejected the hierarchy of the heavens, and his cosmology cast doubt on the purpose of the universe itself: namely, to proclaim the divine handiwork and to serve as a stage for human redemption. Rome soon condemned his treatise and proclaimed his ideas heretical. Italian philosopher Giordano Bruno (1548–1600) pushed Copernican ideas further, proclaiming that the universe was not closed but infinite, that there was not one world but many. Persisting in these ideas, Bruno was condemned by the Catholic Inquisition and burned at the stake. Galileo, too, was compelled by the church publicly to renounce his belief that the earth moved around an orbit and rotated on its axis. Since the church claimed the universe to be a symbolic expression of divine purpose, it could not be passive as scholars began to explain the heavens in a new way. It made little difference that most of the astronomers pursued their investigations from religious motives, precisely to see divine perfection in natural laws; their discoveries still cast doubt on the church's explanations and its intellectual authority.

The ensuing conflict concerned scientific methods as well as conclusions. Galileo and Bacon expressed the scientific spirit that would eventually prevail: one should approach a vision of the whole through the mastery of humbler details, the keys to which were direct observation and repeated experimentation. For the church, however, religious and worldly knowledge were intertwined, and revelation and faith were the keys to both.

Despite Catholic opposition, the scientific revolution continued to reshape the mentalities of educated people. The Protestant Reformation had, after all, removed half of Europe from Rome's spiritual influence. Even in some Catholic states, an anticlerical tradition could protect a university from persecution, as in Padua. And as modern science made headway among loyal Catholics, the church hierarchy found it increasingly difficult to compel belief in old ideas even among its own prelates, priests, and professors.

Protestant reaction to the scientific discoveries was even less coordinated, for Protestantism itself was divided among churches and sects, some less orthodox than others. The major churches, however, quickly took a position of accommodation, admitting that physical science was competent in its limited sphere but insisting that religion held the key to ultimate questions concerning the creation and purpose of the universe. Newton was a religious man as well as a kind of scientific pope in his time: both a member in good standing of the Church of England and president of the Royal Society of London, an association of scientists. The religious faith of most scientists made it easier for the churches to acquiesce to them, to grant the lower realm to scientific laypeople as the clerics retained control of higher spiritual ground.

The Implications of Science: The Enlightenment of the Eighteenth Century

The seventeenth century was the heroic period of the scientific revolution in Europe, for it produced scientists and discoveries that generated the modern conception of nature and human knowledge. Newton's laws of motion appeared to be the culmination of modern science; the universe was a vast, unchanging, and perfectly rational clockwork. With this assumption, in the eighteenth century new discoveries in other fields such as chemistry and electricity followed one upon another and prepared the way for the scientific and technological wonders of the industrial age.

As scientists continued to build on their most recent discoveries, a larger public also became imbued with the scientific outlook. Previously, physical science had touched only a highly educated elite, but in the eighteenth century it began to affect a much wider audience. Although its apparent materialism and impiety continued to provoke cultural and religious opposition, by the late 1600s scientific societies and a popular press proclaimed a new age free from superstitions such as witchcraft—an age of Enlightenment. The Royal Society of London, the Academy of Sciences in Paris, the Berlin Society of Sciences, and the St. Petersburg Academy of Sciences in Russia, together with new libraries and museums such as the British Museum in London, were important institutions that encouraged the international exchange of knowledge and the evaluation and support of research. The Prussian and Russian states, for example, were significant patrons and sought to attract the most promising thinkers. Local scientific societies appealed to enthusiastic amateurs and became markets for a popular scientific literature that not only explained in simple terms the great discoveries of mathematics and physics but also encouraged the application of the scientific method to other fields such as history, politics, and economics.

This steady expansion and sharing of knowledge would hardly have been possible without the printing press. Its invention in the late fifteenth century gave rise to a lively book trade that facilitated a vigorous intellectual exchange in Europe. Not only did scientists now share knowledge with one another through identical printed copies of their own works, but the general public, whose rate of literacy was on the rise, could read simpler versions and commentaries.

The Science of Politics

As the physical scientists were formulating new theories and laws to explain the cosmos, other thinkers wrote about human affairs in a similarly realistic way. An early example is Niccolò Machiavelli (1469–1527), a Florentine diplomat who wrote about politics after being forced into exile. His best-known work, *The Prince,* is a prescription for political success based on observation of Italian politics rather than on idealistic principles. To the question of whether a prince should be feared or loved, Machiavelli replied:

> One ought to be both feared and loved, but as it is difficult for the two to go together, it is much safer to be feared than loved. . . . For it may be said of men in general that they are ungrateful, voluble, dissemblers, anxious to avoid danger, and covetous of gain. . . . Fear is maintained by dread of punishment which never fails. . . . In the actions of men, and especially of princes, from which there is no appeal, the end justifies the means.[3]

Influenced by Greek and Roman classics, Machiavelli believed that the ideal form of government was the republic. But he recognized that conditions were not favorable for a republic in the Florence of his day, and so he proceeded to discuss how an autocratic prince might succeed in retaining power and building the state. He is widely regarded as the earliest modern political scientist.

The English scholar and philosopher Thomas Hobbes (1588–1679) also lived in an age of political turmoil, in this case the sharp conflict between king and Parliament during the English Revolution. He achieved lasting fame with the publication of his political treatise *Leviathan* (1651). Educated at Oxford, Hobbes traveled widely and knew Descartes, Galileo, Harvey, and Bacon. Like the physical scientists, he assumed that there was a natural law that scholars could discover. But from his experience with English political and religious upheaval, he concluded that human life, when unchecked by a powerful monarch, was "solitary, poor, nasty, brutish, and short." People were by nature, he thought, essentially self-centered. For this reason, they gave up their natural freedom along with its dangers and uncertainty to an absolute monarch who provided order and security. Hobbes was a modern thinker in his argument rather than in his conclusions: monarchs owed their position to their usefulness rather than to divine right.

John Locke (1632–1704), a British philosopher who lived during the English Revolution, constructed a different political philosophy, but it too argued from observations of human nature and expediency rather than from religion or tradition. Like Hobbes, Locke proceeded from the state of nature. Although he retained the traditional Christian view of original sin, he was more optimistic than Hobbes about self-government. There was a latent democratic thrust to his *Essay Concerning Human Understanding* (1690), which argued that for everyone, regardless of social class, the mind was a blank slate at birth, that it acquired knowledge through sense impressions or experience, and that proper education could offset sinful human nature. Reasonable and decent men and women required government merely to furnish certain guarantees of "natural rights," namely life, liberty, and property. The contract between ruler and ruled should last only as long as it served the public well.

Jean-Jacques Rousseau (1712–1778) also used the vocabulary of natural law and the state of nature, but rather than justifying the political regimes of his own time, his ideas were more democratic and gave expression to social and political aspirations of the poor and dispossessed. In *Emile* (1762), a short book about the ideal education for a boy, Rousseau argued that nature was a sounder source of guidance than civilization, which was corrupt; whereas nature taught self-reliance and generosity, civilization fostered individual possession, greed, and envy. He believed that in an original state of nature (the hypothetical starting point for most social theorists), human beings lived in small rural communities, held property in common, and were basically good, but that when certain people claimed property for themselves, cities grew and spawned selfishness, inequality, and all the vices.

Rousseau's *Social Contract* (1762) offered the means to regain primordial innocence. Citizens would form a contract, not with a sovereign but among themselves; they, the people, would be sovereign. They would give up the individual liberty of a state of nature but gain security for themselves and their possessions. Further, as sovereign people obeyed only themselves as a group, their liberty, somewhat transformed, would return. Rousseau's social and political thought profoundly influenced educational theory, the rise of nationalism, and eventually the democratic revolutions and socialism. Although his *Confessions* and the novel *La Nouvelle Heloise* made Rousseau a forerunner to romanticism in literature and the arts, he provides a striking example of the effects of the scientific revolution beyond the narrower confines of physical science.

Economics also felt the influence of scientific ways of thinking. The Catholic church had preached against lending money at interest, and governments, such as that of France under Louis XIV, had sharply regulated commerce and industry. But there were no economic laws equivalent to the law of gravity. The physiocrats, a group of French thinkers whose name derives from their intention to link economics with physical science, began to develop economic laws from what they understood to be natural law. But it was the Scottish professor Adam Smith (1723–1790), with the publication of *Inquiry into the Nature and Causes of the Wealth of Nations* in 1776, who became the Newton of economics. He formulated laws that accounted for variations in supply, demand, wages, prices, and interest rates and justified free trade on the basis of its inevitably favorable results for society. So economics joined physics, astronomy, and politics as disciplines to which the scientific method could be applied.

In their different ways, Machiavelli, Hobbes, Locke, Rousseau, and Smith invoked nature, natural law, and the criterion of utility. Like the natural scientists, they appealed to evidence and reason rather than to authority. The British poet Alexander Pope (1688–1744) spoke of this new confidence in human reason in "An Essay on Man":

Know then Thy-self, presume not God to scan;
The proper Study of Mankind is Man.

. . .

Go wondrous Creature! mount where Science
* guides,*
Go measure Earth, weigh Air, and state the Tides,
Instruct the Planets in what Orbs to run,
Correct old Time, and regulate the Sun. . . .[4]

Popularizing Scientific Attitudes

Particularly prominent among the popularizers of modern science were the French writers known as the *philosophes,* a word that came to denote writers on practically any subject who were of independent views and skeptical of authority. Although their influence was felt throughout Europe, their works and their followers were most prominent in England, France, Prussia, and North America, where censorship was mild or unorganized. Elsewhere the writings of the *philosophes* did not penetrate far beyond the drawing rooms of traditional elites.

François-Marie Arouet (1694–1778), better known by his pen name, Voltaire, was the central figure of the French Enlightenment. His essays, poems, dramas, prose fiction, and histories touched practically every issue of the day, popularized modern scientific attitudes and Newtonian concepts, and praised English religious tolerance and civil liberties.

Voltaire had good reason to envy English freedom of the press, for although he was widely read in France his works drew the hostility of individuals, the government, and the church. Yet he did not advocate parliamentary government for France. Voltaire favored absolute monarchy because he believed it could bring rational order to society and encourage the arts and sciences. Not sharing Locke's generous appraisal of human character, Voltaire considered the reign of the absolute monarch Louis XIV to be a golden age. Like other *philosophes,* he idealized China, as it was described to Europeans by Jesuit missionaries, for this autocratic empire seemed to be administered wisely by a scholarly elite selected for their talent. The abundance of Chinese porcelain and furniture in aristocratic households of the eighteenth century suggested a lively admiration for Chinese civilization among a European elite yearning for strong, but enlightened, monarchs.

As for established religion, however, Voltaire's pen was devastating; both the church and the Bible, he claimed, encouraged superstition, ignorance, and immorality. In his *Philosophical Dictionary,* he wrote that a miracle was "a violation of mathematical, divine, immutable, eternal laws . . . a contradiction in terms." He continued, "A law cannot be immutable and violable at the same time."[5] Voltaire's own faith can be described as deism: a belief in a single creator, a rather abstract and logically necessary first cause of the universe, a force that could not intervene in history or tamper with natural law. Voltaire recognized that different cultures would always generate different customs and ideas, and much of his literary effort, in particular the famous satire *Candide* (1759), argued for mutual understanding, tolerance, and cooperation rather than blind dogmatism of any sort. Science and education, then, rather than godliness and prayer, were the source of happiness and virtue. Taken as a whole, the intellectual ferment of the eighteenth century undermined religion, which many intellectuals either dismissed altogether as ignorant superstition or tolerated only as a mild form of deism.

Popular novels and pamphlets proclaimed the merits of science to a wider and less cultivated pub-

VOICES
A Vision of Human Progress

The Marquis de Condorcet (1743–1794), like many other French aristocrats, died on the guillotine during the French Revolution because of his social class rather than his convictions. Soon after, his book The Progress of the Human Mind *appeared to sum up the optimism of the* philosophes *concerning worldly happiness.*

Organic perfectibility or deterioration amongst the various strains in the vegetable and animal kingdom can be regarded as one of the general laws of nature. This law also applies to the human race. No-one can doubt that, as preventative medicine improves and food and housing become healthier, as a way of life is established that develops our physical powers by exercise without ruining them by excess, as the two most virulent causes of deterioration, misery and excessive wealth, are eliminated, the average length of human life will be increased and a better health and a stronger physical constitution will be ensured. The improvement of medical practice, which will become more efficacious with the progress of reason and of the social order, will mean the end of infectious and hereditary diseases and illnesses brought on by climate, food, or working conditions. It is reasonable to hope that all other diseases may likewise disappear as their distant causes are discovered. Would it be absurd then to suppose that this perfection of the human species might be capable of indefinite progress; that the day will come when death will be due only to extraordinary accidents or to the decay of the vital forces, and that ultimately the average span between birth and decay will have no assignable value? . . .

Finally may we not extend such hopes to the intellectual and moral faculties? May not our parents, who transmit to us the benefits or disadvantages of their constitution, and from whom we receive our shape and features, as well as our tendencies to certain physical affections, hand on to us also that part of the physical organization which determines the intellect, the power of the brain, the ardour of the soul or the moral sensibility? Is it not probable that education, in perfecting these qualities, will at the same time influence, modify, and perfect the organization itself? Analogy, investigation of the human faculties and the study of certain facts, all seem to give substance to such conjectures which would further push back the boundaries of our hopes.

Source: Antoine-Nicholas de Condorcet, *Sketch for a Historical Picture of the Progress of the Human Mind,* trans. June Barraclough (London: Weidenfeld and Nicolson, 1955), pp. 199–201.

lic. The American Benjamin Franklin (1706–1790) became the exemplar of the new age to this public on both sides of the Atlantic. His *Poor Richard's Almanac* (1732), quickly translated into French, was full of practical advice that stressed reason, thrift, work, and human values; and his autobiography described his efforts to perfect his own character through the careful organization of his time and the evaluation of its use. A scientist, writer, diplomat, philosopher, and sage, Franklin seemed to be the complete man of his era. He appealed to the masses because he seemed unpretentious, wrote and spoke clearly and simply, and conveyed a cheerful outlook concerning the future of humanity.

Modern secular thought had become so widespread in the eighteenth century that it provoked a popular reaction, which was expressed in such religious movements as English and American Methodism and German Pietism. The well-established churches had learned both to accept the accomplishments of modern science and to maintain their basic religious principles. In general they taught that since God created reason, religious believers could remain true to their faith even while embracing essential tenets of the Age of Reason. Such accommodation between science and religion well suited the educated and prosperous classes, but for many of the common people of the eighteenth century, religion had become too austere, distant, and intellectual. As England industrialized rapidly in the late eighteenth century, many of the new urban workers found solace in their present misery through the promise of salvation in a better world. Methodism generated an especially fervent popular following with its anti-intellectual and moralistic teachings that gave workers a renewed sense of identity and purpose without advocating social revolution.

Many from the educated and privileged classes soon turned against the rational spirit of the Enlightenment, but their revolt usually took a secular form. Romantic literature and art celebrated passion and unique human feeling, which many feared would be lost in the mechanical universe of Descartes and Newton where universal law applied to an essentially uniform humanity. Ever since the Enlightenment, the scientist and the poet, the engineer and the painter, have symbolized for the educated public two contrasting views of the modern world. Much of modern history in the West is about the synthesis of these perspectives.

Science and Progress

As scientific discoveries continued during the eighteenth century, the literate public became ever more aware of the new reasoning formulated by Bacon and Descartes and practiced by Newton and others. In significant numbers, the public adopted this way of approaching the world and applied the scientific method to all fields of investigation. Although no longer at the center of all creation, Europeans had gained confidence in their rationality and in their capacity to understand the world; knowledge and happiness would increase, as would human progress or improvement. The future need no longer resemble the past. Religion remained a comfort for mortals, but God, the author of natural law, had no need to intervene directly.

There were comforting similarities between this new public philosophy and the medieval one. The universe was far more vast and complex, but it was still perceived as fixed and unchanging; it had been created once and for all time. Likewise, the plants and creatures of the earth, including men and women, were considered to be the same as they had been at the moment of creation. The main elements of the Christian worldview could still be assimilated with the scientific worldview, and this was the course the major churches took.

Throughout the nineteenth century, the ideas of progress and human rationality remained dominant in Western society; in the twentieth, they perished amid the flames of world war and genocide. But even before these tragic events, the further development of science itself had begun to undermine some of the confident assumptions of the Age of Reason.

Beyond the Enlightenment: Science in the Nineteenth and Twentieth Centuries

In the industrial era of the nineteenth and twentieth centuries, scientists continued to explore inanimate matter and in the process came up with unsettling theories. They cast doubt on the assumption that the universe, the earth, and living things were unchanging; they undermined the assumption that humans are essentially rational; and they demonstrated that space and time, matter and energy, were not distinct, as Newton believed, but versions of the same phenomenon. By the twentieth century, the confidence of the *philosophes* that the universe was essentially a static mechanical clockwork had given way to the realization that matter and life alike were in continuous flux.

Darwin and Evolution

In 1859, Charles Darwin (1809–1882) published his classic *Origin of Species*. It laid out a complex argument that all of life was in flux, that over millions of years creatures were continuously coming into being and becoming extinct. The book was as shattering to traditional religious views as Copernicus's treatise on the solar system had been. For more than a century, other biologists and geologists had been making observations that undermined the accepted religious explanation of the age of living things. Excavations revealed skeletons of dinosaurs, long extinct; fossils found in different geological strata were not the same, which suggested a correlation between form and environment; cross-breeding produced new varieties of plants and animals, suggesting continuous

Unable to challenge Darwin on scientific grounds, the popular press and general public who could not accept his theories resorted to ridicule as in this caricature of the great biologist.

creation; and fossil evidence of sea life found on high mountains could be explained only by geological change over millions of years. Thus the evidence had multiplied that the earth was far older than had been presumed, that creatures adapted somehow to different environments by changing their characteristics, and that similarities of structure within groups of living things meant a common biological origin. The literal biblical account of creation was inadequate to account for the variety of plants and animals extinct, living, and still emerging. Darwin's achievement was to offer a theory that could explain the changes in living forms in different climates over eons.

In *The Descent of Man,* published in 1871, Darwin went so far as to argue that the appearance even of human beings was the work of evolution through natural selection. Over millions of years, living forms well suited to their environment survived and prospered, whereas those less well suited lost out in a ceaseless competition for mates and sustenance. Thus, men and women were not the products of a sin-

gle act of creation but rather of a long process of competition between animal species. The anthropologist Loren Eiseley noted the public dismay concerning Darwin's brilliant synthesis: "The wonder of the human achievement was lost for a moment in the sick revulsion of the wounded human ego. The fallen Adam had stared into the mirror of nature and perceived there only the mocking visage of an ape."[6]

And yet, for those who did not cling to the literal statements of the Bible, all was not lost for the idea of divine creation. Darwin himself believed God to be the creator; but rather than creating eternal living forms (including humans), he created the material (matter) and the mechanism (natural selection) for life to evolve. Still, the tale of the Garden of Eden had been left far behind.

Social Darwinists went further. They applied Darwin's biological theory to society and international politics. Believing in historical progress, they noted that history rewarded the strong and clever but punished the meek and simple. In nineteenth-century Europe with its competing capitalists, conflicts between workers and factory owners, antagonistic nation-states, and imperialist rivalries, Darwin's scientific theory was appropriated to make commercial, class, and military competition appear not only inevitable but ultimately beneficial. "Survival of the fittest" became a slogan that justified winners. In the century of their global dominance, it permitted Europeans to ignore gentler virtues for the sake of what they judged to be the long-range progress of humankind.

Marx and History

In the realm of social and political theory, Karl Marx (1818–1883) articulated what became a famous view of history. Like Darwin's scientific theories, Marx's social and political theories featured causes and effects based on a struggle for existence and power. In fact, Marx read Darwin's work with great interest, and it is apparent that both were affected by the social conditions of the industrial age and the scientific ethos of modern European culture. But whereas Darwin confined his research to the very long-term biological development of species, Marx studied the recorded history of human civilization. He sought in particular to explain the rise and fall of social classes in order to understand and even predict the course of history.

To each period of history, Marx wrote, there corresponded a certain "mode of production" consisting of technology, the organization of labor, social relations, and political power. In this context, a struggle inevitably arose between two fundamentally antagonistic social classes—one that controlled the means of production and the other compelled to furnish labor to the system. In Europe's Middle Ages, the central social conflict had involved the nobility and the peasantry, both of whom were tied to land and agriculture. In Marx's own era, the major struggle encompassed the urban capitalists (bourgeoisie) and the workers (proletariat), who depended on industrial production and world markets. But Marx believed that the age of the capitalist too would pass, for as wealth inevitably became concentrated in fewer hands, the proletariat just as inevitably would take stock of the unfair situation and "expropriate the expropriators." Chapter 4 explores Marx's economic and social thought in greater detail, including his Socialist ideology, which was a major product of Europe's Industrial Revolution. It is important to note here, however, that Marx was a social theorist marked by the scientific revolution. He based his theory of history on extensive historical research; like Newton and Darwin, he sought to formulate general laws that would explain events in a rational way. Furthermore, he did not believe in divine intervention, chance, or mysterious powers of kings. Rather, in his view, history involved struggle among all the actors, great and small, within particular economic circumstances.

In the world of Darwin and Marx, conflict rather than peace or reason was the very motor of progress. Their work expressed the major themes of the nineteenth century: the ideas of progress, competition, and struggle for survival, and the inevitable character of the historical process. The image of the tranquil, rational, and autonomous individual created by the Enlightenment was fading. Although the idea of progress remained, it had become less intellectual and personal; individuals were seen as caught in vast systems of biological, economic, and social forces.

Freud and Human Behavior

During the first decades of the twentieth century, a Viennese physician claimed that he had discovered the factors that determined human personality and behavior. Sigmund Freud (1856–1939) was not alone in pursuing this kind of research, but through his lectures and voluminous writing, he became the most influential, not only within the medical profession but among the general public as well. He concluded that the rational individual as understood by most of the *philosophes* did not really exist. Instead of being rational at the core, people are motivated by basic drives—sexual and aggressive—about which they have scant knowledge and over which they have little control.

Human behavior, Freud argued, is shaped by the experience of early childhood, the fulfillment of sexual drives, and the conflicting demands of pleasure and conscience. Whereas our quest for pleasure springs from our biological nature, our inner voice of conscience is derived from our social development. In growing up with two parents, the child is caught up in a sort of "lovers' triangle" or "Oedipus complex," which shapes the conscience and censures the drive for pleasure. Part of the conscious mind, which Freud called the ego, engages in a ceaseless struggle to reach accommodation or compromise between the irrational socially formed conscience and the equally irrational biologically based primal drives. According to Freudian theorists, the complex stratagems of the ego to keep the irrational component of the psyche in check are responsible for both the most sublime achievements in literature, music, and art, as well as the most dreadful crimes of individuals and nations.

As a medical doctor, Freud sought not only to account for irrational behavior but also to help the sick patient to become well. In his clinical practice, he alleged that certain repressed experiences caused his patients to exhibit alarming physiological symptoms as well as disturbing social behavior. His therapy, called psychoanalysis, involved talking with patients to make sense out of dreams, slips of the tongue, jokes, and family history. It sought to make the patient aware of unconscious drives that generated painful or unacceptable conscious behavior. Awareness of these unconscious drives could rarely dispel them, but in the most successful cases the patient could devise acceptable ways to divert them or blunt their harmful effects. To Freud, sanity and insanity were relative, since everyone carries neuroses from underlying drives and childhood experiences. Clearly, Freud's imaginative portrayal of the human condition was far different from that of the eighteenth-century *philosophe,* who assumed the citizen to be autonomous and at least potentially rational. Ironically, while Freud and other European thinkers like him claimed their own work to be rational, they cast doubt on human rationality itself.

Einstein and the New Physics

Even the apparently unchallengeable description of the cosmos that Newton had provided in the seventeenth century was fundamentally revised in the twentieth. The revisions became necessary because Newtonian theory no longer accounted for all of the observed phenomena concerning light, energy, and the atom. Albert Einstein (1879–1955), a German-born Swiss citizen who moved to the United States in 1940, was the best known among some dozen physicists who during the first third of the twentieth century provided a new description of matter and the cosmos.

Albert Einstein. *The Granger Collection*

Whereas Newton had assumed that a system of celestial mechanics functioned with respect to a fixed standard of space and time, Einstein demonstrated that this notion of "absolute" space and time stood in the way of understanding. He showed that space and time were equivalent entities, not the distinct realities that Newton had assumed. The perspective of the human observer, moreover, was a partial one, relative to that observer's place in the vast flux of space and time. According to Einstein's relativity theory, in absolute terms, we have no way of knowing our size, place, or velocity.

Just as the cosmos now seemed more complex and less knowable, the nature of matter proved to be equally mysterious. In place of the solid, indivisible atom, scientists found a complex mass of particles that eluded precise definition. Part of the mystery was expressed in Einstein's famous formula, $E = mc^2$, which showed that matter and energy, like space and time, were equivalent entities.

Paradoxically, as physicists in the twentieth century made discoveries that affected everyone's life, their ideas became more abstract and difficult for the public to grasp. Even for the physicists themselves, uncertainty about material reality replaced the relative certainty and simplicity of the Newtonian system. As the twentieth century neared its end, Einstein's successors were still searching for a Grand Unified Theory that would restore the kind of unity and coherence to humankind's conception of the universe that Newton's system could no longer provide.

Whether expressed in terms of biology, history, psychology, or physics, knowledge in the twentieth century seemed relative, contingent, and fraught with uncertain consequences. Atomic energy, for which the new physics paved the way, ironically attested to both the power of modern science and the precariousness of life on the planet.

I Conclusion

Science was never a purely internal affair between the scientist and a set of puzzling phenomena; there were always conditioning institutions and climates of opinion that led to or away from the threshold of discovery. Even as modern science stamped its imprint indelibly on Western culture, so too it was shaped by that culture and its history. The voyages of discovery, the rise of capitalism and the merchant class, the fragmentation of a once-united Christianity, the consolidation of monarchies and state bureaucracies, the Industrial Revolution, and national rivalries—these and other events provide a necessary framework for understanding the evolution of modern science in Europe.

The early success of the scientific revolution in the West gave scholars confidence that they would soon uncover the ultimate secrets of the physical world. However, each new discovery provoked further questions, and final truth has kept receding beyond the scientists' grasp. What endures from the early triumphs of the seventeenth century is not the specific conclusions of the scientists but rather their methods, their criteria for verification, their curiosity, and their attempt to be objective.

The scientific component of Europe's modern transformation fostered continuing change in the West. The more recent European and North American discoveries in basic science have produced a bewildering array of technological advances in fields such as medicine, electronics, space travel, and nuclear power. Moreover, industries in these fields have not only marketed new products but generated new social relations and customs as well. More profoundly, though, the scientific enterprise both re-

quired and nurtured habits of mind that have been critical, analytical, curious, receptive, and daring. These traits have shaped the best of modern scholarship, have challenged ancient religious beliefs, and are the hallmark of serious inquiry concerning the nature and destiny of the human species. At the same time, however, they have left the West a double legacy: increasing our power over nature, but also our anxiety and uncertainty about fundamental matters.

Notes

1. Mark Elvin, *The Pattern of the Chinese Past* (Stanford: Stanford University Press, 1973), p. 179.

2. Quoted in A. R. Hall, *The Scientific Revolution, 1500–1800* (London: Longmans, Green, 1954), p. 248.

3. Niccolò Machiavelli, *The Prince* (New York: New American Library, 1952), pp. 90, 94.

4. Alexander Pope, "An Essay on Man," in *Eighteenth-Century English Literature,* ed. G. Tillotson, P. Fussell, and M. Waingrow (New York: Harcourt, 1969), p. 640.

5. Voltaire, *Philosophical Dictionary,* vol. 2, trans. Peter Gay (New York: Basic Books, 1962), p. 392.

6. Loren Eiseley, *Darwin's Century* (New York: Doubleday, 1961), p. 195.

Chapter 3
The "Hidden Hand": Capitalism and the Transformation of Europe

The achievements of modern science were the work of a very small number of writers and thinkers who transformed European conceptions of the world. At the same time, a far wider group, made up of merchants, bankers, explorers, artisans, manufacturers, workers, and peasants, collectively pioneered the transformation of economic life and, in so doing, gave rise to *capitalism,* a distinct departure from previous forms of social and economic organization. What made capitalism unique? How did it come to replace the old order of feudalism in Europe? In what respects did it transform European society and conceptions of the social order? These are some of the questions that arise in considering this central element of Europe's modern transformation.

Capitalism in World History

Before the triumph of capitalism in Europe, two principles dominated economic life in all human societies. Economies operated by tradition, by a ruler's command, or by some combination of the two.[1]

Under the older of the two systems, the traditional economy, people assumed that life should go on much as it had in the past, that traditions should be passed on from generation to generation. Productive tasks were assigned automatically by birth or social position rather than according to ability or inclination; a potter's son became a potter, and so forth. People's goals in such societies were survival, security, and social stability, not progress or change. Traditional communities did not organize tasks to maximize production, partly because material progress did not seem possible but also because the very attempt would be socially disruptive. A person's work, in short, was part of a social relationship even as it contributed to the material life of the community.

Rewards for work likewise tended to be based more on social position than on production or performance. There was little incentive for the individual to excel in order to claim a material reward, for the group would normally enforce a customary distribution based on a combination of age, gender, and other criteria. In a relatively unstratified society of hunters and gatherers, the successful hunter might gain prestige and a choice share of the prize, but his companions and the rest of the community would claim their prescribed share as well. In a stratified traditional society, such as a feudal manor, the lord likewise owed his power and wealth in large measure to tradition, while the peasant family on the same manor inherited lower status and onerous tasks. However, both lords and peasants, like the hunters and gatherers, lived in accordance with customary rights and obligations to each other: the lord owed his peasants protection in return for farm labor and other service. A purely traditional economy required no elaborate governmental apparatus to enforce its traditions. Family, clan, and village together exercised informal authority over the individual, who had no alternative but to follow the patterns of life and work maintained by the elders. Although such rural societies could harshly exploit individuals and groups, they succeeded for thousands of years in ensuring many people a secure place in a local community.

Command economies arose with urban civilizations such as Egypt, China, and the Roman Empire.

These systems did not eliminate traditions at the village level, but their political leaders consciously formulated broad economic policy, which they enforced with a bureaucracy and, when necessary, with military force. The Roman Empire, for example, was an agricultural society in which an emperor presided over a bureaucracy and an army that together made decisions about the allocation of material resources. Like the Great Wall of China, Roman roads and bridges were proof of the government's power to allocate economic resources. But primitive agricultural technology (by modern standards) and low crop yields dictated that the vast majority of people would cultivate the land, live at the subsistence level, and be compelled to support a ruling class of landlords and a bureaucratic state.

In both traditional and command economies, a third principle of economic life also played an important role. It was the principle of the market, of commerce or trade, of buying and selling to earn a profit. In feudal Europe, states were weak and hence were unable to shape command economies, but a commercial network arose in towns and cities to complement the essentially traditional economy of the countryside. When this mechanism for regulating economic life triumphed over tradition and command, we can speak of the emergence of market or capitalist economies.

Markets and Morals, Commerce and Capital

Commerce—that is, buying and selling—has existed in one form or another everywhere throughout history. By using keen insight into prices and costs, merchants have taken profits while serving the requirements of buyers and sellers. In the great civilizations of premodern times, particularly in China and the Islamic world, many of the elements of a capitalist economy had already developed: private property, economic competition, moneylending, trade between regions specializing in different products, production for the market (rather than for immediate local consumption), communities of wealthy merchants, and the impulse to make a profit.

China, for example, has been described as "one of the most highly commercialized preindustrial soci-

eties the world has seen."[2] Historians speak of a "first commercial revolution" dating from the ninth to the thirteenth centuries, and of a second one from the seventeenth to the nineteenth centuries. In the latter period, Chinese peasants came to rely in part on goods produced outside their region and sold part of their crops on the market. Substantial and often wealthy merchant communities facilitated this growing pattern of exchange. Furthermore, large-scale private entrepreneurs, using hired labor, organized production for the market in large workshops manufacturing paper, textiles, pottery, and other items.

Similarly, in the Islamic world, which covered a vast extent of Afro-Eurasia, regions or towns specialized in producing particular agricultural goods or manufactured products for the market. Merchants conveyed these goods from one end of that world to the other, often accumulating substantial fortunes in the process. Despite the Quran's prohibition on lending money for interest, the practice was widespread in the Islamic world. "We are thus justified," writes one scholar, "in talking of a capitalistic sector within the societies of medieval Islam."[3]

Yet the influence of the market was limited, and capitalist practices and tendencies were hedged about with restrictions. Most production was not for sale on the market but for the consumption of the family or community. Some things, such as land and labor, were not usually for sale at all. Although merchants might facilitate commerce, the process of production was often controlled by independent artisans, landowners, or the state. Thus merchants could not dominate the economy as a whole. Furthermore, they often had lower social standing than landowners and government officials and were frequently at the mercy of the state. Particularly in Confucian China, mercantile values of profit-seeking and the accumulation of money were held in low esteem. And though Islam was more favorable to merchants, the ideals of social justice placed limits on their behavior. Thus, elements of capitalist practice existed in China and in the world of Islam, but neither developed a full-fledged capitalist economy, and the values and influence of merchants did not come to dominate these societies.

However, these changes did occur in Europe, and therein lies its uniqueness in world history. Until 1700 or so, Europe's economic development largely paralleled that of China and the Islamic world. As described in Chapter 1, in the centuries after 1000 C.E., trade and commerce grew rapidly, and after 1500 they came to operate on a global scale. By the eighteenth century, however, the vigorous European market economy was not only expanding in scale but changing in nature as well. Between 1700 and 1900, European societies became capitalist societies, a process that involved a number of related changes.

First, alongside the merchants, who conducted a trade within Europe and throughout the world, there appeared entrepreneurs, who organized the production as well as the sale of goods. They became known as capitalists because they assembled the means of production—capital (such as tools, buildings, and raw materials)—then bought land, hired labor, produced and sold goods, and collected a profit, which they used to repeat and expand the whole process. Whereas merchants had dealt only in the exchange of goods, capitalists gained control of all aspects of the productive process. Especially important was their ability to hire workers for money wages, which meant that human labor, like other commodities, was now available for sale on the market.

While gaining a pervasive influence over the economy, the capitalist class, referred to as the *bourgeoisie,* also gained social and political prominence in a way that had happened nowhere else. Their power grew quickly beginning in the late eighteenth century, when they took advantage of the technological innovations that came out of the Industrial Revolution. The nineteenth century was the age of the bourgeoisie in Europe.

In addition, the growth of commerce and capitalism had profound social and moral implications. Private property progressively replaced communal property, and individualism became admired rather than feared or criticized. The spirit of competition and the habit of seeking greater wealth for oneself weakened older religious and social impulses to generosity, sharing, and service to the community. The values of the merchant, so feared in many premodern societies, became widely accepted and socially sanctioned. The whole process provoked a wide-ranging debate among intellectuals concerning the nature of the good society: Did the new economic system that relied on private property and possessive

An important criticism of the new capitalist economy was that it seduced the pious away from their religious values. Here the wife of a moneylender is distracted from her reading of the Bible by a pile of coins. *Scala/Art Resource*

individualism produce a good society and good people? Many thought that it did not and proposed alternatives, such as socialism or a return to religion and tradition.

Whatever the social and moral qualities of these capitalist societies, they contained the most productive economic system the world had ever known. In some capitalist countries in the twentieth century, agriculture became so efficient and agricultural imports so accessible that the number of people directly involved in food production declined from more than 90 percent of the population to less than 10 percent. People no longer employed on the land were free to do other things. In response to changing and growing markets, both labor and capital resources were concentrated on more specialized tasks, and production mushroomed. Individuals acquired the right to own property, and instead of merely "making a living," a few directed their energies toward achieving great material success in the marketplace.

The main contours of this remarkable transformation occurred in Europe alone. There were indeed "sprouts" of capitalism elsewhere in the world, but only in Europe did these sprouts take root and grow into more fully capitalist economies, which gave rise by the nineteenth century to capitalist societies.

Markets in the Middle Ages

In 1000 C.E., about 90 percent of the European population was engaged in agriculture and lived in a rural and feudal economy that combined traditional and command features. Few people had any idea that their standard of living or way of life could change dramatically. The idea of worldly progress seemed religiously perverse as well as unrealistic.

Yet things did change. Chapter 1 outlines the unique conditions that gave rise to a new civilization after 1000 C.E., and contributed to the prominence of the market in its economic system. In particular, the weakness of the state provided great opportunities for the merchants of Europe's emerging and uniquely independent cities.

The process by which a market economy emerged from the grip of Europe's feudal economy, however, was slow and filled with obstacles. Physical barriers to expanding commercial networks were substantial and only gradually overcome. Only as local roads and transportation improved over many centuries were remote rural areas drawn into the developing market economy.

There were social obstacles as well. With its wealth in land, the nobility who benefited from the traditional feudal economy were severely threatened by the rise of an urban merchant class. As a result, the landed nobles frequently opposed the growth of a market economy. And the urban guilds, which organized and protected craft production in medieval Europe, were more concerned to preserve their way of life and the security of their local markets than to seek greater profit in a less certain world market. We often speak of the "rise of capitalism" as though it were some automatic or painless process, but it took revolutions in seventeenth-century England and eighteenth-century France to overcome the social obstacles of feudalism and to create conditions in which capitalism could flourish.

The medieval church was likewise hostile to most commercial ventures that yielded a profit in excess of fair payment for services rendered. Credit was essential to the growth of business, but the church condemned usury, or the lending of money for profit. In its view, a good Christian could not become a merchant or a banker. Hence, at first, the Jews—a people with ties neither to the church nor (it was believed) to a Christian state—were prominent figures in international trade.

Despite these obstacles, by the twelfth century a commercial revolution was in full swing in Europe. This did not mean that the percentage of Europeans who worked the land had sharply declined, nor that most people turned their full attention to making profits. Rather, it meant that a new class of city dwellers had become economically and socially prominent. Alongside the lord, the peasant, and the priest, there emerged the urban bourgeoisie. It survived by calculating profits and losses in the marketplace rather than according to traditions or the edicts of a lord. Further, its horizons were regional or international rather than local. Its business transcended the political regime of the local prince.

The urban bourgeoisie forged an urban civilization that very slowly penetrated and transformed rural society. Cities furnished oppressed peasants with alternative employment and limited the lord's ability to manage the local economy. As the rise of commerce fostered the minting of coins and the use of money, rural areas slowly shifted from a barter to a money economy. In their desire for cash, landlords permitted their peasants to discharge feudal obligations of service or labor with money payments instead. This process contributed to freeing the serfs in western Europe from legal bondage to a lord. The serfs progressively became tenant farmers or independent farmers in their own right, free to sell their produce at the local market. In short, the urban commercial revolution made its way into the countryside and slowly broke down the traditional relationship between lord and peasant. As feudal bonds and traditions dissolved, both lord and peasant were free to invest, produce, and sell their crop for a profit. The resulting market economy ignored ancient traditions and social hierarchies, rewarding work, efficiency, and intelligence instead. Even in rural areas, astute and productive individuals began to rise in wealth and status.

The Growth of Market Economies: 1400–1800

Nowhere in Europe did capitalism immediately transform human societies or behavior. But the central principle of a market economy—the impulse to make a profit by selling something in a market—became increasingly apparent in the expansion of European commerce, in agriculture, and in manufacturing between 1400 and 1800. These developments laid the foundation for the more thoroughly capitalist societies of the nineteenth century.

Trade on a Global Scale

An expanding commerce led the way to Europe's new economic system. The rise in population and the expansion of European trade, so apparent in the Middle Ages, dropped off sharply after 1348, when the Black Death carried away at least a third of the population. After a generation, the plague subsided, but it took a century for the population to rebound and economic progress to resume. As recovery set in, Europeans looked increasingly to the world beyond their own perimeter for economic opportunities.

The Portuguese took the early initiative and sought a route to India by sailing south around Africa. Such a direct route to the East was commercially advantageous, for it would eliminate the Italian and Muslim merchants who for centuries had controlled the trade. The prospect of profit for the pioneering merchant or monarch who used such a route was most alluring. For more than forty years until his death in 1460, Prince Henry the Navigator led research in shipbuilding and navigation and sent ships down the African coast. He created a tradition of exploration that carried Bartholomeu Dias to the Cape of Good Hope in 1487 and Vasco da Gama around the Cape and on to the Malabar coast of India in 1498.

The Genoan sailor Christopher Columbus was interested in reaching the East by sailing west. He finally gained the support of Ferdinand and Isabella of Spain and set out on his famous voyage on August 3, 1492. Two months later, he touched land in the New World. A materially rich but militarily weak part of the world, utterly unknown to Europeans, was now accessible to them.

Over the next three hundred years, sailors such as Ferdinand Magellan, Francis Drake, and James Cook explored and mapped the oceans and landmasses until only the most obscure corners of the globe remained undiscovered by Europeans. These voyages vastly expanded the stage on which merchants could act. The movement of silver and sugar from South America, furs and fish from North America, gold and slaves from Africa, and spices and textiles from Asia provided enormous new possibilities for Europe's traders. Often aided by their governments, merchant firms such as the British, French, and Dutch East India Companies practiced commerce on a global scale. This international trade in turn stimulated and enriched Europe's domestic economy, frequently at the direct expense of Afro-Asian and Amerindian peoples.

The propensity of the market to foster and deepen inequalities was apparent in the creation of a highly unequal world economic system, with western Europe as its powerful and privileged core. Areas at its near and distant periphery (eastern Europe, the Americas, and Africa) were increasingly relegated to supplying western Europe with raw materials produced with cheap or forced labor.

Land, Labor, and the Market

As regional and international commerce expanded, agricultural production was increasingly oriented toward sale in distant markets rather than for immediate and local use. The significant increase in urban population and the development of river and coastal navigation during the late Middle Ages encouraged greater agricultural production. Here and there, landlords ceased to be indifferent about the productivity of their lands and sought to achieve greater yields for sale in regional and distant markets. Some people began to consider land as more than a family inheritance that brought memories and status; it became a source of wealth that could be developed and evaluated according to its capacity to generate a profit. Despite emotional attachments, astute landlords increasingly sold some parcels and bought others to increase profits.

Much of the pasture and woodland of medieval Europe was used jointly by nobles and peasants according to customs of the village community. As all land became more valuable as a source of profit, however, nobles began to assert their rights to exclusive use based on absolute ownership. As they enclosed grazing land for their own use, small farmers of the village were forced to give up raising livestock of their own. This "enclosure movement" spread irregularly across western Europe from the fifteenth to the eighteenth centuries in response to rising demand (from cities) for agricultural produce.

The livelihood of peasants was frequently a casualty of this process. Although the growth of a money economy had allowed peasants to buy their way out of feudal obligations, the newly freed peasants often lost the economic basis of real independence and became simply farm laborers. As the medieval manor gradually abandoned its traditions of community welfare and solidarity under the lord's authority, peasants became independent farmers in competition with one another as well as with their former lords. In western Europe, the modernizing independent farmers, whether lords or peasants, slowly assumed control of agriculture.

In eastern Europe, however, capitalist agriculture did not lead to the emancipation of the peasantry. Here the noble landlords remained more powerful than their princes and retained absolute control of the land. Since there were few towns where people without land could find employment, the landlords were able to tie the peasants to the land (enserfment), thereby ensuring themselves a supply of cheap labor, and thus produce cash crops for the growing European market. Poland became one of the first underdeveloped areas in the world economy, specializing in a narrow range of products, marketing its produce through foreign merchants, and depending on cheap or forced labor.

However, the labor associated with manufacturing also underwent change as trade increased. During the late Middle Ages, guilds of masters and apprentices controlled most urban manufacturing for the retail trades. These guilds were unions of shopowners and workers, who set prices, wages, and standards of quality for their goods. Such a system offered a protected market for artisans within the jurisdiction of their towns and cities; it did not encourage competition or innovation. But guilds declined as cities expanded and new products appeared in local markets. Some guildmasters themselves ignored their own rules, perfected their methods, hired cheap wage labor, and sold what they could in a growing European market. In those towns that continued to enforce old guild restrictions on manufacture, entrepreneurs took their operations into the countryside, where guild laws did not apply.

Another way to avoid guild restrictions was the "putting-out system." Merchants would invest in raw materials, such as a wagonload of cloth, which they would distribute to several households for cutting into patterns. A week later they would pick up the cut cloth and deliver it to other households, where it would be sewn, and after several steps in the production process, they would sell the finished goods to retailers or wholesalers. This new system of rural manufacturing, which some historians have called "proto-industrialization," took advantage of underemployed and inexpensive rural labor that could become specialized and efficient. Using hand or unmechanized technology, rural families produced yarn, cloth, nails, pins, pots, and other items. Both the merchant and the rural workers (often entire families) bargained over wages, and the outcome depended on the market. Thus, peasants were progressively drawn into a new capitalist world of production for the market, of wage labor in rural manufacturing, and of commercialized agriculture.

As a way to organize production, the putting-out system was a transitional stage between guilds and factories. Some peasant households broke loose from the merchants' control, hired their neighbors, and set up factories of their own. By the nineteenth century, the putting-out system had ceased to be important in Europe because the factory could organize goods and labor more efficiently under one roof. But the status and conditions of labor had changed. Whereas the apprentice or journeyman had been like a family member in the master's shop and house, the factory worker became a factor of production that could be kept or abandoned according to fluctuations in the market. Although guildmasters typically exploited their journeymen and apprentices, they were all artisans who shared skilled work and the pride that went with it. In Europe's emerging capitalist system, the laborer had ceased to be regarded as a full person embedded in a network of social relationships; labor

The making of coins, shown in this sixteenth-century print, was an important element in the growth of a capitalist economy. *The Metropolitan Museum of Art, gift of Harry G. Friedman, 1962 (62.635.20)*

was becoming a commodity to be bought or sold at the most advantageous price.

Additional signs of an emerging capitalism were apparent in the development, in northern Italy, of double-entry bookkeeping; in the growing use of gold and silver currency; in the growth of banks that issued credit; and in the development of various forms of partnership. The sea captains of 1500 typically owned their own vessels, but increasingly they became employees of trading companies owned by the state, several partners, or groups of small investors. Though small entrepreneurs did not disappear, they were increasingly overshadowed in profitable international trade by states and large

companies that could raise capital through investment and credit.

Societies, States, and the Growth of Capitalism

Modern capitalism arose in a highly competitive state system. The civilization that emerged between 1400 and 1800 was religiously and politically heterogeneous but economically interdependent. Religious diversity arose from the success of the Protestant Reformation in attracting the support of roughly half of

Europe. A balance of power that prevented any single state from conquering all of Europe ensured its political diversity. Religious strife gradually subsided after the religious wars of the sixteenth century, but conflict over territory, trade, and power has remained a factor in European history to the present day. Europe's economic vigor was due in large part to its political fragmentation and competition.

Commerce expanded brilliantly in the 1500s as European ships suddenly dominated the trade routes of the world. The resulting rise in prices enriched merchants and bankers. And Europe's population continued to increase and generate higher internal demand for goods. The 1600s, however, were on the whole a different story. The flow of precious metal from the New World virtually stopped, and European prices declined. So did population in many regions, further discouraging investment and commerce. And a long and costly war in Germany drained resources. The period of economic stagnation tested the political and social institutions of nations and shifted the center of power from southern to northern Europe. The Dutch Republic and England developed strong merchant classes and became leading commercial

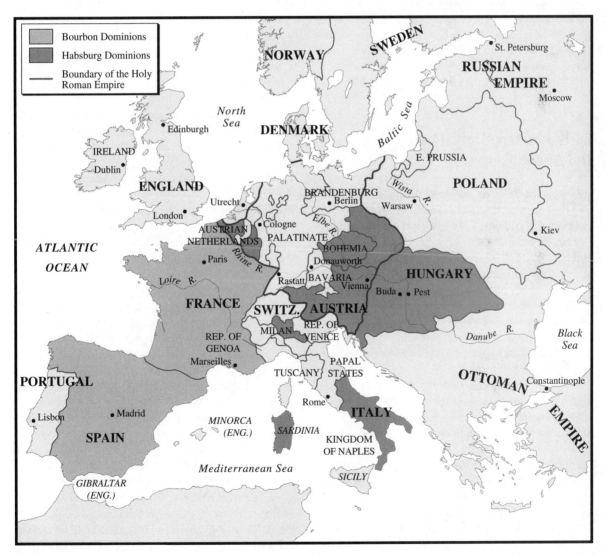

MAP 3.1 Europe, c. 1714

powers in the seventeenth century. But Italy, Portugal, and Spain, the early leaders in trade, exploration, and conquest, could not withstand the economic crisis and fell behind. How can we explain the very different social and economic histories of Europe's various states?

Capitalism, after all, was not simply an economic phenomenon but one that embraced the entire culture. The values of work, thrift, calculation, and profit had to compete with such aristocratic traditions as leisure, hospitality, and the consumption and display of luxury goods. The relative strength of various social classes and the attitudes of governments likewise played a role in shaping the nature and extent of capitalist transformation. Thus, although Europeans shared certain cultural traditions, they were far from homogeneous: each state faced the growth of the market with traditions of its own. Hence, some states responded to the opportunities and crises of capitalism more fully than others (see Map 3.1).

Early Leaders: Italy, Portugal, and Spain

Italy appeared at first the most likely candidate to lead the capitalist transformation in the West. Venice had been the principal European port on the Mediterranean since the Middle Ages, and an ancient tradition of commerce among northern Italian cities sustained their art, science, and technology. Despite these initial advantages, the Italian economy was in decline by the 1600s. Strong craft guilds kept wages so high that finished products became increasingly less competitive in European markets, and new trade routes to the East bypassed Italy. In addition, the Italian cities failed to form a unified state that could defend frontiers, enforce uniform laws, and furnish merchants with a large internal market. Before it achieved national unification in 1860, Italy remained a marginal participant in the world economy.

A second candidate for economic leadership was Portugal. At the intersection of trade routes from the Mediterranean to the North Sea, to the East Indies around Africa, and to the Americas via the Canary and Cape Verde Islands, Portugal was briefly the hub of world maritime commerce. Brilliant exploration and the strategic conquest of trading stations from Africa to the East Indies promised riches for the fu-

ture. But there were liabilities. Portugal was relatively isolated from rich urban markets in the rest of Europe, and its population of only two million was inadequate to support a world power with a global commercial network and simultaneously develop a strong urban manufacturing base. Most important, the country remained semifeudal, its working population tied to subsistence agriculture, mining for export, or the production of port wine. The aristocratic ruling class and the government controlled a trading empire that yielded rich profits and saw little reason to invest capital and labor in manufactures. Hence, a vigorous middle class of artisans and manufacturers failed to develop. Although Portugal continued to maintain outposts and carry on trade in Brazil, Africa, and Asia, by the seventeenth century its role in the rise of capitalism was overshadowed by that of several other European states that fostered industry as well as trade.

For a century following Columbus's discovery of America, Spain was the dominant European power and seemed destined to control world trade as well. Regular cargoes of gold and silver arrived from colonies in America to sustain Spanish prosperity in the sixteenth century. Although the gold and silver were real, the prosperity was an illusion. Chronic debt plagued the Spanish crown and suggested national problems that gold alone could not cure. Spanish land, wealth, and values remained under the control of a leisure class of landed aristocrats who put their stamp on the entire culture. In the *hidalgo,* or aristocratic, tradition, leisure was more honorable than enterprise. Moreover, the monarchy granted aristocrats a monopoly on sheepherding, known as the *mesta,* in return for a tax on exports of wool. Although this measure raised revenue in the short run, it discouraged improvements in farming, such as enclosures, which would have given Spain a stronger and more independent economy. No dynamic middle class, admiring work and thrift, arose to challenge the entrenched *hidalgos,* supported by the government, contemptuous of business, and content to spend their wealth on foreign goods. Like Portugal, Spain spent its wealth of the sixteenth century on imports instead of investing it in domestic industrial capacity.

In addition, Spain's national energy served a crusading religious spirit rather than economic development. Militant Catholicism had rallied and united the country against the Moors, but in European wars and the Inquisition, Spain squandered soldiers and money in a tragic struggle against Protestants and, within its own borders, against nominal Christians of Muslim or Jewish descent. As capitalism spread in areas of growing religious toleration, Spain wore itself out in a doomed attempt to enforce religious uniformity both at home and abroad. While shipments of gold and silver from America lasted, Spain retained a veneer of prosperity but remained weak in technology and production. And then, in the 1600s, the center of world trade shifted from southern to northern Europe.

Protestants and Capitalists: Germany and the Netherlands

The German sociologist Max Weber (1864–1920) noted that the Calvinist version of Protestantism discouraged vain display and inspired sobriety, savings, and hard work. Eager to demonstrate by their worldly success that they were predestined to salvation, people cultivated those traits of character that increased rather than dissipated wealth.[4] To Weber, the histories of Holland, England, northern Germany, and the United States constituted strong evidence of a link between capitalist growth and Protestantism. Yet there are enough examples of Catholic capitalists in Europe to suggest that religion alone cannot account for the rise of capitalism.

Protestant northern Germany was unable for centuries to overcome the economic weakness that resulted from political disunity. During the early modern period, Germany was more of a geographical than a political reality. The Holy Roman Empire was a loose federation of about three hundred German cities, principalities, bishoprics, and states. Catholic and Protestant coalitions fought for control of these territories in the Thirty Years' War (1618–1648), but Germany emerged from that devastating struggle no more united than before. The empire remained fragmented until Prussia forged a united Germany in 1871. Here was a clear illustration of the importance of state-building in economic development, for Germany remained a minor factor in the European economy until its unification in the nineteenth century.

Like most of Europe in the sixteenth century, the Netherlands was torn by religious and political strife. Finally, in 1609, after several decades of war, the predominantly Protestant northern provinces won

formal independence from Spain. Refugees from the Spanish Netherlands, which remained Catholic, fled to the new Dutch Republic (Holland) and contributed significantly to a golden age that encompassed art and science as well as industry and trade. A policy of religious toleration attracted immigrants with valuable technical skills and encouraged new industries to complement the solid agricultural base. Limited in population and land, the Dutch made the most of what they possessed. A critical factor in their rapid success was a maritime fleet that became the largest in the world in the seventeenth century. Made up of small crews and efficient vessels, it imported raw materials and goods for manufacturing and consumption and exported finished products all over the world. With commercial success, the internationally respected Dutch florin made Amsterdam the most important European money and banking center up to the French Revolution. No religious, social, or legal barriers held back Dutch trade and manufactures, and, as a result, a highly enterprising capitalist class arose to set the pace of early modern Europe's economic development. Although France and England had superior resources and dominated world trade after 1700, the small Dutch state continued to accumulate wealth through trade and investment and remained an example of what capitalism could achieve.

Capitalism and the English Revolution

Unlike Germany and the Netherlands, England was spared religious wars in the sixteenth century because its king, Henry VIII (reigned 1509–1547), seized control of the Roman Catholic church in England and renamed it the Church of England. During much of the economically troubled seventeenth century, however, the English wrestled with religious and political issues, endured a revolution, executed one of their kings, and later restored the monarchy. The outcome of this tumultuous century was a social and political system particularly favorable to the growth of capitalism.

Following the death of Queen Elizabeth I (the daughter of Henry VIII) in 1603, two monarchs of the Stuart line tried to reinstate Catholicism as the official religion of the realm, a measure opposed by both Anglicans and other Protestant dissenters such as the Calvinist Puritans and Quakers. The Stuarts posed a political as well as a religious threat, for they sought to wrest power from Parliament, which was controlled by the landed gentry and wealthy merchants and represented the emerging capitalist forces in the country. Open war between Parliament and King Charles I broke out in 1642, and Oliver Cromwell, a commoner, led the parliamentary forces to victory. For the next eighteen years, England was a republic known as the Commonwealth. But the Calvinists ruled by force rather than consent, and soon after Cromwell's death in 1658, the largely Anglican Parliament recalled a Stuart king, Charles II. A generation later, Parliament tired of constant quarrels with its Catholic monarch and, in 1688, invited the Dutch prince William of Orange to become king, with his English Protestant wife, Mary, as queen. Following this particularly bloodless Glorious Revolution that installed William and Mary on the throne, Parliament's Bill of Rights in 1689 stipulated that taxes and standing armies required Parliament's approval, that each subject had the right to due process of law, and that the king had no power to suspend a law of the land. Parliament had declared its political supremacy.

The Glorious Revolution was far from democratic, however. Parliament consisted of prosperous landowners, professionals, and merchants elected by the most prosperous citizens. Democratic ideas were unpopular in part because of their association with some of Cromwell's followers, known as the Levelers, who sought far more radical reform. Furthermore, the revolution brought only limited religious toleration. The Church of England maintained its hold on political offices, and other religious groups—Catholics and Puritans among them—were excluded and denied the vote.

While the issues in the English Revolution were religious and political, the principles it established—religious toleration, supremacy of Parliament, and clear limits on the power of the king—helped create a society in which those of property were secure, powerful, and unlikely to spend their treasure on wasteful religious conflict. Thus, there were powerful reasons for the success of capitalism in England. Following the Glorious Revolution, the country was politically stable and controlled by an unusual alliance of landed and commercial elites, who domi-

nated Parliament until the twentieth century. With the support of Parliament, rural landlords were able to enclose much of the common land to graze their own sheep for the expanding wool market. As a result, the marginal farmers, forced from the countryside to the towns and cities, complained that "sheep were eating men." Unlike Spain, however, England did not neglect agriculture, for enclosed land devoted to crops produced some of the highest yields in Europe. The rural base of England's economy was secure and efficient; furthermore, the countryside supplied a work force to the towns and cities.

With only five million inhabitants in 1600, however, England did not seem destined for leadership in the world economy. But, like the Netherlands, this country made good use of its resources and situation. Scotland joined England in 1707, thus creating the United Kingdom of Great Britain. This island nation required no large land army, and tax revenues consequently went largely to support the Royal Navy, which protected the merchant fleet as well as the coastline. England had become a leading seafaring nation at the moment when sea routes originating in Europe evolved into a global network. Confidence soared in 1588, when the Royal Navy destroyed the Spanish Armada. Even religious strife, which sent Puritans, Quakers, and Catholics into exile to North America in the 1600s, contributed to English economic growth, for the English colonies in America became part of a commercial network that stretched from East Asia to the Caribbean. Loss of the American colonies in the eighteenth century did little to slow the expansion of British commerce throughout the world. In fact, the United States soon became a valuable trading partner.

Capitalism flourished in England as manufacturing expanded. By the seventeenth century, woolen cloth of high quality found a market in Antwerp because of the decline of the Italian cloth trade. Other industries such as coal, iron, armaments, and shipbuilding brought wealth to a growing class of manufacturers. Efficient agriculture furnished a surplus that could support this manufacturing sector of the economy as well as the merchant class.

The three centuries from 1500 to 1800 laid the groundwork in England for the Industrial Revolution that would follow. National unity, political stability, social mobility, trading companies, the navy

VOICES
Revolutionary Dreams in Song

French revolutionaries used music, art, and theater to help shape a new nation and to create citizens who shared common aspirations. While Robespierre had the Cathedral of Notre Dame converted into a Temple of Reason, the following solemn "Hymn to Liberty" nevertheless combined the form of traditional church music with the explicit message of the Enlightenment.

Hymn to Liberty

Oh Liberty, sacred Liberty!
Goddess of an enlightened people!
Rule today within these walls.
Through you this temple is purified!
Liberty! Before you, reason chases out deception,
Error flees, fanaticism is beaten down.
Our gospel is nature,
And our cult is virtue.

To love one's country and one's brothers,
To serve the Sovereign People—

These are the sacred tenets
And the pledge of a Republican.
He does not fear the futile flame
Of a chimeric hell;
He does not wait for the false rewards
Of a deceptive heaven;
Heaven is peace of the soul
And hell is remorse.

Shield the Republic and its children
From ignoble slaves.
Our cause is just, they are brave,
Make them return triumphant.
When the powerless rage of tyrants
Is punished by them.
Let us watch out for them,
And may France on their return,
Offer them a family
United by nature and by love.

Source: From James Leith "Music for Mass Persuasion During the Terror" n.p., n.d. (a collection of texts, tapes and slides, copyright for James A. Leith, Queen's University, Kingston).

and a large maritime fleet, highly productive agriculture, and laws and habits that favored commerce— these elements made Great Britain the leading capitalist country at the beginning of the nineteenth century.

France: The Old Regime, the Revolution, and Capitalism

France was a country of more than fifteen million in 1600, about three times the population of England, and at that point it appeared to be far richer in natural resources. But population, size, and natural wealth were not sufficient to guarantee economic growth. In contrast to England, France was divided by religious wars in the 1500s, and the aristocracy and bourgeoisie failed to form a cohesive ruling class. By the 1600s, the monarchy finally controlled a united kingdom, but French kings, although claiming to be absolute, were powerless to reconcile the rising bourgeoisie with the traditional aristocracy.

France also differed from England in having to support a large army to defend its borders; thus, the military budget could not be devoted almost entirely to the navy. A further drain on national resources was the luxury of the monarchy itself under Louis XIV, from 1643 to 1715. Not only his wars but also his immense chateau at Versailles strained the economy to the limit. As a class the aristocracy was more decorative than functional and lived on rents from land, feudal dues, government subsidies, and tax exemptions. Only a minority of aristocrats became active capitalist farmers in the eighteenth century. So, despite its large population, France remained a country of small farmers who could not generate a brisk demand for consumer goods. Most peasants were free and owned some land, but because of taxes, they could afford to purchase only bare necessities.

Despite the unfavorable conditions for the growth of a capitalist economy, France's sheer size counted for something, and a merchant class steadily grew in wealth and influence. The monarchy had long recognized the importance of commerce and subsidized trading companies, such as the East India Company, and industries, such as tapestries and porcelain. But pressure for a basic transformation of the society could come only from outside the official ruling class. During the Enlightenment, the bourgeoisie and liberal elements of the aristocracy expressed the need for such basic change. A critical minority of *philosophes* and their readers could see that Europe was shrugging off aristocratic values and adopting instead those of the commercial bourgeoisie. Not only Great Britain but also the newly formed United States served as examples of a liberal society in which careers were open to talent. But in France, the monarchy, the aristocracy, and the church were all opposed to the formation of such a society.

This opposition delayed fundamental change in France but could not stop it. Support of the American colonists in their war against Britain exhausted the French treasury, and Louis XVI was compelled to summon the Estates General, a deliberative body dating to the fourteenth century and composed of representatives of the clergy (First Estate), nobility (Second Estate), and commoners (Third Estate). The king had hoped that the nobility, who dominated the first two estates, would consent to paying higher taxes and thus solve the state's financial crisis. Instead, the Third Estate declared itself the National Assembly in June 1789; a Parisian crowd in July stormed the Bastille (a prison and a hated symbol of the regime); peasants throughout the summer pillaged manor houses; and the monarchy collapsed. Political authority passed into the hands of lawyers, notaries, and liberal aristocrats who originally represented the Third Estate and now claimed to speak for the entire nation.

The National Assembly supported a constitutional monarchy and drew up a "Declaration of the Rights of Man and the Citizen," a truly revolutionary document that overturned basic principles of the old order:

> I.   Men are born and always continue free and equal in respect of their rights. Civil distinctions, therefore, can be founded only on public utility.
>
> II. The end of all political associations is the preservation of the natural and imprescriptible rights of man; and these rights are liberty, property, security, and resistance to oppression.
>
> III. The nation is essentially the source of all sovereignty; nor can any individual, or any body of men, be entitled to any authority which is not expressly derived from it.

Thus the aristocracy lost its legal privileges, and civil equality became a central principle of the state.

For the next several years, and even for decades, the French struggled over what the declaration and

The women's march on the King's palace at Versailles was an important event in the revolutionary process of 1789 in France. Note the reluctant participation of the well-dressed woman on the left. *The Bettman Archive*

the slogan "Liberty, Equality, Fraternity" should mean in public life. Since 1789, reaction against the revolution had been building. By 1790, the National Assembly took stock of the Roman Catholic church's hostility to the new regime, placed French priests under government authority, sold church lands to raise revenues, and thereby provoked intense opposition from loyal Catholics. Most aristocrats, who had lost their privileges, also opposed the revolution, especially as it became more radical. So as the revolutionary government tried to mobilize the country against a European military coalition, Catholics and aristocrats led internal revolts, most notably in the Vendée, a western province.

By 1792, there were serious threats to the new French regime, not only from foreign invasion and civil war, but also from peasants and workers, whose economic condition had deteriorated. In this crisis and under pressure from a radical popular government in Paris, a new legislature—the National Convention—took extreme measures that amounted to a sharp break with the past. The legislature abandoned the constitutional monarchy, condemned Louis XVI and Queen Marie Antoinette to death on the guillotine, and proclaimed a republic. The convention's famous Committee of Public Safety, led by Maximilien Robespierre, a provincial lawyer, attempted to silence opposition by terror: revolutionary courts tried "suspects" and sent the guilty, many of whom were aristocrats, to the guillotine. In addition, the committee instituted price controls, required military service, and even imposed a new calendar to proclaim a new era.

During the first five years of the French Revolution, people who had never before participated in politics joined political clubs, took part in marches and demonstrations, served on local committees, and ran for public office. Common people who had identified primarily with their local community now thought of themselves as belonging to a nation. Thus, the political education and awakening of the masses had begun, and in the near future French nationalism would provoke a similar awakening in the rest of Europe.

By 1795, the threat to national security in France had passed, and it was clear that the French had grown weary of the Committee of Public Safety's high-handed methods. Robespierre himself perished on the guillotine, and for the next four years, a more moderate republican government ruled France. But throughout a turbulent decade, France failed to achieve a republican political consensus, and in 1799, General Napoleon Bonaparte, opportunistic and ambitious, seized power and ruled until 1814.

Napoleon (1769–1821) was an autocrat, but he contributed much to the modernization of France by blending traditions of the *ancien regime* with new ideas from the Enlightenment and the French Revolution. Napoleon did not tolerate freedom of speech or the press, but he supported civil equality and promotion according to merit rather than birth. Although he established a new aristocracy based on merit and wealth, neither the new nor the old aristocrats enjoyed special legal privileges. Public honors depended on service to the state or real achievements in the world. Aristocrats still took pride in their titles, but France was no longer an aristocratic society, for careers were open to those with talent.

Despite chronic political strife, France emerged from the revolution and the Napoleonic Empire with new traditions and institutions favoring the bourgeoisie and the development of capitalism. Citizens were subject to taxation on an equal basis by the state alone, and thus property was secure. Guilds were abolished, for they were viewed as a restraint on employment, production, and trade. Uniform weights and measures, a consistent set of laws (the Code Napoleon), a centralized system of education, and a reformed government administration were other enduring accomplishments. France had produced a great reservoir of ideas and institutions that spurred the democratic Republican movement in Europe in the nineteenth century. In 1848, for instance, revolutions echoing 1789 erupted in France, Germany, Italy, and Austria. And in the twentieth century all of the democratic and Socialist movements—in India, Africa, China, Southeast Asia, and South America—could trace their roots to the French revolutionary tradition.

The French Revolution had such an extensive influence because it established an agenda for change that went far beyond reforms permitting the bourgeoisie to compete successfully in a capitalist world. "Liberté, Egalité, Fraternité" became a cry worldwide for people who sought relief from political oppression. In France and elsewhere, the poor would interpret *egalité* as something more sweeping than equality before the law. So although the immediate effect of the revolution in France was to abolish aristocratic privilege and establish a liberal society dominated by successful bourgeois, the revolution also awakened the masses and introduced Socialist ideals that would challenge bourgeois society up to the present day. The French Revolution was more violent than either the English or the American Revolution, in part because it gave sharper expression to more radical aspirations of ordinary people. Its immediate effect, however, was to permit France to establish its own version of a liberal society in which capitalism could flourish.

Toward a Capitalist Society and Culture

What changed in Europe between 1400 and 1800? Although mechanical inventions contributed to rising productivity, the truly dramatic advances in technology would come in the following two centuries. Nor did the ratio of urban to rural population change appreciably: more than 80 percent of Europeans continued to toil on the land. Much of Europe's economic life remained local in character, quite unaffected by the growth of world trade. Still, Europe had changed in important ways. Its largest cities more than doubled in population and formed a commercial network that superimposed itself on the rural world. In the past, wealth had derived principally from the exploitation of rural land, but now manufacturing and trade also produced large fortunes. Cities were no longer isolated, walled enclaves within a society that lived by different values, for urban commercial values increasingly penetrated the countryside. As rural Europe sent larger shares of its produce to urban markets, landlords and peasants learned to farm the land for maximum profit rather than simply to fulfill basic needs.

By 1800, merchants and modern politicians understood that their interests were allied. Now the hereditary aristocracy had competition for the king's favors, and in the case of the Netherlands, Britain, the United States, and France, the bourgeoisie assumed outright political control or gained a preponderant influence in public affairs.

The commercialization and specialization of labor—both agricultural and artisan—began to affect the lives of families in general and of women in particular between 1400 and 1800. Commercial agricul-

Capitalism and industrialization largely destroyed the kind of artisan's workshop depicted here. Critics of capitalism decried the loss of such home and family based production in favor of the impersonal and wholly commercial factory workplace. *Holzapfel-DF*

ture tended to favor farms run by nuclear families rather than those on which extended families carried out a basically subsistence agriculture. But married women on both types of farm continued to carry out traditional tasks, such as caring for cows and chickens as well as helping in the fields, raising children, and cooking. Unmarried women in both rural and urban settings frequently became known as "spinsters," as spinning became a means for women to support themselves or to contribute to family income. But they did much else, and rural manufacturing organized by the putting-out system gave some women an independent income. The new freedom that came with this income alarmed religious and civil authorities, who sought in various ways to push women back into male-headed households. Some historians have suggested that this hostility toward unmarried and more independent women may have played a role in the upsurge of witchcraft accusations and trials, most involving women, that broke out in the sixteenth and seventeenth centuries in parts of Europe.[5]

If the putting-out system of manufacturing offered women new, though quite low-paying, economic opportunities, it also diminished their role in traditional guilds. As guilds faced growing competition from merchant-financed manufacturing, their male leaders acted to restrict women's participation in direct production. But to the extent that urban craft workers lived and pursued their trade in the same building, women still played a role: they were typically in charge of keeping accounts and dealing with clients. Thus, although there was some division of labor based on gender, men and women of the working class did not inhabit those separate worlds that the Industrial Revolution would increasingly create.

Although change occurred slowly, the leavening influence of capitalism had created a new social order and a new conception of society. As the Roman Catholic church lost its monopoly on moral authority, merchants as well as states invoked the principle of self-interest to justify their policy and behavior. The Scottish philosopher and economist Adam Smith (1723–1790) articulated most clearly this radically new view. His *Wealth of Nations* (1776) became the classic defense of the market economy that was transforming the world. Self-interest, Smith wrote, would direct buyers and sellers to the best prices, and assuming that the government did not intervene, prices would fluctuate based on supply and demand. A shortage of labor or goods would immediately affect the price of those items in a free market, and thus the shortage would soon be filled by those eager to make a profit. Once the shortage vanished, prices would return to normal, and self-interested producers and workers would seek similar opportunities elsewhere. In this way, the domestic economy would constantly regulate itself to the advantage of all despite the selfish motives of individuals. Such a system required neither tradition nor political intervention. Nor did it require men and women to be compassionate, just, or concerned with the welfare of their neighbors. It asked them only to pursue their own interests.

Smith also believed that production should be carried out as rationally as possible to maximize output. He observed that a pin factory could turn out more pins if each worker specialized in a small part of the process rather than producing each entire pin before going on to the next one. There should be a division of labor between nations as well, he argued, for if every nation concentrated on what it did best, and if there were no tariffs, then production would reach its optimum, and people would attain the highest possi-

ble standard of living. An "invisible hand" would turn the selfish instincts of individuals and nations into a rising standard of living for the human race. The image of a continually growing and self-regulating economy that Smith articulated was a profoundly new conception of human society.

In a dramatic transmutation of values, the vices of an earlier age had become capitalist virtues. Smith's economic writings reflected important aspects of the cultural transformation of the capitalist era. Absent were religious warnings against usury or greed; on the contrary, the capitalist was urged to make as much money as possible. Nor did Smith uphold the traditions of fine craft work or the regulations of guilds: if mass-produced goods could compete in the marketplace, they should prevail. Rational people should strive for profits wherever they could be found, and rational states should buy and sell freely the goods that they are best suited to produce. These ideas were the culmination of recent economic thought best characterized by the phrase *laissez-faire,* the belief that buyers and sellers should be free to pursue their own interests unregulated by guilds or governments.

Smith's version of economic liberalism became the cornerstone of modern economic theory. However, governments adopted his ideas only selectively as they continued to intervene in the economy to safeguard national interests. The British, for example, generally supported free trade because they could compete successfully in the world market, but many other countries felt obliged to protect their industries by erecting tariff barriers. And how could one sovereign state calmly depend on another to manufacture all of its weapons? As a prescription for international relations, Smith's liberalism was too utopian; it presupposed peace and relative equality among European states over the long term. But states were not equal. And in the nineteenth century, the capitalist system that Smith described and justified—combined now with ingenious technological innovations—sharpened even further the disparities of power among European states and between them and the rest of the world.

Notes

1. These distinctions are spelled out clearly in Robert Heilbroner, *The Making of Economic Society* (Englewood Cliffs, N.J.: Prentice-Hall, 1962).

2. William T. Rowe, "Approaches to Modern Chinese Social History," in *Reliving the Past,* ed. Olivier Zunz (Chapel Hill: University of North Carolina Press, 1985), p. 270.

3. Maxime Rodinson, *Islam and Capitalism* (Austin: University of Texas Press, 1978), p. 54.

4. Max Weber, *The Protestant Ethic and the Spirit of Capitalism* (New York: Scribner's, 1958).

5. Merry E. Wiesner, "Women's Work in the Changing City Economy, 1500–1650," in *Connecting Spheres: Women in the Western World, 1500 to the Present,* ed. Marilyn J. Boxer and Jean H. Quataert (New York: Oxford University Press, 1987), pp. 64–74.

Chapter 4

"The Great Acceleration": Industrialization and Social Change in Europe

Before 1800, the wealthiest capitalists of Europe were typically merchants, who earned their profits from domestic and international trade. Yet despite their success, they had not swept away the traditional economy or society of the Middle Ages. In much of Europe, a dual economy prevailed, in which capitalism, based on profit-seeking through commerce, was the dynamic element prevalent in cities and towns, whereas rural, agrarian society and manufacturing had changed relatively little. Only in certain industries such as mining, iron-smelting, shipbuilding, and weapons manufacture had aggressive entrepreneurs already taken control of the entire process of production. Capitalist practices, values, and institutions had taken root, but nowhere did they dominate the entire society.

After 1800, however, Europe's capitalist transformation entered a new phase, sometimes called *industrial capitalism,* and its historical development began to diverge much more sharply than before from that of China and the Islamic world. During the nineteenth century, production—especially industrial production that required a large capital investment—came to be controlled by a relatively small group of large-scale *capitalists*. Their social class, the bourgeoisie, finally emerged into social and political prominence, and their unique values and outlook came to define European culture. At the other end of the social scale, working for money wages became widespread for the first time. And a flood of technological innovations vastly increased European output. These changes collectively represent the first appearance in history of a thoroughly capitalist society. That process fundamentally transformed all of life

and richly deserves the label so often given it: the *Industrial Revolution.*

Machines and Steam: Perspectives on the Industrial Revolution

Strictly speaking, the Industrial Revolution was a matter of technology: the application of inanimate power (steam or electric) to industrial processes and the conversion from handicraft to machine production. But it was Europe's capitalist framework that provided the incentives to mobilize both capital and human energy on such an enormous scale. Great Britain pioneered this unique combination of elements. Since merchant capitalism in the eighteenth century was most advanced in Britain, the conditions were ripe for new investment and further organizational and technological change. The development of the steam engine and machinery for spinning and weaving triggered Britain's Industrial Revolution from roughly 1760 to 1830. France's development throughout the nineteenth century was far more gradual, unfolding perhaps thirty to fifty years later than Britain's. Germany's industrialization was also delayed, but it was explosive in the late nineteenth century. Nor was the Industrial Revolution limited to Europe. It spread to the United States, Russia, and Japan in the nineteenth century and to much of the rest of the world, in varying degrees, in the twentieth.

Textiles, steam power, coal, iron, steel, and railroads were the primary elements of the first phase, which lasted into the final third of the nineteenth century. Chemical and electrical industries then triggered a second phase. And in the twentieth century, technological innovations came at an accelerating pace with the development of electronics, the internal-combustion engine, nuclear energy, and computers. Thus, the first phase of the Industrial Revolution, begun in Britain not much more than two centuries ago, initiated a process that, like modern science, built cumulatively upon itself and continues to transform human societies today.

Industrialization and Modern History

It would be difficult to overestimate the significance of industrialization in the history of the human enterprise. At the most basic level, it changed the relationship of human beings to nature: industrialized societies gained further mastery over the physical environment, felt superior to it, and proceeded to despoil it. Europeans were optimistic throughout the nineteenth century that science and industry would produce unending progress for the whole human race. Only an undercurrent of critical voices regretted the declining respect for nature and asked how much of this process the earth's thin crust could support and how much the human body could withstand. By the last quarter of the twentieth century, awareness of these unintended and unexpected consequences of economic "progress" had become much more widespread.

The Industrial Revolution also caused shifts in the division of labor and in relative power among human societies. As the first industrialized society, Britain initially seized the lion's share of international trade. Only in the twentieth century did other European states decisively overtake Great Britain in manufacturing and international commerce. Meanwhile, Europe as a whole unequivocally cemented its economic and military domination of the world through industrialization.

Inevitably, Europe's wealth and power provoked both anger and envy in the rest of the world: anger because colonial and nonindustrialized societies were exploited and prevented from industrializing themselves; envy because Europeans had discovered a way to raise their standard of living to unparalleled levels. France, Britain, and the United States served as models to states that had not modernized; they pointed the way to a higher standard of living, greater material security, and even political survival in a highly competitive world. Their very power and success suggested that the future of the world lay in capitalist industrialization.

But in the twentieth century, a number of societies, including Russia and China, sought to separate the twin elements of Europe's economic revolution, avidly accepting its industrial technology while rejecting its capitalist framework. The economic failure of communism by the 1990s raised the question of whether an advanced industrial society could survive outside of a capitalist system. Other critics, focusing on the environmental consequences of industrial development, came to question whether industrial societies in any form represented a viable long-term future for the human species.

Within those European societies that first experienced industrialization, its economic significance lay in an unprecedented increase in total wealth. Production per capita rose sharply, average real income increased, and the material standard of living improved. The middle class expanded in numbers and gained in prosperity as people seized new opportunities for employment and investment. Rising new fortunes amassed by industrial capitalists and the rising standard of living of the bourgeoisie gave substance to the capitalist promise of unlimited growth. And whereas in the preindustrial era, most people assumed that poverty for much of the population was inevitable, the new means of production seemed capable of abolishing it. Although the new industrial working class became the victims of grim working conditions, uncertain employment, and meager wages, even they gradually gained access, largely through their own vigorous efforts, to more of the benefits of Europe's remarkable economic revolution.

New sources of power changed the size and location of the productive units in Europe. Greater power could handle more and larger machines, and their efficient use required the concentration of work in a relatively large building. Thus, the factory became distinct from the owner's house and constituted a separate world with its own logic and routine; here the worker was disciplined to follow the cadence of machine and clock. Nor was the factory anymore tied to a river as a source of power: it could function in a city, where labor was plentiful, or near a supply of raw material such as wood, coal, or iron ore. Some old cities declined or barely sustained their population while others gained dramatically. Increased migration of people within Europe and from Europe to the United States and to colonial territories was a symptom of new conditions and opportunities.

The social significance of Europe's economic transformation lies in changes in both class and gender relationships. Most notably, the peasantry declined as a percentage of the population as the urban working class and the middle class rose. Likewise, landed aristocrats found that they had to share prestige and power with the commercial and industrial bourgeoisie as both were challenged by the demands of the industrial proletariat. Within the family, the economic lives of many women diverged from those of men as the workplace was separated from the home. At the same time, the family probably became a more central factor in the emotional lives of people as they made their way in an often impersonal urban environment.

Such were the profound changes that flowed from Europe's Industrial Revolution. No wonder, then, that historians, economists, and modern policymakers have tried to discover what made it all possible.

Preconditions for Industrialization

Scholars have long debated the mix of elements that initiated and sustained Europe's Industrial Revolution. A narrow explanation focuses on the dramatic technological changes—the steam engine, the power loom, the railroad. But technology became critical only in the context of a broad range of social, economic, and political preconditions.

Population and Technology

Entrepreneurs must have a motive to change their methods and invest in costly new equipment. Taking such risk is justified either by severe competition or by the promise of extraordinary profit. A sharp rise in the European population after 1750 provided both. Increased population spurred demand for agricultural and manufactured goods and thus encouraged investment. Ambitious farmers sought means to extract more from land already under cultivation so as to produce a surplus for the urban market and realize a maximum profit. Some of the increase in rural popu-

Power looms were a central technological innovation of the early industrial revolution. Women could weave at least as well as men and often worked for lower wages. *Library of Congress*

lation was used as farm labor, but many people fled to cities for employment. The rising European population, in short, created both a growing demand for goods and services and a labor force for manufacturing. A significant number of entrepreneurs seized this opportunity to change their methods of production.

As the rising population increased the overall demand for goods, individual manufacturers competed ever more aggressively for a share of the European market. Old handicraft traditions of manufacture, upheld by guilds, gradually gave way to more efficient and cost-effective methods. Entrepreneurs tried to increase productivity, control quality, and lower price by replacing manual labor wherever possible with machines.

Inventors had been devising machines for new tasks since the Middle Ages, but the Industrial Revolution brought the engineer to the center of the stage. Not only were basic inventions such as the steam engine and the dynamo important; their refinements and applications were practically endless in the new commercial environment. Hence, an industrializing society required not merely a handful of inspired inventors but an entire class of engineers and technicians as well. By the late nineteenth century, "pure" scientists from the universities also brought their theoretical knowledge to practical engineering problems; universities and industry began to collaborate, whereas in the past they had shared very little.

Empire and Industry

One of the most sensitive issues involving the origins of Europe's Industrial Revolution is the question of imperialism. Was Europe's economic progress purchased at the direct expense of exploited peoples in Asia, Africa, and the Americas? Did the resources gained from empire provide a crucial boost to Europe's industrial development?

In the three hundred years preceding Europe's industrial takeoff, its well-known voyages of discovery and conquest had established a growing hold on India, a burgeoning slave trade in Africa, and extensive colonial possessions in the Americas. There were at least three ways in which these global connections might have contributed to Europe's Industrial Revolution. The first was plunder. The enormous treasures of gold and silver looted from Aztecs and Incas

and smaller amounts seized in India certainly enriched Europe but were hardly decisive for its industrialization. The continuing economic backwardness of Spain despite its windfall from the New World illustrates the point. However, by adding to Europe's money supplies, imperial treasure increased demand and fostered commerce and so, in general, stimulated Europe's economic vitality.

More important than plunder for Europe's industrialization were the demand and the profits derived from its growing international trade, a clear result of its global expansion. England's colonial trade, for example, exploded in the eighteenth century: exports to North America and the West Indies doubled between 1750 and 1790, and those to India more than tripled. This growing demand from the colonies certainly stimulated England's capitalist economy, even if it was not alone sufficient to trigger an Industrial Revolution. And the profits from the colonial trade in slaves, tobacco, spices, cotton, sugar, and other commodities contributed to the pool of capital from which British and continental industrialists drew as they invested in new machines and factories.

Europe's global expansion also provided real resources: cod from the Grand Banks of Newfoundland; forest products from trade with Russia; sugar, cotton, and rice from the tropical possessions; grain from North America; and human labor from Africa. "An unparalleled share of the earth's biological resources was acquired for this one culture," writes historian E. L. Jones, "on a scale that was unprecedented and is unrepeatable."[1] None of this—plunder, markets, profit, or resources—was alone decisive in triggering the Industrial Revolution, but all contributed to the general economic growth that made possible the industrialization of Europe.

Imperialism intensified during the nineteenth century as the Industrial Revolution spread. Britain tightened its grip on India; Britain, France, Belgium, and Germany seized most of Africa; France took over Indochina; Britain and France forced China to open its ports to trade on European terms; and at the end of the century, the United States seized the Philippines and Cuba and established its own overseas empire. In this environment, imperialism seemed to promise economic advantages for certain industries: the German steel and shipbuilding lobby, for example, successfully argued for a large navy and an aggressive imperial policy. Without taking stock of the cost of imperialism to governments, many industrialists and enthusiasts of empire believed that colonies were essential to European economic progress and acted on that assumption.

Whether colonies were in fact necessary to sustain industrial prosperity is doubtful. Although they furnished raw materials, they were on the whole rather weak markets for finished industrial goods because of the low wages and general poverty of colonial subjects. The industrializing countries themselves, precisely because of their prosperity, were the best customers for their own goods. In fact, most scholars calculate that, on balance, nineteenth-century colonies placed a heavy military and administrative burden on European states, a burden that was not balanced by the economic rewards. Only in indirect ways, perhaps, did nineteenth-century imperialist expansion in Africa, China, and elsewhere assist industrialization. By fostering nationalism, imperialism tended to divert the attention of the working class from its social grievances; colonies provided land, wealth, and administrative employment for traditional elites threatened at home by social and economic change; and the military competition between states for colonial possessions persuaded governments to invest in the latest research and industrial techniques. It is impossible to compile a precise balance sheet of advantages and disadvantages, but once the industrializing process got started in earnest, European imperialism probably cost far more than it earned.

The State and the Economy

Political conditions also played an important role in establishing a climate for industrialization. Since the Middle Ages, European monarchs reclaimed control of their territory from nobilities that had for centuries enjoyed much political autonomy at the local level. As that authority became consolidated around a single figure, responsibility for national welfare also came to rest with the central government. The monarch not only organized military defense but also tried to create the optimum conditions for economic prosperity. Despite Adam Smith's theory of laissez-faire (see Chapter 3), European governments continued to assist their economies: state investment and financial guarantees for railroads, bridges, roads, and harbors; tariffs to protect young industries from for-

eign competition; and tax relief to encourage crucial industries.

But each state and its economy were linked in other ways fully as important. Consolidation of national territory under one government with the same laws, administration, and money meant an internal market where goods and services could flow freely. Lacking this kind of unity, Germany and Italy were left behind, until the late nineteenth century, in the race to industrialize.

National unity was important for industrial modernization, but it was not sufficient. Both France and Britain were unified states in the eighteenth century, but Britain, despite a smaller population, was better suited for economic development. A modernizing elite of landowners and merchants took control of Parliament in the seventeenth century and created favorable conditions for growth. France, by contrast, had to endure a costly revolution a full century later to sweep away feudal institutions that were restraining capitalist expansion. Germany, on the other hand, was able to industrialize rapidly after unification in 1871 without undermining the power of the landed aristocracy.

Thus, there were different paths to industrialization. In some respects, the process of applying machines to production was the same everywhere, but the political and social context and the timing of the transformation varied from country to country.

Separate Paths to Industrialization

Since Great Britain was the first to industrialize, many historians and economists have assumed that other countries would have to replicate the British experience quite closely in order to achieve the same result. Once Great Britain had made the breakthrough, however, the competitive situation in the world had changed. Other countries were suddenly at a severe disadvantage in international trade. Aware of this, their governments sought to catch up with Great Britain by any means available. The historian Alexander Gerschenkron attributes the industrialization of Continental Europe largely to the efforts of governments to overcome economic backwardness with respect to Great Britain.[2] He sees no single set of preconditions for an industrial revolution but a willingness on the part of the state and of a modernizing elite to invest in new technology so as to catch up. Thus, even as Russian agriculture remained backward, Russia began to industrialize in the late nineteenth century; and in the same period, despite semifeudal conditions in the Prussian countryside, Germany too experienced an industrial revolution. In both cases, the state intervened to compensate for deficiencies that might otherwise have prevented industrialization. Still, there were quite different experiences of industrial development in several European countries (see Map 4.1).

Great Britain: The Classic Case

Great Britain industrialized when and as it did because individuals made the most of favorable economic, social, and political conditions. Industrialization happened spontaneously as inventors, engineers, manufacturers, and bankers responded to business opportunities in new ways. It was neither planned nor expected.

An agricultural revolution had prepared the way. Legal acts of enclosure gave a relatively few landlords absolute control of large blocks of land. Freed from the traditions of communal agriculture, many of

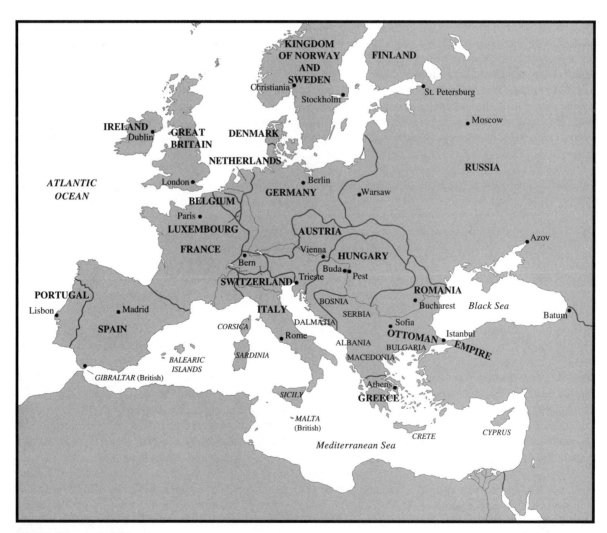

MAP 4.1 Europe in 1871

these landlords, with an eye to urban markets, invested in new equipment and experimented with fertilizer, crop rotation, and animal breeding so as to realize the maximum profit from their investment. These "improving" landlords and farmers raised agricultural production sharply by such methods so that fewer farm workers were required. Many small independent farmers, unable to compete, became laborers on the more efficient larger farms; others went to the cities, where they became urban workers.

Although this process placed the severest hardships on the peasantry, it contributed to the overall wealth of the country. Britain's population spurted from about six million in 1700 to about nine million in 1800. Furthermore, that population gained in disposable income as it rose in numbers. Having paid for better nourishment—meat, fruits, vegetables—the British earned the nickname "Beefeaters" and sought other ways to spend their rising real wages. This reservoir of domestic demand created a potential mass market for inexpensive clothing, which the British cotton industry proceeded to address.

The fly shuttle (invented in 1733 and slowly introduced in the following two decades) speeded up weaving and made the demand for yarn even more acute. A series of inventions in the 1770s drastically shifted the balance so that the hand-loom weavers now could not keep up with the supply of yarn and thread. Then, in 1785, Edmund Cartwright patented the power loom. It mechanized the weaving process and, by 1803, was driven by steam. These and other inventions followed one another in a pattern of challenge and response that caused British production of cotton cloth to soar. There was a market for these goods not only at home but throughout the world.

Britain's commercial connections throughout the globe greatly contributed to the success of the cotton industry. A large merchant fleet protected by the Royal Navy imported raw cotton from India, Brazil, and especially the United States. At the same time, the export of cheap cotton goods to British imperial possessions such as India discouraged even handicraft cotton production and relegated many of these territories to producing less profitable agricultural goods.

Coal, iron, and steel made up another cluster of industries that gave Britain economic leadership in the nineteenth century. Again, a succession of shortages led to innovations that yielded higher produc-

tion and better-quality products at a lower price. Britain's sparse forests could not satisfy the demand for charcoal, thus the rich coal reserves came into play to furnish fuel for heating and coke for smelting ore. Coal mining, however, required transportation both in the mine itself and from the mine to the ports and cities where the coal would be used: hence came the demand for metal rails to carry wagons. As in the cotton industry, a series of key inventions raised output: reheating or "puddling" molten iron (developed in 1784) burned away much of the waste that previously had to be eliminated by hammering; the steam hammer developed in the 1780s by James Watt increased the production of wrought iron; and various strip and rolling operations made finished iron more uniform and abundant.

Steam power was the decisive element in accelerating the supply of manufactured goods; by the 1760s, it had begun to remove the ceiling that human, animal, and water power had placed on production. Steam engines were initially used to pump water from mines and to drive bellows for iron smelters. Other industries progressively adopted this new source of power that could drive heavier and more productive machinery and could be located wherever raw materials and transportation were at hand.

Railroads, made possible by iron, coal, and steam power, not only revolutionized transportation in the nineteenth century but also effectively reduced costs and expanded markets for finished goods. Furthermore, they provided a rich investment for the excess capital amassed in agriculture, cotton, coal, and iron. By 1850, more than sixteen thousand miles of rail lines formed a thickening commercial web throughout Great Britain, and British investors were buying large blocks of railroad stock in Europe and the United States.

After this phase of industrialization, British development ceased to be so unique and merged with that of the continental European powers and of the United States. A cascade of innovations and adaptations transformed practically every field of manufacture as chemical and electrical industries took the lead late in the century. Between 1760 and 1860, agriculture shrank from 77 percent to 36 percent of national wealth, whereas industry, commerce, and transportation rose from 7 percent to 36 percent. By 1900, Great Britain manufactured over thirteen times what it had done a hundred years before, and its exports had increased over twenty-three times.

VOICES
The Life of an English Factory Girl, 1841

William Dodd, a crippled factory worker, traveled around England in the early 1840s observing the factory system and writing letters to Lord Shaftesbury, a member of Parliament who used this information in the campaign leading to the passage of the Factory Act of 1844. That act limited women's working hours to twelve per day and required safety measures for dangerous machinery. In the account that follows, Dodd describes the daily routine of a nineteen-year-old girl with whose family he stayed in Manchester.

At about half past four o'clock [A.M.], a rattling noise was heard at the window.... The watchman or person who performs this duty . . . then went to the next house, and so on through the streets, disturbing the whole neighborhood, till the noise of his "infernal machine" died away in the distance. This machine was made for the purpose of making a great noise on the glass windows without breaking them, and is somewhat similar to a shepherd's crook....

[T]he watchful waking mother, well knowing the consequences of being too late, is now heard at the bedside of her daughter, rousing the unwilling girl to another day of toil. At length you hear her on the floor; the clock is striking five. Then for the first time, the girl becomes conscious of the necessity for haste; and having slipped on her clothes, and (if she thinks there is time) washed herself, she takes a drink of cold coffee, which has been left standing in the fireplace, a mouthful of bread . . . and having packed up her breakfast in her handkerchief, hastens to the factory. The bell rings as she leaves the threshold of her home. Five minutes more and she is in the factory, stripped and ready for work. The clock strikes half past five; the engine starts, and her day's work commences.

At half past seven, and in some factories at eight, the engine slacks its pace (seldom stopping) for a short time, till the hands have cleaned the machinery, and swallowed a little food. It then goes on again, and continues full speed till twelve o'clock, when it stops for dinner. Previously to her leaving the factory, and in her dinner hour, she has her machines to clean. The distance of the factory is about [a] five minutes' walk from her home. I noticed every day that she came in at half past twelve or within a minute or two . . . ; the first thing she did, was to wash herself, then get her dinner (which she was seldom able to eat), and pack up her drinking for the afternoon. This done it was time to be on her way to work again, where she remains, without one minute's relaxation, till seven o'clock; she then comes home and throws herself into a chair exhausted. This is repeated six days in the week (save that on Saturdays she may get back a little earlier, say, an hour or two). Can there be any wondering at their preferring to lie in bed till dinner-time, instead of going to church on the seventh?

Source: William Dodd, *The Factory System Illustrated* (London: John Murray, 1842), pp. 108–10.

What were the social costs of Britain's rapid economic progress? Larger landowners, traditional artisans, and industrial workers on subsistence wages all suffered. The Corn Laws of 1819 temporarily pacified landed interests by imposing high tariffs on cheap foreign grain, but industrial and labor interests organized the Anti-Corn Law League and succeeded in forcing the repeal of these laws in 1846, thereby reducing the price of bread. Cheaper bread, however, benefited the industrialist far more than the worker, whose living wage declined.

The first mass movement to represent the industrial working class was organized around a petition called the People's Charter. Chartists opposed capitalism, publicized poor industrial working conditions, and sought parliamentary reform and universal male suffrage. Parliament rejected their initial petitions but responded gradually to popular protest with a series of Factory Acts, which addressed the worst industrial abuses, and with reform bills in 1832, 1867, 1884, and 1918, which gradually broadened the suffrage. The British political system, in short, responded to popular pressure in such a way as to avoid violent reaction from traditional landed interests and revolution from the new industrial proletariat. However, artisans such as the hand-loom weavers found no relief, their way of life made obsolete by machines and factories.

What were the principal elements of the Industrial Revolution in Britain? Merchant capitalism and the modernization of agriculture had already raised the standard of living and created a demand for manufactured goods. Despite antagonism between agricultural and industrial interests, there was no radical social distinction between agriculture and commerce. Although Britain remained a society with well-defined class distinctions, barriers to social mobility fell, and human resources became available as needs and opportunities arose. Coal, iron, and wool were abundant, and cotton was available from colonial India and the United States. Oceanic transportation was excellent, and internal transportation was efficient due to the long coastline dotted with harbors, the compact shape of the country, and liberal investment in roads. Although it did not sponsor the Industrial Revolution directly, the British government proved to be a valuable instrument of compromise between competing interest groups in this pluralist society. Finally, several generations of mechanics and tinkerers responded to these favorable conditions with their inventions and improvements, and bankers and investors supplied the capital to create factories and railroads.

France: The Persistence of a Dual Economy

Like other continental powers, France was left behind by British industrialization and tried to copy elements in Britain's success that seemed to promise similar results. But neither the starting conditions nor the results were the same as those in Britain. For instance, French political instability, underscored by a succession of revolutions and changing governments, contrasted sharply with the political picture in Britain.

Unlike Britain, France experienced no agricultural revolution that would encourage industrial production. The French Revolution had reinforced the hold of most of the peasantry on small parcels of land. Throughout the nineteenth century, most of the French countryside remained a patchwork of small and inefficient farms run by fiercely independent owners. They sought self-sufficiency more than profit, cooperated little with one another, and as a class remained relatively poor. French law since the revolution decreed equal division of inheritances, which also tended to keep farms small. To prevent further division of farmland, families practiced birth control so effectively that the French population remained stagnant as the population of other European countries rose sharply. This pattern of farming, inheritance law, and population combined to limit domestic demand for both agricultural and manufactured goods.

The Revolution of 1789 affected French industrial development in other ways. Although it swept away the remnants of feudal institutions and provided a legal framework more conducive to business, it also brought a quarter century of war that cut France off from much foreign trade. Thriving ports in Bordeaux, Nantes, Brest, and Marseilles became depressed areas. And by the time Napoleon fell from power in 1815, Britain was far ahead as an industrial nation and had captured most of world trade.

Prerevolutionary social patterns also continued to affect French life long after the revolution had destroyed France's former legal framework. Whereas British merchant, industrial, and landed classes intermarried and mingled socially, their French equivalents tended to remain distinct. A tradition of social hierarchy continued to curtail social aspirations and mobility long after the French Revolution had guaranteed equality before the law. Hence, just as peasants were reluctant to give up their farms to work in factories, both the bourgeois and the notables hesitated to exchange government office, medicine, law, or the management of estates for the uncertain pursuit of profit in business. Between a large peasant class and the upper classes, the typically ambitious and upwardly mobile French middle class was relatively smaller than Britain's and more limited in its prospects.

In the absence of significant demand from this class, French industrial production concentrated on luxury items such as glassware, porcelain, fine leather, high-quality fabrics, silks, and vintage wines for those who could afford them. Although the markup on such items was large, the demand for them was limited. Luxury goods, which required skilled artisans, could not alone generate an industrial revolution.

There were also social and institutional factors that retarded French industrial growth: heavy taxes to support the military and bureaucracy; rigid government regulations affecting banking, mining, and other activities; a low level of savings; a preference for foreign over domestic investment; a thinly developed banking system; and a reluctance to look beyond the immediate family to banks, investors, and mergers for the means to expand and modernize the enterprise.

Given these conditions, French industrial growth was more gradual than that of the British and, therefore, does not merit the term *revolution*. The chief reason for this was the pattern of slow population growth, for although France fell behind in total industrial output, on a per-capita basis it caught up with its German and British rivals by the mid-1890s. By then, electrical, chemical, and aluminum industries had sprung up, and pharmaceuticals, bicycles, and motorcars found a growing market among the general public. Consumer demand, reflected in the rise of the department store, finally became a significant factor in France's economic development.

Both political and economic factors were responsible for this rise in consumer demand. A mandatory public education system, instituted in 1882, began to broaden provincial mentalities and provide avenues for professional advancement. Having earned a state diploma, students became eligible for jobs on the railroad, in the government, or in teaching, which took them to cities far from their rural origins. They constituted a rising professional middle class—in short, urban consumers.

Machines did not replace skilled human labor everywhere. In this French pipe-making firm, the skill of the blacksmith remained important as the work was reorganized to carry out larger projects. *Museé Dauphinois*

An agricultural crisis in the 1880s and 1890s also contributed to the accelerated shift of population to towns and cities. Whereas British peasants more than a hundred years earlier had been chased from small farms by enclosures and by competition from commercial farmers, many French peasants now gave up farming because of a plant disease that devastated vineyards, or because of ruinous competition from foreign produce. Thus began a slow consolidation to produce more economical farms, a painful process that would drag on for almost a century. France brought its dual economy into the twentieth century—part subsistent, backward, and inefficient, and part modern or modernizing.

France began the nineteenth century as the largest and potentially most productive power in Europe; it ended in third place, behind Great Britain and Germany. Urbanization, industrial and agricultural production, and material wealth were not the only valid goals for a nation, but they were crucial for achieving any measure of modernization. According to these indicators, Great Britain had far surpassed France in the nineteenth century.

Germany: Old Bottles and New Wine

The uniqueness of Germany's modern development lies in the relationship of its political and economic elements. After 1840, the German economy industrialized quite rapidly. And particularly after 1870, a very effective system of technical and scientific education helped Germany take the lead in what were then the high-technology fields of chemicals and electricity. The organization of major industries into cartels to protect markets and control production and trade, together with ready access to credit from Germany's banks, provided additional momentum to industrial growth. By the end of the century, Germany had surpassed France and was second only to Great Britain in industrial development. But this rapid economic progress took place in a society and a state that retained many of its premodern patterns: authoritarian government, militarism, and the continued prominence of aristocratic landlords.

One source of Germany's uneven development lay in the lateness of its national unification. Unlike

Great Britain and France, "Germany" in 1815 was not a unified state but a loose federation of thirty-eight states, of which Prussia, in the north, soon emerged as the most important. Even this was an improvement on the three-hundred-some states and principalities that had constituted the Holy Roman Empire before its destruction by Napoleon in 1806.

Thus, unlike Britain, France, and the United States, Germany began to industrialize before it could achieve political unification and without undergoing a bourgeois, liberal, or democratic revolution. In the Europe-wide upheavals of 1848, an assembly of bourgeois liberals from all the German states wrote a constitution but failed to persuade the Prussian king to become a German constitutional monarch. He refused to "accept a crown from the gutter." Two decades later, Prussia's prime minister, Otto von Bismarck, used a series of short wars with Denmark (1864), Austria (1866), and France (1870) to compel the other German states to submit to Prussian authority. So, Germany was unified politically from above, with "blood and iron," rather than from below, as a liberal democratic state.

Within this new German Empire, the Prussian landed aristocracy, known as the Junkers, retained great influence. From privileged positions in the government and the officer corps of the army, this class continued throughout the nineteenth century to oppose and limit the development of liberalism in Germany. Although Germany had a parliament elected by universal male suffrage, that body had little real influence in the affairs of state. Most members of the middle class, proud of Germany's newly established unity and its growing power in the world, were not disposed to challenge vigorously the prerogatives of the state. German nationalism, in short, undermined German liberalism.

In summary, the German formula for industrial growth was unique and complex. Its rapid industrialization caused both the middle class and the proletariat to increase in numbers, but it did not give these classes a significant political voice. The government channeled popular enthusiasm into patriotism and loyalty to the authoritarian regime, or it limited discontent from the proletariat by sponsoring social welfare measures. Lacking a firmly established democratic tradition, Germany responded to the crises of the early twentieth century far differently from its French and British rivals.

Industrial Comparisons and Commonalities

In addition to Great Britain, France, and Germany, lesser European states such as Belgium, Sweden, and Switzerland industrialized and prospered usually by concentrating on neglected niches in the world market. But each country's experience with industrial development was unique. By industrializing first, Britain dominated world trade for most of the nineteenth century. But Britain paid a price for its early lead, for it was committed to machinery that became obsolete as the century progressed. Latecomers such as France, Germany, and Italy invested in more modern equipment and competed successfully in certain industries and markets.

Certain ingredients, however, were everywhere essential: entrepreneurs, a labor force, capital to invest in machinery, and potential demand for industrial goods. Where private investment was weak, the government could subsidize heavy industry, as Italy did for its armaments and shipbuilding firms. But government investment depended ultimately on rising tax revenues derived from increased productivity in agriculture or trade. Only increased productivity, in turn, could furnish higher wages that would spur demand for consumer goods. Hence, industrialization required a political and social climate that encouraged entrepreneurs to accumulate profits and to invest, that permitted social mobility according to merit, and that supported rising real income per capita to increase domestic demand.

Each industrializing European country met these general requirements to differing degrees and achieved different results. Despite the persistent backwardness of certain regions and countries during the nineteenth century, Europe as a whole was launched on an industrial path from which there was no turning back.

Social Change, Politics, and Culture

Among the clearest indications of the social changes emanating from Europe's Industrial Revolution and the political upheavals of the French Revolution were the ideologies spawned during the nineteenth century, some of which still resonate in the late twentieth.

Ideology and Class: Conservatism versus Liberalism

Associated with the older and threatened social groups such as royalty and landed nobility was a view of society that came to be called *conservatism*. Conservative thinkers, such as Edmund Burke (1729–1797) in England and the French writer Joseph de Maistre (1753–1821), defended monarchies, aristocracies, and traditional religious institutions and values against the individualism, liberalism, and secularism of industrial society. Viewing human societies as fragile, they valued institutions that were deeply rooted in history and feared mass participation in public life. In response to the squalor, materialism, and competitiveness of modern life, conservative theorists looked to an idealized version of the Middle Ages—one that was ordered, hierarchical, and organic—as a model for a good society.

The modern ideology of the upper-middle classes—largely business and professional people—was known broadly as *liberalism*. Rooted in the ideas of the Enlightenment, its core value was individualism, and it sought to further individual liberation in every domain of life. Politically, liberals opposed arbitrary royal authority and the domination of society by privileged aristocracies. Intellectually, they sought liberation from ancient superstitions and religions, believing that human rationality was sufficient to penetrate the mysteries of the universe. Economically, they sought an end to restrictions on private property, believing with Adam Smith that the public good would be best served by individuals pursuing their own economic interests.

As the nineteenth century wore on, liberalism expressed the increasingly defensive ideology of a privileged class. Its members were reluctant to extend political rights to the lower classes and to women of any class, and they refused to consider using state power to redistribute national wealth. To liberals, property was almost sacred and nothing should interfere with its use, particularly the growing demands of the industrial working class.

Ideology and Class: Socialism

The working classes of industrial Europe encompassed highly skilled printers and masons, workers and machine tenders in the factories, and unskilled dockworkers and common laborers. What they had in common was a lack of property; they did not own the means of production and had only their labor to sell on the marketplace of a capitalist society. *Socialism,* the ideology associated with this class, achieved its classic expression in the writings of a brilliant intellectual named Karl Marx (1818–1883). In the mid-nineteenth century, Marx began to describe a "scientific" socialism that promised the working class eventual triumph. A German who spent most of his adult life studying and writing in London, Marx collaborated with Friedrich Engels (1820–1895) and wrote constantly and with great subtlety on political economy, society, and history. He articulated a set of ideas that seemed threatening in the extreme to the established order of middle-class industrial Europe.

Like liberalism, Marxist socialism was a modernist ideology. In both systems of thought, capitalism and industrialization were keys to progress, and there was no nostalgic yearning for a vanished past. Both reflected the materialistic, scientific, and optimistic tone of much nineteenth-century European thought. But where liberals saw a world of competing individuals leading to general improvement, Marxists saw struggling classes and growing social conflict.

To Marx, each historical epoch was shaped by its economic system and especially by the clash of its opposing classes. The class struggle between lords and peasants during the feudal period gave way under capitalism to a struggle between the bourgeoisie and the proletariat. In each case, the owners of the means of production (the land or the factory) exploited those compelled to exchange their labor for a bare living. Contradictions, or fundamental conflicts, in the system at each stage gave rise to a new class that pushed aside the old ruling class. Isolated merchants living in the towns during the feudal period may have been necessary to the feudal economy itself, but eventually their descendants—the capitalist bourgeoisie—wrested control of the economy and of political institutions from the landed aristocrats and established an industrial economy.

To Marx, capitalism was a progressive force, and he described its productive virtues in almost lyrical terms. Yet he denied that industrial capitalism, controlled by the bourgeoisie, could bring happiness to the population at large. Despite its enormous increase in human productive capacity, the very logic of the system—competition and the drive for profits—compelled successful capitalists to exploit workers. Marx predicted that this same logic would produce a chain of worsening consequences: an increasing concentration of industry and economic power; the rise in numbers and misery of the proletariat; the drying up of markets for capital investment as industrial goods found insufficient numbers of buyers; and the eventual collapse of capitalism and its ruling class amid a proletarian Socialist revolution.

This analysis of history and prediction of the fate of capitalism drew upon intellectual currents of Marx's time in such diverse fields as philosophy, economics, and biology. It was also based on careful study of industrial conditions. Marx claimed that his ideas were scientific rather than utopian. History it-

A socialist perspective on industrial capitalist society. The caption reads: "If only the chaps at the base, proletarians and peasants, should move . . . and the pyramid crumble!" *Holzapfel-DF*

self, he claimed, demonstrated that the latest unjust social system would be replaced by a classless society without private property in which the enormous wealth produced by modern technology would be used in a planned way to meet the needs of all. In such an egalitarian society, the coercive power of the state, used to maintain ruling classes, would be unnecessary, and the state would "wither away," as would international conflict.

With such claims, Marx became a prophet rather than a historian. Indeed, his own vision of a future society without social classes or class struggle recalls those of utopian thinkers dating back to the prophets of the Old Testament. But in an age when science enjoyed great prestige, Marx gave elaborate scientific justification to the long-term hopes of the working class and provided the foundations for a broad attack on capitalism. In the twentieth century, his ideas proved attractive to oppressed and exploited people worldwide. Claiming Marx as its fundamental authority, twentieth-century communism achieved political hegemony in roughly one-third of the world, though the sway of Marxist ideology began to contract sharply in the late 1980s.

Politics and Social Change

For several centuries before 1800, European merchant capitalists had already challenged landed aristocrats for economic and political leadership, but the Industrial Revolution gave the capitalists far greater leverage than they had before. Although some aristocrats adapted to the new conditions by investing their fortunes in industrial enterprise, as a class the aristocracy continued its decline as capitalism continued its development. The tension between the rising bourgeoisie and the declining aristocracy was expressed politically in liberal and conservative political parties. Both assumed that only men of property and wealth should vote, but they typically disagreed over what sort of wealthy men should rule—landlords, or merchants, bankers, and industrialists? These nineteenth-century liberals and conservatives were but a small minority of the population, and so as suffrage expanded, they had to make political alliances with other social groups, in particular the peasantry and the middle class.

There had always been shopkeepers, small merchants, lawyers, doctors, and officials, but the spread of capitalism caused certain professions to grow significantly, notably those of industrial manager, office worker, state official, teacher, and engineer. This "middle class" included people of both meager and modest wealth who possessed some education, skill, taste, and financial security that distinguished them from the proletariat. Their collective political outlook was democratic but not socialist: they especially insisted on their superiority over the working class and the peasantry. Although the middle classes and the ruling landed and capitalist elites were far apart in wealth, they shared similar values and cooperated politically when socialism posed a threat.

In revolutions that broke out all over Europe in 1848, the middle classes displayed both their aspirations to share power and their willingness to support conservative regimes against more radical threats from the working class. But despite the triumph of authoritarian regimes in 1848, during the next half-century, most industrial states of Europe progressively granted their citizens further civil rights, political representation, and economic freedoms. The middle and upper classes and the peasantry could unite around these broad principles, which left existing social hierarchies of birth and wealth virtually intact. According to liberal ideology, each person living under this system had an equal chance to succeed, and those who did so merited their success. Thus the successful were justified, the less successful could nurture hopes, and social conflict was discouraged.

Nationalism was another facet of nineteenth-century liberalism that made the separate social classes tend to forget their differences. Before the nineteenth century, the great mass of Europeans, largely farmers, were conscious of little that transpired beyond their own village or region, and they felt no social bond with farmers of other regions who obeyed the same king. This provincial mentality changed as Europe modernized. Improved transportation and trade, greater mobility of labor, and representative government with uniform codes of law all contributed to widening the horizon of citizens to the point where they recognized a fundamental tie with other citizens served by the same government. The Burgundian and the Tuscan began to see themselves as French and Italian as well.

The French revolutionaries of 1789 were particularly instrumental in awakening a national consciousness among Europeans. In carrying the message of fraternity, as well as of liberty and equality, the French armies under Napoleon combined liberal ideology with national pride as they claimed to liberate other Europeans from their backwardness. In demonstrating the power of loyalty to an idealized nation, the French aroused a nationalistic response among the Spanish, Germans, Italians, and Russians. Thus early in the nineteenth century, many Europeans learned to embrace this new secular religion that generated its own martyrs, saints, hymns, creeds, and great moments. The nation became an extended family whose real or imagined glory all loyal citizens could share as their formerly closed provincial societies were shaken by external influences. Yet while a shared nationalism tended to weaken antagonisms between social classes within individual nation-states, later it would also exacerbate tensions between such states and become a factor in the outbreak of World War I.

The working class, particularly when its leaders adopted Marxist ideas, posed a threat to each state's liberal and national consensus. As industrial workers grew in number, they became aware that they constituted a distinct and potentially powerful social class. In the late nineteenth century, they won not only the right to vote but also the right to organize in labor unions and to strike. Although only a small minority of workers actually joined labor unions, industrial labor acquired a voice and began to affect public policy. Furthermore, Socialists established political parties in most European states and became affiliated with international Socialist organizations. These parties recruited members, contested elections, agitated for reforms, and in some cases plotted revolution.

Why, then, did industrial workers never become a truly revolutionary force, and why did socialism, as Marx had envisaged it, never come to power in Europe? The workers' unions and political parties claimed to be part of an invincible international movement, but they were organized on national lines and were loyal ultimately to their own nation rather than to an international working-class movement. The moment of truth came in World War I, when European workers rallied to their respective flags and enthusiastically set off to slaughter fellow workers rather than rising up against their capitalist overlords. Nationalism, in short, proved a more compelling loyalty than socialism.

In addition, the workers' movement in each state was split between revolutionaries and reformers, between those who rejected any collaboration or compromise with bourgeois liberals and those who were willing to negotiate for improvements in social insurance, working conditions, pensions, and wages. Success at the polls encouraged most Socialists to believe that they could achieve a Socialist society through education and the ballot box—without a violent revolution. Germany under Bismarck's leadership exploited this split by expanding the state's welfare program, thereby blunting labor's revolutionary zeal. The labor movement gradually forced wages upward, and workers consumed more, felt more secure, and identified with their own nation. Socialist parties and labor unions became entrenched in their own countries and lost the will to risk their positions in a violent international revolution. Despite their revolutionary rhetoric, they came to accept bourgeois society as the workers themselves aspired to become comfortable bourgeois themselves.

Marx had predicted that a Socialist revolution would occur only when industrial capitalism had fully developed and the proletariat had become acutely aware of its exploitation. But Marx did not reckon fully with capitalists and politicians who discovered that they could retain their own hegemony as they purchased social peace with higher wages, welfare programs, consumer culture, and nationalist ideology. Industrial capitalism proved more amenable to reform than Marx had ever imagined. Ironically, socialism triumphed in unexpected areas of the world—in Russia and China, where capitalism was least developed.

Daily Lives: Men, Women, and Children

The changes wrought by industrialization became apparent not only in ideologies, social movements, and political conflicts but also in the lives of ordinary people. For men, Europe's industrial transformation probably altered work more than it did relationships

VOICES
"Only a Weaver"

By the early 1860s, the silk-weaving industry in Coventry, England, was in desperate straits, due in part to a decline in the fashion of wearing silk ribbons. Many individual weavers had to sell their looms to the larger manufacturers who were organizing more efficient production in factories. The song that follows was sung by unemployed weavers as they paraded through the streets of Coventry or were on their way to relief work (often in a stone yard). It reflects the costs of the Industrial Revolution for a body of proud and skilled artisans and their distress at an economic system that seemed to cast them adrift.

Who is that man coming up the street,
With weary manner and shuffling feet;
With a face that tells of care and grief
And in hope that seems to have lost belief?
For wickedness past he now atones,
He's only a weaver that no one owns.

He's coming no doubt from breaking stones,
With saddened heart and aching bones;

But why should he grumble, he gets good pay;
A loaf and sixpence every day.

He thought if he worked both night and day,
He ought to receive equivalent pay;
But he's just an inconsistent man,
Who doesn't understand the commercial plan.

Political economy now must sway
And say when a man shall work or play.
If he's wanted his wages may be high;
If he isn't, why then, he may starve and die.

If you employ him, don't mend the price—
He's starving, you know, and has no choice—
And give him to weave the worst of silk,
For it's only a weaver's time you bilk. . . .

Yet take no heed of his sighs and groans,
His careworn face, his agonised moans;
For wickedness past he now atones,
He's only a weaver that no one owns.

Source: Joseph Gutteridge, *Lights and Shadows in the Life of an Artisan* (1893), p. 153, abridged and adapted in Roy Palmer, ed. *Poverty Knock* (New York: Cambridge University Press, 1974), p. 24.

---

with women and children. Many men continued to pursue their professions as they had before. Doctors, lawyers, and shopkeepers were little affected by the Industrial Revolution, and many skilled artisans continued to practice their trade as before. But factories steadily drove certain artisans out of business— weavers, glass blowers, nail makers, blacksmiths— and compelled them to become semiskilled factory laborers. Although factory discipline was seldom absolutely rigid, factory workers who had been independent artisans lost a way of life that included pride in their skill and the freedom to determine their own rhythm of work. The pocket watch came into general use, made the communal church bell superfluous, and symbolized the contradictions of the new age. People now measured time for themselves, which underscored their individualism, but insistent demands for efficiency tended to make them slaves to the clock.

Women's lives were probably even more radically affected than those of men. Married women had always played several roles: caring for children, maintaining the household, and contributing to the family income. Under the putting-out system and other earlier forms of craft production, women contributed labor at home, but under the factory system it became much more difficult to hold a job and carry on as mothers and homemakers. Likewise, as small farms were absorbed by large ones and formerly independent farmers became farm laborers, their wives could no longer perform all their tasks at home. Many ceased for a period in their lives to "work" like their husbands in the fields or in factories; others, desperate to contribute wages to the family economy, left their children with relatives or nursemaids. Unmarried women, who formerly had worked in the family business or on the family farm, increasingly found employment as domestic servants or in facto-

Child labor, as in this English coal mine, was one of the major abuses of the early industrial revolution. *The Bettmann Archive*

ries such as cotton mills, where they tended spindles and were subject to various forms of exploitation. In any case, the family remained an important focus for women. But whereas formerly women had contributed labor to the family economy, now they increasingly brought in wages that they earned outside the home.

For middle-class women as well, there was a tendency for the workplace and the home to become distinct in the nineteenth century. Wives of small shopkeepers continued to meet customers while their children played in a back room. However, other middle-class women lived in houses or apartments that had no direct function in the marketplace. Those who needed to contribute to the family economy left their children with others and sought employment as teachers, sales clerks, or office workers. Broadening educational opportunities for women in the late nineteenth century gradually permitted a few to aspire to higher positions, even in medicine and law.

Wealthier middle-class women who were not required to contribute to the family economy (except by their dowries) frequently constructed a separate domestic world that had little to do with the industrial and democratic one in which their husbands moved. Their days consisted of raising a family, supervising the servants, calling on friends, carrying gifts to the poor, and attending church. As in earlier times, however, widowhood could propel women of means into the public world to manage businesses left to them by their husbands.

As with adults, children's destinies depended in large part on their social class and their gender. But for them, too, modern society provided new opportunities and constraints. The most obvious of these was education, which became compulsory throughout Europe during the nineteenth century. Factory acts eliminated child labor, and educational reforms sent the young to school for a minimum of about six years to learn to read, write, count, and respect national traditions. Industrial society required obedient and punctual workers, and democratic society required literate and loyal citizens. Compulsory primary education did more than furnish compliant drones to the ruling class; it gave a handful the chance to prove their worth, go on to universities, and rise to higher rank. Separate secondary education for girls permitted a small but rising number to go on to the universities and pursue professional careers. But the educational systems that took shape in Europe during the nineteenth century did little to increase social mobility for the working class and the peasantry. Public education for the masses led to inferior certificates and modest employment, whereas the upper classes used their wealth and cultivation to monopolize the higher schools that prepared for the universities and the most prestigious careers.

Conclusion

By the late nineteenth century, schools, newspapers, and railroads were making all Europeans more aware of a world beyond their villages and towns. The most ambitious seized new opportunities in business, technology, government administration, or politics. Although opportunity smiled most broadly upon the wealthy and well educated, it beckoned the middle and lower classes far more than in the past. Europe was at the height of its power and ruled practically the entire world. Industry, democracy, nationalism, and education had finally awakened the masses, but only the most discerning critics could foresee what that would mean for European society and the world in the twentieth century.

Notes

1. E. L. Jones, *The European Miracle* (Cambridge, Mass.: Cambridge University Press, 1981), p. 82.
2. Alexander Gerschenkron, *Economic Backwardness in Historical Perspective* (Cambridge, Mass.: Harvard University Press, 1966).

Chapter 5
Collapse and Reconstruction:
Europe in the Twentieth Century

In the four hundred years since Columbus stumbled upon America in 1492 and da Gama made his way to India in 1498, Europe had grown in population, wealth, military power, and global influence. The major European states had consolidated their power and competed for territory and hegemony. Science, capitalism, and industrial technology had transformed European society and politics and made Europe the hub of a world economy. More than ever before or since, in 1914 Europeans ruled the world, either directly through their colonial possessions or indirectly through a combination of economic and military power.

Those accomplishments convinced Europeans of their intellectual and moral superiority and, therefore, of their "right" to rule. Although a minority of conservative thinkers maintained that human beings were neither reasonable nor perfectible and that the universe's deepest secrets were unfathomable, the dominant liberals held otherwise. The universe had revealed many of its secrets to European scientists since the Renaissance, and further scientific progress seemed assured. Progress would flow inevitably, the liberals believed, from a combination of free enterprise; education; freedom of speech, press, and assembly; and representative government.

Europeans in 1914 rode a crest of optimism that overshadowed the few who saw flaws in their civilization or threats to their preeminence. Historian Barbara Tuchman, however, describes Europe in 1914 as a "proud tower" whose foundations were already weakened: aristocrats and wealthy capitalists still ruled despite the advance of democracy, but popular discontents and movements threatened their dominance. Behind a facade of power and progress there was rising pressure from the masses for more

radical social change.[1] Furthermore, the military and economic competition between nation-states that for four hundred years had stimulated Europe's rise to preeminence now became bitter and dangerous. And here and there in the world outside Europe, societies long subordinated to Europe's power began to challenge its dominance.

Europe in 1914

Europe itself accounts for less than 7 percent of the world's land area, but in 1914, it had about 25 percent of the world's population. Better harvests and living conditions in the nineteenth century increased life expectancy sharply, and the population jumped from about 188 million in 1800 to 401 million in 1900. Another 50 million people had emigrated: about 30 million to North America, 10 million to Latin America, and the balance to Russia, Australia, New Zealand, and South Africa. They took with them the ideas and techniques that had brought power and prosperity to Europe and in varying degrees implemented these ideas where they settled. Europeans and transplanted Europeans together made a formidable global network.

But the European demographic surge slowed in the late nineteenth and early twentieth centuries as child labor was abolished, as governments provided pensions for old age, and as birth control became widespread. Europeans took about a century to conclude that large families were no longer necessary either to produce living heirs or to provide security in old age. Eliminated from the labor force and compelled to attend school until about age fourteen, children became an added expense to a family rather than an economic resource. Parents cherished their children at least as much as before, but the rational and upwardly mobile middle class in particular tended to have fewer of them. During the twentieth century, Europeans dwindled from 25 percent to 15 percent of the world's population as its growth leveled off and as Africa, Latin America, and Asia underwent an even greater population surge than Europe had experienced in the nineteenth century.

Compared with the rest of the world, Europe stood alone in wealth and power. It could command the natural resources of the entire world. Militarily, European states were vulnerable only to one another. Their schools and universities produced the best-educated citizens and the most advanced scholars and technicians. Despite these accomplishments, most Europeans lived a frugal or impoverished existence. The male peasantry and working class had attained civil and political rights, whereas women had only begun their struggle for these rights. Both lacked the basic economic security attained by successful bourgeois. Europe's modern transformation, in short, undermined the position of some groups, left others unsatisfied, and certainly had not produced social and political tranquility as the twentieth century dawned.

Politics and the Rise of the Masses

Despite democratic revolutions and the spread of democratic ideology in the late eighteenth and nineteenth centuries, by 1914, France was the only great power in Europe to discard its monarchy for a republic. Yet the gains of democracy were evident in the extension of voting rights after 1870, and universal male suffrage became the rule by 1914. Parliaments increased their power while mass political parties and their newspapers drew more of the general public into political debate. Despite the lingering power of monarchies and aristocracies, popular pressure mounted in Europe for a broader democracy that would respond to the needs of the middle and lower classes.

Political parties became more numerous, better organized, and more competitive as suffrage broadened. Conservatives who opposed the expansion of democracy became increasingly isolated, and tradi-

tional liberals who supported laissez-faire economics and a limited suffrage of property owners appealed to a dwindling minority of the electorate. As these parties declined, Socialist parties and middle-class parties variously described as republican, radical, democratic, and progressive took their place. Socialist programs for better working conditions and a more equal society appealed so broadly to the middle and working classes that they challenged other politicians to support government welfare programs, health insurance, and pensions.

In addition to organized political parties that presented candidates at elections, a variety of other movements sought to spread a particular ideology or publicize a particular issue. At the opposite pole from the New Left of organized Socialist parties were the scattered formations of a New Right: groups such as the Action Francaise or the Austrian German-National movement that drew upon mass support, stressed national patriotism, and denounced constitutional democracy and the liberal traditions of the Enlightenment. The anti-Semitism and anti-Marxism typical of such movements expressed social fears that the Industrial Revolution had made more acute. For much of the middle and working classes, unemployment and shifting social status would grow dramatically after World War I and make these reactionary groups an ominous political force.

Feminism was another movement that gained considerable momentum during the two decades before 1914, but its modern origins in Europe went back at least to the Enlightenment. In 1791, Mary Wollstonecraft of England had published her *Vindication of the Rights of Woman,* and in 1793, Olympe de Gouges of France had written *The Declaration of the Rights of Woman and the Female Citizen,* a women's version of the document written by the revolutionaries of 1789. The ensuing era of liberal ideology and revolution provided the atmosphere for early feminist initiatives. Yet it remained clear that women would not easily win civil and political equality with men, for not only did Catholic and Protestant churches forbid or discourage such aspirations, but secular institutions were rarely more sympathetic. Left-wing political parties, led by men, were lukewarm in their support, and a male champion of the women's cause such as the nineteenth-century liberal John Stuart Mill was truly exceptional. Facing this resistance, active feminists had to consider their real possibilities as they pursued their goals. Clara Zetkin, for instance, worked within the German Socialist party in the later nineteenth century and accepted its doctrine that the destruction of capitalism was the precondition for women's liberation. Although she pressed for women's rights in the party and in the workplace, she gave a proletarian revolution precedence over a feminist revolution. Furthermore, despite her political militancy, Zetkin maintained a traditional view of a woman's role in society and opposed other feminists who advocated birth control and cooperative child care.[2] Thus, by the end of the nineteenth century, a sign of the feminist movement's progress lay in its diverse currents.

The movement came together, however, in pushing for political and civil rights in the late nineteenth century following the success of men in gaining these rights. Industrialization had altered the family economy so that more women worked outside the home in factories, offices, and schools. Also, more women were attaining a secondary education, and some were entering universities, earning professional degrees, and competing with men in certain professions. By 1914, women had won the right to vote in national elections in Finland and Norway and in local elections in Denmark, Sweden, and Great Britain. Although the outbreak of war in 1914 initially pushed the feminist movement into the background, women played crucial economic roles in the war effort and gained support for their cause. They won the right to vote in national elections in many countries either during World War I or immediately after it. In France and Italy, however, suffrage was delayed until after World War II, largely because radical and socialist politicians, theoretically the feminists' allies, had feared that a new mass of enfranchised women would use their vote to support right-wing clerical candidates. Yet political feminism was only one aspect of a movement that had far broader aims, such as equal opportunities for employment and equal pay, and that would eventually have a sweeping impact on European society.

In short, European economic and political progress had not produced a tranquil society; instead, it had encouraged new aspirations and generated new fears. As political competition threatened to divide the population of each state, another potent force, nationalism, drew diverse classes and political interests

together. Both the liberal tradition of the Enlightenment—embraced by a relatively small elite—and the Socialist movement had encouraged a generous international spirit and looked forward to a harmonious world community. But the European masses by 1914 had come to identify intensely with their own nations and had become fearful or contemptuous of others. The nation seemed a more concrete and emotionally powerful loyalty than a universal humanity or a worldwide proletariat. So the liberal spirit, an expression of Europe's triumph in the world, fell under attack and began its decline. In its place there had arisen both popular democracy and nationalism. Those forces developed within states that had for centuries been bitter political rivals and more recently extended their economic rivalries to the far corners of the earth. Thus, by 1914, a potent and almost fatal combination of popular democracy, nationalism, and economic competition had set the stage in Europe for two generations of tragedy.

The Coming of the Great War

European nation-states claimed to be "sovereign" in that they not only commanded the loyalty of their citizens but were also absolute masters of their own affairs. No other power, such as a Holy Roman emperor, a church, or an international ruling elite of monarchs and aristocrats, could enforce a higher authority. By the end of the nineteenth century, this need to ensure national security led to a protracted arms race, expressed most clearly in a competition between Britain and Germany to build battleships. Even in peacetime, the European states assembled weapons and conscripted large numbers of men for training, as modern technology—especially the railroad—made possible a rapid attack. Thus, constant preparation for war seemed essential. By 1914, all able-bodied young men were expected to serve two or three years in the army before taking up their careers. Ironically, then, as Europe made industrial and democratic progress, and as its economy became ever more integrated, its separate states grew more suspicious and fearful of one another.

Whatever security Europe could achieve came from the maintenance of a balance of power. When Britain led a coalition that finally defeated Napoleon in 1815, it redressed the balance of power by ensuring that no single state would swallow up all the others. The game had always been intrinsically difficult, but industrialization and imperialism had raised the stakes, and democracy and nationalism had unleashed movements of uninformed and inflexible public pressure.

Futhermore, the unification of Germany in 1871 sharply changed the political situation in Europe. Germany's subsequent demographic and industrial growth confirmed that it was the dominant land power in Europe. Yet for two decades under Chancellor Bismarck, Germany claimed no grand imperial ambitions and succeeded in forestalling the formation of a European coalition hostile to it. Only when Bismarck was forced from power in 1890 did Germany, now in a military alliance with Austria-Hungary and Italy, begin to pursue a more ambitious foreign policy both in Europe and around the world.

Russia and France initially felt most threatened by the growing power of Germany. After prolonged negotiations, autocratic Russia signed a military alliance with republican France in 1894. This unlikely connection showed that the geopolitics of state power counted more heavily than domestic ideology. Russia required foreign investment to improve its military equipment; France needed assurance that in case of a German attack, the Russians would strike the Germans' eastern frontier. So the Franco-Russian alliance gave assurances to each of its signatories, but it caused Germans to feel surrounded and gave its military establishment justification to urge greater preparations for war.

By 1900, Great Britain was the only major European state that had not entered a military alliance with one or more other powers. It typically refrained from committing itself to military alliances, for its navy was sufficient to ensure independence. But when Germany began construction of a large naval fleet in 1898, Britain became wary and moved closer to France and Russia. In 1914, therefore, Europe dominated the world but was dangerously divided. The major states were grouped in two hostile alliances. The Triple Alliance included Germany, Austria-Hungary, and Italy; the Triple Entente joined France, Russia, and Great Britain. And there was no stabilizing "third force" to adjust the balance in a crisis and prevent the outbreak of war. After 1900, the European great powers stumbled from one diplomatic crisis to another, none of them seeking war but not quite knowing how to avoid it.

Strangely enough, it was not the many colonial rivalries in Asia or Africa that plunged Europe into war. The great powers usually resolved such disputes by negotiation and at the expense of Afro-Asian peoples. Instead, rivalries in southeastern Europe and the Ottoman Empire proved to be far more dangerous, for there the national interests of practically all European powers clashed as the decline of the Turks left a power vacuum. Germans had invested heavily in the Ottoman Empire, especially in a Berlin-to-Baghdad railroad, and their influence mounted. Russia claimed to be the protector of the small independent Slavic states, particularly Serbia, and wished eventually to control the straits that led from the Black Sea to the Mediterranean. Austria sought to extend its empire southward into former Ottoman territories so as to silence those states, notably Serbia, that wanted to expand at its expense. Britain and France did not want Russia to become a serious naval power by gaining unlimited access to the Mediterranean and sought to maintain the status quo so that other great powers would not profit from the area's military weakness.

All of the European powers had some vital interest in the Balkans that could not be compensated elsewhere, as the rest of the world had already been largely divided up among them. So when a conflict arose between Austria and Russia over control of Serbia, their respective allies and thus all of Europe were drawn into war. Nationalist sentiment had become so powerful and the systems of alliances and military planning so rigid that a minor crisis was sufficient to trigger a general war.

On June 28, 1914, a Serbian nationalist assassinated the archduke of Austria and his wife. After a month of negotiations, on July 28, Austria invaded this small Balkan country, and within a week, the other great powers of Europe had declared war. Why did such a minor incident provoke general war?

Each state had its reasons. Austria obtained reassurances from Germany before moving its troops. For several decades, Russia had jousted with Austria for power in the Balkans, and so when Serbia asked for support, Russia responded. But Russia, well aware of the German-Austrian alliance, concluded that it was most prudent to mobilize its troops against Germany as well as Austria. This act made it imperative for Germany to put its own mobilization plan into operation. Known as the Schlieffen Plan, it called for a quick strike at France followed by a longer war with Russia on the opposite front. Thus, France, whether it would have respected its alliance with Russia or not, was drawn into war. Finally, Britain used the pretext of Germany's violation of neutral Belgium to rally popular support for entering the war on the side of France and Russia.

This sequence of events masked a highly complicated reality: industrial growth and competition; changes in military technology and the increasing influence of military experts over public policy; the decline of a less aggressive diplomatic tradition in the face of rising nationalism and popular government; and the widespread feeling that survival for nations as well as for the species depended on struggle and conflict. The latest industrial phase of capitalism had made warfare more deadly and required the regimentation of entire populations.

Most businesspeople preferred peace, for war disrupted their worldwide markets. But capitalism was international in scope and had no means of political expression except through individual states. The leaders of these states, many of them from military and aristocratic backgrounds, sought their separate advantage and collectively lost sight of the larger international system in which their particular countries were embedded. Political leaders found no means to escape a chain of events that led to mobilization. And on the whole, Europe's general public faced the prospect of war, not with dread, but with confidence and expectancy, as if the looming conflict might help to solve old social problems rather than create new ones.

I The Collapse of Europe

It began as a European war, but it ended as a global conflict. Britain's dominions, such as Canada, Australia, and New Zealand, joined in defense of the British Empire. In 1917, a reluctant United States entered the war against Germany as did a newly industrializing Japan. British and French colonies in Asia and Africa provided troops for the war in Europe.

Women entered the industrial work force in greater numbers during World War I, as in this French munitions factory. *Museé Dauphinois*

And in the Middle East, the Ottoman Empire joined the war on the side of Germany, while Britain supported both Arab and Jewish nationalists who opposed the Turks.

European states went to war in August 1914 to defend their territory and other national interests. Few could foretell that the war would undermine the power of victors and vanquished alike. German, Austrian, and Russian monarchies collapsed; the Ottoman Empire weakened further; Italian democracy lasted only until 1922; and Britain and France emerged shaken and heavily in debt. The new Soviet regime had to struggle to survive civil war and foreign intervention. Only the United States and Japan immediately enhanced their position as world powers.

The twenty-year truce that followed World War I brought more upheaval to Europe. Communism and fascism undermined democratic regimes, and a series of economic crises, culminating in the Great Depression of the 1930s, further weakened Europe's economic position in the world. Finally, the renewal of war in 1939 brought forth awesome examples of human cruelty and destruction. No foreign invader was to blame; European civilization suffered from its own flaws.

The First World War

Too few foresaw what a general European war fought with modern weapons would be like. In August 1914, the troops left their towns and villages with buoyant spirits, confident that they would be home for Christmas. Very quickly, however, the bitter reality sank in that neither side could achieve a clear advantage, for the machine gun made any attack virtually suicidal. A million soldiers dug hundreds of miles of trenches to protect themselves from artillery fire and watch for any movement from opposing troops. Much of northeastern France became a wasteland, for artillery pounded the opposing lines for days before an attack. The troops received orders to go "over the top" of the trenches, charge ahead, and break through the enemy's defenses. The ensuing attacks were futile on the whole, for eventually the enemy's defenses tightened and machine guns raked the field. Yet the generals were painfully slow to comprehend the situation and persisted in throwing masses of soldiers at deadly lines of defense.

Instead of a war of movement and attack, by 1915, the conflict on both the western and eastern fronts became a war of attrition, for neither side at first possessed any means to penetrate a hail of bullets. In addition, the tank, airplane, and submarine were introduced to military arsenals. Each of these weapons underwent further development after the First World War and played more decisive roles in the Second.

Technology also altered the relationship between the civilian and military populations. The weapons consumed far more men and ammunition than in previous wars. The early estimates of what the war would cost in human and material treasure soon went out the window. About a half to two-thirds of those men aged 20 to 45 were eventually drafted between 1914 and 1918: in France, about one-fifth of the entire population; among all the belligerents, about 60 million men. Modern war also required enormous logistical support: railroads, industrial production, supplies, and capital. In factories, women replaced men who had left for the battlefront, and their general contribution on the "home front" gave women leverage to insist on broader political and civil rights after the war. Labor unions came to agreements with governments to suspend strikes and accept sacrifices in return for a voice in the production and allocation of goods. This war's outcome depended on the ability of each state to mobilize not only soldiers but also the entire population and industrial economy. Democracy, nationalism, and industrialism had produced "total war"—conflict that committed each nation to struggle for survival and victory without compromise. Ominously for the future of Europe and the world, modern warfare regimented and militarized entire populations.

Public opinion, therefore, was a crucial element in each nation's total strength. The masses of every country were asked to make extraordinary sacrifices. Governments justified these sacrifices on moral grounds: propaganda typically depicted a cruel and inhuman enemy who killed innocent children and violated women. How, after all, could one compromise with such evil? The democracies—Britain and France—rallied their citizens behind the war not only by evoking the immorality of the enemy and the justice of their own cause, but also by promising a more just and democratic society after the war. Russia and Austria could not make such promises without undermining their respective regimes, and they failed to rally sustained mass support. In fact, the strain of the conflict led to revolution in Russia in 1917 and the disintegration of Austria into separate national states in 1918. With the entry of fresh American troops in the west, German resistance reached the point of collapse, and the weary powers of the Triple Entente staggered to victory.

A Temporary and Uncertain Peace

Politicians soon arrived in Paris to arrange the terms of peace, but the wounds of war were far too deep for peace to be easily or permanently achieved. In addition to the known dead on both sides, about 7.5 million unrecorded deaths and civilian casualties pushed the toll well over 10 million. In addition, there were the mutilated survivors of the war and women for whom there would be no husbands or children. An entire generation had paid for the war with their lives, wounds, and grief, and many Europeans harbored lasting resentments.

The genie of nationalism, which had broken loose to provoke the war, also affected the ensuing peace settlement. The U.S. president, Woodrow Wilson, sought what he considered a just rather than a punitive peace. Wilson's "Fourteen Points" reflected his theories about the causes of modern warfare: there should be freedom of the seas in peace and war, the abolition of secret treaties and unequal trading privileges, and the establishment of an international organization to resolve disputes before they lead to war—the League of Nations. But another of Wilson's points gave encouragement to nationalism. It held that national groups should have their own governments. Thus, Wilson's published principles encouraged the Poles, Czechs, Yugoslavs, and others, who set up their own states. It also encouraged ethnic minorities to demand separate states or inclusion in a neighboring state of their own nationality. For economic, military, and geographical reasons, most such demands had to remain unsatisfied.

Aside from such practical difficulties, the other victorious powers, Britain and France especially, had suffered too much to be generous toward Germany. So they insisted Germany sign the Treaty of Versailles, which included payment of a large indemnity, or reparations; admission of responsibility for the war; the loss of various territories in Europe as well as overseas colonies; demilitarization of German territory west of the Rhine; and the limitation of German armed forces to one hundred thousand troops. Because most of the war had been fought on French soil, the French demanded that the peace settlement sharply weaken Germany. But opposition from the United States and Great Britain meant that the peace settlement did not weaken Germany drastically, and hence it did not satisfy the French demand for security. At the same time, it infuriated the Germans, who considered many of the provisions too harsh, and a generation later, German soldiers marched into France again to take revenge.

Italy, which had joined the victorious Allies only in 1915, ended up on the winning side but was likewise exasperated by the peace settlement. Few of Italy's demands for territory were met, and Italian prime minister Orlando walked out of the conference. Chronic economic problems fed Italian socialist and nationalist movements; its democratic government lost popular support; and a dictator—Benito Mussolini—came to power in October 1922. His regime was to become a model for Adolf Hitler a decade later.

War perpetuated or created long-term problems that a peace conference could not resolve. Nationalism had grown steadily in the nineteenth century, reached a fever pitch during the war, and continued to smolder afterward. Despite the much-heralded Wilsonian principle that nationalities should have their own states, many Europeans, particularly Germans and Hungarians, were minorities in states such as Poland, Czechoslovakia, Romania, and Yugoslavia. Unsatisfied nationalism remained a volatile ingredient in European politics.

Other factors undermined the peace settlement. No longer could Europe depend on a stable monetary system; bankrupt state economies printed money, caused inflation, and eroded confidence in paper currency. People living on fixed incomes, especially in Germany, saw their savings wiped out and their very survival in jeopardy. Furthermore, the war made European states debtors to the world instead of creditors: whereas in 1914 the United States owed Europe about $6 billion, in 1918 Europe owed the United States about $16 billion. This reversal of fortunes marked the arrival of the United States as a major world power. Meanwhile, the Soviet Union began to build a powerful industrial state and started to affect European politics through its satellite Communist parties.

Nevertheless, for the first decade after the war, many Europeans convinced themselves that peace would last. The victors imagined that reparations from Germany would ensure their economic revival. Only a few economists, such as Britain's John Maynard Keynes, understood that such transfers would undermine the economy all Europeans shared. An impoverished Germany would be a weak market for British and French goods; and, in any case, German payments could only come from the profits of its own brisk trade. Some who understood the problem proposed canceling all war debts, but the United States had become the principal creditor among the Allies, and refused; hence, Britain and France continued to insist on German payments in order to repay the United States. In this way, the war dealt a continuing blow to the European economy.

Military security even for the victorious powers proved to be an illusion. Germany remained the major threat to peace: its population grew from 62 million to 69 million between 1918 and 1939, whereas France's population remained static at about 39 million; German industrial capacity was hardly impaired by the war, most of which had been fought on French soil; and few Germans thought the terms of the Versailles settlement should be respected. Once the war was over, Britain was interested in reestablishing trade with a prosperous Germany so long as the Germans did not again engage them in a naval rivalry. The United States, despite its economic and military capacity, refused to take responsibility for maintaining a world balance of power. The U.S. Senate refused to ratify the Versailles Treaty, and the United States did not enter the League of Nations.

So France soon found itself vulnerable to a resurgent Germany and sought alliances and assurances throughout the 1920s and 1930s. But French alliances with Poland, Czechoslovakia, Yugoslavia, Romania, and Belgium provided only the illusion of security as Germany violated the Versailles settlement by building the core of a modern army and air force in cooperation with Soviet Russia. Sixty-

two countries signed the Kellogg-Briand pact in 1928, renouncing war as an instrument of national policy. But this proved to be little more than a rhetorical gesture unsupported by serious national commitments. Germany meanwhile grew in strength. After January 1933, under the leadership of Adolf Hitler and the National Socialist (Nazi) party, the Germans were determined to revise the Versailles settlement.

Fascism and Modern Europe

In the course of Europe's modern transformation, two major mass movements challenged its dominant liberal, democratic, and capitalist values and institutions. In the nineteenth century, a minority of intellectuals and workers created the Socialist movement in response to dislocations and hardships associated with the Industrial Revolution. This movement gained strength in the twentieth century but split politically between autonomous Socialist parties and Communist parties loyal to the Soviet Union. Twentieth-century fascism, in contrast, was a mass movement that appealed to dissatisfied or unfulfilled people in all social classes, those who felt threatened or left behind by capitalist modernization but unable to embrace Marxist socialism. Thus, it appealed to large fractions of the middle and upper classes who feared the advance of socialism and communism. It was attractive to small-scale merchants, artisans, and farmers who feared the loss of their independence to either big business or Socialist revolution. And it fascinated those who were appalled by the materialism and artificiality of modern life. Fascism reflected a loss of faith in the capacity of liberal democracy and capitalism to create a good society and was therefore most successful where democratic traditions and experience were weakest: in Hungary, Italy, and Germany.

Fascism arose from a pragmatic alliance between upper-class conservatives and discouraged members of the middle class who faced economic hardship and feared Communist revolution. European conservatives had attacked liberal and capitalist institutions ever since the French Revolution. Whereas modern liberals stressed democracy, social mobility, material progress, and competition, conservatives preferred a static world based on traditional spiritual values and economic cooperation between classes that understood and accepted their place in the social hierarchy. The Fascists romantically appealed to this more tranquil "world that was lost" in the smoke of the Industrial Revolution.

Fascist ideology varied slightly from country to country, but everywhere it was nationalistic, condoned violence against its enemies, looked to a charismatic leader for direction, and condemned individualism, democracy, and Marxism. It exalted action rather than thought and reflection. In Italy, anti-Semitism played no important part in fascism at the beginning, but in Germany, it was the most conspicuous aspect of the Nazis' ideology and conduct. Fascism was both revolutionary in its determination to overthrow existing regimes, and conservative in its affirmation of traditional values and its opposition to much of modern life.

Ideology was frequently at odds with conduct as Fascist movements maneuvered for power. In theory, Fascists opposed the capitalist class, which bore modern and liberal values, but in practice, they tended to leave this class undisturbed in return for financial support. Fascist leaders in power soon understood that the industrial capacity that capitalists had created was essential to their own survival. For this reason, European fascism sought to reconcile modern technology and industrialism with its otherwise antimodern principles and to harness industrial and military power to a mass movement that rejected democracy, capitalism, rationalism, and materialism.

While springing from different roots, Italian and German fascism had much in common, and the two countries were allies during World War II. Here Mussolini (far left) and Hitler (center) meet in 1941. *The Granger Collection*

The Italian Precursor

The Fascist movement in Italy brought Benito Mussolini (1883–1945) to power in 1922. Italy had become a unified state only in 1860 and never developed a truly modern and democratic culture. Conservative landlords controlled most of the rural areas both economically and politically. In the north, however, a significant industrial society arose in the late nineteenth century, and with it an industrial proletariat and a large middle class. The war introduced another social element—resentful veterans who lacked both employment and popular respect. During the economic crisis following the war, trade unions and various Communist and Socialist parties threatened the traditional social order from the Left.

At this juncture, Mussolini and his followers, the "Black-shirts," offered an alternative to both communism and ineffective liberal-democratic rule. Fearful of communism, big business threw its support to Mussolini, who promised order in the streets, an end to liberal democracy, and the maintenance of the traditional social order. Although "il Duce" promised his mass following a generous social program, once he attained power, he concentrated instead on building state power. Mussolini diverted attention from real domestic grievances by evoking national traditions, building military power, and carrying out imperial expansion in Ethiopia. He also reconciled the Italian state with the Roman Catholic church, and hence with Italian conservatives, in the Lateran accords of 1929. These agreements recognized the pope's right to rule the Vatican city, compensated the church for property losses under the republic, and ensured religious instruction in the schools. Democracy in Italy was suspended; opponents were executed or imprisoned. Mussolini claimed to speak for all Italians, but he served the interests chiefly of the landed and industrial elites who felt threatened by democracy and socialism.

Hitler and the Nazis

In Germany, there arose a far more terrible manifestation of fascism. As World War I ended, the imperial regime of Kaiser Wilhelm collapsed, and democratic politicians of the new government—known as the Weimar Republic—were left to negotiate the peace settlement. As one scholar has put it, the Weimar Republic was run by social "outsiders."[3] The traditional elites were either disgraced or had withdrawn from public life because their regime had lost the war. However, these defeated leaders, such as General Erich Ludendorff, never explicitly took responsibility for the defeat; instead, they attacked the democratic politicians who had the unfortunate task of signing the peace settlement and enforcing it. In this atmosphere, a myth arose that Germany had not really lost the war but that civilians, especially Socialists, Communists, and Jews, had stabbed the nation in the back.

During the 1920s, liberal political leaders faced the active or silent animosity of much of the German population. Vigilante groups of veterans (the *Freikorps*) assassinated hundreds of liberal politicians, journalists, and supporters of the Weimar regime, and they received only mild punishments from conservative judges who also detested the republic. These small groups of discontented veterans hostile to democracy gradually drew support from the middle classes as well as from conservative landowners because of the ruinous inflation of 1923 and the worldwide Depression that began in 1929. Whereas the war provided the shock that drove Italians to fascism in 1922, the Great Depression of 1929 was the final blow that destroyed the Weimar Republic.

The Depression created massive unemployment (six million by 1932) among the proletariat and the middle class alike. Everyone demanded decisive governmental action. Many industrial workers turned to Socialists and Communists for answers, whereas some abandoned these traditional working-class parties in favor of fascism. Large numbers of middle-class people deserted moderate parties in favor of the conservative and radical right-wing parties, in particular the Nazi party of Hitler. The liberal political center on which the democratic regime depended simply evaporated. After several years of propaganda and street battles with their opponents, the Nazis won about 37 percent of the popular vote in 1932, Hitler became chancellor in January 1933, and in March he assumed dictatorial powers. The Weimar Republic, a democratic regime that never commanded broad support, gave way to the Third Reich.

Adolf Hitler (1889–1945) suppressed all other political parties, abolished labor unions, controlled radio and the press, and in general assumed police power over the society. Yet he had the support of the vast majority of the population. His control would not have endured, however, had he not put unemployed Germans back to work. The government invested first in civil projects such as superhighways and, after 1935, in rearmament. To compensate for the continued weakness of foreign trade due to the Depression, Germany tried to become self-sufficient by developing and manufacturing substitutes (such as artificial rubber) for foreign goods it could not afford. Eventually, however, this solution could not satisfy German needs, and Hitler used his growing military force to expand first to the east, for grain and oil, and then to the west.

For many countries still suffering from the Depression throughout the 1930s, Hitler seemed to have found the secret for recovery: economic planning, controlled wages and prices, government investment, and enforced peace between capital and labor. This was a radical departure from the classical principles of capitalism. Some industrialists had contributed money to the Nazi movement, but the "Nazi revolution" was not essentially a capitalist phenomenon: it sought political power, not the prosperity of an industrial elite. Still, Hitler, like Mussolini, chose not to dispossess the capitalists so long as they cooperated by producing goods that the regime required.

The social and economic reasons for the failure of the Weimar Republic and the rise of Hitler's National Socialists are fairly clear. But Hitler's success was the result of other factors as well. Hitler masterfully invoked rural and traditional values that Germans feared losing in their increasingly urban and materialistic culture. He used Jews as a symbol of the

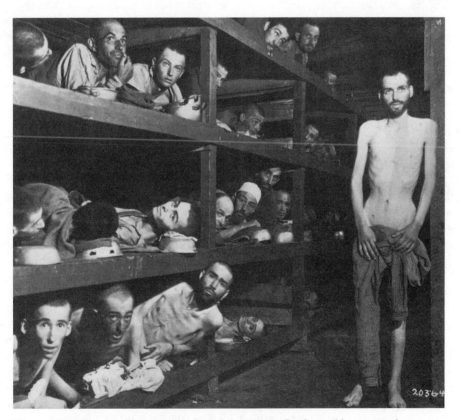

Faces of the holocaust. Slave laborers in their barracks at Buchenwald concentration camp in 1945. *The Bettmann Archive*

urban, capitalist, and foreign influences that were corrupting true German culture. The Nazis reinforced a current of anti-Semitism that had deep roots in Germany and most of Europe. But more than other Europeans, Germans projected all their self-hatred as well as their distaste for modern life and recent German history upon the Jews.

Soon after Hitler came to power he implemented policies prejudicial to Jews, such as exclusion from universities, professional organizations, and civil employment. In 1935, the Nuremberg laws forbade sexual relations or marriage between Jews and other Germans and forced Jews to identify themselves in public by wearing the Star of David. Such ostracism escalated to terror on the night of November 9, 1938, known as *Kristallnacht,* when Nazis smashed and looted Jewish shops. Finally, during the Second World War, Nazi leaders carried their anti-Semitic policy to the extreme by organizing a "Final Solution" to the "Jewish Problem." They created an elaborate system of classification and transportation to bring millions of Jews to death camps in eastern Germany and Poland, notably Dachau, Buchenwald, Auschwitz, and Treblinka. In these places several million Jews were worked to death, shot, and gassed in the final two years of the war. Here a modern administrative and technological apparatus for death served one of Europe's oldest and most traditional hatreds. This tragedy—the Holocaust—took the lives of about six million Jews and ever since has haunted the human conscience.

In schools and in massive torchlight ceremonies, the Nazis expressed their opposition to modernism by stressing the superiority of the German race, folk culture, and ancient heroes. Although Hitler relied on modern technology to create his war machine, in his public speeches he was the mystical leader, the führer whose deeds were beyond the rational understanding of his people. Intuition and force rather than reason and compromise should rule Germany. Hitler's power rested ultimately on the willingness of most Germans to surrender their right to question and analyze; instead, they followed a mesmerizing orator who they believed would lead them to national greatness and personal fulfillment.

The Nazi rise to power thus reflected the crucial flaws of European civilization: an unstable system of sovereign states that both generated and glorified war; the virus of a narrow nationalism defined in terms of race; and a capitalist economy prone to periodic breakdowns, with terrible social consequences.

The Second World War: The End of European Hegemony

German economic and military revival under Hitler effectively upset the balance of power in Europe, much as German unification had done before the First World War. Germany openly violated the Treaty of Versailles in 1935 and 1936, when it began to rearm and to remilitarize the Rhineland. But the rise of the Soviet Union, with its disturbing Communist ideology, made most Western leaders lenient toward Germany: a strong German state would act as a buffer against Soviet expansion toward the West. A major factor in Hitler's rise to power was the belief of most Western liberals that the Communist threat was far more serious than the Fascist threat. Furthermore, during the Depression of the 1930s, Britain and France were preoccupied with the problem of securing food and shelter for their people, and they were not prepared either materially or morally to intervene against a German state that invoked the right of national self-determination—the right of German minorities to be united with the German fatherland.

The Soviet Union did recognize the German threat and encouraged the formation of "popular front" governments consisting of Communist, Socialist, and other left-wing parties in France and Spain. Such governments would prevent further Fascist political victories and bar German expansion. But this tactic made Western moderates and conservatives only more wary of Soviet meddling in their affairs. A Popular Front government in Spain led to a bitter civil war. In France, a Jewish Socialist, Leon Blum, led a left-wing coalition twice between 1936 and 1938, but the rise of the French Popular Front caused many conservatives to mutter nervously, "Better Hitler than Blum."

Hitler understood that Britain and France were in no mood to risk another world war, and so he dared to expand in the south and east. In March of 1938, Germany invaded and annexed Austria, which was mostly German. Later that year, Germany threatened to annex the German-speaking region of Czechoslo-vakia (the Sudetenland), and to avoid general war, France and Britain agreed at Munich that Hitler should have his way. But when the Germans occu-pied the rest of Bohemia and Moravia in March of 1939, French and British leaders finally realized that appeasement was no solution to Hitler's limitless ap-petite for new territory.

Still, both ideology and geography prevented Britain, France, and the Soviet Union from forming another Triple Entente: not only was communism ab-horrent to Western leaders; in addition, Soviet troops would have had to march across either Poland or Ro-mania to engage German troops. Finally, in August 1939, the Soviets signed the Nonaggression Pact with Germany in order to gain territory, temporary security, and time. German troops crossed the Polish border on September 1, and Britain and France belat-edly and reluctantly declared war on Germany two days later. The Second World War had begun, but nationalism kindled less enthusiasm than in the past, for few Europeans had any illusions concerning the suffering that lay ahead.

Germany and the Soviet Union quickly defeated Poland and divided it between themselves. Assured by the Nonaggression Pact, the USSR proceeded to incorporate the Baltic states into the Soviet Union and to invade Finland, as Germany turned its military machine upon the West. Within a month, German troops had defeated French and British forces on the Continent (see Map 5.1). By the summer of 1940, Great Britain was the only European power still at war with Germany. The British Empire, navy, air-force, pride, and geography all helped to preserve British independence until reinforcements arrived from across the Atlantic.

Meanwhile, Hitler attacked the Soviet Union in the summer of 1941, a calculated risk that committed Germany again to a protracted war on two fronts that it could not win. This time, moreover, Russia did not withdraw from the conflict but absorbed the Ger-man onslaught and then counterattacked. When the United States entered the war against Japan and Ger-many in December 1941, it was only a matter of time before Germany and its much weaker Italian ally would have to submit to superior human and material resources. In November 1942, Americans began to move across North Africa and thereby took control of the Mediterranean. In July 1943, American,

British, and Free French forces landed in Sicily and began the invasion of Italy. Finally, on June 6, 1944, a massive Allied force landed on Normandy beaches in France and began to push the German army east-ward. Simultaneously, the Soviet army drove west-ward.

As the Allied land armies converged in the cen-ter of Europe, American and British bombers pounded German factories, railroads, and cities. Even more than in the First World War, the civilian population suffered horribly. British, German, and Soviet citizens were particularly hard hit by aerial bombing. French workers were deported to supple-ment the German labor force. And throughout Eu-rope, the disruption of farming and transportation created food shortages. Including the war in Asia against Japan, about fifteen million soldiers died, of whom almost half were Soviet. There were fewer than a million British, French, and American mili-tary deaths. The civilian and military death toll of the Second World War is estimated at upward of forty million men, women, and children, of whom about six million were Jews and twenty million were Soviets.

Europe itself was impoverished and in ruins, the victim of its own political vices and industrial power. It was clear that European hegemony in world af-fairs was finished and that a strengthened United States and a weakened but determined Soviet Union would define the immediate fate of Europe and the world.

Europe Divided and Reconstructed

The grand Alliance that defeated Hitler soon unrav-eled, as a basic tension between the Soviet Union and the Western democracies became apparent. The So-viet Union sought military security on its western border and a buffer against Western capitalism, whereas the Western victors wished to extend capi-talism and democracy to all of Europe. Both sides agreed that Germany should pay heavily for the war and suffer occupation, but disagreement was sharp concerning Eastern Europe, especially Poland and Czechoslovakia, which had developed democratic

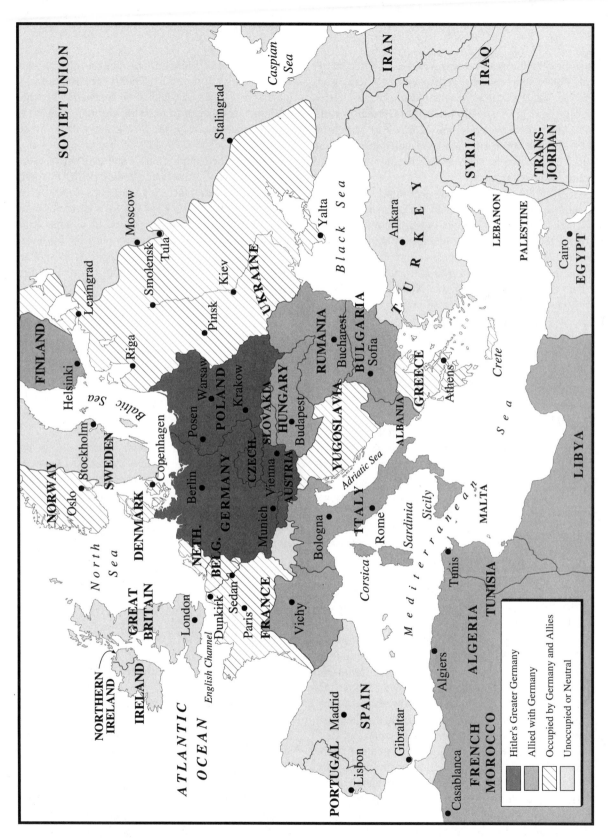

MAP 5.1 Nazi Europe during World War II

traditions of their own. Agreements eventually broke down as each side invoked its own interpretation. Finally, it was the position of military forces on May 8, 1945, when the German army surrendered, that separated Soviet Communist from Western capitalist spheres of influence.

Europe itself was prostrate at the end of the war and could not prevent the United States and the Soviet Union from ruling its destiny either directly or indirectly. The Fascists were defeated, and their political allies were in disgrace, but hunger, disease, poverty, and unemployment had become almost as menacing. The United States, fearing both Soviet expansion and the growing influence of European Communist parties, determined that its own political and economic interests were at stake in the revival of Western Europe and offered generous financial aid through the Marshall Plan in 1947.

The Soviet Union had paid heavily for its share in the Allied victory and demanded a sphere of influence in Eastern Europe, both as a reward and as a guarantee against future aggression from the capitalist West. It responded to the American Marshall Plan with its own system of economic development for Eastern Europe. Thus two separate economies took shape, and tensions between them gave rise to corresponding military alliances (see Map 5.2).

Cold War: The Political Context of Postwar Europe

Europe was not only divided after the war; it was also subject to the intense hostilities generated by the ideological, political, technological, and military rivalry between the United States and the Soviet Union. During the first phase of this *Cold War,* the new superpowers maneuvered for control of sensitive areas such as Berlin, Poland, Czechoslovakia, Greece, and Turkey. Each saw the other as expansionist and threatening to its social system. Since these systems—democracy and market economies, on the one hand, and communism and state managed economies, on the other—were radically opposed, an ideological contest that had originated with the Russian Revolution of 1917 intensified, spread to much of the world, and threatened to trigger another world war. Initially, however, the two superpowers focused their attention wholly on Europe.

As victory over Germany became assured in 1945, American leaders turned their attention to the anticipated Soviet threat. Many feared an outright Soviet invasion of Western Europe, or at least a dangerous political influence. Using the atomic bomb against Japan in 1945 was probably in part an initial effort to warn the Soviets against any such action. The United States also abruptly terminated shipment of Lend Lease supplies to the Soviet Union in May 1945, reduced the amount of reparations it was willing to permit the Soviets to extract from Germany, and pressed to establish democratic regimes in Eastern Europe open to Western economic penetration. Joseph Stalin, the Soviet leader, feared that the capitalist West intended to encircle his country with potentially hostile powers under American leadership.

When the United States set up the Marshall Plan in 1947 to furnish economic assistance to Europe, Soviet fears only increased. As Czechoslovakia, Hungary, and Poland became interested in the plan, Stalin recognized it as a threat to the Soviet sphere of influence. To eliminate any further temptation from the West, in 1948 Stalin replaced the mixed governments in Eastern Europe with Communist party regimes unequivocally loyal to the Soviet Union and cut off the supply route to West Berlin, moves that confirmed to the West that the Soviet Union threatened European security. The United States responded in 1949 by organizing a military alliance of Western states: the North Atlantic Treaty Organization (NATO). In 1955, in response to the rearming of West Germany and to keep its own satellites in line, the Soviet Union organized its own military alliance—the Warsaw Pact. Thus the Cold War had become the central fact of international relations, and each side blamed the other for starting it.

The states of Europe had become largely pawns of the two superpowers. In Eastern Europe, only Yugoslavia, which owed its liberation from the Nazis to its own resistance movement, escaped Soviet control. As the other East European states fell under Soviet political control, their agriculture was collectivized, their private industries were taken over by the state, and their economies were planned to benefit the Soviet Union. Periodic protests against Communist and Soviet domination, particularly in Hungary in 1957 and Czechoslovakia in 1968, were ruthlessly crushed.

Meanwhile, in Western Europe, American hegemony over its Allies was less absolute although quite effective. It was primarily the threat of military conflict with the Soviet Union that kept West European states securely in their military alliance (NATO) with the United States, even after their economies no longer depended on direct American assistance. Extensive trade with the United States was an additional inducement to European recognition of American leadership of the Western Alliance.

Military competition between the United States and Soviet Union maintained a balance of power—or terror—that kept the peace in Europe, but at a high price. American troops and equipment in France, Great Britain, and Germany faced Soviet counterparts throughout Eastern Europe. Most threatening of all were the thermonuclear weapons that both superpowers possessed by 1954. These devices, which could be carried by ever more sophisticated rockets, were hundreds of times more powerful than the

MAP 5.2 "Cold War" Europe

atomic bombs dropped on Japan just a decade before. For almost a half-century after the Second World War, the two superpowers were locked in a nuclear arms race to maintain a military stalemate and thus deter an actual attack. However, by maintaining peace in this dangerous fashion, the superpowers placed a great burden on their economies, with long-term social and political consequences.

The former colonies of the European states became another arena for conflict in the Cold War, but here the weapons were economic assistance, technical advisers, and conventional military hardware. A weakened Europe was in no position to retain its Afro-Asian empires, which were increasingly inflamed with anticolonial nationalism. Moreover, for ideological reasons both the United States and Soviet Union supported the independence of these possessions. But as colonies won their independence from European states and faced problems of economic development and security, they too often became caught up in superpower rivalries. For about forty years, the United States and Soviet Union struggled for the allegiance of developing countries in places as diverse as Cuba and Nicaragua, Angola and Ethiopia, Egypt and Afghanistan, Vietnam and China.

However, on a world scale the struggle between the superpowers for the allegiance of these "new nations" became, like the arms race itself, essentially a stalemate. Furthermore, many of the former European colonies, such as India, remained officially nonaligned during the Cold War.

The Common Market and West European Revival

As West European nations recognized their economic and military vulnerability and surrendered their colonies, they also shed some of their prickly independence and established cooperative rather than strictly competitive economies. A new generation of Europeans began to think in terms of the welfare of Europe as a whole; they recognized that unity could better ensure economic prosperity and the elimination of war. In 1957, six countries—West Germany, France, Italy, Belgium, the Netherlands, and Luxembourg—signed the Treaties of Rome, thus establishing the European Economic Community (EEC), known as the *Common Market*. Through such action, Western Europeans achieved remarkable economic growth during the 1950s and 1960s.

Unlike the leaders of the Eastern bloc states, however, the pioneers of the Common Market envisioned their economic union as a future political force that could rival the superpowers. Although not yet achieved, that goal is in sight. The addition of Britain, Ireland, Denmark, Greece, Spain, and Portugal has made the union far more powerful, and despite setbacks and difficult negotiations, the original vision is very much alive. The early 1990s saw movement toward a true Common Market with uniform external tariffs, common social policies, no special government subsidies to protected industries, and the free movement of goods and labor across national boundaries. In addition, the union is attempting to adopt a common currency. Finally, the direct election of a European Parliament has contributed to a sense of European solidarity and has further undercut the sovereignty of the separate states. In short, the West European states have taken decisive action in order to prosper economically and, as a group, to determine their own political destiny.

In their domestic political and social life, various combinations of Christian Democrats, Socialists, and Communists who had participated in resistance movements during the Second World War swept away the gangster elites of fascism, but there was no broad social upheaval, as in Eastern Europe. Despite the egalitarian ideals of the resistance, the older landed and commercial elites on the whole retained their wealth, joined in the postwar decades by a new class of industrial managers and technicians. But the memories of suffering and insecurity during the Depression and the war led Europeans to demand new social-welfare measures along with economic prosperity. Thus, Western Europeans used their democracies to create modern welfare states—a sharp departure from the world of free but vulnerable individuals that Adam Smith had described.

In doing so Western Europe sponsored a broadening of the "meritocratic" revolution that after the war opened university doors to greater numbers of bright students. Parents of all social classes soon became

The breaching of the Berlin Wall, shown here in process as East German border guards look on, was the central event in the collapse of communism in Eastern Europe in 1989. *The Bettmann Archive*

aware that achievement in school was the major route to social advancement, and they encouraged their children to pursue longer courses of study. More than in the past, Western European families did not accept their social position as fixed: they began to assume that social mobility was possible at least for their children.

Hence, a combination of economic prosperity and new opportunities in Western Europe blunted the appeal of social revolution. In a series of dramatic demonstrations and protests in 1968, university students in France and West Germany attacked capitalism, imperialism, and spendthrift consumer societies, but they also complained of the shortage of jobs appropriate for young graduates whose expectations had soared in prosperous times. With few exceptions, these student revolutionaries of the 1960s eventually made their peace with the new Europe and its consumer culture.

Industrial workers, some of whom joined forces with the students in 1968, were no more willing to undertake a thorough social and political revolution. Contrary to Marx's prediction that they would become an irresistible majority, their numbers stabilized at about a third of the work force. Furthermore, they became acccustomed to welfare states that provided security, employment, and paid vacations, and to a consumer culture that furnished automobiles and television sets. They wished to modify rather than overturn the European version of capitalism. In short, no broad support existed in Western Europe for changing basic institutions. This was the social basis for the gradual accommodation of both Socialist and Communist movements to existing democratic systems.

Thus, Western Europe has taken a new course since the Second World War in two major respects. First, it has carried out a broad social experiment that blends elements of capitalism and socialism. Although some argue that the European welfare state is merely a device for capitalists to prevent real social revolution, the masses of Europeans who now enjoy a high standard of living do not wish to overturn the system. Second, since the high cost of unbridled nationalism became painfully evident in the twentieth century, the Western European states have tempered their traditional independence with a broad plan of economic integration and a vision of political union as well.

Eastern Europe: From Subjection to Liberation

In Eastern Europe, the Communist seizure of power deprived old elites of property, businesses, and influence as a new generation, from modest social origins, assumed leadership positions in both state and economy. Soviet hegemony enforced a social revolution and gave rise to a privileged Communist ruling class, sustained until 1989 largely by military force. Until the 1960s, however, these new societies could not hope to enjoy a higher standard of living, for their economies produced few consumer goods in order to concentrate on heavy industry for Soviet military purposes. Since then a combination of the West's example and popular pressure pushed the Soviet Union and the Eastern bloc to produce more consumer goods and, in countries such as Hungary, to experiment with more liberal and decentralized forms of economic organization. This shift in policy, however, only raised expectations further and fueled the political and social demands that led to the "miraculous year" of 1989 and the collapse of communism.

Whereas after 1945 the United States encouraged the West European states to consolidate so as to revive and exercise some of their former influence, the Soviet Union treated the East European states differently in its Council for Mutual Economic Assistance (COMECON). COMECON discouraged the independent development of East European economies and reinforced their ties with the Soviet Union. The periodic revolts in Eastern Europe in the face of overwhelming military force suggested that the managed economies in these states did not produce a standard of living that could satisfy the populations and certainly did not match that of Western Europe.

Despite Soviet repression, some of the Eastern European states were able to establish a measure of autonomy. Hungary experimented with elements of a market economy; Poland permitted private agriculture and a role for the Catholic church; Romania practiced a relatively independent foreign policy. The final loosening of the Soviet grip on Eastern Europe and the demise of the Communist party throughout the Soviet bloc began in Poland in 1980–1981 with a series of strikes at the Gdansk shipyards. From these there arose a movement known as *Solidarity,* which drew support from all sectors of the population and the Catholic church. As Solidarity's demands escalated to include the right to foreign travel and free elections, the Communist regime once again suppressed the movement by force. Yet Poland's rulers now faced a population conscious of its unity and eager for a future chance to pursue Solidarity's demands.

What made this possible was the transformation of the Soviet Union under the leadership of Mikhail Gorbachev. By the late 1980s he had concluded that the Soviet Union could no longer hold its East European allies by force. In this context, Solidarity's struggle in Poland soon resumed, and in June 1989, in the first free elections, the people resoundingly defeated the Communist candidates. As if a dam had broken, a similar process of popular revolts and weak responses on the part of the Communist regimes took place in Hungary, East Germany, Czechoslovakia, Bulgaria, and Romania. The entire edifice of Communist satellites built in the early years of the Cold War suddenly crumbled as Communist parties were turned out of power and popularly elected governments installed. The breaching of the Berlin Wall, erected in 1961 to prevent East Germans from fleeing to a better life in West Germany, became the symbol of Eastern Europe's liberation from Communist oppression and of the reunification of both Germany and Europe itself.

Another sign that the Cold War was coming to an end was the virtual ending of the arms race between the United States and the Soviet Union. Under Gorbachev's leadership it became clear that the Soviet Union desperately needed relief from the economic strain of military competition, and so he sought a dramatic reduction of armaments with less attention to the military balance. Furthermore, Gorbachev made clear that he no longer considered the Soviet Union to be the mortal enemy of the United States. He backed this up by halting economic assistance to Cuba and giving political support to the United States and its allies in the war with Iraq in 1991. Eastern Europe's liberation, though partly the result of popular resistance, was facilitated by the declining significance of the Cold War in world affairs.

Conclusion

With the demise of the Soviet Union, the end of the Cold War, and the liberation of Eastern European states, Europe faces new challenges that are rooted in old realities. The problem of integrating East European societies into the rest of Europe reminds us that the division of Europe into east and west long predates the Communist seizure of power. The explosion of ethnic nationalism reflected in the disintegration of Yugoslavia, Czechoslovakia, and the Soviet Union represents a renewal of the kinds of conflicts that destroyed the Austrian and Ottoman empires and that contributed to World War I. And the problem of assimilating Algerian immigrants in France, West Indian immigrants in Britain, and Turkish immigrants in Germany represents the consequences of an imperial past. Thus, Europe continues to struggle with the legacy of its modern history in the altered circumstances of the late twentieth century.

Notes

1. Barbara Tuchman, *The Proud Tower* (New York: Macmillan, 1966).

2. Bonnie S. Anderson and Judith P. Zinsser, *A History of Their Own: Women in Europe from Prehistory to the Present,* vol. 2 (New York: Harper & Row, 1988), p. 389.

3. Peter Gay, *Weimar Culture* (New York: Harper & Row, 1968).

SUGGESTIONS FOR FURTHER READING: EUROPE

Adas, Michael. *Machines as the Measure of Men.* 1989. (Shows how Europeans' perceptions of themselves as scientifically and technologically superior shaped their views of other peoples.)

Boxer, Marilyn J., and Jean H. Quataert, eds. *Connecting Spheres: Women in the Western World, 1500 to the Present.* 1987. (A collection of articles that shows how women experienced and contributed to a process of modernization that men largely dominated.)

Braudel, Fernand. *Civilization and Capitalism, 15th–18th Century.* 3 vols. 1975–1984. (A classic work that describes in great detail the social and economic life of emerging capitalist Europe.)

Cipolla, Carlo. *Before the Industrial Revolution: European Society and Economy, 1000–1700.* 2nd ed. 1980.

Gottlieb, Beatrice. *The Family in the Western World from the Black Death to the Industrial Age.* 1993.

Greenfield, Liah. *Nationalism: Five Roads to Modernity.* 1992. (Discusses nationalism as a fundamental theme in the experience of England, France, Germany, Russia, and America.)

Heilbroner, Robert L. *The Worldly Philosophers.* 6th ed. 1987. (A brilliant exposition of the economic principles and ideas that underlay the rise of capitalism in the West.)

Jones, A. L. *The European Miracle.* 1981. (A discussion of why Europe rather than some other culture created the first modern civilization.)

Landes, David. *The Unbound Prometheus.* 1969. (A classic study of Europe's rise and the growth of its industrial societies.)

McNeill, William H. *The Pursuit of Power: Technology, Armed Forces, and Society since AD 1000.* 1982. (Addresses the role of war and technology in the rise of the West.)

Mikyr, Joel. *The Lever of Riches: Technological Creativity and Economic Progress.* 1990. (Argues that invention has been the trigger of economic progress in Europe and elsewhere.)

Moore, Barrington Jr. *Social Origins of Dictatorship and Democracy.* 1966. (A provocative work that traces patterns of modernization to the social evolution of rural societies.)

Payne, S. G. *Fascism: Comparison and Definition.* 1980.

Stearns, Peter, and Herrick Chapman. *The Industrial Revolution in World History.* 1993.

Thompson, E. P. *The Making of the English Working Class.* 1966. (Discusses the transformation of working people into a working class during the Industrial Revolution.)

Tilly, Louise A., and Joan W. Scott. *Women, Work, and Family.* 1978. (Addresses the changing roles of working-class women in France and England as they participated in the Industrial Revolution.)

PART II

INTERSECTIONS AND ENCOUNTERS: GLOBAL CONNECTIONS SINCE 1500

Chapter 6: *Europe and the World: Forms and Phases of Global Expansion*

Comparative Essay: *Paths to the Modern World: Patterns, Themes, and Questions*

Suggestions for
Further Reading: *Europe and the World*

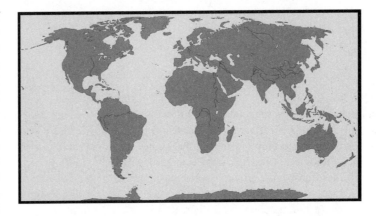

The central encounter of modern world history occurred between the expanding civilization of the West and everyone else. As Part I indicates, that encounter shaped Europe's own historical development in many ways and often to its economic advantage. But Europe's global expansion also created the setting within which, and often against which, all other societies have been compelled to make their way in the modern world. Russians, Latin Americans, Arabs, Indians, Chinese, Africans—these and other peoples found themselves faced with the daunting fact of west European dominance in one form or another. None of them could avoid dealing with it.

Thus, Part II marks a transition between the story of European development, recounted in Chapters 1–5, and the modern histories of the world's other peoples, the focus of the rest of this book. Chapter 6, therefore, asks how and why Europe's global expansion began and how it changed over the course of some five centuries. It seeks to define the changing contours of the modern world system created by Europe's spreading economic networks and colonial empires. And it outlines the contraction and decline of European global dominance in the twentieth century. The Comparative Essay in Part II raises a series of questions about the impact of the world system on the various subordinated peoples encompassed within it and their efforts to respond to it. In doing so the essay introduces the major issues that will be explored in the regional case studies, which constitute the remaining chapters of the book.

Chapter 6
Europe and the World: Forms and Phases of Global Expansion

Historians generally associate the interconnected world of the modern era with the expansion of Europe's influence and empires around the globe. And so they should. But from the perspective of world history, the European-centered world system that arose in the four centuries after 1500 was not a wholly new or unique creation. Rather, it built upon and transformed an already existing world system that had matured in the thirteenth century and then subsequently declined.

The World System in Transition: 1200–1500

By roughly 1300 C.E., the major urbanized societies of the Afro-Eurasian world had come into closer economic contact with one another than ever before.[1] Aided by the spread of Islam and the creation of the Mongol Empire, widespread trading connections by both land and sea linked urban centers and merchant communities from the Atlantic coast of Europe to the Pacific coast of China. It was a cosmopolitan economic system without a dominant political center, for no single region or state controlled this complex network of exchange. Participants included north and south Europeans; Africans from the western interior and the eastern coast; Arabs and Persians from the Middle East; both Hindus and Muslims from South Asia; Malays, Sumatrans, and Javanese from southeast Asia; and, of course, Chinese (see Map 6.1). Along the routes of commerce passed a variety of agricultural and manufactured goods, including gold and salt, textiles of wool, silk and cotton, sugar

and spices, pottery, and much more. It was a sophisticated commercial economy with a number of currencies, various kinds of credit, partnerships for pooling capital and minimizing risk, and bankers and wealthy merchant communities with differing relationships to their respective states. Within this complex system, Europe was clearly less highly developed than its more experienced Asian and Middle Eastern counterparts. It was also the most recent participant, having reconnected with the larger world system only recently and largely as a result of the Crusades in the eleventh and twelfth centuries.

This flourishing system, which had enriched all of its participants, substantially contracted and decayed between 1350 and 1450, just before Europe's voyages of global exploration began. The reasons were various. The political collapse of the Mongol Empire in the mid-fourteenth century thoroughly upset the overland trade route from China through Central Asia to the Middle East and Europe. At the same time, the epidemic known as the Black Death struck with a vengeance, spreading across the sea routes of the world system and wreaking havoc in many of the important commercial cities of China, the Middle East, and Europe.

Another factor in the collapse of the early world system was the voluntary withdrawal of China from active participation. For a time in the early fifteenth century, it looked as if China was on its way to dominating a large part of that system. With the most advanced economy in the world and a strong centralized state structure, China launched a series of massive naval expeditions in the Indian Ocean between 1405 and 1435. Consisting of as many as sixty-two large and well-armed ships in a single expedition, this fleet visited all of the major port cities

110

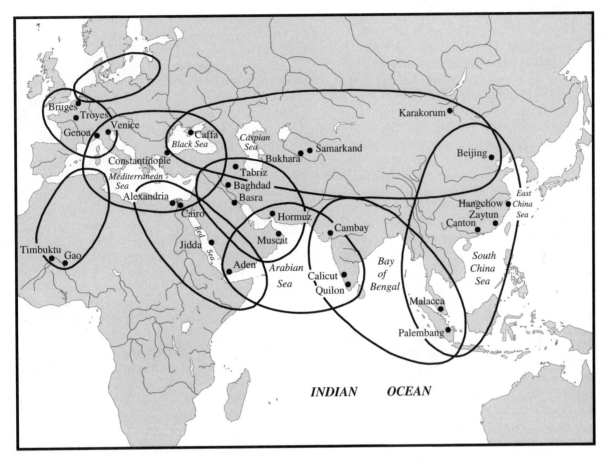

MAP 6.1 Circuits of World Trade, c. 1300. *Source: Janet L. Abu-Lughold,* Before European Hegemony, *New York: Oxford University Press, 1989. p. 37.*

of Southeast Asia, India, Arabia, and the east African coast. But then, suddenly, and for reasons historians still debate, the Chinese government withdrew its fleet and turned its attention almost wholly inward. By the end of the fifteenth century, over half of the Chinese navy had been scrapped.

Thus, when the Portuguese penetrated the Indian Ocean in the early sixteenth century, they encountered a power vacuum rather than the force of a Chinese navy with which they could have hardly competed. The surprising ascent of Europe to global dominance was facilitated not only by its own extraordinary dynamism but also by the collapse of the preexisting world system. Europe was able to take over and reorganize the fragments of the older system and to expand it into a new one centered on Europe itself. "[T]he 'Fall of the East,'" writes one recent historian, "preceded the 'Rise of the West.'"[2]

Remaking the World System: Europe's Early Empires, 1500–1800

If the collapse of an earlier world system helps to explain Europe's success in achieving an unprecedented global leadership, how can we account for its interest in overseas expansion? China's withdrawal from the arena of Indian Ocean competition, even though it had the means to dominate that competition, suggests that the impulse toward expansion and empire is neither automatic nor universal. Europe's advance, like China's retreat, needs to be explained.

"Gold, God, and Glory!" This has been the standard shorthand version of the motives that first drove Europeans, initially the Portuguese and Spanish and then the Dutch, British, and French, to the Old World of Asia and Africa and to the New World of the Americas. "Gold" symbolizes the search for material gain: Asian spices, African slaves, precious metals wherever they could be found, and the profits of trade. It must surely take first place in any assessment of European intentions.

"God" refers to the militant crusading tradition of Christian Europe and especially its fierce antagonism to Islam, which the West had seen for centuries as a mortal threat. The most recent carriers of Islam were the Turks, who conquered southeastern Europe in the fourteenth and fifteenth centuries and were viewed with the same combination of fear and hostility that many Americans felt for communism and the Soviet Union after World War II. Anti-Muslim feeling was at its most savage in the Iberian peninsula, where the Spanish and Portuguese had only in 1492 completed an eight-hundred-year struggle to expel the Muslims. And the frustrating need to rely on Muslim intermediaries to gain access to the highly valued spices of Asia simply compounded that sentiment.

"Glory" reminds us that the new and competing monarchs of Europe were looking for resources and victories abroad to bolster their claims at home. In the process, they enlisted unemployed fighting men and others with unfulfilled ambitions. Over the centuries, many Europeans found in empire a quicker and more certain route to higher status or respected position than was possible in their own countries.

But why did it begin in the fifteenth century? The Vikings had explored parts of North America as early as the ninth century, and the Crusaders had invaded the Middle East in the eleventh and twelfth to recover the Holy Lands for Christendom. Yet neither of these movements led to sustained European expansion. Not until the fifteenth century did Portuguese explorers push down the west coast of Africa and around the Cape of Good Hope to India. Only in 1492 did the Spanish crown sponsor Columbus's attempts to find India across the Atlantic Ocean.

Part of the answer lies in the development of a particular technology—an efficient, full-rigged, ocean-going sailing ship, outfitted with naval guns, that became available in Europe only during the fifteenth century. Although this technology was of little use against the Turks on land, it made possible the remarkable voyages and conquests of the western Europeans. Furthermore, the organizational capacity of the new European states, and a bit later of their trad-

ing companies, had only recently provided the ability to mobilize resources on the scale required for such ventures.

However, it was the economic and social crises of the fourteenth and fifteenth centuries (described in Chapter 1) that best explain the timing of Europe's early overseas expansion. In the wake of these serious setbacks to a growing economy, Europeans of all kinds began to look outward. Consolidating states and national monarchs needed revenue. The landowning nobility needed a new source of wealth, for declining income from feudal dues was eroding its economic base. This was particularly true in a small country such as Portugal with little room for internal expansion. Merchants, especially in Italy, needed investment outlets for their surplus capital, and those from Genoa in particular generously funded Portuguese expeditions.

Furthermore, Europe's economy as a whole was running short of gold needed to finance its growing internal trade and to pay for spices, jewels, and other Asian luxuries for its wealthy elite. The initial motive for the Portuguese voyages, in fact, was to gain direct access not to Indian spices but to west African gold fields, which had long been monopolized by north African middlemen. Finally, Europe's agriculture, based on wheat and livestock, could expand only by adding territory, whereas the more intensive rice agriculture of Asia could increase production by the application of more labor. Thus, the growing desire in Europe generally for wheat, sugar, meat, and fish meant that "Europe needed a larger land base to support the expansion of its economy."[3] Europe turned to the wider world, in short, to solve its internal problems, which had become increasingly apparent following the crisis of the fourteenth century.

In the three hundred years between 1500 and 1800, Europe's expansion gave rise to a new kind of world system quite unlike the earlier one it replaced. This European system differed mainly in that it had a single dominant center, western Europe, whereas the older one consisted of a number of more or less equal participants. But the core area of the world system was hardly a unified whole, for it was laced with bitter rivalries and frequent wars among the major competing west European powers—Portuguese, Spanish, Dutch, English, and French. In fact, it was largely the political competition of the nation-state system and the economic competition of an emerging capitalism

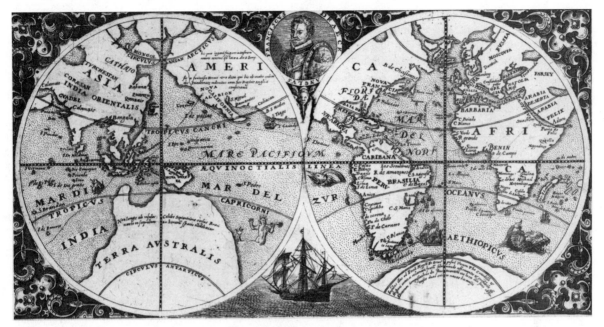

By the end of the sixteenth century, Europeans had added greatly to their knowledge of the world's geography, as illustrated in this map of 1599. *Rare Books and Manuscripts Division, The New York Public Library, Astor, Lenox and Tilden foundations*

that maintained the momentum of European expansion and drove it to the ends of the earth. Unlike China, where the state could make and enforce a decision to pull back from overseas competition, Europe possessed no corresponding single authority.

Europe's expansion during these centuries took a variety of forms. One, of course, lay in the voyages of discovery undertaken by Columbus, Magellan, da Gama, and others. Conquest and political control were also important, especially in the Americas and, by the end of the eighteenth century, in India and Indonesia as well. New cultural connections likewise played a significant role in Europe's early expansion. Settlers in the Americas took their culture with them and tried to practice as much of it as possible in their new setting. Missionaries made strenuous efforts to transmit Christianity but made little headway except among some of the conquered and dispirited peoples of the New World. In a process sometimes called "fringe Westernization,"[4] a few members of African and Asian societies picked up enough European culture—religion, language, literacy—to facilitate their role as brokers or go-betweens in cross-cultural trade.

Even more significant than empire or culture was the emergence of a global trading network, centered in Europe but touching in various ways most of the major culture areas of the world. The Dutch of the seventeenth century provide a telling example:

> [E]verything was grist for the Dutch mill. Who could fail to be surprised that wheat grown . . . in South Africa was shipped to Amsterdam? Or that Amsterdam became a market for cowrie shells brought back from Ceylon and Bengal, which found enthusiastic customers, including the English, who used them for trade with black Africa or for the purchase of slaves destined for America? Or that sugar from China, Bengal, sometimes Siam . . . was alternately in demand or out of it in Amsterdam, depending on whether the price could compete in Europe with sugar from Brazil or the West Indies?[5]

Not all parts of this interacting global economy were affected in the same way or to the same extent. Eastern Europe, especially Poland, was one of the first areas to be connected to the new global commercial system, largely through the export of rye and wheat to western Europe in exchange for herring, salt, silk, wines, and other manufactured goods. The strong demand for grain in western Europe encouraged a powerful landlord class in eastern Europe to produce for this market. In doing so, these landlords found it profitable to reduce their relatively free peasantry to a position of serf laborers. The absence of both strong monarchs and an independent merchant class gave the landlords the political clout necessary to accomplish this "second serfdom." Thus the new world economy pushed eastern Europe into a subordinate and dependent position and gave rise to a quite different kind of society from that of a dynamic and modernizing western Europe.[6] Other more distant peoples likewise found themselves caught up to varying degrees in the new European world system, as the experience of Asia, Africa, and the Americas demonstrates.

Empires of Commerce in Asia

The empires that Europeans initially constructed in Asia reflected the principal economic motives that drove them there—the desire to monopolize, through purchase or plunder, such Asian goods as pepper, ginger, cinnamon, cloves, and other spices, and to do so in an altogether alien cultural setting. Thus, Europeans established "trading-post empires,"[7] for their purpose was not to control territory or large populations but trade routes. Particularly if the routes were oceanic, it was enough to acquire a few fortified coastal locations from which to control seaborne trade.

The Portuguese were the first. Once Vasco da Gama showed the way to India around Africa in 1498, the Portuguese, with their efficient sailing ships and powerful on-board cannon, smashed their way into an ancient and complex trading system that included Arab, Indian, Malay, and Chinese merchants. Had they wanted only to trade, the Portuguese could have competed freely in this open commercial network. But they also wanted to control the trade. The total absence of armed ships in the Indian Ocean following the Chinese withdrawal and the relative lack of interest of the major land powers meant that the Portuguese were able to seize almost complete control of that trading system within fifteen years. With forts at Mozambique in east Africa, Hormuz at the mouth of the Persian Gulf, Goa in India, and Malacca in Southeast Asia, the Portuguese reaped the advantages of dominance in at least three ways. They partially blocked the traditional Red Sea route and carried about half of the spice trade to Europe around the Cape of Good Hope, making handsome profits in the process. They became heavily involved in shipping Asian goods to

Asian ports, using the profits from this "carrying trade" to buy spices. And they required all merchants in the Indian Ocean to purchase a pass, or *cartaz*, and to pay duties of 6 percent to 10 percent on their cargoes.

Despite these impressive accomplishments, the Portuguese did little to alter the Indian Ocean trading system and were unable to monopolize even that limited section directed toward Europe. Furthermore, their military dominance was strictly limited to the sea. The major land powers of Asia—the Ottoman Empire, Persia, India, China, and Japan—were not threatened by the minuscule trading posts of the Portuguese who had extended themselves beyond their capacity. With a small population, Portugal was unable to replace the losses that its forces and fleet inevitably suffered.

Overextended in Asia and without a strong base in Europe, the Portuguese confronted vigorous competition from the Dutch and English in the seventeenth century (see Map 6.2). Operating through private commercial East India companies rather than direct royal control, these rising northern European merchants established their own parallel and competing trading-post empires, with the Dutch focusing on what is now Indonesia and the British on India. Their operations during the seventeenth and eighteenth centuries differed from those of the Portuguese in ways that served to heighten their impact on Asian societies and increase Asian connections to Europe's expanding economy. The Dutch, for example, succeeded in controlling not just the shipping but also the production of nutmeg and cloves by seizing several of the "spice islands" and using force to prevent the growing of these spices elsewhere. An enforced monoculture thus made these islands wholly dependent on the import of food and clothing. A twentieth-century Dutch historian describes the results: "the economic system of the Moluccas was ruined and the population reduced to poverty."[8] It would not be the last time such an outcome followed incorporation into a European economic system.

In the eighteenth century, the structure of trade began to shift as well, with bulk goods such as coffee, tea, and textiles looming much larger than spices. Thus, Asia was beginning to provide Europe with necessities for a mass market, rather than only luxuries for the elite.

However, the most dramatic change lay in the slow transition of trading-post empires into a com-

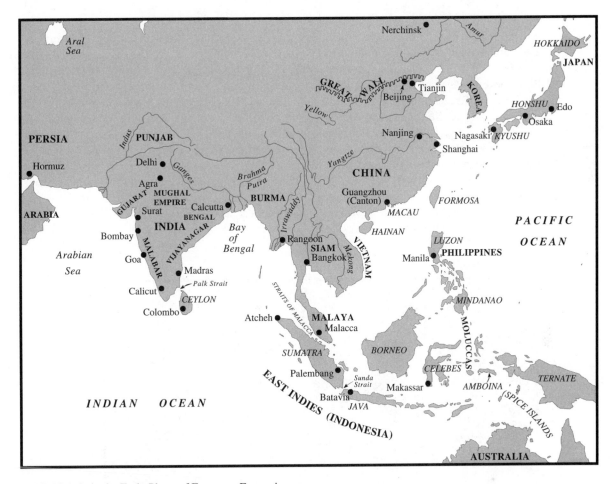

MAP 6.2 Asia in the Early Phase of European Expansion

pletely different form of European control, for by 1800, the Dutch in Indonesia and the British in India found themselves governing large territories with millions of inhabitants. The transition from trading-post to territorial empire was altogether unexpected and certainly unplanned, a classic case of things working out very differently from what had been intended. But it was a sign of the times: the balance of global power was shifting decisively in favor of Europe.

On the whole, Asia before 1800 was more marginal to the global economy than eastern Europe, Africa, or the Americas because relatively little of its land and labor served the new global markets. A major obstacle to developing greater commerce with Asia was the reluctance of Asian societies to purchase European goods; Asians simply wanted little that Europe had to offer. Thus, Europeans had to pay

for their tea, silk, and spices with gold and silver, something they were extremely reluctant to do. But even China, largely isolated in East Asia, was not completely outside the growing world economy, for it had come to depend on American silver supplies for its currency. The interruption of that supply in the 1640s temporarily paralyzed the country's exchange economy, made it difficult to meet the military payroll, and therefore may have contributed to the collapse of the Ming Dynasty in 1644.

Empires of Commerce in Africa

Europe's early intrusion into Africa was similar to its push into Asia, both in form and cast of characters. In each case, the purpose was commerce, with little desire for political control or penetration of the interior.

And in Africa, as in Asia, the Portuguese came first, followed by the Dutch, British, French, and others.

But Europe's contact with Africa began almost a full century earlier than it did with Asia. The state-sponsored Portuguese voyages of exploration along the west coast of Africa started in the early fifteenth century. The most dramatic difference between the two situations, however, lay in the content of the trade, which in Africa centered largely on the commerce in captive human beings—the slave trade. How did this come about? It certainly was not the original European intention, for early Portuguese commerce with Africa sought gold and pepper as well as ivory, gum, beeswax, and timber.

From the beginning, however, slaves were one important item in the Portuguese trade, claiming perhaps 150,000 African victims between 1450 and 1500. But these slaves were destined for the Mediterranean, where slavery had been practiced for many centuries. This ancient slave system was not based on race, and, although Africans were among their number, the great majority of slaves in southern Europe were of Slavic origin, from the area around the Black Sea. (Hence, the term *slave*.) They served their masters as domestic labor, as rowers on galley ships, and increasingly as workers on the sugar plantations of southern Spain, Portugal, and the islands of the Mediterranean, which were established following the

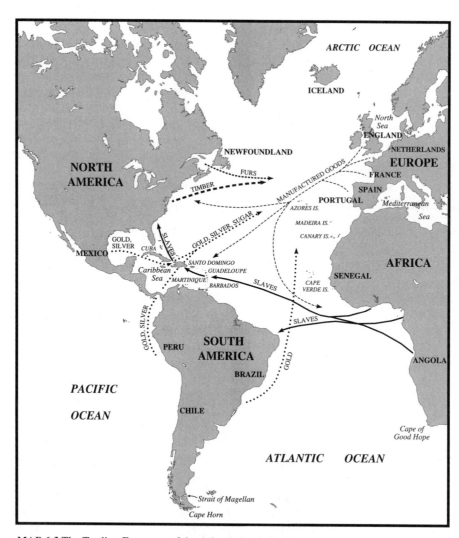

MAP 6.3 The Trading Economy of the Atlantic Basin in the Early Eighteenth Century

Crusades. The Portuguese created similar plantations on the islands off the coast of Africa—on Madeira and São Tomé, for example—as they seized them during the fifteenth century. The demand for sugar was growing rapidly in Europe, and great profits could be made.

The extension of this labor-intensive plantation economy to the New World vastly increased the demand for slaves. And the recognition that Africans survived the tropical American environment better than either Europeans or the native Amerindians eventually made them the almost exclusive target population for American slavery. Thus "black" and "African" became almost synonymous with the status of slavery in the minds of most whites. About twelve million Africans were shipped from their homeland over the four centuries of the slave trade, with the peak coming in the eighteenth and early nineteenth centuries. In the process of capture and transportation to the Americas, probably several times that number perished. The human dimensions of the slave trade were staggering.

The actual operation of the slave trade was broadly similar to that of the spice trade in Asia. European merchants established trading posts along the west African coast, from Senegal in the north to Angola in the south (see Map 6.3). Some of these trading posts were fortified; others were merely a few buildings to store goods and to keep slaves waiting for transshipment; and elsewhere still, Europeans simply traded from their ships anchored off-shore.

Europeans exercised even less political control in Africa than they did in Asia. There was little existing oceanic trade to capture and control, as they tried to do in the Indian Ocean. Where they established permanent trading stations or "factories," it was with the permission of local African rulers and often involved the payment of rent. And fortification provided protection from European rivals rather than from African adversaries. The inland trade, involving the capture, provisioning, and transporting of slaves to the coast, was almost entirely in the hands of African political and social elites, who were often in bitter competition with one another for the trade goods, especially firearms, that Europeans offered in exchange for human merchandise. With the exception of a vague Portuguese control over Angola, nowhere in Africa did the trade in slaves lead to the kind of territorial empires that the British and Dutch created in Asia. And with the exception of a small Dutch out-

A slave market along the coast of West Africa. The process of capture and shipment often included the branding of human beings as illustrated here. *Visual Studies Workshop*

post in South Africa, nowhere in Africa did Europeans settle in large numbers as they did in the Western Hemisphere.

Thus, the slave trade initiated, but did not complete, Africa's integration into the European world system. It began the process of focusing west African economies toward the sea rather than across the Sahara. It gave rise to a partially westernized class of Africans who "brokered" or mediated this trade. And although it expanded the exchange economy and introduced a variety of new commodities, it also increased the violence and insecurity of life and focused attention away from productive work to the wasteful activities of slaving. How the slave trade affected particular African societies is examined in Chapter 21, but from a global viewpoint, its function was to provide the labor force for the growing European settlements of the New World.

Empires of Settlement in the Americas

More than anything else, the incorporation of the Americas into the network of Afro-Eurasian exchange distinguished the European world system from all earlier patterns of cross-cultural encounter. An entire hemisphere was now brought into the orbit of the intercommunicating zone. Two Old Worlds collided, and in the process a single new world system, truly global in its dimensions, came into being.

When Isabella and Ferdinand sent Columbus west to find the East, both they and he anticipated the development of trading connections with the richer civilizations of Asia. From their perspective, the discovery of America was an "immense disappointment, a heart-breaking obstacle on the hoped-for route to the East."[9] And the simple societies inhabiting the Caribbean and the eastern coast of the Americas provided few trading opportunities. But it soon became apparent that other possibilities were at hand—vast expanses of fertile land, a potential native labor force, and heartening rumors of abundant gold and silver. From these possibilities, the Spanish and Portuguese and later the British and French fashioned empires in the Americas that were far different from anything they had constructed in Asia or Africa.

Most obviously, these possibilities involved outright conquest. Attracted by the promise of precious metals, the Spanish led the way. Within fifty years of Columbus's first voyage, they had smashed the complex civilizations of the Aztecs and the Incas and had conquered or claimed a huge territory extending from Oregon, Colorado, and the Carolinas in North America to central Chile and Argentina in South America. None of the imperial powers—Spanish, Portuguese, British, or French—experienced any major difficulty in taking what they wanted from the local people, who proved fatally vulnerable to both European weapons and European diseases.

Isolated for thousands of years from the interacting world of Afro-Eurasia, the inhabitants of the Americas simply lacked immunity to common diseases on the other side of the Atlantic. Smallpox, measles, yellow fever, and malaria swept into oblivion both millions of individuals and many entire peoples in the Americas. A densely populated Mexico declined from perhaps thirty million in 1519, when Hernán Cortés arrived, to about three million only fifty years later. In what would become the United States, there were approximately five million Amerindians in 1492, while by 1800 that figure had dropped to 600,000. Far more than Spanish *conquistadores* or missionaries, the germs of Europe and Africa shaped the trans-Atlantic encounter. This plague of plagues created an enormous labor shortage, which opened the way to massive European and African migration in the four centuries following the arrival of Columbus. It was the largest and most rapid population transfer in world history. More than anything else, the infusion of these new populations gave European empires in the Americas their distinctive quality.

The absolute number of the dominant European immigrants was not large in the early centuries, but their number grew rapidly through natural increase. The Spanish colonies received something under 200,000 immigrants in the first two centuries of occupation, but by the early nineteenth century, there was a white population of over three million. Between 1820 and 1930, the tide of European immigration mounted dramatically as more than fifty-five million people left their former homelands to seek a new life in a new world. The pattern of the slave trade, which brought roughly twelve million Africans to the Americas, had a different timing. It began rather slowly, peaked in the eighteenth century, and then gradually faded away in the nineteenth.[10]

VOICES
Columbus from a Different Perspective

In 1992, the five-hundred-year anniversary of Columbus's accidental discovery of America was the focus of considerable discussion about the man himself and the significance of what he set in motion. Central to this debate were the views of a young sixteenth-century priest, Bartolomé de Las Casas, who transcribed Columbus's journal and witnessed and wrote about the Spanish conquest of the West Indies. In an essentially eyewitness account written in 1542, he accused Columbus and his successors of nothing less than genocide.

[O]f all the infinite universe of humanity, these people [original inhabitants of the West Indies] are the most guileless, the most devoid of wickedness and duplicity, the most obedient and faithful to their native masters and to the Spanish Christians whom they serve. . . . These people are the most devoid of rancors, hatreds, or desire for vengeance of any people in the world. . . . They are also poor people, for they not only possess little but have no desire to possess worldly goods.

Yet into this sheepfold, into this land of meek outcasts there came some Spaniards who immediately behaved like ravening wild beasts . . . that had been starved for many days. And Spaniards have behaved in no other way during the past forty years . . . , for they are still . . . killing, terrorizing, afflicting, torturing and destroying the native peoples, doing all this with the strangest and most varied new methods of cruelty, never seen or heard of before, and to such a degree that this Island of Hispaniola, once so populous (. . . more than three million) has now a population of barely two hundred persons.

The reason for killing and destroying such an infinite number of souls is that the Christians have an ultimate aim, which is to acquire gold and to swell themselves with riches in a very brief time and thus rise to a high estate disproportionate to their merits. . . .

They usually dealt with the chieftains and nobles in the following way: they made a grid of rods which they placed on forked sticks, then lashed the victims to the grid and lighted a smoldering fire underneath, so that little by little as those captives screamed in despair and torment, their souls would leave them. . . .

And because on few and far between occasions, the Indians justifiably killed some Christians, the Spaniards made a rule among themselves that for every Christian slain by the Indians, they would slay a hundred Indians. . . .

After the wars and killings had ended . . . , [the] survivors were distributed among the Christians to be slaves . . . to send the men to the mines to dig for gold, which is intolerable labor, and to send the women into the fields of the big ranches to hoe and till the land, work suitable for strong men. Nor to either the men or the women did they give any food except herbs and legumes, things of little substance. The milk in the breasts of the women with infants dried up and thus in a short while the infants perished. And since men and women were separated, there could be no marital relations. And the men died in the mines and the women died on the ranches from the same causes, exhaustion and hunger. And thus was depopulated that island which had been densely populated.

Source: Bartolomé de Las Casas, *The Devastation of the Indies: A Brief Account,* trans. Herma Briffault (New York: Seabury Press, 1974), pp. 38–52.

The demographic mix within the various European colonies differed substantially and gave rise to several distinct types of colonial society. In the northern colonies of Britain and France, it proved impossible to enslave Native Americans and, apparently, unprofitable to establish plantations with African slaves. Thus, here settlement colonies developed in which Europeans constituted the great majority of the population. In northeastern Brazil, the Caribbean Islands, and the southern United States, plantation colonies combined a dominant stratum of European managers and owners and a large number of African slaves, with little Native American participation at all. And in much of Spanish America, the pattern was one of mixed colonies. There, a substantial minority of white settlers ruled a large Native American population and intermarried with them and with Africans to produce important *mestizo* and *mulatto* groups as well. Although such mixing occurred in North America, the offspring were never recognized as a distinct social category. Why the mixed and plantation colonies of Spanish and Portuguese America slid into economic stagnation and backwardness while the settler colonies of British North America developed rapidly toward industrialization is a major focus of Chapters 7 and 8.

Whatever their particular features, all of these empires of settlement in the Americas had a far more profound impact on indigenous societies than did the trading-post empires of Asia and Africa. Part of this is reflected in the brutal facts of conquest and in population declines of genocidal proportions. Further-

more, the demands of settlers for land and labor dispossessed millions and disrupted traditional societies more than the spice or even the slave trade had done. But the disruption was also cultural, for Christianity spread rapidly among the Native American populations of Spanish America, often mixed with traditional religious symbols and practices.

Plants and animals introduced into the Americas from Europe contributed enormously to the changes transforming the Western Hemisphere and its peoples. The introduction of sugarcane gave rise to the plantation economy and the massive use of African slaves, thus shaping the entire social structure of the Americas. The importation of horses produced ranching economies and cowboy culture in both North and South America and transformed the societies of numerous Native American peoples. Sheep, cattle, goats, and especially pigs also followed the European conquerers and substantially altered both the ecology and the economy of the Western Hemisphere.

This drawing from an Aztec manuscript shows the approach of Aztec emissaries to Cortéz and the Spanish in early sixteenth-century Mexico. *The Bettmann Archive*

Part of the profound impact was a result of much more complete integration into the emerging world economy than was the case in Asia or Africa, and more so in South America than in North America. Precious metals led the way to this dependence. After the initial plunder of Aztec and Inca wealth, mining industries in Mexico, Peru, and Brazil flooded Europe with gold and silver and made extensive use of forced or slave labor. "These circumstances," writes one Latin American historian, "transformed the . . . Spanish colonies . . . from modest but well-balanced, increasingly diversified economies into capitalistic, highly specialized, unbalanced export-oriented economies producing mainly for European markets. This economic dependence . . . was to last for centuries."[11] Extensive sugar plantations, worked by slave labor in Brazil, the Caribbean, and elsewhere, compounded this highly specialized and dependent pattern of development.

However, the "Columbian exchange," as historian Alfred Crosby has called it,[12] was not a one-way street, for the Americas came to have a powerful impact on the Afro-Eurasian world. Nowhere was this more clearly seen than in the influence of crops native to the Americas on societies of the Eastern Hemisphere. The humble potato, originally cultivated in the Inca lands of highland Peru, spread widely in northern Europe by the eighteenth century. Because it produced far more calories per acre than traditional grain crops, it was attractive in areas of rapidly growing population. And because it could be stored in the ground during the winter, it was less vulnerable to pillage and requisitioning during Europe's frequent wars. The nourishment provided by potatoes was absolutely essential in sustaining Europe's rapid population growth after 1750 as well as its industrial development in the nineteenth century. Maize and sweet potatoes, also native to the Americas, played a similar role in China, supporting a rapid population surge that began in the eighteenth century and that has continued ever since. It is estimated that crops of American origin currently provide 37 percent of China's food supply. And in twentieth-century southern Africa these same crops have become a significant element in the diet of a rapidly expanding population.[13]

Thus, in the three centuries following the initial voyages of European discovery, a new world system—centered in a highly competitive western Europe and extending its tentacles literally around the world—began to take shape. In the industrial era of the nineteenth century, however, that system broadened its reach and deepened its grasp on many of the world's major cultures.

Empires of the Industrial Age: The Nineteenth Century

More than any other period, the nineteenth century was Europe's age of global expansion. By the outbreak of World War I in 1914, the ties of trade and investment linked Europe to every corner of the world, including such previously isolated and aloof regions as China. Between 1812 and 1914, millions of Europeans migrated to new homes outside Europe. Missionaries and explorers penetrated the distant interiors of Asia and Africa. Europe incorporated Africa, Southeast Asia, and the islands of the Pacific into its colonial empires and reduced the once proud domains of China, the Ottoman Empire, and Persia to a subservient and dependent status. What led to such dramatic changes in the scope, character, and intensity of European expansion?

Industrialization and Imperialism

Behind every aspect of Europe's nineteenth-century expansion lay the massive fact of its rapid industrialization. This process gave rise to new economic needs, many of which found solutions abroad. Whereas the desire to buy foreign luxury goods propelled Europe's earlier efforts at expansion, the enormous productivity of industrial technology and Europe's growing affluence now created the need for extensive raw materials and agricultural products. Wheat from the American Midwest and southern Russia, meat from Argentina, bananas from Central America, rubber from Brazil, cocoa and palm oil from west Africa, tea from Ceylon, and gold and diamonds from South Africa—the demand for these and other products radically changed patterns of economic and social life in the countries of their origin.

Furthermore, Europe needed to sell its own goods. One of the peculiarities of early industrial capitalism was that it periodically produced more manufactured goods than could be profitably sold at home. By 1840, for example, England was exporting 60 percent of its cotton-cloth production, annually sending 200 million yards to Europe, 300 million to Latin America, and 145 million to India. This last figure was especially significant because for centuries Europe had offered almost nothing that Asian societies were willing to buy. Part of Europe's fascination with China during the nineteenth and twentieth centuries lay in the enormous potential market represented by the huge Chinese population.

Much the same could be said for capital, for European investors often found it more profitable to invest their money abroad than at home. Between 1910 and 1913, England was sending about half of its savings abroad as foreign investment. In 1914, it had about 3.7 billion pounds invested abroad, about half of it in Asia, Africa, and Latin America.

Many Europeans, particularly those with wealth, were aware of the social as well as strictly economic importance of foreign outlets for surplus goods and capital. Without them, many feared, prices would fall, profits decline, unemployment increase, and socialism become more popular. The nineteenth-century British imperialist Cecil Rhodes confided his fears to a friend:

> Yesterday I attended a meeting of the unemployed in London and having listened to the wild speeches which were nothing more than a scream for bread, I returned home convinced more than ever of the importance of imperialism. . . . In order to save the 40 million inhabitants of the United Kingdom from a murderous civil war, the colonial politicians must open up new areas to absorb the excess population and create new markets for the products of the mines and factories. . . . The British Empire is a matter of bread and butter. If you wish to avoid civil war, then you must become an imperialist.[14]

To some people, therefore, imperialism promised to solve the class conflicts of an industrializing society while avoiding revolution or the serious redistribution of wealth. But what made imperialism so broadly popular, especially in the last quarter of the nineteenth century, was the growth of mass nationalism. When the unification of Italy (1861) and then Germany (1870) made Europe's always competitive political system even more so, much of this rivalry spilled over into the struggle for colonies or economic concessions in Asia and Africa. Colonies became a symbol of great power status and their acquisition a matter of urgency even if they possessed little immediate economic value. After 1875, it seemed to matter, even to ordinary people, whether some remote corner of Africa or some obscure Pacific island were in British, French, or German hands. Imperialism, in short, appealed on economic and social grounds to the wealthy or ambitious, could seem politically and strategically necessary in the game of international power politics, and was emotionally satisfying to almost everyone. It was a potent mix.

If the industrial era provided new motives for European expansion, it also provided new means to do so. Steam-driven ships facilitated the penetration of the Asian and African interiors along their river systems, and the discovery of quinine to prevent malaria reduced the risk of an extended stay in Africa from quasi-suicidal to merely dangerous. Breech-loading rifles, which became available about midcentury, and machine guns, in regular use by the 1890s, provided the overwhelming firepower that decided many a colonial conflict. A much-quoted ditty expressed the essential facts of the situation:

> *Whatever happens, we have got*
> *The Maxim gun, and they have not.*

Finally, remarkable improvements in the technology of transportation and communication—larger and more efficient ships, the Suez Canal, underwater telegraph cables, and, of course, the railroad—linked Europe and its dependencies more tightly than ever before.[15]

Industrialization also occasioned a marked change in the way Europeans perceived themselves and others. In earlier centuries, Europeans had defined themselves and others largely in religious terms: "they" were heathen; "we" were Christian. But while holding to their sense of religious superiority, Europeans had adopted many of the ideas and techniques of more advanced societies. Furthermore, they held many aspects of Chinese and Indian civilization in high regard; and some even saw the more technologically simple peoples of Africa and America as "noble savages."

With the advent of the industrial age, however, Europeans developed a secular arrogance that matched or in some cases replaced their notions of religious superiority. They had, after all, unlocked the secrets of nature, created a society of unprecedented wealth, and used both to produce unsurpassed military power. These became the criteria by which Europeans judged both themselves and the rest of the world.

By these standards, it is not surprising that Europeans' opinions of other cultures dropped sharply. The Chinese, who had been highly praised in the eighteenth century, were reduced in the nineteenth to the image of "John Chinaman"—weak, cunning, obstinately conservative, and, in large numbers, a distinct threat, the "yellow peril" of late nineteenth-century European fears. African societies, which had been regarded even in the slave trade era as nations and their leaders as kings, were demoted in nineteenth-century European eyes to the status of "tribes" led by "chiefs" as a means of emphasizing their "primitive" qualities.

Increasingly, Europeans viewed the culture and achievements of Asian and African peoples through the prism of race. Although physical differences had often been a basis of fear or dislike, only in the nineteenth century did Europeans come to believe that these qualities actually determined human capabilities and destiny. Such beliefs, furthermore, were increasingly backed by the prestige and apparatus of science. Phrenologists used allegedly scientific methods to classify the size and shape of human skulls and concluded, not surprisingly, that those of whites were larger and therefore more advanced. Nineteenth-century biologists who classified the varieties of plants and animals applied these notions of rank to varieties of human beings as well. The result was a hierarchy of races, with whites on top and the less developed "child races" beneath them. "Race is everything," declared British anatomist Robert Knox in 1850; "civilization depends on it."[16]

These ideas about race influenced how Europeans viewed their own global expansion. Almost everyone saw it as inevitable, as a natural outgrowth of a superior civilization, particularly after Darwin's theories were popularized. But for many this was tempered with a genuine, though condescending, sense of responsibility to the "weaker races" whom Europe was fated to dominate. Empire and trade, they felt, should bring the blessings of civilization: Christianity, freedom, and material improvement. Rudyard Kipling's famous poem of 1899, "The White Man's Burden," gave this paternalistic idealism its classic expression:

Take up the White Man's Burden—
Send forth the best ye breed—
Go bind your sons to exile
To serve your captives' need;
To wait in heavy harness
On fluttered folk and wild—
Your new caught, sullen peoples,
Half devil and half child.[17]

But another side to the ideology of imperialism derived from a popularization, and a misinterpretation, of the ideas of Charles Darwin—struggle, natural selection, survival of the fittest—applied to an understanding of history. Thus, the war, bloodshed, and brutality associated with imperialism could be seen as natural and even progressive, the means by which superior races established their dominance, sometimes displacing or even destroying backward peoples. This glorification of war and aggression not only served to justify imperial expansion in the nineteenth century, but also became a major element in the Fascist ideologies of the twentieth.

From Informal to Territorial Empires

During the first seventy-five years of the nineteenth century, the economic, technological, and cultural changes associated with industrialization did not produce any dramatic increase in Europe's political control over non-Western peoples. In fact, Europe's dominant power, Great Britain, seemed decidedly reluctant to annex additional territory to its empire. It sought rather to create conditions in which British commerce and investment could flourish without the inconvenience and expense of actually governing large territories and populations. England wanted no more Indias.

Nor did it need them. Britain's immense economic advantage as the first industrialized society and its corresponding military power were sufficient to persuade ruling elites in Latin America, Asia, Africa, and the Middle East to open their societies to European trade and capital. In the process, the major industrial powers created what many historians have called "informal empires." Europeans exercised substantial influence in the affairs of these societies, gradually penetrated and dominated their economies, but allowed the actual operations of government to remain in local hands. They justified such arrangements by referring to the many benefits that European trade and investment were supposed to confer on "backward" societies. The British in particular came to have an almost religious view of free trade, believing it would stimulate stagnant societies, create world peace through international exchange, and bring prosperity to all as each society produced those things for which it was best suited. Any government so obstinate as to refuse to participate in this global economic system, it was argued, deserved to be coerced into cooperation or, if that failed, replaced.

During the nineteenth century, Europeans, joined later by Americans, came to exercise this sort of control over the newly independent states of Latin America, the ancient empire of China, much of the Middle East, and parts of Africa. In the process, these societies lost much of their sovereignty. China, for example, signed treaties surrendering legal jurisdiction over Europeans living in the country. When persuasion and pressure were ineffective, gunboats and troops could be called in. China fought four wars with European powers during the nineteenth century and lost them all as that country slipped ever more deeply into semicolonial status. In the late nineteenth and early twentieth centuries, the United States likewise enforced its informal control over Central America and the Caribbean with repeated military interventions. Under the umbrella of informal empire, these societies became increasingly incorporated into the rapidly growing world system, and their economies were shaped to the needs and desires of Europe. Scholars would later refer to this process as "dependent development."

However, informal empire was a fragile enterprise. It required local elites willing to collaborate with European governments, traders, and investors. And it worked best if competition among the various European countries was muted. After 1875, these conditions no longer prevailed. France, Germany, and the United States increasingly challenged Britain's dominant position in the world. As these and other European states industrialized, they began to compete more effectively with Britain for investment and trading opportunities abroad. A sharp downturn in the European economy between 1873 and 1896 further increased this rivalry. And the rise of a popular and aggressive nationalism made all European governments more receptive to pleas for help from their traders, investors, and missionaries in Asia and Africa. At the same time, at least some societies began to resist European control. In Egypt, for example, the growth of a strongly nationalist insurrection preaching "Egypt for the Egyptians" provoked the British to occupy the country in 1882. Informal empire had collapsed.

The last quarter of the nineteenth century, therefore, saw an enormous wave of territory-grabbing by Britain, France, Germany, Italy, Belgium, Portugal, and the United States. Africa was the major target, and within twenty-five years, a half-dozen European powers divided virtually the entire continent among themselves, with Britain and France reaping the most new colonies. Mainland Southeast Asia and the islands of the Pacific were likewise partitioned, and the United States conquered the Philippines. Often called the "new imperialism," this wave of territorial empire-building represented a new form of European expansion in the highly competitive conditions of the late nineteenth century. It was within the framework of this colonialism that millions of Asians and Africans encountered the modern world in the twentieth century.

Europe's World System under Attack: The Twentieth Century

By 1900, some four centuries of European expansion had given rise to a world system with western Europe and the United States at its core and most of the rest of the world connected in some dependent status. In 1914, Europe and its existing and former colonies covered no less than 85 percent of the world's land area. And most areas that Europe did not directly rule—Turkey, China, Persia, parts of Arabia—had fallen into a semicolonial status.

Less visible but even more powerful economic connections had created an international division of labor that cast Europe and the United States as the producers of manufactured goods, whereas Asian,

TABLE 6.1: World Manufacturing Output,
1750–1980 (percent of total output)

	India	China	Total Developing Countries	Total Developed Countries
1750	24.5%	32.8%	73.0%	27.0%
1800	19.7	33.3	67.7	32.3
1830	17.6	29.8	60.5	39.5
1860	8.6	19.7	36.6	63.4
1880	2.8	12.5	20.9	79.1
1900	1.7	6.2	11.0	89.0
1913	1.4	3.6	7.5	92.5
1928	1.9	3.4	7.2	92.8
1938	2.4	3.1	7.2	92.8
1953	1.7	2.3	6.5	93.5
1980	2.3	5.0	12.0	88.0

Source: Colin Simmons, "Deindustrialization, Industrialization, and the Indian Economy, 1850–1947," *Modern Asian Studies* 19:3 (1985): 600.

African, Middle Eastern, and Latin American countries each specialized in the production of a few raw materials or agricultural products. Table 6.1 illustrates the extent to which the global distribution of manufacturing output changed during the nineteenth century—from a relatively balanced pattern to a highly unbalanced and concentrated one, which has not changed much in the twentieth century.

Thus, the dramatic increase in world trade was accompanied by an equally sharp growth in the degree of economic inequality between Europe and its overseas dependencies. Among the non-Western areas of the world, only Japan was able to begin a substantial and independent process of industrialization during the nineteenth century.

The political and economic linkages of the world system were paralleled by those of culture. By the early twentieth century, the local elites in Asia and Africa had learned European languages and in some cases had adopted Christianity. The ideas of science, nationalism, and modern education had begun to penetrate colonial societies. So too had the concept of progress—the notion that the future could be different from the past, and should be. Such notions later challenged the world system that European expansion had called into being. But in 1900, that system seemed both natural and impregnable, certainly to its creators but also to many of its subjects.

The new century, however, saw that system undermined at its center and sharply attacked from its periphery. What were the movements and forces that challenged what had so recently seemed beyond question? In what ways did the world system change under pressure? How much of it survived as the twentieth century approached its end? These are issues that will arise repeatedly in the rest of this book. However, a brief overview at this point will serve to set the twentieth century in global perspective.

The World System and the Collapse of Europe

As noted in Chapter 5, the collapse of Europe in the twentieth century came as war and depression wreaked havoc in the West between 1914 and 1945. The European heartland did recover, and remarkably so, from that series of catastrophes, but its role in the world changed dramatically. Weakened by the exertions of war and the need for internal recovery, Europe lost its dominant position in the world system it had created. That status passed by default to the United States, which emerged from World War II as the strongest of the capitalist powers and their natural leader. U.S. economic resources helped to rebuild Europe and Japan, and its trade, investment, and foreign aid penetrated many of the developing countries and strengthened the capitalist world economy. In Korea, Vietnam, the Dominican Republic, Iraq, and elsewhere, the United States used its enormous military power, though not always successfully, to defend the interests and the values of the world system. And by the mid-twentieth century, a new and major opponent—the Soviet Union—loomed on the horizon.

The rise of the Soviet Union marked a major change in the evolution of the European world system. Before the Russian Revolution of 1917, the great powers of Europe had competed bitterly among themselves, even to the point of an exhausting war. But they had competed for advantage in a capitalist system whose values and outlook they all shared, however much they quarreled over its spoils. When the smoke of World War I cleared away, Europeans found themselves face to face with a different kind of adversary—a Communist state committed to an alien

Socialist ideology and wholly opposed to the very idea of a capitalist world economy. In fact, the new Soviet state largely withdrew from that economy in the 1920s and 1930s and proceeded to industrialize at a forced pace and in isolation, depending mostly on its own resources.

During World War II, the Soviet Union suffered greatly at the hands of German invaders and contributed much to their eventual defeat. When the Soviets subsequently imposed their control over Eastern Europe, many in the West feared that the Soviets were poised to march on Western Europe and to mount a global challenge to Western interests. Thus, while political rivalries among the major capitalist powers diminished after World War II, they were replaced by what seemed a far greater threat in the shape of Soviet communism. Not since the Muslim Turks invaded eastern Europe in the fifteenth and sixteenth centuries had the West felt so much on the defensive.

Thus, the global conflicts of the twentieth century provided the European world system with a new leader in the United States and a new and hostile ri-

val in the Soviet Union. But the conflicts also stimulated the enormous energy of anticolonial nationalism in much of the colonial world and thereby put Europe on the defensive from a second front.

"Standing Up": The Revolt of the Colonies

Strange as it may seem, few Europeans in 1900 expected their subject people in the colonies or "informal empires" to revolt, and certainly not so soon. In that sanguine expectation, they had history on their side. We often think that imperialism automatically creates a nationalist response as oppressed people assert their "natural" rights to self-government. Yet many imperialisms had not done so. In the empires ruled by the Romans, Arabs, Turks, and Mongols, and in various African dynasties, many millions of people lived for long periods without being greatly distressed that their rulers were culturally different from themselves. They may have protested acts of exploitation or oppression, but it seldom entered

The widespread triumph of anticolonial movements in the postwar world is illustrated by this poster in Leopoldville (now Kinshasa) announcing the date of independence for the Belgian Congo. *UPI Photo*

their heads to object on the nationalist grounds that their rulers were foreigners. "Government by aliens," writes one historian of nationalism, "has been the rule rather than the exception in world history."[18] Why, then, did European imperialism in Africa, Asia, and the Middle East produce such a tremendous nationalist response when other imperialisms had not?

Certainly one answer is that Europe was itself the home of the nationalist idea and could therefore hardly avoid conveying it to the colonies. Thus, when Asians and Africans objected to colonial rule, they quite naturally used the rhetoric of European nationalism. If it was wrong for the Germans to dominate Europe, it was also wrong for the British, French, or Portuguese to dominate Africa. The logic of nationalism, therefore, undermined the moral foundations of colonialism.

But nationalism was also a general blueprint or model for a new society. European colonialism, far more than most earlier imperialisms, had uprooted people from their villages, clans, age groups, and other forms of local community. It had pushed them into societies that demanded or encouraged them to work on settler farms, migrate to distant jobs, live in urban areas, study in missionary schools, and participate in vast trading networks. In such a setting, the idea of belonging to a "nation," however it was defined, created some sense of modern community from the disruptions of the modernizing process. Nationalism, then, responded not only to the fact of foreign rule but also to the social and economic changes occurring within it.

Finally, nationalism was a response to European racism. The French and Portuguese in particular had promised to extend the privileges of citizenship to the people of their Asian and African territories until no essential differences remained between them and the citizens of the mother country. Many among the first-generation elite accepted the implied promise at face value. But as things turned out, European racial exclusiveness overwhelmed these intentions. Nationalism provided a framework in which colonized peoples could create their own modern societies, having been so clearly excluded from those of their European rulers.

In short, nationalism was a European idea that could be turned to a variety of African or Asian uses. As such, it became a tremendously powerful and popular force in the twentieth century throughout the developing nations. In semicolonial countries, such as Mexico, Turkey, and China, it stimulated more vigorous opposition to European control and more aggressive, sometimes revolutionary, efforts to reform and modernize their own societies. In the numerous official colonies of Asia and Africa, it gave rise to successful mass movements that ousted colonial rulers. After World War II, colony after colony achieved independence and joined the ranks of "new nations." (See Map 6.4.)

Did this success mean the end of the European-dominated world system? Certainly direct political control was a thing of the past, for by 1975, Europe's formal empires had almost vanished. It was less clear whether political freedom would enable dependent, impoverished, highly specialized export economies to transform themselves into more prosperous and balanced ones. Continuing or even deepening poverty in the developing nations has suggested to many observers that the unequal economic ties of the world system—reflected in massive indebtedness, frequently declining terms of trade, foreign investment, export of raw materials, dependence on foreign manufactured goods—have survived intact or even been strengthened as the leadership of the capitalist world passed into American hands. The sharp North-South division in the contemporary world is a reminder that the global inequalities fostered by the modern world system still persist as the twentieth century draws to a close.

Conclusion: Toward the World System of the Twenty-first Century

Beyond the massive fact of decolonization, the late twentieth century saw a number of dramatic changes in the modern world system. Among these was the ability of some states to use the leverage of political independence to increase the benefits they derived from participation in the international economy. The oil-rich countries of the Middle East acted politically to take advantage of their economic resources by raising the price of oil in the 1970s. And several East Asian and Latin American countries, including South Korea, Taiwan, Brazil, and Mexico, achieved a sub-

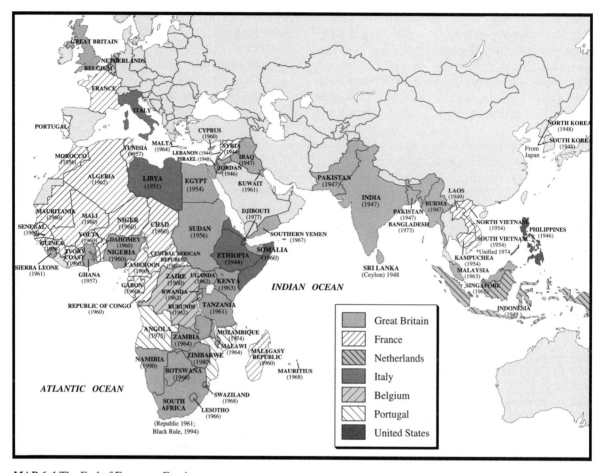

MAP 6.4 The End of European Empires

stantial degree of industrialization within the capitalist framework of the world economy.

Another recent change in the world system was
the withdrawal of a number of countries from active
participation in it. This usually occurred where nationalist movements coincided with massive social
revolution to produce a Communist regime. China
after its 1949 revolution was the most dramatic example, but Vietnam, Laos, Cambodia, Cuba, and perhaps Ethiopia belonged in this category as well.
Combined with the Soviet Union and its dependent
allies in Eastern Europe, this meant that about one-
third of the world's population in the mid-1970s
lived in Communist countries that had largely severed their economic links with the capitalist world
economy and created an alternative economic and
political network among themselves. A second and

competing world system had thus emerged, complete
with its own rivalries, largely between China and the
Soviet Union. Certainly this was a very different situation from that which prevailed at the beginning of
the century.

But that period of withdrawal proved to be short-
lived, for the reform or collapse of Communist
regimes in the 1980s brought almost all of them
scrambling to reenter the capitalist world economy.
The admission of Russia to the International Monetary Fund in 1992 as well as China's growing commercial presence in the world signaled the end of the
division that the Cold War and communism had introduced into the world system.

A final change involved the decline of American
dominance. Since the end of World War II, the
United States had been clearly the predominant eco-

nomic and political power in the world system. In some respects, the disintegration of the Soviet Union seemed to confirm that status, as the United States remained the only real military superpower. But other trends undermined its hegemony, largely because economic vitality was increasingly replacing military force as a measure of global power. The rise of Japan as an economic power; the consolidation of the European Community; the rapid growth of newly industrializing countries in east Asia; the reentry of China's one billion people to active participation in the world economy; the large trade imbalance of the United States—all of this seemed to suggest the return to a multicentered world system, more like that of the thirteenth century than the European- or American-dominated system of more recent times.

Whatever the future holds, Europe's global expansion over the past five centuries has created an increasingly connected but highly unequal world. It has been within this framework that Indians, Chinese, Arabs, Africans, and others have made their own modern histories. They and their European overlords have been intimate, though often involuntary and hostile, companions in the journeys of the past five hundred years.

Notes

1. This section is based largely on Janet L. Abu-Lughod, *Before European Hegemony* (New York: Oxford University Press, 1989).

2. Abu-Lughod, *Before European Hegemony,* p. 361.

3. This paragraph is based on Immanuel Wallerstein, *The Modern World System: Capitalist Agriculture and the Origins of the European World Economy in the Sixteenth Century* (New York: Academic Press, 1974), ch. 1. The quote is from p. 51.

4. Paul Bohannan and Philip Curtin, *Africa and Africans* (Prospect-Heights: Waveland Press, 1988), pp. 330–32.

5. Fernand Braudel, *The Perspective of the World,* trans. Sian Reynolds (New York: Harper & Row, 1984), p. 220.

6. Alan K. Smith, *Creating a World Economy* (Boulder, Colo.: Westview Press, 1991), pp. 125–31.

7. Philip Curtin, *Cross Cultural Trade in World History* (Cambridge, Engl.: Cambridge University Press, 1984), pp. 136–57.

8. Bernard H. M. Vlekke, *Nusantara: A History of the East India Archipelago* (Cambridge, Mass.: Harvard University Press, 1943), p. 139.

9. D. K. Fieldhouse, *The Colonial Empires from the Eighteenth Century* (New York: Dell, 1966), p. 6.

10. Alfred W. Crosby, "Infectious Disease and the Demography of the Atlantic Peoples," *Journal of World History* 2:2 (Fall 1991): 119–33.

11. Guillermo Cespedes, *Latin America: The Early Years* (New York: Knopf, 1974), p. 26.

12. Alfred Crosby, *Ecological Imperialism* (Cambridge: Cambridge University Press, 1986).

13. William H. McNeill, "American Food Crops in the Old World," in *Seeds of Change,* ed. Herman J. Viola and Carolin Margolis (Washington, D.C.: Smithsonian Institution Press, 1991), pp. 43–59.

14. Quoted in Heinz Gollwitzer, *Europe in the Age of Imperialism* (London: Thames and Hudson, 1969), p. 136.

15. The preceding paragraph is derived from Daniel Headrick, *The Tools of Empire* (New York: Oxford University Press, 1981).

16. Robert Knox, *Races of Man* (Philadelphia: Lea and Blanchard, 1850), p. v.

17. Rudyard Kipling, "The White Man's Burden," in *Rudyard Kipling's Verse.* (Garden City, N.Y.: Doubleday, 1940), p. 321.

18. Elie Kedourie, *Nationalism in Asia and Africa* (New York: New American Library, 1970), p. 22.

Comparative Essay

PATHS TO THE MODERN WORLD: PATTERNS, THEMES, AND QUESTIONS

Western Europe's global domination, a process examined in Chapter 6, was a defining element of modern world history. It was important not only as an unprecedented political achievement, but also because it induced such profound changes in the Afro-Asian and New World societies it incorporated into its spreading empires and economic networks. The responses of these societies—their efforts to cope with political subordination and accompanying economic, social, and cultural changes—represent a second major theme in the making of the modern world. The balance of this book deals largely with this issue, as we examine, one after another, the paths to the modern world taken by North and South American societies, by the Russian Empire and Soviet Union, by the peoples of the Islamic world, the South Asian peninsula, the African continent, China, and Japan. In the process, we will highlight the unique features of each region's historical experience and make frequent comparisons among them. But these are not separated and isolated stories; they are instead connected journeys, part of a larger historical picture.

To reinforce this larger context, we offer here an introduction to the rest of the book. It identifies a variety of patterns, themes, and questions that you will encounter in the following chapters.

Confronting the European Challenge

We begin with an elementary reminder—that each region's encounter with Europe was decisively shaped by its own political structures, its cultural values, its historical experience. Despite what Europeans sometimes think, the history of Asia or Africa did not begin with their arrival. The Islamic world, for example, had been central to the intercommunicating zone of Afro-Eurasia for one thousand years before west Europeans posed a serious threat. No wonder Muslims did not at first seriously consider the possibility that they might have something to learn from the infidels. Likewise the Chinese, long accustomed to their dominance in East Asia and easily able to contain European "barbarians" for almost three hundred years after their initial arrival, found it difficult to cope with the changed global balance of power in the nineteenth century. Each of the regional cases illustrates the ways in which earlier patterns of historical development shaped interaction with the intruding Europeans.

In addition, as Chapter 6 indicates, the particular forms of European penetration varied considerably from place to place and over time. The European-induced slave trade in Africa, for example, took shape without general European political control, and direct colonial rule occurred only after that trade had largely died out. Parts of the Middle East and China experienced heavy European economic penetration and sharp limits on the independence of existing states, but without the formal colonial rule that India and most of Africa experienced. And the New World experience of large-scale European immigration in both North and South America distinguishes its modern history from most of Asia and Africa where such extensive settlement seldom occurred.

The impact of European penetration—in whatever form—on the economic and social life of Afro-Asian societies is another common thread in the histories of these regions. The growing importance of a Western-educated class, more rapid urbanization (especially in the twentieth century), the growth of export economies, the decline of earlier forms of manufacturing, the introduction of modern European political ideas such as nationalism and socialism—all of this and much more became part of the historical experience of those peoples connected to the European world system. Historians and others have debated the nature and consequences of this European impact at great length. Did it provoke stagnant societies onto the path of a fruitful modern development? Or did it distort and impede their evolution and thus contribute to their underdevelopment? We will consider this debate, particularly in reference to India, China, and Africa, in later chapters.

For those societies that retained some measure of political independence, the question of how to respond to the European threat became increasingly important. One common pattern has been called "conservative modernization." It refers to the attempt by the governing elite to incorporate enough modern military and economic innovations to strengthen the state against foreign intrusion, but without fundamentally challenging the existing political system, social structure, or cultural values. The most successful and far-reaching effort at conservative modernization occurred in Germany during the latter half of the nineteenth century, when a government dominated by a traditional landed aristocracy (*Junkers*) presided over a process of rapid industrialization that led Germany to the first rank of world powers. At the same time, on the other side of the world, Kings Mongkut and Chulalongkorn of Siam (now Thailand) undertook a series of administrative, economic, educational, and military reforms that successfully protected their country's independence, even as the British and French were reducing the rest of Southeast Asia to colonial status. Chulalongkorn's dynasty continues to rule Thailand in the 1990s.

Elsewhere, three great nineteenth-century experiments with conservative modernization took place under the pressure of European or Japanese aggression in the Russian, Chinese, and Ottoman empires. The Russian and Chinese empires were swept away by vast revolutionary upheavals in the twentieth century; the Ottoman Empire slowly fell apart and then collapsed in the flames of World War I. What these experiments had in common, how they differed, and why they all failed—are important comparative questions in modern world history.

In more recent decades, traditional monarchies in Saudi Arabia, Jordan, and Morocco have retained power while their countries assimilated much of modern economic life. But the shah of Iran and the emperor of Ethiopia, unable to control the process, were ousted in the 1970s. Gorbachev's efforts to revive a Soviet society that had grown stagnant and conservative might be considered in the same category with a similar outcome. All of this points to the great difficulty of limited and piecemeal change, which attempts to preserve the power and privileges of an established elite. Old regimes are never so vulnerable, noted Alexis de Tocqueville, than when they begin to reform.

Revolutions from Below and Above

Far removed from efforts at conservative modernization have been social revolutions. In France, Russia, China, and, more recently, in Vietnam, Cuba, and Nicaragua, massive and popular upheavals have violently overthrown existing governments, largely destroyed the traditional landed upper class, created far more powerful and highly centralized states, and opened the way to more rapid development. Since genuine social revolutions have been quite rare in modern history, historians and others have tried to define the conditions under which they are most likely to occur. Why have some modernizing societies experienced social revolutions and not others?

Certainly the pressures of the modern transformation (population growth, mass poverty and inequality, and foreign aggression) are by themselves an insufficient answer to the question, for many societies have experienced such pressures without succumbing to revolution. In a study of the French, Russian, and Chinese revolutions, sociologist Theda Skocpol[1] points to three factors that in her view combined to produce massive social upheaval. The first was the weakness or collapse of state authority. Particularly prone to collapse under pressure were states whose officials or bureaucrats were recruited directly from large landholders, for they were exceedingly reluctant to undertake reforms that could minimize mass discontent but might undermine their own privileges and wealth. This suggests that it is not so much political oppression, but weakness, rigidity, and incompetence, that breed revolution.

Since all major social revolutions have taken place in predominantly agricultural societies, Skocpol argues, peasant upheavals have been the second major ingredient. Following the collapse of the state, peasants have been most likely to rebel in societies where they traditionally had a good deal of control over their daily lives and work (as in France and Russia) or where landlord power was neutralized by military force (as in China). In any case, massive peasant participation in revolution seems to have been a prerequisite for revolutionary success.

A final element of successful social revolutions according to Skocpol has been an educated elite to provide direction, organization, and an ideology to the revolution. Such leaders have come not from the ranks of merchants, bankers, and industrialists, but from students, teachers, lawyers, and bureaucrats. The role of the "intelligentsia" has been critical in the making of social revolutions.

The Russian and Chinese revolutions, of course, brought to power Communist regimes committed to creating simultaneously both modern industrial economies and Socialist societies. Their respective histories are reviewed in subsequent chapters and in a later Comparative Essay.

Somewhere between conservative modernization and social revolution lies another phenomenon sometimes called "revolutions from above" or "elite revolutions."[2] The revolutionaries in these cases have often been high-ranking military or civil officials in the government who were not economically dependent on traditional landholding or modern business interests. In mid-nineteenth-century Japan and early twentieth-century Turkey, such officials, motivated by an intense nationalist concern for the survival of their societies, were able to seize control of their governments after a brief civil war, to institute major social reforms, and to begin a process of industrialization. In neither case, however, did the revolutionaries attempt to mobilize mass support or provoke mass upheaval. The extraordinary success of the Japanese in industrializing their country and preventing its domination by Europe contrasts sharply with the experience of its larger neighbor China. Explaining that difference is a main theme of Chapter 20. Variations on the theme of "revolution from above" have been experienced several times in Russian history—first in the dramatic modernizing reforms of Peter the Great in the eighteenth century and then under Stalin's brutal efforts to industrialize the Soviet Union in the 1930s. More recent cases include Egypt in the 1950s and Ethiopia in the 1970s.

Afro-Asian struggles for independence after World War II. The most obvious difference, of course, is that the American movements pitted European settlers against European colonizers, while twentieth-century Afro-Asian struggles occurred between culturally different peoples, a fact that gave them a quite distinct flavor and a different set of issues to deal with. The independence movement of the thirteen North American colonies is distinguished from all others by its ability to overcome colonial boundaries and create a larger union, the United States of America. Neither Latin American nor African movements were able to do so, despite similarly artificial colonial borders. The North American colonies, however, had a far greater degree of cultural homogeneity on which to build such a union than either Latin America or Africa.

Among the more recent Afro-Asian independence movements, numerous differences have emerged. Some, for example, achieved independence through a largely political struggle, while others required bloody wars of liberation to expel their European overlords. Some were led by a dominant single party; others were divided among numerous competing groups. Class conflicts in China, religious conflicts in India, and ethnic conflicts in Africa divided their respective independence movements. Furthermore, some experienced a prolonged struggle for independence measured in decades, while others achieved it much more quickly. The ideologies of such movements also varied, ranging from religiously defined struggles pitting, for example, "Muslim" nations against European imperialism, to secular reformist movements, to those identified with communism or socialism. Defining and explaining these variations are important tasks for historians of the modern world.

Getting Out from Under: Anticolonial Movements

The widespread experience of direct European colonial control represents yet another common element in modern world history, as do strenuous efforts to achieve independence from it. Here it is interesting to compare the first wave of independence movements in North and South America in the late eighteenth and early nineteenth centuries with that of

The Challenge of Development

After independence, the "new nations" confronted a set of similar problems: fragile states, weak economies, divided societies, surging population growth, rapid urbanization, continued dependence on the West, and a range of popular demands that few governments could fulfill. Under these conditions, it is perhaps not surprising that many so-called developing countries, especially in Latin America, Africa, and the Middle East, fell under highly authoritarian governments, often the result of military coups. India, however, maintained the world's largest democracy, while in China the Communist party retained its grip on power despite the collapse of communism elsewhere. The revival of democracy on a global scale in the 1980s broke the hold of authoritarian regimes in many places, though how permanently remains unclear.

On the economic front, wide variations have also been apparent, though the impulse toward development has been universal and the process has become independent of its original European stimulus. In terms of economic growth and industrialization, East Asia has fared the best and Africa the worst, with other regions falling somewhere between. The overwhelming nature of the problems and the small size of local business classes initially persuaded many developing countries' governments that they alone were in a position to move their economies forward. Communist states such as the Soviet Union, China, Cuba, and Vietnam largely abolished private property; a party-dominated state tried to organize the entire economy while controlling social, cultural, and political life at the same time. More recently, however, most developing countries, including the Communist states, have rediscovered the virtues of the market and have undertaken to reform their economies along more capitalist lines. Explaining the political and economic variations among the "new nations" and the changes in their policies over time represents a major theme in recent world history.

I Culture and Community

Finally, many developing countries, together with their counterparts in the more highly developed parts of the world, have had to confront the deeply troubling issue of cultural pluralism: how to accommodate a variety of politically articulate cultural groups within a single state. It is an issue common to such diverse countries as Yugoslavia, Nigeria, Russia, the United States, and India.

It is not, of course, a new issue, for most major states in earlier times had also encompassed numerous culturally distinct peoples. But the multiple

changes of the modern era have encouraged the creation of new definitions of community and new, more sharply defined cultural loyalties in many parts of the world. Four such changes are worth noting.

First, the social and economic transformations of the modern era—production for the market, urbanization, industrial development, wage labor, modern educational opportunities, and more—have in many places sharply undermined earlier patterns of social life. Such dislocations and upheavals have created a need for new kinds of communities and new patterns of belonging. Second, the penetration of the world economy into virtually every corner of the globe has brought quite different peoples into close and highly competitive contact with one another, making it necessary to sort out friend and foe, "us" and "them." Third, the growth of mass politics has encouraged would-be leaders to appeal for popular support on the basis of shared culture, often expressed in terms of language, religion, or ethnicity. When such groups express their grievances and make their demands in the political arena, there occurs what some scholars have called the "politicization of cultural differences." Finally, the experience of colonial conquest or humiliation at the hands of Europeans led many people to look carefully at their communities, states, and societies. Sometimes the result was to defend those communities vigorously; elsewhere there were efforts to reform and reshape the societies so as to strengthen them against external attack; and in some cases, people abandoned older patterns of social life in favor of new communities able to cope more effectively with the demands of the modern world.

In response to these changes, new forms of community, new definitions of cultural identity, or new patterns of political loyalty have emerged in many parts of the world. The growth of new ethnic or "tribal" identities in Africa, the emergence of distinct and sharply defined "Hindu" and "Muslim" communities in India, the reassertion of Islam as the basis for modern life in the Middle East and elsewhere, the rise of fascism in Germany and Italy—these are some of the new patterns of cultural identity that have assumed political importance in the modern world. Many of these movements have expressed their demands in terms of nationalism—the quite modern belief, derived from the experience of Europe, that the world is divided into culturally distinct peoples, each of which merits some independent political expression. This notion has played an enormous role in virtually every part of the world and is the subject of the Comparative Essay in Part V.

Other efforts to reintegrate shattered societies and to create new forms of human community have focused more directly on social and economic issues. Arab and African socialism and Soviet and Chinese communism are among such movements, though they too have usually blended their efforts at economic justice with the language of nationalism. In general, it seems clear that cultural definitions of community—those expressed in terms of nation, religion, or ethnic group—have proven more durable than those defined in terms of class or economic status. Precisely why this seems to be the case is yet another question for historical analysis.

Notes

1. Theda Skocpol, "France, Russia, China: A Structural Analysis of Social Revolutions," *Comparative Studies in Society and History* 18 (1976): 175–209.

2. Ellen Kay Trimberger, *Revolutions from Above* (New Brunswick: Transaction Books, 1978).

SUGGESTIONS FOR FURTHER READING: EUROPE AND THE WORLD

Abu-Lughod, Janet. *Before European Hegemony.* 1989. (Addresses the rise and decline of a world system prior to European expansion.)

Adas, Michael. *Machines as the Measure of Men.* 1989. (Discusses the role of technology and science in shaping Europeans' perceptions of other peoples.)

Chinweizu. *The West and the Rest of Us.* 1975. (A highly critical account of European expansion from an African scholar.)

Cosby, Alfred. *The Columbian Voyages, the Columbian Exchange, and Their Historians.* 1987. (A brief interpretative account of the encounter between the hemispheres.)

Curtin, Philip. *The Rise and Fall of the Plantation Complex.* 1990. (Discusses the transfer of slave plantations from the Mediterranean to the Americas.)

Fieldhouse, D. K. *The Colonial Empires.* 1971. (A general overview of European expansion.)

Kiernan, V. G. *Lords of Human Kind.* 1969. (Focuses on changing European ideas about other parts of the world.)

Manning, Patrick. *Slavery and African Life.* 1990. (Explores the course of three distinct slave-trading patterns in Africa.)

Pannikar, K. M. *Asia and Western Dominance.* 1953. (An Asian scholar's assessment of European imperialism.)

Porter, Bernard. *The Lion's Share.* 1984. (An account of the British Empire from 1850 to 1983.)

Stavrianos, L. S. *Global Rift.* 1981. (A history of Europe's global expansion stressing its economic dimension and the creation of a sharply divided world.)

Viola, Herman J., and Carolyn Margolis, eds. *Seeds of Change.* 1991. (A beautifully illustrated series of essays on the encounter of Europe and the Americas.)

Wallerstein, Immanuel. *The Modern World System,* 3 vols. 1976–1989. (A pioneering argument that Europe's global expansion has decisively shaped the economic fortunes of all the societies it touched.)

Wolf, Eric R. *Europe and the People without History.* 1982. (Discusses the impact of European capitalism on African, Asian, and Amerindian societies.)

PART III

EUROPE'S EXTENSIONS: VARIATIONS ON A MODERN THEME

Chapter 7: *European Offshoot or Unique Experiment? The United States in World History*

Chapter 8: *Social Inequality and Dependent Development: The Latin American Difference*

Chapter 9: *The Soviet Alternative: The Rise and Fall of a Communist Experiment*

Comparative Essay: *The Development Debate*

Suggestions for Further Reading: *Europe's Extensions*

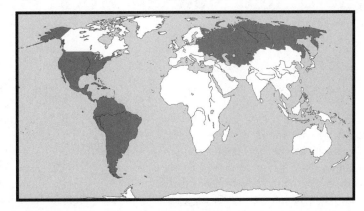

Despite their many differences, the United States, Latin America, and the Russian Empire had one thing in common by the eighteenth century: their populations were dominantly European in ethnic and cultural terms even though geographically separated from Europe's heartland. This was most completely the case in the United States, where a transplanted European population largely eliminated the Native American peoples and harshly exploited a substantial community of African slaves. In Latin America, where considerably more racial mixing occurred, the European element nonetheless remained generally dominant. To the east of heartland Europe, a Russian elite assimilated elements of western European culture and the Russian state came to dominate an enormous geographical area.

These three extensions—or outliers—of European culture provide a basis for comparing the modern transformation in very different social settings and historical circumstances. Chapter 7 compares the historical experience of the United States with that of western Europe. Chapter 8 asks why Latin America's modern trajectory differed so sharply from that of its North American neighbor despite roughly similar colonial beginnings. Finally, Chapter 9 explores the uniquely Russian path to the modern world with a special focus on the rise and fall of the twentieth-century Soviet experiment in communism.

Chapter 7
European Offshoot or Unique Experiment? The United States in World History

The colonies of North America that later became the United States were founded by men and women who left Europe to escape its social, economic, or religious limitations. Yet no sooner had they arrived than they began to create institutions that resembled those they left behind. By 1700, English visitors to Philadelphia, North America's largest city, would have felt right at home: the language was the same, the economy was similar to that of any large city in England, the political institutions were patterned on those of the British "Mother Country," and the most respectable people in town belonged to the Church of England. Most Philadelphians, when asked their nationality, would have responded "English."

Yet, if our visitors had traveled one hundred miles into the interior, they would have found a vastly different situation. The prevailing language might have been Iroquoian or Algonquian, French or German. The economy might have centered on the sale of beaver skins, wampum, or even human beings. Political and religious institutions would have been even less recognizable. Generally speaking, the farther inland one went, the less "European" the culture.

This illustrates the central problem facing historians who wish to incorporate the history of the United States into the larger pattern of world history. Is American civilization best understood as an offshoot of Europe, as our visitors might have believed had they stayed in Philadelphia? Or is it better perceived as a unique mixture of many cultures, as those visitors might have concluded after venturing inland? "What is the American, this new man?" asked the French-born American essayist, Hector St. John de Crèvecoeur just before the American Revolution. Historians have been asking the same question ever since.

A century later, a young historian from Wisconsin, Frederick Jackson Turner, thought he had the answer. The key to the American experience, he wrote in 1893, was the frontier—the line at which European civilization and the American wilderness confronted one another. In the ensuing clash, whether it took place in Virginia in 1607 or Oklahoma in 1885, both would be changed. This was the heart of Turner's argument:

> The frontier is the line of most rapid and effective Americanization. The wilderness masters the colonist. It finds him a European in dress, industries, tools, modes of travel, and thought. It takes him from the railroad car and puts him in the birch canoe. It strips off the garments of civilization and arrays him in the hunting shirt and the moccasin. It puts him in the log cabin of the Cherokee and Iroquois and runs an Indian palisade around him. Before long he has gone to planting Indian corn and plowing with a sharp stick; he shouts the war cry and takes the scalp in orthodox Indian fashion.[1]

Then, however, the frontier retreated. Schools and churches replaced cabins and wigwams; trails and paths became streets and roads; forests fell before factories. This process, repeated over and over in succeeding generations, is what "explains" American history. "American democracy," Turner concluded, "was born of no theorist's dream; it was not carried in the *Susan Constant* to Virginia, nor in the *Mayflower* to Plymouth. It came out out of the American forest. . . ."[2]

However, Turner's ideas have never lacked critics. Millions of free European and enslaved African newcomers never saw the frontier. The Founders of the American Republic would be surprised to learn that the Declaration of Independence and the Constitution "came out of the forest." Yet there is no escaping the fact that American history and the culture that it produced were hardly carbon copies of Europe.

This raises a related question: To what extent has American history followed the European pattern of development? In its comparatively brief span of less than four centuries, did it repeat the feudal (traditional) to capitalist (modern) journey, or did it skip the feudal stage and plunge into modernity right from the start? How can we explain the emergence of the United States as the world's most powerful—and most modern—nation by the mid-twentieth century? Can those from other nations with vastly different histories learn anything useful from the Americans?

Colonial Beginnings

The settlement—or "invasion"—of North America took place at a critical point in the history of England. In the 1620s, Puritans who believed too many compromises had been made with the Catholic church, and merchants and middle-class landowners who resented the power of the titled aristocracy, challenged King Charles I's claims to supremacy and "divine right." The result was a generation of civil war and revolution. While other European monarchs in the seventeenth century were consolidating their powers, the English executed one king in 1649 and expelled another in 1688. In so doing, they justified their actions in terms of the immutable common law of the land, natural rights, and ultimately, the right of revolution itself.

Twelve of the thirteen original colonies were settled during these tumultuous decades. Sometimes the colonists were led by friends and allies of the Stuart monarchy, as in most of the southern colonies; other times by the king's critics and enemies, as in the Puritan colonies of New England. Therefore, it is difficult to generalize about what the several hundred thousand English colonists had in common. Adventurers seeking more economic opportunity than that offered at home, religious zealots seeking to practice a faith not tolerated by the government, workers choosing to become temporary servants in the New World rather than permanent drudges in the Old—all of these were represented. But most were, in one way or another, "outsiders." As such, they were poor ma-

terial for re-creating a traditional society, whatever may have been their intent.

The first waves of English invaders and colonists found themselves face to face with cultures vastly different from any that Europeans had seen before. In contrast to the complex Aztec and Inca civilizations of Central and South America, the indigenous peoples of eastern North America organized themselves into numerous small communities and lived by a mixture of hunting, fishing, and farming. Often nomadic, they possessed no written language and were unskilled in metallurgy. The arrival of the European had devastating effects on nearly every aspect of the Native Americans' existence.

Like the Portuguese and the Spanish, the first Virginians hoped to use the Native Americans either as slaves or cheap labor. Neither plan worked. Far less numerous than their counterparts in Latin America, and unused to European ways of agriculture, the Native Americans made poor slaves, for it was all too easy for them to disappear into the forest.

The northern colonists were less interested in the Native American population as a domestic labor force. Lacking the missionary zeal of their Catholic counterparts in Latin America, the Puritans were content to observe a few legal amenities whereby they "purchased" their land from local Native American groups, and then for the most part ignored them. The two cultures lived uneasily together until the steady growth of the New England colonies threatened to overwhelm the original inhabitants. Then, as in the southern colonies, fierce and brutal conflict resulted, sometimes wiping out whole Native American communities. The survivors were forced to retreat in the face of the white man's agriculture, which drove away their wild game; the white man's technology, for which their arrows and clubs were no match; and the white man's diseases, which ultimately destroyed whole societies and decimated others.

Still, the Native Americans left their mark on Europeans. French settlers in the Mississippi Valley, mainly hunters and trappers like the natives, were less hampered by racial prejudices than the English and often married and allied themselves with the native peoples. New methods of warfare developed, suited to the tangled underbrush of the American forest rather than the open battlefields of Europe. New words of Native American origin enriched the European languages spoken in North America—*tobacco, succotash, toboggan, moccasin, powwow*—while place names, from Massachusetts to Mississippi, remained behind long after their originators had disappeared.

Slavery in the Land of the Free

The colonists came to America with certain social, economic, or political blueprints to which they presumed the colony would conform.[3] Virginia was expected to become a thriving business enterprise, exploiting the gold that would be found with the help of the Native Americans. Massachusetts was to be the "city on a hill," to which the rest of the sinful world would eventually turn for salvation. Maryland was conceived as a refuge for English Catholics and as a gigantic feudal manor, complete with peasants, country homes, and coats of arms. William Penn's blueprint for Pennsylvania called for a Quaker commonwealth based on brotherly love, religious toleration, and mutual forbearance. In each case, however, the original intention was substantially altered in the face of geographic and cultural realities.

In Virginia, so confident were the original Virginia Company investors in their ultimate success that the first boatload of settlers included a wig-maker, a perfumerer, and a goldsmith, to serve the needs of the upper class that was expected to result from the wealth generated by the enterprise. Disaster followed when no gold was to be found and no Native Americans could be coerced into supporting the colony. What saved the colony was tobacco, the so-called noxious weed. Tobacco-growing became so popular that laws were passed requiring colonists to grow corn on some of their lands, lest the people starve in the winter. Labor at first was provided by white indentured servants and later by African slaves.

The origins of slavery in a country that would later describe itself as "the land of the free" are not clear. Although the first Africans "sold" in North America arrived in Virginia in 1619, it is by no means certain what that meant. They may have been treated as indentured servants, serving for a fixed period of time, and then receiving land of their own. There are records of free blacks owning land in the years following 1619. But by 1650 they had disap-

peared, and servitude for Africans in America had become fixed and inherited. Neither of these conditions ever applied to Europeans and rarely to Native Americans.

By 1700, there was no doubt about the status of African Americans in the southern colonies, where white supremacy and black subordination became part of the legal and social order. Because tobacco, and later indigo, rice, and cotton, were most profitably grown on large plantations, cheap labor was in demand. That demand was fulfilled by Africans, vulnerable as they were in a hostile New World. In 1600, the idea of slavery repelled most English men and women, but a century later it had come to be accepted with varying degrees of enthusiasm. Thus soil, climate, and the unsuitability of Native-American forced agricultural labor conspired to produce a society quite different from that envisioned a century before by the Virginia Company investors. The Virginia countryside indeed sprouted stately homes that often were copies of English estates, but they were not examples of inherited privilege. Rather, they were the product of slavery, sharp practice, shrewd marriages, and luck. English civilization had met the New World frontier, and the result was neither English nor wilderness.

Puritanism and Religious Freedom

To the north, where climate and geography conspired against the plantation system, there was less demand for cheap labor. Also, the first generation of northern settlers often had their minds on other things. In the 1620s and 1630s, thousands of Puritans arrived in New England, convinced that God's wrath was about to descend on Old England. Led by John Winthrop, they believed that the Stuart monarchy had compromised the true Protestant faith in favor of a "Church of England" that was too close to the hated Roman Catholic church. But in seeking freedom to pursue their own austere religion, it never occurred to Puritans to tolerate others. Catholics, Quakers, and other dissenting Protestants had the liberty, Puritans said, to "stay away from New England."

Yet, as in the case of Virginia's economy, circumstances worked against the Puritan religious blueprint. Although the first generation may have been committed to Winthrop's vision of an orthodox "city on a hill," those who came later were motivated by more worldly concerns. With the economic growth and physical expansion of the New England colonies, church membership declined in many towns.

The presence of so much available land and the inability of the Native Americans to prevent European settlement made it difficult to enforce orthodoxy. Dissenters who did not wish to be martyrs could move away and form a separate community, as did Roger Williams and his followers in what was to become Rhode Island. By the end of the seventeenth century, some Puritan ministers were already preaching religious toleration. Whatever the original intent may have been, the openness of the continent eroded the concept of "one society, one faith." Religious freedom came to America not by design, but by circumstance.

Europe and America

If in Europe the possession of land was still the key to prestige and power, its abundance and fertility in America promised these to nearly every citizen. To a European visitor, the lines between the social classes, while always visible, were nonetheless blurred. Children and grandchildren of the servant class often acquired wealth and standing in English North America with an ease unknown elsewhere. The status of women, while remaining legally and politically subordinate to men throughout the colonial period and beyond, nonetheless improved. In the southern colonies, where fewer women emigrated, women took advantage of their scarcity to bargain for their rights. Wealthy widows, inheriting the lands of their late husbands could and did enter the business community and become established figures. Among the settlers at large, the descendents of Europeans in North America ate better, grew taller, married earlier, had larger families, and lived longer than their cousins on the other side of the ocean.

Can we thus conclude that Frederick Jackson Turner was right in his "frontier thesis"? Was it the frontier that liberated men and women from the yoke of Old World orthodoxy and feudalism? Did democracy really come out of the American forest? Three considerations should caution us before we accept Turner's argument completely.

First, the erosion of Old World practices and institutions took place over the opposition of a good portion of the colonial community, who regarded it as a sign of decay, not progress. There is something both quaint and pathetic in the attempts by the authorities in Virginia to limit horseracing to "men of the better sort," or the laws enacted in Massachusetts against ordinary men and women wearing fine clothes that implied a higher social status. But these regulations, and dozens of others like them, reflected a deep-seated class consciousness that most citizens shared well into the eighteenth century.

Second, the opportunities offered by the frontier and the abundance of cheap land did not always result in the freeing of the human spirit. Thousands of African slaves could attest to that. And finally, the long survival of Catholic orthodoxy in French Quebec and aristocratic dominance in Latin America suggest that the frontier did not have the same effect everywhere. The "cultural baggage" of settler communities has on occasion proved as important as the environment in which they sought to fashion new societies.

By the eighteenth century, then, American society was a distant outpost of the growing British Empire that showed signs of both uniqueness and conformity to European norms. Like Britain, it was a rural, agricultural society. There is also evidence that the social mobility often found in seventeenth-century America was diminishing. Most of the good land east of the Appalachians was occupied. By 1750, America had its own elite, recognizable by the powdered wigs and knee buckles worn by its members in imitation of the latest styles in London and Paris. The governing bodies in each of the colonies showed the same family names recurring from generation to generation. For some historians this was evidence of an emerging American "aristocracy." They point to the laws requiring landownership to vote, and even larger amounts to hold office, as proof that early America was only a reflection of the Europe from which its citizens emigrated.

Perhaps. But land was still cheap by European standards and more readily accessible to those who wished to enter public life. That certain families had emerged as a social elite was true enough, but they held their position not by title but by virtue of their wealth and long-term residency. Moreover, they were always making room for newcomers.

Eighteenth-century America has been called a "deferential" society: one in which political and social leadership was held by an elite, not as a result of legal titles or feudal privilege, but through custom and tradition. Most eighteenth-century Americans assumed that those who had the education, the leisure, and the experience that came with wealth made good leaders. While the electorate may have been large, real power and responsibility gravitated to a relatively small number of people. Thomas Jefferson, who was one of them, would later refer to the elite as a "natural" aristocracy.

The deferential society of eighteenth-century America was thus neither wholly traditional nor wholly modern. Its flexibility made it unlike anything in Europe at that time, but its class structure prevented it from being democratic in any twentieth-century sense. This was the society that produced the so-called Founding Fathers, who defined much of the political system under which Americans have lived for more than two hundred years.

The American Revolution: The First Watershed

Eighteenth-century America was different from the Old World in other ways as well. Owing to earlier marriages, larger families, a lower mortality rate, a better diet, and continued immigration, the North American colonies grew faster than any other part of the world. Whereas in 1630 there were only 5,000 colonists in all of the English mainland settlements combined, a century later there were 629,000. On the eve of the American Revolution, there were close to 2.2 million. The colonies were doubling their population every twenty-five years. In 1750, this population explosion caused the energetic printer and politician Benjamin Franklin to exult in the future of America, looking forward to the day when there would be more Englishmen living in the New World than in the Old. Independence had not yet occurred to him. Instead, the loyal Franklin saw the flourishing colonies bringing greater glory for the British Empire, with the center of power moving inexorably from east to west.

With a relatively empty continent blessed with abundant natural resources, population growth fostered even greater economic growth. From 1700 to the eve of the Revolution, exports to Britain increased seven times. Since the economy grew faster than the population, per-capita wealth steadily increased, providing the foundation for American industrial development.

Another distinguishing feature of eighteenth-century America was the system of self-government under which its citizens lived. Because the English monarchy and Parliament were engaged in a power struggle throughout much of the seventeenth century, they paid little attention to the internal affairs of the colonies. So, while England was occupied with its own problems, a remarkably uniform and independent pattern of government emerged in North America. Each colony had a governor, usually appointed by royal authority, who in turn was advised by a "council" of prominent citizens, also appointed. In addition, there were the increasingly powerful "lower houses" elected by the landholders. Until the 1760s, these self-governing colonial bodies operated without much interference from England.

While the colonial system of government resembled that of England, there were also subtle differences. The electorate was proportionally greater in America. There was no legal aristocracy that guaranteed membership in the upper house. And the royal governors found themselves increasingly handcuffed by the elected assemblies, which jealously protected and expanded their powers, especially those involving taxation. Many colonial citizens came to view their version of "balanced" government as more open, more responsive, less corrupt, and therefore better than the English original.

If the American colonists in the eighteenth century were prosperous and well governed, how can we explain the American Revolution? For many historians, this question has not been easy to resolve. Scholars no longer refer to "bad" King George III and his evil advisers as a major factor. Rather, they point to attempts by the Crown, beginning in 1763, to rationalize and consolidate the British Empire along the lines already followed by Spain and France. The Navigation Acts, initiated in the 1660s to confine American trade to the British Empire, were now to be enforced. For the first time, the colonies were expected to provide revenue to Britain in order to main-

The battle of Lexington, depicted here, began the Revolutionary War. *The Bettmann Archive*

tain and protect the empire and to help pay its debts. These attempts, which included the infamous Sugar Act, Stamp Act, and Townshend Duties, were accompanied by ham-handed tactics and ignorance on the part of the king's ministers and the parliamentary leaders. For most eighteenth-century Americans, long accustomed to local government and self-taxation, the proposed changes and arbitrary behavior reeked of tyranny. The result was a revolution.

It would be easy to dismiss the colonial revolt as a stubborn determination to preserve local privileges in the face of an imagined "conspiracy" to take them away. But to do so would ignore the profound impact that the British attempt at consolidation had on the American consciousness. In defying the new taxes and regulations, the colonists defined themselves in ways not contemplated before. They came to see themselves as "republicans," defenders of a "new order in the world," which the Old World—the British government—was trying to destroy. This was what John Adams meant when as an old man he wrote that the real Revolution was not the war against England;

rather, it "was in the minds of the People . . . before a drop of blood was drawn at Lexington."[4]

The American Revolution was the first major watershed in American history. Before its inception, the colonists saw themselves, as the young Benjamin Franklin did, as part of a larger whole. They shared most of the characteristics of the "mother country," and were proud of it. But afterward, Americans, like the older Franklin, concentrated instead on their differences with Britain, defining their political, social, and economic values in opposition to Britain and the rest of the Old World. Others went further, confronting the obvious inconsistency between revolutionary rhetoric and American slavery. In the years immediately following independence, slavery was abolished in all states north of Maryland, though it had never played a significant economic or social role there. The Revolution also accelerated incremental changes in the legal status of women, especially in the areas of marriage and divorce.

In 1788, a national constitution was adopted, based in part on "the right of the People . . . to institute new Government" when the old one no longer protects their rights. But at the same time, the U.S. Constitution made no attempt to alter or abolish the existing social or economic system. Slavery was maintained south of Pennsylvania, and voting remained the privilege of property holders, which almost invariably meant white males.

Four features of the American Revolution distinguish it from the French and Russian revolutions with which it is often compared. First, it was directed primarily against an external enemy, the British Crown, rather than against a domestic monarchy or a local ruling class. Second, it was led by neither oppressed workers and peasants nor more affluent bourgeoisie. Rather, its leaders were a colonial elite: George Washington, John Adams, Thomas Jefferson, and John Hancock were not unwashed upstarts. Third, where other revolutions sought to consolidate and strengthen governmental power, the revolt of the American colonies was triggered by a reaction against centralization. Some Americans saw the new Constitution of 1788, with its enhanced federal government, as a betrayal of revolutionary intent. Finally, the American Revolution preserved as much as it destroyed. Ideas of local autonomy and "no taxation without representation" were long-held traditions in the colonies, and in American eyes it was the British who were the agents of dangerous innovation.

The Revolution also bears comparison with Afro-Asian nationalist movements of the mid-twentieth century. Like many of them, the leaders of the American Revolution sought no major social upheaval, but a change in political status for their country. However, American anticolonialists did not have to confront the racial and cultural issues so central to the more recent independence movements. Nonetheless, the rhetoric of the American Revolution has been echoed more than once in the twentieth century.

The Case for American Exceptionalism

In many respects, the United States in 1776 was still closer to a traditional agrarian society than to a modern industrial one. The vast majority of citizens earned their living from the land. Manufacturing played no significant role in the economy. In spite of such cities as Philadelphia, New York, and Boston, urban life was known only to a few. There was no national market system; most products were either consumed locally or exported to Europe. Yet in the century and a half following its independence, the United States would become the leading example of a modern society. In time, the words *modern* and *America* would become almost synonymous, as many came to believe that the United States was the prototype for all societies seeking to modernize in the future.

Not all scholars agreed, however. Those who believe in American "exceptionalism"—that the development of the United States was substantially different from that of other nations—suggest it is a difficult, and possibly dangerous, example to imitate. Some of their reasoning we have already anticipated. The absence of a genuinely feudal system and the availabilty of cheap land to a good portion of the citizenry were conditions not found in other societies. Furthermore, the United States possessed a measure of "free security." Whereas most European and Asian states had to be constantly wary of threats from external enemies, Americans generally enjoyed the luxury of isolation from Old World ambitions and rivalries. American growth and development thus proceeded without interference or competition from outside powers.

Born Equal?

In the early 1830s, the young French aristocrat Alexis de Tocqueville toured the United States and made the classic case for American exceptionalism. Unlike the French, he observed, the Americans did not have to fight a bloody revolution to destroy hereditary privilege. The Americans were a nation "born equal."

Of course, Tocqueville could not have meant that phrase literally, in the midst of slavery and the continued subjugation of American women. Moreover, the deferential society permitted revolutionaries such as Alexander Hamilton and John Adams to endorse the rule of "the rich, the well-born, and the able." Even Thomas Jefferson fretted occasionally about the "mobs" of the cities. Indeed, of the first six presidents of the United States, all but Washington were college educated; all had served extensively in a va-

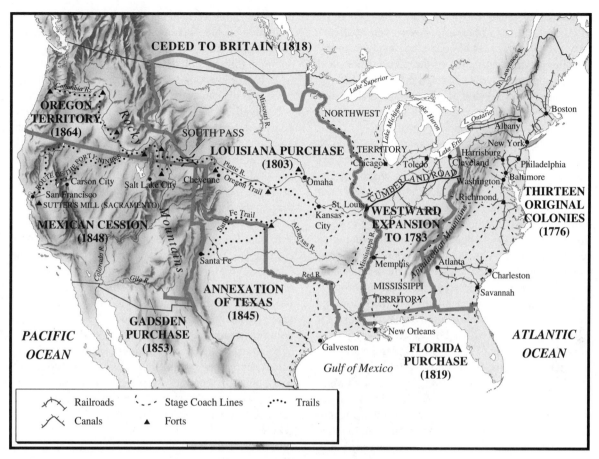

MAP 7.1 United States Expansion and National Integration through the Nineteenth Century

riety of political positions before becoming president; all were born into wealth.

Yet by the time of Tocqueville's visit, that situation had changed. President Andrew Jackson was a military hero with no formal education, and his successor, Martin Van Buren, was the son of a New York taverner. The nation's highest political offices seemed to be available to a much broader social spectrum than would have been the case a generation earlier. This was accompanied by the rise of mass political parties, the first anywhere in the world. By mid-century, the deferential society was being eroded. "Universal" white male suffrage was proclaimed nearly everywhere as conservatives and democrats alike applauded the alleged absence of social class in America, which allowed the Jacksons, the Van Burens, and the Lincolns to attain its highest office.

Open Spaces and Free Security

When President Thomas Jefferson bought the Louisiana Territory from Napoleon Bonaparte in 1803, he extended the boundaries of the United States from the Atlantic to the Rockies. In 1819, Secretary of State John Quincy Adams negotiated the cession of Florida from Spain and simultaneously extended American claims to the Pacific. Then, in the late 1840s, the United States wrested Texas and California from the Mexicans and divided the Oregon Country with the British. In one lifetime, the United States had nearly tripled in size (see Map 7.1).

Unlike Europe, most of the new land lay in the public, not private, domain. Thus Congress facilitated the rapid settlement of the West by steadily lowering the price that pioneers and speculators paid for the land.

By the 1860s, land was being given away to those willing to settle it. Furthermore, government at all levels acted as a promoter of economic development by assisting in the construction of turnpikes, canals, and railroads. From the 1820s through the 1880s, the continent was bound together to a degree unmatched anywhere else in the world, and with enormous consequences for American economic development.

No ancient titles or landed estates lay in the path of the westward expansion of white civilization. Only the Native Americans, many of them pushed across the Mississippi in Andrew Jackson's day, and later hemmed in by white farmers, ranchers, and miners, stood in the way. Although Native Americans occasionally slowed the settlement process and scored an occasional victory—as at Little Big Horn in 1876—they steadily weakened. Confronted by the transcontinental railroads that carved up their hunting grounds and accelerated the white settlement of the Plains and mountains, Chief Joseph of the Nez Percé spoke for most of his people when he declared a year after Custer's Last Stand, "I will fight no more forever."

After the War of 1812, only the relatively underpopulated Canada to the north and a weakened Mexico to the south were left as obstacles to U.S. expansion. Many Americans assumed it was only a matter of time before they too were annexed to the United States. By the mid-nineteenth century, the term *manifest destiny* summed up the vague set of religious, political, and racial imperatives that justified U.S. expansion. "Make way, I say, for the young American Buffalo," shouted an expansionist to a partisan convention in 1844. "He has not yet got land enough. . . . He shall not stop his career until he slakes his thirst in the frozen ocean."[5] Such spread-eagle oratory was typical of the era, and it encouraged many Americans to imagine a United States that stretched from the Arctic Circle to Panama. Whereas other nations had jealous rivals to check and throw back their advances—often at great cost—the United States, now attracting hundreds of thousands of European newcomers every year, had the field virtually to itself.

"A House Divided": The Second Watershed

The Civil War of 1861–1865 was the second great watershed in American history. It was a critical turning point in the drive toward modernization and consolidation in the United States, and has often been compared to other wars of modernization and consolidation in Europe: in Italy in the 1850s and in Germany in 1870, for example. But beyond that, the American Civil War also answered decisively two questions left unresolved by the Founders: Was American slavery consistent with American democracy? Was the Union a voluntary league of sovereign states—like the present United Nations—from which a state might leave peacefully at any time? By answering both questions in the negative, the Civil War marked the end of an era and the beginning of a new one.

However, historians disagree about the relationship between modernization and the Civil War. According to the early twentieth-century historians Charles and Mary Beard, the Civil War was a "Second American Revolution . . . in which the capitalists, laborers, and farmers of the North and West drove from power in the national government the planting aristocracy of the South."[6] More recently scholars have argued that northern economic and political supremacy was all but achieved by 1860, and that southern secession was a counterrevolutionary reaction against northern modernization. Thus some scholars have viewed the Civil War as the means by which the United States achieved modernization, whereas others have maintained that it was a last-ditch attempt by the South to prevent modernization. Still others have argued that the differences between North and South have been exaggerated, and that the causes for the war must be sought in human folly, and in the breakdown of political institutions that failed to preserve the Union.

It is clear that by 1861 the North led the South in the usual indices of modern development. The North had 86 percent of the country's manufacturing establishments and 71 percent of its railroad mileage. Its degree of urbanization was double that of the South, and its literacy rate was far higher. In the years following the adoption of the Constitution, American social and economic development had been distinctly uneven, and with that unevenness had come diverging views about the future of such "feudal" institutions as slavery. In those differing views lay the root cause of the American Civil War.

When Abraham Lincoln was elected president in 1860, it was as the leader of a new political party, the Republicans, who, unlike any of their predecessors, focused their appeal to only one section, the North.

That appeal was to the conviction of the majority of white northerners that slavery should not be allowed to expand further. By restricting the growth of slavery, the North was implying that slavery had no place in America's future, regardless of the role it had played in its past. It was the unwillingness of the South to accept this restriction that provoked secession in 1860–1861. It was the unwillingness of northerners to accept secession that brought on the Civil War.

The American Civil War was the first modern war. The line between soldier and noncombatant was blurred. Public opinion and propaganda—essential in a democracy to sustain support for war—played a significant role in the war's outcome. New technologies—railroads, rifle barrels and minié balls, ironclad naval vessels—combined to change the nature of war, to make it more efficient and more deadly. The nation had changed; a second watershed had been passed. Whatever chance there had been to alter or slow down America's rush to modernization was destroyed with the fall of the Confederacy. Yet that was not all that was destroyed. Years later, the poet Stephen Vincent Benét would sum it up in his epic *John Brown's Body*:

> *Bury the bygone South*
> *Bury the minstrel with the honey-mouth . . .*
> *Bury the whip, bury the branding-bars*
> *Bury the unjust thing . . .*
> *And with these things, bury the purple dream*
> *Of the America we have not been,*
> *The tropic empire, seeking the warm sea*
> *The last foray of aristocracy. . . .*[7]

I Industrial America

The years following the Civil War saw an explosion of American industrial power. A national market system, already in embryo before the war, was born with the completion of the first transcontinental railroad in 1869. Railroads stimulated other industries, notably steel, coal, and lumber, which in turn relied on the railroads to transport their products. Successive administrations, usually controlled by the business-oriented Republican party, continued to promote economic growth through railroad subsidies: they granted more than one hundred million acres of public land—an area equal to the German Empire—to corporations such as the Union Pacific Railroad.

As before, technology promoted economic growth and development. The telephone, the refrigerated boxcar, the Westinghouse air brake, and new techniques of steel-making made their impact within a generation. By the end of the nineteenth century, the United States had become the world's leading industrial nation. By 1910, it produced more iron and steel than Britain, France, and Germany combined. Whereas in 1880, the United States accounted for less than 15 percent of the world's manufacturing, by 1913, that figure had more than doubled.

Ironically, much of the capital needed to generate industrial success had come from Europe. By 1914, nearly $12 billion had been invested in the United States by British, French, and German capitalists. Like many former colonies in the twentieth century, the United States relied on foreign capital for its development. But its overall economic strength was sufficient to avoid the dependency and underdevelopment that more recent emerging nations have so frequently experienced.

Production figures could not be denied, and they led many Americans to proclaim the "Gospel of Wealth." It was, declared Henry Ward Beecher, formerly a radical abolitionist, the duty of everyone to get rich: poverty was evidence of sin. In America, at least, there was no excuse for failure, unburdened as it was by the archaic class systems of Europe and elsewhere. "I defy any man," said industrialist Andrew Carnegie in 1887, "to show that there is pauperism in the United States."

Yet even as Carnegie spoke, the evidence was mounting that the wealth generated by the American economy was increasingly maldistributed. Preindustrial America had prided itself on its lack of European-style slums. But by the 1850s, and even more so by the 1890s, a gap had opened between the poor and the working class on one hand and the middle class and the rich on the other. Around Carnegie's Homestead plant near Pittsburgh lay thousands of workers' shacks. Employees worked every day of the year except Christmas and the Fourth of July, often for twelve hours a day. In crowded Manhattan, the first (and sometimes the last) stopping point for millions of European immigrants, many lived in the infamous "dumbbell" tenements: five- or six-story buildings with four families and two toilets on each floor. Yet in every large city these slums existed within walking distance of the mansions of the well-to-do. Some maintained the contrast was a disgrace to the economic system that produced it; others held that it was a natural result of competition and the "survival of the fittest." Social Darwinism and the Gospel of Wealth provided both comfort and justification for those who enjoyed the fruits of industrialism in America.

Reform without Socialism: The Great Evasion?

By the turn of the century, critics of American industrialism were increasingly outspoken. In Europe, critics of capitalism formed a powerful Socialist movement that aimed at the redistribution of wealth and the ultimate replacement of capitalism by public ownership and collectivism. America, too, had its Socialists, but the movement never attained the significance that it did in Europe and elsewhere.

Explanations for this form of American "exceptionalism" generally fall into three categories. First, historians often point to the long tradition of social mobility in America that had its roots in the seventeenth century. Immigrants, whether English Protestants in 1700 or Italian Catholics in 1900, expected to improve their status by coming to America. If they did not, certainly their children would. And there was always just enough evidence, from Benjamin Franklin through Abraham Lincoln to Andrew Carnegie, to justify this faith. The fact that the rags-to-riches ideal celebrated in the novels of Horatio Alger was statistically out of reach for most Americans made little impact.

Second, the wide variety of ethnic and cultural differences in America tended to soften or undermine what radicals called "class consciousness." In the early nineteenth century, divisions existed between Protestants and Catholics. Later, friction developed between "old" immigrants (Irish, German) and "new" immigrants (Slavs, Jews, Italians), between Christians and non-Christians, and, most devastating of all, between whites and blacks. Thus, while the more homogeneous working classes of Europe were drawn together by the inequities of modern industrialization, producing class-oriented political parties and a Socialist labor movement, these developments were largely absent in the United

A country of immigrants. Here an Italian mother and her three children arrive at Ellis Island after making the transatlantic passage in steerage. *The Bettmann Archive*

States. Third, the remarkable growth of the American economy, at least through the 1920s, tended to undermine critics of the system. Growth meant progress for the vast majority of American families and blurred the sharp edge of social conflict.

However, the seamy side of industrialism in America did not go unnoticed, unchallenged, or unabated. Between 1880 and World War I, two political movements emerged that, though hardly Socialist, were nonetheless critical of the trends toward economic inequality and the concentration of power. The first, known as *populism,* was centered in the farming areas of the South and Midwest. The second, *progressivism,* had its greatest appeal to middle-class Americans in most regions, particularly in the cities. Of the two, the Populists were the more radical, at least in their rhetoric. They systematically denounced banks, industrialists, monopolies (especially railroads), the existing money system, and both major political parties, which they saw as controlled by the corporate interests of the East. But populism, after reaching a high point in the mid-

1890s, had little appeal in the growing industrial areas, even among the workers at whom much of its rhetoric was aimed.

The Progressives, who claimed presidents Theodore Roosevelt and Woodrow Wilson among their number, had more success, especially after 1900. Unlike the Populists, few Progressives questioned the overall structure of the economy or looked backward to America's allegedly more innocent agrarian past. Rather, they sought to remedy the ills of industrialization through reforms, such as wages-and-hours legislation, better sanitation standards, and antitrust laws. Thus they called for greater governmental intervention in the economy. Theodore Roosevelt's presidency (1901–1909) saw the creation of a Food and Drug Commission and the passage of a Meat Inspection Act. Woodrow Wilson's first term (1913–1917) saw the enactment of an income tax amendment to the Constitution, the creation of both the Federal Reserve System of national banking and a Federal Trade Commission, and the regulation of hours for railroad workers. Progressives were sometimes attacked as "Socialists" and "radicals" by defenders of traditional laissez-faire economics, but nothing could have been further from the minds of men like Roosevelt and Wilson.

Imperial America

The late nineteenth century witnessed other results of America's surge toward industrialism: the nation became an exporting rather than an importing system, a creditor rather than a debtor. From colonial times through the Civil War, Americans had bought most of their manufactured goods abroad. Now, however, the products not only of America's farms but also of its factories began to descend upon Europe, Latin America, even Asia. Foreign markets, and the need to sustain them, played an increased role in the thinking of American business leaders as the factories poured out more goods than most U.S. citizens could afford to buy. This was accompanied by a revival of expansionist thinking reminiscent of the manifest destiny era. By the 1890s, Americans were looking west beyond the Pacific and south to Latin America for potential markets. And some argued for an expanded navy with which to protect American commerce abroad.

The Spanish-American War of 1898 was the most visible result of the new U.S. interest in expansion. The United States wound up in possession of Guam, Puerto Rico, and the Philippine Islands. In a separate action, Hawaii was annexed in 1898. The United States thus entered the twentieth century as the newest of the imperial powers.

But the new imperialism did not come without challenge. Just as Americans had once prided themselves on the absence of slums and paupers, so too had they distanced themselves from Old World colonialism, against which in 1776 the nation had rebelled. To anti-imperialists such as Mark Twain and labor leader Samuel Gompers, the nation was turning its back on its heritage. Others scoffed at such notions. Senator Albert J. Beveridge of Indiana, thrilled listeners with his oration "The March of the Flag," an updated version of manifest destiny with more than a tinge of racism:

> God has not been preparing the English-speaking and Teutonic peoples for a thousand years for nothing but vague and idle self-contemplation and self-admiration. No! He has made us the master organizers of the world to establish a system where chaos reigns.... He has made us adept in government that we may administer government among savage and senile peoples.... We are the trustees of the world's progress, guardians of its righteous peace.[8]

Looking to the future, Beveridge later added, "the twentieth century will be American. American thought will dominate it. American progress will give it color and direction. American deeds will make it illustrious."[9]

However, the United States seemed hesitant to go beyond the acquisitions of 1898. With the exception of the Panama Canal zone (created in 1903 by a treaty with the new nation of Panama after its U.S.-encouraged rebellion from Colombia), no further colonies were acquired. Instead, in Central and South America, the United States practiced a form of noncolonial imperialism, or informal empire, in which nations nominally independent nonetheless were actually dominated by U.S. mining, agricultural, and commercial corporations. Thus, both sides of the imperialism debate were satisfied. No more colonies were established, but U.S. economic and political interests, occasionally with the help of the Marine Corps, prevailed throughout Central and parts of South America.

When the United States entered World War I in 1917 on the side of Britain and France, it took another step away from the isolationism that had characterized its nineteenth-century foreign policy. President James Monroe, in his famous doctrine of 1823, had proclaimed the essential separateness of the Old and New Worlds, pledging noninterference in Europe's quarrels in exchange for Europe's isolation from the Americas. When President Woodrow Wilson threw the weight of the industrial might of the United States on the side of the Allies in World War I, clearly a break had been made with the past.

The United States, having already established its economic leadership, now assumed a diplomatic and political role equal to that of the other great powers of the day. Critics of Woodrow Wilson's diplomacy maintained that the United States had no vital interest in the power struggle in Europe, and that by taking sides the nation had lost its claim to separateness and moral leadership. Wilsonians, however, believed that entry into World War I had made it possible for the United States to assert its moral leadership and bring a breath of fresh air to the corrupt world of European diplomacy. Announcing an idealistic set of "Fourteen Points" at the war's end, Wilson sailed for Europe, intending to rewrite the rules of diplomacy and redraw the map of Europe.

Although Wilson was received with near-religious fervor by the masses in Italy, France, and Britain, his hopes were blasted, first by the cynical— or realist—Allied leaders with whom he dealt, and second, by his own country's unwillingness to join the new League of Nations, through which he had hoped his ideas would be established. The Treaty of Versailles proved unsuccessful in preventing a recurrence of war in Europe and the world. Wilson left office in 1921 a broken man, but his conviction that the United States, because of its uniqueness and its power, had a mission to lead the rest of the world to a new level of order and stability, lived on in subsequent generations of American leaders.

American Prosperity and the Great Depression

If the 1920s were a period of growing political tension and economic instability in Europe, the "Roaring Twenties," as they came to be called by Ameri-

cans, saw a surge in the U.S. economy and an alteration in U.S. industrialism. Formerly concerned mostly with manufacturing and production, American business leaders now turned their attention to advertising and sales. Although it was not the first nation to industrialize, the United States was the first to achieve what economist W. W. Rostow has called "the age of mass consumption."

The automobile, symbolized by Henry Ford's inexpensive and well-promoted Model T, did for the economy of the 1920s what the railroad had done in the 1880s. By 1929, there were more than twenty-three million private automobiles in the United States, six times as many as the rest of the world combined. The motorcar industry in turn stimulated the steel, rubber, glass, petroleum, electrical, and highway construction industries, creating hundreds of thousands of new jobs. Mass advertising, spawned by the radio and new methods of journalistic photo reproduction, encouraged peoples' appetites not only for automobiles but also for such labor-saving devices as refrigerators, washing machines, and vacuum cleaners; such personal items as toothpaste, deodorants, and cigarettes; and such luxury items as furs, jewelry, and vacations.

Increased leisure for the middle classes was accompanied by cultural changes as well. American women, after several generations of agitation, acquired the vote by 1920, along with women of several European nations. Although their enfranchisement had little immediate effect on American politics, the newly emancipated woman of the 1920s challenged conventional notions of "woman's place." The youthful, high-heeled, short-skirted, cigarette-smoking "flapper" became as symbolic of changed gender roles as the Ford's Model T was of the changing economy. Another change was foretold as thousands of African Americans began to forsake the rural South for the greater opportunities offered by the burgeoning factories in and around northern cities. Middle-class Americans everywhere took part in a wider world as they flocked to the new movie theaters and gathered around their new radios. The nation was binding itself together, not only by the railroads and turnpikes of the past, but by wires and airwaves as well.

But for all its promise, the decade ended in the economic disaster of the Great Depression. Its causes are still in dispute. Some historians have argued that the prosperity of the decade masked a growing inequality reminiscent of the previous century. The agricultural sector, which had enjoyed unusually good times since 1900, began to lag. The South continued as the nation's most poverty-stricken section. Large parts of the West and Midwest were still without electricity in 1929, which meant that the gaudy new world of household appliances meant nothing to them. Workers, despite some gains in real wages, also did not share equally in the economic boom. Although a mere $2,000 in 1929 provided the basic necessities for a family, nearly 60 percent of America's families did not earn that much. They too were not in a position to consume much of what was being produced. The income of the richest 1 percent of the population, however, went from possessing 12.2 percent of all U.S. income in 1919 to 18.9 percent in 1929. Much of the wealth accumulated at the upper end of the scale found its way into the stock market instead of being used for consumer goods.

Other historians and economists have placed the Great Depression within a world setting. Staggering from the effects of world war, the major European powers were unable either to produce or to buy the consumer goods that typified the United States. This meant that once American manufacturers had satisfied the domestic market for American-made automobiles and other durable goods, there were few other markets to be found. Compounding the problem was the raising of tariff barriers by Congress in the late 1920s, which reduced the sale of foreign-produced goods in the United States. This in turn prevented potential European consumers from acquiring the dollars needed to buy American goods and thus perpetuate American prosperity.

Regardless of its causes, the Great Depression of the 1930s proved to be a catastrophe of unprecedented proportions, especially among the industrialized powers of the United States, Great Britain, and Germany. Moreover, unlike previous slumps and recessions, the Depression confounded the belief of classical economists that capitalism was a self-correcting system. In spite of bold predictions, it grew steadily worse. By 1933, one out of every four American workers was unemployed. Farmers watched the prices of their products plummet. Middle-class savers lost millions of dollars as banks collapsed under the burden of unpaid debts. Never before had there been such a crisis of confidence in a land whose economic system had known almost nothing but success when measured with those of other nations. Americans increasingly looked to the federal government, never seen before as an agent for guaranteeing stability and prosperity, as the only institution capable of restoring faith in the American economic system and in capitalism generally.

Depression and World War: The Third Watershed

Like the American Revolution and the Civil War, the combined experiences of the Great Depression and the Second World War defined the values not only of that generation but of succeeding ones as well. President Franklin D. Roosevelt presided over the entire period, and thus remains a pivotal figure in twentieth-century American history. During the Depression, he broke with the past when he argued that the role of government, especially the federal government, had to be expanded beyond anything envisioned by the Populists or the Progressives. Roosevelt's radicalism has been exaggerated by both his friends and his critics, but there is little doubt that the Depression converted the role of the federal government in the United States from that of a mere regulator of the economy, occasionally punishing wrongdoing and breaking up monopolies, to that of a guarantor, whose function it was to create and maintain prosperity, and to intervene whenever prosperity was threatened.

Roosevelt's New Deal was a complex tangle of reforms intended to restore pre-Depression prosperity and to prevent future calamities. How successful it was in achieving these ends is still in dispute, but all agree that it permanently altered the relationship among government, the economy, and the individual citizen. Through programs of public spending, it hoped to "prime the pump" of the economy, reduce unemployment, and restore prosperity. Through such reforms as the Social Security system and various relief and welfare programs, it attempted to build an economic "floor" below which the poor, the unemployed, and the elderly could not fall. By giving support to the organization of labor unions, it strengthened their hand against business. Through farm subsidies it created a permanent agribusiness that made possible continued production without the risk of falling prices. And through a vast array of government agencies, it instituted a new degree of regulation and supervision of the economy.

Critics of the New Deal, both then and later, assailed its lack of consistency, its cost, and its failure to put an end to the Depression. In 1937, some 7.7 million Americans were still unemployed. Production was still below pre-Depression levels. Socialists and other radicals pointed out, correctly, that the New Deal did nothing to alter the fundamentals of capitalism; indeed, it probably strengthened them. The primary beneficiaries of the New Deal were the middle classes and the organized sectors of the labor and business community. Unorganized Hispanic farm workers in the West, tenant farmers in the South, and African Americans generally, failed to benefit economically from the New Deal. However, conservatives maintained, also correctly, that by assuming responsibility for the welfare of individuals, the federal government was exchanging the principle of "rugged individualism," inherited from the nation's frontier past, for that of the "welfare state."

While the United States struggled with the Depression through the New Deal, other nations resorted to increased totalitarianism and repression. As they had in the past, Americans avoided formal ideological solutions to their economic and social problems in favor of what Roosevelt liked to call "experimentation." For better or for worse, the New Deal restored the confidence of most Americans in their political and economic system. And it enabled them to play a greatly enlarged role in an increasingly dangerous world.

What ended the Great Depression in America was not the New Deal but World War II. Even before U.S. entry into the war, Roosevelt urged that the nation become "the great arsenal of democracy" by providing assistance to the Allies, principally Great Britain but later the Soviet Union as well. Thus, spending for tanks, planes, and naval vessels in 1940 and 1941 dwarfed the amounts spent earlier to combat the Depression, creating far more jobs than all the earlier programs combined. Although by early 1941 Roosevelt fully expected a second war with Germany, America's entry into World War II was occasioned instead by a surprise attack from Japan following his decision to virtually isolate that expansionist nation from its supplies of raw materials. Hitler and his Italian ally Mussolini obligingly declared war on the United States in the aftermath of Pearl Harbor. For the second time, the United States cast its lot with the industrialized democracies of Eu-

This famous photograph came to symbolize for many the agonies of the Great Depression and the apparent failure of capitalism in the United States. *The Granger Collection*

rope, and with a new totalitarian ally, the Soviet Union.

After Pearl Harbor, unemployment in the United States virtually disappeared as millions of Americans of both sexes and all races streamed into the armed forces and the factories that sustained them. If World War I established the United States as a co-equal with the great powers, World War II made it a superpower. Again, its civilian casualties were negligible and its combat deaths were proportionately lower than those of the other participants. Despite the loss of 405,000 men and women around the globe, the United States was the only nation to emerge from the conflagration more powerful than when it entered. As the end of the war came in 1945, the atomic bomb symbolized virtually unlimited American power.

The American Century?

In 1941, even before the United States had entered World War II, the publisher Henry Luce, whose *Time, Life,* and *Fortune* magazines had become mainstays of American popular culture, repeated the claim of Senator Beveridge that the twentieth century would be "the American Century." "Our Bill of Rights, our Declaration of Independence, our Constitution, our magnificent industrial products, our technological skills" would be shared by all peoples, he declared. The United States must become the "training center for the skilled servants of mankind."[10] To what extent has the latter half of the twentieth century fulfilled Luce's prediction? What kind of role has America played in the world? And how has that global involvement shaped American life and institutions at home? These are central questions in understanding America's place in modern world history as the twentieth century draws to a close.

By the end of the war, the "American Century" seemed to have arrived. The industrial, military, and political power of the United States was unmatched anywhere in the world. Large portions of Europe, the Soviet Union, China, and Japan lay in ruins, while the American flag flew triumphantly in Berlin, Rome, and Tokyo. Great Britain and France, along with the Dutch and Portuguese, were in the process of losing their colonial empires. The United States, in contrast, was the world's largest creditor, controlled two-thirds of the world's gold, and accounted for half the world's manufacturing and shipping. Of all the world's currencies, only the U.S. dollar was universally trusted.

American postwar diplomacy was in marked contrast to the aftermath of World War I. In 1919, the U.S. Senate rejected the League of Nations; in 1945, there was little opposition to American membership in the new United Nations. Indeed, its permanent headquarters was soon established in New York City. Far from withdrawing from international affairs, the United States took advantage of both its own strength and the weakness of its allies and enemies to expand its political and economic influence to a degree far surpassing that of any previous great power.

In western Europe, the United States took the lead in aiding recovery through the Marshall Plan, which provided loans and credits to those war-torn nations that chose to participate. In Japan, Americans virtually dictated the rebuilding of that shattered nation, imposing a Western-style constitution on the existing economic system. In Latin America, untouched by the war, the power and influence of American banking, mining, agricultural, and petroleum interests remained unchallenged.

In the wake of American influence came heavy doses of American culture as well. American movies attracted and influenced millions. The works of American authors were translated into dozens of languages. American music, particularly jazz and later rock and roll, became a major form of entertainment for young people the world over. And the brand names of American products, such as Jeeps, Spam, Kleenex, and Coca-Cola, entered the vocabulary of many languages as common nouns. While the masses tended to embrace these American cultural exports, a vocal minority of writers, intellectuals, and political leaders in Europe and elsewhere objected to the new "cultural imperialism" and to the "Americanization" of their countries.

The growing U.S. role in the world was sustained by unparalleled economic growth and middle-class prosperity at home. Private spending for housing, automobiles, and durable goods, as well as public spending for schools, superhighways, and the Cold War armaments industry spurred this remarkable growth. The suburbanization of America, begun in the 1920s by Henry Ford and his Model T but delayed by the Great Depression and World War II, resumed in the 1950s. Low-cost modular housing and an explosion in new thruway construction separated more and more Americans from their place of work. American women reentered the work force at a rate that eventually surpassed that of the World War II years. Baby boomers—children born during or just after the war—began moving through the elementary and secondary schools.

Cold War and Containment

There was one serious challenge to the "American Century": the apparently spreading ideology of communism backed by the growing power of the Soviet Union. From Berlin to Korea, from Cuba to Vietnam, the two superpowers, with their various allies and surrogates, confronted one another in what quickly came to be known as the *Cold War*. The Soviet Union's insistence on protecting itself from a real or imagined threat from the Western powers by dominating Eastern Europe—and the ruthlessness with which the Soviets were prepared to do so—was incompatible with the American view of expanding liberal capitalism throughout the world. Furthermore, the growing attraction and influence of communist development models among some of the new nations of Africa and Asia raised the stakes to global dimensions. And the possession of nuclear weapons by both sides set the stage for confrontation and potential catastrophe.

From the 1940s through the 1960s, the U.S. posture toward the Cold War and the Soviet Union was guided by the doctrine of containment, which assumed that Moscow was the hub of a vast and coordinated revolutionary expansionism aimed at Western institutions and interests, not unlike Nazi Germany in the 1930s. Accordingly—and in contrast to 1930s' diplomacy—that expansionism had to be confronted at every opportunity.

Containment emerged first in the Truman Doctrine of 1947, in which the United States pledged support for virtually any government threatened by Communist aggression or subversion. The Marshall Plan soon followed, as did the American-led North Atlantic Treaty Organization (NATO), designed to counter any Soviet military threat to Western Europe. In 1950, after Communist North Korea attempted to overrun South Korea, Americans again took the lead in combatting Communist expansion. For the next three years, American and South Korean forces, under the U.N. flag, engaged the armies of both North Korea and China. The Korean War ended in a stalemate, but with the loss of over 54,000 American lives.

In the 1950s, the containment policy led to the creation of the Southeast Asia Treaty Organization (SEATO) in 1954, and the Central Treaty Organization (CENTO) in 1959. In addition, the United States actively engaged in the overthrow of democratically chosen but leftist governments in Iran (1953) and Guatemala (1954). Yet containment had its limits. It did not, for example, challenge Soviet control over nations adjacent to the Soviet Union itself. In Eastern Europe, when anti-Soviet Hungarians temporarily overthrew their government in 1956, they received no aid from the United States. Nor did Czechoslovakians in 1968.

Most Americans agreed with the goals of containment. There seemed to be consensus on domestic policy as well. The Republican Eisenhower administration (1953–1961) accepted most of the New Deal reforms and a correspondingly larger role for the state in public life. Throughout the 1950s, political discourse was largely limited to which party or candidate could best maintain prosperity at home and containment abroad.

No one summed up the containment philosophy better than the young Democratic President John F. Kennedy in his stirring 1961 Inaugural Address, in which he pledged that Americans would "pay any price, bear any burden, meet any hardship, support any friend, and oppose any foe to assure the survival and success of liberty." It was during Kennedy's brief administration that the Cold War came the closest to ignition. In 1961, Soviet and East German forces faced Americans and West Germans across the newly built Berlin Wall, erected to halt the flow of refugees from the Communist sector of that divided city. In 1962, Kennedy and Soviet Premier Nikita Khrushchev confronted one another over the placement of Soviet strategic missiles in Cuba. Though neither crisis escalated to war, the world had come perilously close to nuclear holocaust.

America in Turmoil

When Lyndon Johnson succeeded John F. Kennedy as president following the latter's assassination in 1963, he pledged to continue the policy of containment, especially in Vietnam, a former French colony in Southeast Asia threatened with a Communist takeover. Those who supported intervention in Vietnam did so largely on the basis of containment. They argued that Ho Chi Minh, the revolutionary leader of Communist forces in the north, was an aggressor and an agent of the Soviet Union and China, both of which were giving him substantial aid. Once again, analogies were drawn between the 1930s and the 1960s. This time, however, a formidable opposition developed, especially in American colleges and universities. Opponents of the war in Vietnam not only rejected the analogy with Nazi Germany but also began to challenge the whole philosophy of containment itself. For one thing, it was clear by 1965 that China and the Soviet Union were no longer allies but rivals competing for leadership in the Communist world. If there ever had been an international Communist conspiracy coordinated in Moscow, it was clearly over. It was also clear, at least to the war's critics, that the Vietnam conflict was not a case of external aggression but a protracted civil war, in which the United States had chosen the losing side.

The Vietnam War divided America as it had not been divided since the Civil War. It split families and

The war in Vietnam sharply polarized American society, as this confrontation between peace demonstrators and the military police in 1967 illustrates. *The Bettmann Archive*

friendships, churches and political parties. It alienated the United States from many of its traditional allies. It provided a platform for a growing number of critics, both at home and abroad, who had come to resent the American cultural and economic hegemony of the post-1945 world. It coincided with the struggle of African Americans and their white allies to end racial oppression in the South and elsewhere. It stimulated a new sense of activism among the newly arrived baby boomers in the nation's colleges and universities. And it gave rise to charges that the Cold War had undermined American democracy by promoting an overly powerful or imperial presidency, by creating a culture of secrecy and an obsession with national security, and by limiting political debate in the country. Many recalled President Eisenhower's prophetic warning about the misplaced power of a "military-industrial complex," and not a few came to see America itself as an imperialist power. All of this caused many Americans to reexamine not only their place in the present world, but their past as well. Perhaps America was not so exceptional after all.

As Americans reexamined their history, a substratum of violence and oppression appeared: the institu-

tion of slavery and its continued legacy of racism, the subjugation and near eradication of Native American societies, the exploitation of America's underclass. American prosperity was shown to be flawed, distributed unevenly and to the disadvantage of ethnic minorities and the working poor. There had always existed, said the Socialist writer Michael Harrington, the "Other America," which those in power had largely ignored.

Ironically, President Lyndon Johnson, more committed to domestic reform than perhaps any other president in U.S. history, shared many of Harrington's views. He hoped to remedy many of the country's ills through what he called the *Great Society:* a dazzling array of reforms and expenditures designed to pick up where the New Deal left off a generation before. He even announced a *War on Poverty.* But his other war, in Vietnam, came to overshadow all other considerations. In the end, the opposition to the war in Vietnam persuaded Johnson not to run for re-election.

The failure of the Great Society reforms to produce the results they promised marked the beginning of the breakdown in the liberal consensus that had controlled American domestic policy since the

1940s. Conservatives who had never been comfortable with the Great Society, as well as liberals and radicals who thought it had not gone far enough, pronounced it a failure. But no new consensus arose to take its place. Similarly, containment suited neither conservatives who wished to see communism overthrown, nor liberals and radicals who had come to see containment at best as unworkable and at worst a cloak for imperialism and expansion.

By 1970, the United States had more than a million soldiers in thirty countries, participated in five regional military alliances, had defense treaties with over forty nations, and was committed to various forms of military or economic aid to nearly one hundred countries.[11] Despite President Kennedy's soaring rhetoric of a decade before, were Americans really prepared to "pay any price" or "bear any burden" in pursuit of the war in Vietnam? In the early 1970s President Richard Nixon concluded that they were not, and gradually extricated the United States from that destructive conflict. It cost more than fifty thousand American lives and many times that number of Vietnamese.

The defeat left the United States weakened at home both economically and psychologically. A nation whose history had appeared to be unique, untrammeled by failure or humiliation, now seemed no different from any other. Although the war had ended, the bitter debate over America's role in the world did not. Was the "American Century" over? Was the United States a great power in decline?

On the international front, the evidence was mixed. The chasm between the Soviet Union and China enabled President Nixon to restore American diplomatic relations with China and to negotiate a strategic arms limitation agreement with the Soviet Union that many expected to slow down or end the arms race. At the same time, a series of apparent Soviet gains in the developing nations during the late 1970s and a growing belief that the United States was slipping behind the Soviet Union in the arms race provided ammunition for those concerned about America's declining role in the world.

But the United States already had been declining in relative economic terms for many years. As Europe and Asia were still recovering from the effects of World War II, America's economic, military, and political preeminence remained unchallenged outside the Communist bloc. But the recovery of Western Europe and Japan, the accelerated industrialization of new nations such as Taiwan and South Korea, and the increasing importance of the oil-rich Middle East were combining to create a multipolar world of several powers that would replace the bipolar world of only two superpowers. And while U.S. industry bestrode the world in 1945, controlling 50 percent of capacity, it slipped to 45 percent by 1953 and to 32 percent in 1980.

The post–World War II boom had ended, a victim of the inflation touched off by spending for the Vietnam War and Great Society programs without corresponding tax increases. Unemployment had increased, along with prices, a puzzling phenomenon to most economists. A series of oil shocks in the 1970s, generated by the mostly Middle Eastern oil-producing countries (OPEC), tripled the price of imported oil and doubled that of gasoline. In politics, the Watergate scandal had destroyed the presidency of Richard Nixon in 1974, calling into question the integrity of the entire U.S. political system.

Conclusion: The Cold War's End Brings Victory and Uncertainty

In late 1979, the Soviet Union, in hopes of maintaining a friendly and stable government in neighboring Afghanistan, undertook an invasion of that country. At about the same time, Islamic militants in Iran invaded the American embassy in Tehran and proceeded to hold a group of American diplomats and their families hostage for over a year. These two events seemed to support conservative contentions regarding the decline of the United States in world affairs. Moreover, they combined with a surge in U.S. inflation and unemployment, bringing to fruition a reaction against the welfare state that had been growing since the late 1960s. The new conservatives drew their strength from resentments of both middle-class and working-class Americans, mostly white, who believed themselves threatened by militant blacks, liberated women, and liberal intellectuals. Hit by the economic stagnation and high unemployment, they felt ignored by those who sought to remedy past and present racial injustice through affirmative action programs in employment. Deeply religious, they resented the trend toward public secularism, especially regarding education. Culturally traditionalist, they fought against the changed roles and increased liberation of women symbolized by the proposed Equal Rights Amendment and the removal of restrictions on abortion. Militantly nationalist, they agreed with those who believed America's decline was the result of poor leadership and a failure of nerve.

Under a new president, Ronald Reagan, the 1980s thus saw a resumption of the rhetoric of the Cold War reminiscent of an earlier period. For years Reagan had been a critic of accommodation with either the Soviets or the Chinese, had supported the Vietnam War, and had opposed the liberal consensus. He promised to reverse the pattern of government spending established since World War II, reduce taxes, balance the federal budget, increase military spending, and restore America's place in the world. Referring to the Soviet Union as an "evil empire," Reagan doubled military spending over five years from its 1980 level. Along with his successor George Bush, he dispatched American forces to Grenada in the Caribbean, Panama in Central America, and to Lebanon and the Persian Gulf. Increased support also went to authoritarian anti-Communist governments in El Salvador and Guatemala, as well as to conservative anti-Communist insurgents in Nicaragua, Angola, and Afghanistan.

When communism collapsed in Eastern Europe and the Soviet state disintegrated in the early 1990s, Reagan and most Americans were quick to claim victory in the Cold War, and with some justification. The Soviet Union had failed to keep its promise of a better life without capitalism. The market system and political democracy proved to have greater appeal and staying power than many had believed. Many Americans argued that Reagan's accelerated military spending and confrontational tactics had worked, that they had pushed the Soviet Union into political and economic bankruptcy and had exposed its weaknesses for all to see.

Yet the 1980s exposed weaknesses in the American economy as well. It stagnated, and the national debt more than tripled. Once the world's leading creditor, the United States now became the world's leading debtor, with much of that debt held by interests in Europe, Japan, and the Middle East. The U.S. dollar now competed with the yen, the mark, and the franc. At home, average incomes of Americans declined. Relatively high-paying manufacturing jobs were replaced with lower-paying service positions, resulting in lowered expectations, especially for young people. By the end of the decade, economic expansion came to a virtual halt. Moreover, the abrupt end of the Cold War meant sharp reductions in military spending and severe dislocations in many parts of the economy. All of this contributed to the election of Bill Clinton to the presidency in 1992. As a baby boomer who had actively protested the Vietnam War, Clinton was the first American president to be born after World War II. It would be his task to define America's place in the world at the end of the twentieth century.

If the "American Century" had not turned out precisely as promised by Albert J. Beveridge and Henry Luce, surely no other nation could lay claim to it. But America now faced painful paradoxes. For three hundred years economic growth had been the key to prosperity and had offset the inequalities of wealth and income to which Socialist critics had called attention. Now growth was slow, and even the idea of unlimited growth was challenged by environmentalists. But without economic growth, the division between the haves and have-nots would surely become more painful.

In a world that was multipolar, America was still the only superpower. If its economy was increasingly penetrated by foreigners, never had the rest of the world been so influenced by Americans. Asian-built cars and trucks might crowd America's highways, but McDonald's restaurants generated huge lines in Moscow, American rock music was heard in Bombay, Coca-Cola was still being sold in Caracas, and American communications satellites literally circled the world. Despite the agony of the Vietnam War and over twenty years of declining economic expectations, Americans were as successful as ever in exporting their culture to distant places.

But what was that culture? Americans were no longer sure. Defined at the beginning of the twentieth century in terms of the dominant white Anglo-Saxon Protestant Christianity, such a conception was even less accurate at the century's end. The proportion of Americans of white European background was declining; the role of African Americans in American history and politics was now widely recognized; and the political and economic power of new arrivals from Latin America, the Middle East, and Asia was growing. Thus many proclaimed America to be multicultural, a unique mixture of many ethnic and religious heritages in which none could or should receive preference. Others, aware of the lesson of the Tower of Babel, insisted on defining and promoting a common culture beneficial to all.

Most Americans have believed, or have tried to believe, that diversity brings strength. But are there limits to that diversity? The early 20th-century poet, William Butler Yeats, had once written with foreboding that "Things fall apart; the centre cannot hold. . . ." Might this description be applied to the late twentieth-century United States? Of all the challenges Americans have faced in "their" century, this might prove the greatest.

Notes

1. Frederick Jackson Turner, *Frontier and Section* (New York: Prentice Hall, 1961), p. 39.

2. Ibid., pp. 100–01.

3. This concept is borrowed from Daniel Boorstin, *The Americans: The Colonial Experience,* vol. 1 (New York: Random House, 1958), pp. 1–143.

4. Adams to Jefferson, 14 Aug. 1815, in Lester Cappon, ed., *The Adams-Jefferson Letters,* vol. 2 (Chapel Hill: University of North Carolina Press, 1959), p. 455.

5. Quoted in Albert K. Weinberg, *Manifest Destiny* (Baltimore: The Johns Hopkins University Press, 1935), p. 119.

6. Charles A. Beard and Mary R. Beard, *Rise of American Civilization,* vol. 2 (New York: Macmillan, 1927), p. 54.

7. Stephen Vincent Benét, *John Brown's Body* (New York: Rinehart, 1928), p. 374.

8. Quoted in Claude Bowers, *Beveridge and the Progressive Era* (New York: The Literary Guild, 1932), pp. 121–22.

9. Quoted in John Dos Passos, *U.S.A.: The 42nd Parallel* (New York: Modern Library, 1937), p. 5.

10. *Life,* 17 Feb. 1941.

11. Paul Kennedy, *The Rise and Fall of the Great Powers: Economic Change and Military Conflict from 1500 to 2000* (New York: Random House, 1987), pp. 389–90.

Chapter 8
Social Inequality and Dependent Development: The Latin American Difference

When the British colonists constructed their first building in Jamestown in 1607, the Spanish had already established nearly a dozen major cities, two viceroyalties in Mexico and Peru, many great universities, hundreds of churches and missions, and a sophisticated network of regulated commerce. Unlike the British, the Spanish found advanced Native American civilizations with great cities, spectacular works of art and architecture, and enormous accumulations of wealth. In addition, the Spanish soon discovered rich mines of gold and silver beyond anything found in North America before the nineteenth century. And Spain's profits from sugar and other agricultural products exceeded even those from precious metals.

Given Latin America's apparent advantages and its headstart, why did its historical development diverge so sharply from that of North America despite broadly similar beginnings as European settlement colonies? Why did the former Iberian colonies become relatively underdeveloped, impoverished, dependent on external technology and investment, undemocratic, and politically volatile in comparison to the wealth, power, and democratic stability of their North American neighbors? These are central comparative questions in the history of the Americas.

Aztecs and Incas: Latin America before the Spanish

Large areas of Latin America had been the domain of highly developed Native American civilizations with authoritarian religious and political structures and a submissive population engaged in sedentary agriculture. Their economies could feed warriors, priests, architects, engineers, astronomers, poets, and others who did not contribute to the food supply. At Teotihuacán, in central Mexico, a culture that preceded the Aztecs by more than a dozen centuries had established a city of at least sixty thousand people. The construction of the huge Pyramid of the Sun in the first century C.E. probably engaged ten thousand Native Americans for ten years, an organizational feat that sixteenth-century Europeans would have been hard put to emulate.[1]

The Maya of southern Mexico and Guatemala had constructed huge pyramids and palaces decorated with magnificent sculptures and mural art. Their "scientists" had discovered the concept of zero before the Arabs introduced that mathematical notion to Europe, and the Mayan calendar was more accurate than the Roman one then used in Europe.

The Aztec peoples of central Mexico, although noted more for their fighting skills, absorbed the best of the various cultures they conquered. With an elaborate hierarchy of priestly and civil rulers, the Aztecs by the 1300s developed complex class structures and harnessed hundreds of thousands of workers under an authoritarian system of social control capable of directing enormous work projects and great wars. Tenochtitlán, on whose ruins the Spaniards constructed Mexico City, may have been five times the size of Henry VIII's London and was certainly cleaner, more beautiful, and far better organized than any city the *conquistadores* could have seen in all of Europe. Yet the Europeans had nothing to compare with the grisly human sacrifices of hundreds of thousands of victims, an Aztec religious practice that so

159

The ruins of a Mayan temple in Guatemala. *James Horn*

shocked the Spanish they were convinced that these were works of Satan that had to be uprooted.

The Inca civilization held sway in the Andean highlands from present-day Ecuador to southern Chile. The Incas were similarly advanced in art and architecture and produced great wealth. Chief Atahualpa tried to secure his freedom from Francisco Pizarro by delivering enough gold objects to fill a large room. Inca buildings and roads were of such solid construction that they have survived to this day, even though earthquakes have destroyed more modern structures. The presence of such societies in Latin America meant that the relatively small number of Spanish settlers could, and did, incorporate large Native American populations into their economic, social, and political systems, whereas the larger population of British settlers to the north either evicted or exterminated the less highly developed Native American societies among whom they had settled.

In addition to these complex civilizations, large areas of Latin America were peopled by seminomadic tribes—hunters and gatherers with less sophisticated cultures and little accumulated wealth who often offered stubborn resistance to conquest. The Aztecs failed to extend their rule into the far-northern regions of Mexico, and the Inca never sub-

dued southern Chile. The Spanish conquerors and later the independent republics fought Native American wars well into the nineteenth century, eventually destroying the Native American heritage and making places like Argentina largely European in ancestry.

The Colonial Epoch in Latin America: 1500–1800

Despite their numbers and cultural achievements, sedentary Native American populations were conquered with relative ease by a handful of Spaniards, and, in the case of Brazil, by the Portuguese. In 1519, for example, with a force of only six hundred soldiers, Hernán Cortés conquered the powerful Aztecs, who had a population of perhaps twenty-five million. Superior Spanish technology—steel swords and shields, armor, cannon, gunpowder, cavalry—helps to explain the ease of conquest. But the Native Americans also lacked the Spaniards' command structure and battle strategies. Their military concentrations and mass battle formations made subjugation easier, whereas a guerrilla-style warfare might have decimated the Spaniards by attrition.

Oppression by their own rulers and the apparent superiority of Spanish gods caused thousands of Native Americans to change masters and ally themselves with Cortés. Pizarro likewise benefited from a civil war between rival heirs to the Inca throne. Luck and religion also played a part. Moctezuma II believed Cortés was the legendary Quetzalcoatl, a light-skinned, bearded god predicted to return from exile in the east to reclaim his throne precisely the year Cortés arrived. But far more important was an unexpected Spanish ally: epidemic disease. Native Americans were decimated by epidemics of typhus, influenza, smallpox, measles, and other illnesses to which the Spaniards had developed immunities. What followed the initial contact with Europeans, therefore, was a demographic disaster. Central Mexico, for example, lost over 90 percent of its approximately thirty million inhabitants in less than a century after the Spanish arrival.

In relatively short order, then, the Spanish found themselves masters of vast domains and millions of subjects (see Map 8.1). Portuguese expansion in Brazil occurred more slowly, focusing initially on a narrow coastal band where large-scale sugar plantations were established. Not until the eighteenth-century discovery of mineral wealth in the interior did the frontier move substantially inland.

Whether Spanish or Portuguese, colonial life in Latin America differed greatly from that in British North America—in patterns of landholding, economic growth, racial mixture, social structure, relationship of church and state, and much more. In those differences, many of which persisted well after independence, we may find the origins of the diverging historical trajectories of the two areas.

The very different character of colonial societies in North and South America owed much to the differences between Spain and England themselves. Despite Spain's military and maritime achievements, its overall accomplishments were built on a weak foundation. By the sixteenth century, Spain's economic development lagged well behind that of England. And despite a theoretical monopoly on trade with its colonies, Spanish industry and commerce could not supply what the colonies needed, and foreigners came to dominate trade.

Historical timing was also important, for sixteenth-century Spain was sparsely populated, politically authoritarian, institutionally semifeudal, and zealously, some would say fanatically, Catholic. But

when England began its colonial ventures in the seventeenth century, it had experienced a Protestant Reformation, the rise of an incipient capitalism (reflected in joint-stock companies, for example), the growth of a major cloth industry, the emergence of a Parliament and popular checks on authoritarianism, a growing population, and the breakdown of feudalism in general. England's was an altogether more dynamic society.

These unique characteristics of both Spain and England were reflected in the ambitions and expectations of the settlers they sent to the Americas. The Iberian colonists arrived in a time of population scarcity at home; they were disdainful of manual labor and expected to become aristocratic landlords by exploiting the energies of pacified Native Americans or slaves from Africa. In contrast, the North American colonists fled a land-scarce and population-swollen Europe, eager to work an abundance of land available at cheap prices almost beyond belief in the Old World. The southern gentry in the English colonies, like the Hispanic landlords to the south, did establish large estates with involuntary labor and imitated the social and cultural values of aristocrats in the homeland. But they were not the driving force of colonization and expansion in North America, where a growing class of small-scale independent farmers and tradespeople stamped the colonial experience with a dynamic and democratic character. The Iberians, in contrast, remained an aristocratic and ruling minority in their colonies.

Peons and Slaves: Patterns of Labor Exploitation

In governing its New World possessions, the Spanish crown took great care to preserve royal prerogatives. The colonies were the monarch's personal property, not that of the nation, and Castilian nobility predominated in political offices as well as in the church hierarchy in the New World. The monarchs who had so recently subdued the competitive power of feudal lords in Spain were not about to allow the creation of an independent nobility in America. Hence the concern for a variety of checks on and reviews of colonial administrators' performance and financial records. Virtually all viceroys and other high officials were peninsular Spaniards whose families and

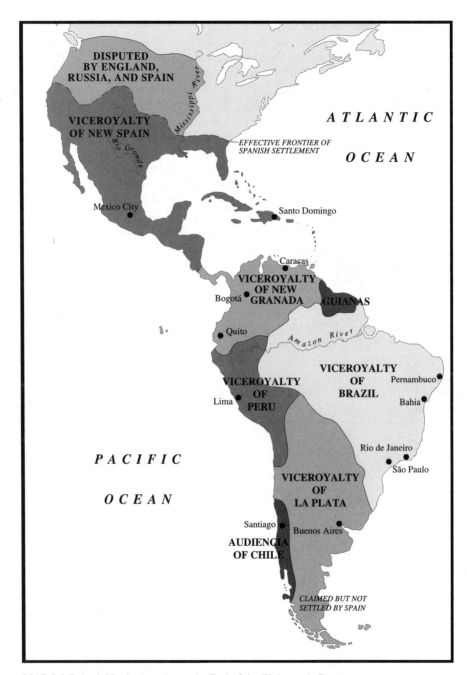

MAP 8.1 Colonial Latin America at the End of the Eighteenth Century

estates in Spain could be held hostage to imperial authority.

But transoceanic distances and the remoteness of colonial outposts restricted the crown's ability to control its colonies tightly. Because of the small numbers of colonists—probably fewer than 200,000 immigrants in the first two centuries of colonial rule—and the crown's dependence on the wealth they produced, it was unwise to alienate them by royal decrees too narrowly limiting colonial prerogatives. Furthermore, rampant nepotism and flagrant corruption characterized government at every level, a pattern that long persisted in many Latin American bureaucracies. A landed ruling class (though not a titled nobility) gradually emerged as the dominant force in local affairs, often with economic interests that went well beyond their own estates. Ultimately, they posed the kind of political threat the crown had feared and came to spearhead movements for independence.

To encourage occupation and exploration of the colonies, the crown had granted large landholdings to the sons of noble, military, and professional families. Such land was of little value without a labor force, a problem solved in various ways with different economic and social implications for modern times.

In highland areas of great wealth and concentrated population, Spanish colonizers merely replaced the existing hierarchy with their own authoritarian rulers, who continued to exploit local labor in extracting mineral wealth, in agricultural production, and in workshops. Here the emphasis on Native American labor continued into the twentieth century despite the shrinking native population. As a result, the racial composition of the highlands to this day includes whites, natives, and those of mixed blood, called *mestizos,* with few people of African ancestry, since slaves were not needed.

In these highland areas, Spanish authorities settled on the *encomienda* as the dominant labor pattern. A certain number of Native American laborers were "commended" in trust to an *encomendero,* who was also responsible for their physical and spiritual welfare. These native laborers made possible the great highland estates, some producing for export, others providing cattle and grain to sustain the cities and mining areas. Other Native Americans toiled to premature death in grueling mines, like those at Guanajuato, in northwest Mexico, and Potosí, in present-day Bolivia, whose enormous output financed Spain's imperial ventures and wars of European domination.

By the seventeenth century, the *encomienda* was being replaced by a system of debt peonage and the emergence of the *hacienda,* whose powerful owners also challenged crown authority at the local level and eventually sought independence. Debt peonage was a system by which landowners extended loans to Native Americans for such needs as seed, equipment, and household necessities, to be repaid by native labor. Wages were kept so low and taxes so high that

the debts could not be repaid. Legal restrictions that required even the children of debt peons to remain on the estates guaranteed a captive labor force. Although permitted the use of land to grow food for themselves, peons may have ended up working longer and eating less than slaves.

Lowland areas, by contrast, were populated largely by nonagricultural nomadic or seminomadic societies. Such people were unaccustomed to field labor and resisted enslavement. Here the Iberian policy toward Native Americans was similar to that practiced later in the North American colonies— expulsion or extermination. Where export agriculture held promise, as in the vast lowland sugar estates, African slaves replaced Native Americans, and thus slavery became an important institution in many Latin American societies until its abolition in the nineteenth century.

Europeans saw Africans as a more effective labor force because of their prior agricultural experience and their relative resistance to European diseases. Hence, lowland areas like northeast Brazil, coastal Colombia, Venezuela, and Ecuador, as well as Central America and the Caribbean islands, depended on slave labor, and their racial composition today includes whites, blacks, and *mulattos* with little trace of Native American culture. In these areas as well, slave-owning landlords achieved local autonomy, for no one challenged the authority of the master on his plantation.

Both highland and lowland labor systems created classes of impoverished, illiterate, mostly darker peoples, lacking freedom, resigned to domination by a small class of whites, and possessed of little prospect for any improvement in their lot. Although considerable production was required for local consumption, much of the economy focused on exports, such as gold and silver, sugar, tobacco, cotton, and later coffee, rubber, and bananas. Thus, at an early date, a significant portion of Latin America's economy was tracked into a pattern of production for the needs of distant markets.

By contrast, because of scarce labor and abundant land on the frontier, the British in their New England and Middle Atlantic colonies generally did not establish the large estates favored by the status-seeking Spanish *hidalgo* class of aristocratic gentlemen. Instead, they emphasized small-scale agriculture in which the main source of labor became a large class of free, white yeoman farmers. They developed a far more diversified economy, including ironmaking, textiles, and a substantial merchant marine.

In their southern colonies, however, the British could grow cash crops for a larger market in Europe. Hence, production for export and large plantations worked by black slaves predominated. The social and economic results were more like those of lowland Latin America—a privileged white minority dominating an impoverished majority of unfree blacks (and mixtures that were classified as blacks). Moreover, the emphasis in England's southern colonies on large-scale agriculture for export and dependence on manufactured imports and external sources of capital paralleled similar economic weaknesses in Latin America. Thus, areas whose readily available wealth and accessible labor supplies made them early subjects for intense exploitation were drained, rather than developed, by their colonizing countries. "It is not accidental," writes historian L. S. Stavrianos, "that the most profitable New World colonies of the past are now among the most underdeveloped members of the Third World (West Indies and northeast Brazil) and that the least profitable colonies have become leaders of the developed world (Canada and the United States)."[2]

Colonial Society in Latin America

The economic structures of colonial Latin America gave rise to a distinct social hierarchy. Whites of Spanish ancestry were on top of the hierarchy, though those born in the New World (*creoles*) were less favored politically than those born in Spain (*peninsulares*). Next came the people of mixed racial background, primarily *mestizos* and *mulattos*. They were the product of an initial scarcity of "respectable" white women capable of providing the aristocratic Spaniards, obsessed as they were with genealogy, a proper lineage for their offspring. Miscegenation and a large mixed-blood population were the natural and inevitable results. At the bottom of the social hierarchy were people of Native American and African origin.

Actually, Spaniards and Portuguese recognized a wide variety of different racial combinations, each with a specific name. Forty different terms emerged in one study in Brazil, with no universal agreement on what the terms meant. This was a situation far different from that in North America, where women

A portrayal of Spanish colonialism by the Mexican painter Diego Rivera. *James Horn*

joined the colonial migrations at an early date. Thus, there was less racial mixing and certainly less willingness to recognize the offspring of such unions and to accord them a place in society. No confusion about color existed in North America, for anyone with even partial black parentage was automatically classified as black and subject to the discriminations that applied to all blacks.

In highland areas, *mestizos* may have had considerable Native-American physical features, but because they adopted many aspects of Spanish culture, they were not classified as Native Americans. But physical similarities allowed the most ambitious or aggressive Native Americans, fortunate enough to acquire education and shrewd enough to acquire dominant white behavior patterns, to pass for *mestizo*. Thus, the better educated, more capable, luckier Native Americans and *mestizos* "whitened" as they improved their economic position. Although a few rose to positions of political importance, they were clearly the exceptions; poverty and social degradation remained the fate of the overwhelming majority of Native Americans and *mestizos.*

In lowland Latin America, where blacks were a major element of the population, a complex social system developed in which discrimination came to be based more on class than on race. Initially, people of African descent were slaves and were treated harshly, perhaps more so than their counterparts in North America. By 1750 or so, slaves in the United States had become self-reproducing and a century later almost all North American slaves had been born in the New World. That was never the case in Latin America, where importation of new slaves continued well into the nineteenth century. Brazilian slave owners in fact calculated the useful life of their slaves at just seven years!

But if the institution of slavery was even more in-humane in Latin America than in the United States, there was not the same feeling about blacks simply on the basis of their skin color. Far more slaves were voluntarily set free by their owners in Brazil than was ever the case in North America. And far greater economic opportunities were available to blacks and *mulattos* in Brazil than in North America, where rigid and exclusive racial categories existed. Color was one criterion of class status, but it was less important than education or economic standing. Preju-dice clearly existed in the sense that "white" charac-teristics and features were regarded more positively than those of "blacks." But, according to anthropolo-gist Marvin Harris, it was "not accompanied by sys-tematic racial segregation and discrimination."[3] White Brazilians did not fear and despise darker-skinned people nearly as much as did their counter-parts in the United States.

Harris points to demographic and economic fac-tors to explain the difference. In North America, a large group of white indentured servants preceded the introduction of large-scale black slavery and in-creased the numbers of the independent-white-yeoman class that performed the economic tasks filled by mixed bloods in Brazil. In lowland Latin America, by contrast, where whites were a smaller proportion of the population, a large mixed-race population filled the essential economic and mili-tary roles that whites concerned with status would not perform—artisans, blacksmiths, peddlers—and for which slaves were inappropriate—overseers, fugitive-slave hunters, muledrivers, and cowboys, for example. As with *mestizos,* an improved eco-nomic position produced a perception of a "whiter color." But to be accepted by the dominant white class still required acceptance of white social values as well, and consequently, alienation from their own cultural heritage. The requirements of economic suc-cess and social acceptance meant imitation of whites rather than resistance to them, acquiescence rather than reform. Leaders of social revolution were un-likely to emerge from such a group.

That the white elite co-opted and absorbed some people of racially mixed ancestry did not substan-tially lower barriers to social mobility, which re-mained pervasive and persistent. The social legacy of colonial Latin America is preponderantly one of the dominant and dominated, patron and client, full of the prejudice and discrimination that flowed in-evitably from the ruthless exploitation of labor, whether the debt peonage of the *hacienda* or the slav-ery of the plantation.

These social patterns have weakened national stability, past and present, and contribute still to Latin America's relative backwardness compared to the United States. The status-oriented Hispanic elites created a society that accentuated class differ-ences to safeguard their privileges. The degraded lower classes encountered onerous obstacles to self-improvement and social mobility. The oppressive class consciousness, elitist educational system, and restricted access to political participation placed a significant segment of the population on the margins of society. Their poor health and resignation limited their productivity, and their paltry incomes curbed demand and restricted the size of the domestic mar-ket, surely disincentives to industrialization. Govern-ments today divert large portions of their scarce de-velopment capital just to pay for the damages caused by social neglect—debilitating disease and epi-demics, physical and mental retardation, chronic al-coholism, crime, and illiteracy—all of them obsta-cles to productivity.

Mercantilism and Dependency

As the social, cultural, and political atmosphere sti-fled the individual, the crown's economic policies enfeebled the potential of the colonies at large and led to a deepening pattern of dependency that still marks the boundaries of development.[4] That the colonies existed for the benefit of the metropolis was an idea unchallenged in an age of expansionist imperialism. By policies later called *mercantilism,* Spain and the other colonial powers sought to control industry and commerce throughout their colonial systems. But Spain's own economic weakness meant an inability to provide the products needed by the colonies or to absorb colonial exports. Nor was Spain itself able to benefit much from the great wealth of its Latin American colonies. Much of the wealth stayed in Spain only long enough to raise prices before flowing out to finance military campaigns to defend the empire and to purchase foreign-manufactured goods for sale in the colonies, thus stimulating the economic development of Spain's neighbors and eventual rivals.

In the colonies themselves, the *creole* elite of large landowners and mining interests chafed under the crown's restrictions but lacked the power to alter a system that, with all its flaws, remained intact for three centuries. State monopolies and regulation of all enterprise, together with policies that limited colonial production to raw materials, provided a poor foundation for future growth. While Spain lacked the power of vigorous enforcement in such a vast empire, particularly in frontier areas, the predominant economic pattern was the export of raw materials and the purchase of imports rather than the development of internal industry. In some areas such as Argentina, British imports were smuggled in at prices cheaper than products available through Spain or domestic manufacture. Great Britain could not enforce its colonial economic regulations rigorously either, and later efforts to tighten restrictions helped alienate its colonies further on the eve of independence.

Spain's semifeudal institutions and state economic policies had prevented the rise of incipient capitalist institutions such as joint-stock companies, which provided venture capital to British and Dutch colonists. The Spanish *hidalgo* tradition of seeking wealth and status through large estates discouraged the emergence of ambitious groups, such as independent prospectors, traders, small manufacturers, and other enterprises tainted by manual labor—demeaning tasks fit only for the poor white and mixed-blood populations.

Spain's zealous pursuit of religious orthodoxy had resulted in the expulsion of the Jews from the peninsula and their exclusion from the colonies. In fact, experienced financial and commercial groups of any kind were noticeably absent among colonial settlers.

Nor were independent banking and commercial institutions part of the orthodox Iberian heritage. On the eve of independence, then, Latin America had fewer of those progressive economic forces that ultimately triumphed in North America. And independence from Spain left the elite landholding class and the export-dependent economy intact. This was a weak foundation on which to build more modern structures.

Church, State, and Schools

The centuries-long struggle to reclaim Spain from the domination of the Muslims (711–1492 C.E.) did not end until the very eve of the discovery of the New World. Thus, the militant and zealous representatives of crown and clergy looked upon the conquest of the Native Americans as an extension of that struggle against the infidel. The Catholic church became a primary instrument for "civilizing" and "Christianizing" the Native Americans, as well as for harnessing them to the yoke of Spanish political control and economic enterprise. The colonization of Latin America, in short, was as much a religious as a military conquest.

In that enterprise, church and state worked closely together as Catholicism and Spanish national identity were scarcely distinguishable. The state sanctioned and controlled the church, forbidding nonconformity, collecting the tithe, and administering its distribution. In return, the church sanctified and supported the crown and its officials, even to the extent of arguing during the wars for independence that opposition to the crown was not merely treason but heresy.

The religious conversion of millions of Native Americans and their incorporation into the lower rungs of Hispanic society were labors that fell largely upon the church and that required an extensive clergy. Members of religious orders and secular clergy in Mexico, for example, constituted perhaps 10 percent of the population. Financing such a huge religious establishment fell upon the colonists and added to the burdens of the Native Americans.

Although the church spoke out on behalf of Native Americans' rights, particularly in the early years of colonial rule, it also benefited from Native American labor. The church shared in the grants of *encomienda,* received other lands as gifts or bequests, and supervised the work of hundreds of thousands of native laborers on church-owned estates and frontier

A Spanish mission church built in 1699 in what is now New Mexico. *Robert W. Strayer*

missions. By the time of independence in the early nineteenth century, the Catholic church owned half or more of all the productive land. From these resources, it supported schools, hospitals, asylums, and orphanages. Whatever social services were available owed their existence to the work of the friars.

As an integral part of the colonial establishment, the Catholic church opposed land reform and allied with large landowners and other conservative defenders of the status quo. Liberals and reformers who battled conservative elements throughout the nineteenth and twentieth centuries thus placed anticlerical measures high on their reform agenda. The separation of church and state that evolved and strengthened in North America makes it difficult for North Americans to grasp the depth of the struggle that ensued in Latin America. The Spanish effort to achieve political unity by demanding religious conformity was an impossible goal for the British, since no one denomination controlled all the colonies. Although religious intolerance and persecution certainly occurred in North America, nonconformists could usually find haven in a more tolerant colony or could pioneer a new settlement.

British colonies were hardly immune to religious interference in politics. But the diversity and unofficial status of the churches made their voices less powerful than in Latin America, where varying degrees of church power have continued in most coun-

tries even to the present time, one of the more persistent legacies of colonialism. Hence, the political power and exclusivity of the Catholic church, its enormous landholdings, and its opposition to reform made it, until the 1960s, a powerful defender of the status quo and an obstacle to development, handicaps the British colonies escaped.

Divergent educational histories also help explain differences in patterns of modern development. By 1551, the Catholic church had founded the University of Mexico and that of San Marcos, in Lima, and a dozen such institutions provided higher learning by the time the first North American college opened at Harvard in 1636. But Latin American education consisted of classical training for the elite and little more than catechism for the masses. Denial of primary education became a major obstacle to improving income and social status for the great majority of the population. After three centuries of church-sponsored colonial education, illiteracy rates may have exceeded 95 percent throughout Latin America, and independence from Spain did nothing to diminish the church monopoly on education at every level.

In the Protestant colonies of North America, literacy was more common in part because ability to read the Bible was deemed essential for spiritual growth, if not for salvation itself. The drive for self-improvement that characterized parts of the early Republic led to a growing secularism in the United States.

But in Latin America, as in the antebellum South of the United States, agriculture on large estates made few educational demands on the work force, and the social values of the elites concurred that education spoiled a good field hand. Modern republics with scarce capital and weak traditions of public schooling continued to short-change modern education, especially in rural areas. Studies conducted in the 1970s found areas of rural Brazil where no education existed beyond fourth grade and 76 percent of the teachers had less than an eighth-grade education.[5]

Furthermore, formal education in Latin America was almost exclusively restricted to males even into the nineteenth century. Women's roles were confined to marriage and child-rearing or the nunnery and, in the case of poor Native-American or mixed-blood women, to fieldwork and other tasks unknown to their Hispanic counterparts in the dominant classes. Thus, the limited and elitist nature of colonial Latin American education persisted into modern times as an obstacle to development.

Toward Independence

Between 1810 and 1825, the colonies of Latin America fought a series of wars that resulted in their independence. The background to these events lay in the eighteenth century, when a new line of French kings, called the Bourbons, ruled Spain and implemented a series of economic and political reforms designed to make the colonial system more efficient administratively and more productive economically. But these reforms also sharply curtailed the economic independence of the colonies and thus created a long list of colonial grievances. At the same time, *creoles* had improved their economic position, but access to political power in both church and state bureaucracies was still limited largely to peninsular Spaniards. Liberal ideas of the eighteenth-century Enlightenment also stimulated the *creole* yearning for change. No amount of censorship could keep out the writings of Montesquieu, Rousseau, Locke, and others who contributed to popular notions embodied in the French Revolution.

Like the English colonists in North America, the *creole* intellectuals of Latin America discussed ideas of liberty, freedom from monarchical oppression and economic restrictions, and greater access to political power. But these ideas were never as widely popularized in Latin America as they had been in North America. No Thomas Paine emerged to propagandize notions of egalitarianism. Instead, the independence movement was the province of the *creole* elite, who feared unruly masses might challenge their privileges—fears heightened by the violent turn the French Revolution took and by several outbreaks of social upheaval in Latin America itself.

Despite their growing disenchantment, the *creoles* did not so much lead a revolution as have one thrust upon them by events in Europe. Napoleon Bonaparte's occupation of Portugal and Spain in 1807, part of his effort to conquer all of Europe, caused the Portuguese crown to move the entire court to Brazil and instigated a rebellion in Spain led by juntas loyal to deposed King Ferdinand VII. In New Spain, a disgruntled parish priest, Miguel Hidalgo, launched an unintended social revolution when he rallied Native Americans and *mestizos* against the authority of an alien crown. Aroused by anarchy and fearful of losing their privileges, the *creoles* raised an army and suppressed the revolt. But by 1822, the same *creoles* teamed up with clergy and elements of the earlier revolutionaries to create an independent monarchy under *creole* General Agustín Iturbide. The incompetence and extravagance of Emperor Agustín I led to his deposition and replacement by a republican form of government just a few months later.

With its vast geographic diversity, deep regional differences, and poor communications, South America saw no united or orderly movement for independence. There was no Continental Congress and no single recognized leader such as George Washington. Those handicaps explain the many reverses and the long delays that preceded independence despite the weakness of the Spanish crown. Independence was not a national movement, as in the United States, but a series of regional exploits by now-famous generals, such as Simón Bolívar, José de San Martín, and Bernardo O'Higgins.

Lacking any leadership role, Native Americans, blacks, and mixed bloods became cannon fodder on both sides of what became civil wars. And with few exceptions, the masses were not the beneficiaries of these elite-dominated revolts. The new governments were directed by a minority anxious to preserve its privileges. The victors had led narrowly based political revolts, not social revolutions, and many peninsular Spaniards, unlike English royalists, stayed on to reinforce the status quo.

In Brazil, prince regent João returned to Lisbon after the defeat of Napoleon, leaving his son prince Pedro as regent, with the advice that he should ride and direct the independence movement rather than be swept aside by it. Thus he came to lead Brazilian patriots in launching independent Brazil. Dom Pedro was crowned constitutional emperor in 1822, but the masses never participated in this transition. The weakness of Portuguese resistance and the role of Dom Pedro made the process of independence less violent and more orderly than that of Brazil's Spanish neighbors. But the social, political, and economic beneficiaries were a similar, narrow elite.

After Independence: The Persistence of Colonialism

Any hopes for change the oppressed masses might have entertained were quickly dashed as the privileged few consolidated their rule and expanded their share of land and wealth. Except for Hidalgo's abortive revolt in Mexico and a slave revolt in Haiti, social revolutions were postponed interminably, not to erupt again until the twentieth century, where they usually have been frustrated.

Nor did political changes in colonial capitals alter the configuration of power in the interior. Although slavery generally ended by the 1830s, in such places as Cuba and Brazil masters retained their plantations and slaves into the late nineteenth century; almost everywhere, *hacendados* kept their estates and their peons; and traditional elites held their grip on the local economies. With peninsular officials ousted from their posts, *creole* elites eventually played a larger role in local and regional politics, bringing their political influence more in line with their economic dominance.

English Economic Imperialism

International economic patterns also remained largely intact despite independence from Spain. But in the new circumstances of the nineteenth century, it was a rapidly industrializing England, not Spain, that played the dominant role. No longer confined to smuggling or quotas, English traders began flooding the Latin American market with manufactured goods priced lower than those of any domestic producers. Local manufacturers could not compete with the longer-established, more efficient British, who could produce in much larger volume for a far greater market. Latin American economic independence would have required long-range planning and promotion of protective tariffs and domestic manufacturing such as that of the United States. There, too, large planters in the South opposed tariffs and emphasized free-trade policies beneficial to the export of their agricultural commodities. But the balance of political forces in North America favored economic nationalists and protectionists, led at first by Alexander Hamilton, whose ultimate victory guaranteed more successful industrialization.

In nineteenth-century Latin America, no cohesive governments emerged, and no consensus of political forces held sway for sufficient time to plan a coherent, independent economic policy. In many nations, different factions of the elite battled for control with no popular participation. In fact, due to literacy and property requirements, class rigidity, and racism, only 2 percent to 4 percent of the male population participated in electoral politics throughout the nineteenth century. More common were revolving governments of either military officers or *caudillos* (strongmen), and political factionalism was endemic.

In the absence of concerted opposition, the victory in economic policy went to commercial and large-scale agricultural interests, who favored expansion of Latin American integration into the world free-trade system rather than economic independence and industrialization. That victory was due in part to a very small internal market. The social patterns discussed earlier meant that the masses lacked sufficient purchasing power to create consumer demand sufficient to stimulate native industry. And without protectionism, there was no competing with cheap English manufactured goods anyway.

With expanding English trade came increased investments. English capitalists financed the expansion of mines and smelters, railroads to carry ore to the sea, ports to facilitate shipping of mineral and agricultural commodities, and various urban services needed to support the cities that served the export economy. Thus, England was able to erect a system of dependency in Latin America—economic colonialism without outright possession of territories. Often called *neocolonialism,* this is one of the persistent legacies of the nineteenth century that Latin America continues to confront. Some argue that it remains the major obstacle to economic development.

Yankee Imperialism

In the last quarter of the nineteenth century, U.S. industrial and financial interests began to displace Britain's grip on the Latin American economies. By the late 1890s, a "new manifest destiny" preached the inevitability of American domination of the Western Hemisphere. The Spanish-American War in 1898 gave the United States the beginnings of a colonial empire, but more important was informal U.S. colonialism in Latin America, encouraged by both strategic and economic interests. The Panama Canal, completed in 1914, was the most prominent example of these interests. It was a vital trade link and a key element in protecting the United States' growing economic stake in Latin America. Since debt collection had been the primary motive for European interventions in the hemisphere, President Theodore Roosevelt issued a corollary to the Monroe Doctrine in 1904, arguing that "chronic wrongdoing" could force the United States to the "exercise of an international police power" in the hemisphere. Repeated military interventions in the decades that followed proved that this was no idle threat.

By the first quarter of the twentieth century, the United States had become the dominant trading partner and the prime source of Latin American loans and investments. Latin Americans now sold primary commodities to the United States to earn the dollars essential to service its debts and purchase manufactured goods. Uncle Sam had become the beneficiary of Latin American dependency.

In many respects, these relationships continued into the latter half of the twentieth century. By the 1960s, far more dollars flowed out of Latin America in the form of principal, interest, and profits than new dollars entering in the form of loans and investment. Critics complained that Latin America was contributing to the development of the United States. Deteriorating terms of trade, exacerbated by world recession in the 1970s and 1980s, also contributed to Latin America's economic difficulties. Fidel Castro provided an example of such difficulties when he noted that in 1959, Cuba could purchase a 60-horsepower tractor for 24 tons of sugar, but by 1982 it

needed 115 tons of sugar to buy the same tractor.[6] Such conditions provided the raw material for Latin American economists to argue that their problems were largely the fault of the world economy, rather than their own policies, and they provided political support for anti-American feeling on the continent.

During and after World War II, many Latin American nations attempted to industrialize, manufacturing those consumer goods they had previously imported. Such import-substitution industrialization was usually associated with heavy state control, if not outright ownership. Mexico, Brazil, and Chile, for example, industrialized considerably, improving employment and wages for the laboring classes. But development capital for the region at large continued to be scarce and predominantly external.

Some economic improvements occurred in the 1970s but those gains were eroded during the "lost decade" of the 1980s. Huge increases in world oil prices in 1973 and 1979 triggered a worldwide economic contraction. Most countries to the south had to increase indebtedness just to maintain development programs. But the recession in industrial countries cut demand for raw materials, causing the prices of Latin American commodities to fall precipitously. By the late 1980s, the average price of over thirty commodities had fallen by 40 percent and terms of trade declined to levels nearly as poor as during the Great Depression.

Industrial countries raised interest rates to combat oil shock-related inflation. Such high interest rates to the north, combined with lack of confidence in southern economies, prompted wealthy Latin Americans to invest their money abroad, further retarding growth. Latin American nations had to increase short-term borrowing at outrageous interest rates just to service existing debt and avoid default. By 1985, Mexico and Brazil, the largest debtors, were each paying about $250 million a week in interest payments alone.

With Latin American borrowers on the verge of default, money for new loans largely dried up. Refinancing agreements monitored by the International Monetary Fund required "adjustment programs," which amounted to programed recessions. Governments cut subsidies for basic food items and transportation for the poor, slashed social service budgets, raised the costs of services, halted construction projects, and restricted wage hikes, causing a regional decline in purchasing power on the order of 40 percent. Evidence of a return to economic growth, meager as it was, did not appear until the early 1990s.

Reform, Revolution, and Repression in the Twentieth Century

Social upheaval and efforts to cope with the problems of inequality, dependency, and underdevelopment have punctuated the history of Latin America in the twentieth century, but no movement has succeeded in writing a prescription for change that other countries have been eager to follow. Early in the century, a genuine social revolution challenged the old order in Mexico but subsequently lost much of its revolutionary vigor. The Great Depression elicited a variety of political responses, mostly authoritarian, but paternalistic reformers such as Getulio Vargas in Brazil and Juan Domingo Perón in Argentina represented new and more populist approaches, which involved mobilizing the workers and peasants, though without sharing real power.

In the 1950s, notable revolutions occurred in Bolivia and Guatemala, though both were soon replaced by conservative military regimes, which flourished in many countries in the 1960s and 1970s, often with American support or assistance. Overtly Socialist governments came to power in Castro's Cuba (1959), briefly in Chile (1970–1973), and in Sandinista Nicaragua (1979–1990). By the 1980s, years of austerity, economic sacrifices, and mounting joblessness caused a loss of faith and challenged the legitimacy of governments everywhere in the region. Economic shock may have been the final straw for teetering military and autocratic regimes, giving rise to a wave of popular demands for democratization. Democracy returned to Argentina, Brazil, Chile, and Peru, among others. But continued sacrifices enforced by austerity programs inspired social instability that threatened political gains. An attempted military coup in Venezuela and presidential suppression of the legislative body in Peru in 1992 raised grave concern for the durability of democracy.

Perhaps the most striking stimulus to reform, at least since the mid-1960s, has been the altered posture of the Catholic church. In marked contrast to its traditional image as a stout defender of the status quo, a vocal minority of religious and laypersons spoke out clearly for change. Professing "liberation theology" and promoting a "Church of the Poor," many church leaders sharply criticized existing social inequities both domestic and international, defined those injustices as a form of "institutionalized violence," and called for dramatic change. The murder, arrest, or torture of more than 850 bishops, priests, and nuns in the 1970s testified to the threat that this new and critical stance posed to established and highly privileged elites. At the local level, impoverished peasants and the urban poor created tens of thousands of "base Christian communities" in which the poor met regularly to study the Bible, discuss their common problems, and devise strategies of local action. As Latin America's most powerful nongovernmental organization, the church's shifting position became a major pressure for reform in the 1970s and 1980s, and it contributed to the movement for democratization. But continued austerity and the reemergence of market economics and privatization shifted political priorities away from social reforms by the 1990s.

The twentieth-century experience of Mexico, Brazil, and Cuba, briefly summarized here, illustrates both the variety of efforts to cope with Latin America's problems and the limits of these countries' ability to do so (see Map 8.2).

Mexico

A violent social revolution shook Mexico beginning in 1910, the product of rapid economic growth, a growing middle class with no political outlet, endemic mass poverty, and an intrusive U.S. presence. Among the outcomes of that upheaval was the new, progressive Constitution of 1917, a landmark document designed to win the support of workers and peasants. It provided a legal framework for land reform, seizure of foreign holdings, limits on church influence, and social legislation for workers, while permitting unionization, collective bargaining, maximum-hour and minimum-wage laws, and health and compensation programs.

The Mexican Revolution succeeded initially in breaking the power of traditional elites—the landed aristocracy, the church, and the military. But from the ruins of the old order arose a new class of bureaucrats and their allies, who created a one-party author-

MAP 8.2 Contemporary Latin America

itarian state and whose leaders became distinctly more conservative as their economic fortunes improved. Continued reforms posed a threat to their newfound privileged status.

An exception was Lázaro Cárdenas (president, 1934–1940), a Tarascan Native American whose compassionate social ideals and economic nationalism reinvigorated the revolution during the difficult years of the Great Depression. Cárdenas was among the first Latin American politicians to recognize the political usefulness of the masses, mobilizing peas-

ants and workers behind his political and economic agenda. Recognizing that modernization of agriculture depended on reforms in the traditional agrarian establishment, Cárdenas promoted the *ejido,* the communal village land organization rooted in pre-Hispanic times. The popular president distributed twice as many holdings to landless peasants as did all his predecessors combined. But changes in ownership did not necessarily mean improved productivity, and peasant gains required their dependence on an agrarian bureaucracy that eventually checked further reforms. Cárdenas also encouraged a more militant union leadership and improved wages and labor conditions for the working classes.

In nationalizing the railroads in 1937 and the foreign oil companies in 1938, Cárdenas did give a solid boost to Mexican economic independence. But most of the mining industry remained in foreign hands, and, after 1940, foreign capitalism increased its penetration of the Mexican economy, dominating its most dynamic sectors.

Beginning in the 1940s, when the revolution began its shift to the Right, government policies increasingly favored the new Mexican elites that grew out of postrevolutionary economic changes. The new bureaucrats have been as obsessed with self-enrichment as their colonial-era counterparts, undermining earlier efforts to promote a more equitable distribution of wealth and opportunity. A 1967 U.N. report noted that despite its social revolution, Mexico's income distribution was "significantly more unequal than that of most countries of Latin America," countries that lacked a similar revolutionary experience.[7]

Despite severe inequities, real economic growth continued through most of the 1960s and 1970s until mismanagement and deepening indebtedness put Mexico on the verge of default in 1982. The painful austerity of the adjustment policies of the 1980s induced a recession and negative growth rates for several years, including a significant decline in the standard of living for a majority of Mexicans. The resulting stress on the social fabric led to increasing discontent and a political challenge to the ruling party.

By the late 1980s, Mexico embarked on political and economic liberalization. President Carlos Salinas recognized that political reforms were essential if his party was to contain discontent and compete successfully in a more open electoral system. He saw that an economic turnaround was essential to his party's political fortunes and gambled on drastic changes, privatizing hundreds of state enterprises and opening the economy to foreign investment and greater competition. To offset leftist critics, he increased social spending for the poorest groups in society.

Economic reforms helped Mexico win debt concessions and private investment, and the economy began to turn around with positive growth rates by the early 1990s. Meanwhile Salinas had staked Mexico's economic future and perhaps its political stability on negotiating a free-trade agreement with the United States and Canada. Opposition to that agreement was one element in a peasant rebellion that erupted in early 1994 in southern Mexico. That upheaval raised troubling questions about the country's democratic processes, its political stability, and its treatment of impoverished and Native American peoples.

Brazil

In Brazil, it was the economic traumas of the Great Depression that brought to power a paternalistic reformer, Getulio Vargas (1930–1945, 1951–1954). He grasped the political potential of the growing working class and dominated the political scene for a generation. Like Cárdenas in Mexico and Perón, later, in Argentina, Vargas granted labor paternalistic benefits and reforms but not real freedom of action or a voice in decision making. He suppressed strikes by nonapproved unions and repressed radical reform movements, which he labeled subversive.

Unable to harmonize the many conflicting voices in any kind of democratic concert, Vargas in 1937 imposed his dictatial *Estada Novo* (New State), which resembled Fascist experiments in contemporary Europe. Vargas did give a major boost to economic nationalism, imposing controls on foreign interests in the mining and energy sectors and in industries deemed vital to national defense.

In attempting to modernize Brazil, Vargas brought improvements to workers and some other nonprivileged groups, but he contemplated no significant restructuring nor any changes as radical as land reform. Yet his shift to the Left after the war raised fears and opposition in the United States and distrust in the Brazilian military, which forced his resignation in October 1945. Vargas was reelected president in 1951, but, unable to reconcile conflicting interests, betrayed by his friends, tainted by scandal, opposed by the United States, and threatened by the military, he committed suicide in 1954.

João Goulart, a political heir to the Vargas tradition, succeeded to the presidency in 1961. Goulart appealed to workers and peasants in what the military feared could lead to a leftist alliance and a class conflict unacceptable to the middle class and its military protectors. With U.S. knowledge and approval, the military resolved the political crisis in a brutal coup in 1964, followed by a wave of repression.

The "military modernizers" and technocrats who dominated Brazil for the next twenty years represented a serious setback to any hopes for major reform. Despite economic growth rates described as a "Brazilian miracle" and the development of a major industrial sector exporting manufactured goods, an economic model favoring growth over social welfare resulted in deteriorating standards of living and disastrous social conditions for the majority of the population, who did not share in the miracle.

The military regimen succumbed to its economic and social failures and to the wave of democratization sweeping Latin America in the 1980s. But the civilian presidents were unable to surmount the crushing indebtedness, scarce investment capital, and chronic hyperinflation that continued to afflict the economy. Income distribution remained among the most inequitous in the world and the civilian administrations showed no more commitment to social reform than their military predecessors. Moreover, they failed to clean up chronic violations of human rights by the military, the police, and vigilante groups.

Disillusion with democratic government deepened as the civilian governments displayed a disappointing lack of leadership skills and ethical conduct. Corruption charges and personal scandals exacerbated the malaise. Brazilians and outside observers had to wonder how a country so rich in natural and human resources could prove so unable to govern itself wisely. There was little cause for optimism for Brazil in the 1990s.

Cuba

The most radical and deep-seated social change in Latin America occurred in Cuba after Fidel Castro ousted longtime dictator Fulgencio Batista in 1959. Castro exploited the Cold War and sought Soviet aid as a way to break the economic stranglehold of the United States, which he viewed as incompatible with real independence.

Cuba and the United States reacted to each other's inflamed rhetoric and political responses. As Castro turned more and more to the Soviets, socialized the economy, strengthened the military, and threatened neighboring dictatorships, U.S. hostility mounted.

Cuban leader Fidel Castro. By the early 1990s, his beleaguered regime was one of the few remaining Marxists states in the world. *The Granger Collection*

The CIA's attempt to overthrow the Castro regime by arming and training an army of Cuban exiles met humiliating defeat at the Bay of Pigs in 1961. Subsequently, Castro's revolution turned more extreme. Political opponents were exiled or imprisoned, and denial of human rights resembled the pattern of the right-wing dictatorships that Castro had rebelled against.

Castro's present-day international supporters prefer to emphasize the success of his social reforms. Even critics admit that Cuba had the most equitable distribution of social services in the hemisphere, featuring free education for all, the best literacy rate in Latin America, and social security for virtually the entire population. Improved equity and free public-health and medical programs combined to raise life-expectancy levels to those of most developed countries. Cuba does not have the high rates of infectious, parasitic, and nutritional disease common in even the most advanced Latin American countries. These conditions have assisted Cuba in cutting sharply the spiraling population-growth rates that imperil development elsewhere in Latin America.

VOICES
Land Reform in Song

The reform of Latin America's highly unequal pattern of land ownership has been among the persistent demands of the poor. This song, sung widely by peasants in Chile, Equador, and other countries in the 1950s to 1970s, both conveys some of how peasants perceived their situation and represents part of their protest against those conditions.

The Agrarian Reform

All the peasants
want an "Agrarian Reform":
so that it is the cows that
are milked . . . not the tenants.

When the sow gives birth
my heart aches:
the son of the landlord
eats my piglets.

We will no longer be serfs,
there will be no pariahs,
when the peasantry
makes an "Agrarian Reform."

The bull is fattened up
and the foal is provided for,

but rations are denied
to the peasants.

The landlord's wife
gave me half a plot [of land];
I did the work
and she took the product.

The boss goes by car
we travel by cart;
these are the delights
of our landlord's rule.

The boss is well-heeled
we walk about in sandals.
The boss is well dressed;
we are without a stitch. . . .

The poor work harder
even than oxen;
the rich do not work;
and live like kings.

The priest from my village
told me to wait. . . .
But I cannot endure any more
I want an "Agrarian Reform."

Source: "Peasants Speak," *Journal of Peasant Studies* 4:2 (1977): 225. Reprinted by permission.

But Cuba's reliance on Soviet aid had not resulted in freedom of action despite the country's break with Western colonialism. Cuba remained as economically dependent on sugar as it was before the revolution. Poor planning and policy decisions, excessive militarization, and other factors had prevented any real takeoff in the Cuban economy.

So the Cuban ship of state was already listing when the collapse of the Soviet Union in the early 1990s battered its fragile stability. The economy reeled as Cuba lost Soviet aid and trade, especially subsidized petroleum on which it was so dependent. As the economic crisis lowered levels of consumption and set back social progress, discontent within the island mounted and Cuban exiles in the United States gloated over the regime's approaching collapse. Yet Castro hung on to power and even ap-

peared to tighten his grip. The country scrambled to forge new trade ties with the fragile republics in the former Soviet Union and Eastern Europe, and reluctantly in 1993, the government authorized some market-oriented reforms including consultation with officials from the previously despised International Monetary Fund (IMF). But the international backlash against communism resulted in little sympathy and less economic assistance, and the island faced its greatest crisis since the early years of the revolution.

Reform in Perspective

Reform tendencies in the 1960s and 1970s generally succumbed to military regimes or other forms of authoritarianism. Such efforts also had to confront frequently the hostility of the United States. Thus, the democratically elected Socialist government of Salvador Allende in Chile in the early 1970s was reversed by military coup after just three years. Repression and inequity gave rise to leftist insurgencies in Central America, bringing a *Sandinista* victory in Nicaragua, but protracted civil war or guerrilla struggles in El Salvador and Guatemala achieved no such success.

By the 1990s, peace and a commitment to electoral democracy seemed to be breaking out in Central America, but the legacy of civil war was compounded by economic difficulties that deepened the fragility of the emerging democracies. After a decade of bloodshed, the only thing certain was that the poor were poorer for the experience. Nowhere in the hemisphere had any regime except Cuba achieved significant social reforms, and that experience was tarnished by its economic and political failures.

Thus, the record of social reform in Latin America has been a dismal one. Whereas radicals have been quick to identify economic dependency and U.S. influence and intervention as the major obstacles to development, gross internal inequalities of wealth and power have an equal claim to attention. The composition of the elites may have changed since colonial times, but the persistence of their opposition to real structural reforms has not. A number of Latin American countries—Mexico, Brazil, Argentina, Chile—have industrialized substantially in the twentieth century, and in terms of per-capita income, Latin America is considerably better off than most of Asia or Africa. But this growth has often been accompanied by increasing inequality. Modern development in North America has produced a far more equitable distribution of wealth than in Latin America. Such inequality threatens political stability and in some cases seems to limit further economic growth. Most important, it forces millions of Latin Americans to live in conditions of extreme poverty and social degradation.

Social Dimensions of Underdevelopment

In the century after independence, the masses in Latin America had not increased their share of the economic pie. In some countries, the poor were worse off in 1900 than in 1800. After independence, large landholders actually increased their share of the land, dispossessing Native American villages and noncompetitive independent farmers of what little land they had.

Nor did independence from Spain alter the traditional role of women. In the frontier society of the United States, women worked hand in hand with men, at least until industrialization separated the home and the workplace. The status-conscious Spanish and Portuguese males had a deeper tradition of patronizing women, embodied in the cultural trait of *machismo,* one expression of which was the male obsession with proving his masculinity and a strong sexual double standard.

Gradually, the independent republics recognized the need to educate women, but usually this was to provide better training for only slightly expanded notions of women's work, such as teaching and, later, nursing. Not until the late nineteenth century did growing cities begin to provide poor women the chance to escape domestic service for factories and textile sweatshops.

Later modernization and the longer grip of traits like *machismo* explained delays in female suffrage and political participation. Ecuador (1929) and Brazil (1932) led the way in granting women the right to vote, but most countries did not follow suit until the late 1940s and early 1950s, and Paraguay held out until 1961. With suffrage, women entered politics and won minor offices with gradually increasing frequency. The first female chief executive, María Estela Martínez de Perón, succeeded to the presidency of Argentina upon the death of her husband, Juan Perón, in 1974. But with few exceptions, contemporary Latin American women tend to hold relatively low positions in the appointed bureaucracy and elected offices, even in Cuba, which has made the greatest strides in advancing women's economic and political equality.

By the mid-twentieth century, inability to compete with large landholders and the squalor of the countryside drove millions of landless workers and small farmers to abandon rural Latin America in hopes of better opportunities in the cities. Huge slums characterize every city of present-day Latin America. Perhaps 40 percent to 50 percent of urban populations lack adequate housing, water, sanitation, and social services. Population-growth rates of over

3 percent per year in the 1960s and 1970s added significantly to the social burdens of already impoverished governments.

Even in good years, Mexico created only about 500,000 new jobs while 800,000 to a million new people entered the job market each year. Unemployment and underemployment together affected 40 percent to 50 percent of the work force in the 1980s. Yet the existence of schools, health facilities, and menial jobs continues to draw people from the even more impoverished countryside.

Meanwhile, large estates continued to expand, including the growing holdings of multinational agribusinesses. In Brazil in 1980, for example, about 5.3 percent of the farms controlled over 70 percent of the land. But landholding patterns also contributed directly to food shortages and malnutrition. Modern agriculture requires large investments for tractors and harvesters, fertilizers and pesticides, fuel, and other capital that cannot be paid for by growing beans for the poor. Hence, vast tracts of land that once produced food crops were now devoted to soybeans to feed chickens in other countries or carnations for flower markets in New York. The world's largest grain-exporting region in the 1930s, Latin America was a net importer in the 1980s. National policies compounded the problem, since governments encouraged agricultural exports to earn the dollars needed to repay loans and foster modern development.

Meat prices have risen dramatically in most of Latin America, since so much of the stock is exported. Yet cattle production diverts millions of acres of land from the production of food. In Mexico, 60 percent of all grain production ends up as forage, and animals consume more food than twenty million *campesinos*.

The poor can scarcely afford this kind of modernization. In Latin America, a significant proportion of all deaths still occur among children under five. Studies of childhood mortality have identified malnutrition as a contributing cause in more than half of all deaths. Among poor children, most deaths result from infectious diseases that would not be fatal in well-nourished children. Measles is still among the top ten causes of death in many countries of Latin America.

Malnutrition is a function of inequitable income distribution, and severe inequities are a result of the continued grip of a privileged minority on governments throughout the hemisphere. These narrow elites drive Rolls-Royces while the poor lack bus service; they expect their hospitals to have expensive CAT-scans when millions are dying from diarrhea because they lack pure drinking water. In Brazil, half the population lacks regular medical attention, but Rio de Janeiro is the plastic-surgery capital of the world, the site of more than twenty thousand operations a year.

Many scholars view recent social unrest in Latin America as the reemergence of reform aspirations postponed by the *creole*-led victories at the time of independence. They view modern revolutions as an attack on centuries of colonial and neocolonial social, economic, and political structures.

Conclusion

Latin American underdevelopment is the consequence of a variety of factors. The acquisition of vast mineral and agricultural riches encouraged exploitation and export rather than development for domestic use and, in the nineteenth and twentieth centuries, led to neocolonialism rather than economic independence. The labor systems devised to facilitate these economic patterns limited personal freedom and led to sharp class distinctions, arrested social mobility, and grossly unequal distribution of wealth.

Cultural differences played a role as well. The immense power of the Catholic church eventually became an obstacle to development in Latin America. The elitist educational system constituted a barrier to social mobility. The status-seeking *hidalgo* ethic demeaned manual labor, in contrast to the work-oriented Protestant ethic in the United States. The corrupt and highly bureaucratic institutional framework and limited political participation provided no solid foundation for democratic tradition.

These conditions help to explain the distinct modern histories of North and South America. The modernization of Latin America modified and built upon colonial and neocolonial structures but did not destroy or replace them. Neither reformist regimes nor those that continued to play by traditional rules have succeeded in completely escaping the colonial legacy.

Notes

1. Eric Wolf, *Sons of the Shaking Earth* (Chicago: University of Chicago Press, 1959), p. 10.

2. L. S. Stavrianos, *The Global Rift* (New York: William Morrow, 1981), p. 98.

3. This section is based largely on Marvin Harris, *Patterns of Race in the Americas* (New York: Walker, 1964). The quote is from pp. 60–61.

4. This and other sections on Latin America's external economic relations draw heavily on Stanley J. Stein and Barbara H. Stein, *The Colonial Heritage of Latin America* (New York: Oxford University Press, 1970).

5. Inter-American Development Bank, unpublished project report, 1982, cited in James J. Horn, "Brazil: The Health Care Model of the Military Modernizers and Technocrats," *International Journal of Health Services* 15:1 (1985): 57.

6. Fidel Castro, *The World Economic and Social Crisis; Report to the Seventh Summit Conference of Non-Aligned Countries* (Havana: Council of State Publishing Office, 1983), p. 62.

7. U.N. Economic Commission on Latin America, "Income Distribution in Latin America," Oct. 1967, cited in James J. Horn, "The Mexican Revolution and Health Care, or the Health of the Mexican Revolution," *Latin American Perspectives* 10:4 (Fall 1983): 24–39.

Chapter 9
The Soviet Alternative: The Rise and Fall of a Communist Experiment

Although much of Russia was culturally a part of Western civilization, its modern experience diverged sharply from that of Western Europe and the United States. Its long tradition of absolute monarchy, for example, lasted well into the twentieth century, whereas its industrialization began only in the late nineteenth century. That process was then interrupted by a powerful revolutionary upheaval in 1917, the first in world history in which a factory working class played a major role.

The new Soviet Union that emerged from the revolution was the first society to withdraw from the capitalist world economy, to industrialize rapidly under direct state control, and to commit itself to the creation of a Socialist society, led and dominated by a Communist party. In doing so, the Soviet Union pioneered a new model of modern development, became the post–World War II leader of a Socialist bloc of nations, and thus posed serious threats to Euro-American world dominance and the capitalist world system. But the Soviets also constructed a system of political oppression and state control so pervasive as to warrant comparison with Hitler's Germany. Whereas Western Europe's capitalist development was generally accompanied by the growth of political democracy, civil society, and individual freedom, the Soviet Union's socialist development witnessed no parallel trend.

Then, in the late 1980s and early 1990s, an alternatingly bold and timid attempt to reform a stagnant Soviet regime brought the entire system—ideology, state, party, and economy alike—to a dramatic collapse. The Soviet experiment had failed, and the new leaders of a non-Communist Russia sought to redirect their country onto the Western path of a market economy and democratic politics, although amid enormous difficulties and much confusion.

This very different trajectory of Russia's modern history has presented historians with three major problems of explanation. First, why did Russia experience a Socialist revolution while the rest of Europe avoided that fate? Here scholars argue the relative weight that should be given to a variety of factors: the lateness and rapidity of Russia's industrialization; the weakness of the Russian middle class; the unwillingness of the tsars to permit real political reform; the attractions of socialism for Russia's revolutionary elite; and the vast misfortune of the country's participation in World War I.

The second major issue involves understanding the tremendously repressive and authoritarian character of the Soviet experiment, particularly in its Stalinist phase. Who or what was responsible for the enormous human suffering the regime imposed? Historical debate pits those who focus on Russia's autocratic tsarist past against those who blame the Socialist revolution and its Leninist leadership. Historians who stress the tsarist tradition locate the origins of Stalinist oppression deep in the Russian past. Historians who hold communism responsible argue that it was an inherently despotic system, for by eliminating private property, it removed the economic basis for opposing total state control. In this view, Lenin's fanaticism, his use of violence, and his insistence on Communist party dominance doomed the country to a repressive and highly authoritarian political system. Still other historians point to the context, or historical circumstances, of modern Russian/Soviet development as a primary explanation for its unique history. Seeking to preserve its independence and its Socialist revolution, the Soviet Union was determined to catch up to its far stronger Western rivals through rapid industrialization. Perhaps any such government would be driven to authoritarian methods. Is it possible to mobilize a whole society and its resources while facing the overt hostility of the capitalist world and still adhere to democratic practices? In this view, the requirements of national survival, rather than those of communism or tradition, best explain the Soviet political system.

The third major question, and one with which historians will be struggling for some time, involves explaining the quite sudden and relatively peaceful disintegration of the entire Soviet system. Was the Socialist experiment flawed from the very beginning? If so, how did it last so long? If not, what happened to erode its basis of support so thoroughly by the 1980s? Did the Gorbachev reform effort contribute to the country's collapse, even as it tried to revive socialism? These are some of the questions we will confront in tracing the unique contours of Russia's path to the modern world.

I Mother Russia

The earliest Russian state emerged during the tenth and eleventh centuries, and its history followed a very different course from that of its European neighbors to the west. At least in part, those differences reflected a particularly harsh physical environment. Situated in the central and eastern sections of the vast Eurasian plain, Russia lacked natural barriers to the frequent invasion of stronger peoples or, once started, to its own expansion. Furthermore, its extreme northern location meant that much of the country was unsuitable for agriculture and the rest had a short growing season and long, harsh winters. The combined effect of these conditions was very low agricultural yields. By the mid-nineteenth century, Russian farmers were only one-quarter to one-third as productive as their counterparts in western Europe. This meant general economic stagnation, a continuing search for new and more fertile lands to cultivate, and, by late in the nineteenth century, economic crisis. By 1914, Russia had Europe's highest rate of population growth and its lowest rate of agricultural productivity. In these conditions lay some of the roots of Russia's explosive revolution in 1917.

Russia was different from Europe not only in its geographical setting but also in its cultural development, for Christianity came to Russia, in the tenth century, in a Byzantine Orthodox rather than a Roman Catholic version. This had the effect of separating Russia from the mainstream of Western religious and cultural development. Russia did not participate in the intellectual revival of the late Middle Ages or in the Renaissance, Reformation, and scientific revolution—all of which promoted the autonomy of the individual and secular attitudes in Europe. While the Western churches accommodated themselves to modern science and sought to address the needs of the emerging new society, the Russian Orthodox church emphasized personal conversion, mysticism, and renunciation of the world. And whereas Western churches generally kept their independence from the state, in Russia the Orthodox church was closely identified with and controlled by the government.

Europe remained free of barbarian invasions until after roughly 1000 C.E., but steppe nomads frequently attacked the exposed principalities of early Russia. The most destructive and influential of these invaders were the Mongols, who, as part of their general conquest of nearly all Eurasia, devastated Russia between 1237 and 1241. Not for more than two hundred years would the Russians completely regain their independence.

The Mongol impact was profound. It imposed political unity on the many feuding states of medieval Russia and provided a common enemy around which the idea of Russian nationality took shape. It contributed much to the notion that the ruler exercised unrestrained and absolute power, as the Mongol khans had done. As Mongol rule came to an end in the fifteenth century, the princes of Moscow, already calling themselves "tsar," emerged as their successors. Over the next several centuries, they consolidated their control and in the process created a state and a society far different from those developing in western Europe.

In the rest of Europe, rulers generally respected the property rights of their subjects while trying to monopolize political power. But Russian tsars, following the Mongol model, claimed total authority over the territory and people of their country. While that control was never fully established, the Russian state came to exercise a far greater authority over individuals and society than was the case in western Europe. A long and bloody struggle removed the nobility as an obstacle to royal authority and required them to render service to the tsar in return for their estates and the right to exploit their peasants. Members of the urban merchant class, few in number and

MAP 9.1 The Growth of the Russian Empire

far removed from the main routes of international commerce, had learned that "the path to wealth lay not in fighting the authorities but in collaborating with them."[1] It was an attitude far different from that in western Europe and offered little basis for a capitalist-democratic society like that of England or France.

As the nobility and the bourgeoisie came under the control of an increasingly powerful state, so too were the ancient privileges of the peasantry undermined. From early times, Russian peasants had been tenants, free to move from one landlord to another. But when, in the sixteenth century, large numbers of them took advantage of this right to move into the recently conquered and fertile "black soil" region, the state acted to enserf them and to forbid their leaving the estates of their landlords. Serfdom was created by government decree in Russia just as it was declining in western Europe. The church, the nobility, the bourgeois, and the peasants all had to submit; the state, as historian Richard Pipes remarks, had "swallowed society." It was a powerful legacy on which

Russia's twentieth-century revolutionaries would later build.

Accompanying the creation of Russia's unique political and social system was its enormous geographical expansion. While western Europeans built empires across the seas, the Russians, driven by the tsars' desire for ever larger territories and peasants' need for cultivable land, expanded across the vast Eurasian plain to construct the world's largest contiguous land-based empire.

Until 1550, the strength of the steppe nomads limited Russian expansion. But in the century that followed, Russians explored and conquered Siberia all the way to the Pacific (see Map 9.1). It was a remarkable feat, similar to but far more rapid than the westward movement in America. Both were continental in scope and involved the incorporation of territories sparsely populated by much weaker societies. In the Russian case, the initial economic motive was the rich trade in furs, which long provided the most important source of revenues for the government. But some 400,000 settlers also migrated to the region in the centuries that followed. Russian expansion continued in the eighteenth and nineteenth centuries as Alaska, the Amur River Valley, the Ukraine, the Caucasus, and the ancient Muslim kingdoms of Central Asia were incorporated into the Russian Empire.

Thus, Russia became a huge multiethnic empire covering no less than one-sixth of the world's land area, within which Russian and non-Russian peoples were almost equal in number. The needs of expansion and colonization required, or at least served to justify, a powerful state and an extremely large military establishment. War was frequent, and its threat was constant. To their many weaker neighbors, the Russians no doubt appeared as a threatening power. But remembering the Mongol invasions and the many nomadic incursions, the Russians more often felt themselves to be victims rather than aggressors. The growing strength of Europe during and after the seventeenth century provided additional evidence of Russia's vulnerability and stimulated efforts at reform that eventually led to revolution.

Reformers and Revolutionaries: Old Russia and the West, 1700–1900

Russia was among the first of the world's major societies to perceive itself as weak and backward in comparison to the West. A growing awareness of Europe's dynamic society, punctuated by periodic military defeats, posed the central dilemma of modern Russian history: how to catch up with the West, preserve Russian power, and yet protect the position of its ruling elite. Those concerns persisted into the twentieth century to motivate both Stalin's brutal regime and Gorbachev's efforts at reform.

Peter the Great: A Revolution from Above

The first major effort to cope with the dilemma is associated with Tsar Peter I, or Peter the Great, who reigned from 1689 to 1725. An extended trip to western Europe early in his reign convinced Peter of the backwardness and barbarity of almost everything Russian and of his need for European institutions, experts, and practices. If he needed concrete proof of Russia's weakness, it was provided on the field of battle, where Russia had been defeated by Poland, Sweden, and the Ottoman Empire. A huge and energetic man, Peter determined to haul Russia into the modern world by creating a state, based on European models, that could mobilize the country's energies.

Even a short list of Peter's reforms conveys something of their enormous scope. Much of this effort was aimed at increasing Russia's military strength. He created a huge and professional standing army for the first time, complete with uniforms, modern muskets and artillery, and imported European officers. Absorbing some 80 percent to 85 percent of government revenues, the army was proportionately almost three times the size of western European forces. A new and more efficient administrative system, based on written documents, required more serious educational preparation. Thus Peter created a variety of new and largely technical schools and tried to impose at least five years of education for the sons of nobles. A decree of 1714 forbade noblemen to marry until they could demonstrate competence in arithmetic and geometry. To staff the new bureaucracy and the army, Peter bound every nobleman to life service in the state and actively recruited commoners as well. State power and compulsion were also applied to the economy. Aware of the backwardness of Russia's merchants and entrepreneurs, Peter established two hundred or more manufacturing enterprises, particularly in metallurgy, mining, and textiles, with the government providing overall direction, some of the capital, and serf labor.

In cultural matters, Peter and his successors, especially Catherine the Great, tried vigorously to foster Western manners, dress, and social customs. Forcing the nobility to shave their beards became a hated symbol of this effort. Finally, he built a wholly new capital, St. Petersburg, in the far north of the country on the Gulf of Finland. European in its architecture, the city was to serve as Peter's "window on the West," the place where Europe's culture would penetrate the darkness of Russian backwardness.

During Peter's reign, Russia became one of the great powers of Europe, but at a great price. Government revenues grew by over five times between 1680 and 1724, placing an enormous burden on an already impoverished peasantry. Later tsars required the landlords to collect the taxes, thus increasing their control over the serfs. By pushing Western education and culture so vigorously, Peter fostered an elite class largely cut off from its own people. The educated nobility spoke French, were familiar with European literature and philosophy, and often held Russian culture in contempt. Under the influence of Western liberal ideas, some of this group came also to oppose the regime itself; among these were the revolutionaries of the nineteenth century.

Peter's reforms—in fact a revolution from above—were imposed ruthlessly, often against violent opposition. Their emphasis on the creation of a powerful central government gave rise, in the words of one historian, to a "huge state establishment [which] seemed to float in mid-air, unconnected to the population or the country at large."[2] Whereas Europe's economic development was largely a matter of private initiative percolating up from below, in Russia, only the state had the capacity and the motivation to undertake the apparently necessary but painful work of social and economic transformation. It was a lesson not lost on Peter's twentieth century successors.

Serfs and Industry

Russia's modern development, like that of developing countries in the twentieth century, was undertaken with a constant eye on the West. But since the West was itself growing rapidly in strength and wealth, this was like aiming at a moving target. Napoleon's invasion in 1812 and the British and French victory over Russia in the Crimean War of 1854–1856 demonstrated the apparent hollowness of Russia's claim to real "great power" status. In an age of industry, more than 90 percent of Russia's population lived in rural areas, and most still derived their living from a very inefficient agriculture; in an age of democracy and capitalism, the Russian state still dominated virtually every aspect of social life but was unable to tap the energies of its people. A growing awareness of this widening gulf between Europe and Russia stimulated a series of major reforms during the latter half of the nineteenth century, but, far from creating a new stability, these reforms generated pressures that led to revolution in the early years of the twentieth.

The first of the reforms was the abolition of serfdom in 1861, just a few years before the freeing of the slaves in the United States. For a half-century or more, thoughtful Russians had felt that serfdom, almost indistinguishable from chattel slavery, was incompatible with modern civilization and held back the country's overall development. But only the shock of defeat in the Crimean War was enough to overcome the objections of the landlords. Although emancipation gave the peasants both legal freedom and more than half the arable land in Russia, it caused their economic condition to deteriorate even further. In addition to regular taxes, peasants now found themselves saddled with "redemption payments," and many fell deeply into debt. Furthermore, peasants no longer had access to the meadows and forests they had previously shared with their landlords, and as population rose sharply while yields remained low, their standard of living actually dropped. When the monarchy faltered and then fell in the early twentieth century, it is hardly surprising that the peasants were among the rebels.

Despite the freeing of the serfs, Russian agriculture stagnated. But from the 1860s on, its industrialization began to take off. In the absence of a vigorous capitalist class, the government, as in Peter's time, took the initiative largely for reasons of state power, with railroad construction and heavy industries leading the way. Under the leadership of Sergei Witte, the minister of finance, Russia experienced a remarkable spurt of industrial growth in the 1890s. Convinced that nothing less could keep Russia a great power, the government spent two-thirds of its revenue on economic development between 1892 and 1900 and opened the country to a vast influx of foreign capital.

The results were dramatic. Russian industrial growth exploded at an average rate of 8 percent per year during the 1890s. By 1900, Russia ranked fourth in the world in the production of steel and had developed major industries in coal, textiles, and oil. A substantial urban working class, numbering some 2.3 million by 1900, suddenly emerged, concentrated in large factories in Moscow, St. Petersburg, and a few other cities. A growing bourgeoisie, largely dependent on the state, added to Russia's social complexity.

Further reforms convinced some that Russia was moving toward a Western-style society. Tsar Alexander II had created in 1864 a system of district and provincial councils, called *zemstva*, to encourage some local public service outlet for members of the

Scene from a rural village in early twentieth-century Russia. The land hunger of such villagers played a major role in the revolution of 1917. *Visual Studies Workshop*

peasant, middle, and upper classes. Some easing of censorship, a greater freedom accorded to universities, and a more independent court system provided further encouragement for those seeking a European-style society based on social classes rather than legal estates. But after the assassination of Alexander II in 1881, constitutional reform largely ended. Already, however, the reluctance of the regime to accommodate the political demands that its own reforms had set in motion persuaded some among the educated elite that revolution was the only alternative.

Revolutionaries before the Revolution

Given the overwhelming domination of Russian society by the state, the representatives of its various classes—nobility, bourgeoisie, and peasantry—were either unable or unwilling to mount an effective op-

position to the tsarist regime. That task fell instead to a group known as the *intelligentsia*. Well-educated individuals often drawn from the nobility or emerging professional groups, these people argued passionately about the nature of Russian society and the programs necessary for its regeneration. Western-style liberalism, with its emphasis on majority rule, constitutional government, and open politics, had some support among the *intelligentsia*. But since the government allowed no legal outlet for political expression, most members of the *intelligentsia* committed themselves to revolution by the mid-nineteenth century and to a form of communal peasant socialism, commonly called populism.

Despite a tradition of periodic peasant upheavals, the peasants of nineteenth-century Russia refused to cooperate in this idealized scheme. When in 1873–1874 thousands of students and intellectuals sought to rouse and enlighten the peasants, they found the peasants suspicious and inclined to turn their uninvited guests over to the police. And when small bands of frustrated revolutionaries turned to terror and assassination a few years later, the peasants still did not respond, not even when Tsar Alexander II was killed, in 1881. Here was the central problem of Russia's revolutionary elite: they could find no base of mass support able to turn their visions into reality.

No wonder, then, that the ideas of European Marxism were appealing when they began to circulate among the radical *intelligentsia* in the 1880s, for Marxism promised the growth of a class that would make the revolution: the urban industrial workers. Accepting that message meant giving up the utopianism of the Populists and dependence on the peasants. It also meant abandoning the use of terror and assassination and waiting for capitalism to develop modern industry and, with it, a revolutionary working class. But many were willing to make the adjustment, largely because Russia's own history seemed to be fulfilling Marx's prediction. As its industry grew, so too did the urban working class. Employed in large plants where they worked under horrendous conditions, the Russian proletariat of the 1890s became particularly militant and revolutionary, often engaging in large-scale strikes. Since the government frequently intervened in labor disputes on the side of factory owners, the workers soon demanded political change as well as economic gains. Marxist intellectuals, illegally organized in the Russian Social-Democratic Labor party (RSDLP) in 1898, soon became involved in workers' education, trade-union organizing, and, by 1905, insurrection.

But before it had to confront a real revolution, this embryonic party had to face the difficulties of applying Marx's theories, developed in Europe's most advanced industrial societies, to the conditions of a relatively backward country on the European periphery. In doing so, the party split irrevocably, with fateful consequences for the future.

The Marxist theory of history generally taught that all human societies moved in stages from feudalism through capitalism to socialism. Since Russia was, in this scheme of things, still in the feudal stage, Socialist revolutionaries should first work to establish a fully capitalist society by supporting, in Marxist terms, a bourgeois rather than a proletarian revolution. One faction of the RSDLP, known as the Mensheviks, or "minority," was willing to accept this uncomfortable role: to build a large, broadly based Socialist movement; to ally with the bourgeoisie to overthrow the tsar; and to create a liberal-democratic-capitalist regime. Only later, when Russian industrialization had been completed under capitalist auspices, would the country be ready for a Socialist takeover.

The other Marxist faction, called the Bolsheviks, or "majority," was led by Vladimir Ilyich Ulyanov, better known as Lenin. Born into a solid middle-class family and a lawyer by training, Lenin had been a man of ferocious revolutionary will ever since his brother was executed for conspiring to assassinate the tsar. Temperamentally unwilling to wait for history to unfold, Lenin sought to force its pace, to seize the moment, and to prepare actively and constantly for revolution. To this end, he advocated a small, highly disciplined party of dedicated professional revolutionaries who could act quickly, decisively, and ruthlessly. In part, this conception of the party was a response to existing conditions in Russia, where open political activity merely invited arrest. But it also reflected Lenin's distrust of the working class, which, he feared, could be lured away from revolution and socialism by mere economic gain. The party thus claimed to act as a "vanguard" of the proletariat and in the workers' best interests as interpreted by the party's leadership.

Nor would Lenin work with the bourgeoisie, for whom he had an active contempt and who were in any event a weak and timid force in tsarist Russia. Rather, he argued, Russia's small working class should find its allies among the peasantry, whose revolutionary potential he recognized. Thus, Lenin adapted Marxism to the unique conditions of Russia and so positioned the Bolsheviks to take advantage of the revolutionary moment when it arrived in 1917.

The Coming of the Revolution

By 1900, the strains of rapid change and continued intransigence by the state had reached the bursting point, and in 1905, following its defeat in a war with Japan, Russia erupted in spontaneous insurrection. Workers in Moscow and St. Petersburg went on strike and created their own representative councils, or "soviets." Peasant uprisings, student demonstrations, revolts of non-Russian nationalities, and mutinies in the military all contributed to the upheaval.

Recently formed political parties, representing intellectuals of various persuasions, came out into the open.

The 1905 revolution, though brutally suppressed, forced the regime to make more substantial reforms than it had ever contemplated. It granted in effect a constitution, legalized both trade unions and political parties, and permitted the election of a national legislative body, called the Duma. Further reforms followed. The tsar's chief minister, Petr Stolypin, took steps to foster an independent and prosperous class of peasant capitalist farmers, and by 1914, many peasants had consolidated their scattered holdings and begun to operate outside of the traditional village commune. Peasants' taxes were reduced and their redemption payments eliminated. Lenin feared that these reforms might create a conservative peasantry attached to the regime and thus doom the chances for revolution. Industrial development likewise continued at a rapid rate, so that by 1914, Russia stood fifth in the world in terms of overall output. Censorship was eased, and plans were under way for universal primary education.

Did 1905 mark the beginning of Russia's evolution into a constitutional monarchy and a capitalist democracy along European lines? Had it not been for the "accident" of World War I, which placed overwhelming pressures on this new and fragile order, might Russia have stabilized its society and avoided the trauma of revolution?

Probably not. Such an argument underestimates the profound fissures and conflicts of Russian society in the decade preceding World War I. Tsar Nicholas II dissolved the first two Dumas when they failed to agree with his programs, and he changed the electoral laws to favor the landed nobility. Thus, Russia still lacked a political system in which the people, even the middle class, had an effective voice. The representatives of the privileged classes had become so alienated by the government's intransigence that many felt revolution was inevitable.

Furthermore, in the major cities, industries grew rapidly, and labor unrest increased dramatically after 1910. In the first half of 1914, approximately 1.3 million workers, representing about 40 percent of the entire industrial work force, went out on strike. And among these increasingly militant workers, the more radical Bolsheviks were gaining support at the expense of the more moderate Mensheviks. The growing polarization of Russian society made it likely that revolution of some kind was not far off even had World War I not engulfed Russia and the rest of Europe.

1917: From March to November

The pressures of World War I provided the occasion, if not part of the fundamental cause, of the Russian Revolution. Crushing defeats, millions of casualties, and utterly incompetent leadership soon prompted calls for a new government, and by early 1917, major cities erupted in insurrection. When bread riots broke out in early March in the capital city of Petrograd (later renamed Leningrad), workers joined the street crowds, and soldiers sent to restore order refused to fire. There was simply no one left to defend the bankrupt regime. On March 15, 1917, the tsar abdicated the throne, and Russia entered a new era.

That Old Russia had collapsed amid the flames of war was not so surprising. More remarkable was that the revolution catapulted the Bolsheviks to power, for they were only one of many active political groups. Few would have predicted this outcome in March 1917. And many have subsequently charged that the Bolsheviks essentially "stole" the revolution by using their highly disciplined and well-organized party to seize power illegally, thus subverting what might otherwise have been a liberal-democratic revolution. This view of Russia's modern transformation serves to raise, though not necessarily to answer, the question of why the revolution turned out as it did.

Toward the Bolshevik Revolution

When the Russian monarchy fell, power was assumed by the Provisional government, which shortly became a coalition of leading liberals and representatives of the moderate Socialist parties. These leaders recognized themselves as only a temporary government and called for an elected Constituent Assembly to draw up a new constitution for the shattered country. Almost everyone expected that this would result in a European-style democratic government controlled by a coalition of the major parties, both Socialist and non-Socialist. In the meantime, the Provisional government proceeded to dismantle the old system and lay the foundation for a liberal order. All citizens received equality before the law; personal freedoms, including those of speech, assembly, religion, and the right to strike, became real for the first time in Russian history; local government was made more democratic; the eight-hour workday was declared for some workers; ethnic minorities were promised autonomy. It seemed as if Russia was finally on the road to a Western-style regime. But the Provisional government was unable to stabilize the country, and in less than a year the possibility of a democratic capitalist society in Russia had been swept away. Why?

Basically, because the fall of the old regime had unleashed a massive torrent of social upheaval, an elemental popular demand for radical change, with which the government proved unable to cope. In the face of this spontaneous upsurge of revolutionary fervor, the generally moderate and well-educated leaders of the Provisional government hesitated, acted indecisively, and by November were swept aside. The Bolsheviks who replaced them had certainly not created this mass convulsion, but they, and they alone, proved able to ride the tidal wave to power.

In the face of overwhelming demands for peace and increasing rates of desertion from the military, the Provisional government determined to continue the war and defend the homeland. As peasants began to seize the estates of the landlords, the government again temporized, urging them to wait until the Constituent Assembly could arrange for an orderly transfer of land. But the peasants would tolerate no delay, and throughout Russia in the summer and fall of 1917, they acted spontaneously through their village assemblies to seize landlords' estates and to distribute these lands according to traditional communal principles, with the poor and landless peasants receiving the greater share. Within a few months, the old nobility simply ceased to exist as a viable social group. The peasants in Russia made their own revolution, largely apart from urban-based political parties.

The popular mood in major industrial cities was equally revolutionary. The Petrograd Soviet, a body of about 1,500 deputies elected from the factories and military units of the capital city, regarded itself as a watchdog of the revolution and frequently coun-

Soldiers in St. Petersburg (then Petrograd) in 1917 hail the overthrow of the tsar with a sign reading "Down with the Old World." *The Granger Collection*

termanded or undermined the actions of the Provisional government. Local "soviets" appeared all over the country in an explosion of grass-roots organizing. New trade unions sprang up, and at the plant level "factory committees" began to exercise worker control in what were still privately owned businesses.

In an atmosphere of growing radicalism, the Provisional government seemed immobilized. The alliance between its liberal and Socialist members was increasingly strained. It faced threats from conservative forces eager to crush the radicals and from the street crowds equally eager for drastic revolutionary action. It was this situation that gave the Bolsheviks their opening. Untainted by association with the government, the Bolsheviks were growing rapidly in popularity and in numbers of party members. Their program, drawn up by Lenin, was far closer to the mood of the masses than that of the Provisional government. It called for immediate peace, confiscation of landowners' estates, and workers' control in the factories. In its slogan "All power to the Soviets," the

Bolsheviks were calling for the overthrow of the Provisional government and the beginning of class warfare. In November 1917, the Bolsheviks were probably right in thinking that they spoke for the working class. On that basis, Lenin insisted that the Bolsheviks seize formal state power from the increasingly unpopular Provisional government. On the night of November 6–7, they did precisely that.

The Legacy of 1917

The Bolshevik coup effectively ended any chance Russia may have had to establish a Western-style, bourgeois-capitalist regime. In any event, the rapidity of social change, the growing radicalism of the masses, and the weakness of Russia's middle class rendered that possibility unlikely.

But did the Bolshevik takeover lead directly and inevitably to dictatorship, terror, and the pervasive intrusions of the secret police? Did Lenin, in short, make Stalin necessary? Many scholars, first in the West and more recently in Russia itself, have argued the case. Lenin's concept of a single centralized and disciplined party; an "ends justify the means" morality; the early use of terror to defend the revolution; the urge for a total transformation of society; an unwillingness to enter coalitions with other parties— these have been cited as the seeds of Stalin's enormously oppressive dictatorship and his ruthless policies of development in the 1930s and later.

But the Bolshevik party was hardly monolithic. It was described by one of its leading members as a "negotiated federation between groups, groupings, factions and 'tendencies.'"[3] Furthermore, a considerable tradition of "proletarian democracy" within the party allowed for the expression of widely varying views. And on many important questions, such as an economic program for Socialist modernization, Lenin and the party had no clearly developed ideas at all upon coming to power. They spent the decade following 1917 hammering out such policies amid bitter internal disputes. Furthermore, many of their early decrees on the role of rural land committees, urban factory committees, and people's courts were quite democratic, although short-lived. What emerged as Stalinism in the 1930s was in many respects a sharp departure from the theory and practice of early Bolshevism.

Bolshevism, in short, put out many seeds.[4] Some flourished; others were nipped in the bud; and still others never took root at all. To understand the Stalinist outcome, we need to remember Russia's historical autocracy and the circumstances, both domestic and international, in which the Bolsheviks attempted to govern and transform their country.

From Lenin to Stalin: Building Socialism in the Soviet Union

From the perspective of world history, the Russian Revolution has had a double significance. First, it represented a direct challenge to the system of global imperialism erected by European states since the sixteenth century. The Russian Revolution sent a shudder of fear running through the capitalist world, and opposition to Bolshevism became the rallying cry of conservative forces almost everywhere. The forcible expansion of the Soviet system to Eastern Europe after World War II helped to trigger the Cold War. But the revolution was also an inspiration to those who were hostile to capitalism and those who sought to throw off European imperialist control. To both groups, socialism was now a massive political fact, embodied in a huge state, not simply a theory or movement. Lenin firmly believed that Russia was inaugurating a world revolution that would soon spread into the strongholds of capitalism in the West. The establishment of the Communist International in 1919 reflected that belief.

At the same time, the Soviet Union pioneered a new road to economic and social development that held out the promise of catching up to the West in short order and avoiding the inequalities and exploitation of capitalism in the process. Therein lay part of its attraction to many poorer societies. Because the Soviet Union was still extremely backward, the Bolsheviks, now called Communists, had to be modernizers concerned with industrial growth. Because they were Marxist revolutionaries, they were equally committed to creating a Socialist society. How to combine these two tasks was the central problem of Soviet history over the next three decades.

Civil War: 1918–1921

For the first three years of the new regime, everything took a back seat to mere survival as the country plunged into a bitter civil war. So unpopular had the Provisional government become that there was little initial resistance to the Bolshevik takeover. But when, in January 1918, the new government disbanded the Constituent Assembly, which had been called to draw up a constitution, it signaled its intention to create a one-party state and to establish "class rule" of the proletariat rather than majority rule involving several political parties. Soon the Bolsheviks' many enemies, ranging from reactionary tsarist officials to moderate Socialists, began largely uncoordinated military actions against the Communist government.

While the Communists, almost miraculously, emerged victorious by 1921, the civil war decisively marked the new regime. Since a number of Western powers, including Britain, France, and the United States, briefly entered the conflict against the government, the Communists came to fear capitalist encirclement, and in the decades to come they often used the threat of foreign intervention against the revolution to justify harsh internal policies. Furthermore, the experience of civil war made a heavy military imprint on what had been a largely civilian party and thus contributed to its authoritarianism, its inclination to use force, and its willingness to rule by decree. The revival of a secret police, the *Cheka*, and its use as an organ of terror, summary justice, and political control was an ominous sign of things to come, though regarded by the Communists as a temporary expedient.

The practical demands of the civil war and the ideological desire to move quickly to a Communist society combined to produce a highly centralized economic system called "war communism." It involved nationalization of large-scale industry, the abolition of free trade, and the forced requisition of grain from the peasants. But the system far outran the government's limited administrative capacity. Furthermore, the civil war had devastated the country's economy, sent industrial production plummeting to 20 percent of its 1913 level, scattered half of the urban working class to the villages, and created widespread famine. Active opposition from peasants, workers, and soldiers alike soon prompted the victorious but beleaguered Communists to change their strategy decisively.

"Liberal" Communism in the Making?

Lenin called it the New Economic Policy, or NEP, and it represented a sharp reversal of the policies followed during the civil war. Forced requisitions from the peasants ended, replaced by a system of regular taxation. Some twenty-five million peasant families were guaranteed tenure on their land, held as private property. Whereas the state controlled large-scale industry, banking, transportation, and foreign commerce, private merchants dominated retail trade; many small businesses were returned to private hands; and foreign investors were invited to participate in mining and manufacturing enterprises. Here was the world's first peacetime "mixed economy," combining some state ownership and overall government control with substantial elements of private enterprise. Rapid economic recovery ensued, with production reaching prewar levels by 1926.

As the state granted more freedom in the economic realm, it tightened Communist control over politics by effectively outlawing other parties and cracking down on dissent within the Communist party itself. But leadership was in the hands of an oligarchy of leading Communist party members, and they vigorously debated a wide range of issues.

Also associated with NEP was a far more relaxed cultural and intellectual climate, with much experimentation in theater, art, literature, and film-making. Utopian thinking and social experimentation proliferated as many people seemed to feel that the revolution had made all things possible. The whole atmosphere of NEP was one of gradualism and social harmony rather than radical upheaval and class conflict. In the aftermath of Stalin's harsh dictatorship of the 1930s, many remembered the 1920s as a golden age when a humane and relatively free Socialist society seemed possible. But could it last?

Certainly, many people welcomed NEP as a respite from the convulsions of revolution and civil war. Until his death in 1924, Lenin himself accepted the reformist and peaceful approach of NEP and said that it would be required "for a long time." To the program's major architect and spokesman, Nikolai Bukharin, NEP was necessary because it retained the support of the peasant majority and enabled the Soviet Union to "grow into socialism." It was desirable to Bukharin because it avoided the growth of an oppressive state apparatus.

Others had their doubts. To those Communists who remembered the bold action of November 1917 and the epic struggle of the civil war, NEP seemed tame and hardly revolutionary by comparison. Worse yet, it fostered a kind of creeping capitalism. Bukharin had told the peasants, "Enrich yourselves," and many dedicated Communists deeply feared that a class of rich peasants, or *kulaks,* was emerging. Finally, many believed that NEP meant a very slow pace toward industrialization and socialism. Bukharin had spoken of "tiny steps" and of moving "at a snail's pace," hardly encouraging to those with a vision of rapidly transforming their society.

Events further undermined support for NEP. A momentary threat of war with the capitalist powers in 1927 focused attention on the need for rapid growth in heavy industry, to meet military requirements. And a crisis in the procurement of grain in 1927–1928 raised questions about peasant hoarding and the productivity of small-scale agriculture. Internal and external threats coincided to produce widespread support within the party for more drastic and revolutionary action and a sharp change of course. In the rise to power of Joseph Stalin, that sentiment found a spokesman.

Many economists, then and later, felt that the New Economic Policy could have moved the Soviet Union toward modern industrialization and socialism just as quickly and with far less trauma than did Stalin's program in the 1930s. But political realities in the late 1920s did not permit the experiment in "liberal" communism to continue, and the Soviet Union moved to a "second Bolshevik revolution."

| Stalin and Stalinism

Unlike most other early Bolshevik leaders, Joseph Stalin (1879–1953) was from a humble background and had a limited education. He was rough and uncultured, whereas Lenin and Bukharin were cosmopolitan and intellectual. But Stalin was a shrewd and ambitious politician, and in the bitter factional struggles that followed Lenin's death, he used his position as general secretary of the party to eliminate his rivals. By 1929, he had emerged as the party's dominant leader.

The profound upheavals that Stalin set in motion in the late 1920s have often been described as a "revolution from above." Perhaps any minority party seeking to transform society radically, and particularly to create industrial socialism in an overwhelmingly peasant country, would be led to drastic actions and authoritarian policies. In that sense, Stalin was working out the "logic" of Lenin and the revolution of 1917–1921.

But Stalinism as a social and political program was something more than the legacy of Lenin. It had a quality of "excess," of "extraordinary extremism," that set it apart from early Bolshevism.[5] In this respect, Stalin perhaps drew on an even earlier Russian tradition, that of the reforming tsars, in his efforts to force the pace of change. Like Peter the Great, he sought frenetically to catch up to the West and to bind the country's population to the service of the state at the same time. In this sense, Stalinism was as much Russian as it was Marxist.

Rural Revolution from Above

The first major break with the gradualism of the NEP era was the decision in late 1929 to collectivize Soviet agriculture immediately. The Bolsheviks had always believed in large-scale collective farming as the ultimate Socialist goal, but throughout the 1920s, almost everyone agreed that this should be pursued gradually, peacefully, and voluntarily. However, the grain crisis, and its apparent threat to prospects for rapid industrialization, convinced Stalin that the state needed to seize control of agriculture. Local party and government officials were ordered to "persuade" village peasants to abandon their homesteads and join large collective farms. Where persuasion was not enough, the military arm of the secret police was called in, and by 1936, some 90 percent of the Soviet Union's peasants had been reorganized into some 200,000 collective farms. Singled out for particular attention were the *kulaks,* or rich peasants, who represented about 5 percent of the population and were frequently little more than hardworking and thrifty farmers. They became the objects of class warfare,

Joseph Stalin, leader of the Soviet Union from 1929 to 1953. *The Bettmann Archive*

were excluded from the collective farms, and were deported in large numbers to distant work locations, where many died.

To all of this there was massive resistance, which often took the form of killing large numbers of farm animals. But no coordinated peasant uprising occurred, and the government was soon collecting set amounts of grain and "industrial crops," which it used to feed urban workers and to export in exchange for industrial machinery. High grain quotas, particularly in the Ukraine, triggered famines in which millions perished during 1932–1933. For many, it was a second serfdom.

The Communist leadership no doubt believed that this enormous human suffering was a necessary price for economic progress. After all, the capital, or savings, necessary for industrial expansion, even in cap-

italist countries, had often been squeezed from the peasants, and the enclosure movement in England had displaced and uprooted many of them. The tragedy of Soviet collectivization is all the more poignant in light of modern scholarship, which suggests that this economic disaster required more resources than it generated and thus slowed down Soviet industrialization.[6]

Soviet-style Industrialization

Creating modern industry had always been a Bolshevik priority, both as a means of strengthening the country militarily against its capitalist neighbors and of increasing the social weight of the proletariat in a dominantly peasant society. But during the NEP years, a moderate pace of industrial growth prevailed, and production focused largely on consumer goods. By the late 1920s, Stalin had determined to break out of this gradual approach and launched a massive drive to "put an end to [Russian] backwardness." "We are fifty or one hundred years behind the advanced countries," he declared in 1931. "We must make good this distance in ten years. Either we do it or we shall perish."

The means to this great leap was state planning, total nationalization of industry, and a commitment to heavy industry as a first priority. It was the world's first modern industrial command economy. Thus, Soviet economic development differed sharply from that of the rest of Europe, which had relied largely on the market and private enterprise. Treating the country's economy as a whole, a first Five-Year Plan (1929–1932) and then a second (1933–1937) established overall goals and determined what items should be produced, in what quantities, and at what price. Based on estimates of requirements from local factories, the planning agency (*Gosplan*) tried to make available the right amount of raw materials, workers, and equipment. It was an enormous undertaking, and made even more so by political pressure to increase production targets unrealistically. The first Five-Year Plan, Stalin demanded, must be completed in four.

By any economic measure, it worked. Soviet industrial growth rates in the 1930s were high. Between 1928 and 1938, iron, steel, and coal production almost quadrupled. New cities and whole industries were created, and the urban work force grew rapidly. Much of this growth took place in the previously backward areas of Siberia and east of the Urals. By the end of the 1930s, the Soviet Union was clearly one of the world's modern industrial states. What had made this remarkable transformation possible?

In strictly economic terms, it was a matter of using labor and machinery more efficiently. Underutilized factories now operated twenty-four hours a day, and almost all able-bodied women worked full time outside the home. Furthermore, the planning process and an authoritarian state allowed the Soviet Union to concentrate its resources on heavy industry while sacrificing housing and other consumer production. Standards of living in both rural and urban areas fell sharply as the surplus for industrial investment was squeezed from the Soviet people. But there was also much genuine enthusiasm, as many workers and managers felt themselves part of a gigantic national effort to create a new Socialist society. Finally, there was the compulsion wielded by an all-powerful government and an omnipresent party. Managers who failed to meet quotas could be accused of sabotage or even treason, and millions found themselves in the forced-labor camps of the *Gulag,* which were administered by the secret police and were responsible for mining, construction, and industrial projects in the remote reaches of the Soviet Union.

The Modernization of Autocracy

Forced collectivization and the drive to industrialize were two legs of the Stalinist system; a third was the enormous growth and pervasive influence of centralized state power. Both state and party bureaucracies mushroomed, as did the secret police. Open debate within the party and press came to an end as ultimate power was centralized in the hands of Stalin, around whom a quasi-religious cult developed.

To some extent, political Stalinism is reminiscent of the autocracy of the tsars. Stalin himself believed that the Soviet people needed a "tsar substitute," and there is considerable evidence for widespread popular affection, even adulation and reverence, for the dictator. Russia's autocratic tradition meant that the concentration of power by itself was unlikely to provoke opposition, as the habit of deference to state authority was deeply ingrained in Russian political culture.

Furthermore, in Lenin's position as dominant leader of the party and in the Bolshevik conception of a highly disciplined and centralized organization, there was precedent for Stalin's growing dominance. And as the effort to mobilize the population and regulate the entire life of a huge country got under way in the 1930s, an authoritarian and intrusive state of some kind was almost inevitable.

But there are dimensions of Stalinism not fully explained by reference to Russian tradition, the legacy of Leninism, or the demands of the 1930s. Most notable was the Great Purge of 1936–1939, in which hundreds of thousands, and possibly millions, were arrested on charges of disloyalty (usually trumped-up charges) and then tried, convicted, and either executed or sent to the labor camps. In the process, virtually all of the old Bolsheviks associated with Lenin in 1917 were eliminated, as were the great majority of the leadership in government, party, industry, army, and police bureaucracies. An enormous and self-perpetuating wave of fear engulfed the country in 1937 and 1938, as citizens denounced one another for fear of being denounced themselves. A series of fantastic show trials featured prominent party officials confessing to a variety of horrendous and altogether unlikely crimes.

Explaining Stalin's terror has been difficult because it went so far beyond what was necessary to secure his power. There had been earlier party purges of politically unreliable people, and terror had been used against "class enemies," especially during the civil war, but never on such an enormous scale nor against the party's most dedicated members. Some were, of course, opposed to Stalin's policies, and there were efforts to remove him from office in 1934. Thus Stalin's own paranoia and drive for total power played a central role in creating the terror. But the purges developed their own momentum, for a large number of lower-ranking party elite benefited as their seniors were denounced and eliminated. Furthermore, the secret police sometimes had "quotas" of arrests that they were expected to fulfill. Real economic problems, a widespread belief in conspiracies to "wreck" the fragile Soviet economy, and antimanagerial feelings among factory workers all contributed to this Soviet horror of the 1930s.[7]

VOICES
Stalin's Victim

In the "thaw" that followed Stalin's death in 1953, the Soviet people and the world at large learned more about the horrors associated with his years in power. In the following account, Irina Kakhovskaya, an ardent revolutionary though not a member of the Bolshevik party, describes her arrest and interrogation. Like thousands of others, she was caught up in the terror of 1937–1938. After seventeen years in prisons and forced labor camps, she was freed in 1954. She wrote an account of her experiences, which she sent to Soviet authorities.

Early on the morning of February 8, 1937, a large group of men appeared at the door of our quiet apartment in Ufa. We were shown a search warrant and warrants for our arrest. The search was carried out in violent, pogrom-like fashion and lasted all day. Books went pouring down from the shelves; letters and papers, out of boxes. They tapped the walls and, when they encountered hollow spots, removed the bricks. Everything was covered with dust and pieces of brick. . . .

[At the prison] everything was aimed at breaking prisoners' spirits immediately, intimidating and stupifying them, making them feel that they were no longer human, but "enemies of the people," against whom everything was permitted. All elementary human needs were disregarded (light, air, food, rest, medical care, warmth, toilet facilities). . . .

In the tiny, damp, cold, half-lit cell were a bunk and a half bunk. The bunk was for the prisoner under investigation and on the half bunk, their legs drawn up, the voluntary victims, the informers from among the common criminals, huddled together. Their duty was never to let their neighbor out of their sight, never to let the politicals communicate with one another . . . and above all to prevent the politicals from committing suicide. . . . The air was fouled by the huge wooden latrine bucket. . . . No books were allowed and . . . prisoners had to sit on the bunk facing the guard's peephole so that authorities could be sure the "enemies of the people" never slumbered or dozed.

The interrogation began on the very first night. . . . Using threats, endearments, promises and enigmatic hints, they tried to confuse, wear down, frighten, and break the will of each individual, who was kept totally isolated from his or her comrades. . . . Later stools were removed and the victim had to simply stand for hours on end. . . .

At first it seemed that the whole thing was a tremendous and terrible misunderstanding, that it was our duty to clear it up. . . . But it soon became apparent that what was involved was deliberate ill will and the most cynical possible approach to the truth. . . .

In the interrogation sessions, I now had several investigators in a row, and the "conveyor belt" questioning would go on for six days and nights on end. . . . Exhaustion reached the ultimate limit. The brain, inadequately supplied with blood, began to misfunction. . . . "Sign! We won't bother you any more. We'll give you a quiet cell and a pillow and you can sleep. . . ." That was how the investigator would try to bribe a person who was completely debilitated and stupified from lack of sleep.

Each of us fought alone to keep an honest name and save the honor of our friends, although it would have been far easier to die than to endure this hell month after month. Nevertheless the accused remained strong in spirit and, apart from the unfortunate Mayorov, not one real revolutionary did they manage to break.

Source: Excerpts from "Our Fate" by Irina Kakhovskaya are reprinted from *An End to Silence: Uncensored Opinion in the Soviet Union* from Roy Medvevev's underground magazine *Political Diary,* edited by Stephen F. Cohen, translated by George Saunders, by permission of W.W. Norton & Company, Inc. Copyright © 1982 by W.W. Norton & Company, Inc.

Assessing Stalin's Revolution

To what extent did Stalin's revolution from above succeed in ending Soviet backwardness and in creating socialism? After centuries of frustrating efforts to catch up to the West, Stalin brought the Soviet Union decisively into the ranks of the world's great powers by modern industrial and military standards. The supreme test of that success was, of course, World War II, in which the Soviet Union suffered far more than most others, endured the worst that Germany could inflict, and pushed the Nazis back into central Europe and defeat. The Soviet Union emerged from that conflict one of two superpowers and maintained that status for forty years, though at the price of its consumer economy. Despite the horrors of the 1930s, many ordinary Soviet citizens took great pride in this accomplishment. Success in war legitimized the Stalinist system even as failure in war had earlier undermined the tsarist regime.

Other aspects of Soviet modernization also moved forward rapidly. Within a generation, the percentage of urban dwellers jumped from 15 percent to 55 percent, an accomplishment that took fully a century in the United States. Literacy rates rose from 51 percent in 1926 to 81 percent in 1938, as a network of elementary schools covered the country. However, Soviet agriculture remained stagnant and inefficient, and living standards recovered only slowly from their precipitous fall in the 1930s. Table 9.1 provides some indication of Stalinist economic priorities and of who paid for rapid industrialization.

Whatever its achievements, Soviet industrialization imposed enormous human suffering: the agonies of collectivization, the forced labor camps, the Great Purge, falling standards of living, the almost complete absence of personal freedom, and sharp restrictions on cultural expression. It also exacted a huge environmental cost. A commitment to rapid development of gigantic enterprises, a belief that the country's huge size minimized ecological damage, a state-dominated society that allowed little critical feedback, the widespread use of toxic agricultural chemicals—all of this contributed to enormous environmental damage that became widely known only much later. By 1990, some seventy million Soviet urban dwellers had to breathe seriously polluted air, while 75 percent of the country's surface water was polluted.[8]

Table 9.1: Soviet Development, 1928–1940

Category	1940 Output (as a percent of 1928)
Industrial production	263%
Industrial materials	343
Ferrous metals	433
Electric power	964
Chemicals	819
Machinery	486
Consumer goods	181
Agricultural production	105
Crops	123
Animal products	88
Individual consumption per capita	93
Real wages	54
Capital stock	286
Urban housing space per capita	78

Source: David Mackenzie and Michael Curran, *A History of Russia and the Soviet Union* (Chicago: Dorsey Press, 1987), p. 670.

Did Soviet economic success, at whatever cost, add up to socialism? In substituting state planning and ownership for the market mechanism, Stalin's regime had eliminated capitalism. In doing so, it eliminated or minimized some of the evils of early industrial capitalism—cycles of expansion and contraction, unemployment, and child labor. While the capitalist West was enduring the Depression of the 1930s, the Soviet Union was moving dramatically ahead in industrial growth. Furthermore, the working class gained considerably in terms of social mobility, and in the early 1930s alone, probably 1.5 million workers moved into white-collar jobs. These were among the beneficiaries and supporters of the Stalinist regime.

However, the elimination of capitalism and the fostering of social mobility do not by themselves create the kind of Socialist society that Marx and Lenin had envisaged. The ending of class privileges and a steady movement toward social equality have always been touchstones of socialism. By that standard, Stalinism fell far short. Although inequalities due to unearned income no longer existed, Stalin encouraged inequalities among workers by paying skilled labor at a far higher rate and by using piecework and bonuses to encourage production. Furthermore, earnings on collective farms were far lower than those of urban workers. After Stalin's death in 1953, those inequities narrowed. But a new and highly privileged class of party leaders, industrial managers, and high-level bureaucrats also arose. With a far higher standard of living and considerable prestige, they were the new elite of Soviet society. But their status was highly insecure, for it rested on their official positions, which could be taken away, rather than on private property, which supported the capitalist elite of the West.

Another Socialist ideal has been internationalism. Blaming national rivalries on capitalist competition, Marx and others assumed that revolution would diminish narrow and antagonistic nationalisms. Lenin and the early Bolsheviks all believed that their revolution would trigger Socialist upheavals in the more advanced states of Europe and thus give rise to a Socialist commonwealth. As it became apparent that no such things would happen, the Soviet Union had to depend wholly on its own resources to create a Socialist society. Surrounded by hostile capitalist nations, it drew increasingly upon its Russian past. Stalin saw himself in the tradition of the tsars Ivan and Peter, who were now interpreted in Soviet history books as Russian heroes and early modernizers. And in the flames of World War II, it was the call to defend traditional Russia rather than the revolution that produced the heroic resistance of the Soviet people.

Most of the non-Russian people within the Soviet Union had only a weakly developed sense of nationality in 1917. But Soviet policies themselves helped to create growing national consciousness, rather than the all-Soviet patriotism that had been expected. The principle of nationality was embedded in the very structure of the country, for each of the fifteen "union republics" was associated with a particular national group. Furthermore, the literacy campaigns of the Stalinist era made use of local languages, though requiring Russian as a second language. And the Communist party encouraged the growth of national elites in the various republics. As national consciousness grew, so too did grievances against the central government, which seemed to be run largely by Russians. These tensions, kept under strict control during most of Soviet history, exploded in the Gorbachev era and contributed much to the collapse of the Soviet Union.

Finally, Socialists since Marx imagined that the state would wither away in the aftermath of revolution and that personal freedoms and democracy would be enlarged. But in the Soviet Union, an enormous growth of state functions and power was the primary means for creating socialism itself. Here was perhaps one of the tragedies of Soviet socialism. Coming to power *before* capitalism had created a modern industrial society, the Socialist regime was required to undertake that onerous task itself, and in the process it created an all-powerful state that undermined the very possibilities of a free, humane, and democratic socialism.

From *Gulag* to *Glasnost*

Even within the limits of the Soviet Union's "premature" socialism, there had been alternatives—the relatively moderate and reformist policies of the NEP era and the harshly repressive dictatorial regime of Stalin. After Stalin's death in 1953, the struggle between these two approaches represented the major conflict in Soviet political life.

The reformist tradition surfaced in the years of Nikita Khrushchev's rule (1954–1964), during which the most repressive aspects of the Stalinist system were dismantled. In a dramatic speech in 1956, Khrushchev openly denounced many of the crimes, excesses, and errors of Stalin to a stunned audience of party leaders. A few years later, the Central Committee removed Stalin's body from the mausoleum, where it had lain alongside that of Lenin. Accompanying these measures of de-Stalinization were the end of mass terror, the release of millions from the prison camps of the *Gulag,* and the exoneration of millions of others, now dead, from crimes they had never committed. Khrushchev's efforts to revitalize the Communist party and to increase its responsiveness to the people involved the ousting and reshuffling of many officials and frequent attacks on bureaucrats who refused to dirty their hands with day-to-day problems. He moved the entire Ministry of Agriculture from Moscow to a state farm some one hundred kilometers from the capital, to ensure that officials were in closer touch with the real life of Soviet farmers. The relaxation of controls on cultural and intellectual expression were likewise part of a limited "thaw" associated with Khrushchev's years in power. For many, those reforms recalled the policies of the NEP and the less oppressive atmosphere of the 1920s.

In the economic realm, consumer industries and agriculture were given a higher priority than ever before, which set the stage for substantial increases in Soviet standards of living over the next several decades. Wages rose; health and education services expanded; the workweek was shortened and vacations were extended; and economic inequalities narrowed. What made these gains possible was a quite rapid rate of economic growth in the 1950s and 1960s. As part of his effort to foster rapid growth, Khrushchev pushed a spectacular decentralization of the administrative bureaucracy that managed the Soviet economy, and he even permitted discussion of experimenting with the profit motive.

Although none of these reforms called into question the basic elements of the Soviet system (central planning and the dominant role of the Communist party), they were more than enough to provoke a widespread conservative opposition to Khrushchev. A violent anti-Communist uprising in Hungary in 1956 seemed to suggest that political reform could easily get out of hand, and administrative decentralization proved threatening to established bureaucratic elites. Experiments with market mechanisms and economic liberalization likewise offended orthodox Communists who greatly feared any compromise with capitalist practices. And many in the party hierarchy were increasingly uneasy with Khrushchev's impulsive style of leadership and "harebrained" reforms. This conservative backlash to Khrushchev's regime, together with the Soviet Union's humiliation in the Cuban missile crisis in 1962, contributed to his peaceful removal from office in 1964.

What followed was "Russia's first truly conservative era since the revolution."[9] The dramatic, if often ill-planned, reforms of the Khrushchev years ended. A crackdown on Soviet intellectuals followed. Under the slogan of "stability in cadre," officials in party and government bureaucracies were guaranteed almost lifetime positions, a security for which they desperately yearned after the upheavals of the Stalin and Khrushchev eras. This resulted in a Soviet gerontocracy, and by the 1970s, much of the leadership of the country was in the hands of men in their sixties and seventies. An important expression of this new conservatism in Soviet life lay in a partial rehabilitation of the discredited Stalin. Books, articles, and the public media praised his wartime leadership and the heroic accomplishments of Soviet industrialization, while omitting almost completely any reference to the purges, terror, and crimes that Khrushchev had so clearly revealed.

But Khrushchev's successor, Leonid Brezhnev, was no Stalin, and there was no return to the days of mass terror and the *Gulag*. It was rather a regime of bureaucratic privilege, widespread corruption among officials, and great cynicism and disbelief among the educated public. The increasingly apparent discrepancy between the official Soviet ideology of Socialist progress and the reality of official privilege drained away much of the regime's support and caused many people to lead almost schizophrenic lives, mouthing the party line in public, while harboring private doubts at home.

Beneath the stable surface of the Brezhnev regime, however, lay a number of trends that produced a revival of Communist reform in the 1980s. The most important was a slowing of economic growth—from more than 5 percent a year in the 1950s and 1960s to almost zero by the 1980s. The need to import substantial amounts of grain from the early 1970s on testified to the continuing inefficiency of Soviet agriculture. Other signs of economic stagnation could be found in growing infant-mortality rates, long lines in front of stores, a flourishing black market, and considerable dissatisfaction with an economy that could not provide the goods that the Communist party continued to promise. What had happened?

Maintaining its status as a military superpower required the country to spend over 20 percent of its GNP (gross national product) on the military, which was a drain on economic growth, especially in the consumer sector. So too were heavy government subsidies for cheap apartments and inexpensive food. It was perhaps good socialism, but poor investment policy. A highly centralized and bureaucratized economy may have worked in the early stages of heavy industrial growth, but mass consumption, electronics, and computerized information systems required decentralized decision making and individual creativity, far removed from the rigid Soviet system. It was possible to command the construction of effective steel mills, but not the writing of imaginative computer programs. Finally, there were few incentives for hard work in a system where wages were relatively fixed, jobs secure, and goods in short supply. A famous Soviet quip about the relationship between the state and its employees made the point: "We pretend to work and they pretend to pay us."

But while the economy was stagnating, the Soviet Union was becoming a much more highly educated and urbanized society, quite different from the largely rural and peasant society over which Stalin and even Khrushchev had ruled. A growing professional middle class sought a much greater degree of personal freedom and in so doing created a variety of unofficial organizations to express their new desires. Informal contacts among scholars, thousands of jazz and rock music groups, associations of private tutors in major cities, the passing of banned manuscripts from person to person, coalitions of writers and officials concerned about ecological issues, groups of political dissidents to monitor human rights violations, to say nothing of a vast and ingenious underground economy—all of this reflected a dynamic social vitality that contrasted sharply with the stagnation of the official ideology and economy. Here was a basis of social support for the initial stages of the Gorbachev reforms.

A variety of international conditions also strengthened the hand of reform elements within the Communist party. In both Eastern Europe and China, Communist regimes had undertaken substantial reforms or were under pressure to do so. Furthermore, Brezhnev's expansionist foreign policy and his military buildup contributed to a new round of Cold War hostilities in the early 1980s, to a further spiral in the arms race, and to the country's deepening isolation in the world.

The Second Russian Revolution

The continuing strength of the reformist wing in Soviet official circles became apparent after the death of Brezhnev in 1982, and particularly with the rise to power of Mikhail Gorbachev in 1985. Much younger and better educated than the Brezhnev generation, Gorbachev proclaimed *glasnost* ("openness") and *perestroika* ("restructuring") as his central themes and promoted reforms that recalled in some respects those of the Khrushchev years. *Glasnost* meant a candid admission of the corruption, inefficiency, and stagnation of Soviet society and economy generally,

as well as the need for substantial changes to address problems of crime, poverty, health care, and education that amounted to a national crisis. Books, plays, and films, many of them highly critical of the Stalinist and Brezhnev regimes, were presented to a public hungry for the truth about their country. Cultural and intellectual life became more open than at any time since the 1920s, with everything from religious literature to pornography available on the streets. The cumulative impact of these revelations eroded what little legitimacy the Soviet state still had.

To shake up an entrenched party bureaucracy and a major obstacle to reform, Gorbachev promoted a kind of democracy that included, by 1989, multicandidate elections for a new parliament in which many big Communist bosses lost decisively. The televised sessions of this Congress of People's Deputies, full of vigorous debate and open conflict, held the nation spellbound. When Article 6 of the Soviet constitution was abolished, the Communist party lost its legal standing as the sole political party in the country. The declining prestige of the party was reflected after 1989 in a growing exodus of its members.

To create an international environment conducive to the renewal of Soviet society, Gorbachev acted to revive détente with the West and made substantial concessions in arms-control agreements with the United States. He eased the country out of its debilitating entanglement in Afghanistan and sought to cooperate with the United States in other regional "hot spots" in the developing nations. Most importantly, he permitted, even encouraged, the East European revolutions of 1989, which swept away Soviet-imposed Communist governments and tore down the hated Berlin Wall, perhaps the most potent symbol of the Cold War.

At the heart of the Gorbachev reform program was economic revival. It began slowly, with an effort to tighten up the old system and make it more efficient. But by 1987, more substantial measures emerged as the party approved major reductions in the role of the central-planning bureaucracy and granted much greater authority to the managers of the country's 48,000 enterprises. In addition, small privately owned businesses were permitted, as were joint ventures with Western firms. Permission to lease agricultural land on a long-term basis was established, though few people had the incentive or sufficient confidence in the government to be-

Thousands of Muscovites defended the Gorbachev regime against the instigators of the August 1991 coup. Here they build barricades around the Russian parliament building, known as the "White House." *The Bettmann Archive*

come private farmers. In 1989–1990, there was widespread discussion of even more radical reforms that would lead to a full market economy with private property and free prices. By then, however, substantial opposition to the reforms had gained momentum.

Like Franklin Roosevelt during America's Great Depression, Gorbachev sought to save the Soviet system by purging its abuses and renewing it from within. He certainly never intended to destroy it. But his efforts to reform the country provoked sharp opposition, especially from the party hierarchy that had benefited most from the old system and was in a position to delay or sabotage reformist efforts. Furthermore, by 1989, the economic situation began to deteriorate sharply as goods became more scarce, prices higher, and lines longer. The old command economy gradually eroded, though a functioning market economy was by no means available to replace it. In such a setting, Gorbachev was vulnerable to criticism for going too fast and for not going fast or far enough. Growing numbers of people sought not simply to reform communism, but to end it. Gorbachev's "revolution from above" had opened the door for contradictory forces from "below."

In addition, ethnic tensions within the multinational Soviet Union mounted rapidly. Democracy and *glasnost* provided an opportunity for non-Russian nationalities to express a variety of long-held grievances: the Baltic republics of Lithuania, Estonia, and Latvia had been conquered by Stalin in 1939 after a cynical deal with Hitler and insisted on official recognition of that fact; extensive cotton cultivation in Uzbekistan had created ecological disaster; within the borders of Azerbaijan lay a substantial number of Armenians who desperately wanted to be part of the neighboring Armenian Republic; Ukrainians feared losing their language and culture in a slow process of Russification; some twenty-five million Russians lived, frequently as privileged minorities, outside the borders of the Russian Republic. These and many other fears were expressed in a rising tide of demands for greater autonomy or complete independence. Critics could argue that the Gorbachev reforms not only undermined socialism and ruined the economy, but also put the unity of the country itself at risk (see Map 9.2).

In the face of these criticisms, Gorbachev vacillated, sometimes siding with the conservatives and other times seeking even more radical reforms. Matters came to a head in August 1991, when a group of

MAP 9. 2 The "Former Soviet Union"

party conservatives, backed by elements of the armed forces, staged a coup and detained Gorbachev himself. Faced by considerable public opposition in Moscow and St. Petersburg and universal international condemnation, the poorly planned coup collapsed within only three days. But by the end of the year the country and the Communist system had collapsed as well. The events of August 1991 completely discredited the old system and its defenders. They also gave a great boost of confidence and momentum to radical reformers within Russia, led by Boris Yeltsin, as well as to various nationalist movements that wanted out of the Soviet Union altogether. The Communist party was soon dissolved and the various republics of the old Union declared their independence, joining only in an amorphous Commonwealth of Independent States to coordinate military

and economic policy. When the red flag of the Soviet Union was lowered for the last time from the Kremlin on December 25, 1991, one of the modern world's great states and a seventy-four-year experiment in Communist modernization came to an inglorious end.

Explaining the Soviet Collapse

Why did the Soviet Union collapse? And how did it occur so peacefully? A starting point in dealing with these questions is to ask how the system managed to last so long. After all, the Soviet Union was the world's last empire, and its survival in an era of fierce nationalist passions is remarkable. What held the Soviet Union together, of course, was the Communist party and its pervasive control over all aspects of life. When Gorbachev sought to revitalize a stagnating economy, he found it necessary to attack the party leadership, which controlled and benefited from the existing economic arrangements. *Glasnost* and democratization were his means of loosening party control over the economy, but they also weakened and divided the only institution that provided the glue for an extremely varied society. When frightened party conservatives launched the abortive coup in August 1991, they soon discovered they had little active support among the general public or even in the security forces of the country. Thus, there was no way to counteract the nationalist and anti-Communist forces that had grown so rapidly in the Gorbachev era. The Soviet system died; it did not have to be killed.[10]

The significance of the Soviet collapse and the issues it raised can hardly be overestimated. It disclosed the bankruptcy of highly centralized Socialist approaches to economic development and, at least for the moment, left liberal democratic capitalism triumphant in the global competition of social systems. It brought an end to the Cold War that had structured so much of international life since 1945. But did that mean the North–South division between rich and poor nations could be addressed more decisively or be more readily ignored?

Furthermore, the disappearance of the Soviet Union and of its control in Eastern Europe unleashed furious national and ethnic passions that had been heretofore submerged, posing the question of political order in a vital region of the world. How would the world deal with close to twenty new states emerging from the confines of the former Soviet Union, Yugoslavia, and Czechoslovakia, many of which had serious ethnic problems themselves? There emerged as well a new and enormous item on the historical agenda of the 1990s and beyond: Can former Communist states make an effective transition to a market economy and to a democratic political system? Finally, the Soviet collapse reminded us, should we need the lesson, of the impermanence of human social creations and the unexpectedness of the historical process. For a central fixture of the modern world—the Russian Empire and Soviet state—had vanished.

Notes

1. Richard Pipes, *Russia under the Old Regime* (New York: Scribner's, 1974), p. 220.

2. Mark Raeff, *The Well-Ordered Police State* (New Haven: Yale University Press, 1983), p. 217.

3. Quoted in Stephen F. Cohen, *Bukharin and the Bolshevik Revolution* (New York: Knopf, 1973), p. 5.

4. For this analogy and general line of argument, see Stephen F. Cohen, *Rethinking the Soviet Experience* (New York: Oxford University Press, 1985), esp. chap. 2.

5. Ibid., p. 48.

6. James Millar, *The ABCs of Soviet Socialism* (Urbana: University of Illinois Press, 1981), chap. 1.

7. J. Arch Getty and Roberta T. Manning, eds., *Stalinist Terror: New Perspectives* (New York: Cambridge University Press, 1993), pp. 1–18.

8. Murray Feshbach and Alfred Friendly, Jr., *Ecocide in the USSR* (New York: Basic Books, 1992), pp. 2–3.

9. Stephen F. Cohen, *Sovieticus: American Perceptions and Soviet Realities* (New York: Norton, 1986), p. 53.

10. Theodore Draper, "Who Killed Soviet Communism?" *New York Review of Books,* 11 June 1992, pp. 7–14.

Comparative Essay
THE DEVELOPMENT DEBATE

Development is apparently the one thing on which virtually all modern societies agree. Everyone wants it. At least since World War II, many countries, particularly in the developing world, have sought this elusive quality quite deliberately. It has been considered the key to national independence or even survival in a highly competitive world; it has been the means to a higher standard of living; it has been a major source of legitimacy for governments everywhere; and it is at the heart of what it means to be modern. But there has been considerable debate about what development means and how to measure it, let alone about how to achieve it. How can we tell if a society is developing? How can we compare various societies in terms of achieving development?

The earliest and still the most prominent of the measures created by economists involves per-capita gross national product (GNP). It is a dollar figure that represents the quantity of goods and services per person produced in one year in a particular country. Thus, according to World Bank statistics, in 1990 Mozambique had the world's lowest per-capita GNP at $80, while Switzerland had the highest at $32,680. But often we are less interested in the size of per-capita GNP than in how rapidly it is growing. Between 1965 and 1990, for example, China's economy grew at an average per-capita rate of 5.8 percent per year, and India's at 1.9 percent, whereas the large

African country of Zaire had a negative annual growth rate of 2.2 percent.[1] This means that Zaire's economy contracted sharply over this period of time. Table 1 presents the recent growth experience of major areas of the world.

However, many scholars are critical of defining development solely in terms of economic growth as measured by GNP. Such figures, they argue, fail to consider subsistence production that is not marketed as well as much of women's household work. Even more important, per-capita GNP says nothing about who benefits from economic growth. By the 1960s, it was apparent that economic growth alone failed to improve the actual living conditions of impoverished people in many developing countries. According to economist Dudley Seers:

> The questions to ask about a country's development are therefore: What has been happening to poverty? What has been happening to unemployment? What has been happening to inequality? If all three of these have declined from high levels, then beyond doubt this has been a period of development. If one or two of these central problems have been growing worse, especially if all three have, it would be strange to call the result "development" even if per-capita income doubled.[2]

Other measures have been created to assess the extent to which economic growth is making a dent in mass poverty. The most important of these are measures of infant mortality, life expectancy, and illiteracy rates. These "welfare indicators" provide a more

Table 1 Growth of Real Per-capita Income in Industrial and Developing Countries, 1960–1990

Country Group	1960–1970	1970–1980	1980–1990
High-income countries	4.1%	2.4%	2.4%
Developing countries	3.3	3.0	1.2
Sub-Saharan Africa	0.6	0.9	−0.9
Asia and the Pacific	2.5	3.1	5.1
East Asia	3.6	4.6	6.3
South Asia	1.4	1.1	3.1
Middle East and North Africa	6.0	3.1	−2.5
Latin America and the Caribbean	2.5	3.1	−0.5

Source: World Bank. *World Development Report, 1992* (New York: Oxford University Press, 1992), p. 32.

direct measure of the extent to which economic growth is translated into a better life for the vast majority of the population. In addition, the impact of development on women has been a growing concern among scholars and officials alike, as women's organizations and movements have increasingly made their presence felt. Table 2 presents some recent data on various indicators for a number of countries.

In recent decades people have become more sensitive about the ecological consequences of modern development. As a result, economists and others have struggled to find ways to take account of environmental damage, deforestation, and polluted waters in their thinking about development. By the 1980s, the term *sustainable development* had become a shorthand way of describing a pattern of economic growth that could minimize mass poverty and respect the environment at the same time. Today it represents development for "meeting the needs of the present generation without compromising the needs of future generations."[3] Thus it injects the issues of gen-

erational justice as well as social justice into the development debate.

A final element in the development debate revolves around the question of human rights and political freedoms. While China's performance on most measures of economic development and social welfare has been substantially better than India's (see Table 2), its highly controlled and repressive political system has not permitted the free expression of individual views. Indian democracy, despite sometimes violent conflict among its culturally diverse peoples, has generally protected the political and civil rights of its people. But it is difficult to factor these important differences into an overall evaluation of Indian and Chinese development.

To complicate matters even further, there is considerable disagreement as to the meaning of "human rights" and their relationship to economic development. The West has generally defined such rights in terms of political and civil freedoms, including the right to vote and organize politically, the right to free

Table 2 Development Indicators for Several Countries

Development Indicator	Country							
	China	India	Republic of Korea	Nigeria	Zaire	Egypt	Mexico	Brazil
Average annual population growth, 1980–1990 (percent)	1.4%	2.1%	1.1%	3.2%	3.2%	2.4%	2.0%	2.2%
Per-capita GNP, 1990 ($U.S.)	$370	$350	$5,400	$290	$220	$600	$2,490	$2,680
Average annual growth in per-capita GNP, 1965–1990 (percent)	5.8%	1.9%	7.1%	0.1%	−2.2%	4.1%	2.8%	3.3%
Life expectancy (years)	70	59	71	52	52	60	70	66
Infant mortality (number of deaths before age 1 per 1,000 live births)								
1965	90	150	62	162	141	145	82	104
1990	29	92	17	98	94	66	39	57
Adult illiteracy (percent)	27%	52%	0%	49%	28%	52%	13%	9%
Urban population (as a percent of total)								
1965	18%	19%	32%	17%	26%	41%	55%	50%
1990	56%	27%	72%	35%	40%	47%	73%	75%
Population per physician, 1984	1,010	2,520	1,160	6,410	13,540	770	—	1,080
Females per 100 males in secondary school								
1965	47	35	59	43	15	41	53	93
1989	71	54	87	75	43	77	90	—

Source: Adapted from World Bank, *World Development Report, 1992* (New York: Oxford University Press, 1992).

expression of religious and political views, and the right to be treated equally under the law. Human rights, in the Western view, are fundamental to a good society, whatever its economic and social conditions. Furthermore, some argue that these rights provide a means for poor and oppressed people to gain a greater share of their country's wealth by putting political pressure on the established system. The improvements in the lives of working people in Europe and the United States under the pressure of collective bargaining and political action are a case in point. Restrictions on freedom of expression have arguably worsened conditions of famine or environmental disaster by preventing authorities from getting accurate information and by eliminating public pressure at the ballot box. China's famine in 1958–1960 and Russia's terrible ecological situation have no doubt been exacerbated by the absence of democratic feedback.

However, many spokespersons in developing countries have argued that for societies attempting to overcome poverty, the legacy of colonialism, and an unfair world economy, the meaning of "human rights" lies not so much in individual political and civil freedoms but in economic and social development. Especially before 1945, Japanese authorities justified an authoritarian state on the grounds that it promoted efficiency and public order, which made rapid economic and military growth possible. African leaders after independence often criticized political democracy for encouraging ethnic conflict and thereby undermining the possibilities of economic growth. In a 1991 statement, the Chinese government claimed that the "foremost human right" was the right to subsistence and that enabling people "to eat their fill" was the primary duty of developing countries.[4] All of this implied that the Western view of human rights was culturally biased and that political and civil rights might have to be curbed to fulfill more pressing social and economic rights. In practical terms, many leaders of developing nations deeply resented Western efforts to link progress on human rights issues with economic aid and trade relations.

In some ways the development debate is but a continuation of that ancient philosophical discussion about the nature of a good life or a good society. It raises questions about the relative importance of material well-being and personal freedom and about the relationship between them. It touches on the enduring tension between the aspirations of the individual soul and the claims of society. And it provokes reflection on the possibility of defining universal human values, as opposed to those associated with particular cultures or historical situations. The debate continues.

Notes

1. World Bank, *World Development Report, 1992* (New York: Oxford University Press, 1992), p. 32.

2. Dudley Seers, "The Meaning of Development," *Eleventh World Conference of the Society for International Development* (New Delhi, 1969), p. 3.

3. World Bank, *Report, 1992,* p. 8.

4. *Human Rights Tribune* 3:3 (Fall 1992).

SUGGESTIONS FOR FURTHER READING: EUROPE'S EXTENSIONS

The United States

Bluestone, Barry, and Robert Harrison. *The Deindustrialization of America.* 1982. (An analysis of the weakening of the American economy.)

Boorstin, Daniel. *The Americans: The Colonial Experience.* 1958. (An imaginative survey of North American colonial culture that centers on the impact of the American wilderness on European "blueprints.")

Brown, Richard D. *Modernization: The Transformation of American Life, 1600–1865.* 1976. (A controversial attempt to explain most of American history up to the Civil War in terms of a single concept.)

Genovese, E. D. *Roll Jordan Roll.* 1974. (A survey of slavery in American history.)

Heilbroner, Robert, and Aaron Miller. *The Economic Transformation of America.* 1984. (A highly readable narrative of American economic history.)

Phillips, Kevin. *The Politics of the Rich and the Poor.* 1990. (An analysis of the growth of inequality in the United States during the 1980s.)

Tocqueville, Alexis de. *Democracy in America.* 1956. (A classic study of American "equality" from the perspective of a young French aristocrat writing in the 1830s.)

Woodward, C. Vann, ed. *The Comparative Approach to American History.* 1968. (A series of essays that place the American experience alongside that of other societies.)

Zinn, Howard. *A People's History of the United States.* 1980. (A survey of American history emphasizing the sweep of popular forces and de-emphasizing the achievements of "great men.")

Latin America

Black, Jan Knippers, ed. *Latin America: Its Problems and Its Promise.* 1984. (A collection of readings covering the themes addressed in this chapter.)

Burns, E. Bradford. *Latin America: A Concise Interpretive History.* 1986. (A convenient, comprehensive, and up-to-date reference.)

Cardos, Fernando Henrique, and Enzo Faletto. *Dependency and Development in Latin America.* 1979. (The basic work on dependency theory applied to Latin America.)

Donghi, Tulio Halperin. *The Contemporary History of Latin America.* 1993. (A historical account from a Latin American perspective.)

Harris, Marvin. *Patterns of Race in the Americas.* 1964. (An anthropologist's provocative comparison of race relations in the United States and Latin America.)

Hemming, J. *Amazon Frontier.* 1987. (Chronicles the defeat of native peoples in Brazil.)

Josephy, A. M., Jr. *America in 1492.* 1992. (An examination of Native American peoples of both North and South America.)

Leon-Portilla, M., ed. *The Broken Spears.* 1961. (Contains documents that provide an Aztec point of view on the conquest of Mexico.)

Morner, Magnus. *Race Mixture in the History of Latin America.* 1967.

Stein, Stanley, and Barbara Stein. *The Colonial Heritage of Latin America.* 1970. (A thorough analysis of impediments to Latin American development and their roots in the colonial experience.)

Russia/Soviet Union

Buckley, Mary. *Women and Ideology in the Soviet Union.* 1989. (Addresses changing Soviet policies on women.)

Cohen, Stephen F. *Rethinking the Soviet Experience.* 1985. (A revisionist history that is critical of standard Western interpretations.)

Crummey, Robert O. *The Formation of Muscovy, 1304–1613.* 1987. (Covers the origins of Russian autocracy.)

Daniels, Robert V. *The End of the Communist Revolution.* 1993. (An analysis of the collapse of the Soviet Union in light of its history.)

Fitzpatrick, Sheila. *The Russian Revolution, 1917–1932*. 1982. (A short account of the revolution with an emphasis on social history.)

Getty, J. Arch, and Roberta Manning, eds. *Stalinist Terror*. 1993. (Addresses new perspectives on the purges that focus on factors other than Stalin's leadership.)

Hoskings, Geoffrey. *The First Socialist Society*. 1993. (One of the best textbooks on Soviet history.)

Medvedev, Roy A. *Let History Judge*. 1971. (Describes Soviet history through the eyes of a dissident Soviet Marxist.)

Reed, John. *Ten Days That Shook the World*. 1919. (A classic eyewitness account of the Russian Revolution.)

Riasanovsky, N. V. *The Image of Peter the Great in Russian History and Thought*. 1985. (Focuses on the continuing legacy of the great reformer.)

Thompson, John. *Revolutionary Russia, 1917*. 1989. (A short and useful summary of the revolution.)

Tucker, Robert C. *Stalin in Power*. 1990. (A detailed and well-written account that focuses on the 1930s.)

Von Laue, Theodore H. *Why Lenin; Why Stalin; Why Gorbachev*. 1993. (A clearly written attempt to explain Soviet history.)

PART IV

FROM THE MIDDLE LANDS TO THE MIDDLE EAST: ISLAM AND THE CHALLENGE OF THE WEST

Chapter 10: *Religion, Empire, and Hemispheric Civilization: The Making of the Islamic World*

Chapter 11: *Reversal of Roles: The Middle East and the West, 1500–1900*

Chapter 12: *Nationalism, Modernity, and Islam: The Middle East in the Twentieth Century*

Comparative Essay: *Industrialization in the Developing World*

Suggestions for Further Reading: *The Middle East*

The civilization of Islam joins those of India, China, and Europe as the four great centers of human achievement on the Eurasian landmass. But while the other three are identified with particular geographical areas, the civilization of Islam is not. Although its heartland lies in the area now known as "the Middle East," Islamic civilization has extended well beyond that region, incor-

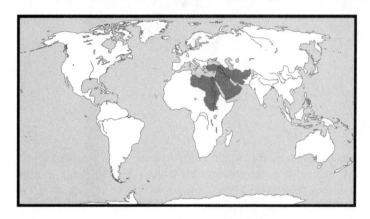

porating or connecting parts of the other three civilizations as well as numerous other areas. The three chapters in Part IV focus largely on the Middle Eastern heartland of Islamic civilization, though with periodic reference to the larger Islamic world.

In its modern history, the Islamic Middle East joins China and India as ancient and highly developed civilizations that encountered an expanding and aggressive Europe. However, its encounter differed from these others' in one fundamental respect. Neither India nor China had much direct knowledge of or contact with Europe before 1500. But Christian Europe and Islamic civilization had been "old acquaintances, intimate enemies, whose continuing conflict derived a special virulence from their shared origins and common aims."[1] Furthermore, the larger process of Europe's global expansion had begun in response to the Muslim challenge. It was no accident that the year 1492 saw both the reconquest of the last Muslim state in Spain *and* the launching of Columbus's epic voyage across the Atlantic.

Our consideration of the Middle Eastern region begins, in Chapter 10, with the making of the Islamic world—its origins as a new religious community in Arabia, its development as an enormous Arab empire, and its transformation into a cosmopolitan world civilization linking the major centers of the Eastern Hemisphere. This chapter thus provides a useful context for understanding the history of Europe, India, and Africa as well as that of the Middle East. Chapter 11 details the changes and responses within the Middle East provoked by Europe's growing domination of the region, especially in the nineteenth century. Chapter 12 extends the discussion of the Middle Eastern struggle into the twentieth century, with a special emphasis on the region's return to a more independent and prominent position in the world. A major theme of these chapters involves the various ways in which Muslim societies and their leaders understood their Islamic heritage and adapted it to the changing circumstances of the modern world.

Notes

1. The part introduction is based on Bernard Lewis, *Islam and the West* (New York: Oxford University Press, 1993). The quote is from p. 17.

Chapter 10
Religion, Empire, and Hemispheric Civilization: The Making of the Islamic World

For many Westerners, the "Middle East" triggers images that are negative, threatening, and exotic—religious fanatics, ferocious warriors, seductive harems. This package of stereotypes often lumps together Muslims, Arabs, and Middle Easterners in a "negative muddle" of images with little or no connection to historical reality. Such broad-brush myths and cultural misunderstandings have long poisoned relations between the Middle East and the West, and they still do. What are their origins?

The answer lies in fourteen centuries of interaction between peoples of the Middle East and those living to the north and west. Trans-Mediterranean interaction was at times peaceful, involving trade, adventure, intellectual and cultural exchange, and religious pilgrimage. But there were also periods of warfare when the fear of being overwhelmed or the reality of being invaded produced mutually reinforcing distortions. Six major phases of conflict during these fourteen centuries have added layer upon layer of negative images that became imbedded in the language, the literature, and the collective memories of Western and Middle Eastern cultures.

First, the explosive military and political expansion from western Arabia during the seventh and eighth centuries C.E. brought the "holy land," North Africa, Spain, and even parts of France under Arab-Muslim control. The Christian Occident was placed on the defensive, sowing seeds of fear and mistrust between Western Mediterranean Christians and Eastern Mediterranean Muslims during formative stages of both civilizations. Subsequent western European military thrusts from the late eleventh century to the late thirteenth century (the Crusades) established temporary European control over parts of the "holy land," casting Europeans as the aggressors, and etching more deeply the mutual hostility of European Christians and Middle Eastern Muslims. Then, between the fourteenth and sixteenth centuries, the dramatic Ottoman Turkish expansion into southeastern and central Europe and into the western Mediterranean sowed genuine fears in Western Christendom of being overrun by the formidable Muslim Turks.

The age of European imperialism—from about 1800 through the 1950s—gave rise to further cultural images that helped to justify European expansion and domination. Middle Eastern culture, and Islam in particular, appeared to Europeans as inherently antimodern—fatalistic, stagnant, and backward. In the twentieth century, the struggle over Palestine and the creation of Israel in 1948 made the Jewish state in large measure the Western window on the Middle East. Israeli perceptions of the Islamic Middle East, and in particular of the Arab world, as intolerant, violent, and threatening, influenced and reinforced Western thinking in general, while Arabs saw Western support for Israel as an extension of centuries of imperialist aggression. Finally, the resurgence of militantly traditionalist Islamist movements and their overt anti-Westernism, most notably the Khomeini-led revolution in Iran in 1979, reinforced negative Western images of "Islamic religiosity."

Such patterns of historical conflict have led many in the West to ignore the enormous and creative role in world history that Islamic civilization has played as well as to minimize that civilization's contribution to Europe's own development. Those attempting to study the history of the Middle East must be constantly aware of the heavy cultural baggage of igno-rance and distortion that has for so long shaped the relations between the Middle East and the West, be-tween Christendom and the world of Islam.

Lands, Peoples, and Historical Change

The *Middle East* as a geographic term clearly repre-sents a European perspective. Europeans had long re-ferred to the Islamic world as the "Orient" or the "East," but when they became involved with India and China, which lay even further to the east, the Is-lamic heartlands became the "Near" or "Middle" East, distinguished from the "Far" East, largely associated with China and Japan. In contemporary usage, the Middle East refers to a region that includes Arab North Africa (although northwest Africa—the Maghrib—is sometimes excluded), Turkey, Iran, the Arabian Peninsula, and the lands to the east of the Mediterranean Sea.

The Arab world comprises only part of the Middle East. *Arab* is an ethno-linguistic term that identifies people primarily as speakers of the Arabic language, although most Arabs also view themselves as sharing a common past, and a minority of Arabs have come to perceive themselves as a nation awaiting eventual unification into a single pan-Arab state. Though Arabs are the largest ethno-linguistic group in the Middle East, there are many others as well—Turks, Persians (speakers of Farsi), Israeli Jews (speakers of Hebrew), Kurds, Armenians, and Berbers, to men-tion a few. The two most widely shared features of Middle Eastern culture, the Arabic language and the Islamic faith, have spread from their Arabian home-land during the past fourteen centuries.

Although the vast majority of people living in the Middle East call themselves Muslims (Islamic be-lievers), the Islamic world has long extended far be-yond the Middle East. Less than one-third of the one billion Muslims living today reside in the Middle East. The four largest Muslim countries—Indonesia, Pakistan, Bangladesh, and India—all lie farther to the east. Furthermore, sub-Saharan Africa hosts a large Muslim population, as does China and the countries of the former Soviet Union. Nevertheless, the spiritual or symbolic center of the Islamic world remains, as it always has, in western Arabia. It is to Mecca, birthplace of Muhammad, that millions of Muslim pilgrims flock each year, and it is toward Mecca that hundreds of millions of Muslims face in prayer each day. Mecca, Medina, and Jerusalem remain the three most sacred cities to the Muslim faithful.

Geography of the Middle East

Two central features of physical geography have profoundly influenced the history of the Middle East and its relationship with other world regions. The first is desert. Lying in the arid belt between 20 and 40 degrees north latitude that encircles the globe, much of the Middle East lacks substantial or regular rainfall. Thus, in the great deserts of the Sahara and the Arabian Peninsula, human population is ex-tremely sparse or nonexistent. But in the higher ele-vations of the north (where mountains wring the moisture from the atmosphere), and along some of the coasts, both rainfall and population density are higher. The Nile Valley in Egypt, although lacking in rainfall, is one of the most densely populated regions in the world. Egypt has long been known as "the gift of the Nile," since the water and silt brought annually by floods from Northeast Africa facilitated the devel-opment of irrigated agriculture, dense populations, and advanced civilizations over the past five thou-sand years. Even earlier, during the fourth millen-nium B.C.E., a similar pattern of irrigation farming, population growth, urbanization, and centralized state formation took shape in the Tigris-Euphrates flood plain (Mesopotamia) of southern Iraq.

The other geographical feature is location. The term *Middle East* may reflect a recent Eurocentric point of view, but the region does lie at the intersec-tion of Africa, Europe, and Asia. These "middle lands" have long been a crossroads of peoples, armies, goods, technologies, ideas, crops, microbes, and institutions. Hence, the history of the Middle East has often been intimately linked with that of sur-rounding regions, serving both as a source of power and innovation and as a bridge between other regions of the Afro-Eurasian world. Whether it was the tran-sition from hunting and gathering to agriculture, the development of irrigation farming, the rise of cities, the growth of complex civilizations, the smelting of iron, or the introduction of the phonetic alphabet, the Middle East has been the scene of some of the most important developments in the human story during the past ten thousand years.

The Birth of a World Religion

Monotheistic religions also first arose in the Middle East. Three closely related faiths—Judaism, Christianity, and Islam—which took form in that order, have been of enduring importance; nearly two-fifths of humanity identifies with one or the other, the vast majority being split about evenly between Christianity and Islam. Each of the three religions is founded on a belief in one universal and just God who has been revealed to humankind through time. For Jews, that revelation came by way of a historical dialogue with a chosen people seeking to fulfill a covenant with God. For Christians, that revelation took human and divine form in a person, Jesus Christ, born in Palestine, whose life, death, and resurrection offer redemption for all of humanity. For Muslims, the fullest expression of God's revelation is a book, the Quran (or Koran), the literal message of God as revealed to Muhammad, between 610 and 632 C.E., that provides the blueprint for a just world.

The Islamic venture is a remarkable story. A small group of dissidents in a remote western Arabian town established in the early seventh century C.E. a new community. It rapidly expanded into an Arabian state, then into an empire reaching from the Atlantic to China, and finally into a world civilization linking distant peoples from one end of the intercommunicating zone to the other, all within a few centuries.

Arabia, a peninsula whose central region was largely inhabited by desert nomads known as Bedouins, sat on the edge of the ancient civilizations of Persia and Byzantium. Caravan routes crisscrossed the peninsula, linking the agricultural heartlands of Syria and Iraq with the Yemeni highlands in the southwest corner of the peninsula. Bedouin peoples were fiercely independent, often worshipping a variety of deities and nature spirits, although Jewish and Christian communities were scattered across the peninsula. The encounter between traditional Arab culture and the influences of surrounding civilizations was especially stark in the commercial town of Mecca, a major stopping point for caravans following the north–south route running down the western coast of the peninsula. Here in the early 600s the cosmopolitan spirit of a merchant center challenged traditional Bedouin values.

Muhammad: Revelation and Revolution

Muhammad was born in Mecca around the year 570 C.E. Orphaned early in life, he was adopted by an uncle, became a merchant, and married a wealthy widow, Khadijah, who provided him with financial and moral support and played a key role during his critically important years at Mecca. Muhammad possessed a rare combination of shrewd pragmatism and deep spiritual sensitivity. He withdrew on occasion to meditate in the arid mountains surrounding Mecca. According to Muslim tradition, in 610 C.E., Muhammad was visited by the angel Gabriel, who commanded:

Recite in the name of your Lord who has created,
Created man out of a germ-cell.
Recite for your Lord is the Most Generous One
Who has taught by the pen,
Taught man what he did not know.[1]

Over the next twenty-two years, Muhammad continued to have experiences that he and and a growing group of followers affirmed as revelations from Allah (the Arabic word for God). With support from Khadijah and other believers, Muhammad became convinced that he had been chosen as the last in a line of prophets to deliver a message to humanity. The revelations received in Arabic between 610 and 632 C.E. were written down shortly after they were received. The definitive version of the Quran (meaning "recitation") was compiled about two decades after Muhammad's death.

Muhammad's message was of the one God, lord of creation and source of all law and judgment, who would judge injustice harshly. It soon caused controversy in Mecca. A few Meccans were initially attracted, but many were repelled by Muhammad's exhortations, for Mecca was not only a commercial town but the focal point for polytheistic cults as well. Muhammad's stern warnings threatened those who

This painting depicts the holy city of Mecca and, at its center, the Black Stone, or Ka'ba, a pre-Islamic shrine that was transformed into the holiest of Muslim places. *The Library of Congress*

enjoyed the benefits of the status quo. Opposition to Muhammad and his followers became so strong that he accepted an invitation to migrate to Medina, a town several hundred miles to the north. This flight (the *hijra*), which occurred in 622 C.E., is one of the most important events in the history of Islam. It marks the beginning of the Islamic lunar calendar.

Invited to Medina as mediator among feuding clans, Muhammad saw his role shift from political dissident to political and religious leader, and by 630 C.E. he was able to return in triumph to his native city. He continued to gain the support of surrounding Bedouin peoples. His prophetic inspiration and political skills succeeded in unifying most of western Arabia under his leadership by the time of his death in 632 C.E.

The message Muhammad preached was revolutionary. For those who accepted the message, it meant a transition from a pagan society, defined by kinship, rival clans, and local enmities, to a single community (the *ummah*), defined by common belief and submission to the one God, Allah. Within that community, all believers were equal, at least in principle, before Allah. This included women as well as men, although women and men performed different roles within the community. In general, each believer had an obligation to help those who were less fortunate by providing protection and assistance to the weak and needy. It was a profoundly religious message, but one that called for the creation of a new society.

For Muslims, the years 610 to 632 C.E. mark the most important era in human history, since the complete message (the Quran) from God was then received by the final messenger or prophet (Muhammad). Although the theological, legal, and institutional features of Islam would require centuries of experimentation and elaboration, their foundations were laid in Mecca and Medina in the early seventh century. Muhammad's words and deeds, recorded later in the "traditions" (*hadith*), became the patterns by which subsequent generations measured their piety, although the Quran remained the wellspring of truth. Written in poetic style and organized by length of chapters (*suras*), the Quran was, however, silent on many issues that later Muslims faced.

Over the centuries, an elaborate literature of interpretation and commentary was drafted by members of the *ulama* (the learned elite), articulating what was required, recommended, optional, discouraged, and forbidden for Muslims. This huge body of writing, centered on the Quran and elaborated by resorting to the *hadith,* came to be known as the *Shariah* (divine law). More than in Christendom, Islamic law defined, at least in principle, the totality of social and political life for Muslim believers. For while Christianity struggled against the state for the initial centuries of its growth, Islam was almost immediately embodied in a community, state, and empire.

Islamic Belief and Practice

Despite the great diversity of peoples within the Islamic world, five central requirements, known commonly as the "five pillars," have bound Muslims together over the centuries. The first pillar is a simple but fundamental profession of faith that affirms the central tenets of Islam—absolute monotheism and a final revelation: "There is no god but the one God (Allah), and Muhammad is the messenger of God." The second pillar is prayer, preferably five times a day at prescribed times facing toward Mecca. The third pillar requires generous giving of one's wealth to maintain the community and to help the needy. The fourth pillar calls for a month of fasting—no food, drink, sexual relations—from sunup to sundown during *Ramadan,* the ninth lunar month of the Islamic calendar. The fifth pillar urges a pilgrimage to Mecca for those who are financially and physically able to do so. Over the centuries, hundreds of thousands, and more recently millions, of Muslims from around the world have gathered at Mecca each year during the month of the pilgrimage. A moving display of religious devotion, the *hajj* or pilgrimage has fostered the unity of a very diverse Islamic world and the exchange of people, ideas, goods, and institutions.

Crisis and Expansion: The Early State

The roles that Muhammad played from 622 to 632 C.E., serving as religious prophet, administrative coordinator, and military mobilizer, established the principle of unified cultural, economic, and political authority that became an integral part of Islam. At the time of his death in 632, the community he had established faced serious challenges—who would provide leadership, what would hold the community together, and how would it resolve questions not addressed by the revelations?

The issue of who would succeed Muhammad as leader of the *ummah* led to a deep split that has divided the Islamic world ever since. In the years following Muhammad's death, one section of the community came to regard Ali, Muhammad's cousin and son-in-law, as the legitimate successor (*khalifa* or caliph) to Muhammad. But Ali was passed over during three succession crises and was eventually assassinated when he did briefly attain that office. After Ali's reign as caliph (656–661 C.E.), the era of the *Rashidun* (the "rightly guided caliphs") came to an end. Sunni Muslims, as the followers of the early caliphs were called, came to view this period, along with Muhammad's time as leader, as the nearest to perfection reached by any society in history. But those faithful to the defeated Ali, later known as Shi'ites, remained unreconciled. They were led by successive generations of *imams* (religious leaders). The Shi'ites believed their *imams* inherited mystical powers that allowed them alone to reveal the true meanings of the Quran and the wishes of Allah. Later the Shi'ites split among themselves as to which claimant was the legitimate *imam.* The unity of the Islamic community, so important to Muhammad, had been lost.

From Arab Empire to World Civilization

Following Muhammad's death in 632 C.E., Bedouin groups began to reassert their traditional autonomy. The Muslim community that Muhammad had assembled appeared to be on the verge of disintegration. Instead, however, it underwent a dramatic political-military expansion over the following decades as horse-mounted warriors swept out of Arabia to the north, east, and west, creating a vast empire. Historians have identified a variety of reasons for this sudden restructuring of the Middle Eastern political order—the mobility and discipline of nomad warriors, their zeal provided by the new unifying faith; the promise of plunder and the need for material resources; the stresses caused by short-term climatic fluctuations; the exhaustion and vulnerablity of the nearby Sasanian and Byzantine empires following their destructive struggles for regional dominance; the receptivity of populations tired of oppressive rule; and the extraordinarily effective leadership demonstrated by early Arab military and political authorities.

After several major battles and sieges, Palestine, Syria, Iraq, Egypt, and Persia came under Arab-Muslim rule. The Byzantine Empire was forced back to the walls of its capital, Constantinople, while the Persian Sasanian Empire was utterly defeated. Meanwhile, the struggle for power intensified at the center of this growing empire, based in western Arabia. When the dust settled, the caliphate was in the hands of the Umayyad Dynasty based in Damascus. The victory of the Umayyads over Ali's Shi'ite followers in the late 650s C.E. signaled both the beginning of the age of imperial Islam and a shift in the political center of Islam from western Arabia north to Damascus in Syria. The Umayyad Empire, although ruled by an Arab elite whose ancestry traced back to western Arabia, incorporated many of the administrative institutions it encountered in Persia and Syria.

Military successes on far-flung frontiers continued, though revolts by Shi'ite and other groups continually challenged Umayyad rule. Arab forces swept across north Africa, reached Tunisia by 700 C.E., and crossed into Spain in 711 C.E. Also in that year Muslim forces conquered the Hindu-Buddhist society of Sind in western India. At the same time, Arab armies were occupying oasis towns of central Asia, reaching the frontiers of Chinese authority, and in 751 C.E., a decisive Arab victory over Chinese forces in central Asia opened up a vast region of Turkish-speaking peoples to Muslim influence. It also fostered commerce on the silk road linking the Middle East with China.

Thus, in little more than a century a vast region covering much of the intercommunicating zone had been incorporated into an Arab-Muslim Empire based in Syria but drawing its inspiration from the revolutionary ideas that had emanated from western Arabia in the early seventh century. Seeds of instability lay both in the core and at the periphery of this vast empire. At its center lay a contradiction between the egalitarian principles of the Quran and the privileged Arab oligarchy that was reaping the fruits of the imperial state. Shi'ites and other dissident groups challenged the legitimacy of the Umayyad state. At the periphery of the state, given the technological limits on communication and transportation, governors of outlying regions soon began asserting their autonomy from the central authority.

The Formation of Islamic Civilization

The eighth and ninth centuries witnessed political changes stemming from both internal and external forces. Around the year 750 C.E., the Umayyad regime was overthrown by members of the Abbasids, a rival lineage whose ancestry traced back to Muhammad's uncle Abbas. Although they maintained many of the ruling institutions inherited from the Umayyads, the Abbasids also brought long-lasting changes. The center of political power shifted again, this time from Damascus east to Iraq, where the Abbasids built the thriving capital city of Baghdad. The Arab oligarchy of Umayyad times was transformed into a more inclusive system that incorporated non-Arab Muslims, especially Persians, at high levels of power.

Baghdad rapidly emerged as the cultural and commercial center of the world's largest empire. Its explosive growth in size, reaching an estimated population of half a million (ten times the size of the Sasanian capital), mirrored an extraordinary economic, cultural, and political florescence that subsequent generations have looked back on as the "golden age" of Islamic civilization. By the early ninth century, Baghdad was among the world's largest cities, comparable to the Chinese Tang capital of Changan (Sian) or the Byzantine capital of Constantinople. Expanded irrigation, introduction of new crops, development of new technologies, extension of commercial networks, rapid urbanization, increased state revenues—all of these contributed to a period of extraordinary growth, vitality, and innovation. Islamic caliphs patronized arts, crafts, and intellectual pursuits, resulting in some of the most refined works of high culture of any region of the world.

The legal, philosophical, and economic aspects of Islamic civilization began to take shape during the early Abbasid period. The spiritual revolution started by Muhammad evolved into the cultural foundation of a world civilization that brought many of the older traditions of the Afro-Eurasian world into contact with each other for the first time or in new ways. Islam as a civilization was more than a synthesis of earlier traditions, but it was founded on such a synthesis. Administrative procedures and monarchical rituals of the Persians, philosophical and scientific breakthroughs of the Greeks, ethical and spiritual traditions of Judaism and Christianity, mathematical and medical knowledge of the Hindus, technological innovations of Confucian China—all of these strands were eventually woven into the fabric of Islamic civilization.

Developments in agriculture, industry, and commerce contributed in fundamental ways to this flowering of Islamic civilization, fostering population growth, increased productivity, and intensified exchange across the Eastern Hemisphere. Extensive trading links among the Middle East, Africa, India, China, and Europe laid the foundations of an early world system many centuries before the Western voyages of exploration.

Muslim naval forces dominated the Mediterranean, while Middle Eastern merchants organized long-distance commercial ventures elsewhere—up the Volga River to the Baltic region, down the east coast of Africa, across the Sahara into west Africa. A Muslim trading colony was established at Canton in China by the mid-eighth century. These caravan routes and sea routes carried a continuous flow of raw materials and finished commodities that made much of the intercommunicating zone a single network of exchange, tied together in large part by Muslim merchants seeking profits in long-distance trade. Baghdad was the commercial as well as the cultural center of the world's largest empire.

The vast expanses of Islamic civilization (see Map 10.1) also facilitated a substantial exchange of agricultural products and practices from one region to another, the largest such transfer in world history prior to Europe's encounter with the Americas. The mid-eighth century Muslim conquest of northwest India opened the Middle East (and, by extension, Africa, Europe, and even East Asia) to a veritable treasure-trove of crops that had been domesticated long before in South and Southeast Asia—rice, sugarcane, new strains of sorghum, hard wheat, bananas, lemons, limes, watermelons, coconuts, spinach, artichokes, and cotton.[2] Both cotton and sugarcane, associated with complex production processes and a corresponding need for large amounts of labor, came to play central roles in the formation of the modern global system during the following millennium. These new crops and the development of intensified agricultural techniques that often accompanied them contributed to increased food production, population growth, urbanization, and industrial development characteristic of the Muslim Middle East in early Abbasid times.

The central location of the empire and the innovative spirit of the period accelerated the development and dissemination of new technologies in transportation, navigation, shipbuilding, cartography, and geography. Techniques of manufacturing paper, for example, were brought to the Abbasid Empire from China in the eighth century, with paper mills soon operating in Iran, Iraq, and Egypt. From the Middle East this revolutionary technology, which everywhere served to strengthen bureaucratic governments, spread into India and Europe over the following centuries.

Patterns of Islamic Culture

The Islamic pattern of borrowing, assimilation, innovation, and diffusion transformed Middle Eastern culture. Here the greatest impact came through contact with Hellenistic and Indian fields of knowledge and methods of inquiry. Already under the Umayyads, philosophical debates between Muslims and Christians linked elements of Islamic theology with Greek concepts, and Greek architectural styles can be detected in such celebrated Umayyad monuments as the Dome of the Rock Mosque in Jerusalem, built at the end of the seventh century. From the Greeks and Indians came analytical and empirical traditions that paved the way for breakthroughs in the natural and life sciences. With the establishment of Baghdad as the Abbasid capital, Muslim intellectuals translated, studied, and built upon Greek, Syriac, Sanskrit, and Persian works in medicine, astronomy, mathematics, and other fields of science and thought.

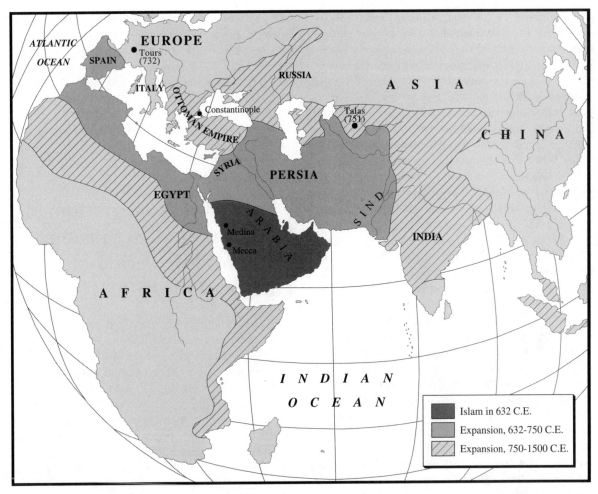

MAP 10.1 The Expanding World of Islam, 632–1500 C.E.

From Indian mathematics, Middle Eastern thinkers developed the revolutionary method of counting using the concept of zero. These "Hindi numerals" later came to be known as "arabic numerals" when incorporated into Europe via Islamic Spain. Utilizing principles of Indian arithmetic and Greek geometry, the Arab mathematician al-Khwarizmi developed the system known as algebra. Another intellectual giant whose breadth of interests spanned the sciences was al-Biruni, who in the eleventh century combined careful observation, measurement, and a knowledge of geometry to calculate with great precision the circumference of the earth. Medical treatises by al-Razi (d. 925) and Ibn Sina (980–1037, known in Europe as Avicenna), not only pioneered the analysis and treatment of disease but became stan-dard works that were translated into Latin and utilized as basic texts in Europe for centuries.

In the realm of theology and law, several centuries of intense discussion and debate established the main tenets of Islamic thought, much as Christian orthodoxy had been painfully hammered out several centuries earlier. An important issue among scholars of both faiths concerned the value and limits of reason in exploring and conveying the truth of divine revelation. During the intellectual flowering of the eighth and ninth centuries, Muslim scholars enjoyed a high degree of freedom in the individual application of reason (*ijtihad*) to theological and legal questions. An important part of this process was the development of the four major Sunni schools of Islamic law (the Shariah). Rooted in the Quran and the *hadiths,* these bodies of legal thinking also used arguments by analogy to solve problems not directly answered in the Quran or *hadiths*. As consensus gradually developed on many issues, individual interpretations, or *ijtihad,* became less acceptable.

Over the first three Islamic centuries, the Shariah grew into a comprehensive system that defined religious belief, ritual practice, personal relationships, political order, crime and punishment, and much more. While it never resulted in a formal legal code, the Shariah was a "discussion of how Muslims ought to behave," an effort "to show man what he must do to live righteously in this world and prepare himself for the next."[3] It was, of course, never perfectly enforced, but the Shariah remained a powerful ideal, beckoning many to bring their personal lives and their societies into conformity with its precepts.

However, the legalistic forms of Islam that prescribed patterns of abstract belief, ritual, and behavior did not necessarily satisfy the heart-felt craving for personal spiritual experience, and the tension between these two emphases sharpened as elaborate legal and theological systems were formalized. Since the absolute transcendance of Allah and his final revelation through Muhammad became fundamental tenets of the Islamic faith, the desire of certain believers to experience intimate contact with Allah always risked going too far—that is, of claiming to be one with the divine or having received additional revelations. A variety of influential voices emerged during the early centuries of Islam that tested the limits of acceptability even as they helped define those limits.

Among the early influential Muslim mystics known as *Sufis,* was a woman, Rabi'al'Adawiya (d. 801), who had been born in Basra (now in Iraq), kidnapped as a child, then enslaved and finally set free. Reclusive and celibate, Rabi'a drew a circle of disciples attracted by her charisma and devotion. The spirit of early Sufism is conveyed in her much repeated prayer:

> O my Lord, if I worship Thee from fear of Hell, burn me in Hell; and if I worship Thee from hope of Paradise, exclude me thence; but if I worship Thee for Thine own sake, then withhold not from me Thine Eternal Beauty.[4]

The tension between these two emphases of Islam—established doctrine versus personal spirituality—culminated in the famous martyrdom of al-Hallaj in 922 C.E. Born in Persia, al-Hallaj traveled to India before settling in Baghdad, where he attracted a growing group of followers. Obsessed with the desire for union with the divine, al-Hallaj was condemned for heresy, publically tortured, and executed. It was not until the following century that one of the most influential intellects in Islamic history, al-Ghazali (1058–1111), would work out an accommodation between formal doctrine orthodoxy and Sufi spiritualism.

Political Disintegration and Cultural Expansion: The Middle Period of Islam, 950–1500

The early centuries of Islam had created political connections on a vast Afro-Eurasian scale. A variety of cultural traditions had been woven into a single comprehensive Islamic civilization characterized by widespread economic growth and prosperity. But beginning around the mid-tenth century, signs of political decay and economic contraction became evident in the Islamic world. Intensive irrigation, necessary for crops that had been imported from the high rainfall regions of India, accelerated both the depletion of soils and fresh water and the salination of irrigated areas. Thus, by the early tenth century, the Mesopotamian breadbasket was producing less than it had a generation earlier. And with declining production came declining government revenues.[5]

Politically, by the mid-tenth century, the vast empire that the Abbasids had inherited from the Umayyads two centuries before was falling apart. In Spain, Tunisia, Egypt, and elsewhere independent states had been formed during the eighth and ninth centuries, and by the early ninth century ambitious leaders were declaring their autonomy from Abbasid authority on the eastern fringes of the caliphate. Many of these political upheavals drew their inspiration from the Shi'ite branch of Islam. Little by little, then, the prestige of the caliphs, inheritors of Muhammad's mantle of divinely sanctioned leadership, eroded.

The transformation of Baghdad from a hemispheric center of culture, power, and wealth into a provincial town reflected this decentralization of

Muslim power and the political and economic decline of the Arabic-speaking regions. While the Arabs had given Islam to the world and created its early empires, other peoples, especially the Persians and the Turks, would exercise leading roles in the Islamic world of the future.

Paradoxically, this "decline" in political unity and Arab dominance occurred simultaneously with a continuous expansion of Islam—as a religious faith and as a high civilization. Although the Islamic world lacked an overarching political framework after the mid-ninth century, a shared culture and economic connections made it a distinct, coherent, and growing civilization. In that sense, it resembled Western civilization in the modern era—politically fragmented but possessing a recognizable cultural identity rooted in a religious tradition.

One indication that Islamic civilization could thrive without a unified political structure during the centuries after 1000 C.E. was the vigorous spread of the religion well beyond the Middle East, associated variously with expanding commercial networks, the emotional fervor of Sufi preachers, or on occasion military conquest. Thus Islam entered India, where it took root in the west (Punjab and Sind) and in the east (Bengal), both frontier areas that had been only lightly touched by Hindu culture and where settled agriculture was only beginning. The spice-producing regions of Southeast Asia, where trade expanded rapidly in the fourteenth and fifteenth centuries, also became incorporated into the world of Islamic civilization. So did the interior of west Africa, home to large trading empires with contacts across the Sahara, and the coast of east Africa, where Swahili city-states took part in the world of Indian Ocean commerce. Thus the religion of Islam "came closer than any had ever come," according to a leading historian, "to uniting all mankind under its ideals."[6]

Turks, Mongols, and Christians: The Middle East and Its Invaders

Between roughly 1000 and 1500, Middle Eastern peoples confronted a series of nomadic migrations and military invasions. Of particular importance for the next millennium of the region's history was the gradual movement of Turkish-speaking peoples westward and southwestward from their homeland in the central Asian steppes. Some gradually migrated

This mosque in the Ethiopian city of Harrar illustrates the spread of Islam all across the Afro-Eurasian world. *Robert W. Strayer*

as tribes, while others were intentionally imported by Abbasid authorities as slaves known as *mamluks* (literally, "those who are owned"). The practice of recruiting such slaves from distant regions, and training them for military and administrative service, became institutionalized first among the Abbasids and then among successor states across the region. By the early tenth century, Turkish forces in Baghdad had attained enough influence to manipulate and even depose some of the Abbasid caliphs.

The growing Turkish influence in the region culminated with the capture of Baghdad in 1055 by the Seljuks, a Turkish-speaking clan originally from the central Asian steppe. The Seljuk rulers called themselves *sultans* (Muslim rulers) rather than caliphs, preferring to keep the Abbasid caliph as titular head of the Islamic world. In 1071, in a pivotal battle at Manzikert in eastern Anatolia, the Turks defeated a Byzantine force, opening the Anatolian peninsula to large-scale Turkish settlement over the following centuries. This was historically important, for that peninsula became the base from which the Turkish Ottoman Empire later reunified the Middle Eastern heartland of Islam. Thus the Turks began the process whereby they became the third great carriers of Islam, following the Arabs and the Persians.

Far more destructive than the coming of the Turks was the invasion of the Mongols, the last great movement of nomadic steppe peoples into the civilized heartland of Eurasia. In addition to their conquests of China and much of Russia, the Mongols arrived in the Middle East in the thirteenth century with unprecedented ferocity and destruction. Early in the century, Mongol tribes in central Asia had been welded together by Genghis Khan. It was his grandson, Hülegü, who led the invasion of Islam's agrarian heartland, culminating in the sacking of Baghdad in 1258, the killing of the last Abbasid ruler, and the disrupting of the delicate irrigation system that had been the basis of Abbasid prosperity. Not until 1260 was the Mongol juggernaut stopped by a Mamluk regime in Egypt. The year 1258 marked the official end of the Abbasid caliphate, although that once-great empire had long since disintegrated, and the power and influence of the "successors to Muhammad" had dissipated.

The Mongol impact on the Middle East, as on much of the intercommunicating zone, was complex and paradoxical. The havoc and destruction, particularly in areas dependent on irrigation, may have permanently damaged agricultural productivity in parts of Iran and Iraq. Politically and culturally, the Mongol Empire was ephemeral; the Mongols assimilated into much more advanced cultures in China and the Middle East, and the vast empire they created rapidly unravelled. At the same time, the Mongols succeeded in establishing a network of communication, the "Pax Mongolica," which drew the intercommunicating zone together in new ways and contributed significantly to the establishment of economic and cultural ties all across Eurasia.

Unlike the Turks, who retained their identity and became one of the leading peoples of Islam, or the Mongols, who were assimilated and largely disappeared as a separate people in the Middle East, the Christian invaders from the western Mediterranean were simply expelled, following a brief occupation of the "holy lands." The end of the eleventh century saw Christian Europeans advancing militarily against Muslim-controlled territory on several fronts, including Spain, Malta, and Sicily. In 1095, Pope Urban II declared the First Crusade to free the Christian shrines in Palestine from Muslim rule. A Crusader state was established in 1096, and Jerusalem fell to the Franks in 1099. Within the context of Middle Eastern history, the Crusades appear less important than they are commonly perceived in the West, since all of the territories brought under Frankish control reverted to Muslim control within two centuries after Urban's first call. Nevertheless, this period of interaction, characterized by alternating phases of warfare and peaceful coexistence between Christians and Muslims, did shape enduring images and attitudes between Western Christians and Middle Eastern Muslims. Moreover, from the standpoint of world history, the Crusaders brought back crops, technologies, institutions, and ideas that profoundly influenced the subsequent development of Europe.

An Islamic World System

While the Islamic world between 1000 and 1500 came under the political control of numerous military leaders, a distinctively Islamic social order also evolved that transcended the boundaries of any particular state. Three major institutions contributed to this uniquely Islamic hemispheric order, which drew much of the intercommunicating zone into a network of interaction in the thirteenth and fourteenth centuries.[7] The first institution was the elite class of religious and legal scholars known as the *ulama* (literally, "the learned"), who staffed the legal, educational, and administrative institutions. Respected because of their knowledge of the Quran and the Shariah, they often legitimized the rule of military elites, but their positions in society were not necessarily dependent on the rulers. These "men of the pen" played an essential role in preserving the idea of a connected Islamic community that transcended particular states, regions, classes, or nations. They passed on their knowledge to future generations of *ulama* by teaching in their homes, in mosques or shrines, or in formal schools called *madrasas*. Thus a complex educational network further integrated the Islamic world as dedicated students sought out the most learned teachers wherever they could be found.

The second institution that contributed to the cosmopolitan web connecting distant regions involved

A sophisticated network of educational institutions, illustrated by this drawing of a small Quranic school, helped to create an Islamic civilization incorporating numerous cultural traditions. *Visual Studies Workshop*

the Sufis, linked together in hundreds of *tariqah* orders, many of which had branches scattered across the entire Islamic world. These orders had been established by outstanding spiritual leaders, or *shaikhs,* and attracted disciples eager to learn their unique devotional practices or way of approaching God. Shrines of the founding saint, together with a hierarchy of lesser shrines, became focal points of pilgrimages associated with particular orders. These Sufi orders sprang up all over the Islamic world and, through their passionate preaching and exemplary living, contributed much to the continuing spread of the faith in regions such as west Africa and South Asia.

Several aspects of Sufi belief and practice brought them into conflict with the *ulama.* One, of course, was the Sufi claim to know Allah through direct personal experience rather than through study of the Quran, Shariah, and Islamic theology. Another was the veneration of Sufi masters, which, the *ulama* feared, could turn into the worship of these men and thus compromise the strict monotheism of Islam. And some Sufi thinkers verged on pantheism, the belief that "everything is God." Such a notion seemed to undermine the transcendence of Allah and to minimize the importance of the Quran as God's final and authoritative revelation to humanity. Finally, Sufi practice often incorporated aspects of local pre-Islamic culture—singing, dancing, and occasionally more exotic feats such as walking on fire—which to the *ulama* seemed to deviate from the pure faith of the early Islamic community.

But the worlds of the Sufis and the *ulama* were by no means always in conflict. Intellectually, these two elements of Islamic belief and practice were brought together by al-Ghazali, the great synthesizer of Shariah-based Islam and Sufi-based Islam. In doing so, he is often viewed as contributing to the development of Islamic thought as a closed system. By formalizing mystical expressions of Islamic faith and making them a part of established doctrine, al-Ghazali helped define the boundaries of what was acceptable while also opening up mainstream Islamic practice to individual expressions of spirituality. In general, the period from the eleventh century on lacked the impressive spirit of innovation and creativity that had characterized the cultural flowering of early Abbasid times, although there were important exceptions to this generalization in many fields of study. But the usual metaphor for the eleventh century is the "closing door of *ijtihad*" (independent reason) and its replacement by "imitation" (*taqlid*).

The third institutional web stretching from one end of the intercommunicating zone to the other involved the merchants, who carried high-value, low-volume goods by land and by sea in hopes of making a profit. These interregional trading networks often flourished even when political unity was absent. One recent view holds that a world system of eight interconnected trading networks and an "archipelago of hinterlands" took form between 1250 and 1350, linking much of the intercommunicating zone.[8]

Thus the three circulating elites—the *ulama,* Sufis, and merchants—established an unprecedented scale of cultural uniformity during the centuries prior to European expansion. The reality of a far-flung Islamic civilization was perhaps best expressed in the pilgrimage to Mecca, which served as an annual mechanism for drawing the faithful from distant regions together in one place.

The World of Ibn Battuta

No single person illustrates more vividly this remarkable period in world history than Ibn Battuta, whose fourteenth century travels spanned the intercommunicating zone. Ibn Battuta was born in Tangiers, Morocco, in 1304, and he died in 1368 or 1369. By some estimates, he traversed nearly 75,000 miles during his extraordinary travels, which took him from west Africa to central Asia, from Spain to Southeast Asia, and from east Africa, it is believed, to China. His remarkable success was a product of skill, determination, and luck, for he happened to be traveling at a time of unusual security made possible by the "Mongol peace." But it was also the result of his membership in all three elites: he was a religious scholar and member of the *ulama,* a member of Sufi networks, and, at times, a merchant. The unity of the Muslim world, extending from the Atlantic to southeast Asia, is best illustrated by the fact that this Moroccan served for a time as a Muslim judge in India. He well understood that:

> The learned man is esteemed in whatever place or condition he may be, always meeting people who are favorably disposed to him, who draw near to him and seek his company, gratified in being close to him. . . . A scholar's education is greatly improved by traveling in quest of knowledge and meeting the authoritative teachers (of his time).[9]

Ibn Battuta also encountered the other great contributor to this early world system—China. Sung China's "green revolution" during the eleventh and twelfth centuries not only increased food production and population, but also paved the way for a premodern industrial revolution that created demands for Chinese products in an enlarged system of exchange. Through the expanded merchant networks, Chinese innovations and inventions moved west; the compass was being used by the Arabs by the end of the eleventh century. Gunpowder, likewise a Chinese invention, was to play a particularly important role in the divergent paths that these regions subsequently followed. Ibn Battuta was deeply impressed by the beauty and sophistication of Chinese civilization, which was precisely why he found it so disturbing.

Unlike other areas of the world he visited, where the level of cultural sophistication seemed to be in direct relation to the influence of Islam, he could not explain the prosperity and security of China in terms of Islam. China challenged his assumptions about the intrinsic superiority of his Islamic culture:

> I was greatly troubled thinking about the way paganism dominated this country. . . . That disturbed me so much that I stayed indoors most of the time and only went out when necessary. During my stay in China, whenever I saw any Muslims I always felt as though I were meeting my own family and close kinsmen.[10]

The spectacular Indian Ocean voyages organized by the Chinese admiral Cheng Ho during the first third of the fifteenth century demonstrated that the Chinese state possessed the human and material resources to organize a global system of exchange had the Chinese decided to continue sponsoring such naval expeditions. The sudden Chinese withdrawal from the Indian Ocean sea lanes in 1433, at the very moment that the Portuguese were beginning their maritime ventures down the coast of west Africa, remains one of the great ironies in world history. Although the interconnected world that Ibn Battuta knew disintegrated under the pressures of the Black Death, the Chinese withdrawal, and the collapse of the Mongol Empire, it provided the elements from which Europeans subsequently constructed the modern world system.

Conclusion: The Islamic World in 1500

In the years after 1500, the political fragmentation of the Middle East, which had followed the collapse of the Abbasid Empire, was being replaced by two remarkable empires—the Turkish Ottoman Empire and the Persian Safavid Empire. Further afield in the Islamic world, the Mughal Dynasty brought political order and Muslim rule to much of the South Asian peninsula, while the Songhai Empire incorporated a large area of west Africa and blended Islam with local African cultures. Thus, the political power of the Islamic world was being reconstituted, even as Europe was beginning its journeys of global exploration. These two processes set the stage for the modern encounter of these neighboring civilizations.

Notes

1. *Quran,* 96:1–5.

2. Richard M. Eaton, *Islamic History as Global History* (Washington, D.C.: American Historical Association, 1990), p. 23; and Andrew Watson, *Agricultural Innovation in the Early Islamic World* (Cambridge, Mass.: Cambridge University Press, 1983).

3. Francis Robinson, *Atlas of the Islamic World since 1500* (New York: Facts on File, 1982), p. 30.

4. Quoted in Margaret Smith, *Readings from the Mystics of Islam* (London: Luzac and Company, 1972), p. 11.

5. Marshall G. S. Hodgson, *The Venture of Islam,* vol. 1 (Chicago: University of Chicago Press, 1974), p. 485.

6. Ibid., p. 71.

7. See John Voll, *Islam: Continuity and Change in the Modern World* (Boulder, Colo.: Westview Press, 1982), pp. 15–17.

8. Janet Abu-Lughold, *Before European Hegemony* (New York: Oxford University Press, 1989), pp. 33–34.

9. Quoted in Ross E. Dunn, *The Adventures of Ibn Battuta* (Berkeley: University of California Press, 1989) pp. 13, 27.

10. Quoted in Dunn, *Adventures*, p. 258.

Chapter 11
Reversal of Roles: The Middle East and the West, 1500–1900

For more than a thousand years the Islamic world had been the dominant feature of the intercommunicating zone, and the Middle East had been at its center. But by the end of the fifteenth century, events were occurring elsewhere that were to influence profoundly the future role of the Middle East in world affairs. The voyages of Bartholomeu Dias (1487–1488) and Vasco da Gama (1497–1498) opened a new age of eastern hemispheric interaction by sea. And midway between the voyages of Dias and da Gama, a journey of even greater consequence occurred—Columbus's 1492 encounter with the Americas. No longer did Middle Eastern states and merchants enjoy a monopoly of trade passing between East and West as an ever-increasing number of ships took advantage of the Cape route between Europe and Asia. Traditional Muslim involvement in the Indian Ocean long-distance trade networks continued, but now there were new competitors, some of whom were arriving with more effective gunpowder weapons. And with the inclusion of the Americas, the intercommunicating world had been substantially enlarged.

Thus, from about 1500 on, the history of most world regions requires a different and larger context. The Middle East, long the center of interaction within the Old World, became increasingly marginalized by the genuinely global long-distance trade networks that emerged over the following centuries. The impact of these developments was, however, by no means sudden. Rather, the changing balance of global power worked itself out over several centuries. Far more important in the decades surrounding the year 1500 was the creation within the Islamic world of three powerful and adjoining empires—the Ottoman, Safavid, and Mughal—which stretched from the Balkans to Bengal, based, respectively, in

present-day Turkey, Iran, and India (see Map 11.1). Among them it was the Turkish Ottoman Empire that gave new political shape to the Middle Eastern heartland of the Islamic world. And it was within that framework that much of the Middle East eventually confronted the new reality of Western imperialism.

The Rise of the Ottoman Empire

When Ibn Battuta traveled through Anatolia in the early 1330s, he was witness to an extraordinary moment in history. The Ottoman Turks were beginning a military expansion that would strike fear in the hearts of Western Europeans over the following two centuries. In the process this family of Turks established one of the longest-lasting imperial dynasties in world history.

During the fourteenth through sixteenth centuries, the Ottoman Turks advanced from their base in Asia Minor to incorporate much of southeastern Europe (the Balkans), north Africa, and the Fertile Crescent. The long-held dream of capturing the Byzantine capital, Constantinople, was achieved in 1453 under Mehmed II, sending shock waves through Western Christendom. Continuing Ottoman expansion challenged Christian control both on land, in central Europe, and on sea, in the western Mediterranean. The discipline and organization of their elite military units, the *janissaries,* were probably unmatched in the world at that time. These units, along with the use of gunpowder weapons, made the Ottomans fearsome adversaries. Venice was forced to accept a tributary status and, in 1480, Ottoman forces landed at

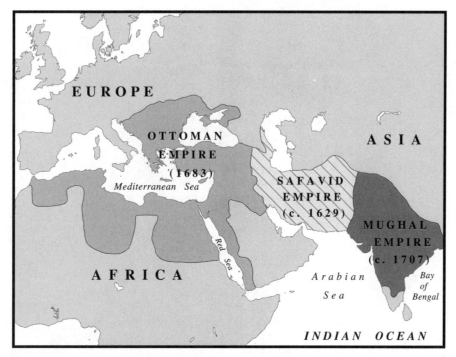

MAP 11.1 Empires of the Islamic World

Otranto, at the heel of the Italian peninsula. The pope prepared to flee Rome. Little wonder that Christopher Columbus, a young mariner from Genoa growing up in the latter half of the fifteenth century, was preoccupied with what appeared to be a hemispheric struggle between Christendom and the Islamic world.

Throughout the sixteenth century, the Ottoman Turks were formidable military rivals of the emerging European monarchies. Spain and the Ottomans struggled for supremacy in the western Mediterranean, while the great Ottoman Sultan Suleyman (1520–1566) began his reign with a drive into central Europe, the conquest of Hungary in 1526, and the unsuccessful siege of Vienna soon after. The Ottomans also gained control of the ancient Arab lands of the Middle East. Their victories brought Syria and Egypt into the Ottoman realm and placed the holy shrines of Christianity (Jerusalem) and of Islam (Mecca and Medina) in Ottoman hands. (See Map 11.2.) All of this took place as Martin Luther launched his challenge to the Catholic church, as Ferdinand Magellan set off on his round-the-world voyage, and as Hernán Cortés landed in Aztec Mexico.

The Ottomans were a formidable naval power as well, controlling the eastern Mediterranean during Suleyman's reign. Ottoman forces challenged the Portuguese in the waters east of Suez, establishing control over the region of Yemen and the Horn of Africa, but the Portuguese maintained their foothold at Hormuz, gateway to the Persian Gulf. Commerce remained active as trade routes continued to crisscross the Middle East. But by the end of the sixteenth century, English and Dutch merchants were penetrating the Iranian silk trade from Persian Gulf ports, much as French merchants were setting up ports of trade along the north African coast.

The expanding Ottoman Empire met its military needs by conscripting Christian boys from rural areas of the empire, converting them to Islam, and then rigorously grooming them for service to the Ottoman state. This system delivered a continual supply of recruits, with absolute loyalty to the sultan, some of whom rose to the highest positions within the bureaucracy. Most found a place in the elite fighting corps, the *janissaries*. The growing numbers and expenses of the *janissaries,* and their role as a central support of the regime, drove the process of Ottoman expansion.

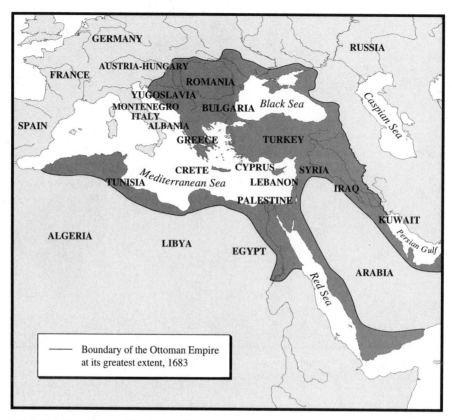

MAP 11.2 The Ottoman Empire in 1683

The brilliant successes of the Ottomans were due in part to their efficient administration. Following the conquest of Constantinople, which became the Ottoman capital Istanbul, Mehmed II acknowledged the civil and religious authority of the Greek Orthodox patriarch over the Orthodox Christian subjects of the empire. Thus there developed a system of organizing religious communities (*millets*) as largely self-governing entities within a relatively tolerant imperial structure. To Arabs, the Ottomans were at least fellow Muslims in an age when religion counted for more than nationality. But the Turks were essentially a military elite, spread thinly over a vast non-Turkish empire. The subjects, governed largely through traditional local leaders, felt no special loyalty to the Ottomans and sometimes resented their powerlessness.

Ottoman achievements involved more than military power and political sophistication. One of the keys to Ottoman power and stability was the relatively harmonious relationship between the *ulama,* as interpreters and transmitters of the Shariah, and the Ottoman administration. A simple but effective phi-losophy of government emerged that emphasized the interdependence of the Shariah, the *ulama,* the sultan, the military, and the populace. With the Shariah as the basis of the Ottoman state, the entire educational and administrative establishment was self-consciously Islamic. At the same time, the flexibility of the Shariah and its explicit sanctioning of protection for non-Muslim "people of the Book" allowed a high degree of tolerance for Christian and Jewish minorities.

The elaborate Ottoman educational system, which groomed the best and the brightest for official service, also supported creative and innovative work in astronomy, mathematics, and medicine. Literary, historical, and artistic masterpieces rival the sophistication of other sixteenth-century civilizations. Little wonder that Western Europeans who visited the court of Suleyman marvelled at the power and grandeur of the sultan and his empire. A Flemish noble, serving as Habsburg ambassador to Istanbul between 1555 and 1562, made the following striking assessment:

It makes me shudder to think of what the result of a struggle between such different systems must be; one of us must prevail and the other be destroyed. . . . On their side is the vast wealth of their empire, unimpaired resources, experience and practice in arms, a veteran soldiery, an uninterrupted series of victories, readiness to endure hardships, union, order, discipline, thrift and watchfulness. On ours are found an empty exchequer, luxurious habits, exhausted resources, broken spirits, a raw and insubordinate soldiery, and greedy quarrels; . . . and worst of all, the enemy are accustomed to victory, we to defeat.[1]

A century and a half later, Lady Mary Wortley Montagu, wife of the English ambassador to the Ottoman state, still extolled the virtues of Ottoman society and government. In a 1717 letter to her sister from Constantinople, Lady Montagu wrote:

As to their morality or good conduct, I can say . . . the Turkish ladies don't commit one sin the less for not being Christians. Now I am a little acquainted with their ways. . . . It is very easy to see they have more liberty than we have. . . . It is true that their law permits them four wives, but there is no instance of a man of quality that makes use of this liberty, or a woman of rank that would suffer it. . . . The smallpox, so fatal and so general amongst us, is here entirely harmless by the invention of engrafting (which is the term they give it). . . . There is no example of anyone that has died in it, and you may believe that I am very well satisfied of the safety of the experiment since I intend to try it on my dear little son. I am patriot enough to take pains to bring this useful invention into fashion [in] England, and I should not fail to write to some of our doctors very particularly about it if I knew anyone of them that I thought had virtue enough to destroy such a considerable branch of their revenue for the good of mankind. . . .[2]

The Ottoman victory over the Hungarians at the Battle of Mohacs in 1526, depicted here, shows that Muslim Turkish forces posed a real threat to central Europe even as Europe's journeys of exploration, discovery, and conquest were beginning. *Giraudon/Art Resource*

The Safavid Empire of Persia

Another impressive sixteenth-century Muslim empire took shape in Persia, which had been ruled during the middle period by a variety of Turkish and Mongol conquerors, most of whom were rapidly acculturated to the highly developed Islamic-Persian culture. Some of the greatest intellectual and artistic achievements of Islamic civilization, a veritable Persian renaissance, took form between the thirteenth and fifteenth centuries. Rashid al-Din's *Collection of Histories* was a landmark in historical studies and one of the greatest Persian works of prose. Persian language and culture thus became dominant in much of Muslim Asia; after Arabic, it was the second major language of the Islamic world.

The political reunification of Persia arose from an unlikely source—a small Shi'ite brotherhood on the shores of the Caspian Sea. Its leader became Shah Ismail, the founder of the Safavid Dynasty, around the year 1500. Shah Ismail expanded the boundaries of his state to include much of Iran and parts of Iraq, bringing the dynamic state into conflict with the Ottoman Empire. Although the Ottoman-Safavid rivalry was largely a struggle for influence and territorial control over the lands that lay between them, the fact that the Ottomans were officially Sunni and the Safavids officially Shi'ite gave a religious flavor to the conflict, leading to purges of suspected sectarian dissidents.

The second decade of the sixteenth century witnessed continuing military victories by Ottoman forces. But the Safavid Empire remained intact, reaching its peak of political and military power under Shah Abbas the Great, who ruled from 1588 to 1629. Abbas built a splendid new capital at Isfahan, with elegant palaces, mosques, and royal tombs. He made Isfahan an artistic and commercial center, developed trade relations with British and French companies, and proposed a military alliance with the pope against their common enemy, the Ottoman Empire. Safavid power declined after Abbas, but as was the case with Ottoman decline during the same period, it is difficult to distinguish the internal signs of decay, the alcoholism of its rulers, for example, from the external forces that were sapping its strength. Would the Safavid Empire have passed through a natural process of political decline regardless of its increasing subjugation to outside forces, represented by growing English and Russian power in the seventeenth and eighteenth centuries? The answer remains elusive. What is clear is that by the early eighteenth century, the Safavid ruling establishment was losing control of Persia and soon after collapsed.

The "Decline" of the Ottoman Empire

The Middle East was not militarily overrun by Europeans, as was Africa at the end of the nineteenth century. Nor was it assembled into an empire, as the British did in India. Rather, a growing European penetration coincided with an internal "decline" of the major Middle Eastern states, resulting in a wide variety of outcomes in the nineteenth and twentieth centuries.

Central to this entire story was the growing weakness of the Ottoman Empire, a long process usually seen as beginning after the death of Suleyman in 1566. The successors to Suleyman seemed to lack the leadership qualities of the first ten members of the dynasty. But it is difficult to determine which was cause and which was effect. Was the Ottoman

decline a result of weakening leadership at the top, or was the weakening leadership a reflection of deeper problems within the vast empire? And were these deeper problems the inevitable result of a fast-growing empire that finally reached the technological limits of control and confronted the social and economic costs of its military successes? Or were they instead the consequence of a new global system in which emergent European centers of power were able to compete with and even exploit an increasingly vulnerable empire?

If great battles are the turning points of history, then the 1571 Battle of Lepanto looms large in the history of the Middle East and its relationship with the West. Up until that great naval battle, Ottoman fleets had dominated the eastern Mediterranean. Then, however, a Christian alliance supported by Spain, Venice, and the pope decisively defeated the Ottoman naval fleet off the coast of Greece. Ironically, the defeat led to a consolidation of Ottoman control over the sea route between Egypt and Istanbul and over north African territories. Nevertheless, the destruction of two-thirds of the imperial fleet was a major blow to an Ottoman regime that previously had known only victories. An enormous ecological price was exacted by this naval battle as well. Entire forests had been cut down to construct the great galleys. More forests fell as Selim II set about rebuilding his shattered fleet, and an enormous financial strain was placed on the treasury.

Other events, much less spectacular in appearance, may have had longer-lasting consequences. One year after the Battle of Lepanto, a supernova appeared in the heavens. Fascinated by this unexpected "star" in 1572, the Danish noble Tycho Brahe began his life-long obsession with astronomy, taking careful measurements of heavenly bodies and conducting fundamental research later utilized by Kepler, Galileo, and Newton. If the development of European science was the critical ingredient in the rise of the West compared to other world regions, then the events of the 1570s hold special significance, not only for what happened in Europe but also for what did not happen in the Middle East.

Muslim scientists and political patrons had long recognized the importance of precise astronomical observations, having centuries earlier made major breakthroughs in this and related fields of study. In 1577, the Ottoman Sultan Murad III sponsored the building of an astronomical observatory with instruments as sophisticated as any in Europe at that time. When an epidemic of the plague broke out shortly thereafter, the leading member of the *ulama* interpreted the outbreak as a sign of God's displeasure with those who were seeking to penetrate his secrets. He petitioned to have the observatory dismantled; the *janissaries* wasted no time in leveling the observatory to the ground. Was the Muslim world thereby denied its own Galileo? Had there been a Galileo in Istanbul in the seventeenth century, would the Middle East and Europe have remained equally powerful over the following centuries?

There were voices that spoke out in favor of reopening the door of *ijtihad* (the path of reason and critical inquiry) within Islam. An Ottoman official Kateb Chelebi, for example, writing in the mid-seventeenth century, warned his compatriots of the consequences of cultural conservatism and geographical ignorance:

> For the man who is in charge of affairs of state, the science of geography is one of the matters of which knowledge is necessary. If he is not familiar with what the entire earth's sphere is like, he should at least know the map of the Ottoman domains and that of the states adjoining it, so that when there is a campaign and military forces have to be sent, he can proceed on the basis of knowledge. . . . Sufficient and compelling proof of the necessity for [learning] this science is the fact that the unbelievers, by their application to and their esteem for those branches of learning, have discovered the New World and have overrun the ports of India and the East Indies.[3]

But the general spirit among the intellectual elite within both the Ottoman and Safavid domains remained profoundly conservative.

For historians who emphasize the flow of capital as the moving force of history, the increasing diversion of trade to North Atlantic centers of commerce by Dutch, English, and French merchants during the seventeenth and eighteenth centuries may well have contributed to Ottoman economic decline. The influx of gold and silver from European colonies in the Americas caused considerable inflation in the Middle East, devalued Ottoman currency, raised the prices of Ottoman goods, and made their products less competitive on global markets. Thus, new products appeared in the Middle East, reflecting an increasingly global network of production and distribution. Tobacco from the Americas, for example, was initally rejected as an unacceptable innovation, but growing popular demand finally overcame the attempts by the *ulama* to draw the line.

The conflicts between the Ottoman and Safavid empires from the sixteenth to eighteenth centuries further sapped their energies when faced with the growing challenges from western Europe. Thus, the latter half of the seventeenth century saw both military setbacks and victories for the Ottomans. They organized their last offensive into Hungary, reaching Vienna in 1683. But their subsequent withdrawal was followed by a string of defeats at the hands of the Habsburgs and the Russians, culminating with the humiliating loss of territory in the Treaty of Karlowitz of 1699.

The shock of losing territory sparked some piecemeal attempts at reform during the eighteenth century within the Ottoman ruling elite. But heavy tax burdens provoked periodic revolts, which in turn required expensive investments to suppress. The outlying provinces in north Africa, Egypt, and Baghdad were asserting, and gaining, greater autonomy from Istanbul.

The Balance Shifts

In retrospect we can see that a shift in the relationship of Muslim and Christian civilizations had been underway for some time, though a widespread awareness of that shift did not occur until the mid-eighteenth century or later. By then, dramatic events made it hard to avoid. The Ottoman Empire, for example, found itself increasingly on the defensive in the face of growing Russian encroachment, aided at times by English intervention. A series of Russian-Ottoman military encounters ended in 1774 with the treaty of Kuchuk Kaynarja, ceding territorial and administrative rights to Russia. And a lengthening set of "capitulations," similar to the "unequal treaties" later signed with China, gave foreign merchants immunity from Ottoman laws and legal procedures, exempted them from internal taxes, and limited import and export duties on their products. Foreign consuls could grant these privileges to Ottoman citizens, and hundreds of thousands of them, usually Jews, Greeks, and Armenians, received this privileged status, which effectively removed them from Ottoman control and greatly enhanced European penetration of the

Ottoman economy. All of this gradually drained the proud sovereignty of the once mighty empire.

Nor was this all. In 1798, French troops under Napoleon Bonaparte occupied Egypt, shaking up the region and leading to an energetic Westernization process under the leadership of Muhammad Ali. In 1816, British naval forces bombarded the port of Algiers in north Africa and did so with impunity. Within another fifteen years, Western forces had come to the aid of Greek rebels who successfully wrested their independence from Ottoman rule. And in 1830, French forces captured Algiers, beginning a process of creeping colonization that profoundly shaped the next century and a half of north African history. Further east in the Islamic world, the British by 1800 exercised effective authority in the south Asian peninsula recently ruled by the Muslim Mughal Empire, while the Dutch consolidated their hold on Indonesia. The Middle East was no longer a hub of power and innovation; rather, it had become a region whose location and resources were coveted by Europeans who had unlocked new secrets of global influence, control, and domination. The "middle lands" were becoming the "Middle East."

Certainly the internal condition of Middle Eastern empires explains much of the epic shift in the global balance of power. The Safavid regime, for example, collapsed in the early eighteenth century, leaving the region in political disarray. The Ottoman Turks retained most of their empire—the Arab lands, Anatolia, and a corner of southeast Europe—but their political control over territory and subjects gradually weakened from the late sixteenth century onwards. Parts of Iraq and Persia, once the center of a proud and prosperous Islamic empire, lay uncultivated in the late eighteenth century. Many towns and cities of the Middle East, having once lain on the bustling trade routes that crisscrossed Afro-Eurasia, saw their commercial life-blood drained away, bypassed by busy sea lanes that connected European ports with distant regions. All of this made the states and peoples of the Middle East ever more vulnerable to the aggressive designs of an increasingly powerful Europe as the nineteenth century dawned.

The West presented many different "faces" to peoples of the nineteenth-century Middle East. For some, the initial face of the "modern" West was the soldier; for others it was the government official; for still others the merchant, missionary, or settler. But behind them all was the powerful reality of Europe's

industrial transformation, which provided both the motives and means of global expansion during the nineteenth century. Some of the "tools of empire" that led to the dramatic reversal in the global balance of power are obvious. Changes in weapons design and manufacturing led from the flint-lock musket to the modern Maxim machine gun by the 1880s. The introduction of steamboats, railways, and telegraphs, and the spectacular completion of the Suez Canal in 1869, all lowered the cost of European expansion and control.[4] Less obvious but equally important were breakthroughs in the struggle against disease. The successful extraction of the malaria prophylactic, quinine, paved the way for European colonization of Algeria beginning in the 1840s.

Just as the "faces" of the West varied greatly, so too did the responses of Middle Eastern peoples and their leaders. Muslims around the world faced the same dilemmas as other regions at the periphery of the world system—how to respond to the challenge of alien control so as to increase their political and economic independence without sacrificing the essence of their cultural identity. Did the answers lie in a wholesale imitation of Western culture, a careful selection of the keys to Western power, or a complete rejection of the modern Western package of institutions, ideas, and technologies? Was Islam inherently incompatible with this package, or was a synthesis possible, desirable, perhaps necessary? These were serious questions that tormented and divided intellectual and political leaders throughout the Islamic world and beyond.

Historians meanwhile have struggled to sort out the answers that Middle Eastern societies articulated. One approach distinguishes four major styles of action: an *adaptationist* style that attempted to synthesize positive elements of both Western and Islamic cultures; a *conservative* style willing to accept a limited degree of change but only within the context of traditional Islamic law; a *fundamentalist* style that promoted a rigorous and uncompromising return to the fundamentals of the Islamic faith; and a personal *spiritualist* style that focused attention on individual piety and charismatic leadership.[5] Such styles mixed and blended in a variety of patterns as political authorities, religious leaders, intellectuals, merchants, and ordinary people sought to cope with the intrusive presence of the Europeans.

In the process of confronting Western encroachment, Middle Eastern societies had to decide what it

The telegraph and effective firearms were among the "tools of empire" with which Europe established its hegemony in the Middle East and elsewhere, as illustrated in this drawing showing the British takeover of Egypt in the early 1880s.

was they were defending or transforming. Sometimes it was an existing state, such as the Ottoman Empire. Later in the nineteenth century, some movements defined the community at risk as a "nation," expressed in ethno-linguistic terms such as Turkish or Arab. Others identified with the Islamic world as a whole and spoke or acted in terms of a pan-Islamic identity. And not a few social movements, often led by *ulama* or Sufis, sought to transform their local societies in accordance with the prescriptions of Islam in order to confront internal decline and external aggression. Thus, in facing the European intrusion, Middle Eastern leaders and movements were defining and redefining the communities in which they lived. And since Islam was so central to all of Middle

Eastern life, they were necessarily redefining their relationship to Islam as well.

The balance of this chapter, and the next, outline a variety of Middle Eastern efforts to respond to growing European domination, to define and defend their communities, and to adjust their religious traditions to the new circumstances of the modern era. In this chapter we examine four cases—Arabia, the Ottoman Empire, Egypt, and Algeria—each of which confronted a somewhat different "face" of European imperialism. Collectively, these efforts represented the latest phase in the long encounter of Islamic and Christian civilizations, which stretched back to the seventh century. A proud civilization, long accustomed to a dominant role in the Afro-Eurasian world, was struggling to find a new internal balance and a new basis for relating to a very different international order.

The Impulse to Return: Islamic Revival and Reform

The impulse to reform and renew Islam long preceded the European threat. In the seventeenth and eighteenth centuries, and in some places much earlier, scholars and religious leaders across the Islamic world had increasingly called attention to the ways in which the practice of Islam had come to deviate from the original teachings of the prophet. Such deviation was perhaps inevitable as Islam was adapted to a variety of cultural settings across the Afro-Eurasian world. But many found the deviations intolerable and sought to rectify them. From the mid-eighteenth century, traditional Sufi orders increasingly served as instruments of reform, sometimes turning against the more pantheistic mystical expressions of Islamic religiosity practiced by some Sufis themselves. Neo-Sufi reform movements such as the Tijaniyya, which originated in eighteenth-century north Africa and spread widely in Islamic Africa, represented a shift back toward a more moderate mysticism that did not compromise the transcendent grandeur of Allah. In India, some Muslim leaders protested against the compromises that had been made with Hindus and their religious traditions.

The internal decline of Muslim power further strengthened the case for religious reform and revival. And Muslims who understood history as the triumphal march of Allah's faithful were dismayed by the string of military and political setbacks in the eighteenth and nineteenth centuries at the hands of European Christians. A young Muslim theologian, Abd al-Wahhab, argued in the eighteenth century that the declining fortunes of the Islamic world were the result of a gradual process of decay that had crept in over the centuries, as Muslims allowed themselves to be drawn away from the essentials of the faith as revealed in the Quran and the *hadith,* the two fundamental sources of the Shariah. Abd al-Wahhab was a link in a long line of puritanical reformers extending back to Ahmad Ibn Hanbal, founder of the most fundamentalist of the four Sunni legal traditions in the eighth and ninth centuries. Living in Arabia, not far from the spiritual center of the Islamic faith, Abd al-Wahhab was in an opportune location to spread his puritanical ideas. He began preaching among the tribes of the Arabian Desert in the mid-eighteenth century, calling for a return to a doctrinaire Islam with an austere and puritanical life-style, in strict accordance with the Shariah. Such austerity often meant that women were expected to subject themselves even more strictly to the traditional patronage of husbands and male relatives. Abd al-Wahhab especially denounced the widespread veneration of Sufi saints, which he regarded as a dilution of the absolute monotheism of authentic Islam. He even opposed the veneration of Muhammad's tomb at Mecca.

When in the 1740s Abd al-Wahhab joined forces with Muhammad ibn Saud, a sympathetic local chieftain, the movement took on a political dimension and soon became a state. By the early nineteenth century, this new reformist state encompassed much of central Arabia, drawing support from tribes whose economic fortunes had fallen as British control of commerce in the Red Sea and Indian Ocean directed trade away from Arabia. Mecca itself came under Wahhabi control in 1806.

Although an Egyptian army broke the military power of the Wahhabis in 1818, the movement's influence continued to spread across the Islamic world. Politically, the ibn Saud dynasty reemerged in the early twentieth century to establish the foundations of modern Saudi Arabia. But even more important, Wahhabi ideas contributed to revivalist movements all across the Muslim world. In Sumatra (now Indonesia), an Islamic reformist movement that sought to correct moral laxness and impose the veil on women and Arab dress on men became a war of resistance to Dutch penetration in the early nineteenth century. The eighteenth and nineteenth centuries likewise saw a wave of revivalist movements in west Africa aimed at purifying and extending Islam, which resulted in the creation of several large Muslim states. Similarly, in India, parts of China, the Caucasus, and the lower Nile Valley, the revivalist impulse surfaced during the nineteenth century, sometimes directed against local deviation from prescribed Islamic practice and sometimes against European invaders. While each had local roots and grew out of unique circumstances, many were linked through a variety of neo-Sufi orders, thus illustrating the continued connectedness of the Islamic world and the continued importance of the *ulama* and the *tariqah* orders. In the face of both internal decay and external aggression, many Muslims sought to reinvigorate and renew their societies by returning to the roots of Islam. That impulse, of course, persisted into the twentieth century and found a growing audience in the 1970s to 1990s.

The Ottoman Empire in Crisis

If the Wahhabis and others represented an effort to renew Islamic societies through religious revival, the leadership of the Ottoman Empire took a different approach in its efforts to revive the fortunes of this increasingly beleaguered state. At the beginning of the nineteenth century, the Ottoman Turkish Empire remained the world's foremost Islamic power, despite its decline during the seventeenth and eighteenth centuries. That decline owed much to weaknesses in the ruling dynasty, loosening administrative controls, factional rivalries, and the growing autonomy of provincial governors who in some cases ruthlessly exploited their subjects. The *janissaries,* the feared vanguard of Ottoman military organization during the sixteenth century, became reactionary defenders of the status quo, their military ineffectiveness increasingly obvious. The stagnation of agriculture and commerce stood in stark contrast to the dynamism of western Europe. Furthermore, by the end of the eighteenth century, the Ottoman Empire had lost much of its territory to the Austro-Hungarian

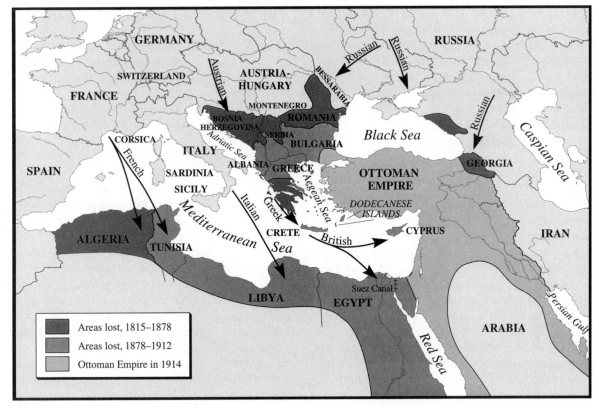

MAP 11.3 Contraction of the Ottoman Empire

and Russian empires and had lost effective control of its north African domains. The continued independence of the Ottoman state depended substantially on the inability of the European powers to agree on how to dismember it (see Map 11.3). And European commercial penetration increased the empire's dependence on its European adversaries.

Ottoman Reforms

In response to the deepening crisis, the political leadership of the Ottoman Empire set in motion a series of increasingly substantial reforms designed to preserve and strengthen the state. It was an effort at conservative modernization paralleled in many other parts of the world in the nineteenth century (Russia and China, for example), where established states found themselves severely threatened by the global shift in the balance of power. In the Ottoman case, that effort to reform the state raised deeply troubling

questions about the role of Islam in public life and about the very identity of the state itself.

The first serious efforts at reform occurred between 1789 and 1807, when Sultan Selim III attempted to set up new military and administrative structures alongside traditional institutions as a means of enhancing state power. Selim sent ambassadors to the courts of Europe, imported European technical advisers, and studied the administrative methods of Europe's "enlightened despots." But even these modest innovations stirred the hostility of powerful factions among both the *ulama* and the *janissaries,* who saw them in conflict with Islam. Opposition to Selim's reforms was so strong that he was forced from power in 1807.

His successor, Sultan Mahmud II, gradually centralized his political control and established an alternative military force until he was strong enough in the 1820s to destroy the *janissaries* and to suppress other resistance forces, ruling until 1839. During Mahmud's reign, early movements of ethnic nationalism overtly challenged Ottoman control. The Serbs rose in revolt between 1815 and 1817, and in 1821, Greek rebels waged a struggle for autonomy with the help of Western forces, gaining their independence in 1830. In the face of such setbacks, Mahmud pursued further Westernizing reforms, especially in the military and administrative areas, in an effort to create a centralized state ruled by an absolute monarch. In the process, the role of the *ulama* was weakened as Islamic institutions came under increased state control.

In 1839, the reform process deepened to include economic, social, and religious matters in addition to military and administrative concerns. A series of reform decrees under Abd al-Majid (1839–1861) and Abd al-Aziz (1861–1876) were the fruit of both internal pressures for change and demands for reform by European powers. In an effort to integrate non-Muslim subjects more effectively into the state, the principle of equality of all citizens before the law was accepted. Christians welcomed the abolition of the special tax to which they had been subject, but were less enthusiastic about being newly eligible for military conscription. A land law of 1858 transformed the traditional tax-farming system into a system of free-hold titles. Corruption may have decreased, but new forms of exploitation emerged with growing divisions between a landlord class and a sharecropping peasantry. Furthermore, Western-style legal codes and schools were introduced. Some of the technological innovations of the industrial age now spread to the Ottoman Empire. The telegraph was introduced in 1854 and, together with steamship lines and foreign-financed railroads, helped to establish a more efficient infrastructure of communication and transportation. Although this increased the efficiency of centralized administration, it drew the Ottoman economy more fully into the global system as an exporter of raw materials and an importer of manufactured goods from western Europe.

The Ottoman state borrowed heavily from European banks to sponsor its ambitious efforts to modernize Ottoman society and to enhance government control. The growing burden of debt required increased taxes on the populace, provoking rebellions, particularly among Christian subjects in the Balkans who maintained long-held grievances against Ottoman Muslim rule. When the Ottoman government attempted to repress popular uprisings, the Russian tsar threatened to intervene on behalf of his Slavic "brothers."

The Problem of Cultural Identity

The reform process raised, though failed to answer, profound questions about political and cultural identity. The Ottoman leadership, while affirming its Islamic identity, nonetheless minimized the role of the *ulama* in public life and began to substitute Western legal and educational institutions for those more directly associated with Islam. In declaring the equality of all subjects, both Muslim and non-Muslim, the reformist leadership sought to substitute loyalty to a dynastic empire for the earlier Islamic foundations of Ottoman rule. The empire would be primarily an Ottoman state rather than an Islamic state. This was one answer to the problem of identity.

Another answer was offered by a group of younger intellectuals, products of the reform process itself. Calling themselves "Young Ottomans," they favored extending Westernizing reforms to the political system itself and rejected the despotism of Ottoman rulers in favor of a constitutional regime like that of Great Britain. Moreover, they believed it was possible to find in Islam itself the basis for a commitment to freedom, progress, rationality, and patriotism. Islam, if so interpreted, supported the principles of Western liberalism. It was not necessary to choose. The growing influence of the Young Ottomans was reflected in the adoption of a short-lived constitution for the empire in 1876, which limited the authority of the sultan and established a representative government.

No sooner had Sultan Abd al-Hamid II (1876–1909) accepted the constitution than he suspended it and purged his government of the more radical reformers, using the occasion of a Russian invasion to act decisively. For the next three decades, he ruled as a reactionary autocrat, suppressing liberal and nationalist sentiments among his diverse and restive subjects, though continuing many of the educational, economic, and technical reforms of the earlier era. He sought to bolster his authority by reactivating an old claim that the Ottoman rulers, in inheriting the caliphate line from the Abbasids, spoke for the entire Islamic world. Here was a third answer to the question of identity. The Ottoman Empire would be a despotic state with a pan-Islamic identity. Thus, Abd al-Hamid II restored the *ulama* to a position of prestige, if not real power, and reintroduced the distinction between Muslim and non-Muslim subjects.

However, the decrepit empire ("the sick man of Europe," as it was known in the West) remained torn by internal divisions and pressured from without. The seeds of future tragedies were sprouting in the last decades of the nineteenth century as groups tied together by language, religion, and/or history (Armenians and Kurds, for example) began asserting rights of national self-determination, much as the empire's Balkan subjects had done earlier. And pockets of disaffected "young Turks" appeared among college students, army officers, and Turkish emigrés in western Europe. Abd al-Hamid's repressive measures only heightened their determination to reform or overthrow the regime.

In 1908, an army faction mutinied, the revolt spread, and the sultan was forced to yield power to a constitutional assembly, a sequence of events similar to the political upheavals in Persia and Russia a few years earlier. The outcome was similar as well, as the intoxicating atmosphere of individual freedom and optimism about the future turned out to be short-lived. Turkish army leaders intervened to "guide" the process of reform, maintaining an oppressive state control. Meanwhile, the Christian European powers continued to chip away at Ottoman sovereignty and territorial integrity until the empire collapsed altogether in the flames of World War I (see Map 11.3).

The "young Turks," at least some of them, began to articulate yet a fourth answer to the question of identity. Perhaps the Ottoman regime should be considered neither a dynastic state nor a pan-Islamic empire, but a Turkish national state. This was a revolutionary notion, drawn from the surging nationalism of their subject peoples and ultimately from Europe itself. It went against the grain of Islamic thinking generally, which focused loyalty on a community of faith, not of ethnicity. And it challenged the longtime Ottoman practice of incorporating a variety of cultural groups into a common political system. Furthermore, there was at the time little popular consciousness of a distinctly Turkish ethnic identity. But by the beginning of the twentieth century, a number of writers and intellectuals began to articulate the notion of a "Turkish nation" and to define its unique character. To the writer Ziya Gokalp, Turkish nationality was based fundamentally on language and expressed in folk stories and popular songs. It was compatible with both the Islamic religion and Western values and institutions. It was this conception of the identity question that would largely guide the

new state, which emerged from the ashes of the Ottoman Empire after World War I.

Egypt: From Independent Development to Colonial Rule

One of the most dramatic demonstrations of the changing global power structure occurred in 1798, when Cairo, the cultural and political capital of the western Islamic world, was occupied by a French military force. Napoleon Bonaparte's motive was not to enlarge French territory, but to strike at British interests by controlling the strategically important Suez land bridge that linked Britain with its Indian colony. The accompanying boxed excerpt illustrates how a well-educated Egyptian Muslim, al-Jabarti, viewed the French scientists, scholars, and researchers in Cairo in 1798. He was forced to the disturbing conclusion that a culture he deemed inferior had superceded the technological and intellectual achievements of his own culture, a reaction similar to that of Ibn Battuta to Chinese cultural sophistication in the fourteenth century. But al-Jabarti reacted in a quite different fashion to another face of the West encountered during 1798—the arrival of the French occupying army:

> the French entered the city [Cairo] like a torrent rushing through the alleys and streets without anything to stop them, like demons of the Devil's army. They destroyed any barricades they encountered. . . . And the French trod in the Mosque of al-Azhar with their shoes, carrying swords and rifles. . . . They plundered whatever they found in the mosque. . . . They treated the books and Quranic volumes as trash. . . . Furthermore, they soiled the mosque, blowing their spit in it, pissing and defecating in it. They guzzled wine and smashed bottles in the central court. . . .[6]

Neither the French soldiers nor the scientists remained long in Cairo, yet their brief stay there is often viewed as the beginnning of the modern age in the Middle East. Once in control of Egypt, Napoleon posed as a protector of Islam and a liberator of the Egyptians; he formed a local governing council, launched an ambitious public works program, founded a cultural institute, and encouraged research in Egyptian antiquities. Napoleon had hoped to es-

VOICES
An Encounter with European Science

When the French landed in Egypt in 1798, among the observers of their arrival was a well-educated, sophisticated, and perceptive Muslim named Abd al-Rahman al-Jabarti. Here he reflects on his encounter with European science and in doing so illustrates the cultural and technological gap that had arisen between Islamic and Western civilizations.

The French installed . . . a large library with several librarians who looked after the books and brought them to the readers who needed them. . . . If a Moslem wished to come in to visit the place he was not in the least prevented from doing so. . . . The French especially enjoyed it when the Moslem visitor appeared to be interested in the sciences. They welcomed him immediately and showed him all sorts of printed books with maps representing various parts of the world and pictures of animals and plants. . . . One was positively astounded at the sight of all these beautiful things.

I had occasion to visit this library quite a few times. I saw there, among other things, a large volume on the history of our Prophet (may God bless him). . . . Some among [the French] had also learned verses of the Koran. In short, they were great scholars and loved the sciences, especially mathematics and philology. They applied themselves day and night to learning the Arabic language and conversation. . . .

An astronomer and his students had very precise astronomical instruments. One saw among them instruments constructed in absolutely remarkable ways and which were obviously very expensive. All of these instruments were composed of many parts. . . . They also had telescopes which contracted and closed themselves in little boxes. They helped to observe the stars and determine their distances, volumes, conjunctions, and oppositions. They also had all sorts of time devices, including very valuable clocks which indicated the second very precisely, and many other instruments. . . .

One of the assistants in the laboratory took a bottle containing a certain liquid and poured a part of it into an empty glass. Then he took another bottle and poured another liquid into the same glass. It gave off a colored smoke, and when the smoke cleared, the liquid had solidified and had a yellowish color. I touched this solid mass and found it to be hard as a rock. The same demonstration was repeated with other liquids and one got a blue stone, and a third time when one got a stone as red as a ruby. Then the assistant took some white powder and placed it on an anvil. He struck it with a hammer and there was a great explosion like that of a gunshot. We were terrified, and that made the assistants laugh. . . .

We also saw a machine in which a glass went around which gave off sparks and crackled whenever a foreign object was brought near it. . . .

We had other experiences even more extraordinary than the first ones, and untutored intellects like ours could not conceive how they happened or give any explanations for them.

Source: Quoted in James Kritzeck, *Modern Islamic Literature* (Orlando: Holt, Rinehart and Winston, 1970), pp. 18–22.

tablish French influence in the Arab world and perhaps march on to India, but the British ousted French forces from Egypt in 1801. Nevertheless, by shaking up the Egyptian political and cultural order, the French invasion precipitated far-reaching changes both in Egypt and in the Middle East generally.

An Experiment in Independent Development

Turkish forces occupied Egypt when the French left. The military then mutinied and drove out the Ot-

Muhammad Ali, Egyptian leader, 1805–1848. *The Library of Congress*

toman governor. In the struggle for power that ensued, a shrewd and ambitious Albanian officer, Muhammad Ali, seized control of the government. The Ottoman sultan confirmed him as governor in 1805, but in reality, Muhammad Ali paid only formal allegiance to Istanbul and ruled Egypt as an independent state until his death in 1848.

Muhammad Ali and his successors launched Egypt on a path of state-controlled reform designed to secure the modernization and independence of the country. It was similar to the Ottoman reform program, though considerably more extensive and produced a far more profound social upheaval. It also had a different outcome, for Egypt was occupied by British forces in 1882 and ruled as a British possession thereafter.

Soon after seizing power, Muhammad Ali disposed of his rivals in a bloody purge and gained control of most of their lands. Although not highly educated, Muhammad Ali was a clever political manipulator and possessed a broad vision of what he wanted Egypt to become. He had seen enough of Eu-

ropean armies to grasp the significance of military technology and organization. Like Peter the Great of Russia a century earlier, Muhammad Ali embarked on a program of military reorganization, conscripting the sons of peasants into the army and importing European officers (mostly French) to train them. He devised a new administrative network for Egypt and expanded irrigation networks to increase agricultural production. Land was distributed to peasants under the condition of growing cash crops, especially cotton, for export. The resulting revenue was used to finance these reforms, which included rudimentary factories for armament production and textiles for army uniforms.

Muhammad Ali cautiously opened Egypt to European influences. He hired European experts such as engineers and educators, founded colleges and printing presses, and sent selected Egyptian youths to Europe for study. Both European and Egyptian business enterprises were encouraged. As a result, Egypt's commercial and intellectual elites became more Europeanized than those of other Middle Eastern areas. Traditional Middle Eastern industries and guilds, unable to compete with cheaper imported goods from Europe, gradually declined during the middle decades of the nineteenth century. Muhammad Ali's economic policies also produced a new dominant class of large landowners, many of whom became military officers and bureaucrats. The religious leadership—both the *ulama* and Sufis—was brought under state control.

Muhammad Ali's reign represented a pioneering effort to achieve a measure of modern development and to secure Egypt's political and economic independence at the same time. Its goals were similar to those of Japan, which substantially transformed its economy and society later in the century and successfully avoided European domination. Why was Egypt not able to do the same?

The Suez Canal and Egyptian Debt

One answer is that Egypt lay directly in the path of major European interests, particularly the route to India, which guaranteed intensive British and French concern about its affairs, whereas Japan was more marginal to major European interests. The limits of Egypt's ability to develop as a regional military power became apparent as Muhammad Ali and his new army conquered the Sudan to the south, and brought parts of the Arabian Peninsula under Egyptian control. When he invaded Syria and threatened Ottoman interests in 1839, Britain and France intervened to protect the Ottoman Empire, viewing it as a buffer against Russian expansion, and forced Egypt's withdrawal. The main route from Europe to Asia had been shifting from the South African Cape to Egypt and the Red Sea, and the British were worried about some rival blocking access to India. Furthermore, the extension of the Anglo-Ottoman Commercial Treaty of 1838 to Egypt facilitated the importing of manufactured goods and contributed to growing Egyptian dependency, based in particular on the export of cotton to the European "workshop."

Muhammad Ali's successors were increasingly seduced by European tastes and products, and Egypt fell more and more deeply into a semicolonial relationship with Britain and France, something the Japanese leadership later avoided. Ismail, grandson of Muhammad Ali, assumed power in 1863. Enamored with European culture, he hired European experts and administrators, granted concessions to European businesspeople, and invited European missionaries to open schools for Egyptian children. He spent lavishly to make Cairo a modern capital, with gas lines, waterworks, and even an opera house, leaving Egypt deeply indebted to European creditors. Ismail's greatest achievement was the completion of the Suez Canal in 1869, built at enormous human cost by conscripted Egyptian laborers with capital invested by a European syndicate. Meanwhile, Egyptian revenues were being drained by corruption, court extravagance, and various costly and foolish projects. Cotton exports, Egypt's main source of foreign currency, dropped sharply in price following the end of the American Civil War. By 1876, the Egyptian economy was hopelessly bankrupt.

Since most of the debt was owed to British and French banks, these two governments forced Ismail to turn over control of Egypt's finances to their representatives. The measures ordered by these foreigners to "stabilize" the Egyptian economy stirred popular resentment, as economic austerity fell more heavily on the average Egyptian. Traditionalist members of the *ulama,* liberal intellectuals, and nationalist army officers were outraged at the weakness of the government. The Egyptian masses benefited little from the glittering projects for which they were paying. Growing anti-European resentment crystalized around a nationalist Egyptian army officer, Colonel Ahmed Urabi. In 1881, Urabi's troops, backed by popular outcries, rebelled and forced the weak Khedive Tawfiq, who had replaced Ismail in 1879, to appoint a pro-nationalist administration.

Spreading popular protests erupted into riots in some areas, leading to attacks on Europeans in Alexandria as symbols of Egyptian humiliation and exploitation. In response, the British fleet bombarded Alexandria and then landed troops to "restore order." Urabi brushed aside the weak khedive, seized control of the government, and declared war on Britain. British forces soon crushed the Egyptians and occupied Cairo. Urabi was captured and sent into exile, but the memory of his uprising remained an emotional chord waiting to be played by later nationalists.

The British military occupation of Egypt turned out to be long-lasting, primarily because the Suez Canal was the chief route to India, Britain's most important colonial possession. The khedive was restored as a figurehead, with effective governing power placed in the hands of a British governor, Evelyn Baring, later known as Lord Cromer.

From 1883 to 1907, Cromer served as de facto dictator of Egypt. Brilliant, decisive, aloof, and ruthless, he reorganized the administration, regularized the finances, and established economic reforms that served British interests. Arrogant toward those whom he considered "the lesser races," Cromer rejected growing demands from Egyptian intellectuals and politicians for a gradual sharing of authority. Only on some distant day, when the Egyptian people had reformed their society and shown greater capacity for self-rule, could such a radical proposal be considered. Egypt, once a pioneering experiment in independent development, had been transformed into a colonial dependency under British rule.

Islam and Egyptian Reform

The creation of a new bureaucracy, the emergence of a Westernized intellectual class, the growing presence of foreign merchants, the subordination of Islamic religious leaders to the state, and the British occupation—all of this represented a powerful challenge to Egyptian society. Two major intellectual responses—Islamic modernism and Egyptian national-

A political cartoon from Egypt illustrating the nationalist perception of British and French imperialism in North Africa. *The Library of Congress*

ism—sought to understand the changes and chart a course to the future.

Islamic modernism was similar in approach to that of the Young Ottomans in the Ottoman Empire. Its primary spokesman, both in Egypt where he lived during the 1870s and in the Islamic world generally, was Jamal al-Din (1839–1897), known commonly as al-Afghani. A fiery preacher and writer who traveled tirelessly throughout the Muslim world, al-Afghani stirred Muslims against European political, economic, and cultural encroachment. He advocated a pan-Islamic unity that would transcend the regional, national, and ethnic differences that divided the *ummah.* He urged Muslims to organize and work for the political revival of Islam, utilizing armed struggle if necessary. But it was also necessary to reform Islam and Islamic societies, ridding them of corruption, irrationality, passivity, and resignation. Only then could Islam become the basis for new societies, able to assimilate the technical and scientific knowledge of the West while rejecting its materialism. Al-Afghani mobilized support for the Urabi revolt in Egypt in the early 1880s and helped organize a boycott against Western tobacco concessions in Persia in the 1890s.

Al-Afghani's major Egyptian disciple was Muhammad Abduh (1849–1905), a prominent thinker and writer who played a leading role in articulating a synthesis between Islamic and Western intellectual traditions. He reaffirmed both the truth of Islamic revelation and the truth as derived through rational analysis, arguing that when properly understood and interpreted, the two were entirely compatible. British authorities exiled Abduh after his activities in support of the Urabi revolt, but he later returned to Cairo and rose to the influential position of *mufti,* or senior interpreter of Islamic law, in 1899. Abduh's efforts to reinterpret Islam to meet the challenge of a changing world influenced thinkers throughout the Muslim world.

Alongside Islamic modernism, Egyptian nationalism emerged in the latter nineteenth century with a somewhat different understanding of Egypt's situation. While Islamic modernists such as al-Afghani and Muhammad Abduh saw a reformed faith as the foundation for political revival, nationalists such as the Egyptian lawyer Mustafa Kamil (1874–1908) viewed Islam as a largely personal matter and sought political salvation for Egypt in a more secular and national identity. This was similar to the situation in the Ottoman Empire, where the nationalism of the Young Turks replaced earlier religiously based conceptions of Ottoman identity. In Egypt, however, there was a more solid historical foundation for a distinctive national consciousness. Many Egyptian thinkers had become more aware of the unique heritage of Egyptian civilization as a result of nineteenth-century archeological discoveries. The Urabi revolt and opposition to subsequent British rule enlarged the constituency for this kind of thinking as Egypt entered the twentieth century.

Algeria: Settler Colonization and Muslim Resistance

Already by the late eighteenth century, the Maghrib, known also as the Barbary Coast, had become an irritant to European powers due to privateering and demands for tribute, both of which interfered with the free flow of Mediterranean commerce. Furthermore, a long-standing dispute over payments for shipments of wheat, which Algeria sold to France during the Napoleonic wars, led to conflicts between the two governments and precipitated the French conquest of Algiers in 1830. There followed a gradual but costly extension of military control over the coastal region, as Algeria became a French colonial territory. Thus the Algerian experience with European imperialism was quite different from that of Arabia, the Ottoman Empire, or even Egypt.

The French destroyed or dismantled most of the administrative institutions they found at Algiers in 1830. The Turkish-speaking military elite, along with many of the Arabic-speaking *ulama,* either were exiled or chose to emigrate to the east, leaving the French occupiers to set up an administrative structure from scratch.

In addition, French-occupied Algeria saw the influx of a substantial European settler population beginning in the 1840s. Among the various faces represented by Europe in the Middle East, the most disruptive was that of the settler, the immigrant who came to stay. Although these immigrants arrived from a variety of European countries, they came to view themselves as French Algerians and expected the colonial state to provide them easy access to Algerian land and labor. By the 1840s, the continual French military campaigns to expand territorial control were leading to revolutionary changes as Muslim Algerians, both Arabs and Berbers, faced political subjugation, land expropriation, and new forms of taxation. Algerians who lay in the path of

the expansionist colonial state were forced to eke out an existence on the least productive land (since the best land had been taken over for the settlers) or to go to work as wage laborers on settler plantations.

Not surprisingly, many Algerians resisted the radical changes brought about by French colonization, although their responses covered a wide spectrum from cooperation to tenacious opposition. Dozens of rebellions erupted in the four decades following 1830, many of them tribally based. Movements that launched their appeal in the name of Islam stood the best chance of gaining widespread support. The most successful and enduring of the movements was led by a Sufi *tariqah* leader, Abd al-Qadir, from 1832 to 1847.

A brilliant military tactician and shrewd political leader, Abd al-Qadir held the French at bay for fifteen years, alternately negotiating with and fighting the colonial regime. He organized an effective administrative structure that governed a substantial part of the interior. In Abd al-Qadir's movement lay the origins of a modern Algerian state as well as an embryonic sense of national identity in which Islamic solidarity played an important part. By 1847, French military superiority, together with ethnic divisions in Algerian society, led to Abd al-Qadir's defeat and exile. Though he never set foot in Algeria again, the memory of his resistance movement remained deeply embedded in Algerian culture. In the 1950s, that memory was resurrected as a potent national symbol during Algeria's war for national liberation from France.

In the nineteenth century, Abd al-Qadir's movement was one of many others that organized resistance to French colonization. At times a common Islamic identity superceded linguistic divisions and ethnic allegiances of this largely rural society. But some Algerian groups found Abd al-Qadir's state-building efforts a greater threat than the French colonial regime. Thus there was no single Islamic response to French colonialism.

As the Muslim population of Algeria came under increasing pressure from the growing influx of European settlers, periodic outbursts of millenarian fervor erupted in which a charismatic leader would predict an imminent climactic struggle leading to a utopian future. There were long-standing Muslim traditions that provided justification for such mass movements—from the "renewer" of the faith who was to return each century to the *mahdi* (messiah) who would establish a perfect theocratic order.

The most dramatic expression of *mahdism* occurred not in Algeria but in the Sudan, which had been conquered by Egypt earlier in the nineteenth century. A variety of local grievances fueled resentment against Ottoman-Egyptian rule. Sudanese Muslims were offended by the imported *ulama* from Egypt and by the "worldliness" of Egyptian administrators; those with an economic interest in the slave trade resented Egyptian efforts to curb it. In 1881, Muhammad Ahmad, a pious and ascetic Muslim who had been associated with a local Sufi order for twenty years, declared himself the *mahdi* and initiated a holy war against the Egyptian regime. With growing popular support, he established a theocratic regime consciously patterned after the early Islamic state of the Prophet Muhammad. It lasted until 1898, when it fell to British forces.

Meanwhile, in Algeria, overt mass resistance to the colonial order had been crushed by 1871. A two-caste society became increasingly rigid as the privileged and comfortable European settler minority exploited the impoverished and frustrated Muslim majority. At the end of the nineteenth century, the settlers looked back with pride at what they had accomplished in Algeria over the previous half-century. They little suspected that they were sitting atop a sleeping volcano that would erupt into a bitter war some fifty years later. After World War II, some saw that struggle as a renewal of the militant opposition pioneered by Abd al-Qadir.

| Conclusion

By the end of the nineteenth century, no part of the Middle East remained untouched by a global economic system whose central features involved the export of raw materials to Europe and the import of manufactured goods from Europe. The closer the relationship with industrializing Europe, the more extensively were traditional forms of industrial production undermined—weaving, metallurgy, manufacturing—as locally produced goods could no longer compete with the cheaper mass-produced imports from Europe. The spread of modernity, from this angle of vision, often meant the deindustrialization of the Middle East.[7]

Similarly, no part of the Middle East remained untouched by the cultural imprint of the West, although here the impact was quite uneven. Despite energetic missionary efforts, the conversion from Islam to Christianity had been negligible. However, mission schools in Cairo and Beirut trained a body of Western-educated students, who played prominent roles in the intellectual and political history of the region through much of the twentieth century. Enlightenment ideas of natural rights of individuals and nineteenth-century notions of nationalism sowed the seeds of future upheavals and demands for change in the colonial order.

The political impact of the Western challenge was also highly varied by the end of the nineteenth century. Some areas remained nominally independent of foreign control. Britain and France had propped up a weakening and shrinking Ottoman state as a buffer against Russian expansion. Morocco, though still independent, was coveted by several European powers and would become a French protectorate in the early twentieth century. Persia came under increasing pressure from Russia and Britain but managed to escape formal colonization. Parts of Arabia were simply ignored initially because they seemed of no geopolitical importance to European strategists, though the Persian Gulf region was of growing importance. The British colonial protectorate in Egypt was similar to the French system of indirect rule in Tunisia. Algeria, the most intensively colonized region, was considered part of France.

By the turn of the century, Western technology, organization, and assertiveness had become so overwhelming that the entire world appeared at Europe's disposal. Beyond the Middle East, Muslim territories and peoples in Africa, central Asia, and South and Southeast Asia likewise found themselves under alien control. Little wonder that Europeans felt smugly confident that the traditional rivalry between Christendom and the "lands to the east" had been decisively altered in their favor.

As European leaders exulted over the collapse of Islamic power, they easily overlooked the continuing spread of the religion to new areas and the reaffirmation of Islam in long-established Muslim regions. In Africa and Asia, people continued to join the *ummah,* largely at the expense of traditional localized religions. The link between a growing Islamic identity and resistance to European hegemony would shape Middle Eastern history throughout the twentieth century.

Notes

1. Quoted in C. T. Forster and F. H. B. Daniell, eds., *The Life and Letters of Ogier Ghiselin de Busbecq,* vol. 1 (London: Kegan Paul, 1881), rpt. in Philip Riley, *The Global Experience,* vol. 2 (Englewood Cliffs, NJ: Prentice Hall, 1987), p. 39.

2. Quoted in Lord Wharncliffe, ed., *The Letters and Works of Lady Mary Wortley Montagu,* vol. 1 (London: Henry G. Bohn, 1861), pp. 298–300, 307–309.

3. Quoted in Norman Itzkowitz, *Ottoman Empire and Islamic Tradition* (New York: Knopf, 1972), p. 106.

4. Daniel R. Headrick, *The Tools of Empire* (New York: Oxford University Press, 1981).

5. John Voll, *Islam: Continuity and Change in the Modern World* (Boulder, Colo.: Westview Press, 1982), pp. 28–31, 146–47.

6. Quoted in Magali Morsy, *North Africa: 1800–1900* (London: Longman, 1984), p. 79.

7. Charles Issawi, *An Economic History of the Middle East and North Africa* (New York: Columbia University Press, 1982), chap. 8.

Chapter 12

Nationalism, Modernity, and Islam: The Middle East in the Twentieth Century

During the nineteenth century, the Middle East had shared the fate of India, China, Africa, and other major world regions in falling under European control. In the twentieth century, it joined them in casting off that control, in reshaping its societies along new lines, and in regaining a more independent and prominent role on the global stage.

The twentieth-century Middle Eastern revival was expressed in numerous ways. Among the most prominent were the emergence of powerful nationalist movements and the creation of corresponding nation-states in Turkey, Egypt, Algeria, Iraq, and elsewhere. These movements broke Europe's political hold on the Middle East and gave rise to strong states committed to the modernization and economic development of their societies. By the 1960s, a number of these states (Egypt and Algeria, for example) had governments proclaiming allegiance to an even more radical transformation of society under the banner of "Arab socialism." And in the 1970s, the oil-producing states in the Middle East took dramatic advantage of their political independence and sharply raised the price of this precious commodity, thus gaining a measure of revenge on the West for centuries of economic exploitation. Meanwhile, the competing claims of Palestinian and Israeli nationalisms made the Middle East a focal point of the Cold War, providing Arabs in particular and Muslims generally a focus for united action and feeling, a means of overcoming, at least occasionally, their many divisions.

Throughout this process of Middle Eastern revival, and especially by the 1970s and 1980s, a growing number of Muslims began to feel that something precious had been lost: the centrality of Islam in public life. Islam had always claimed to provide a blueprint for all of life—political structures, social relationships, legal codes, and economic policy as well as the more personal relationship between the individual and Allah. But the various twentieth-century nation-states into which the region was divided proclaimed ethno-linguistic loyalty (Turkish, Arab, Egyptian, Algerian)—not religion—as the primary basis of political identification. State-led programs for modernization were, explicitly or implicitly, secularizing and Westernizing. Shariah courts lost out to Western legal systems, and religious leaders and institutions were brought under state control. When Islam was invoked at all, it was to mobilize the masses on behalf of some nationalist movement or political program. Religious faith, long at the heart of Middle Eastern life, had been relegated to the personal domain or removed to the margins of public life. And the presence of Israel, heavily supported by the United States and Europe, served as a reminder of a continuing "imperialist" presence in the Middle East. Finally, these secular, nationalist, or socialist regimes often seemed inadequate to the tasks at hand, unable to provide political stability or to solve the overwhelming problem of massive poverty amid rapidly rising populations.

These conditions combined to generate renewed movements of Islamic assertion, often called Islamic fundamentalism, that referred back to the Wahhabis and other movements of Islamic revival in the eighteenth and nineteenth centuries. In the twentieth century, this style of thought and action became particularly prominent in the 1970s to 1990s, achieving political power in Iran in 1979 and gaining considerable support elsewhere, both in the Middle East and in the broader Islamic world. Such movements represented yet another element in the continuing struggle of Middle Eastern and Islamic societies to find their place in the modern world. That struggle is the main theme of this chapter.

Arab Nationalism and the Arab Revolt

The rise of nationalism over the past two centuries has been one of the most powerful forces in world affairs. In the Middle East and other parts of the colonial world, *nationalism* sometimes refers to any anticolonial movement. The nineteenth century witnessed dozens of such movements in the Middle East, starting with the Egyptian response to the French invasion at the dawn of the century, continuing with Serbian nationalism in the teens, Greek nationalism in the 1820s, and Algerian nationalism beginning in the 1830s, to highlight a few. But if nationalist movements rejected colonial rule, they usually did so by affirming a new definition of community—the nation, associated with a particular territory. As elsewhere in the colonial world, the idea of the nation as a primary political or cultural loyalty was a new conception, derived from nineteenth-century European usage. It usually began among members of the literary elite, who sought to identify the supposedly unique roots of the nation in its language, its folk customs, or its historical heritage. Gradually, the various nationalisms of the Middle East—Turkish, Arab, Egyptian, Algerian, Iranian—gained the emotional support of larger circles of people.

But nationalism in the Middle East had to contend with two important cultural realities unique to the region. One was that the Arabic language was spoken widely in the Middle East and certainly was not limited to a single state. This gave rise to a pan-Arab nationalism that transcended any particular state. A politically conscious resident of Algiers, for example, might well have identified with an emerging Algerian national consciousness while simultaneously feeling part of a larger Arab nation. The other complication for nationalists in the Middle East was, of course, Islam, which had always defined fundamental loyalties in cosmopolitan religious terms, transcending particular linguistic or ethnic communities.

Here was a tension that Middle Eastern political and cultural leaders could not avoid. Some came to think in terms of a larger pan-Islamic "nation"; others emphasized specifically Islamic elements in their particular national identities; and still others sought to limit Islam to the realm of private life while focusing attention on the ethnic or linguistic basis of national identity. All of this meant that emerging national identities in the Middle East were fluid and overlapping.

Ironically, certain European innovations fostered the very nationalism that became the vehicles of resistance against Western dominance. The printing press allowed increased diffusion of ideas; Western missionary schools such as the Syrian Protestant College (later the American University of Beirut) produced educated persons familiar with European political ideas; and modern techniques of transportation and communication accelerated the exchange of people, products, and ideas. These and other innovations contributed to the growing strength of nationalist sentiment during the nineteenth and twentieth centuries. Among these movements was Arab nationalism, which initially had an interesting double focus—directed against both Ottoman Turks and Europeans.

Despite their status as the original Muslims in whose language the Quran was written, Arabs had lost much of their distinctiveness as Islam became a cosmopolitan faith in which other people came to play the leading role. Ever since the fifteenth century, the Ottoman Turks had been the most formidable military defenders of the Islamic world, and many Arabs were among their subject peoples. For the most part they had viewed the Ottomans as legitimate protectors of their interests as fellow Muslims. But by the early twentieth century, such sentiments were changing due to increasingly reactionary Turkish rule and Ottoman ineffectiveness in countering growing European influence. Ahmed Urabi's revolt against the British in Egypt in 1881–1882 had stimulated Arab nationalist feeling directed at both European and Turkish domination. And the seizure of power by the nationalist Young Turks in Istanbul in 1908 increased the sense of both alienation and hope for change by subject peoples, emotions felt all the more intensely because Greeks, Serbs, and others had already gained their national independence.

Of special importance for the growth of Arab nationalism was the emergence of a politically and culturally self-conscious Arabic-speaking literary elite in Damascus and Beirut. Some of these people came to feel that Islamic leadership belonged in Arab hands since it had been the Arabs who had fostered the rise and spread of Islam. Proposals for an actual political movement—an Arab revolt—centered on Sharif Husayn. He was a descendant of Muhammad and an Ottoman-appointed governor of Mecca and Medina, where the sacred sites of Islam were located. Among Arab leaders at the time, Husayn came closest to claiming a widespread allegiance and he hoped to translate this support into a renewed Arab kingdom with himself at its head.

World War I provided the opportunity. The Turkish army, armed and trained by the Germans, entered the war as an ally of the kaiser. The Ottoman attempt to rally support among his subjects by declaring the war a *jihad* was less than convincing among large numbers of his subjects, particularly those who had craved greater autonomy if not complete independence from Istanbul's oppressive control. With the inducement and blessing of the British, Husayn and his sons launched an Arab revolt against the Turks in 1916, based on vague promises of support for Arab independence. When the momentum finally turned in favor of the Allies in 1917, the Arab forces led by Faysal, son of Husayn, combined with the British to force a Turkish retreat from Arabia north to Syria.

But the British had made other promises during this long war. Even earlier they had signed a secret pact (the Sykes-Picot agreement of 1916) with their French and Russian allies to carve up most of the Ottoman Empire among themselves after the war. And in 1917, the British government issued the Balfour Declaration, publicly supporting the establishment of a "national home for the Jewish people" in Palestine, on the condition that such a home not infringe on the rights of the non-Jewish majority residing there.

The Balfour Declaration was a major victory for the Zionist Organization that had been working for twenty years to cultivate Great Power support for a migration of Jews to Palestine. Theodor Herzl, a Jewish Hungarian journalist, was responsible for transforming the age-old dream of returning to Zion (Jerusalem) from a vague spiritual wish into a practical political solution to the recurring cycles of anti-Semitism that had subjected Jewish minorities to persecution for centuries. His influential pamphlet, *Der Judenstaat* ("The Jewish State"), published in 1896, persuasively argued the case for political Zion-

ism, and Herzl convened the first Zionist congress in Basel, Switzerland, the following year. Twenty years later, British government leaders, fighting desperately for wartime survival, saw the Balfour Declaration as a means of winning Jewish support for the war effort, of helping to assure British control of the Suez region, and of atoning for centuries of European anti-Semitism.

Thus, Palestine, long known as "the promised land," became cynically referred to as "the much-promised land." Both Arabs and Zionists (Jews supporting the establishment of a state in Palestine) looked to the wartime promises as important steps toward their nationalist dreams.

In the 1919 peace conference at Versailles, where the victors laid the groundwork for a new geopolitical order, Emir Faysal presented his case for the establishment of a united Arab nation. But the Arabs were bitterly disappointed by what they regarded as a betrayal of the wartime agreements and of the promises contained in Woodrow Wilson's famous "Fourteen Points." Much of the Middle East was divided along the lines of the Sykes-Picot agreement largely under British and French control (see Map 12.1). This occurred under the auspices of the League of Nations' mandate system, in which the lands were to be governed by the Allied powers and prepared for eventual independence. The British assumed control of Palestine (the land west of the Jordan River), created a new Arab kingdom of (Trans)Jordan (east of the Jordan River), and oversaw the placing of Faysal on the throne of Iraq. The French, by force of arms, took over control of Syria, carving out Lebanon in the process. Written into the mandate over British-ruled Palestine was the Balfour Declaration, which provided international sanction for Jewish immigration and land purchase. The Arab population, although poorly organized and ethnically divided, quickly grasped the significance of the new order, and growing tensions among Arabs, Jews, and the British administration, marked by occasional outbursts of violence, became the hallmark of the interwar period.

Meanwhile, in Mecca, Sharif Husayn was independent but frustrated. Not only was his pan-Arab dream in tatters, but his own control over the Hijaz (western Arabia) was soon challenged by the expansionist Abd al-Aziz ibn Saud, who united most of the Arabian peninsula under his personal control during the 1920s and 1930s. Thus the Arab revolt, which

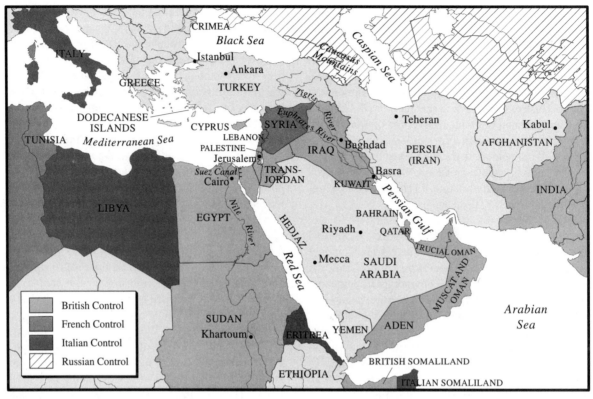

MAP 12.1 The Middle East between the Wars

had aimed at freeing and unifying the Arab nation, did neither. Instead it left the Arab lands fragmented and under various levels of direct and indirect European control in the wake of Ottoman political collapse.

The Rise of the Turkish Nation

Far more successful than the Arabs in throwing off European control and fashioning a new society were the Turks. As the First World War ended, the Ottoman Empire lay in ruins before the victorious Allies, who stripped off its Arab provinces and attempted to carve up Anatolia itself. But out of the ashes of the Ottoman Empire arose a unified Turkish nation-state that managed to defy and reverse the humiliating conditions imposed by the Allies at the postwar conferences.

In the face of far-reaching Allied demands, the Ottoman Turkish sultan, eager to save his dynasty, accepted the harsh terms handed to him by the Allies. But when the Greeks—former subjects and age-old enemies of the Turks—occupied the western region of Anatolia, a determined Turkish movement of national resistance arose under the leadership of a wartime general, Mustafa Kemal. In the early 1920s, Kemal led a military campaign that forced the evacuation of Greek forces from Anatolia and tenaciously held out for more favorable terms by the Allies. In no mood to continue the fight and exhausted by the war, the Allies accepted the unification of Turkey. This was greeted enthusiastically all over the Muslim world, as a victory for Islam as well as for the Turkish nation. But for Christian Armenians who had been promised an independent state in eastern Turkey, the Lausanne Treaty of 1923, which recognized the independence of Turkey, was a bitter betrayal and a continuation of their tragedy, after having endured unspeakable suffering during the war years.

Led by the dynamic Kemal, the new Turkish National Congress declared the Ottoman Empire abolished and the Turkish state a republic. Kemal then pushed for radical reforms in Turkish society, politics, and culture, continuing in a more thoroughgoing fashion the modernizing reforms of the Ottoman Empire in the nineteenth century. Seeking far more than national independence, he wanted to create a thoroughly modern Turkish society and viewed traditional Islamic institutions, beliefs, and rituals as obstacles. Within a few years, the caliphate had been officially abolished, Sufi orders disbanded, and the Shariah replaced by Swiss legal codes. A new state agency exercised control over the religious endowments called *waqf*, which had been the traditional source of independence for the *ulama*. In 1932, the government even ordered that the call to prayer should be made in Turkish rather than Arabic. Although the mosques remained open and Kemal justified his reforms as being in tune with the spirit of Islam, the material base of much of the Islamic establishment was taken away, considerably increasing the power of the state. Islam had largely lost its position as the foundation of public life. In Kemal's view, Islam should become a modernized personal religion, accessible to the individual citizens of a secular Turkish state.

Mustafa Kemal's radical reforms were the most ambitious attempts at social and cultural engineering in the Middle East. For Kemal, modernizing meant a thorough Westernizing of Turkish society. Like Japan in the late nineteenth century, Turkey's transformation was largely an "elite revolution" led by military and civilian officials unburdened by close ties to traditional landholding groups. State-organized enterprises were set up with centralized economic planning on the Soviet model, though without the redistribution of wealth and social revolution that were part of the Soviet experience. A secular educational system was devised. The Turkish language, "purified" to eliminate words borrowed from Arabic and Persian, was now to be written in the Latin instead of Arabic script. In 1935, Turks were asked to rename themselves, assuming surnames as in the West. Thus Kemal became Kemal Ataturk. The traditional headdress known as the *fez* was replaced by legally required brimmed hats. As Kemal explained to a Turkish audience:

A civilized, international dress is worthy and appropriate for our nation, and we will wear it. Boots or shoes on our feet, trousers on our legs, shirt and tie, jacket and waistcoat—and of course, to complete these, a cover with a brim on our heads. . . .[1]

Turkish women gained new legal rights under Kemal's reforms. Polygamy was abolished. The husband's right to repudiate his wife or wives, a tradition that had invited abuse, was taken away. Under the European-modeled legal codes, women achieved equal rights to divorce, child custody, inheritance, and education. By the mid-1930s, they had been granted the right to vote in national elections. Although many Turkish women led the struggle to achieve these reforms, one woman in particular gained international stature as a writer, an intellectual, and a symbol of the new Turkish woman. Halide Edib had been influenced earlier in the century by the nationalist ideology of Ziya Gokalp. Edib's writings explored in depth the political, social, and cultural dilemmas faced by Turkey during the interwar period, providing special insights into changes and continuities in the lives of women.

Despite these dramatic changes, there was no social revolution in Turkey. Landlords kept their lands; most property was owned privately; and there was no effort to mobilize the masses for drastic political action. In fact, there was considerable continuity with earlier patterns of Turkish life. Despite the imitation of Western European parliamentary politics, the Turkish government remained authoritarian. Despite the attacks on Islamic symbols, Turkish society at the local level remained firmly attached to Islamic traditions. And despite the efforts at developing a Turkish-controlled industrialization, the country remained in a largely dependent relationship with the more highly industrialized regions of the world.

After Ataturk's death in 1938, some of his more radical decrees were moderated, and a multiparty parliamentary system was allowed to develop. In 1950, the opposition Democratic party came to power and restored Arabic as the language of calling the faithful to prayer. A variety of other movements and parties emerged, calling for the restoration of Islam to a more prominent role in society and the state. But behind the democratic veneer and the chronic threat of political instability stood the military, ready to intervene when politicians appeared to lose control or yield to religious pressures.

Nevertheless, the Turkish Republic under Kemal Ataturk and his successors provided a distinctive answer to the question of what it meant to be modern in an Islamic setting. While modern Turkey was the

Mustapha Kemal Ataturk and his wife Latifah. *The Bettmann Archive*

first Islamic state to successfully defy European political power, it was also the first to embrace Western culture and civilization in public life and to relegate Islam to the sphere of private life. Clearly, large numbers of Turkish and other Muslims did not find that a satisfactory answer.

The Second World War and the Crumbling of Imperialism

Despite Turkey's dramatic example of independent development, much of the Middle East, though officially "independent," remained under various degrees of European control during the years between the two world wars, even as movements of national

self-determination became increasingly assertive. Iraq became nominally independent when Britain gave up its mandate in 1932, but remained in the imperial shadow through a defensive treaty. Egypt remained occupied by British troops, and the descendants of Muhammad Ali, now monarchs instead of khedives, jostled with the nationalist politicians of the assembly for popular support. In turbulent Syria, the French suppressed a bitter insurrection and sliced off Lebanon as a separate territory, with carefully manipulated boundaries that provided for a Christian majority. Iran remained independent, with the British controlling the oil-producing southwest region of the country. A period of political instability ended with a takeover by an ambitious and ruthless army officer, Reza Khan, in 1921, who declared himself the founder of the Pahlavi dynasty in 1925. The Arabian peninsula was largely controlled by a Saudi dynasty that revived its eighteenth-century claims to the area. Only in north Africa did traditional colonies of France and Italy remain intact.

Palestine was opened to Zionist settlement by the British in accordance with the League of Nations' mandate of 1920. Thousands of Jewish settlers arrived annually, adding to the strength of the Yishuv, the Zionist community, although Jews remained outnumbered by the Muslim and Christian Arab population. As Jewish and Palestinian nationalism arose in opposition to each other, tensions increased, erupting at times into violence. Zionist immigration increased dramatically following Adolf Hitler's 1933 rise to power in Nazi Germany, and Arab fears of being overwhelmed by an alien influx increased correspondingly, leading to an Arab uprising in 1936 that was harshly suppressed by the British.

In 1939, as the shadow of war hung over Europe again, the British reversed their traditional support for Zionist immigration and land purchase in Palestine. At stake were the potential alienation of vital Arab areas and an increasingly important supply of oil from the Middle East. Now it was the Zionists' turn to feel betrayed by the British. But with the rising threat of Nazi Germany, they had little choice except to swallow their disappointment.

World War II (1939–1945) broke the European imperial grip on much of the Middle East, as it did in Asia and Africa as well. The brief occupation of Middle Eastern regions by Fascist and Allied armies accelerated demands for change following the war. For example, north African soldiers who fought in

Europe were resentful when asked to accept their prewar status as colonial subjects. The end of the war left the European powers weakened and unable in some areas to reassert their control. Thus the mandate system lapsed, and Syria, Jordan, and Israel emerged as independent states. The global wave of nationalist movements spread across the formal colonial regimes of north Africa, with Libya achieving independence in 1951, Tunisia and Morocco in 1956, and Algeria, following a long and bitter struggle, in 1962.

Thus, the Middle East emerged from over a century of European political domination to chart new political courses. In the process, emerging leaders faced a number of daunting questions. What kind of accommodation would Muslims work out with the increasingly technical global system? Was Islam compatible with liberal democracy, secular nationalism, or revolutionary socialism? How would Muslims accommodate the increasing recognition of equal rights and obligations for women? Would the *ummah* reconstitute itself, or were localized nationalisms and separate states permanent features of the political landscape? Would Muslims, Christians, and Jews be able to live side by side in peace, or would they make exclusive claims to truth, to personal allegiances, and to territorial control? These have been among the issues with which Middle Eastern societies have struggled in the latter half of the twentieth century.

Arab Socialism and Nasser's Egyptian Revolution

As independence dawned on Middle Eastern states following World War II, quite a number of them (Iran, Iraq, Jordan, Saudi Arabia, Egypt, Libya, Morocco) were ruled by monarchies of one kind or another. They were concerned with problems of national unity, with the promotion of modern development, and, of course, with preserving their own regimes. Jordan, Saudi Arabia, and Morocco have been sufficiently successful to maintain their dynasties into the 1990s.

Elsewhere economic failure or political conflict resulted in the overthrow of the initial independence regimes and their replacement by others espousing a more radical transformational approach known generally as Arab socialism. Stressing the importance of Arab unity and vigorous opposition to Western control, such movements also argued for a more radical Socialist approach to the transformation of their societies under state control. But they vigorously rejected communism as a foreign ideology, incompatible with Muslim values. They sought to find an indigenous basis for radicalism in Islam itself, focusing especially on its teachings about equality, community, and brotherhood, while rejecting Muslim institutions and practices connected with traditional society. It was an effort to gain popular support for a radically modern program of action by linking it to Islamic or Arab values. By the mid-1960s, governments guided by such ideas were in power in Syria, Iraq, Egypt, and Algeria, while movements with this general orientation were active elsewhere as an opposition force. Here we shall look more closely at the Egyptian example of this broad Middle Eastern tendency.

As the most populous and modernized of Arab nation-states, Egypt had long been an influential voice in the broader Arab and Islamic worlds. The British had occupied Egypt militarily in 1882, maintaining a strong influence even after Egypt was declared "independent" in the years following World War I. With increasing demands for full independence after 1945, the British withdrew their forces to the strategically important Suez Canal Zone. The occupied Canal Zone was an emotional symbol of imperialist humiliation for many Egyptians, much as the influence of the British-controlled oil company played a similar role in Iran in the years after 1945. Demonstrations were organized in Egypt by the Muslim Brotherhood, an Islamist network popular among university students that combined Islamist zeal with determined anti-imperialism. The disastrous Palestine war of 1948–1949, following the creation of the state of Israel, exposed the ineptitude and corruption of King Faruq's regime, the monarch himself having gained a reputation as a dissolute playboy. In 1952, as the regime lost control of the streets, the army intervened, seizing power and sending Faruq into exile.

Prominent among the military leaders of the coup was a young army officer named Gamal Abd al-Nasser, who would later combine nationalism, pan-Arabism, and socialism into a unique political program. Shrewdly working his way to the top of the political hierarchy, Nasser attempted major reforms

Egypt's Gamal Abd-al-Nasser and India's Jawaharlal Nehru, pictured here, helped to create the concept of the "Third World," a bloc of newly independent nations aligned with neither of the Cold War powers. *United Nations*

by breaking up large landed estates and distributing land to peasants, while building roads, schools, clinics, and small industries in the rural areas. He also seized foreign-owned businesses and expanded the state-controlled sector to include banking, foreign trade, construction, transportation, and most industries. This activist and state-led approach to economic development was intended to free Egypt from foreign economic control and to spur economic growth.

A tireless proponent of Arab socialism, Nasser also became the spokesman for pan-Arab nationalism. One of its rallying cries was the recovery of Palestine, which for Israelis meant the destruction of the Jewish state. Another was the liberation of the Suez Canal, which Nasser nationalized in 1956. British, French, and Israeli forces soon invaded Egypt in a coordinated attempt to remove Nasser as a threat, each government having its own reasons for fearing him. Nasser was saved by a rare moment of Cold War cooperation between the two superpowers, which jointly condemned the invasion and pressured the three forces into a humiliating withdrawal. Nasser, meanwhile, saw his political popularity skyrocket as he became a symbol of defiance against European imperialism.

Nasser urged other peoples in developing nations to follow Egypt's lead and organize Socialist revolutions. Egypt, he wrote, was the cornerstone of three overlapping worlds—Muslim, Arab, and African— and was destined to play a leading role in all of them. He supported revolts in Iraq, Yemen, Libya, and Algeria. His pan-Arab rhetoric took concrete expression in the union with Syria from 1958 to 1961, known as the United Arab Republic. However, what was designed to be the first step in the eventual unification of the "Arab nation" instead fell apart, with only one member, Egypt, left by 1961, thus exposing the shallowness of pan-Arab ideology. Despite his radical rhetoric, which tempted American policymakers to view him as a Soviet stooge, Nasser ruthlessly suppressed the Communist party in Egypt.

Nasser's visceral perception of Israel as a Western imperialist dagger in the heart of the Arab nation dragged Egypt and other Arab nations into a disastrous military defeat in 1967. Although Nasser never recovered from the humiliation of this defeat, he retained a remarkable hold on the imagination of the Egyptian masses and of Arabs generally, as demonstrated by the outpouring of sentiment following his death in 1970.

Nasser's legacy has been complex. His nearly twenty-year rule in Egypt led to social improvements in some areas—public health, education, and limited land redistribution. But it did not make a major dent in the massive poverty of the country's vast majority. Overly ambitious goals, bureaucratic inefficiency and corruption, heavy defense spending, the embarrassing defeat in the 1967 war with Israel, and surging population growth undermined Egypt's Socialist experiment. The Aswan High Dam, whose disputed financing led to an estrangement with the American government soon after the Suez War, increased Egypt's electric power supply and extended irrigated farming, as had been intended. But it also created major ecological headaches—reduction in downstream silt, erosion of river banks, decline in the Mediterranean sardine industry, increased dependence on expensive petroleum-based fertilizer, and the spread of the snail-borne disease schistosomiasis in some areas. And while Nasser's Arab socialism had intellectual roots in Islamic values, his government acted in many ways to offend Muslim leaders and institutions. He outlawed the Muslim Brotherhood, brought religious endowments and private monasteries under government control, and changed the curriculum of Egypt's al-Azhar university.

Following Nasser's death in 1970, his successor, Anwar al-Sadat, proceeded to surprise most observers by reversing Nasser's state-oriented economic policy and opening up the Egyptian economy to private enterprise and foreign investment. On the international front, in a sudden turnaround, Sadat expelled many Soviet advisers in 1972 and looked to the United States for economic aid and political support in resolving Arab-Israeli disputes. Frustrated at the lack of response following his risky turnabout, he orchestrated a surprise attack on Israeli forces in the occupied Sinai in October 1973 that ended in a stalemate. But by 1979, Sadat had become the first Arab leader to visit Israel and then to sign a peace treaty with Egypt's long-time enemy.

The Middle East on the Global Stage

While Egypt and other countries were sorting out their domestic priorities, larger historical forces after 1945 shifted the Middle East from a "peripheral" region back to an increasingly central role in global affairs. The Cold War, the establishment of the Israeli state, and the world's growing dependence on Middle Eastern oil all played critical roles in this process.

Competing Nationalisms: The Palestinian-Israeli Conflict

By 1945 the situation in the Middle East, as in the world at large, was radically different from what it had been in 1939. The horrors of the Holocaust placed the Zionist dream of a Jewish state in Palestine in a new light for both Jews and non-Jews. What had once appeared as an option to many Jews now became an urgent necessity, even a matter of survival. The moral argument for the establishment of a Jewish state in Palestine derived from several sources. For many religious Jews, and for some Christians, Zionism drew its legitimacy from an Old Testament promise by God to the descendants of Abraham. Some secularized Jews rejected the relevance of a divine promise, but argued that the long historical connection of Jews to Palestine justified a political title to the land. Other Zionist voices emphasized the obligation of the international community to fulfill commitments made in the Balfour Dec-

The state of Israel took shape from thousands of European Jewish settlers such as those pictured here in an early tent settlement. *Robert W. Strayer*

laration and the post–World War I mandate system. For still others, the most persuasive case for the establishment of a Jewish state was based on natural law—the Jews were a nation like any other nation and, without a state of their own, they would be subjected to persecution and perhaps even attempts at extermination, as the Holocaust had so tragically demonstrated.

Palestinian Arabs contested each of these claims. From their point of view, Zionist immigration and land purchase leading to a Jewish state were not the legitimate fulfillment of the right to nationhood, but rather the last gasps of a European colonial mentality that saw the world as awaiting "development" at the hands of Europeans, the "natives" fit to be either displaced or exploited by an alien power. The chance of finding a middle ground between these diametrically opposed views was slim at best.

When Zionists tried to smuggle European Jewish refugees into Palestine at the end of the war, Arab groups organized themselves in opposition. The situation in Palestine following 1945 gradually devolved toward civil war with the British caught in the middle between two communities, each creating fearsome images of the other. Extremist Zionist paramilitary groups organized attacks on British installations. Unable to control the situation, the British government handed it over to the newly created United Nations to resolve, promising to withdraw all British forces by 1948.

In a confused and chaotic situation and under heavy American pressure, a majority of the members of the United Nations proposed in 1947 a partitioning of Palestine into two states, one Arab and one Jewish, with international control over Jerusalem (see Map 12.2). Zionist leaders accepted it as a first step toward their aims, while the Arabs rejected it as patently unfair, for the proposed boundaries had been drawn so as to grant the Jewish minority a majority of the territory west of the Jordan River.

As the date for British troop withdrawal approached, Palestine became the scene of civil war with atrocities on both sides. Jewish leaders declared the new state of Israel on May 14, 1948, and it was immediately recognized by the United States and the Soviet Union. Backed by military contingents from five Arab states, Palestinian Arabs fought to prevent the partition of Palestine. Although outnumbered, Jewish military forces (now the Israeli Defense Forces) were motivated by the thought of their fate if they lost, a scenario made all the more compelling by the recent memory of the Holocaust in Europe. Zionist forces captured additional territory, and when the United Nations finally arranged an armistice in 1949, the new state of Israel controlled about one-third more territory than had been allocated by the 1947 partition resolution, including west Jerusalem. The remaining territories came under Jordanian control (the West Bank, including east Jerusalem) and Egyptian control (the Gaza Strip).

For Israelis it was Herzl's fifty-year-old dream come true; for Palestinian Arabs it was their worst nightmare. Hundreds of thousands of Palestinians found themselves refugees, having fled or been forced from their homes by advancing forces. Some eventually settled in other Arab countries, while others remained in refugee camps, often serving as political pawns in Middle East politics. There they waited, as first years, then decades passed, deeply resentful about their harsh fate at the hands of an uncaring world, made all the more bitter by the influx of Jewish immigrants from Arab lands and elsewhere who were immediately welcomed as Israeli citizens. A sense of Palestinian identity and nationalism grew among Arabic-speaking refugees. They were not simply an Arab nation; they were a uniquely Palestinian nation.

Relations between Israel and its Arab neighbors remained hostile in the decades following its establishment, with periodic guerrilla operations and Israeli military retaliation along border regions with Jordan, Syria, Lebanon, and Egypt. More important were a series of Arab-Israeli wars in 1956, 1967, and 1973, made all the more dangerous by their connection to the global U.S.-Soviet rivalry. By the mid-1960s, the United States had become deeply committed to Israel, while the Soviet Union increasingly backed Egypt, Syria, and Iraq. These connections flooded the Middle East with arms and turned a local conflict of competing nationalisms into a global crisis with the distinct threat of war between the superpowers.

These wars settled nothing fundamental. In the 1967 conflict, Israeli forces wrested control of the West Bank from Jordan, the Golan Heights from Syria, and the Sinai Peninsula from Egypt, tripling in a few days the total land area controlled by Israeli forces. The United Nations tried to arrange negotiations and withdrawal, according to Security Council Resolution 242, which called for Israeli withdrawal from occupied lands in exchange for peace. But deep-seated hostility and suspicions on both sides prevented such an outcome.

Meanwhile, Palestinians were determined to take matters into their own hands. Having witnessed two decades of futile Arab rhetoric and Israeli expansion, many Palestinians had concluded that only through their own efforts could their national aims be fulfilled and their dignity restored. Their instrument was the Palestine Liberation Organization (PLO), founded in 1964, and chaired by Yasser Arafat, leader of the largest faction within the umbrella organization. The PLO won the support of most Islamic governments and gained much sympathy in the developing countries, culminating in Arafat's invitation to speak at the United Nations in 1974.

In some ways the PLO proved more dangerous to its Arab host countries than to Israel. Cross-border guerrilla raids and rocket attacks often provoked explosive retaliation by Israeli forces. The assertiveness of Palestinian militia forces upset the fragile political balance in Jordan in 1970 and then in Lebanon, helping to precipitate that country's 1975 civil war. Occupation by both Syrian and Israeli forces followed, as did involvement by American troops, hostage taking, and a seemingly interminable cycle of instability and crisis.

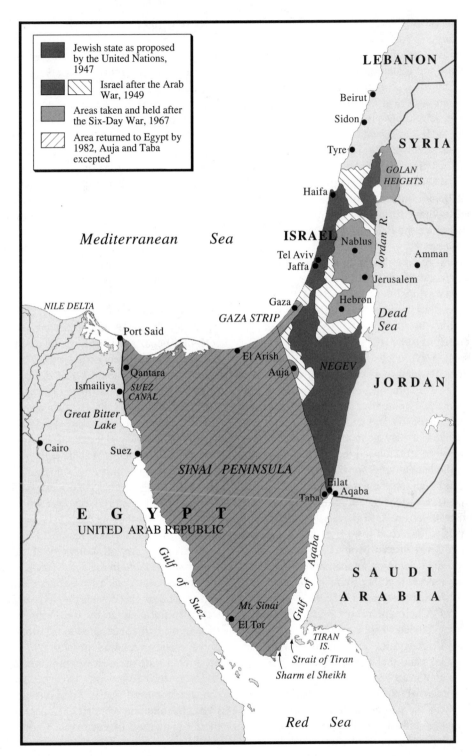

MAP 12.2 Palestine and Israel in the Twentieth Century

The first major break in that cycle occurred in late 1977, when Egypt's Anwar Sadat shocked the world by accepting an invitation to visit Israel. He raised hopes for some and fostered bitterness for others by recognizing Egypt's archenemy. The changed atmosphere led to an American-brokered peace between Egypt and Israel signed in 1979. Although this breakthrough led to Israeli withdrawal from the Sinai and a cold peace with Egypt, it failed to resolve the central issue of Palestinian rights and control of the West Bank and Gaza. Israel's "creeping annexation" of the West Bank continued. In 1978, and again in 1982, Israeli military thrusts into southern Lebanon sought to neutralize the Palestinian political and military infrastructure.

As the mainstream Palestinian leadership moderated its position during the 1980s, accepting officially a two-state division of Palestine by the end of the decade, various factions continued acts of violence, sometimes directed at rival forces within the PLO. In the fall of 1987, the powder keg of frustration and tension exploded into the *intifadah*, daily confrontations between rock-throwing youths and Israeli soldiers that resulted in a rapidly growing toll of Palestinian deaths. Eventually, the *intifadah* was superceded by more costly and widespread violence as the Iraqi invasion of Kuwait in 1990 and the Allied war against Iraq in 1991 placed the issue of Palestinian rights in the background, for the time being. The end of the Cold War and the defeat of Iraq facilitated long-awaited face-to-face negotiations between Israelis and Palestinians in 1991. It was a small but important step in a long road toward compromise and reconciliation between two peoples, alienated from each other by their common attachment to the same piece of land. Pushed together by their common fear of the rising Islamist challenge in the West Bank and Gaza Strip, PLO Chairman Yasser Arafat and Israeli Prime Minister Yitzhak Rabin negotiated an agreement of mutual recognition and limited Palestinian autonomy in Gaza and the West Bank, which began to be implemented in 1994.

The Palestinian-Israeli conflict propelled the Middle East back to the center of world attention because it resonated with so many larger issues: echos of the Holocaust; perceptions of continuing Western imperialism in the region; Muslim humiliation at the hands of outside forces; Cold War hostilities of the United States and Soviet Union; rivalries within the Arab world; and finally, but by no means of least importance, the question of oil.

The Question of Oil

The prominence of the Middle East in world affairs after 1945 is closely related to economic geography. Its location as the "middle lands" between Africa, Europe, and Asia assured its continuing importance in the strategic calculations of the great powers (see Map 12.3). But there was a new factor of even greater significance that proved to be both a blessing and curse for millions of people in the region—the abundance of oil, energy life-blood of the global economy.

Major oil reserves were found in Iran (Persia) during the first decade of the twentieth century, with substantial exports flowing to Europe before World War I. The British began tapping Iraqi oil fields during the interwar period, and Saudi Arabia, with the largest oil reserves in the world, emerged as a major producer after World War II. The Western world converted its navies and home furnaces from coal to oil, then began gulping huge quantities of gasoline for its growing fleets of automobiles and airplanes. Since Western companies had discovered, pumped, refined, and marketed the oil, they reaped most of the profits through long-term concessions. This soon stirred popular resentment. In 1951, the Iranian regime seized the properties of the Anglo-Iranian Oil Company. Two years of strife followed, in which the popular prime minister, Muhammad Mossaddiq, drove the shah, Muhammad Reza Pahlavi, from the throne. He was restored to power with the help of the American CIA; then he clamped martial law on Iran, arrested Mossaddiq, and reached a compromise settlement with the oil company. Iran's bargaining power was limited in the early 1950s by the ability of the United States, as a net exporter of oil, to fill the gap created by the Western boycott of Iran. The austerity brought about by the Western embargo on Iranian oil had contributed to Mossaddiq's fall from power. The weakness of acting alone as an oil-producing state in the developing world was obvious.

Over the following two decades, important changes occurred in the world oil market. In 1960, five oil-producing countries formed their own cartel, the Organization of Petroleum Exporting Countries (OPEC), to counteract the power of seven major Western oil companies. The addition of new members to OPEC during the 1960s and 1970s increased the organization's potential political and economic clout.

Further shifts in the global economy gave oil producers in the developing world new advantages in

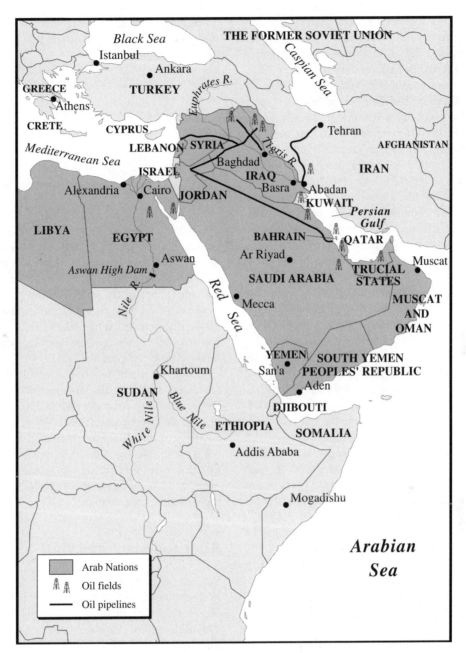

MAP 12.3 The Contemporary Middle East

their demands for higher revenue and greater control over their oil industries. Around 1970, the United States, due to increased oil consumption and declining production, moved from being a net oil exporter to a net oil importer, losing the excess production capacity that helped bring Iran to its knees in the early 1950s. In addition, the booming economies of both Western Europe and Japan were by this time deeply dependent on continuous supplies of Middle Eastern oil, especially from the Persian Gulf.

OPEC, and the Arab oil countries that constituted a majority of its members, were now in a position to extract economic and political concessions from countries dependent on the petroleum lifeline. Ever since the late 1940s, American foreign policymakers had feared the potentially explosive convergence of two issues—U.S. support for Israel and Western dependence on Arab oil. In October 1973, the dreaded scenario unfolded. Egypt's surprise attack on Israeli forces in the Sinai precipitated an Arab oil embargo against countries considered unfriendly to Arab interests. For the first time since World War II, American consumers saw lines waiting at the gas pump, and there were panicky predictions of economic depression and even calls for an invasion of the Middle East to assure "American" supply lines.

The economic effect of the embargo and uncertainty surrounding the war's impact quadrupled the price of crude oil, benefiting both Arab and non-Arab, OPEC and non-OPEC producers of oil. Although the sudden price increase contributed to inflation, gloomy predictions of the demise of the world economic system turned out to be exaggerated as governments and consumers discovered ways to conserve and to find alternative energy sources.

Billions of "petrodollars" flowed into OPEC treasuries, leading to a windfall for oil-producing economies. Much of the oil wealth was squandered, much of it was reinvested in Western economies, but a substantial part of it went toward raising the standard of living of Middle Eastern peoples, surrounding many for the first time with the material trappings of modern life.

Oil revenues offered unparalleled opportunities for rapid social and economic development in Arab states as well as in Iran. But there were costs to this windfall of liquid wealth. Some governments were more prudent than others in investing their resources in long-term productive enterprises. Both Libya and Kuwait had small enough populations that they could afford to provide a comfortable life-style for their populations. The Libyan leader, the mercurial Muammar Qaddafi, however, had an ideological agenda as well. As a believer in pan-Arab revolutionary nationalism and the global struggle against Western imperialism, Qaddafi provided financial backing for a variety of revolutionary movements. Kuwait, perched between more powerful neighbors, paid its dues to Palestinian and other Arab causes, but also invested a great deal in education, technical training, and a modern infrastructure. Saudi Arabia, the most influential member of OPEC, came to follow a moderate course in trying to avoid radical increases in oil prices so as to assure the economic and political stability of the region and the larger world economy. But the sudden and disorienting social changes in oil-rich societies led to unpredictable eruptions that surprised even the most astute students of Middle Eastern societies.

The Islamic Resurgence

Nationalist movements, Socialist regimes, economic development, the Arab-Israeli conflict, and the politics of oil—these have been among the dominant themes in the history of the Middle East in the twentieth century. But alongside them, and increasingly prominent in the final third of that century, has been yet another theme: the vigorous reassertion of Islam as the foundation on which modern Middle Eastern societies should be constructed. "It was no longer enough," commented one historian "that the European ruler had been expelled; now those aspects of his civilization which had taken firm root in Muslim soil—western laws, godless learning, decadent culture—must also be grubbed up."[2]

It was in many respects a revolutionary quest, seeking to realize in the modern world something of the ideal society created by Muhammad at the beginning of the Islamic age. The common element across a variety of so-called fundamentalist movements was not a wholesale rejection of modernity but an assertion that Islam was profoundly relevant to all of life, even, or perhaps especially, in societies undergoing rapid modernizing change.

Roots of Islamic Revival

Since Islam had been from the beginning embodied in a community and a state, its leaders had never accepted the sharp distinction, so familar to Western Christian culture, between church and state or religion and society. Thus Islam had always contained the potential for movements of renewal, as the historical evolution of Muslim societies departed from the ideal community described in the sacred writings and, according to Muslims, practiced in the early years of the Islamic era. Movements of Islamic renewal, such as the Wahhabis in the eighteenth century, had expressed this impulse well before European imperialism became a serious threat.

It was the revival of the Wahhabi-Saudi power in Arabia between 1902 and about 1930 that produced the first successful case of Islamic revivalism in the twentieth century. Established by the remarkable Abd al-Aziz Ibn Saud (1880–1953), this newly established state controlled much of the Arabian peninsula, basing its authority initially on highly puritanical military-agricultural settlements. The state itself was rooted firmly in Islamic law and provided the *ulama* with financial support and an influential role in government. As one of the few genuinely independent states in the Middle East and as the protector of the holy places in Mecca and Medina, the Saudi state enjoyed considerable prestige in the region.

Even more remarkable has been the ability of the Saudi dynasty to retain its power and its traditionalist Islamic policies while becoming enormously wealthy through oil exports since the 1960s. Modern cities, transportation networks, industries, and universities have flourished alongside laws prohibiting gambling and drinking, sharp limitations of the behavior of women, Quranic punishments for adultery and theft, and a legal system controlled by Wahhabi *ulama*. Furthermore, the Saudi dynasty has cultivated an Islamic rather than an Arab nationalist identity, offering support to a wide variety of Muslim causes. Here, then, is a case of "pragmatic fundamentalism," which has sought to blend a strictly Islamic foundation with all that modern economic opportunity can offer.

Another early twentieth-century expression of Islamic revival was the Muslim Brotherhood, an organization established in 1928 by an Egyptian teacher, Hasan al-Banna. Organized in local cells or chapters, the Brotherhood set up schools, clinics, and cooperative workshops and sent its missionaries to preach in mosques and public places throughout Egypt. Its message was one of a Muslim government based on the Shariah, of an economy regulated by Islamic principles, and of a society informed by Islamic morality. It was a message that drew support not only from more traditionalist rural people but also from students, teachers, civil servants, and office workers who had some exposure to Western or modern life and sought an Islamic identity at the same time. An alternative to Western liberalism or communism, Islam would provide the foundation for a modern Egypt.

The Muslim Brotherhood became politically active in the 1930s in support of Palestinian Arabs, fought against British rule in Egypt in the 1940s, and came into sharp conflict with Nasser's regime in the 1950s and with every subsequent Egyptian government as well. Though it has never achieved state power, it has not shrunk from violence or armed struggle and remained in the 1990s an important element in Egypt's growing Islamic fundamentalist movement.

Until the 1970s, however, revivalist Islam remained a minor current in a Middle East dominated by the more secular concerns of nationalism, socialism, and economic development. Since then, however, the fundamentalist style of Islamic reassertion has become a powerful element in Middle Eastern political and cultural life. Governments committed to the Islamization of public life have come to power in Libya, Iran, and Sudan. Growing movements of Islamic revival have challenged existing governments in Egypt, Algeria, and elsewhere. In early 1992, for example, the fundamentalist Islamic Salvation Front in Algeria seemed on the verge of winning parliamentary elections, provoking the military to cancel the elections and to take vigorous action against the movement. Islamic groups responded with an armed insurrection that killed some two thousand people by early 1994. Even in Turkey, the most avowedly secular of the Middle Eastern states, the fundamentalist National Salvation party won almost 12 percent of the vote in 1973. Other examples of Islamic reassertion were evident in the farther reaches of the Islamic world, including west Africa, Pakistan, and Indonesia.

Responding to these concerns and pressures, both radical and conservative governments have drawn more heavily on Islamic themes in their efforts to mobilize popular support. Nasser's successor in Egypt, Anwar Sadat, laced his speeches with references to Islam, supported constitutional changes giving a prominent role to Islamic law, and was careful to appear publicly at Friday prayers. Nonetheless, he was assassinated by members of a radical Islamic group in 1981. The reassertion of Islam was also felt at the international level, where the Islamic Conference, established in 1969, brought together the leaders of some forty-three Islamic countries to take common action on issues of concern to Muslims. And at the level of personal behavior during recent decades, many urban middle-class women have voluntarily adopted the veil and other aspects of religiously approved dress.

How can we explain the rapid growth of this fundamentalist style in Middle Eastern life since the late 1960s?[3] One point of view sees the revival of Islam in the context of Muslim successes in the twentieth century: achieving political independence and, through the oil price increases, a measure of economic independence for some. The reassertion of Islamic faith follows, then, as the cultural dimension of this general Muslim revival.

Others have viewed it as a response to the disappointments of more secular ideologies such as nationalism or socialism and to the continuing elements of Western domination in Middle Eastern life. Some Muslims were repelled by the growing materialism and destruction of traditional values and life-styles associated with oil wealth and modern Western culture generally. Secular education, unaccompanied and "scantily clad" women, Western-style cinemas, abolition of Shariah courts, political leaders who gave only lip-service to Islam, rapidly growing cities such as Cairo and Tehran with impoverished populations—all of this and more made many people sympathize with the cry of the early twentieth-century Indian Muslim writer Muhammad Iqbal:

> *Turk, Persian, Arab*
> *Intoxicated with Europe*
> *And in the throat of each*
> *the fish-hook of Europe.*[4]

Furthermore, the presence of Western military bases, Cold War rivalries in the Middle East, and especially the state of Israel and the Arab defeat in the 1967 war provided humiliating reminders that the heartland of Islam was still not completely free. In this view, movements of Islamic assertion represent a continuation of the anti-imperialist struggle and a simultaneous effort to find a more satisfying Islamic foundation for modern development.

An Islamic Revolution in Iran

Nowhere has the force of Islamic reassertion been felt more powerfully than in Iran. It was also Iran that experienced the most dramatic repercussion of the oil revolution. Muhammad Reza Shah had used the massive oil revenues to develop the economy and to build up Iranian armed forces. The shah also received considerable support from the United States, which increasingly saw him as the protector of American interests against Soviet encroachment and Arab radicalism in the region. Between 1956 and 1976, Iran's urban dwellers grew from 31 percent of the population to 47 percent, and the military ballooned to a force of over 400,000. But part of the country's oil wealth was skimmed off for the shah and his retinue of privileged and ruthless leaders. And the heavy-handed brutality of his secret police alienated many in Iran.

Opposition to the shah's regime crystalized from a variety of quarters for diverse reasons. Some still resented his coming to power at the hands of the British during World War II and the British-U.S. intervention to save his throne in 1953. His land reform program alienated landowners and upset traditional village life. Small merchants, shopkeepers, and artisans were threatened by modern stores, large government agencies, and imported foreign goods. Rural migrants to the rapidly growing cities, especially Tehran, lived an insecure life, coping with inflation, unemployment, and falling standards of living. Furthermore, the shah had provoked the Shi'ite religious establishment by attempting to redistribute religious lands; by initiating reforms that offered women greater rights and a literacy program that threatened to replace religious schools; and by permitting the growth of Western political, economic, and cultural influences in the country. His decision to replace the Islamic calender with one derived from Persian imperial history further alienated his subjects, as did the building of a Hyatt Hotel (serving foreign wines and liquors) near a religious sanctuary in the city of Meshed.

In a tightly controlled political system, the one institution in which opposition could express itself relatively unhindered was the mosque. Unlike their counterparts in the Ottoman Empire, the Shi'ite *ulama* of Iran had maintained their independence from the state and had often criticized both the royal government and Western intervention in Iranian affairs. While the shah attempted to restrict the influence of the *ulama,* he had not been able to uproot the religious establishment as Ataturk had done in Turkey. Thus, the Shi'ite leaders increasingly became the voice of opposition. One elderly cleric in particular, the Ayatollah Khomeini, organized opposition from exile and became the focal point of a growing movement demanding that the shah give up power. His taped messages, distributed through a network of local religious leaders, triggered massive

These women wearing the traditional *chadur* participated as guards at a rally at Tehran University in 1979. Note the flowers in the barrels of their guns to show their peaceful intentions. *AP/Wide World Photos*

urban demonstrations that paralyzed the government and strikes that shut down oil production. As the nation revolted and slipped into anarchy, the shah abdicated his throne and fled into exile with his family in January 1979. Ayatollah Khomeini returned to Iran to a hero's welcome and appointed his own government. In a striking departure from most Muslim practice, the religious leadership itself had seized power in an Islamic society.

This Islamic revolution signaled the abolition of the monarchy and the establishment of an authoritarian state with little tolerance for opposition. Widespread purges, aimed at Islamicizing the bureaucracy and the army, resulted in hundreds of executions and thousands of discharges, with Islamic activists taking the place of those removed from their positions. Within the *Majlis* or Parliament, a Council of Guardians supervised the legislative process to ensure conformity to the principles of Islam. State-appointed prayer leaders in local mosques became

an important means of mobilizing popular opinion behind the new government.

Culturally, the new regime sought the moral purification of the country under state control. Discos and bars were closed; alcoholic drinks were forbidden; co-education was eliminated; women were required to take the veil. In the early years, revolutionary groups patrolled the streets in an effort to identify and punish improper behavior, while "Islamic societies" were established in many organizations to enforce conformity with Islamic standards. In 1982, an Islamic penal code was introduced and all existing non-Islamic laws were suspended while the *ulama* came to dominate the judicial system. In the educational system, textbooks were revised under clerical supervision, and ideological commitment became a criterion for admission to universities. In other respects, however, the new regime was less than revolutionary. Despite some efforts to respond to the demands of the poor for social justice, no class

CONTRASTING VOICES
Islam, Modernity, and Relations with the West

Since the late 1970s, the debate about the relationship of the Islamic world and the West has intensified, as has discussion about the compatibility of Islam and modernity. In part, this is a continuation of controversies stretching back through the age of Western imperialism and even earlier. The following are two quite different contemporary voices that convey parts of that debate. The late Ayatollah Khomeini was both a leader and a symbol of the 1979 Iranian revolution as well as an inspiration for many Muslim fundamentalists into the 1980s and 1990s. Anwar Ibrahim, a finance minister from Malaysia, has been a leader within the World Council of Mosques and the Islamic Development Bank.

Ayatollah Khomeini

Islam is the religion of those who struggle for truth and justice, of those who clamor for liberty and independence. It is the school of those who fight against colonialism. . . .

The homeland of Islam, one and indivisible, was broken up by the doings of the imperialists and despotic and ambitious leaders. . . . And when the Ottoman Empire struggled to achieve Islamic unity, it was opposed by a united front of Russian, English, Austrian and other imperialist powers which split it up among themselves.

Moslems have no alternative, if they wish to correct the political balance of society, and force those in power to conform to the laws and principles of Islam, to an armed holy war against profane governments. . . .

What do you understand of the harmony between social life and religious principles? And more important, just what is the social life we are talking about? Is it those hotbeds of immorality called theatres, cinemas, dancing, and music? Is it the promiscuous presence in the streets of lusting young men and women with arms, chests, and thighs bared? Is it the ludicrous wearing of a hat like the Europeans or the imitation of their habit of wine drinking? . . . Let these shameful practices come to an end, so that the dawn of a new life may break!

Islam has precepts for everything that concerns man and society. . . . There is no subject upon which Islam has not expressed its judgement.

Anwar Ibrahim

The state of the Muslim world, so dismally revealed during the Persian Gulf crisis and its aftermath, may be summed up in a single phrase: a collapse of moral initiative. . . .

Instead of honestly addressing the central issue that faces the Ummah, or Muslim community, our leaders have engaged in emotional exploitation . . . like Saddam Hussein's cant against Western imperialism and his call for a Muslim *jihad* (holy war). . . .

There is, of course, truth in the Muslim criticism of the West. The West has not shown a moral consistency in dealing with the Muslim world. It is this disillusionment with the West which is partly responsible for the current state of affairs. . . . [T]he recent events in the Persian Gulf tell us that the Western bogey is invoked by tyrants and aggressors to perpetuate their hold on their own people. . . .

Muslim leaders must take the initiative to get out of their predicament by appealing to reason and moral principles. . . . We have failed to recognize that the rampant corruption, chronic poverty, disregard for fundamental human rights, denial of opportunities for women, economic inequality, illiteracy and tolerance of . . . tyrannical systems are not symptoms, but the cause of our decay. . . .

It makes little sense to curse the materialism of the West and sanctify anti-materialism when the majority of Muslims cannot afford the basic amenities of life. . . .

In today's world, Muslims are marginalized. They are excluded from advanced technological society, which, to a great extent, will determine our political fate. The devastating effectiveness of Western military technology in the Persian Gulf War provided fresh evidence of this actuality. . . .

In our efforts to regain moral initiative and re- solve the identity crisis of the *Ummah,* we must push aside symbols and rhetoric to embrace the Is- lamic commands that bind us as a community. These commands enjoin good and forbid evil, and call for the improvement of our socioeconomic condition. They enjoin us to defend the rights of the poor and the oppressed, refrain from economic exploitation and strive for a socially just society.

On the global scene, Muslims must develop the confidence to become actors rather than passive spectators. . . . To begin, we should accept the re- ality of a pluralistic world. Within Muslim his- tory, pluralism is far from an alien concept. Any doctrinaire rigidity that runs counter to Islamic principles of accommodating others should be re- jected. . . .

Intellectual reconstruction, which can only be based on free expression, is every bit as urgent in the wake of the Gulf War as repairing the material and environmental devastation. Only under the free flowering of the Muslim intellect can we jet- tison the rigid polemics and intolerance of thought and develop credibility with the rest of the world community. . . .

We must develop the potential to construct and maintain an economic infrastructure which is self- reliant as well as globally competitive. Only on that basis can we begin to improve the living con- ditions of our people and provide them with the basic amenities of life.

Then we can realistically aspire to fulfill the moral imperatives of Islam—the promotion of universal education, prudent management re- sources, respect for basic human rights and fair distribution of wealth.

Sources: Quoted in *Sayings of the Ayatollah Khomeini* (New York: Bantam Books, 1980), pp. 3–29, and Anwar Ibrahim, "Muslims Must Stop Blaming the West for All Their Problems," *Houston Chronicle,* 9 June 1991. Copyright © 1991 by Anwar Ibrahim

---

upheaval or radical redistribution of wealth fol- lowed; private property was maintained and a new privileged elite emerged.

Internationally, the Khomeini regime overtly challenged American interests. The arrival of the for- mer shah in the United States for medical treatment precipitated the seizure of American diplomatic hostages, who were held for a year before being re- leased in 1981. This violation of international diplo- matic norms isolated the Khomeini regime; it also etched long-lasting and negative images about Islam in the minds of many Americans.

The Iranian revolution inspired and supported radical Islamist movements elsewhere, especially in Shi'ite areas such as Lebanon. There Iranian-inspired guerrillas known as Hizb-Allah (party of God) cap- tured and held Western hostages and organized suicide attacks on American installations following the Israeli invasion of the country in the early 1980s. In 1981, Anwar Sadat of Egypt was assassinated by Islamic radicals in his own army. Even in cosmopolitan Cairo, young women began adopting the traditional body-length garb that had been re- jected earlier by many of their mothers and grand- mothers.

"Revolutionary Traditionalism": Iran in Comparative Perspective

It is fascinating to compare this Iranian upheaval with other radical or revolutionary movements in modern world history.[5] Unlike the collapse of the French, Russian, and Chinese monarchies, for exam- ple, the shah's regime fell without being defeated in war, without a corresponding peasant upheaval, and without the disintegration of its army. It was the gov- ernment's almost total loss of popular support, espe- cially in the urban areas and within the bureaucracy, that led to its downfall. Furthermore, while the French and Russian revolutions were made by secu- lar revolutionaries against the combined power of state and church, in Iran it was the religious leader- ship itself that led the assault on the state. Finally, in France, Russia, and China, class conflict was an im- portant element in the revolution, but Iranian revolu- tionaries sought to be inclusive and to integrate all classes into a national community defined by Islamic principles.

In this limited respect, the Iranian revolution has been similar to European Fascist movements earlier in the twentieth century. Both emphasized culture rather than economics as a basis for revolutionary action. Both sought to provide a new sense of community for societies undergoing rapid and highly disruptive social change. And both articulated their movements as "revolutionary" while simultaneously appealing to tradition—to older and allegedly purer values—in their effort to gain mass support. In these ways the Fascist and Islamic revolutionary movements differed from Communist ideologies, which located the ideal society in the distant future rather than in the past. However, while the Nazis invoked vague, romantic, and racist images of a preindustrial rural Germany, the Ayatollah Khomeini spoke in the name of a highly specific and distinctly religious tradition—that of Shi'ite Islam. In doing so, he defined a movement that was genuinely "revolutionary" and authentically "traditional" at the same time.

I Conclusion

The encounter of the Middle East with modern European civilization demonstrated not so much a "decline" in cultural vitality during the eighteenth and nineteenth centuries as a technological gap and a political collapse. Islam, as a faith, a culture, and a civilization, has shown remarkable durability and capacity for revitalization. It provided the basis for movements of resistance against European domination; it became an important element in the nationalist identities of Arab, Turkish, Kurdish, and Iranian peoples; it provided in some cases an indigenous basis for Socialist movements promoting an egalitarian social order; and it has enabled millions to embrace the modern world while retaining roots in their own traditions. Clearly, at least in the Middle East, modernity has not meant secularism.

Equally clear, however, is that Islam has not provided a solvent for the Middle East's many internal divisions. During the 1980s, much of the energy of the Khomeini regime was consumed in a bitter and costly war, initiated by Saddam Hussein's Iraq in an attempt to establish Iraqi regional hegemony. Saddam's ambitions backfired, however, leaving both countries exhausted and willing to accept an uneasy armistice in 1988. The financial strains of the war set the stage for the Iraqi invasion of oil-rich Kuwait in 1990, followed by the humiliating defeat of Sad-

dam's army in 1991 by an American-led coalition. The fluctuations in world oil prices triggered by war in the Persian Gulf helped to destabilize other oil-producing nations, paving the way for new political initiatives. When Algeria permitted multiparty elections in the early 1990s, for example, the Islamist movement there advanced its political program by taking advantage of the economic austerity resulting from declining oil prices as well as the corruption of the ruling party in a largely secular Socialist state. Here was the complex interaction of Islamic revivalism, political liberalization, and the dynamics of the world economy.

It is difficult to determine precisely which currents of change sweeping the Middle East and the larger Islamic world in the 1990s will prove ephemeral and which will prove enduring. Will the wave of Islamic revolution in Iran and elsewhere lead to a thorough transformation of public life in the Middle East, or will it represent only a temporary reversal in a long-term process of secularization? Few serious scholars of the Middle East would feel confident in making a definitive prediction. After all, many ideologies and political programs have emerged during the twentieth century, ranging from the radically secular nationalism of Ataturk's Turkey and the Arab socialism of Nasser's Egypt to the "revolutionary traditionalism" of Khomeini's Iran. Others may still emerge. The Islamists of Algeria promised a fundamentalist regime compatible with democracy. But the Algerian military snuffed out their experiment in 1992, just as they were on the verge of gaining power through free elections. Little wonder that many find armed struggle a compelling alternative.

In the Western world and particularly in America, some, especially in the popular media, have perceived an "Islamic threat." While such a "threat" may be largely imaginary, deriving from the need for an external "enemy" in a post–Cold War world, such images have a way of becoming self-fulfilling and therefore deserve careful analysis. A recent scholar has pointed out the challenges that the current situation presents to both the West and the world of Islam:

Contemporary Islam challenges the West to know and understand the diversity of the Muslim experience. It challenges Muslim governments to be more responsive to popular demands for political liberalization and greater popular participation, to tolerate rather than re-press opposition movements and build viable democra-tic institutions. At the same time it challenges Western powers to stand by the democratic values they embody and recognize authentic populist movements and the right of the people to determine the nature of their gov-ernments and leadership.[6]

Notes

1. Quoted in Bernard Lewis, *The Emergence of Modern Turkey,* 2nd ed. (London: Oxford University Press, 1968), pp. 268–69.

2. Francis Robinson, *Atlas of the Islamic World since 1500* (New York: Facts on File, 1982), p. 165.

3. For several interpretations of recent Islamic reassertion, see John Voll, *Islam: Continuity and Change* (Boulder, Co: Westview Press, 1982), pp. 349–57.

4. Quoted in Robinson, *Atlas of the Islamic World,* p. 163.

5. This section is based largely on Said Amir Arjomand, *The Turban for the Crown: The Islamic Revolution in Iran* (New York: Oxford University Press, 1988), pp. 189–210.

6. John L. Esposito, *The Islamic Threat: Myth or Reality?* (New York: Oxford University Press, 1992), p. 209.

Comparative Essay

INDUSTRIALIZATION IN THE DEVELOPING WORLD

Since England's breakthrough in the late eighteenth century, industrialization has become practically synonymous with modern life and greatly desired almost everywhere. However, the English Industrial Revolution was the unexpected and unplanned outcome of a long process of economic growth, capitalist development, and technological change. In the rest of the world, industrialization has appeared as something borrowed, and much more deliberately and urgently sought, often with substantial government involvement in the process. This was the case in the second wave of industrialization, which took place in Germany, the United States, Japan, and tsarist and then Soviet Russia in the late nineteenth and early twentieth centuries. And it has characterized developing countries as they emerged from colonial or semicolonial domination to chart their own modern courses.

Can these late twentieth-century industrializers repeat the process that transformed their predecessors? Can they find the necessary capital, shift their material resources and labor from agriculture to industry, and direct the benefits of industrial growth to ending mass poverty in their countries?

Certainly, developing nations have faced a formidable array of obstacles in the attempt. Most have begun the industrializing process at a far lower level of economic development than was the case in Europe, for they did not experience the long and slow accumulation of wealth that characterized Europe since the Middle Ages. Thus, developing countries have been capital poor in an era when the establishment of modern factories with competitive and up-to-date technology has required far more capital than in the nineteenth century. Furthermore, these later modernizing societies have confronted a world economic system whose long established division of labor has cast them as producers of agricultural goods and raw materials. Entering the industrial game has meant competing against the already wealthy and advanced industrial countries, many of whose enterprises have been organized in huge multinational corporations.

Finally, the internal poverty of most developing societies, their great social inequalities, and in many cases their small size have ensured a limited domestic market for their manufactured goods, and this too has inhibited industrialization.

It comes as no surprise, then, that when measured by the standards of the West, industrialization in developing countries as a whole has been quite modest. In 1980, these nations accounted for only 12 percent of total world manufacturing output, though this figure was up from a low of 6.5 percent in 1953. And while the industrial democracies of the West average only 7 percent of their labor force in agriculture, that figure for most of the larger Afro-Asian countries (India, China, Nigeria, Ethiopia) still stood at 70 percent or more in the 1980s. Clearly, no general breakthrough to fully industrialized societies seems on the horizon in the developing world, and many wonder whether widespread industrialization will be possible there at all.

When measured against the conditions of 1900 or 1950, however, industrial growth in the developing world seems much more substantial. Between 1965 and 1973, industrial production grew at an impressive rate of almost 9 percent a year in the developing nations as a whole, and from 1973 to 1984 it maintained a respectable rate of around 5 percent a year despite a slowdown in the world economy. Moreover, these growth rates were much higher than those of developed countries. Today, a growing number of developing countries produce manufactured goods, not only for their own consumption but for export as well. Industrialization has become a global process.

But this general picture covers up a lot of variation among developing countries both in the industrializing strategies they have employed and in the outcomes they have produced. For example, even the two developing regions regarded as most successful—Latin America and East Asia—have very different industrial histories.

Latin American developing countries, especially Mexico, Brazil, and Argentina, were the pioneers in industrialization. Stimulated by the Great Depression of the 1930s, they determined to reduce their dependence on the uncertain world economy by processing their own raw materials and producing their own consumer goods behind high tariff barriers if necessary. This strategy is known as *import substitution* because it aims to produce locally and for a domestic market many previously imported manufactured items.

Brazil[1] has been the most successful practitioner of the import substitution strategy, supplying by the 1980s about 90 percent of its consumer goods from domestic manufacturing. Generally, authoritarian governments provided credit through state-owned banks, operated some industries themselves, built the necessary infrastructure, and kept wages low and labor unions under control. Within this framework, Brazil's industrialization spurted dramatically, especially during the years 1968–1974, when growth rates exceeded 10 percent a year.

But Brazil's industrial miracle has a dark underside as well: it has increased the country's dependence on and vulnerability to the world economy. Brazilian industrialization has been accompanied by massive investment by multinational corporations and massive debt owed to foreign lenders. Moreover, since the whole process has occurred in the absence of serious social reform, especially in land holding, it has produced tremendous regional and class inequalities. The growth of a large and wealthy "middle class" in Brazil means that most current production is aimed at the top 20 percent of the population. More than anything else, social and economic inequities hold back Brazil's development into a balanced and modern industrial society.

Even more impressive than Brazil has been the experience of two newly industrializing countries (NICs) in East Asia: Taiwan and South Korea.[2] Since the mid-1960s, their GNP growth rates have averaged about 10 percent a year, while their manufacturing production has often increased at an incredible rate of 20 percent a year. By most economic indicators, Taiwan and South Korea were, by the mid-1980s, developed, not developing, countries. Like their Japanese neighbor before them, they had scrambled into the industrial club. How had they done it? And could the East Asian model be transplanted elsewhere in the developing world?

These questions have intrigued scholars and politicians alike. Some have noted that Taiwan and South Korea, like Japan and an impressively growing China, have been greatly influenced by Confucian culture. They have speculated that Confucian values—social discipline, hard work, and an orientation to this world—may have fostered economic growth in East Asia much as Protestantism did in Europe. But such a view does little to help us understand why economic growth took off in East Asia in the 1960s or in China in the 1980s and 1990s.

Perhaps a better starting point for explaining the remarkable industrial development of Taiwan and South Korea lies in their common colonial experience. Both countries spent the first half of the twentieth century under Japanese, rather than European, colonial rule. While Japanese colonialism was deeply resented, it did far more to deliberately foster modern economic growth than most of the European powers. The Japanese modernized Taiwanese agriculture, increasing the cultivated land by some 40 percent and eliminating absentee landlords. For military reasons, the Japanese also located some modern heavy industries in the colonies, including steel, chemicals, and hydroelectric facilities. By 1945, when Japanese rule came to an end, Taiwan and Korea were already among the most highly developed of the developing countries. They possessed not only an impressive industrial base but also a tradition of strong state involvement in the development process.

Another unique feature was shared by these East Asian industrializers. Unlike Brazil, Taiwan and South Korea had substantial land-reform programs in place prior to their rapid industrial growth of the 1960s and later. The postwar South Korean and Taiwanese governments redistributed large amounts of land and created in rural areas a great number of small owner-operated farms. Both countries were threatened by nearby Communist states and pressured by an American government eager to limit the potential attractiveness of communism. The land reforms laid the foundation for a far more egalitarian industrialization than anywhere in Latin America.

Furthermore, by 1960 the East Asian industrializers adopted a fundamentally different strategy than their Latin American counterparts. Rather than focusing on production for domestic consumption, they chose to specialize in particular products for an export market—textiles, leather goods, electronic goods, and later even automobiles. Much of this was labor-intensive industry, which drew large numbers of women into the work force and thus distributed the benefits of industrial growth quite widely even though wages were low. In Brazil, by contrast, the emphasis was on heavy and more capital-intensive industry, which used proportionately fewer workers. Until the 1980s, moreover, Brazilians produced primarily for a domestic market whose purchasing power was limited by a highly unequal distribution of income.

In addition, the East Asian approach to industrialization was facilitated by favorable international circumstances. Japan's colonial empire had been destroyed by 1945, and Taiwan and South Korea soon after became important parts of the U.S. presence in East Asia and benefited from a great deal of American aid. Furthermore, the booming world economy of the mid-1950s to the mid-1970s greatly assisted East Asian exports. Unlike the Latin American import-substitution approach, the East Asian "export-led" industrial strategy depended very little on direct foreign investment, though it was highly dependent on the economic vitality of the rich countries that purchased most of their exports.

A final factor contributing to East Asian industrialization was the presence of strong, authoritarian, and intrusive governments. Unlike most other developing nations' governments, those in South Korea and Taiwan were not beholden to particular economic interest groups such as local capitalists, labor movements, or multinational firms. They were thus in a position to organize and coordinate the activities of all these groups in the interests of overall industrial growth and to adjust rapidly to shifts in the world economy on which they were so dependent. Until the late 1980s, they also acted to repress dissent and offered only very limited opportunities for democratic participation.

Is the East Asian model of rapid growth, production for export, strong state involvement, and relative equality itself exportable? Elements of that strategy have been adopted with considerable success in other parts of East and Southeast Asia, such as in Thailand, Indonesia, and China, where industrial growth in the 1980s and 1990s has been strong.

Elsewhere the picture is not so promising. The particular conditions that gave rise to the East Asian approach, especially a rapidly growing world economy, no longer hold. The contraction of that economy since the mid-1970s sharply slowed even Korean growth in the early 1980s and stimulated considerable social and political conflict that until 1987 was harshly repressed. Furthermore, few developing states have had the political capacity to manage a complex economy effectively, and most have not been subjected to the kind of external pressure to enact land reforms that Korea and Taiwan experienced. Most important, however, is the question of whether the world could even absorb the increased volume of exports if the East Asian model were replicated many times over. Thus, slow and unbalanced industrial growth seems a more likely future for most developing countries than the dramatic spurt of East Asia's recent experience.

Notes

1. This discussion of Brazil draws heavily from Tom Kemp, *Industrialization in the Non-Western World* (London: Longman, 1983), chap. 6.

2. This section on East Asia is drawn heavily from Frederic C. Deyo, ed., *The Political Economy of the New Asian Industrialism* (Ithaca, N.Y.: Cornell University Press, 1987).

SUGGESTIONS FOR FURTHER READING: THE MIDDLE EAST

Ahmed, Leila. *Women and Gender in Islam: Historical Roots of a Modern Debate.* 1992. (A historical survey of the role of women in Middle Eastern societies.)

Burke, Edmund III, ed. *Rethinking World History: Essays on Europe, Islam and World History.* 1993. (A series of essays that reconsider Middle Eastern and Islamic history in a world historical context.)

Dunn, Ross E. *The Adventures of Ibn Battuta.* 1986. (The remarkable travels of a Muslim scholar illustrate the fourteenth-century intercommunicating zone and the Islamic webs that united it.)

Esposito, John L. *Islam: The Straight Path.* 1988. (A concise and balanced introduction to the faith and society of Islam in both historical and contemporary contexts.)

Hodgson, Marshall G. S. *The Venture of Islam.* 3 vols. 1974. (A masterful integration and analysis of Islamic civilization set in a global context.)

Hourani, Albert. *A History of the Arab Peoples.* 1991. (A masterful survey of the Arabic-speaking world.)

Humphrey, R. Stephens. *Islamic History: A Framework for Inquiry.* 1988. (An introduction to the historiographic issues and debates surrounding Islam and the Middle East.)

Issawi, Charles. *An Economic History of the Middle East and North Africa.* 1982. (Emphasizes the economic and political challenges of the last two centuries.)

Lapidus, Ira M. *A History of Islamic Societies.* 1988. (An overview from the time of Muhammad to the late 1980s.)

Lewis, Bernard. *The Muslim Discovery of Europe.* 1982. (A historical survey of one thousand years of evolving perceptions between two civilizations.)

Richards, Alan, and John Waterbury. *A Political Economy of the Middle East.* 1990. (A systematic study of the relationship between socioeconomic and political forces in the contemporary Middle East.)

Robinson, Francis. *Atlas of the Islamic World since 1500.* 1982. (A beautifully illustrated text that covers the history of the entire Islamic world both before and after 1500.)

Shaw, Stanford J., and Ezel Kural Shaw. *History of the Ottoman Empire and Modern Turkey.* 1976–1977.

Smith, Charles D. *Palestine and the Arab-Israeli Conflict.* 1992. (A balanced survey of a deeply divisive issue.)

Voll, John O. *Islam: Continuity and Change in the Modern Middle East.* 1982. (A well-informed and balanced study of Muslim leaders and institutions and their responses to the modern Western challenge throughout the Islamic world.)

PART V

COMMUNITIES AND STATES: INDIA IN MODERN HISTORY

Chapter 13: *Experiments in Diversity: States and Societies in Early Modern South Asia*

Chapter 14: *India and the British Raj*

Chapter 15: *Democracy, Development, and Cultural Pluralism: India since Independence*

Comparative Essay: *Nationalisms in Modern World History*

Suggestions for Further Reading: *India*

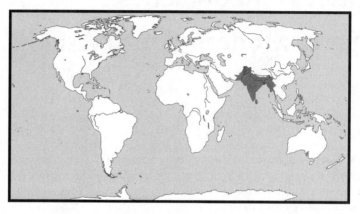

The South Asian peninsula, like its West Asian or European counterpart, has long been home to a vast diversity of peoples and cultures, a historical pattern that contrasts with the relative cultural homogeneity of Chinese or Japanese civilization. That highly pluralistic subcontinent evolved a unique civilization of its own; it was also, subsequently, incorporated first into the Islamic world system after 1000 C.E. and then into the European world system after 1750. Both of these processes gave new shape and definition to the multiple communities that populated the South Asian peninsula. It should come as no surprise that this enormous diversity has, since ancient times, posed great challenges to those—whether indigenous or invader—seeking to build large and inclusive political systems in India.

The changing patterns of India's cultural diversity and recurrent efforts to encompass that diversity within wider state structures are two related themes that link the subcontinent's early history with its contemporary experience. Chapter 13 outlines the roots of India's highly textured civilization and looks more carefully at two attempts—in the south and the north, often labeled "Hindu" and "Muslim," respectively—to establish powerful states on the subcontinent. As India succumbed to Europe's widening imperial networks, the British took their turn in trying to create political order amid South Asia's many cultures, classes, and communities. That attempt, and the responses it provoked in India, are the focus of Chapter 14. The final chapter in Part V, Chapter 15, takes up the story following India's independence in 1947. It chronicles the shifting and conflicting understandings of what it means to be "Indian" in a state that is simultaneously attempting to maintain the world's largest democracy, create a modern industrial society, and preserve political unity.

Chapter 13

Experiments in Diversity: States and Societies in Early Modern South Asia

Loose-knit and diverse, Indian civilization emerged gradually over long periods of time on the South Asian peninsula. Migration and conquest brought to this area an incredible mixture of peoples with different languages, customs, cultures, and religions. From this diversity there emerged a religious tradition now known as *Hinduism.* It had neither a single founder nor a clearly articulated creed; rather, it evolved over the centuries and evolves still, expressed in a multitude of philosophical tendencies, devotional practices, and sectarian communities. At the local village level of society a complex and fluid system, known to the West (somewhat misleadingly) as *caste,* organized people into separate groups around the ideas of occupation, rank, pollution, and purity. A variety of state structures rose and fell at the local, regional, and all-India levels of organization. These states had to confront the problem of incorporating communities representing prolific cultural and social diversity into a common political structure. The art of political incorporation, and the process by which groups defined themselves as particular communities, are the themes that give the kaleidoscopic history of the South Asian peninsula a certain unity over the course of many centuries.

Indian Beginnings

The area generally known as India (composed of the contemporary states of Pakistan, India, and Bangladesh) forms a subcontinent separated from the rest of the Asian landmass by mountains, jungles, and the sea (see Map 13.1). Often more than 20,000 feet high, the Himalayas in the north provide an awesome barrier, 100 to 200 miles wide, to the rest of Asia. On the northwest, the barrier turns southward in a swathe of dry, mountainous country through which have come repeated incursions of new peoples and conquerors. Below the Himalayas stretches the vast alluvial plain of the Ganges River and its tributaries; village upon village dot the flat and lushly planted plain. This Indo-Gangetic Plain gives way, in turn, to the Deccan Plateau, demarcated for 600 miles by the ridges of the Western Ghats on one side and the Eastern Ghats on the other. With its hills arising abruptly along the tableland, the Deccan is punctuated by long, eastward-flowing rivers—the Godavari, the Krishna, and the Cauvery. The peninsula is ringed with narrow coastal strips beyond the Ghats to both the east and the west. From these coastal areas merchants carried Indian culture and trade to nearby Sri Lanka as well as to much of Southeast Asia.

South Asia's natural environment includes a warm climate that permits several harvests a year, coal and iron ore that are available in some abundance, and good conditions for irrigation. The uneven quality of the soils has contributed to high population densities in the fertile river valleys, leaving vast stretches of hilly or heavily forested land practically uninhabited. Until fairly recently, Indian agriculture depended largely on the monsoons—heavy seasonal rains that fall unevenly across the subcontinent from June through September. Failure of the monsoon meant hardship, perhaps even famine, distributed unevenly throughout South Asia.

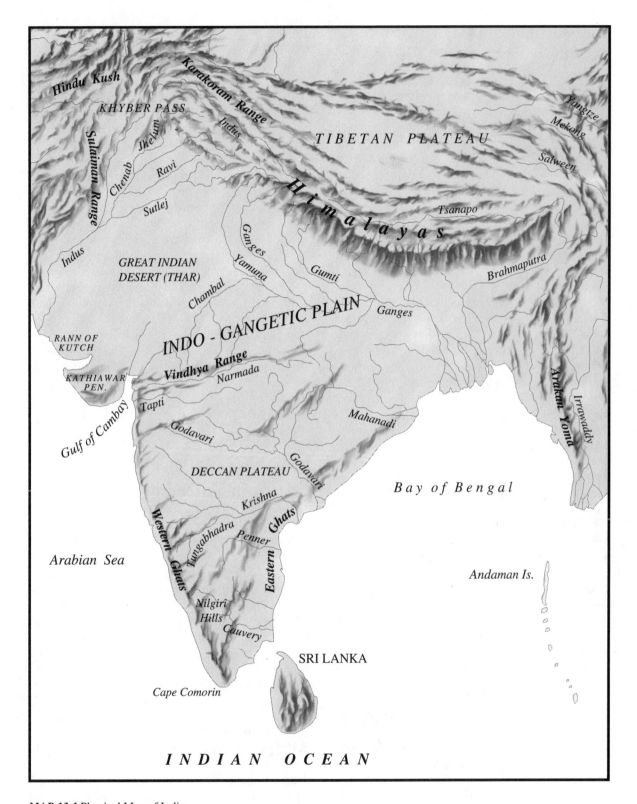

MAP 13.1 Physical Map of India

Cultural Foundations of Indian Civilization

India's cultural diversity has a very long history. An early and sophisticated civilization in the Indus River Valley (2500–1500 B.C.E.) was overrun by nomadic Aryan invaders from the northwest and thereafter numerous peoples from central Asia migrated or invaded the Indian subcontinent through the mountain passes. The Aryans spoke an early form of the Sanskrit language and, like their remote cousins who settled in Greece and Italy, had a religion based on nature gods and ritual sacrifices to them. Ultimately they also had the Brahmans, a hereditary class of priests, who developed rituals of supposedly great supernatural powers. Their prayers, hymns, and connected narratives were gradually organized into the four books of the Vedas, which much later, in written form, became the sacred scriptures of the high-culture religion now known as Hinduism. From these ancient times to the present, Brahmans have been the carriers of this Indian high culture and have diffused its ideas and practices throughout a culturally diverse and politically fragmented subcontinent.

In the sixth century B.C.E., growing resentment against Brahmanism gave rise to a new body of sacred literature, the Upanishads, which provided this religious tradition with a lofty moral and philosophic outlook, focusing on the essential oneness of all things. Enlightened persons, who realized this profound truth, sought an escape from the cycle of rebirths that kept their souls imprisoned in this painful world. They longed for release, for salvation, to have their souls finally absorbed in the Ultimate. To achieve this final release, people had to lead a pure and righteous life (or series of lives), fulfilling their designated roles. This law of *karma* (action or duty), together with the idea of reincarnation, helped people to accept their lot in life because it assumed a universe of stern mechanical justice in which deeds performed in this life determined one's position in the next.

Buddhism also emerged at this time as a simpler, more individualistic, and egalitarian religion. Its founder Siddhartha Gautama (c. 563–483 B.C.E.), soon to be called the Buddha ("enlightened one"), taught that individuals, though burdened by the sins of past lives, could work toward their own salvation through restrained and modest living and the suppression of distracting desires and passions. Instead of the multiple social distinctions of Indian life, the Buddha preached essential equality to the disciples who gathered around him.

Buddhism became a major religion through the patronage and promotion of the most powerful monarch in early Indian history, the Emperor Ashoka (273–232 B.C.E.), and through the widespread support of merchant groups, who benefited from the expansion of trade. Monks and merchants helped to spread Buddhism well beyond its Indian homeland—to the island of Sri Lanka, to Southeast Asia, central Asia, and China. It became one of the major connecting links of the ancient world, even while it was fading in the land of its birth. Buddhism had begun as a revolt against the Brahman establishment, but it developed an establishment of its own, including temples and monasteries generously endowed by kind and wealthy merchants. It coexisted so peacefully with the Brahmans that eventually it lost its separate identity and slipped into the mainstream of religious tradition. Some temples even housed images of Buddha beside those of Hindu deities. But the impact of Buddhism remained, in India as in China, in the idea of individuals working out their own salvation, instead of relying entirely on the prayers and rituals of priests or the support of an eternal social order.

The Classical Indian Pattern

The classical period of Hindu-Buddhist civilization—when the culture, society, and state developed and flourished in established patterns—occurred between the fourth century B.C.E. and the seventh century C.E. in northern India and about five centuries later in the southern region. This implies neither political unity nor a society frozen in time, but it did mean that kings fighting battles or collecting taxes, merchants pricing goods, peasants sowing crops, and Brahmans chanting prayers were expected to conform to proper and well-established traditions.

The Making of an All-Indian Tradition

Whatever defined Indian civilization, it was not the ethnic or linguistic homogeneity of its people. Unlike China, the vast majority of whose population were ethnic Chinese, India has had since very ancient times an incredibly diverse society of peoples of all descriptions who filtered into the subcontinent across the northwest passages from central Asia. Furthermore, southern India had its own traditions that varied significantly from those of the North. It had never been conquered, nor had its people been displaced by the early Aryan invaders. The languages of most southern Indians are those of the Dravidian linguistic group, which are unrelated to the Aryan. Yet cultural patterns from the north did infiltrate the south to mix with the already well-developed Dravidian culture. Thus, in terms of its ethnic and cultural diversity, historical India was more similar to medieval Europe than to China.

What connected such diverse peoples and made them part of some larger whole that was recognizably Indian? One answer to that question is a highly flexible cultural and religious tradition that accommodated infinite variation. Unlike Christianity or Islam, the Indian religious tradition never required its adherents to assent to a particular creed; it focused attention not on theological beliefs but on social behavior. Similarly, the Indian political structure could always make room for another successful military leader, and its social structure accommodated new groups as they migrated into an area.

During the classical period, the form of elite or high-culture religion stabilized somewhat as a multitude of local traditions and divinities were fitted around the gods Brahma, Vishnu, and Shiva. Each group of devotees followed its own practices and worried little about the diverse practices of others. The Brahmans gradually accepted these cults and merged them with their own Vedic rituals. In this way the all-India high-culture religious tradition that we now know as Hinduism slowly developed and gradually incorporated larger areas and more people.

A vital influence in creating this all-India tradition was the remarkable power of two epic poems, the *Ramayana* and the *Mahabharata.* Both were collections of legends from a remote "Heroic Age," tales of adventure overlaid with moral and religious lessons. Stories from these two great epics spread throughout India and provided a measure of common culture to its diverse peoples.

Patterns of Society: Caste and Class

Developing along with this all-Indian religious tradition was an elaborate network of supposedly fixed social relationships that we now refer to as the caste system. It has been seen as a device by which the Aryans tried to preserve their racial purity amid the numerous darker-skinned peoples around them; a means by which the Brahmans tried to enhance their status and power; and a way of distributing surplus foodgrains by ritually bartering them for services.[1] There is probably some truth in each of these explanations. But the caste system's dominant historical function in India has been to integrate diverse peoples and cultural groups into a common social framework, while preserving their separate group identities.[2]

In the late eighteenth and early nineteenth centuries, British scholars discovered and translated certain classic texts that became identified as the *canon* defining Hindu culture. In these texts written by Brahmans, caste was treated as an unchangeable system of unequal relationships, based on the economic functions of various groups. The whole arrangement was justified by concepts of pollution and purity applied to these social groups. One of the texts, known as *The Code of Manu,* used an analogy to liken society to the body of a man; it was then divided into four main parts called *varna,* which have often been translated as caste. The highest *varna,* corresponding to the head of a man, were the Brahmans, priests considered to be the most ritually pure; the upper torso represented the *kshatriya varna,* warrior chiefs or kings; the lower torso depicted the *vaisyas,* merchants and craftspeople; and the feet were *shudras,* peasants and laborers. The first three groups were regarded as "twice-born" castes, more ritually pure than the *shudras.* Outside this whole structure resided the Untouchables—those who performed tasks considered ritually unclean and polluting. The inequity from birth that this picture of society expressed was explained by the good and bad deeds done in one's former lives (*karma*), which automatically rewarded or punished the individual in this life.

However, the ritualistic and idealized pattern hardly represented real life in India, where there were thousands of separate hereditary occupational groups called *jatis* (a term also translated as caste), each with its own unique *dharma* or duty. This was the group into which people were born, and which determined their role and status in society—always in relationship to the other *jatis* in the local community. Indians generally married within their *jati* and preserved their purity by dining only with *jati*-fellows. Before modern times, most people worked

Bathing in the sacred Ganges River at Banaras has long been an important Hindu religious ritual. *Visual Studies Workshop*

at a hereditary caste or *jati* occupation. To violate these rules was to risk being shunned or made an outcast and to lose whatever social and family status one had. Even the Untouchables were divided into hundreds of separate castes or *jatis,* each with its own occupation and rank. A particular village might have thirty to forty *jatis,* ranked in a hierarchy known to everyone. Theoretically, each *jati* was associated with one of the *varna* categories, but even the British administrators who sought to use classical texts to impose order on the complex society they ruled, recognized that local social organization did not perfectly reflect the division of society into five neat categories.

Thus, local society was not as fixed, rigid, and inflexible as the *varna* theory suggested. New *jatis* were established to accommodate immigrant or invading groups; old ones died out; many people worked at occupations not originally associated with

their *jati;* and over time the *jatis* could rise and fall in the status hierarchy of the local village or region. A peasant *jati* associated with the *shudra varna* might gain access to land or render particular service to a local ruler and thus gradually come to be recognized as part of the *kshatriya varna.* It was a complex, fluid, and changing society, far removed from the immobility of the *varna* theory.

We often see caste as a unique Indian institution, and in some respects it is. But the extreme inequalities that it structured and the sharp limits on career opportunities and social mobility that it enforced were part and parcel of all ancient civilizations. These hierarchical divisions in India, as in societies everywhere, exploited those least powerful: dominant groups in a village took advantage of cheap labor from those beneath them; urban elites extracted produce and taxes from the villages to support elaborate religious festivals and lavish life-styles; rulers extracted surplus and support from their chiefs to exercise control over other areas. The uniqueness of the Indian situation lay in the ideology that justified those inequalities—notions of rebirth, ritual impurity, and the assumption of inherent spiritual inequality among whole groups of people. All of this contrasted sharply with Islamic and Christian philosophy regarding the basic equality of all, though practice, of course, was a different matter.

Patterns of Political Authority: Indian Empires and Local States

The political shape of India was a kaleidoscope of almost constant change. States expanded and were smashed, dynasties rose and fell, invaders disrupted and were absorbed. The rule of a king hailed as "lord of the universe" was far from absolute. He was limited by shared notions regarding the duties (*dharma*) of a righteous king toward his people. If the king failed to protect his people against bandits, administer proper justice, or patronize the temple at festival times, or if he tried to interfere with established social relationships, the people were not obliged to obey him, at least in theory. The frequency of dynastic warfare, of assassinations, and of seizure of thrones showed the hazards awaiting kings who turned tyrant or lost their popular support.

Only twice in its early history were large parts of India incorporated into a single state—once in Ashoka's era and again in the Gupta Empire of the fourth and fifth centuries C.E. The more familiar pattern of political life involved local or regional centers of power based on the control and subdivision of landholdings by warrior elites. Rivalries based on various regional cultures and dynasties, or on identities linked to tribes, castes, and sects, worked against a unified imperial state, though the memory of Ashoka's empire persisted and the ideal remained.

All of this contrasts sharply with the experience of China, where effective and centralized bureaucratic government persisted over many centuries, brought political unity to Chinese civilization, and, through its official Confucian ideology, defined proper behavior in many spheres of life. In India, the early state was far less central in defining standards of conduct and generally played a much less significant role than the state did in China. Local social groups with dominant political power structured daily life so tightly that states and dynasties could come and go without greatly affecting people at the village level.

An elaborate commercial network had developed by classical times, with merchants and craftspeople organized into guilds. Large workshops, owned by guild cooperatives or individuals, produced cotton and silk cloth, ceramic goods, and ironware. Their products, as well as sugar, copper, spices, herbs, dyestuffs, gems, and semiprecious stones, were shipped around India by ox-cart caravans or along rivers and overseas by flotillas of ships. Cotton cloth, especially, found a ready market in other parts of Asia and east Africa, and it was India's staple export for many centuries.

Culturally diverse, religiously inclusive, politically fluid, and structured by caste—this was the India that faced a new and severe challenge from beyond the mountains. It was in part the challenge of a new religion, Islam, but also that of military rulers accustomed to a different way of organizing society and structuring a kingdom, drawing on long established Middle Eastern traditions. This was the "Islamicate" world system into which South Asia was increasingly incorporated.

South Asia and the Wider World

This process of incorporation into the larger Islamic world occurred in several ways. Muslims came first as merchants, extending the trade and economic relationships that characterized the Islamicate world system. But they also came as conquerors. In the eleventh and twelfth centuries, Muslim Turk and Afghan warriors, through their vigor, discipline, and effective cavalry tactics, defeated large, unwieldy Indian armies commanded by quarreling princes. They ultimately placed their capital at Delhi and sent forces to establish their rule down the Ganges Valley and later in central and southern India. At first it was a "garrison state," as the conquerors kept to their strongholds and let the countryside run itself. But gradually these Muslim rulers learned to accommodate local elite groups, whose administrative, professional, and commercial skills they needed. By far the most impressive effort to weld Indians and foreign Muslims into an effective partnership was the

Mughal Empire, one of the Islamicate "gunpowder empires" that controlled much of India from its founding in 1526 well into the eighteenth century. The courtly culture of the Mughals attracted soldiers and administrators from older centers of Islamic culture such as Persia and Turkey. For them India was a place of opportunity. From their ranks there emerged a high-born community of Muslims called *ashraf,* who prided themselves on their foreign ancestry.

Accompanying both merchants and soldiers were Sufis, or holy men, who settled into the countryside and by exemplary behavior, spiritual power, and philosophical teachings attracted believers to Islam. India has always respected "god-filled men," and the Sufis, singing and praying and preaching the love of Allah, won converts. Many came from low castes or from the Untouchables, who were attracted by Islam's ideals of equality and brotherhood, or from groups who were on the margins of classical Hindu culture.

The presence of a competing high-culture religious tradition helped to define more concretely the outlines of Hindu belief and practice. Caste rules were tightened up to guard against personal pollution. Respectable upper-class Hindus began secluding their wives, just as Muslims did. Hindu devotional cults, like the Sufis, served as vehicles for the adoration of the divine. One was Sikhism, which borrowed certain features of Islam and gradually evolved into a separate religion.

Hindu and Muslim communities established their own boundaries, their own equilibrium in each locality. But there was never a complete wall between them. Social and economic relationships often crossed religious lines, and a composite Indo-Persian high culture, often called Hindustani, developed. It found expression in the emerging literary language of Urdu, which linked Hindustani language and Persian literary forms in an Arabic-related script. And it emphasized the role of kingship, the values of Islam, and the aristocratically supported arts of painting, poetry, and architecture. The contributions of foreign Muslims distinguished this high culture dramatically from its predecessors.

India in 1500

Indian society continued to be composed of many communities. By the sixteenth century, a number of distinct cultural regions, frequently associated with major languages, had crystallized (see Map 13.2). Punjab in the northwest served as home to Hindus and Sikhs, large numbers of Muslim peasants, and various administrative elites (both Muslim and Hindu) of the dominant Mughal Empire; most spoke Punjabi, but Urdu served as an important literary language. The Gangetic Plain was dominated by settled agriculturalists who spoke various forms of Hindi; the elite groups included substantial numbers of traditional Hindu merchants and landlords as well as Muslim courtiers and landlords, many of whom contributed to a cultural renaissance associated with Urdu. Bengal in the east had a Muslim peasant population and a (largely) Hindu elite, both of whom spoke Bengali—a language with a well-developed literary tradition. The Deccan Plateau encompassed several cultural zones: the northern area became a Marathi-speaking core region now known as Maharashtra; Andhra was a Telegu-speaking area in the eastern part of the plateau; and a Kannada-speaking area became known as the Karnataka.

In the far south of India, Tamil and Telegu speakers vied for dominance in a shifting series of kingdoms, characterized by a distinctively Hindu concept of kingship and large temple complexes; another region of the south was Kerala, a southwest coastal trading area that served as an entry point for Islamic culture and Christian missionaries. Within each cultural region there was great diversity of political, economic, and social organization—ranging from tribal groups in Assam on the east and pastoralists in Sind on the west, to the settled agriculturalist areas of the Gangetic Plain and the seafaring communities of each coast.

In this extraordinarily diverse section of the world, there have occurred in the past five centuries a series of efforts to incorporate some or all of this diversity into more highly centralized and enduring political systems. These efforts have been undertaken by Hindu rulers in southern India, by Muslim rulers in the Mughal Empire of northern and central India, by the British during their roughly two-hundred-year domination of the peninsula, and, since 1947, by the governments of independent India, Pakistan, and Bangladesh.

Such experiments are not, of course, unique to India. The blending of Spanish and various Native American and African cultures in Latin America; the multiethnic pluralism of the United States; the great kingdoms of west Africa; the empires of Turkey, Russia, and Austria—these and other experiments

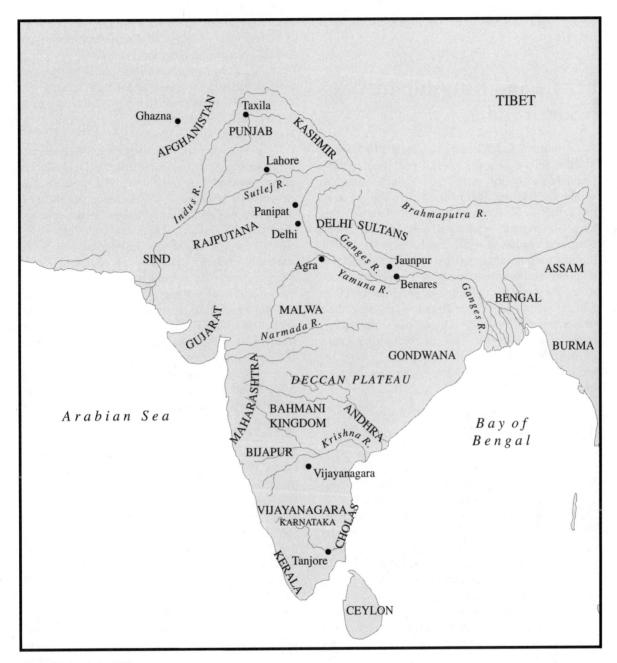

MAP 13.2 India in 1500

have struggled with the central issue of the modern world: How can large and inclusive political systems accommodate the diverse societies encompassed within their borders? In considering this question, we confront the processes by which groups of people define themselves as members of particular communities. Religious movements, connections to the world

of Islam, colonial rule, modern economic development, and the rise of nationalist ideologies have all played a role in shaping distinct cultural identities in modern times. Since South Asian peoples have been confronting these dilemmas for a very long time, their "experiments," which we will explore in this and subsequent chapters, have a global and contemporary significance as well as an Indian and regional importance.

State and Kingship in South India

With northern India largely dominated by various Muslim rulers after the twelfth century, it is not surprising that the next great Hindu kingdom would arise in the south. Known by the name of its capital—Vijayanagara, or "city of victory"—this kingdom or empire represented a new kind of Hindu state in the south. Together with the more famous Mughal Empire in the north, it gave rise to political traditions and practices important for modern South Asia. These political traditions provided both the foundation on which the British later built their Indian empire and the cultural basis for Indian rejection of British rule. Thus, in examining the evolution of Vijayanagara and the Mughal Empire, we are looking at the historical roots of contemporary India.

The Vijayanagara Experiment

The kingdom of Vijayanagara, established on the Deccan Plateau of southern India, arose around 1340. Under its third dynasty, established by the Tuluvas in 1505, Vijayanagara achieved its greatest territorial reach. Consciously patterning their capital city after an earlier south Indian kingdom, Vijayanagara's kings created a massive, fortified city of stone that stretched for miles amongst reddish hills and giant outcroppings of rocks.

But the architecture of the new capital showed that Vijayanagara was quite different from earlier Hindu states in the region. Previous kings had more or less "lived on the road," taking with them mobile trappings of rule; when they held audiences with their subjects, all met on an open field or under elaborately decorated tents. Permanent architecture, patronized extensively by these earlier kings, had housed the gods, not the temporal rulers. At Vijayanagara, by contrast, during the relative peace and prosperity of the early sixteenth century, royal buildings built of stone proliferated to the point that a distinct civic center emerged. The design of these royal buildings showed a deliberate blending of temple architecture characteristic of Tamil south India and courtly architecture from the Muslim-ruled states to the north. It was an effort to integrate both regional cultural differences (Tamil and Telegu in south India, and the Deccan regions of Karnataka and Maharashtra) and the emerging gulf dividing Hindu and Muslim cultures.

This self-consciously integrative Vijayanagara kingdom has been seen as distinctively Hindu because it was based on the uniquely Hindu philosophical concept of *dharma*—the separate and different duties imposed on individuals or groups according to their place in society. These ideas had been elaborated during the earlier classical period, and by the sixteenth century, the duty of the king—*rajadharma*—occupied a central place in political and religious philosophy. It was the exercise of proper and virtuous kingship that enabled various communities of the realm to fulfill their own *dharma* and thus to form a society that was greater than its several parts. While these ideas were distinctively Hindu, in the sixteenth century that term had little of the sharply defined and exclusive connotations that it has acquired in more recent times.

Politics and Ritual in Vijayanagara

The role of the king as an agent of social integration was expressed through royal patronage of art (for instance, the carvings typical of Hindu temples transferred to the faces of many Vijayanagara buildings) and, especially, through a new festival called Mahanavami. Observance of the annual nine-day Mahanavami festival brought to the capital city the chiefs who owed allegiance to the dynasty; they set up temporary pavilions in front of the great platform erected in the royal center of the city, and participated in a series of processions and ceremonies designed to involve all representatives in the realm. Focused on the reigning king, the festivities—processions, displays, games—enabled the king to receive homage and gifts from his notables, and to return to them gifts and honors that underscored their status in his kingdom. Central to these observances was *puja* (worship) of the king's guardian deities; the sacred aspects of kingship were reinforced by connecting Vijayanagara's rulers to both Rama (an incarnation of Vishnu who stands as the model of a good god-king) and to the goddess Devi or Durga (known for her power to destroy).

Thus, the Mahanavami festival represented a ceremonial integration of gods and king with the various communities of Vijayanagara. This expressed a new conception of the king as centralized ritual integrater of the realm, differing sharply from the earlier south Indian pattern in which a number of localized rulers each functioned as the center of his own smaller kingdom, with none being superior to the other. But it was different also from European notions of centralized kingship, which were becoming in the sixteenth century much more autocratic, bureaucratized, and absolutist, attempting to suppress local centers of power. The Mahanavami festival under the Vijayanagara kings ritually recognized the rights of local communities and systematically parceled out political and economic authority to their leaders.

Finally, the Mahanavami ceremonies provided an opportunity for the Vijayanagara state and its elite to support a number of *bhakti* or devotional movements that were proliferating throughout India in the sixteenth and seventeenth centuries. *Bhakti* emphasized the personal relationship between the god or goddess and the individual believer. Cults grew up around particular local or regional deities. Equally important, new texts—written in local everyday or vernacular languages, rather than in classical Sanskrit—told favorite stories about the gods. Such texts made these religious stories accessible to pious individuals, who no longer needed to rely on ritual intermediaries such as Brahmans. *Bhakti* thus provided an avenue for believers, previously excluded by a Brahmin-centered ritual religion, to receive recognition and status on the basis of the support they contributed to the movement; these patrons included large numbers of merchants and women. Indeed, south Asian women have been a central element of *bhakti* movements throughout the last four centuries; they have found in it both a religious expression appropriate to their activities at home and an opportunity to exercise public roles in shrines and local temples.

The major devotional movement was associated with the god-king Rama as expressed in the epic *Ramayana*. The characters of Rama's story came to stand as exemplars of certain roles: Rama's wife Sita became the model for the perfect virtuous wife; Hanuman, the king of the monkeys, stood for the perfect follower, a brave warrior, and a pure-hearted devotee; Rama's brothers demonstrated the virtues

of kinship and perfect loyalty. Rama himself, through the trials of losing and then regaining his kingdom and his wife, illustrated how the perfect king should behave. The adventures of this appealing band inspired and galvanized devotees. Performances of Rama's story were supported by individual patrons as well as elite sponsors in a multitude of localities. Proliferation of devotional activities for Rama expanded until, in the eighteenth century, widespread public ritual reenactments of Rama's story took place in cities and towns throughout the subcontinent. Rulers as well as local elites joined in patronizing these ritual reenactments. In supporting such cultural events, the authority and legitimacy of the state thus became linked with the new emphasis on personal devotion.

The rise of Vijayanagara's new form of state was also connected to important economic changes. One was expansion of cultivation, as the rulers and chiefs supported the building of tanks to store water, which enabled mixed "wet" (irrigated) and "dry" areas to be cultivated even without regular rainfall. As one historian has noted, "state building and tank building had become a single process."[3] As agriculture expanded, new communities not previously engaged in cultivation were organized around strong local leaders, often those who had first distinguished themselves in battle for local kings. The early dynasties of Vijayanagara awarded to these leaders increased control over resources and the privileges of political power while insisting on their subordination through attending the Mahanavami festival.

Equally important to economic change was an expansion of overseas, coastal, and inland trade, all of which were supported by political authorities at various levels of the Vijayanagara state. Tax revenue derived from the expanded trade went to many overlords in the empire, and the king benefited as well. Increasing urbanization accompanied the expansion of cultivation and trade. In new cities, groups of merchants, artisans, and others organized to regulate their internal affairs and to conduct both urban-based commerce and long-distance trade. Towns in the south had long emerged around temple complexes, but now, in the fourteenth to sixteenth centuries, a substantial number of urban sites were established for secular, commercial purposes. In the process, new groups such as large landlords, merchants, and traders emerged to claim their rights and to exercise power under Vijayanagara rule.

This 1902 photograph of Indian women grinding their grain reflects patterns of economic life and gender roles that have persisted for generations. *Library of Congress*

In cementing ties with these new groups as well as with the older authorities from an earlier era, Vijayanagara rulers emphasized the values they shared: the sense of an ordered realm, in which many groups shared in political power; the emphasis on *dharma* and, especially, on the need for a virtuous and valiant king to fulfill *rajadharma*. An expanded understanding of patronage became part of this system—in which the king, local rulers, military chiefs, merchants, some peasant groups, and some upper-class women all participated through their support of personal devotionalism and of locally and regionally recognized gods and temples. Such individuals or groups, seeking to maintain or improve their social and political position, often donated land, cattle, or rights to income from particular villages to one or another temple. In return they were honored at annual temple festivals, which served to integrate and to rank the various communities of the realm.

Beyond these south Indian Hindu features, the rulers of Vijayanagara also drew on the military and artistic styles of Muslim states of northern India. They sometimes hired Muslim mercenaries (gunners and footsoldiers) as part of Vijayanagara military forces. And they adopted Muslim architectural patterns such as domed ceilings, piers, and arches, thus calling attention to the more highly centralized kingship models established by Islamic states.

Community and State

In local villages and small towns, people lived in face-to-face relationships, embedded within kinship and *jati* networks. Lower caste families traditionally performed certain functions for more highly ranked families and received prescribed payments in return. It was possible for members of various caste groups to achieve social status and locally powerful positions by their distribution of resources to various clients. All of this was then ritually recognized through temple ceremonies emphasizing purity and pollution. Though the sharp inequalities in the relationships appeared solid and timeless at any given moment, the fate of particular groups and families did change over time as access to power and resources fluctuated.

Beyond the local community, political structures operated around various levels of lordship. While the preeminence of the Vijayanagara king became established by the sixteenth century, that process by no means neutralized the independence of the various chiefdoms scattered through the realm. To the contrary, at the heart of the Deccan style of kingship lay a somewhat fragmentary exercise of rule, in which all lordships became strengthened simultaneously. Since frequent succession struggles at the top marked Vijayanagara politics, kings could not afford to permanently disarm or too strenuously limit the power of their supporters. Instead, the exercise of kingly rule meant frequent "tours of conquest," in which the king established his personal rule over the great and little chiefs of his realm through military confrontation and the exaction of tribute and homage.

The ceremonies resulting from the tours cemented the personal relationship between king and chief. Chiefs worshiped the king as a god and the king awarded chiefs with symbols of lordship. *Puja* ceremonies and gifting processes thus stood at the heart of the political relationships that constituted kingship in early modern South Asia. Once this relationship had been established, chiefs operated to a large extent on their own—maintaining order, fostering trade, extending cultivation, collecting land revenue, patronizing religious institutions, and encouraging devotional activity.

Vijayanagara represented a new kind of kingdom in the south, quite different from the political system that preceded it. And its style of kingship also characterized the numerous smaller kingdoms that followed Vijayanagara after its military defeat and disintegration in the mid-sixteenth century. These successor states often called themselves Hindu. But in the relationship of the state to its various communities, the Muslim Mughal Empire in north India followed a similar pattern. Here was evidence of a uniquely South Asian approach to the problem of political order amid vast cultural diversity, one that was often able to avoid or transcend the divisions and conflicts that have so troubled India in the twentieth century.

The North Indian Model: The Mughal Empire

The rise of the Vijanayagara kingdom in south India was paralleled in the north by the creation of a new, more centralized and bureaucratized Muslim state known as the Mughal Empire (see Map 13.3). It was established in 1526 by a central Asian military leader named Babur with a force of only 12,000 but armed with the new technology of muskets and artillery. Babur's grandson, Akbar, however, laid the real foundations of the Mughal Empire during his long reign from 1556 to 1605. In Akbar, India found one of the great emperors of the world: a brave and resourceful military commander, an efficient and innovative administrator, and a visionary of a broad, inclusive empire. His military successes greatly expanded the boundaries of the Mughal Empire throughout north and central India. Building on the simpler administrative systems of earlier states, he sought to incorporate the many communities he ruled into a single, uniquely South Asian political system.

Akbar operated within an "Islamicate" world, which incorporated not only Islamic religious values but political and cultural influences from other traditions as well. Both the regional states that had preceded the Mughals in north India and the world system within which Akbar operated provided him with Islamicate models. In India, however, the majority of the population—and the predominant princes of Akbar's realm—were not Muslim. Earlier rulers had rested fairly lightly on this population, though they had destroyed a number of temples and had imposed taxes on non-Muslims. But in Akbar's more central-

ized political system, it was necessary to address the concerns of non-Muslims more concretely. Akbar did this in three ways: he created a philosophy of state focused on the ruler that accepted both Hindu and Muslim aristocrats into the new empire; he pursued policies of cultural and devotional patronage that undergirded the blending of multiple cultures; and he developed an administrative-military system to extend his vision far into the outlying provinces.

At the heart of the new Mughal state lay the *mansabdari* system. It placed all members of the elite (as *mansabdars*) within a hierarchically ranked structure and paid them through standardized awards of *jagirs* (assignments of revenue collected from specific villages). As members of a military aristocracy, the *mansabdars* were expected to provide the emperor a specified number of cavalrymen when called upon. However, they also formed a civil administrative system, with responsibility for maintaining order, punishing criminals, collecting the revenue that constituted their salary, and forwarding to the emperor his portion. The *mansabdari* system carefully ranked its members, and provided regular opportunities for promotion, particularly in times of war. Akbar prevented this elite, always relatively small in number, from establishing local power bases by rotating them from one *jagir* to another. Thus the administration served to sustain the loyalty to the person of the emperor himself. Akbar's only exception was his treatment of the Rajput princes, a group of powerful military chiefs located in the Rajasthan desert area of north India: the Rajputs were left in place if they swore allegiance to the emperor. Akbar married several Rajput princesses and encouraged his courtiers to intermarry as well, thus building new kinship alliances, always an important feature of Indian political life.

In this way the most influential existing power brokers were integrated into the Mughal system both culturally and administratively. To this military-administrative structure dispersed throughout the empire was joined both a central administration at the court and a system of urban rule, which rested on key officers appointed in each city. Altogether, these elements comprised a much more centralized and bureaucratized form of rule than the subcontinent had witnessed before.

As in Vijayanagara, the ability of the Mughal state to incorporate its diverse communities rested largely on the exercise of patronage. Lacking the large tem-

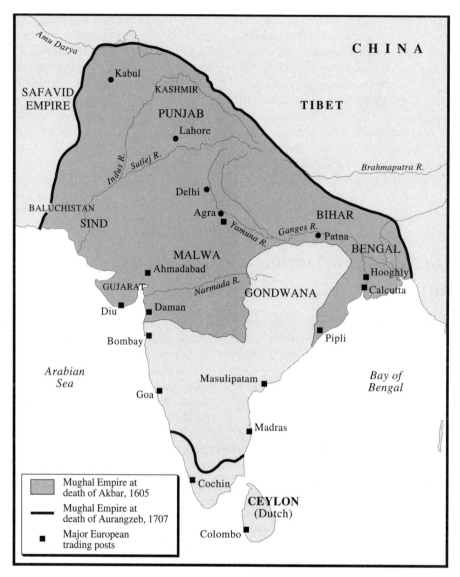

MAP 13.3 The Mughal Empire

ple complexes and water storage tanks of the south, Akbar and his courtiers supported the building of palaces and forts, mosques, tombs, even Hindu temples. The architecture and decoration of these buildings often combined Hindu and Muslim styles, deliberately designed to suggest a culturally inclusive realm.

Beyond architecture, imperial and subimperial patronage encouraged the arts of painting and poetry. The growth of these art forms during the height of Mughal rule created unique artistic styles and a Persian-derived but distinctive style of poetry written in Urdu. The courtly literary language of Urdu had

emerged in this period to become one of the symbols of a shared elite culture fostered by the Mughals. Persian artists and writers were welcome in the Mughal Empire, and under Akbar's patronage the *Ramayana* was translated into Persian, and Persian classics were translated into Sanskrit and Hindi. Profoundly interested in philosophical debate, Akbar also attracted leading intellectual and religious leaders to the court.

Ultimately, Akbar forged his own religious cult, the Din-i-Ilahi ("divine faith"), which emphasized the person of the emperor and blended elements of many faiths into one. Once again, Akbar's concern was to focus the attention and loyalty of the ruling elite on the Mughal dynasty rather than on competing ideologies. In an effort to incorporate non-Muslims more fully into the realm, he ended a ban on the construction of temples and abolished the head tax on nonbelievers. These policies were highly controversial among the Islamicate elite, for they directly contradicted the duties of a good Muslim ruler. They were clearly aimed at creating a state in which the *ulama* (men learned in Islamic law) and immigrants from the other Islamic states exercised much less influence than did the emperors and their loyal, local followers. It was the *ulama* and Iranian immigrant elites who protested strongly against such integrative imperial policies.

The combination of far-sighted administrative structures, successful territorial expansion, cultural patronage to support an inclusive state ideology, and a long life enabled Akbar to provide a solid basis for the Mughal Empire. The empire was further blessed by two able successors to Akbar—Jahangir (1605–1627) and Shah Jahan (1627–1658), both born of Rajput mothers. Both emperors successfully waged military campaigns to contain the empire's enemies, and Shah Jahan, especially, proved an able diplomat as well as warrior. But both of them concentrated first and foremost on the development of a blended culture as the basis for an inclusive state. Their patronage created large workshops of talented painters at the Mughal court that were replicated at the courts of Mughal subimperial rulers. They supported poetry so extensively that it became, in the later period of Mughal decline, the single most important activity of the elite in maintaining their self-respect and identity. The most dramatic architectural creation was undoubtedly the Taj Mahal, the tomb built by Shah Jahan to honor his wife. Although the Mughal state continued to operate within the Islamicate world system, this extensive cultural patronage proved extremely important in providing the basis for a shared high culture in which members of the Mughal elite, whether Hindu or Muslim, could participate. There was enough flexibility in this blended culture so that regional representatives of the Mughals could legitimately patronize explicitly Hindu gods or festivals.

Economic success facilitated the growth of this Indo-Persian culture. As in Vijayanagara, trade—both internal and foreign—expanded, fostered by participation in the larger Islamicate world system. This stimulated more extensive cultivation and agricultural production for sale in distant markets. Fur-

thermore, in urban workshops and rural households additional production for the market took place, especially of textiles. Particularly significant was the growth of rural manufacturing, a development paralleling Europe's "putting-out" system. All of this created a closer cooperation between the government and merchants, and economic partnership led to a more market-oriented or commercialized agrarian society. The increased availability of credit, standardization of currency, and the collection of the land revenue in cash were all part of a more commercialized economy.

These economic changes reinforced an already centralizing imperial state. They also represented a kind of proto-capitalism, resting on production for the market, similar to what was happening in Europe at the same time.[4] But India's embryonic capitalism did not develop into a full-blown industrial capitalism; that transition occurred only in Europe. The most common explanation has been the dominating presence of a powerful state that emphasized the accumulation of wealth for military purposes, thus preventing enough reinvestment to foster industrial growth. Others have pointed to the political turmoil that accompanied the "decline" of the Mughal state in the eighteenth century and the subsequent British takeover. And, finally, much of the capital generated in this period was devoted to luxury production and cultural patronage rather than productive investment.

Community and State

Local rural society in the Mughal Empire was similar to that in Vijayanagara. Village life was ordered by kinship ties and by the fluid hierarchies of caste or *jati*. The position of women in society depended equally on class and location. In both city and countryside, poor women had greatest mobility because they needed to move freely to earn money—in the villages as agricultural laborers, domestic servants, producers of rural handicrafts, or piece workers in cottage industries. Although wealthier women in the countryside did less visible labor as a sign of their status, they still moved relatively freely to perform domestic tasks, including marketing and the rituals necessary to preserve the family from harm. By contrast, urban women became increasingly secluded, as the practice of upper-class Muslim women began to be adopted more widely by Indian elites. While they maintained close ties with other women across the rooftops of their row houses and within the narrow lanes of their neighborhoods, they seldom ventured out into the streets. Indeed, Indian housing in cities made as clear a distinction as the owners could afford between public spaces and private, family space. This reflected a strong division between a domestic world dominated by women, and a public world run by men in which women symbolized values to be protected.

Linking the village and the state was a layer of society located below the *mansabdari* administrative elite. In their effort to implement a centralizing state, the Mughals soon encountered a layer of local powerholders often called *zamindars* who, from their mud forts in the countryside, resisted too great an incursion by the state. Permanent residents in the locality (as compared to the rotating *mansabdars*), and members of regional warrior aristocracies, *zamindars* sought to control both the people and produce of the countryside through the use of armed retainers; they probably controlled larger armed forces than were available to the emperor through the *mansabdari* system. It was largely *zamindars* who kept peace in the villages and collected the taxes that were sent forward to the center. And it was usually the *zamindars* who fomented and supported resistance to the empire. Some 140 such revolts have been counted during Akbar's reign alone. These were quickly suppressed, however, and by the early seventeenth century, most of the *zamindars* had evolved into "a semi-official, collaborating class in rural society," able to mobilize support for the state rather than for revolt.[5]

When necessary, the Mughals razed the mud forts of rebels. But they also awarded tax-free land grants to loyal servants of the empire in order to create a class of people (a service gentry) in the countryside who were loyal to the dynasty. Some of these were *zamindars;* others were upper-class Muslims claiming descent from the Prophet's family, many of whom exercised religious leadership in the countryside; and still others were Hindus literate in Persian who had performed valuable administrative services for the Mughals.

Another link between the Mughal regime and society at large lay in the renewed emphasis on devotionalism that characterized both Hindu and Muslim religious life. As in Vijayanagara during the sixteenth and seventeenth centuries, the proliferation of elaborate festivals provided occasions for Hindus to

The seventeenth century Mughal ruler Shah Jahan meets with Muslim scholars and theologians of his realm.
The Granger Collection

express their devotion to particular gods. It also provided a point of contact with Islam in its Sufi form. From the fourteenth through the seventeenth centuries, the various groups of Sufi mystics in Islam had been migrating to India, bringing with them their distinctive religious culture—the direct appeal to God through ecstatic practices, instruction by the shaikh, and the establishment of a shrine and a community of believers at the shaikh's tomb. All of this provided a powerful entry point into Islam for Indians, already accustomed to worshiping at shrines and treating saintly figures as intermediaries. Saints' shrines soon covered the landscape and Akbar pursued a deliberate policy of providing patronage for Sufi shrines as a counterbalance to the influence of the official *ulama.*

In the rapidly growing cities of the seventeenth and eighteenth centuries, Mughal authorities sought to rest their administrative system on top of an already complex network of self-regulating structures. Within cities there were specialized bazaars—of jewelry makers, textile merchants, or foodstuffs—clustered around the great houses of members of the elite and their dependents. At a greater distance from the city center, neighborhoods grouped themselves by occupation: weavers, toy makers, courtesans. As people moved into the city from the surrounding countryside, they sought out others from their village or those who spoke their language. Thus cities encompassed a number of smaller communities that regulated their own affairs. Neighborhoods, for instance, banded together to hire night watchmen. Great men and their dependents sponsored floats and performers to participate in processions during festivals. Occupational groups not only recruited new workers from the countryside and negotiated with employers, but also joined together to sing devotional songs. These forms of community also provided a basis for protesting or resisting an overlord or a rival community.

Above these self-regulating communities rested the Mughal urban officers: the *qazi*, learned in Islamic law, who served as the local legal officer and a symbol of the empire as an Islamic state; the revenue officer who collected taxes; the *kotwal* who maintained the peace. The *kotwal,* for example, might accommodate the desire of prominent Hindus that no cow sacrifice take place in that city, while enabling Muslim elite families to make the necessary sacrifices out of sight. Thus the idea that was explicit in the Vijayanagara empire—that the king and his representatives enabled the constituent communities to fulfill their own *dharma*—indirectly informed the Mughal Empire as well, but within an Islamicate setting.

The Beginnings of Mughal Decline

By the mid-seventeenth century, under the reign of Aurangzeb (1658–1707), the Mughal Empire began to experience the strains associated with the enormous diversity of the realm and its integrative political philosophy. From the time of Akbar on, the policy of cultural synthesis had provoked strong criticism at the court, especially by the *ulama* and recent emigrés from other Islamicate states. As an austere man who devalued many forms of art and who was faced by rebel challenges, Aurangzeb responded to these criticisms by emphasizing military values and following the model of the ideal Islamic king. He

invested state resources, not in paintings and poets, but in military efforts to defend and expand the empire. Expensive patronage was spent on *mansabdar* awards offered to those resisters he wished to lure into the Mughal aristocracy. The result was to swell dramatically the number of elite families looking to the empire for support; yet all of this occurred without significant expansion in the amount of good land available to be awarded as supporting *jagirs*. He reimposed the tax on non-Muslims and razed certain prominent Hindu temples. The creative tension that had earlier balanced the multiple communities of the empire began to come apart, and regional power centers became more prominent. The need to respond militarily to these challenges required increasing amounts of revenue collected from the land, which, in turn, put pressure on the fragile relationships between the center and the outlying areas of the empire.

A sign of these strains was the revolt of *zamindars* of the Maratha region, led by Shivaji in the 1660s. His military victories did serious damage to the Mughals' prestige. Furthermore, he had established a sufficiently elaborate bureaucracy to justify calling his regime a state, not just a band of rebels. And by presenting his new state as a successor to Vijayanagara and invoking Hindu ideals of kingship, he presented an image of a revived Hindu state in ideological opposition to the Mughals. The inclusive cultural pluralism of the earlier Mughal Empire was clearly weakening.

The Eighteenth Century: Decline or Creativity?

As the center of Mughal Empire weakened, new social, economic, and political patterns began to emerge. Older historical accounts have described this process as one of decline and disarray from which India was saved only by British colonial rule. But more recent historians have described it in terms of creative change and adjustment to new circumstances, including the unraveling of the Islamicate world system and the rise of European trading efforts that led eventually to a scramble for colonies.

Perhaps the most profound change in this period was the shift in political power from the center to the locality. Merchant bankers, the Mughal service gentry in the rural areas, and local landholders all began to consolidate their power at the expense of the central government. Local institutions of self-regulation became more independent and more highly developed as they took over various functions previously left to officers of the empire. For example, revenue farmers, entrepreneurs who combined military power with expertise in managing cash and local trade, increased their influence and strength in the eighteenth century as the Mughal state declined. They were private tax collectors hired by various political authorities. They also became the source of rural credit on a much greater scale.

Thus, in the new circumstances of the eighteenth century, a political system far different from the centralized Mughal Empire emerged—one in which "there were many sharers in the dignity and power of kingship with overlapping rights and obligations."[6] At the top, though with diminishing authority, were the Mughals; below them were regional states such as Bengal, Hyderabad, Awadh and others that had broken free of the Mughal Empire; below them were the heads of large holdings that were ostensibly subservient to these regional states; and the layer below this held a wide assortment of *zamindar*-types, fighting from their mud forts for autonomy and power over the countryside, as well as urban merchants and moneylenders exercising power in the cities. But the lines distinguishing the levels were blurred, and the right combination of military force and access to resources could propel a leader from one level to the next. Political boundaries and political authority remained extremely fluid in this century. Commercialization meant that it was possible to buy many aspects of kingship, such as tax collection, military forces, and cultural patronage. And a great many more entrepreneurs and leaders in South Asian society gained the wherewithal to pay the price.

Many new claimants to power and authority tried to buttress their legitimacy through cultural patronage. In the process, they helped to create a number of distinct regional cultures within India. The Marathas, for instance, fostered the development of the Marathi language through literary patronage, and a regional identity emerged that combined an emphasis on Marathi and Hindu religious devotionalism. Similarly, Awadh—whose ruling family was Shia—created a particular form of north Indian Muslim elite identity, rooted in the literary language of Urdu. The Sikh kingdom in the Punjab emerged, using resistance to the Mughals to define Sikhs as a religious community distinct from Muslims and expressing this identity through art and popular culture.

Changing Society in the Eighteenth Century

Much else was changing in India in the eighteenth century. Trading patterns shifted, partly in response to altered political boundaries as regional states emerged, and partly as a reflection of the new importance of European trading centers. As a result, the largest cities of the Mughal Empire—administrative centers of half a million residents or more such as Lahore, Delhi, and Agra—shrank to half their former size. Other urban sites, located on the new trading routes, grew substantially, the largest ones—such as Banaras—averaging around 200,000 inhabitants. Production for the market continued to expand during the eighteenth century, with rural industries and urban artisan communities gaining in wealth. The major beneficiaries of these processes were various moneylenders and merchants, who provided the economic resources used to support new regional states and provincial magnates.

As political and economic power shifted to regional and local levels of Indian society, so too did the exercise of cultural patronage, so important in Indian life. Previously, it had been kings in both Vijayanagara and the Mughal Empire that took responsibility for sponsoring religious rituals and cultural events that brought the realm together. Now that responsibility began to be shared by an ever-larger number of leaders in South Asian society.

One consequence of this process was the elaboration of Hindu and Muslim festivals in this period. Patrons found that they could buy status and express influence by patronizing such festivals. For instance, two public ceremonial observances that focused around processions—one Muslim and the other Hindu—became widespread in their observance in the eighteenth century. Under Muslim patronage, Muharram—the ten-day telling of the story of the martyrdom of Husain—expanded greatly. Although the origins of the story lay in the Shia branch of Islam, in India it became an expression of Muslim identity more generally. Ramlila, a Hindu enactment of the story of the good king Rama, was performed in many of the same cities or neighborhoods as Muharram. The two often competed in terms of putting on a good show and attracting audiences from long distances. Urban neighborhoods, organized groups of merchants, and others seeking greater prominence or political influence were among the patrons of such

The British East India Company depended on private military forces, such as those shown here in Bombay in 1767, to establish their presence in India. *Hulton Deutsch Picture Collection*

events. So too were the rulers of the new regional states that emerged from the declining Mughal Empire. By sponsoring these ceremonies, the new rulers could establish links to the populace and thus legitimize and publicize their new regimes. The newly autonomous kingdom of Awadh in north India, for instance, heavily patronized Muharram, creating a form distinct from observances in other Muslim states. Similarly, the nearby Raja of Banaras chose to patronize various forms of the Ramayana story and developed a thirty-one-day version of the Ramlila that continues to this day.

Intellectual and philosophical discussion followed a similar pattern. Decentralized to more regional centers and encouraged by the patronage of more localized leaders, a number of South Asian scholars and writers began to rethink their traditions. Several centers of philosophical Hinduism fostered reinvigorated learning in these regional states. Among Muslims, the decline of the Mughals and other Islamicate empires represented a challenge to intellectuals. Under the direction, especially, of Shah Wali Ullah, South Asian Muslims began to consider a self-sufficient world without the benefit of Muslim rulers in which the old hostility between Sufi saints and the official *ulama* was overcome. Indian Islam thus began to create new patterns of behavior for the good Muslim that took into account the absence of a Muslim ruler. It was this changed and changing India that European trading companies encountered in the eighteenth century.

European Traders in a Changing South Asia

Textiles—fine cottons and silks—as well as agricultural produce—indigo, cardamom, pepper, and other spices—attracted the Portuguese, the Dutch, the French, and the British to India. The Portuguese had established a dominant position in the sixteenth century, working through coastal settlements such as Goa on the western coast. The other companies began to challenge this dominance during the seventeenth century. Under the Mughals, these European traders even began to affect the inland trade through their purchases in silver bullion, derived from Latin America, as well as Japanese copper and, occasionally, gold. Given Mughal India's cash economy, and the premium put on cultural patronage and display, these precious metals were in great demand, for the subcontinent produced little of its own. This demand, coupled with the need for coin in the internal economy of the Mughal Empire, made a place for European traders, and linked India to the newly emerging world economy centered in Europe.

The trading companies operated with one eye on their European competitors and another on their Indian collaborators. Established as monopolies in their home countries, the companies competed in an international context in which success in Asian trade was an important element in military and political competition in Europe. The Dutch soon focused their attention on Indonesia and the pepper trade, while the British and French companies began to seek out collaborators in the Indian subcontinent. The bases established by each company took the form of factories, or small forts housing the mercantile staff engaged in seeking out and recording trade. In their search for lucrative trading partnerships, the European trading companies often affected local power arrangements as they sought out Indian middlemen and profitable deals with groups of producers, reaching ever more deeply into the hinterland.

The different experiences of the British East India Company in western India and in Bengal illustrate how this process worked. In western India the British had a freer hand. Gujarat figured importantly in international trade, but did not have a strong local ruler to contain the political maneuvering of the trading companies. Surat, a major port city, had begun to lose its prominence because the merchants living there could not be confident of receiving protection. The British established a new port city down the coast at Bombay, and began attracting Surat's merchants by offering some protection from the attacks of the Marathas and the Mughals. The lesson here was that the armed ships and fortified factories of the European trading companies offered a protection to Indian merchants that the shifting Indian political scene could not provide.

On the eastern coast of India in Bengal, the British East India Company was awarded the privilege of free trade by the Mughal emperor. But it was prevented from taking much advantage of this by the obstruction of the greatest merchant of the area and by the distrust of Murshid Quli Khan, the Mughal governor of the province who ruled as though independent of the Mughals. Nevertheless, the British established a lucrative trade in Bengal in the early eighteenth century: from factories in the interior, company agents contracted directly with weavers to create textiles corresponding to changing fashions in England. This increasing intervention and the presence of fortified settlements made Murshid's successors very uneasy. The ruling governor in the 1750s lacked the military or political skill of his predecessors, however, and when he rashly attacked the British, they defeated him in the Battle of Plassey in 1756. The Mughal emperor, pleased at the defeat of his upstart provincial governor, awarded to Britain's East India Company the civil administration (diwani) of Bengal. Although the Company had misgivings about this new administrative role, it finally agreed.

In return, the Company received from the Mughal emperor the right to the revenue of a lucrative area of Bengal; this provided an economic hedge against the vagaries of trading profits and gave the Company a land base in the subcontinent—thus beginning the British transition from a private seafaring company focused on trade to a government ruling a huge territory. It was a historic turning point.

The activities of the British and French East India trading companies altered profoundly in the latter half of the eighteenth century, as European traders competed more directly among themselves and intervened more actively in the subcontinent. To protect their efforts in the violent and uncertain world of a declining Mughal Empire, the East India companies all developed Indian infantries armed with European artillery and trained in European methods of war. The Europeans who headed the companies had no qualms about using these forces to further their business, though their boards of directors at home had serious reservations. The companies also forged shifting alliances with Indian rulers, to gain more profitable arrangements and to tip the balance of power toward rulers considered sympathetic to their interests. European intervention was made easier by the decline of the Mughal Empire and the commercialization of kingship. If political power was for sale, Europeans were increasingly willing to pay the going price to assure their economic and political positions. When the British chased the French out of India in 1761, the stage was set for the British to try their hand at assembling India's enormously diverse cultures into a larger political framework.

Notes

1. Morton Klass, *Caste: The Emergence of a South Asian Social System* (Philadelphia: Institute for the Study of Human Issues, 1980), esp. pp. 179–80.
2. Irawati Karve, *Hindu Society: An Interpretation,* 2nd ed. (Poona: Deshmukh Prakashan, 1968), esp. pp. 109–10, 127.
3. Burton Stein, *The New Cambridge History of India: Part I*, vol. 2, *Vijayanagara* (Cambridge, Mass.: Cambridge University Press, 1989), p. 24.
4. Frank Perlin, "Proto-Industrialization and Pre-Colonial South Asia," *Past and Present* 98 (1982): 30–95.
5. J. F. Richards, "The Imperial Crisis in the Deccan," *Journal of Asian Studies* 35:2 (Feb. 1976): 256.
6. C. A. Bayly, *Indian Society and the Making of the British Empire* (New York: Cambridge University Press, 1987), p. 13.

Chapter 14
India and the British Raj

From roughly 1800 to India's independence in 1947, the British were the dominant power on the South Asian peninsula. In several important ways, British rule there differed from European domination in other parts of the world. In contrast to the Americas where large numbers of Europeans settled permanently, the British in India represented a very thin layer of officials, businesspeople, and missionaries who governed a huge population of people very different from themselves and who expected to return "home" when they retired. And while Europeans exercised only informal control in the Ottoman and Chinese empires, the British governed India directly and formally. Finally, whereas the colonial experience in Africa was compressed into the first sixty years of the twentieth century, it lasted over twice as long in South Asia.

In terms of the subcontinent's long history, British rule, grandly called the *Raj,* followed Vijayanagara and the Mughal Empire in its attempt to fashion the area's tremendous cultural diversity into a single political unit. But British rule in South Asia changed the way its many peoples defined their communities and sharpened the conflicts among them. All of this undermined the foundations of colonial rule, and the British were forced to withdraw from a much transformed subcontinent in 1947.

The Establishment of the Raj

British power in South Asia was initially created by a private trading enterprise—the East India Company (EIC)—rather than directly by the British government. This process involved the defeat of their European rivals and the forging of military alliances with various Indian regional rulers. Some have described

it as an "absent-minded" imperialism, since the EIC initially sought to expand trade, not territory. In fact, British authorities in London generally took a dim view of the aggressive strategies pursued by their agents in India. But distances were great, and delays in communication were long; so official disapproval frequently arrived after expansion was an established fact.

The award of the *diwani* of Bengal gave the EIC its first experience administering a territory to acquire revenue, rather than conducting trade to make a profit. It did not instill confidence. Employees of the EIC, who already conducted extensive private trade in addition to their official duties, skimmed off huge personal fortunes even as they collected the land revenue for the company. Many profited enormously, with Robert Clive, the company leader, acquiring a fortune virtually overnight. This "rape of Bengal," followed as it was by a monsoon failure in 1769 and a terrible famine in 1770, showed British rule at its worst. Pressure from Parliament, however, soon forced the EIC's governors to create an administration more appropriate for controlling territory. Lord Cornwallis (1786–1793) established a prestigious Covenanted Civil Service that reined in the abuses of EIC employees and developed a reputation for professionalism and incorruptibility. Lord Wellesley (1797–1805) founded a college in Calcutta to train these new civil servants.

But Cornwallis also aggressively sought out confrontations with Indian regional rulers in an effort to secure British dominance. Whether administering territory or pursuing trade, the East India Company found itself persistently concerned with conflict among competing Indian rulers, some of whom seemed a threat to the British themselves. In this situation there were many incentives for conquering and administering large territories. These included the making of political alliances with various regional rulers, the creation of a successful military establishment (based primarily on native troops, or *sepoys*), the ability to trade more easily where direct control could be exercised, the desire to establish firm bases especially in port cities, and the need for cash to finance all other activities. The shift to British domination was hastened by the arrival in the late 1790s of Lord Wellesley, whose instructions from London when he came to serve as governor general explicitly ordered the defeat of all Indian rulers with prior connections to the French. This he proceeded to do. With the final defeat of the Marathas in 1818, the British had eliminated all major threats to their domination of the subcontinent.

The EIC annexed some territories to govern directly. Most of the remaining princes signed "subsidiary treaties" that recognized the company as the "paramount power" in India. They surrendered control of their external relations and received in return an adviser ("resident") and a body of British-led troops to "protect" their thrones and states. The British governed about one-third of India through these princes as "native states," a system of indirect rule that they later used for Malay sultans and African chiefs and kings (see Map 14.1).

Domesticating India

During their early decades in power, the British did not seek to reshape the subcontinent in their own image. The EIC proved quite conservative in the territories it ruled, seeking to maintain local political and economic structures. Often standing in for the Mughal emperor and replacing regional rulers, the EIC also confirmed patronage concessions for Hindu temples and used existing political symbols to legitimize its local rule.

Despite this effort to become just one more ruler on the South Asian landscape, the emerging British Raj represented something quite new on the subcontinent. Since trade, not military conquest, had initially brought the British to India, they had "invaded" not through the Himalayan passes—as had all previous conquerers—but from the coastline, moving inland. Consequently, their bases of power were not military urban centers in the north, but new port cities they created along the coast: Bombay on the west coast, Madras in the south, and Calcutta in the east. These served as the main administrative points for the three provinces into which British India di-

vided. Nonetheless, the fiction remained that the British were acting in the name of the Mughal emperor who lived in the city of Delhi.

As the British consolidated their rule, a number of changes already underway in the eighteenth century accelerated. One was the shift from a state dependent for its revenue on tribute or trade to one that derived its revenue primarily from taxes on land. Such a state gave agrarian society and its leaders a privileged position and motivated the British to seek out allies, whom they called "natural leaders," in the countryside. Another change was the increasing autonomy of urban corporations drawn from the Hindu merchant classes and displaced Mughal courtiers. They operated in the new port cities and urban centers on the emerging trade routes and thus gave these cities a new significance. Together these developments presented the British with a continual tension between the need for a secure rural base and the intellectual and political challenges to their rule generated in the cities.

The process of raising taxes from the land fostered further changes. The EIC initiated land surveys to determine ownership, crop yield, and customary rates of taxation with the goal of creating a class of "improving landlords" such as they imagined existed in England. In the so-called Permanent Settlement of 1793, Cornwallis introduced in Bengal a fixed rate of revenue to be collected from each landholder into perpetuity, while also establishing "ownership" of the land. Acting on their assumptions about property rights in England, the British wanted to deal only with those who held proper "title" to the land. This award of permanent title greatly benefited the *zamindars,* giving them increased control over the land and its tillers. The real losers in the Permanent Settlement were various levels of undertenants who, in Bengali notions of land control, previously enjoyed certain rights or interests in the land. These nuances were lost as the British imposed their own definitions of property. In this way the British "domesticated" large landlords. The new Raj provided the *zamindars* with legal security and recognition of their status in the countryside, in return for which the *zamindars* gave up much of their military capacity. Thus the British gained security in the rural areas.

The EIC also acted to domesticate other powerful groups. Various regional rulers or "princes" gained the support of the EIC only by agreeing to give up the independence they had previously enjoyed.

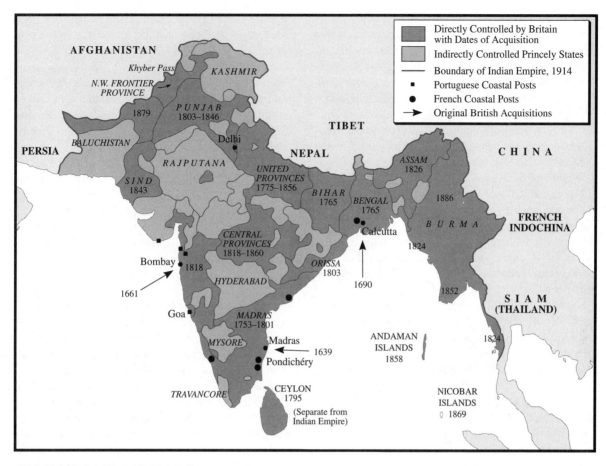

MAP 14.1 The Making of British India

Moreover, their intermittent payments of tribute gradually became a regular tax. In British thinking, all of this was part of the concept of "paramountcy": as the paramount or dominant power in the subcontinent, the British Raj limited the rights of Indian princes to deal independently with each other and ended their ability to wage war. In return, the princes received from the government a carefully graded recognition of their respective ranks (for example, in the number of rounds fired from guns in salutes), along with the assurance that their lines of succession would continue.

In the cases of landlords and princes, domestication brought a hardening of what had been a more fluid society. In the past, those gaining control of resources by military means had moved into positions of power in the countryside, and from there into positions of local rule. Most of the princely rulers,

for example, headed relatively new states that had begun to claim a place in the Indian sun only in the eighteenth century as the Mughal Empire declined. This avenue of social mobility was cut off by the British, and those currently in place were frozen into the social positions they occupied when the British Raj emerged.

In addition, the British sought to subdue other sources of power and social mobility. In the 1830s, for example, they discovered the Thags—bands of highway robbers who seasonally left their villages to prowl the main highways of the subcontinent, preying on merchants and soldiers on leave. To the British, the Thags represented a form of insurrection and a threat to their rule. In the course of suppressing them, the British came to view the Thags as characteristic of the whole of Indian society: they were superstitious, using omens from the ferocious goddess

Kali in deciding who to attack; they were untrustworthy liars, pretending to be ordinary peasants when not out on forays; even worse, they had corrupted local powerholders who shielded them from the government's eye; they attacked innocent property owners and therefore cast doubt on the effectiveness of the government; and through the caste system (that is, by apprenticing youngsters on each annual outing), they perpetuated themselves from generation to generation. By making their case against the Thags, the British Raj also made a case for itself: only an enlightened ruler from civilized western Europe could hope to suppress such primitive behavior. To deal with the Thags, the British created a special legal structure in which it was possible to convict an entire gang of a crime, without establishing individual guilt. This reflected the growing, but erroneous, British belief that Indian society consisted of fixed groups or "castes" into which individuals were born and from which they could hardly deviate. Such a notion became an important element in Britain's understanding of India and in the relationship between the colonial state and the communities that emerged under its rule.

In some places, the East India Company also tried to win over other Indians located at different places in the power structure. For instance, they introduced a second model of land revenue settlement into Madras in the early nineteenth century. Called the *ryotwari* system, it was organized on entirely different assumptions than the *zamindari* system of Bengal. It bypassed large landholders entirely, viewing them as parasites on the land. Instead, the government entered into direct relationships with the *ryots* or peasant cultivators, evaluating the taxable potential of each plot of land and settling with the peasant owners on a tax rate that could be revised periodically. Thus the government could increase its tax yield over time, but in return the peasants received title to their land.

India in Rebellion

Early efforts at securing British control focused primarily on the Indian countryside, but it was also from the countryside that the major opposition to British rule emerged. The uprising of 1857, often called the Indian Mutiny, was the most important example of Indian resistance. Its suppression represented the final consolidation of British rule in South Asia, a process that had lasted well over a century.

Resistance movements were endemic to South Asia, as the Vijayanagara, Mughal, and British imperial rulers, along with many local authorities, had all painfully discovered. In the north Indian area known as Awadh, resistance emerged in reaction to specific exploitive British policies of the 1850s. Although the British had confirmed the Nawab of Awadh as an ostensibly independent princely ruler, their own greed forced the Nawab to extract more and more revenue from the countryside to meet British financial demands. This situation created profound dislocation and opportunities for corruption that continued for several decades in the early nineteenth century. Not surprisingly, then, when an observer for the British toured the princely state in midcentury, he found rack-renting and "exploitation" of the peasants everywhere. After much debate, the British used these findings as grounds to dispossess the Nawab and to administer the territory directly, introducing a *ryotwari*-like revenue settlement that completely bypassed the local landlord class, known as *taluqdars*. These actions deeply offended two groups upon whom the British depended more heavily than they realized: the *taluqdars*, who were responsible for maintaining relative peace in the countryside, and the *sepoys*, who were recruited heavily by the British as soldiers.

The mutiny of the Bengal Army, composed of *sepoys* recruited from Awadh, triggered the Indian uprising. Changing recruitment policies that expanded the range of castes and groups enlisted into the army had reduced the privileged position of the north Indian *sepoys*; and at about the same time, their pay had been reduced. They also received the news that *sepoys* must be willing to fight in far-flung places, thus risking ritual pollution. Finally, it was rumored that bullets for the new Enfield rifles were packed in animal fat from cows and pigs. The first animal was sacred to Hindus and the second deeply offensive to Muslims. This provided the final impetus for open revolt. In early May of 1857, the mutineers marched on Delhi, hoping to place the Mughal emperor at the head of their revolt. They presented their movement as an effort to revitalize the defunct Mughal Empire and thereby attracted all those with strong grievances against the British Raj: princes whose states had been annexed, landlords deprived of their estates or their rent, peasant followers of dispossessed chiefs, religious leaders threatened by missionary activities.

Ultimately, the EIC forces suppressed the rebellion. In Britain, however, this challenge to imperial control finally forced Parliament to confront the question of governing all of India through a commercial company. Parliament decided to replace the remnants of EIC rule with a crown-appointed secretary of state for India in London and with a viceroy of the queen to rule in India. Thus, India officially became a colony, the "jewel in the British Crown."

The Captive Jewel

The substitution of the Crown for the East India Company as ruler of Britain's India empire completed the process by which a trading enterprise became a ruling authority. Frightened by the recent uprising, Crown rule was consistently more conservative and cautious than its predecessor in introducing change. But substantial change continued nonetheless and affected education, cultural patronage, the economy, the legal system, and political structures. Taken together, these changes contributed to the development of a modern society in India, with the selective importation of western European values and understandings. However, because the modernization process occurred within an imperial system designed for exploitation, it produced an Indian society different from its west European counterpart.

Understanding and Misunderstanding India

The British recognized early on that to control India they would have to know it better. Through land revenue surveys, a regular census after 1870, and the research of local administrators, the British had accumulated an enormous quantity of data about India by 1900. Much of this data was compiled in a prodigious series of gazetteers that brought together every kind of information a local administrator would need. Motivated both by the academic curiosity of learned societies in Britain and the needs of a ruling power, this process of "getting to know" India reflected the capacity of the imperial state to reach ever deeper into the communities it governed.

But knowing India required fitting this mass of information into some analytical framework, a process that has profoundly affected both Western and Indian understandings of what India was and is. There was nothing implicitly "correct" or "accurate" about the way the British came to understand India; it was simply the understanding of a dominant imperial power.

How would the British find an organizing principle or a rational social system among the enormous variety of Indian customs, traditions, and practices that their research had disclosed? The answer came from the work of British scholars known as Orientalists, who had rediscovered India's classical past during the late eighteenth century. Led by Sir William Jones, a judge in Calcutta on the EIC's High Court, these scholars had learned Sanskrit and had translated a number of ancient classical texts with the help of literate Brahmans. In these ancient works, the Orientalists found an idealized description of the caste system, based on the notion of four ranked *varna,* that made it possible to bring order out of the apparent chaos of India. The notion of a hierarchical caste system proved appealing to the British for two important reasons. First, it provided a theory of social organization that enabled the British to define a separate role for themselves at the top. In the classical texts, the king did not need to be part of the society he ruled; he simply claimed a place at the top of that society and gained legitimacy by protecting the separate communities that ranked beneath him. Second, the *varna* theory fit neatly into the new pseudo-scientific ideas of Social Darwinism, which were increasingly popular in late nineteenth-century Europe. Thus, the British came to see castes "as races, separate populations within the population."[1] Indeed, by 1915, the head of the census operation was able to argue that social status could be determined at a glance in India, by looking at "the mean relative width of their noses."[2]

Thus, the British came to understand and value highly what they referred to as "traditional" India—a conservative society organized hierarchically through the caste system and dominated by a "natural" ruling group, the Brahmans. The British much preferred and sought to preserve this idealized traditional India over the newer forms of social organization emerging in the cities. And they came to see as distinctly non-Indian the new elite, educated in European schools and enthusiastic about European val-

Indian princes, such as these splendidly attired men, played a major role in the governing of colonial India. *Bettmann*

ues. This was a kind of "Brahmanization," for the British had sought the assistance of literate Brahman scholars in developing their understanding of India, and the view that emerged from their collaboration reflected the interests and ideals of the Brahman elite.

Governing India

At the same time, however, the British realized they could not rule India alone and that collaboration with the Brahman elite, princes, and *zamindars* was not enough. They needed Indians who had been trained in Western rationalist thought and could therefore be trusted to use "knowledge" in the same way British administrators did. The foundation for such a collaborating class was a decision, hotly contested, about government funding of education made in the 1830s

for higher education and extended to the primary grades in the 1850s. Thomas Babington Macaulay, a member of the Governor General's Council in India, had proposed that the government support a system of Western education in English that would include the new scientific and rationalist thought characteristic of western Europe at this time. The Orientalists opposed this suggestion, arguing that the classical world they had recently uncovered was so valuable that educated Indians should be equipped to work with the classical texts; this required training in Sanskrit, not English. Though the debate often pitted the relative merits of European culture against those of classical South Asia, the outcome turned on the pragmatic need for educated people to staff the empire. Western education won the day, with Macaulay arguing the need to "form a class who may be interpreters between us and the millions whom we govern; a class of persons, Indian in blood and color, but English in taste, in opinions, in morals, and in intellect."[3]

The decision in favor of English education was momentous, for it meant India's future leaders would be trained in English-type universities and familiar with European culture. In India and throughout the colonial world, people schooled in the language and culture of their foreign rulers emerged as the leading critics of Western imperialism and organizers of the mass movements that eventually toppled colonial regimes. This impact was even more impressive because very few Indians were so trained. The decisions to focus on education in English and to reject the use of vernacular languages clearly meant a very limited spread of education. At independence in 1947, some 88 percent of the Indian population was still illiterate. Nevertheless, a certain amount of "trickle-down" did take place, for it was often these same English-literate intellectuals who translated Western scientific and philosophical materials into vernaculars and who, more generally, fostered the development of vernacular languages and literatures. More important, however, the decision to follow Macaulay's recommendation created a sharp distinction between the state and public life—conducted in English on the basis of Western traditions—and the private lives of Indian intellectual and public leaders—conducted in other languages and referring to indigenous values that often varied greatly from place to place.

Constitutional developments reinforced this outcome as the British began in the 1860s to allow some participation by Indian elites in political life. The most important innovation came in the 1880s with the Local Government Act, which created municipal committees that allowed for significant participation by local Indian leaders as a means of legitimizing increased local taxation. The result was to introduce at least some Indians to the ideas and procedures of British political life. While the British members of these municipal committees retained control, they selected representatives of the important communities within the city to accommodate all influential local interests.

However, the new political life of these official "representatives"—their alliances, factions, and maneuverings—often seemed quite different from the older informal politics of local communities. These differences were sharpened by the Indian Councils Act of 1909 (known as the Morley-Minto Reforms), in which the principle of election replaced appointment for seats in the provincial and governor-general's councils. The act placed a new emphasis on the number of supporters a representative could muster. At the same time, the British began to recognize a number of comprehensive "communities," such as Hindu and Muslim, which implied that all members of such groups had overriding commonalities. In this legislation Muslims were also given "weightage" in areas where they were a minority—that is, more seats were reserved for them than their numbers in the population would have warranted.

Yet the categories the state created were artificial and often obscured profound differences behind the labels. In the case of Muslims, for instance, the composition of this "community" differed profoundly among regions. Muslims along the south coast were predominantly merchants whose ancestors had arrived as early as the 1500s, and who participated in certain civic ceremonies connected to goddess worship. Further up the western coast in Kerala, by contrast, lived the Mappilahs, descendants of the first Muslims in India who had arrived in the 700s. They had become agricultural and, by the nineteenth century, had labored under predominantly Hindu landlords, against whom the Mappilahs had developed a strong tradition of *jihad*—a "holy war" that was also a class war. In the western port city of Bombay, one prominent Muslim pointed out in 1908 that "the most essential fact to be learnt about the Mahomedan community of Bombay is that there is no such community. There are various communities in the city which

profess this religion."[4] And in the Muslim majority areas of Punjab and Bengal, the diversity was even more pronounced. In Punjab, Muslims were large landlords, peasants, nomadic tribespeople, and urban artisans. In Bengal, they made up the majority of the peasantry and practiced a distinctly Bengali way of life that encompassed goddesses and had no word for monotheism. Perhaps the only common characteristic shared among all of these groups was a profound split between the "well-born" members of society (the *ashraf*) and those of the lower classes (often called the *ajlaf*). The lower classes generally shared much more with their Hindu fellows than they did with members of the so-called Muslim elite. The *ashraf,* united by the shared Indo-Persian culture they had absorbed under the Mughals, valued literacy and education in Arabic or Urdu, artistic accomplishments, the holding of administrative positions in nearby Muslim-ruled states, the study of Islamic law, and Muslim reformist activities. It was this small group to which the British referred when they used the category "Muslim," but when they counted up the numbers of such Muslims, they included all the lower-class groups as well. Thus, the creation of new political structures representing these arbitrary, even partially artificial "communities" served to redefine and sharpen the differences among social groups in India.

The legal system that developed in British India likewise reinforced the new definitions of "community." The civil law code, for example, defined inheritance according to Hindu classical texts for Hindus and according to Islamic law or customary practices for Muslims. Furthermore, the British developed a separate criminal code for dealing with certain "criminal tribes" based on their earlier dealing with the Thags, treating the participants as members of a caste-like group whose genetic makeup supposedly caused their criminality.

All of these developments served to emphasize the importance of simplified definitions of "community" for ruling India more efficiently than would have been possible otherwise. But in this colonial setting the British had largely invented these communities; they had not emerged from within the local society. And the British were in a position to reward people who made use of the new categories. The leader who claimed to speak for "the Muslims," for instance, or later for "the Untouchables," gained greater influence, stature, and recognition from the

British than did one who spoke on behalf of the neighborhood or a voluntary worship group, though these forms of social organization often possessed greater meaning for their participants than did the new and broader categories created by the British. In time, of course, the new definitions of community took on a greater reality and became meaningful for more people, particularly in the political arena. Nevertheless, the lack of fit between the political labels created by the British and the actual communities created by Indians represented a continuing tension in colonial India and beyond.

Indian Experiments under the Raj

Indians themselves, as well as their British rulers, were creating new institutions and new definitions of "community" within the Raj. For example, the first public "societies" and institutions created by Indians focused on education, literary interests (including translations of Western writings), and social reform. In establishing such organizations Indians were not only responding to British pressures, but were also creating for themselves new and more meaningful views of the world. Among the earliest of these organizations was the Brahmo Samaj, founded in the 1820s by the Bengali intellectual Ram Mohan Roy. A major figure in the nineteenth-century renaissance of Hindu culture, Roy emphasized the philosophy of the early sacred texts, the Vedas, to deny the validity of certain later Hindu practices that had been harshly criticized by Westerners. He was especially opposed to the practice of *sati*, in which widows were expected to mount the funeral pyres of their husbands. He espoused a monotheistic form of Hinduism and opposed what he saw as the idolatry of later Hindu practice. He saw no contradiction between modern education and science, on the one hand, and authentic Hinduism, on the other: India could be modern and Hindu at the same time. Roy combined the role of a journalist with that of a political organizer, using newspapers and the Brahmo Samaj organization to influence Indian upper-class public opinion.

Somewhat later, a similar reform movement emerged in the west and the north—the Arya Samaj, founded in Bombay in 1875. Under the leadership of Dayanand Saraswati, the Arya Samaj also concentrated on creating an alternative philosophy that integrated modern Western intellectual concerns with preservation of the central values of Hindu culture and religious belief. It found a large following among educated Indians who worked for the imperial state. It appealed most widely in the Punjab, where it adopted a combative stance vis-à-vis traditionalist Hindus, Muslims, and Christians.

Both the Brahmo Samaj and the Arya Samaj prompted a conservative resistance, which similarly acted through educational institutions, journalistic efforts, and public societies. Much of the debate between the reformists and their opponents focused on the role of women. Indeed, the status of women in Indian society formed the heart of social reform efforts, with reformers bent on eradicating or minimizing child marriage, *sati*, and the prohibition on widow remarriage. Women's lives had become increasingly circumscribed and controlled, especially in the late eighteenth-century Indian society that felt itself so much under assault from both internal and external changes. The expansion of *purdah* was a case in point. This practice of keeping upper-class women secluded in the home and behind the veil had been adopted by Hindu upper castes from the Muslim elites. Rapid and threatening change had prompted efforts to more closely control women and the world they represented—that of kinship, devotion, and local ties. But when Indian reformers addressed women's issues, it was men who took the lead. Even those women who took heroic stands—by remarrying after being widowed, for example—often did so as a result of their fathers' decisions. And despite substantial memberships in reformist societies, very few widow remarriages took place, and the campaign to raise the age of marriage took most of the century. Stimulated by Roy's opposition to *sati*, the British made the practice a criminal offense, as part of their campaign to eradicate supposedly "primitive" customs.

Although the reform movements had political implications, strictly political organizations emerged somewhat later. First among them was the Indian National Congress, whose seventy-two members, mostly educators, lawyers, and journalists, met initially in Bombay in 1885. Inspired by Western political ideals, this organization later led the drive for India's independence and became a model for anticolonial movements in Asia and Africa. Initially, however, the Congress sought to create and express public opinion and to influence the colonial state on behalf of a moderate agenda: more Indian representatives on legislative councils, an inquiry into government finances, reduced military spending, and civil service exams held in India as well as England. From the beginning, the Congress emphasized secular values in order to underscore the ability of all Indians—whatever their religious or cultural "community"—to take part in the public life of a modern society. In its early years, however, the Congress focused primarily on the narrower concerns of an elite group consisting of upper-caste male Hindus (especially Brahmans and merchant castes) with a Western education. Relatively few Muslims participated; instead, Muslim intellectuals, who had largely rejected Western education, debated the "fit" among Urdu literary learning, Islamic education, and Western rationalist thought in separate organizations such as the Aligarh Muslim University.

Despite its attempts to be inclusive, the Indian National Congress did not convince all activist Indians that it spoke for them. By the early twentieth century, a number of other political experiments had been launched, including the Muslim League (1906) that argued against a "secular" approach which ignored the special issues confronting Muslims. Regional parties in the south and west gave voice to the non-Brahman movement, such as the Justice party in Madras, founded in 1916. Such groups sought to counteract the domination by Brahmans of emerging nationalist politics. Other regional parties spoke for the interests of landlords and occasionally peasants.

From its inception, then, political activity in British India reflected a diverse society. Competing groups, based on differing definitions of community, sought to capture the public interest. They utilized all available means of publicity—from journalism to processions in the streets—to shape and express public opinion. But colonial rule set distinct limits on Indian political participation, and these limits became apparent in the proposed Ilbert Bill of 1883. This was a bill that would have given senior Indian judges and magistrates the authority to hear criminal charges against Europeans as well as Indians. It unleashed a firestorm of pointedly racist protest by many British residents in India. Mass meetings were held, funds raised, and newspapers filled with crude insults, aimed especially at Bengalis and at the idea of letting Indians judge members of the "conquering race." The form of the protest—utilizing petitions, the press, protest meetings—served as a valuable lesson to Indians in how to bring public pressure to bear on

the state. More important, however, was another message—that a racially defined colonial state would not permit genuinely representative government. Colonial India was not England.

The Imperial State and Indian Culture

British India differed from earlier South Asian political experiments (such as Vijayanagara and the Mughal Empire) in the relationship of the state to cultural expression. Previous empires regarded it as part of the kingly role to patronize a wide range of religious institutions and cultural activities, and thus defined a good ruler as one who kept the world in balance, enabling various communities to pursue their own interests effectively. Furthermore, the ruler was expected, when possible and auspicious, to be present at religious activities.

But the British redefined religious ceremonies and cultural patronage as private activities, and the state remained aloof from them in order to objectively mediate among its various communities. The state did not actively attempt to integrate the society. Thus, at the height of imperial rule, the Raj did not provide financial support for cultural and religious activities, and it did not send representatives of the colonial government to attend these observances. Instead, the British supported only a very narrow range of cultural activities, primarily those that expressed and celebrated the imperial state. It held, on occasion, imperial *durbars* that, like the Mughals, summoned and then carefully ranked—through the number of gun salutes and value of the gifts bestowed on them—the rulers of princely states, influential landlords, and other "natural leaders" under the Raj. In the early nineteenth century, the colonial government also sponsored a new style of painting, known as "Company Painting," which served to illustrate, catalog, and define the various caste, occupational, and tribal groups. Similarly, the buildings sponsored by the colonial state had a distinctly imperial (and aloof) appearance, and all served official and public purposes: schools, railway stations, libraries, memorials, and government buildings.

The withdrawal of state support for a wide range of cultural expressions created a vacuum, increasingly filled by those seeking local power and honor in the new circumstances of the British Raj, particu-

This 1875 woodcut shows British officials being entertained by an Indian prince and fanned by one of his servants. It illustrates the social hierarchy of colonial India. *Bettmann*

larly members of the Mughal courtier class and leading Hindu merchants. Cultural patronage reinforced their legitimacy as local leaders. However, because the activities were specific to certain communities, and because they so often used a religious vocabulary, the British viewed them as "private" rather than "political" activities and happily abandoned them to local leaders. But in this judgment, based on their experience in England, the British were wrong (and so are scholars who have focused only on the political-constitutional side of Indian history). In India, the alternative world of cultural expression and the official public world of politics went hand in hand.

The political importance of cultural movements can be seen in the efforts of many late nineteenth-century Indian intellectuals to reassert the validity and worth of the Hindu religious tradition. Among the most significant was the Bengali spiritual and intellectual leader Sri Ramakrishna (1836–1886). A pious mystic who lived in a temple near Calcutta, Ramakrishna deeply felt the pervasive presence of the divine and maintained that all religions were essentially the same, offering a message of universal compassion and brotherhood. Thus the Indian religious tradition, and especially the devotional tradition of Bengali culture, had as much validity as any other.

He provided spiritual leadership for a generation of Bengalis whose professions involved them deeply in the Western world of the colonial state and offered them a new model for living. They could simultaneously participate in the Western world and remain devout and active Hindus.

The connection between the "private" world of devotional religion and the "public" world of political activity was even more apparent in the work of Bengali intellectual Rabindranath Tagore (1861–1941), the first Indian to receive, in 1913, the Nobel Prize for Literature. He worked to revive and develop Indian arts and culture and established a university at his country estate for that purpose. In an 1899 poem Tagore predicted that in the new century, the greedy nations of the West would destroy one another in a bloody war and then India's offerings of peace, freedom, and spiritual fulfillment would be appreciated. In emphasizing India's unique and special qualities, Tagore was building the cultural foundations of Indian nationalism.

Tagore wrote of the early nationalist struggle in *The Home and the World* (1919), a novel that chronicles the agony of Bimala, the good wife of a *zamindar* and a symbol of the homeland, "Mother Bengal," as she emerges from the women's quarters of the house into a larger world swept by political protest. In the novel and in reality, the protest movement that engages Bimala attracted mass support because it combined political and economic causes with passionate, selfless devotionalism. The devotional practices of the home, seen as crucial to protecting domestic and family life, were now writ large to protect the "nation" or the world of Bengal. "Religion," then, was something more than the private exercise of personal belief, and its intertwining with political activity gave Indian nationalism a religious flavor largely missing in China and Africa.

This passionate exercise of individual devotionalism could be harnessed quite easily to the activities of local groups as well as to those of larger anticolonial movements. Thus, various religious or cultural movements competed in mounting public processions on city streets and staging new ceremonies in bazaars or at temples, shrines, and mosques. Here was a realm in which Indians could freely experiment and even compete in expressing their various understandings of the new world introduced by the imperial order without attracting the intervention of or even much interest from the colonial state.

In the Mughal city of Agra during the late nineteenth century, for example, competition between local branches of the reformist Arya Samaj society and the more traditionalist Sanatan Dharm Sabha was expressed through rival festivals and processions. Here was culturally staged competition between reformist and more conservative Hindu groups. But when the Sanatan Dharm Sabha created new festivals that paraded richly decorated cows through town, accompanied by temple music, Muslims were offended. The new festival coincided not only with the Muslim mourning ceremonies of Muharram but also with a politicized movement for the protection of sacred cows. The conservative Hindu society sought to resist the slaughter of cows for meat and the sacrifice by Muslims of cows for religious purposes.

Leadership in these competitions was drawn from lower-class or caste groups in urban neighborhoods, where status depended more on religious devotion and commitment to the cause than on education or occupation. This made it very difficult for the British to discover what was really happening, as none of the participants qualified as "natural leaders" in British terms and the action took place in the alternative cultural realm outside of official political channels.

The kinds of groups that took part in the festivals and celebrations were quite different from the rigid caste or religious communities in which the British imagined Indians to live. Various kinds of kinship groups, worshipers of the same saint, neighborhood and occupational groups—all of these and others took part in local and often competitive cultural activities. Indirectly, such activities resisted British conceptions of Indian society.

At the same time, these local cultural activities became a meeting ground for the new middle class and for the mass of ordinary people. Some Hindu merchants and displaced Mughal officials chose involvement in such activities instead of official state-fostered organizations. Others operated in both worlds simultaneously. For the throngs of ordinary people engaged in local cultural and religious activities, this was the center of their lives. The legislative councils and newspapers, recently introduced by the British, had little significance for them. But in this diverse and competitive world of local cultural expression, the great gap between the Western-educated elite and the mass of ordinary Indians could be overcome. It was a lesson that later nationalist leaders, particularly Gandhi, learned well.

The Economics of Empire

The various cultural, social, and political developments in India were clearly connected to economic changes. New economic opportunities provided the wealth for cultural patronage. Charges of British economic exploitation provided grist for the mill of nationalist propaganda. And closer links to the world economy provided a mix of advantages and impoverishment to various Indian groups.

Some Indians clearly benefited economically from British rule. In the late eighteenth and early nineteenth centuries, this included particularly members of the merchant community, who used the profits they gained from collecting revenue and financing armies to invest in land rights in the countryside and in cultural patronage in the cities. But Indian entrepreneurs were slowly squeezed out of shipowning and shipbuilding, prevented from entering the new railroad industries, and restricted in the profitable export trade—primarily because they lacked access to credit, insurance, technology, and information about the world market. These were largely monopolized

Artisans such as these spinners and weavers frequently had their livelihood endangered by the competition from cheaper machine-made textiles imported from England. *Visual Studies Workshop*

by European interests in the British port cities of Calcutta, Bombay, and Madras. Indian entrepreneurs continued, as they had in past centuries, to develop inland trading routes, selling cloth for the masses and luxury goods for the new middle class.

India's growing connection to world markets also produced changes in agricultural production. Cotton production shot up to meet international demands when American cotton disappeared during the American Civil War, and remained at a much higher level. The demand for grain likewise increased when it could be shipped more quickly through the Suez Canal. And India's opium production flourished, especially after Britain forced the Chinese to open their markets to the sale of the drug in the 1840s.

An internal market expanded to meet the needs of Indian consumers. Entrepreneurs developed rural industries such as sugar-making and rice-husking. Although much cloth production was destroyed by the influx of mass-produced English cloth, the high end of this market—especially that of silk saris—continued to thrive.

The economic impact of British rule has been hotly debated by scholars and politicians alike since the late nineteenth century. The central question in that debate has been the degree of British responsibility for Indian poverty. Clearly, the British did not create that poverty, for India's low level of technical development and great inequalities long predated the British takeover. But equally clearly, two hundred years of colonial rule by the world's first industrial power did not make a substantial dent in that poverty, for India achieved independence in 1947 as one of the poorest of underdeveloped countries. No transformation along Japanese lines took place under colonial auspices, either in India or anywhere else.

The benefits of political stability, improved transportation and irrigation, and access to the European market meant that overall production kept up with or slightly exceeded population growth during the colonial era. One recent estimate put the average annual per-capita growth rate at about 0.75 percent between 1868 and 1920.[5] But this modest increase in national wealth was very unequally distributed, as British policy did little to modify the inequalities of Indian society. In many places a "rich peasant" class emerged in response to new opportunities for cash-crop farming and better channels for marketing agricultural produce. Yet the numbers of the landless and the deeply impoverished peasants likewise increased because indebtedness and commercialization of land meant that poor farmers often had to sell their plots to meet their obligations. British dependence on the well-to-do rural elites ensured that they would not sponsor any comprehensive land reform programs.

The urban and industrial sector of the Indian economy presents a similarly mixed picture. Mughal India had a major handicraft manufacturing industry and was an exporter of manufactured goods. But a flood of cheap machine-made goods from England's new and mechanized industries poured into India and, by the mid-nineteenth century, had put many thousands of Indian handloom weavers and other artisans out of work. The changing tastes of the new elite also diminished demand for the products of India's traditional industries. Thus, critics charged that England "deindustrialized" India. The country's exports in the nineteenth century were primarily agricultural products such as tea, cotton, jute, wheat, and especially opium. A century earlier it had been cotton textiles.

Furthermore, modern industrial enterprises did not compensate for losses in the traditional industrial sector. Compared to the rapid industrial growth of late nineteenth-century Japan and Russia, the pace of India's industrialization was slow. By 1900, India had perhaps one million industrial workers in a population of 350 million. Scholars have argued much as to the reasons for this slow growth. Many have focused on internal factors such as the poverty of the internal market, the continuation of rural mentalities among workers, and inadequate Indian entrepreneurs. Critics of British imperialism have pointed to the almost religious belief in free trade and the political influence of English manufacturing interests, which produced a virtual refusal to provide tariff protection for India's infant industries. Certainly, the unwillingness of the British government of India to actively foster industrial growth (as the governments of Germany, Japan, and Russia were doing in the late nineteenth century) played an important role in its retarded industrialization.

Yet another inhibition of British colonial rule on India's economic growth lay in the substantial wealth the British carried home from India, which drained the country of investment capital needed for development. Some of this drain came in the form of profits made by British banks and corporations, some as pensions sent to retired soldiers and officials, and some as various expenses that the British government charged off to the Indian treasury. Indian taxpayers had to foot the bill, for example, for the Indian army, which was used, in places as far away as China and Ethiopia, to further British imperial interests. While the size of this drain is in dispute, its existence is not.

By the end of the nineteenth century, politically active Indians, educated in Western schools, participated in debates about the colonial economy and propagated their views through the new communications networks introduced by the British. They also became part of the anti-imperialist and nationalist movements that were gaining strength in India as the twentieth century dawned.

Community and Nation in the Struggle for Independence

The first collective actions to resist the imperial state took place in Bengal. In 1905, the government of India divided this large, culturally homogenous province into two separate units, partly to administer it more efficiently, but also to buttress the power of a small Muslim elite against that of the politically troublesome Bengali intelligentsia, now seen as "Hindu." Bengali resistance to the partition was immediate and passionate. Led by Hindu *bhadralok*—a class of landowning intelligentsia—it indelibly stamped the Indian nationalist movement.

Initial reactions to the partition closely paralleled earlier British protests against the Ilbert Bill—"monster" meetings, petitions, press editorials, and marches. But soon Bengalis turned to other forms of protest, including both terrorism and an economic boycott. Known as Swadeshi, the boycott first targeted British manufactures, such as cloth, sugar, and salt. Tagore's fictional character of Bimala would have joined thousands who gathered around bonfires in the countryside to burn consumer goods that symbolized Bengal's economic enslavement. Soon the *bhadralok* began to boycott education, the judiciary, and the administration, while ordinary people found their own forms of protest: "washermen refused to wash foreign clothes, cobblers to mend foreign shoes and cooks to serve masters who used foreign goods."[6] Moreover, those who refused to support the movement were, in turn, boycotted. At this point there was little difference between the economic and political woes of British India generally and the Bengali homeland in particular. As Nirad Chaudhuri, a Bengali who was then a boy, recalls, "When the anti-partition agitation began there were no ready-made songs embodying the sense of grievance. . . . We had to fall back on the patriotic songs composed in the preceding era, many of which were by Tagore and breathed a lyrical love for our country, both India and Bengal. . . ."[7] The "country" hailed in these songs was *Bande Mataram* ("Mother India")—an evocative but Hindu image casting the homeland as a goddess. In this patriotic imagery the private world of religious devotionalism and the public world of political activism were immediately fused.

Yet, as Chaudhuri observed many years later, defining the connection between the home and the nation in this highly emotional way necessarily placed some people outside the boundaries of the "nation":

> There was a number of Muslim lawyers in our street, whom we respected as much as any other colleague of my father. With their sons and nephews we were as friendly as with the children of our Hindu neighbours. . . . A very large number of our school-fellows were Muslim. . . . We worked, talked, and played with them quite naturally. . . . It was from the end of 1906 that we became conscious of a new kind of hatred for the Muslims, which sprang out of the present and showed signs of poisoning our personal relations with our Muslim neighbours and school-fellows. If the sprouting enmity did not go to the length of inducing us to give up all intercourse with them, it made us at all events treat them with a marked decline of cordiality. We began to hear angry comment in the mouths of the elders that the Muslims were coming out quite openly in favour of partition and on the side of the English. . . . We also noticed that our Muslim school-fellows were beginning to air the fact of their being Muslims rather more consciously than before and with a touch of assertiveness.[8]

Thus the categories of "Hindu" and "Muslim"—largely created and rewarded through British policy

decisions—began to assume political and emotional meaning for larger numbers of Indians.

Prolonged protest, and the coming of a more liberal British administration, led to the repeal of partition in 1911 and the transfer of the capital of British India from Calcutta to Delhi. But the lessons of the partition agitation were learned well. Nationalists noted the success of the Swadeshi movement in connecting political causes with the alternative world of cultural activity and the usefulness of devotionalism as a way of incorporating mass support. Moderates, who had earlier petitioned for minor political concessions, now began to think more concretely about self-rule, previously the cry only of the extremists. Muslims concerned about their declining influence in the government saw the importance of numbers and popular protest.

These lessons were played out in various political organizations. The Indian National Congress adopted self-rule or independence within a kind of commonwealth as its goal. But at least of equal importance was the establishment of the All-India Muslim League in 1906. Although the League remained for some years an elitist organization, it contradicted the Congress's claim to represent all Indians. And within it, Muslims began to consider more directly antigovernment and anti-Hindu strategies. Among them was the increasing demand for separate electorates as a permanent recognition of the importance of Muslims in India, regardless of their numbers. Indeed, by 1916, when the Congress and the League joined forces in the Lucknow Pact, their joint demands to the government included the immediate aim of self-government as well as the continuation of separate electorates in provincial assemblies, weighted in some cases to favor Muslim voters. Thus, "religious" definitions of political organizations were becoming entrenched in Indian political life.

Equally important, the lessons of the Bengal partition were also played out in the alternative cultural realm. In 1911, for instance, administrators in north India became concerned about the "innovations" being introduced into urban tellings of the story of Ram. The processions of the annual Ramlila performances in cities across the north now included a number of new figures—women labeled *Bande Mataram* and the Rani of Jhansi (a heroine of the revolt of 1857) riding a horse with a British soldier transfixed on her spear. Large pictures of current nationalist leaders were also held aloft like banners. All of these figures marched in the army of Ram, the quintessential god-king of India. Here was a message that integrated the political and cultural realms, but at the same time implicitly excluded Muslims since the religious vocabulary was largely Hindu.

It was increasingly possible to identify local community values and interests with those of the "nation." Each separate community saw itself resisting the imperial state. Thus, anti-imperialism gradually became nationalism. In the process, a greatly disputed question arose: Exactly who or what was the "nation"?

Mahatma Gandhi

By the 1920s, British India stood at the threshold of a genuinely mass-based nationalist movement led predominantly by a Western-educated middle class. And while that movement aspired to represent all of India, it too had to confront the sharpening tensions among its many cultural communities. One leader proved particularly able to bridge these social and cultural divisions: Mohandas K. Gandhi (1869–1948). A shy and not particularly successful lawyer trained in England, Gandhi moved to South Africa in 1893, where he developed his concept of an Indian nation and the strategies of peaceful protest that he would later use in India. In addition, Gandhi built on earlier lessons about using religious devotionalism for purposes of political activism. Because he formulated a political philosophy based on distinctly Indian religious traditions, he struck a responsive chord deep within many ordinary Indians.

Gandhi's radical political philosophy, known as *satyagraha* (or "truth force"), involved a nonviolent resistance to specific laws, which, nevertheless, accepted the punishment imposed by the state, and therefore respected the lawful structuring of society by the state. It was an active approach to political protest. "Non-violence," Gandhi argued, "means conscious suffering. It does not mean meek submission to the will of the evil-doer, but it means the pitting of one's whole soul against the will of the tyrant. . . . [I]t is possible for a single individual to defy the whole might of an unjust empire to save his honour, his religion, his soul."[9]

The radicalism of *satyagraha* was not simply that it provided a new form of activism distinct from protest meetings and terrorism; it also represented a fundamental rejection of Western political thinking and put Gandhi in the tradition of earlier Indian thinkers who had presented South Asian philosophies to the West. Swami Vivekananda, a student of Ramakrishna, had attended the First World Parliament of Religions held in the United States in 1893, and widely popularized the assumption that "the East" was "spiritual" while "the West" was "material." Even Tagore, as he gained fame in the West, championed the arts and culture of South Asia as an alternative to the greedy materialism of the West, predicting that India would long outlast the political systems founded on Western materialism and rationalism. Within this context, Gandhi's rejection, for instance, of industrialization in favor of harmonious, self-sufficient villages was fundamentally a rejection of the modern and rationalist assumption that progress was linear, that life would be improved through the application of scientific and materialistic innovations. To many ordinary people Gandhi possessed magical power and produced miraculous events. He was the Mahatma, the "Great Soul."

Both Gandhi's political philosophy and his strategies of mass protest emerged in South Africa. There Gandhi worked for twenty years with Indians—mostly Muslims and merchants—in resisting the racist regime. And there he developed a vision of "India" that included Hindus and Muslims alike and that emphasized a shared identity forged in opposition to the imperial state.

Gandhi returned to India in 1914, and rose rapidly in the leadership of the Indian National Congress. After early experiments in applying *satyagraha* to groups of indigo workers, peasants, and millworkers, Gandhi organized a major campaign in 1919. He proposed a one-day strike, or day of mourning, in which Indians across the subcontinent would cease their normal activities: all shops and businesses would shut, schools and colleges would close, government offices and courts would be boycotted. Gandhi saw this campaign as an experiment, in which he could measure success by the numbers who joined in the strike. But before the movement could prove itself, disaster struck. In Punjab, more than twenty thousand people gathered in a large public meeting place in Amritsar; without provocation, the provincial governor, intent on repressing revolt, had his troops fire on the crowd, killing over three hundred people. The outrage provoked by the Amritsar Massacre mobilized public opinion as never before. But despite the new willingness of people to protest, Gandhi called off the *satyagraha,* arguing that the use of violence by the crowds made it clear that they did not understand his tactics or his philosophy.

Hindus and Muslims

Within two years of the Amritsar Massacre Gandhi again summoned India to action. In his judgment, the credibility of the imperial government had been completely eroded, in part by its attempt to justify the massacre. But even more important was British policy regarding Turkey during and after World War I. As the home of the caliph—spiritual leader for Muslims and the remaining symbol of the once-dominant Islamicate world system—Turkey carried special importance for Indian Muslims. However, Turkey had joined the war on the side of the Germans, and the British therefore took a hard line against the caliph, including plans to end his control over the holy places in Arabia.

The result in India was a surge in Muslim support for the Turkish caliph. Gandhi worked with the leaders of the Khalifat movement as they blended anti-imperialism, pan-Islamism, and Indian nationalism into a single movement, based on the premise that only in a free India could Muslims work for Islamic causes. Together Gandhi and Khalifat leaders launched the first mass movement on the subcontinent. In the process, the Indian National Congress was transformed from an elite-based annual conference to a mass-based political party. A "four anna" membership fee (equivalent to perhaps five cents) permitted mass membership. Parallel local cells were established across India for both the Congress and the Khalifat committees. Strategies to gain mass support, strengthen India, and undermine the Raj were developed: handspun, handwoven cotton produced in India should replace boycotted British textiles; unity among Hindus and Muslims should be promoted, especially through Hindu support of the Khalifat movement; treatment of Untouchables should be improved; picketing of liquor shops would discourage consumption and deprive the government of tax revenue. Women played a key role in the Khalifat movement, attending political meetings in large numbers and serving as volunteers for demonstrations and processions. Their immediate access to jewelry and cash made them effective fund-raisers. And they assumed leadership roles when the male leaders were imprisoned.

Despite heavy government repression and considerable violence that eventually led Gandhi to call off the movement, this first noncooperation movement had clearly succeeded. It had been able to draw support from an extraordinarily broad spectrum of Indians, including Muslims and Hindus, urban dwellers and peasants, middle-class intellectuals and artisans, conservatives and extremists. But this kind of unity was also fragile. The variety of local groups that espoused the movement frequently gave it a parochial character. Many came to equate their own communities with "the nation" and to define others as falling outside its boundaries. Furthermore, Gandhi had insisted that other kinds of conflict—between landlords and tenants, between a Brahman upper class and a non-Brahman lower class—should be ignored in favor of shared resistance to the British. Thus, soon after the protest was called off, a welter of localized riots and protests emerged in which Indians struck out against each other more often than against the colonial state. And when the new Turkish government itself abolished the caliphate in 1924, Muslim enthusiasm for joint action with Hindu politicians waned.

About the same time, many Congress leaders decided to enter the political institutions that the British had created. Some hoped to "wreck" the system from inside by noncooperation; others saw hope for reform from within. But in both cases the mass base of the nationalist movement was neglected.

Into this vacuum moved politicized religious reform movements. Both Hindu and Muslim organizations undertook conversion campaigns, concentrating generally on those who had been neglected in earlier times, particularly the Untouchables. They also organized community defense activities, sometimes quite literally teaching their followers the martial arts and then parading in the streets, other times leading early morning singing processions through the neighborhoods or having stump orators speak informally at bazaars or other public spaces. Believers were encouraged to practice their religion and to support its principles and values publicly and politically. But because this reformism often took the form of Hindu populism, it had little positive meaning for Muslims.

Thus, by the time Gandhi convinced other political leaders to use noncooperation yet again, little good will remained. It was increasingly difficult for him to emphasize either improving the status of Untouchables or Hindu-Muslim unity. Nevertheless, the Congress launched a second noncooperation movement in 1930. This civil disobedience campaign received great support because it coincided with economic distress in the rural areas and with worker unrest in the cities. Brilliantly conceived, the campaign focused on a simple, illegal act: protesters would boil seawater to make salt, thus breaking the laws that made the manufacture and sale of salt a government monopoly. Since salt was essential to life and the tax fell disproportionately on the poor, the issue served as an ideal symbol of British exploitation. Gandhi began a 240-mile march to the sea on 12 March 1930; his march took him through village after village where he was greeted with wild enthusiasm. He reached the beach on the anniversary of the first major *satyagraha* and, holding aloft a handful of mud, he signaled people all over India to "manufacture" salt in defiance of the British Raj.

The Indian National Congress now organized the same kind of early-morning neighborhood singing groups used by religious reformists; the lyrics spelled out how to become a good citizen through purified behavior and by working for an independent India. On strike days, youthful volunteers picketed to ensure that all shops closed; public transport was shut down; processions coursed through the streets of India's towns and cities. Initially an urban movement, the protest soon spread into the rural areas. Under the leadership of Indian nationalist Jawaharlal Nehru, peasants in the Gangetic Plain undertook an antitax campaign. But despite the much broader base of the second noncooperation movement, relatively few Muslims became involved. On the contrary, as merchants were forced to shut their shops and as members of councils became unable to participate in local government, Muslims and others who disagreed with the Congress's tactics often suffered at the hands of nationalist enthusiasm.

Reluctantly, the government of India began to consider the new constitutional structures necessary to prepare for independence. A series of Round Table Conferences held in London between 1930 and 1932 (but essentially boycotted by Congress leaders) created an outline of a new constitutional structure. It took shape in the 1935 Government of India Act, which provided for elected legislatures at the provin-

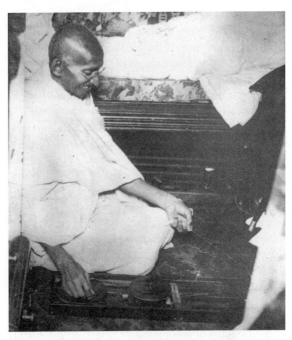

Gandhi's simplicity of dress and his daily practice of spinning on a primitive wooden spinning wheel represented elements of his challenge to both the British empire and the modern industrial world. *Bettmann*

cial level. Elections in 1937 revealed a new political landscape: a number of regional parties had emerged out of peasant or landlord combinations; and non-Brahman parties, depicting the Brahmans as "foreign" oppressors from the north, had emerged in the south and west.

Another contender, the Muslim League, adopted an increasingly separatist position, calling for a territory largely autonomous of the center; it would be composed of Muslim majority provinces in the north and west, including the Northwest Frontier, Punjab, Sind, and Baluchistan. They even gave it a name: *Pakistan*, "land of the pure." But the Muslim League was divided and still elitist in structure. Its tactics included both cooperation and conflict with the Congress. And in the 1937 elections it made a poor showing against powerful regional parties in the Muslim majority areas.

The competition among these political groups quickly moved, in the early 1930s, outside the political arena and into the streets. Civic ceremonies in public spaces became sharply politicized. Conflict—between Hindus and Muslims, between Sunni and Shia Muslims, between Brahmans and non-

Brahmans—spread from cultural activities to wide-spread riots in many Indian cities. Peasant-landlord conflicts broke out in some rural areas. As India moved ever closer to independence, Indians fought more and more over who would be included in that nation, whose "interests" would be protected by it, and who would control it.

After the 1937 elections most people still expected the Congress and the League to cooperate in forming new provincial governments. The League had done reasonably well, especially in Muslim minority areas; the Congress, however, had achieved spectacular successes in each province where it contested. Thus it decided to form governments that included only those who were members of the Congress. In effect, this denied any Muslims who had worked for the League a role in the new semi-democratic structures of government. Many Muslims saw this decision as an alarming indication of the kind of treatment they could expect at the hands of the Indian Congress party. When these provincial governments immediately moved to enforce the teaching of Hindi in schools and to protect cows from slaughter, their worst fears were confirmed. The result was to galvanize the Muslim League, which now became a mass organization like the Congress. And it launched a campaign that highlighted how the Congress's provincial governments disadvantaged Muslims.

Dramatic external events soon intruded into Indian political life. The impact of World War II, including Japanese aggression and the Chinese Revolution, had transformed Asia and galvanized new independence movements in places such as the Dutch East Indies and Burma. In India the impact of the war took many forms. Britain's declaration of war on Germany on behalf of India infuriated nationalists who had been fighting for two decades to be taken as partners in the governance of India. There was also the issue of nonviolence: Did Gandhi's *satyagraha* preclude participation in the war effort? By late 1939, the faction of the Congress led by Jawaharlal Nehru and Congress President A. K. Azad (a Bengali Muslim) had convinced the organization to support nonviolence for achieving independence, but without preventing Indians from taking up arms in the national defense. At the same time, the Congress continued to apply pressure, especially through staged protests in the streets, to force the British to concede more independent self-government.

The End of the Raj

By the end of World War II, the British had become convinced that they should withdraw from South Asia. In part, their decision resulted from the postwar victory in Britain of the Labour party, which had long supported Indian independence. Furthermore, war-ravaged Britain could no longer afford an empire; it was a drain on the country's resources. In order to assess the relative strengths of the various contending parties in India, the government decided to hold a general election, the first since 1937. The stakes were high. Campaigning focused almost solely on the claims of the Congress that India was a united and secular state, versus those of the League that an Islamic state of Pakistan should be created. The results of the 1946 election thus differed dramatically from those in 1937: the regional and minority parties were virtually eliminated, while both the Congress and the League made good their claims to popular support. At the national level, the Congress won all of the general seats with 91 percent of the votes; the League won all of the Muslim seats with 86 percent of those votes. Similar results emerged from provincial elections, though the League gained enough support in only two provinces to establish its own government, while the Congress ruled in eight provinces.

The 1946 elections showed the depth of the gulf between communities now defined as Hindu and Muslim as well as the impossibility of reconciling these communities within the political structures of British India. The Congress's assertion that it would create a secular state did not convince minorities—especially Muslims and Untouchables—that secularism would restrain Hindu populism in a state with a Hindu majority. Muslim activists argued that only a separate Islamic state could protect those who identified themselves as both Indians and Muslims.

The British government made one more proposal for a constitutional arrangement that would leave India intact as a single state by creating a weak center and strong, autonomous provinces, including several Muslim majority provinces. Although both the Congress and the League grudgingly accepted this proposal, they each tried to bargain away the protections provided for the other. By mid-1946, the League had backed out of the proposal, calling for "direct action" instead. Its strikes, public meetings, and processions represented a clear attempt to link constitutional demands to the realm of cultural values. Peacefully conducted in most parts of the subcontinent, the protest emerged as fierce communal violence in Bengal. More than four thousand people, mostly Muslims, died over three days in what became known as the Great Calcutta Killing. Retaliations occurred in the surrounding countryside by Muslim peasants against Hindu landlords and the police.

Further communal violence erupted in early 1947, and by the time the British pulled out in August of that year, Hindu-Muslim conflagration had engulfed much of the subcontinent. Vast migrations followed as millions sought protection among members of their own communities. But this mass exchange of populations led to thousands more violent deaths.

During 1947, these outbreaks of violence served as a tragic counterpoint to the orderly "division of the spoils" that the British sought to undertake. The division of the country was announced by Viceroy Louis Mountbatten in June; two months later the arrangements were completed, and on 14 August 1947, the British left the subcontinent to the two independent countries of India and Pakistan.

I Conclusion

The violence of partition cast a shadow on the triumph of India's independence. It demonstrated clearly how cultural identities had become the basis of political action. Despite the partition, the diverse peoples of India had not settled their relationship with the state or with each other. Now, however, Indians themselves would come to grips with this dilemma. As Nehru, the first prime minister of independent India, put it at the moment after midnight on the day of independence: "Long years ago we made a tryst with destiny, and now the time comes when we shall redeem our pledge, not wholly or in full measure, but very substantially. . . . A moment comes, which comes but rarely in history, when we step out from the old to the new, when an age ends. . . ."[10]

Notes

1. Christopher Pinney, "Colonial Anthropology in the 'Laboratory of Mankind' " in *The Raj: India and the British, 1600–1947*, ed. C. A. Bayly (London: National Portrait Gallery Publications, 1990), p. 253.

2. H. H. Risley, *The People of India*, 2nd ed. (Delhi: Oriental Books Reprint Corp., 1969), p. 29.

3. 1833 "Minute on Education," quoted in William T. de Bary, ed., *Sources of Indian Tradition*, vol. 2 (New York: Columbia University Press, 1958), p. 49.

4. Rafiuddin Ahmed, letter to the editor, *Times of India*, 18 Feb. 1908, quoted in Jim Masselos, "Power in the Bombay 'Moholla,' 1904–15," *South Asia* 6 (Dec. 1976): 75–76.

5. C. A. Bayly, "State and Economy in India over Seven Hundred Years," *Economic History Review* 38 (Nov. 1985): 393.

6. Jim Masselos, *Nationalism on the Indian Subcontinent*, 2nd ed. (Melbourne: Nelson, 1991), p. 89.

7. Nirad Chaudhuri, *Autobiography of an Unknown Indian* (London: John Farquharson, 1968), p. 221.

8. Ibid., p. 229.

9. Quoted in Jim Masselos, *Nationalism on the Indian Subcontinent* (Melbourne: Nelson, 1972), p. 122.

10. Jawaharlal Nehru, *Independence and After* (New York: John Day, 1950), p. 3.

Chapter 15
Democracy, Development, and Cultural Pluralism: India since Independence

A pioneer on the road to independence and an inspiration to many Afro-Asian nationalist movements, India has also been of worldwide significance as an independent state since 1947. Most notably, perhaps, it has built and maintained the world's most populous Western-style democracy. A system of free, peaceful, and regular elections with competing parties and universal suffrage has given India relative political stability and has avoided the military coups, revolutions, and frequent changes in government that have afflicted so many states in Africa, Latin America, and the Middle East. This democratic political system has encouraged the expansion of a lively Indian *civil society,* a term describing those social groups, organizations, and communities that exist independent of the state and that participate openly in debating public issues and in shaping the structure and policies of the state. Such a civil society had begun to emerge in India under British colonial rule, but since independence it has flourished far more than in most developing countries.

India's approach to modern development has frequently been compared to that of China, and the two countries' relative achievements have been a matter of much debate. Both proclaimed socialism as their national goal, but the Chinese version directly confronted the country's ancient inequities, substantially reduced them by revolutionary means, and made regional and social equality a hallmark of its development policy. But these accomplishments occurred within a state dominated by the Communist party, which overrode both individual rights and opportunities for the free expression of public opinion. No independent civil society could emerge in such a setting, though pressures in that direction appeared in the 1980s. India's "socialism," in contrast, has been gradual and reformist and, to some critics, often merely rhetorical. This reflected a society of highly politicized cultural groups in which many feared that decisive action by the state would threaten the country's democracy and fragile unity.

But to both India and China, socialism has meant industrial growth and a planned economy, and both countries have created substantial industrial sectors. But in Communist China, which initially abolished private property, central planning could be far more extensive than in India, which retained most private property rights and limited government ownership to large-scale industries. In the 1980s and 1990s, both nations sought to reduce the role of the state and to rely more heavily on the market as a mechanism for economic development.

In the relationship of the state to a variety of culturally different communities, India has confronted problems common to many new nations as well as a number of old ones. How can civil societies be created amid vast cultural diversity? How much protection should a state offer its minority communities and how much recognition and support should be accorded to dominant majority groups? Does a democratic political system exacerbate the tensions of culturally diverse societies or facilitate their resolution? These and similar questions have faced most developing countries and, as communism has collapsed in eastern Europe, such issues have exploded in Yugoslavia, Czechoslovakia, and most of the republics of the former Soviet Union. The problem of cultural pluralism has risen to the top of the global agenda as the twentieth century draws to a close.

India has had a very long history of dealing with such problems. The Vijayanagara kingdom, the Mughal Empire, the British Raj, and independent India—each of these states and their numerous culturally defined communities have had to find a means of accommodation. That long effort, conducted in a variety of historical circumstances, is what gives India's current struggles their significance, both for South Asia and for the larger world.

I Launching a Republic

How does a country move from being a colony in an imperial system to an independent nation-state in the twentieth-century world? In 1947, South Asian leaders concentrated on creating constitutions and shaping economic development to break the pattern of international economic exploitation. But they soon found themselves confronting the old problem of India's great cultural diversity in the new setting of an independent democratic state.

During the nationalist struggle, the Congress party had insisted that it represented a vision of a secular India, in which various kinds of Hindus—as well as Muslims, Christians, and others—could participate with security. But as the Congress made the transition from a nationalist movement to a governing political party, it found its members at odds over the meaning of a secular state. Gandhi and Nehru came to symbolize these differences, which continue to the present day. Gandhi's vision encompassed self-sufficient villages, supported by cottage industries and characterized by harmonious social relationships, which accepted many of the hierarchies of caste. By contrast, Nehru's rationalist view was based on a Westernized notion of the state, largely separated from religious concerns and devoted to reducing social and economic inequalities and promoting modern economic growth. It is Nehru's vision that dominated in India in the early decades of independence. This meant that, after creating a new constitution, the state focused its energies on economic development and foreign policy. The political leadership simply assumed that most people shared a commitment to secularism in public life. Increasingly, however, that assumption has been sharply challenged.

In many respects, the transition to an independent nation-state was easier for India than for many other new nations. Communication and transportation networks remained intact, as did much of the administrative structure and its personnel, especially officers serving in the civil service and the army. India also emerged, in 1947, with significant industrial and scientific sectors in certain specialized areas. In comparison with other parts of the developing world, its educated middle class was relatively large and included a substantial entrepreneurial segment. Furthermore, India's dominant political party, the Congress, had considerable experience in governing, having assumed control of many provincial governments during the late 1930s. It was an "umbrella" party, including representatives of many regional, ethnic, class, and caste groups. And its leaders, especially Nehru, had a towering stature in India. They had earned their authority as "freedom fighters"; they had suffered long stays in British Indian prisons; and they shared in the prestige of the martyred Gandhi, who had been assassinated by a Hindu extremist shortly after independence. It was with these assets that the new state confronted its initial tasks—integrating the princely states into the Indian nation, creating a new constitutional structure, and finding a place in the world system.

Even before independence, much discussion had smoothed the way for most of the 570 princes to accede to the new state that surrounded them, either India or Pakistan, in return for state support equivalent to that provided earlier by the British. Only three princely states created real problems after partition; these were the two largest states, Kashmir and Hyderabad, and one small state, Junagadh. The last two had Muslim rulers, though the vast majority of their populations was Hindu. Unwilling to see them join Pakistan or retain independence, India forcibly incorporated these states into its territory. Kashmir proved an even knottier problem. Its population was 75 percent Muslim, but its ruler was a Hindu maharaja whose dynasty had purchased the *gaddi* ("royal seat") from the British in the mid-nineteenth century. The strategic position of Kashmir between Pakistan and India made its eventual accession of great importance, and neither nation has been willing to allow Kashmir to join the other. This issue occasioned a number of wars since 1947, with no resolution yet in sight.

The same national security concerns that prompted India's hostility to princely states interested in Pakistan also motivated its antagonism to France, which controlled the small enclave of Pondicherry in the south, and to Portugal, which still retained the states of Goa, Diu, and Daman on the western coast. France turned over Pondicherry in 1954, but the incorporation of the Portuguese territories occurred only in 1961, when India finally launched an "invasion of liberation" against Portuguese Goa. The subcontinent then belonged wholly to South Asians (see Map 15.1), though they would still fight among themselves for territorial control.

The next task was constitutional. Written between 1946 and 1949 under the leadership of B. R. Ambedkar, the visionary spokesman of India's Untouchables, the new constitution created a federal system with a strong central government. Substantial issues, however, such as education and agriculture, were reserved for the regional states to control. Parliamentary in structure, the government was run by the dominant party and headed by a prime minister. The legislature consisted of two houses. The people directly elected representatives to the lower house *(Lok Sabha),* while representatives to the upper house *(Rajya Sabha)* were selected by the regional state legislatures, thus ensuring attention to local interests at the center. It was a strikingly Western-style document and nowhere more so than in its commitment to universal suffrage. Implementing this kind of democratic participation in such a huge and largely illiterate society has meant assigning a ballot symbol to each political party, and a more prolonged period of voting than is often the case in the West.

India quickly became active in creating a new role for post-colonial states in the emerging world order of the mid-twentieth century. Working with Egypt's Nasser and Indonesia's Sukarno in the 1950s, Nehru helped to form a new "nonaligned" bloc that could, they hoped, hold the balance of power in global politics of the Cold War. This bloc, drawing on its experience of colonial economic exploitation, championed the cause of African and Asian nations that emerged into freedom during the 1950s and 1960s.

In the West, and particularly in America, India's efforts to steer an independent course in world politics have been viewed with considerable suspicion, and particularly its close ties to the Soviet Union. But the formulation of nonalignment as a philosophy and new political position gave India a moral and intellectual respectability in world forums otherwise dominated by the powerful voices of the Western and Communist blocs. This was especially the case in the so-called Third World, subject to the continued economic exploitation by Western industrialized nations as suppliers of raw materials and cheap labor in the world economy. Ironically, in India at least, these unequal economic relationships do not stem from a lack of educated people or technological expertise. Many Indians have received training in the West and in India's many universities, which encouraged significant economic advances. But the "brain drain," in which far too many educated scientists, engineers, and intellectuals remained to take jobs in the West, illustrates the disadvantages that India still suffers in the world economy. These international disadvantages have done much to shape Indian foreign policy and its often critical view of the West.

Creating a New Economy

India's disadvantages in the world economy also shaped economic policies at home. The socialism that provided the political philosophy of the new state of India also directed its economic planning. The fundamental starting point was the assumption that the economy should be centrally planned, with the center exercising strong control over industrial and agricultural development, as well as public services. Entrepreneurs, especially large industrialists, had an important role, since they had actively supported the nationalist movement. They retained much control over medium- and small-scale industry and business enterprises; but even here they were expected to cooperate with the state, and to follow the policy goals articulated in the center's planning documents.

India's Second Five-Year Plan (1956–1961) established its overall strategy. Aiming to create quickly a modern industrialized society and military power, this strategy knowingly produced a temporary reliance on imports, foreign exchange, and foreign aid. Although it alarmingly echoed the economic dependence of colonialism, it was justified by the long-term goal of industrial self-sufficiency.

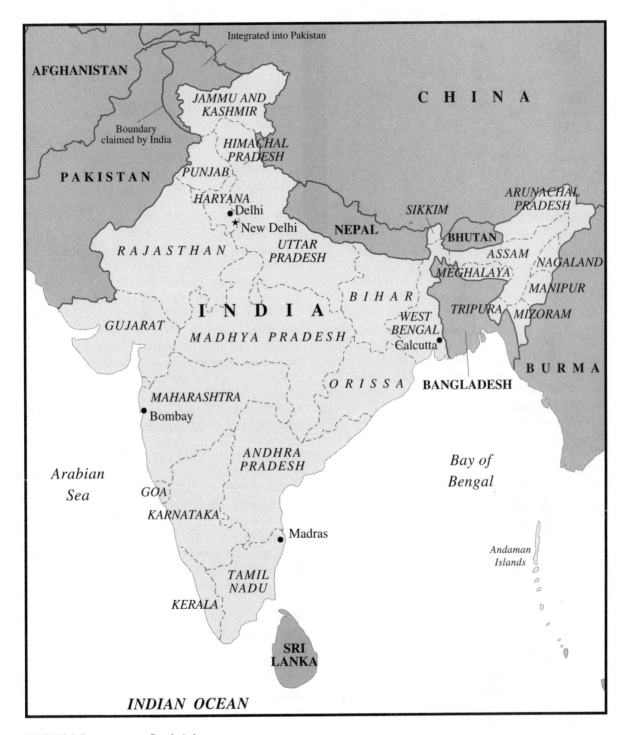

MAP 15.1 Contemporary South Asia

From the mid-1950s to the mid-1960s, India captured vast foreign aid resources from both the Communist and the capitalist blocs, enabling it to put in place a substantial industrial base. Thereafter, India maintained a reasonable rate of economic growth, though less than half that of China and the newly industrializing countries of East Asia.

By the early 1990s, India ranked behind only the United States and Soviet Union in its number of scientists and engineers, and it had acquired a substantial industrial sector that produced high-technology items such as electronic equipment, nuclear power plants, ballistic missiles, and computers. Indian-made goods such as electrical appliances won acceptance on the domestic market, where competition from abroad was restricted, as well as in parts of Asia, Africa, and the Middle East. Furthermore, Indian firms have won contracts elsewhere in the developing countries for major construction and industrial projects. Mahatma Gandhi had largely opposed industrialization as socially corrupting and morally inferior to village life, but modern India has moved dramatically into the industrial age, sometimes in cooperation with foreign corporations and often with the help of foreign-trained personnel.

Urbanization, consequently, has proceeded rapidly, with 27 percent of India's population living in urban areas by 1989. People flock to the cities, abandoning town and village in search of a better job or a better life. This places a tremendous burden on public facilities. Many people jam into wretched slum housing, and many others construct ramshackle squatters' huts or just live on the sidewalks. The unemployment and underemployment can hardly be measured accurately. But the cities also show the wealth of the new India. Sleek new high-rises house elegant apartments and air-conditioned corporate offices, often on land that held huts or swamps not long before. Luxury hotels, restaurants, and shops proliferate. Calcutta opened India's first subway in 1984.

A variety of social indicators likewise demonstrate considerable progress. Life expectancy at birth rose from only thirty-three years in 1941–1951 to fifty-nine years in 1989. Infant mortality declined from 150 per thousand in 1965 to a still very high 95 per thousand in 1989. In both of these critical areas, however, China's record was much better (1989 life expectancy of seventy years and infant mortality rate of thirty). Such comparisons have fueled the debate about the merits of the two nations' respective development strategies and the relative importance of economic growth and political democracy in making a good society.

Agriculture and Inequality

India's emphasis on industrial development, which relied greatly on the Soviet model, minimized other aspects of the Nehru program—agricultural self-sufficiency, balanced regional development, and improved lives for the rural poor. Agriculture, for example, had been so neglected that, by the mid-1960s, India was heavily dependent on the United States for food aid. Thus, there arose a political debate about appropriate economic policies. An alternative approach, which became defined as a Gandhian philosophy, emphasized small-scale agrarian self-sufficiency and the need to provide employment opportunities for the abundant labor force (rather than efficient large-scale farming techniques typical of industrialized Western countries). Supporters of such an approach had an opportunity to implement their policies when the Congress temporarily lost power to the Janata party from 1977 to 1979. The Janata devised an entirely different strategy that focused on agricultural and rural development, creation of employment opportunities for the rural poor through small-scale industries in the countryside, and the diversion of state resources from heavy industry into these new programs. But the Janata party did not remain in power long enough to firmly establish this new approach.

Instead, the pattern continued to be set by the Congress, though under pressure from the alternative policy, through the administrations of Nehru's successors—his daughter, Indira Gandhi (1966–1977; 1980–1984), and her son, Rajiv Gandhi (1985–1989). Nevertheless, a rethinking of economic priorities was prompted in the late 1960s by reductions in foreign aid on which the country had become so dependent. A shift in emphasis toward agriculture coincided with the arrival of new agricultural technology. During the 1960s, the world's agronomists had bred, tested, and begun spreading new, fast-ripening varieties of wheat and rice. Now a peasant could get two or even three crops a year from a field that had yielded only one before. Cautiously, then with increasing speed, the new varieties came into use in India. They became the centerpiece of a "green revolu-

VOICES
"The Young Men Speak"

One evening in 1960, a group of eight young Indian men from the small north Indian village of Karimpur sat down with a trusted American anthropologist and missionary friend. What they said reflected both the achievements and the difficulties of promoting rural development during the years immediately following India's independence. Here is a part of what they said:

We who are farmers or artisans have to work hard and have little time or energy to think, or plan how we can make things better. We have always found something or someone other than ourselves to blame for our lack of progress. . . .

When we see a police constable or a deputy's assistant in the village, we know that someone is going to be threatened and will have to part with some of his money. Who are the men who own watches and live in brick houses? Not one of us here thinks he can afford a watch, it is in the luxury class. . . . Who pays for all of this? We do!

We sometimes take the initiative in offering a bribe to a government man to further our own ends. All of us here know the saying that is popular these days about our government officers. "If you offer me a bribe, I overlook your misdeeds. . . ."

We do not like to see someone better off than we are. If my father has just one thousand rupees and knows that Shankar's uncle has twenty thousand, he will make a false charge against [him] or find some other way to force him into court. Our fathers choose to go on wasting money on these cases . . . and we could make good use of that money in improving our land or buying better animals. We do not need to stay so poor. . . .

We know that we lavish far too much money on the weddings of the girls in our families because everyone is afraid to be the first to spend less. . . . Most of us want to get all that we can when we bring home a bride. We not only want her to help in the work of the courtyard, but also we want all the money we can get out of her parents in expensive dowry gifts, in cash, and in elaborate feasts and entertainment. . . . We like the feasts, but they help to keep us poor.

But there are good things in our village as well as bad. . . . We are even learning ways of cultivating some of the land that we once considered useless. We have different seeds . . . different kinds of fertilizer, and more water for irrigating our fields. . . . We have the help of our village companion and the block officers. . . .

There are fewer caste restrictions than there used to be. Now we young men can do most things together, without considering our caste, like sitting here and talking to each other. Being in classes together in schools is one of the biggest helps. Just two caste conventions remain that separate us. We do not yet feel free to accept food from someone belonging to a caste lower than our own, and we do not consider marrying anyone outside our own caste. . . .

There are some things we should like to have. . . . We should like more games. . . . If we had a newspaper, we would read it ourselves and read it aloud to others. . . . We would like books. . . . We are trying to get permission for enough electricity to have a mill for grinding flour. . . . Why should all the mills be in Mainpuri? We are just as clever as the people there. . . . Most of all we want walls of baked brick for our houses and sound roofs. We are tired of mud-plastering our walls year after year. . . .

Source: William and Charlotte Viall Wiser, *Behind Mud Walls: 1930–1960.* Copyright © 1963, 1971 by The Regents of the University of California Press. Reprinted by permission of the publisher.

---

tion" that included reliable water supplies, chemical fertilizers and pesticides, efficient mechanized equipment, and expert technical advice—taken into the villages by a network of government agents and supported by credit made available to farmers. Agricultural production grew steadily from about 1965 on, and by the early 1980s, India was feeding itself and even exporting rice. The age-old threat of wide-

These Indian women are protesting rising food prices in Delhi in 1952. Note the cordon of women police officers who form a barricade in front of the protesters. *UPI/Bettmann*

spread famine was apparently gone. By 1985, the Indian population had doubled since independence, but food production had *tripled.*

Despite its success in raising overall grain production, the green revolution did little to address the problem of rural inequality. The highly profitable new seeds required extensive irrigation, fertilizer, and insecticides, which the poorest farmers could seldom afford. A 1991 U.N. report estimated that 410 million Indians, out of a total population of 850 million, lived below the poverty line.

The Socialist Nehru had long been concerned about India's massive social inequalities. And the national leadership generally agreed that ceilings should be imposed on the size of landholdings and that state policies and laws should work toward reducing exploitative economic relationships. But agriculture was one of the subjects reserved to the regional states, where political power was held by local dominant castes who had long controlled the land. Moreover, foreign development experts consistently advocated agricultural practices that benefited from large and consolidated holdings. The result has been

that some groups—notably Sikh farmers in the Punjab and dominant agrarian castes in the Gangetic Plain—have prospered greatly. These middle-class farmers, in turn, have retained control of local and regional political and governing structures. The self-interests and ideological commitments of this elite group have worked against the center's commitment to social justice, particularly since regional state governments retained control of the collection and distribution of land revenue taxes needed to fund agrarian development. Over the years, this tension between the regions and the center has become an increasingly prominent feature of India's political life.

Limitations on the government's ability to implement its Socialist commitments reflect a deeply rooted pattern in South Asian history. Holding the country together has always depended on a skillful balancing of local and regional interests or ideologies with all-India ones, and on the ability of the center to create a shared culture for the elite. Since independence, the central government has tried to accommodate three major elite groups that together constitute about 20 percent of the population—the urban industrial class, the professional classes, and the rich farmers of the countryside. Doing so has meant postponing or minimizing the leadership's commitment to social justice and greater equality.

Both domestically and internationally, the early 1990s brought changes that made Nehru's conception of India even more difficult to attain. A new generation had come to power, less committed to Socialist and secularist idealism. The worldwide shift toward a free market economy occasioned by the collapse of communism further diminished support for a Socialist India of any kind. In 1992, the government adopted the first budget to place the private sector in a dominant position. It included measures to reduce public investment and customs duties to foster expanded private enterprise and attract investment from multinational corporations. Furthermore, successful Indian professionals and businesspeople, now dispersed in many parts of the world, frequently returned substantial funds back to India through overseas remittances and investments in various cultural and economic activities in India. Their influence in shaping a vision of "India" and of "Hinduism" represents a new factor in the public life of the country.

Women and the New India

Economic and political developments have brought uneven changes to the lives of India's women.[1] In constitutional terms, women gained with the advent of universal suffrage: they not only won the vote but have been elected to the legislature in numbers slightly larger than their counterparts in the West. One woman, Indira Gandhi, was the country's powerful prime minister for many years.

However, independent India has continued the British practice of relating to individuals through the communities with which they are associated. Thus, women identified as part of caste Hindu society are protected by the "Hindu Marriage Code," adopted in the mid-1950s against considerable resistance, for it prohibits polygamy and provides for mutual divorce. Muslim women, by contrast, are governed by a distinct "Muslim law" created by the British in consultation with Muslim *ulama*. Under its provisions, polygamy is permitted, and there has been considerable controversy as to the security provided to women in marriage and inheritance.

This practice of providing different protections for different communities reflects a real dilemma—while it recognizes the substantial cultural diversity of India, it also inhibits the full development of a civil society in which the state treats all individuals equally. Perhaps the most dramatic illustration of this tension in recent years involved the case of a Muslim woman named Shah Bano. In 1985, she sued under the Indian penal code for support from her former husband, an entitlement she would not have received under Muslim law. The court sided with Shah Bano, awarding her financial support and treating her as any citizen suing in the court. The judgment provoked strong protest from orthodox Muslim political and religious leaders, who probably represented a minority opinion among Indian Muslims. In an effort to placate the most orthodox leaders of religious pressure groups, the government supported a bill misleadingly labeled "Muslim Women's (Protection of Rights on Divorce) Act," which prevents Muslim women from addressing marital issues outside that law. Thus, the government's need to retain the political support of religiously defined communities resulted in actions that limited the legal remedies open to Muslim women.

Such controversies resemble the social reform and political agitation of the nineteenth century, for in each case "women's issues" served as a rallying point for both those advocating and resisting major change. Thus, in independent India, issues surrounding marriage remain very important. Despite efforts by reformers to dissuade families from insisting on dowries, the practice of payments to grooms has actually increased in recent decades. Paying dowries has been a means of upward mobility for certain groups seeking to use their newly acquired wealth to marry into higher-status families. It has led to a new urban phenomenon in which husbands have killed their wives, disguising the deaths as accidents, in order to keep their dowries and become available to attract new ones. This shows the extent to which marriage remains an economic transaction in modern South Asia and illustrates how modern economic development, in the context of sharp gender inequalities, can lead to behavior that exploits and endangers women.

Modern scientific techniques can have a similar outcome. With the advent of amniocentesis, Indians can now test to determine the sex of the fetus; estimates are that up to 99 percent of aborted fetuses are female, strongly suggesting that this new scientific procedure is being used in support of an ancient Indian preference for male children.

Equally alarming has been the new glorification of *sati,* part of the growth of Hindu religious nationalism and personified by the recent case of Roop Kumar. In 1987, this eighteen-year-old widow mounted the funeral pyre of her husband of six months under rather dubious circumstances. It is not clear whether she was coerced; however, the local police did not intervene despite a crowd of ten thousand viewers. In the aftermath of her death, the heroism and saintliness of *satis* as role models for Hindu women has been widely proclaimed in the press. Despite legislation to prevent future *satis,* the site of Roop Kumar's death has become the focal point of pilgrims, and a shrine was under construction there.

Such threats to the position of women have prompted strong protests that, quite often, have forced the state to take action. In 1975, for example, the government appointed a Committee on the Status of Women, which reported, among other things, that the ratio of women to men in India had dropped from 971 per thousand in 1901 to 931 per thousand in 1971. Such revelations, together with the widely publicized abuses mentioned previously, stimulated women themselves to become active in fighting for women's causes. To a large extent the leadership of this women's movement in India has been drawn from urban middle-class professional women; they have benefited most from the political and economic changes of independence. But most of the organizations they have established attempt to reach out to and improve the lives of lower-class and rural women. The All India Women's Conference (AIWC), the oldest forum for women in India, "has on its agenda such diverse activities as publishing, working with destitute women, operating a women's hostel, campaigning and working with the government on women's issues."[2] Perhaps the most visible of the new organizations is the Self-Employed Women's Association (SEWA). Its creation reflects the fact that most women's labor is in the informal sector of the economy. SEWA has worked hard to mobilize women for protests and to give them greater clout in their economic relationships with employers.

Such organizing provides evidence that Indian women who were economically and socially disadvantaged have not been powerless. Other evidence emerges from anthropological research. For example, one scholar has closely examined the life of Jayamma, a brick worker in Kerala, revealing that she was the economic mainstay of her family and its primary decision maker. Her husband, who had been

This street scene in Bombay illustrates the continuing reality of massive urban poverty despite much modern development. *Sygma*

a boatman, stayed home and raised goats. She had been working for thirty years in the same brick kiln, run by an ex-military sergeant. As the anthropologist explains, "She feels that it is better to work for the same brick kiln. Then she cannot only be sure of work but also can expect to get a small loan in an hour of crisis. Also her children are assured of employment."[3] The work at the kiln was strictly defined in gender terms, with women doing the carrying of bricks from one part of the yard to another; "the day she was strong enough to cart twenty bricks on her head she had reached the limit." Because of her experience, Jayamma was occasionally asked to do male work as well (such as the skillful tossing of bricks along a row of men until they were stacked), but without additional pay. It was she who decided to accept the offer of a dowry marriage for one of her sons, and she arranged for the employment of her other children at the kiln. She was also scrupulous in preventing one daughter and her common-law husband from living with the extended family under her roof, because the husband was from a lower caste. Thus, Jayamma retained responsibility for the social and economic well-being of her family. As her four children reached adulthood, she began to put her hopes for her own social security in her youngest son, placing him in the best-paying position she could find so that he could take care of her when she became too old to work at the kiln.

Short stories, fictionalizing women's efforts to retain power over their lives, likewise offer insights into both the changing and continuing patterns of women's lives in contemporary India. "Giribala," written in Bengali in 1982 by Mahasweta Devi, tells the story of a mother who, like Jayamma, tries to achieve economic security by working in a wealthy house, protecting her family from her ganja-addicted husband, and saving money for her daughters' dowries. As the first daughter reaches puberty, however, her husband sells the girl for a "bride-price," ostensibly to an organization recruiting brides for the region of Bihar, but actually for prostitution. Giribala is devastated but continues as before, attempting to protect her second daughter. Once again, however, the husband takes the daughter away. At last Giribala makes a stand for herself and her youngest children, leaving the economic security of the big house to escape from her husband.

> People were so amazed.... What kind of woman would leave her husband of many years, just like that? ... And Giribala? Walking down the unfamiliar roads and holding Muruni on her hip and Rajib by the hand, Giribala only regretted that she had not done this before ... then Beli would not have been lost, then Pori would not have been lost.

From such courageous acts of independence, women in India are trying to create circumstances in which their daughters will have greater opportunities.

Civil Society and Competing Identities

Under British rule, many Indians had begun to define their communities in new ways. As noted in Chapter 14, there evolved two separate realms in which these communities could pursue their interests: the realm of political institutions and the alternative realm of cultural activity. The British had insisted that the cultural realm was "apolitical" or "private" because it dealt with activities specific to local communities and because it so often used the language of religion. The nationalist movement focused generally on the development of political institutions, such as parties, to meet and resist British rule, and neglected (except at certain notable moments) to integrate the emerging alternative realm of cultural activity. In part this reflected elite uneasiness about mobilization of the masses; in part it expressed a conscious desire, by Gandhi and other leaders, to play down the religious and regional forms of community identity that had begun to emerge in this alternate realm. Thus, the relationship between the state and its constituent communities remained unresolved when independence arrived. The cultural realm continued to express forms of community that competed with the nation-state for the primary loyalties of many Indians. Three major issues—language, caste, and religion—serve to illustrate the tensions between the state in independent India and the various communities or societies with which its citizens identified.

Language and Identity: The Redrawing of Regional Boundaries

As late as 1945, the Congress had urged that states or provinces within a federal structure should be drawn along linguistic lines. After partition, however, the government's concern to foster national integration increasingly led it to resist the appeal of language as a basis for political organization. The early 1950s saw bitter struggles around this issue as various regional movements pushed to redraw state boundaries along lines coinciding with linguistic identity.

In many parts of the subcontinent, and particularly in the south, language was an important element of regional identities. India had no common language, but more people spoke some variant of Hindi, a north Indian language, than any other. The constitution writers embraced the Hindi cause on grounds of national unity and directed that it be phased in for official purposes. The regionalists were furious. Massive demonstrations, riots, passive resistance, and fasting to death followed. In south India, Hindi was considered a foreign language; how could southerners compete if university and civil service exams were held in Hindi? Official use of Hindi in Madras in the

1960s led to bloody riots against "northern Hindi imperialism." The southerners wanted to let each state use its own language and continue English as the "link language."

The experience of the Tamil-speaking region of south India illustrates the role of language in the formation of regional identities. There the Congress provincial government elected in 1937, although composed of Tamil leaders, had introduced policies—such as compulsory Hindi instruction in the schools—that provoked a distinct Tamil identity. Between 1937 and the mid-1950s, the central state began to lose the support of Tamil speakers, who increasingly identified with an alternative Tamil "nationalism" rather than the all-India nationalism fostered by the center.

The development of Tamil identity brought together ethnic issues (Tamils were of Dravidian, not Aryan, background), class or caste issues (opposition to Brahman domination), and religious issues (the predominance of goddess worship in the south versus Ram and Krishna worship in the north). All of this came to be associated with the Tamil language, which was presented as a goddess (Tamilttay) and an endangered mother. She resisted the encroachments of Hindi, depicted as a demoness invading from the north who was intent on imposing northern culture on the south.

Tamil resistance to north Indian culture and to the power of the center was also expressed through a retelling of the epic *Ramayana*. The non-Brahman leader E. V. Ramasami, for example, reversed the usual treatment of Ram as a heroic god-king and presented him instead as a repressive, boorish invader from the north. His enemy, Ravana, was no longer a demon in this telling; instead, he represented a victimized local ruler of a south Indian kingdom that was being invaded and taken over. In Tamilnad, this view of Ram provoked well-publicized disagreements and led, in the 1950s, to protests, arrests, and heavy newspaper coverage. These alternative tellings of Ram's story thus became a way to argue about who constituted "the nation," with regional and India-wide forms of identity in competition.

Similar patterns had developed in other parts of the country. Perhaps the earliest and most dramatic was the competition, in the late nineteenth and early twentieth centuries, between Hindi and Urdu—a form of linguistic competition that became connected to the conflict between Hindus and Muslims.

It was particularly striking because both had shared the Urdu literary culture under the Mughals. Similarly, when linguistic boundaries began to be drawn in independent India, the competition between Gujarati and Marathi speakers in the Bombay area led to demands that each linguistic group control its own territory.

To create a national policy, the government appointed a commission to advise on regional states' reorganization. Its recommendations, adopted in 1956, called for state boundaries to be redrawn on linguistic lines; boundaries have continued to be redrawn on that basis ever since. But while the commission supported *linguistically* organized regional states, it opposed religious reorganization. Thus, it recommended against the restructuring of the Punjab because, it argued, the movement there had nothing to do with language (Punjabi) and everything to do with religion (Sikhism). This national policy of refusing to recognize religion in defining regional states has been in effect since independence.

The ability of language to express alternative "national" identities has had foreign policy implications in the subcontinent as well. Hindi chauvinists in India have often treated Urdu as a stand-in for the culture and the political threat of Pakistan. Equally, the battles between the dominant Sinhalese and the minority Tamil in the neighboring country of Sri Lanka often appeared to be an extension of the Tamil nationalism of south India. This conflict resulted in the assassination of Rajiv Gandhi by disgruntled Tamil nationalists from Sri Lanka during the elections of 1991.

Ethnicity, Class, and Identity: The Case of Ex-Untouchables

Perhaps the most unresolved issue at independence involved Untouchables, those groups located at the bottom of the Hindu social and economic hierarchy. Ambedkar's influence during the writing of the constitution resulted in the legal outlawing of Untouchability and provided certain "reserved seats" in the legislature for the "Scheduled Castes and Tribes," as Untouchables and certain rural tribal groups were now officially called. But constitutional change alone could not substantially change the lives of these people on the margins of Indian society. What, then, was the state's responsibility for these least privileged of its citizens?

In general since 1947, the Indian state has defined the issue in class terms and has tried to address it by changing the economic status of "Scheduled Castes and Tribes." Land reform was to assist depressed rural groups in these categories, and the reservation of a percentage of government jobs and places in schools has provided greater opportunities for urban Untouchables.

But Untouchable activists themselves made their claims in terms of cultural identity, referring to distinct caste and ethnic groups. In 1956, Ambedkar gathered together thousands of his Untouchable followers and exhorted them to "change their religion" if they would remedy their social and economic woes. In doing so he was following the general trend of Indian electoral politics that increasingly appealed to voters in terms of their cultural, rather than class, identities. Since this dramatic event, large numbers of ex-Untouchables have converted to Buddhism. A religion regarded as egalitarian and alien, Buddhism had been invisible in the subcontinent for centuries and thus represented an alternative to the Hindu social order. Ambedkar intended conversion as a first step to forming a new political movement as well. Yet those who did convert and assume a new identity as Buddhists were, in effect, penalized by the state, for self-described Buddhists became ineligible for affirmative action governmental support. Ex-Untouchables have seen this policy as discriminatory support by the government for Hinduism.

In 1981, mass conversion to Islam by more than a thousand ex-Untouchables in Meenakshipuram (Tamilnad) prompted dramatic riots of repression by Hindus in higher social positions. Since conversion to Islam was viewed as much more threatening than conversion to Buddhism, the state renewed its affirmative action policies to bring ex-Untouchables up on the economic scale and back into the fold of Hinduism. It reserved a much greater proportion of educational and employment places for Untouchables than had previously been the case. And it did so on the basis of their caste identity, not their economic status. All of this has been highly controversial because it reduced the opportunities available to other, higher-status groups in Indian society.

These events triggered a series of intense conflicts and debates about community identity and state protection. High-caste intellectuals and professionals expressed their outrage at special treatment for Untouchables in economic terms, protesting the government's job and education reservations and other affirmative action policies as immensely threatening to themselves—a group already overqualified for the limited number of professional positions available. But cultural issues were also important. An umbrella organization (the Virat Hindu Samaj) was established to coordinate the reconversion of Indian Muslims to Hinduism. This reassertion of Hindu identity, and the sense of threat felt by majority Hindus, have played an important part in shaping an aggressively pro-Hindu political ideology called "Hindutva." Since the late 1980s, communal parties motivated by that ideology have worked hard to ensure national protection for Hindu interests. The entire process has both sharpened conflict and blurred the distinctions among religious, ethnic, and class forms of identity.

Religious Nationalism

If religious rhetoric has been used to express linguistic and class identity, it is partly because religious nationalism has been a feature of Indian public life for more than a century. Yet religious identity has only intermittently dominated public attention. The early years of independence, for example, saw few outbreaks of "communal" violence. No doubt the staggering toll of religiously inspired killing at partition accounted in part for this reluctance to express communal aggression publicly. So too did the severe public disapproval of the Hindu communal organization, the RSS (Rashtriya Swayam Sevak Sangh), which was responsible for Gandhi's assassination in 1948. Moreover, in this early period, the shared vision of a secular state led most people to expect even-handedness from the state toward various religious groups. Thus, the new Indian government, like the British Raj before it, refused to recognize political claims based on religious identity.

By the 1967 election, however, as the Congress began to lose supporters to various competing parties, it also began to make exceptions to this policy as a means of keeping various groups within the party. Under the leadership of Indira Gandhi (Nehru's daughter), and particularly after she returned to power in 1980, the Congress began to rely more heavily on Muslims and Sikhs and to treat them as minority interest "voting blocs" that might be ap-

Indian security forces used tear gas to disperse Hindu militants attempting to storm a disputed mosque at Ayodhya in 1990. They later succeeded in destroying the mosque. *AP/Wide World Photos/Barbara Walton*

peased by certain state actions. The Congress also tried to "divide and conquer" by supporting certain contenders against others within those communities.

The results of these strategies have been particularly dramatic in the Punjab, where the Congress has always competed with the Akali party for the support of the Sikh religious community. By the 1980s, the Congress began to aggressively compete with the Akalis for Sikh support; thus, it picked out and promoted a little-known Sikh priest, Sant Bhindranwale. But he soon went further in agitating for Sikh causes than the Congress could support and began to stockpile arms in the Golden Temple, the most important religious building for Sikhs. By 1984, the state found itself forced to launch a military action to force Bhindranwale and his Sikh militants out of the Golden Temple. That the government would militarily attack a religious building shocked most Sikhs, as well as many other Indians. It led to the assassination of Indira Gandhi by her Sikh bodyguards and broadened

support for terrorism and Sikh fundamentalism in the Punjab, as more people came to favor Sikh identity over that of the Indian "nation" as a whole.

Thus, while the government *spoke* in favor of a secular state and against the exercise of religion in political life, it also extended, selectively, special protections to Sikhs, Muslims, and ex-Untouchables. Such policies encouraged more aggressive action during the 1980s by a variety of political and religious groups claiming to speak for the country's 726 million Hindus, who made up 83 percent of the population. For the first time since independence, political parties with a religious or communal ideology became major players in Indian political life. Perhaps the most important was the BJP (Bharatiya Janata party), which became in the early 1990s a major opposition to the governing Congress party. A strongly Hindu isolationist party, the BJP argued in favor of arming India with nuclear weapons, of sharply limiting foreign involvement in the economy, and of promoting a distinctly Hindu identity in religion, education, and culture. Its program opposed the state's standing aloof from religion and urged state protection and special consideration for Hinduism as the only indigenous and "natural" identity in the subcontinent.

The rise of "Hindu nationalism" since the mid-1980s has, for the first time, connected political parties with the pursuit of Hindu cultural identity. The BJP won elections to control the governments of four regional states following a sustained campaign, launched with other communal parties in April 1984, to "liberate" a temple in Ayodhya, the ancient north Indian pilgrimage center considered to be Ram's birthplace. Also present on this site was a mosque, said to be built by the Mughal Emperor Aurangzeb, a historical figure used to represent Muslim bigotry. The presence of this mosque was used to justify militant Hindu "protection" of Ram's birthplace, and became the focal point of Hindu activism. To dramatize the case of the temple, which had been closed to worshipers since the 1920s, the communal parties in 1985 organized processions across north India using techniques associated with cultural activities. Public devotional activities, enacted in various towns along a route of political pilgrimage, reminded the faithful of the Ayodhya problem. The protest extended even to the capital at New Delhi as a means of bringing pressure on central government officials.

This appeal to deeply felt cultural values turned the issue into an all-India one that was embraced by activists throughout the subcontinent. In December 1992, activists launched an attack that leveled the offending mosque at Ayodhya, led to weeks of violence and over three thousand deaths, and left the central government scrambling to find an effective response. It did finally promise to rebuild the mosque, to ban five major communal parties, and to declare martial law in the state of Uttar Pradesh, taking control of the state government away from the BJP. None of these actions, however, addressed the fundamental question in a systemic way: To what extent should the religious convictions of the majority of Indians affect the state's relationship with minority communities?

The changing relationship between the Indian state and its various constituent communities has led, in the 1990s, to a fundamental rethinking of basic questions. What does it mean to be an Indian citizen, to be Hindu, and to be a member of Indian civil society? Are these various identities compatible with one another? In the process of this rethinking, some basic assumptions of Indian democracy have been called into question.

Secularism in political life, for example, was generally viewed positively in India at independence. It implied that government was an objective force separate and distinct from its member communities and their religious practices. By the late 1980s, however, even some of India's most respected intellectuals had begun to reject this view of secularism. As one of them wrote, secularism "as a generally shared credo of life is impossible, as a basis for state action impracticable, and as a blueprint for the foreseeable future impotent."[4] But such intellectuals have begun to warn against "majoritarianism" as another way of talking about the dangers to democracy that Hindu religious nationalism poses. If they can no longer successfully urge state action in support of secularism, they now urge it against the domination by a majority intent on suppressing the rights of minorities as citizens to express and practice their beliefs.

Conclusion:
India in the 1990s

To what extent, then, did India by the 1990s realize the Congress's nationalist vision for the country at independence? In keeping with its modernizing commitments, India had created a substantial industrial sector, made considerable gains in agricultural production, and generated a growing middle class representing roughly 15 percent to 20 percent of the population. And it had retained its status as the world's most populous democratic country where the army stayed out of political life. But these economic and political achievements had done little to reduce the country's ancient inequalities or the poverty experienced by so many. And in circumstances of entrenched local privileges, a newfound respect for free markets, and the discrediting of socialism in the former Soviet Union, the efforts of those seeking to preserve the Indian socialism of the early independence period have been ignored.

Perhaps even more important, by the early 1990s India had moved a considerable distance away from the early nationalist conception of a single, secular, democratic state that permitted the private expression of various cultural traditions. Religious rhetoric had become the major means of expressing resistance to the state and its nationalized all-Indian culture. Consequently, many local communities expressed their identities in sharply religious terms, even if the original basis of their protest was linguistic or economic. Although partition had removed millions of Muslims from the body politic of India in 1947, the clash between Hindus and the remaining Muslims, some 120 million, had sharpened to the point of widespread violence by the 1990s. Furthermore, some of these communities had come to see themselves in fundamental opposition to the all-Indian state, while others rejected the state's initial secularism and sought to remake it in a distinctively Hindu mold. Yet India's older traditions were hardly dead, and state elections in late 1993 revealed declining support for the more extreme Hindu nationalist parties.

Thus, India still struggles to create a civil society and a state system that provide room for various communities to pursue and protect their particular regional, religious, ethnic, and class identities. While the British tried to separate politics and culture into two distinct realms, their post-colonial successors must find ways to integrate them. In this effort, the earlier experience of Vijayanagara and the Mughal Empire may prove useful, for the competing claims of India's vast and ancient cultural diversity and its efforts at political unity have for centuries been central to the history of the subcontinent.

Notes

1. This section has benefited from Barbara N. Ramusack, "Women in South and Southeast Asia," in *Restoring Women to History* (Bloomington: Organization of American Historians, 1990).

2. *Sunday,* 14 March 1992.

3. Leela Gulati, "Female Labour in the Unorganized Sector: Profile of a Brick Worker," in *Profiles in Female Poverty* (New Delhi: Hindustan Publishing, 1981), pp. 35–62.

4. T. N. Madan, "Secularism in Its Place," *Journal of Asian Studies* 46:4 (Nov. 1987): 748.

Comparative Essay

NATIONALISMS IN MODERN WORLD HISTORY

I t would be difficult to identify a more powerful force in the modern world than *nationalism*—the popular belief that one's own people share a common and unique culture and deserve an independent political status. Frequently nationalism has also suggested that the nation has some special destiny or historical mission. Such sentiments drove European rivalries in the nineteenth century and produced two world wars in the twentieth; they undermined the empires of Austria, Turkey, Great Britain, France, and Russia; they provoked hostility and even war among supposedly fraternal Communist allies in the 1960s and 1970s; and they have bedeviled efforts to achieve unity and stability in many states around the world.

Although nationalists everywhere proclaim the antiquity of their nations, this kind of political or cultural identity is very recent in world history, dating back little more than two centuries in most places. Before that, most people felt themselves to be members of small local communities such as clans or villages. Where they were bound to larger structures, these were usually religious groupings (Buddhist, Muslim, or Christian, for example) or imperial states (Turkish, Mughal, or Austro-Hungarian empires, to mention only a few). Many people lived in political systems that were governed by rulers culturally different from themselves. Some European monarchs were unable even to speak the language of their subjects. In short, people defined neither their cultures nor their states as "nations."

The emergence of what we now recognize as national identity occurred first in Europe as the old order was eroded by the modern transformation. Science and rationalism weakened traditional religious loyalties. The emergence of separate states (Spain, Prussia, England, and France) undermined dynastic political systems in which a sacred monarch ruled over a variety of culturally different peoples. The invention of printing standardized a vast variety of tongues and dialects into a smaller number of modern European languages and permitted the literate classes to imagine themselves members of a common linguistic group to an extent not possible before. Capitalism, industrialization, urbanization, and population growth uprooted millions from long-established traditions and so created a need for new forms of community. And many of these people began to feel that they had a right to participate in political life and did so through revolutions, elections, and parties.

This was the brew from which nationalism emerged, first in France and England where the modern transformation was most highly developed. In these countries, vernacular languages largely coincided with political boundaries, making the transition to a nation-state easier. The political and economic success of these west European nations—especially the conquests of Napoleon—soon gave the ideas of nationalism and the nation-state a great appeal in central and eastern Europe, where dynastic empires still held sway. There, during the nineteenth century, a distinctly national consciousness dawned for peoples who, unlike the French and the English, had no states of their own. Urban intellectuals—linguists, historians, writers, students of folklore—took the lead in creating German, Italian, Hungarian, Czech, Bulgarian, Ukrainian, and many other nationalisms. Drawing on local folk-cultures and selected aspects of their historical experience, these intellectuals shaped a conception of the nation that appealed to a widening circle of people. The process did not so much reawaken ancient national feelings as it invented or constructed new political loyalties—the "imagined communities" of the modern era.[1]

In Germany and Italy scattered members of the so-called national community gathered into unified states, a process largely completed by the early 1870s. Elsewhere newly conscious "nations" sought greater political independence from the ramshackle Austro-Hungarian, Turkish, and Russian empires. Not until World War I shattered these empires could the new nation-states fully emerge.

For the rest of the world, the nationalisms of Europe had a complex impact. The rivalries of European nations gave energy to their empire building, which carved out a variety of colonial states in Asia and Africa. But the ideology of nationalism also undermined colonial rule by giving the leaders of anti-colonial movements a set of ideas with which to protest European domination. In 1913, for example, the Dutch colonial regime in what is now Indonesia organized celebrations to mark the independence of the Netherlands from France one hundred years earlier. It did not take long for Indonesian intellectuals to draw the logical conclusion: If the Dutch nation had liberated itself from France, why should Indonesians not free themselves from the Netherlands?

However, the anticolonial nationalisms of Asia and Africa were frequently quite different from those of Europe. While European nationalisms often had their cultural basis in a common language, that was impossible for the linguistically diverse societies of India, Indonesia, Nigeria, and Zaire. Rather, the common experience of a colonial educational system and the common hostility to foreign rulers bound together the nationalist elites of the colonies. In Europe, an emerging national consciousness sought political expression in new nation-states, whereas in Asia and Africa, nationalists seized the existing colonial states and tried to create a sense of shared culture within them.

The attempt to create nations within the framework of colonial states has been difficult in part because the ideology of nationalism found a receptive audience among many of the separate peoples of these states. If a wholly artificial political unit such as Nigeria could claim nationhood, why not the millions of Igbo-speaking people who populated its richest region? If Iran, Iraq, and Turkey were nations, what about the Kurds who lived as a minority within each of these countries? Thus were born the ethnic nationalisms that have so troubled the political life of many Afro-Asian states.

Yet the anticolonial nationalisms of the developing countries have served as a model for minority groups in the West as well. The Scots and Welsh in Great Britain, French-speaking Canadians, Native Americans and African Americans in the United States, Slovaks in Czechoslovakia, Croats and Serbs in Yugoslavia, and any number of peoples in the former Soviet Union all have used the language of these nationalists, have thought of themselves as "internal colonies" and have sought a separate state or greater political autonomy. Ethnic nationalism is by no means limited to Asia and Africa.

While most nationalisms have had or sought a territorial base or an independent state, there have also emerged in the past century or more several broader cultural nationalisms that have transcended state boundaries altogether. In the nineteenth century, a pan-Slavic movement cast the Russians as protector of smaller Slavic nations in Europe and purported to find some uniquely Slavic characteristics that distinguished them from the other peoples of Europe. In the twentieth century, pan-Arabism asserted a common cultural tradition and political destiny for Arabic-speaking peoples from Morocco to Iraq. And pan-Africanism sought to connect the experience of colonial oppression in Africa with that of New World blacks.

Nationalism has thus given meaning to life and inspired enormous sacrifice in many diverse settings, but it has had no consistent political philosophy. Conservative monarchs of nineteenth-century Europe claimed to speak for the "nation" in order to bolster their faltering regimes. The Romanov dynasty of the Russian Empire, which had itself adopted and encouraged French culture in the eighteenth century, was by the end of the nineteenth actively attempting to "Russify" many of its non-Russian peoples.

Nationalism can also fuel the most radical of revolutionary movements, as the example of China so clearly demonstrates. There the humiliations of nineteenth-century imperialism persuaded young Chinese nationalists in the early twentieth century that the old order had to be destroyed and a new one constructed if the Chinese nation were to survive. In 1949, Mao Zedong announced the victory of the Communist revolution in the tones of a nationalist: "Ours no longer will be a nation subject to insult and humiliation," he declared. "We have stood up."

Nationalism has served more moderate masters as well. In mid-nineteenth-century Europe, it inspired liberal and democratic movements. In twentieth-century India, it was associated with Gandhi's efforts to raise the status of Untouchables while winning independence from Britain through nonviolent protest.

But in the experience of Nazi Germany, nationality was defined partly in racial terms to justify the physical extermination of whole categories of people—Jews, Gypsies, and Slavs. Here nationalism, which normally emphasized cultural and linguistic differences, was altogether compatible with pseudo-scientific racism. The ferocity of Serbian nationalism in the early 1990s, associated with "ethnic cleansing," rape camps, and enormous violence in the former Yugoslavia, testified to the continuing ability of nationalism to fuel the most horrific and inhumane behavior.

Socialist movements or Communist regimes, allegedly committed to international solidarity with one another, have not been immune to the nationalist virus. Despite the pleas of some Socialist leaders, most Socialist members of European parliaments in 1914 endorsed the war efforts of their respective countries and sent their worker-soldiers to slaughter one another by the millions. The well-known conflict between the Soviet Union and China is but another example of the triumph of nationalism over Communist ideology, as was the war that erupted between China and a Communist Vietnam in 1979.

Nationalism, it seems, traveled easily from its point of origin in Europe to the colonial empires of Asia and Africa and back again to Europe as the twentieth century drew to a close. In the process, it was adopted by monarchs, democrats, Fascists, and Communists. It strengthened some states and shattered others. The "communities" whose identities nationalism articulated may initially have been "imaginary," but they have since become a powerful source of human solidarity and a central element in the making of the modern world.

Notes

1. Benedict Anderson, *Imagined Communities: Reflections on the Origins and Spread of Nationalism* (London: Verso, 1983).

SUGGESTIONS FOR FURTHER READING: INDIA

Basham, A. L. *The Wonder That Was India.* 1968. (A classic attempt to reconstruct and explain Indian civilization on the basis of literary and other evidence.)

Bayly, C. A. *Indian Society and the Making of the British Empire.* 1988. (A view of British India reflecting contemporary scholarship.)

Brown, Judith. *Modern India: The Origins of an Asian Democracy.* 1985. (Covers the past two hundred years of India's history.)

Charlesworth, Neil. *British Rule and the Indian Economy, 1800–1914.* 1982.

Frankel, Francine R. *India's Political Economy, 1947–77.* 1978. (An integrated economic, political, and social history of India in its first thirty years of independence.)

Hardgrave, Robert, Jr., and Stanley A. Kochanek. *India: Government and Politics in a Developing Nation.* 1986. (A study of India's post-independence politics.)

Klass, Morton. *Caste: The Emergence of the South Asian Social System.* 1980.

Kumar, Dharma, and Tapan Raychaudhuri, eds. *Cambridge Economic History of India.* 1982. (Includes chapters on the economy of medieval and modern India by a group of noted scholars.)

Liddle, Joanna, and Rama Joshi. *Daughters of Independence: Gender, Caste, and Class in India.* 1986. (Places the contemporary women's movement in the context of India's caste system, of British colonial rule, and of the emerging class structure.)

Mandlebaum, David G. *Society in India.* 2 vols. 1972. (A study of the changes and continuities in Indian society in recent times.)

Masselos, Jim. *Indian Nationalism.* 1991. (An analysis of the struggle for independence.)

Miller, Barbara Stoler, ed. *The Powers of Art.* 1992. (A study of cultural patronage in Indian history.)

Mitchell, George. *The Vijayanagara Courtly Style.* 1992. (Shows how the state of Vijayanagara synthesized various architectural styles into its own buildings.)

Panikkar, K. N., ed. *Communalism in India.* 1991. (A discussion of how politics and culture have intersected in Indian history.)

Sarkar, Jadunath. *The Fall of the Mughal Empire.* 1988.

PART VI

EAST ASIA AND THE MODERN WORLD: COMPARING CHINA AND JAPAN

Chapter 16: *The Middle Kingdom: The Making of the Chinese Empire*

Chapter 17: *"Foreign Devils": China and Western Imperialism, 1500–1900*

Chapter 18: *Nationalists and Communists: The Chinese Revolution, 1900–1949*

Chapter 19: *Socialism, Development, and Politics: The People's Republic of China*

Chapter 20: *Japan: An Authoritarian Road to Capitalism*

Comparative
Essay: *Comparing Revolutions and Communist Regimes: Russia and China*

Suggestions for
Further Reading: *China and Japan*

The East Asian cultural region was, for most of its history, a world apart, less connected to the wider linkages of Afro-Eurasian interaction than Europe or the Middle East. At its center and overshadowing all other cultures in the area was China, and its splendidly attractive civilization. Around its periphery three other civilizations developed—in Japan, Korea, and Vietnam—that derived much of their culture and political organi-

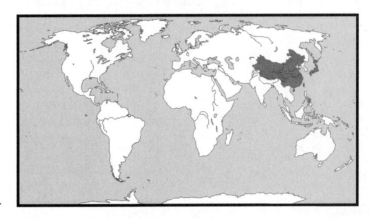

zation from China. The nomadic peoples to the north and west of China were likewise strongly attracted toward China and sometimes assimilated into it.

Part VI focuses primarily on China itself, because of its size, its huge population, and its great significance in modern world history. But the part also looks carefully at Japan, both because of its contemporary significance and because its recent history provides a sharp contrast with that of its larger neighbor on the East Asian mainland.

Like the other great civilizations of Asia, China confronted an aggressively expanding Europe with ideas and institutions that had evolved over many centuries. But China's modern experience provides numerous contrasts to that of other Asian societies. China agonized for over a century in violent internal conflict and under imperialist domination, whereas its island neighbor of Japan modernized rapidly, maintained its political independence, and became an imperialist power itself. Unlike the societies of India and the Middle East, China's modern history pivots on a profound and revolutionary social upheaval, and its subsequent efforts at development took a distinctly Socialist form. Although it shared this revolutionary and

Socialist heritage with the Soviet Union, China departed, quite deliberately, from the Soviet model and sought to forge its own path to the modern world. Thus, defining and explaining China's distinctive history are the primary goals of the next four chapters.

Chapter 16 begins with the evolution of China's unique civilization, and with the particular condition of that civilization at the time of its encounter with an expanding Europe. Chapter 17 traces the decline of China into a semicolonial relationship with the Western powers and the failure of its traditional political and cultural elite to prevent or reverse this humiliating situation. By the early twentieth century, a number of young Chinese had concluded that revolution was the only real alternative. How the Chinese Communist party was able to ride this revolutionary wave to power by 1949 is the main theme of Chapter 18, while Chapter 19 traces the changing contours of the party's efforts since 1949 to build a modern and Socialist society from an ancient Chinese culture. Finally, Chapter 20 examines the very different historical experience of Japan, contrasting it with that of its Chinese neighbor.

Chapter 16
The Middle Kingdom:
The Making of the Chinese Empire

Understanding China's place in world history is important not only because China now represents over 20 percent of the world's population, but also because its path of historical development contrasts sharply with that of other major civilizations. Throughout most of its history, China has been a large and relatively centralized empire with an agrarian economy at least partially controlled by its political authorities. Thus, its history has revolved around the formation and dissolution of an empire. Europe, by contrast, had an imperial past—the Roman Empire—but when it disintegrated, it was never reconstituted; rather, it was followed by a feudal and then a modern capitalist society and the creation of many separate nation-states. Alone among the great civilizations of premodern history, China embodied and expressed its civilization in a state whose duration was measured in millennia (thousands of years) rather than in centuries.

For nearly two millennia, China was the center of an East Asian world system, exercising direct control over numerous peoples within its own borders and dominant cultural influence well beyond those borders. The Japanese, Koreans, and Vietnamese, for instance, all borrowed their written language from China. China's claims to be the center of the universe were believable to peoples living within its shadow.

In contrast to the volatility of Europe's highly competitive interstate system that emerged in the centuries after 1500, China moved to the rhythms of empire for over two thousand years and in the process succeeded in finding a political, social, economic, and cultural balance that led to stability over long periods. It maintained this imperial structure during the four hundred or so years after 1500, when Europe's modern transformation increasingly altered the global balance of power.

The Dynamics of Empire

China's history unfolded in a distinctive and highly diverse geographic setting (see Map 16.1). From the Himalayan Mountains and Tibetan Plateau in the west, China slopes eastward to the Pacific Ocean. Mountains, covering a third of the country, and other nonarable lands, limit cultivation to about 12 percent of its current area, nearly all located in the eastern third of the country. The major rivers, the Yellow in the north and the Yangzi in central China, run west to east, as do the major mountain chains, thus dividing the country geographically on a north–south axis. The frost line, which runs approximately halfway between the Yellow and Yangzi rivers, further divides China into north and south. In northern China, the four seasons mark the passing of time, whereas the southern region rarely sees frost.

Northern China is primarily a wheat-growing region; rice is the main crop in the south. In the north, winter wheat is followed by a crop of vegetables, whereas southern farmers can get two or sometimes three crops of rice from the same plot of land by double-cropping or interplanting. The common vision of China covered with rice paddies and terraces is accurate for the south, but the northern plain—flat and covered with wheat—resembles the American Midwest. It is interesting, therefore, that early Chinese civilization developed not in the warmer south but on the north China plain.

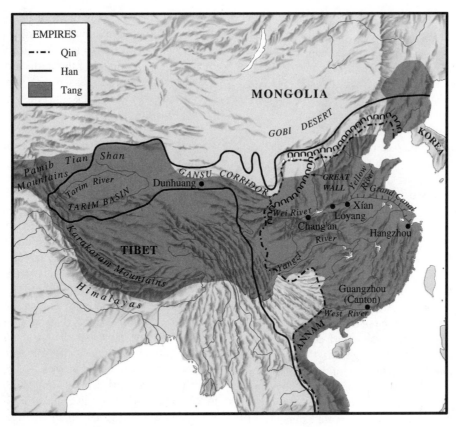

MAP 16.1 Imperial China

China incorporates considerable geographic variety which has shaped the cultures of its different peoples. Northern and southern China, despite their differences, both supported settled agriculture and major cities. In the steppe zone, "beyond the Great Wall," nomadic peoples raised livestock, moving their portable dwellings called *yurts* from one grazing area to another. Throughout much of Chinese history, the nomadic way of life sharpened the war-making skills of these nomadic peoples—horseback riding, herding, archery, and hunting—frequently threatening the settled agriculturalists who lived to the south. In the mountainous regions in the far west, defined by the Himalayan Mountains and the Tibetan Plateau, a mode of life combining mountaineering with herding and agriculture developed. And in the mountainous areas of southwestern China, native peoples practiced a rudimentary agriculture.

Over one billion people—more than one-fifth of the world's total population—live within the boundaries of China in the early 1990s. While 90 percent of these people are ethnic Chinese called *Han,* the remaining one hundred million are composed of nine other major ethnic groups (and countless minor ones) speaking over thirty different languages and scores of dialects. Although China appears ethnically homogenous, especially in comparison to the great cultural diversity of India, we should not overlook its many "national minorities," as they are called. Most live on the periphery of China, in the steppes and mountainous regions that form the borders with other countries. The Han Chinese dominate the core regions of China, having extended their agrarian way of life through centuries of migration from north China south through river valleys and lowlands, assimilating the non-Chinese natives of those areas or pushing them into more remote regions.

The Imperial Chinese State

China's history is conventionally divided into the periods shown in Table 16.1. During the ancient period, lasting from about 1750–250 B.C.E., many characteristic features of Chinese civilization emerged. Settled agriculture supported cities from which aristocrats ruled peasant producers; Chinese writing evolved to the form still used today; and Chinese philosophers, starting with Confucius, began to address questions about the proper social order and mode of governance. The next period, imperial Chinese history, spans over two thousand years, from the establishment of the first imperial dynasty in 221 B.C.E. to the demise of the last dynasty in 1911 C.E. This long era can be further subdivided into the early, middle, and late empire. During the late imperial period, China collided with the expansive and aggressive Europeans, setting off a series of changes and conflicts that led to the overthrow of the last imperial dynasty in 1911, which in turn set the stage for China's twentieth-century struggles.

The creation and maintenance of the Chinese Empire over a two-thousand-year period stands as one of the great accomplishments in world history. It expanded from a core area on the north China plain to about its current size by the eighteenth century; and during the imperial period, the Chinese population increased from fifty million around 200 B.C.E. to perhaps five hundred million in 1900 C.E., and to well over one billion at the end of the twentieth century.

TABLE 16.1 Main Periods of Chinese History

Historical Period	Dynasty	Dates
Ancient China	—	1750–250 B.C.E.
Imperial China	—	221 B.C.E.–1911 C.E.
Early empire	Qin	221–207 B.C.E.
	Han	202 B.C.E.–220 C.E.
Middle empire	Sui	589–607 C.E.
	Tang	608–907
	Song	960–1279
	Yuan	1279–1368
Late empire	Ming	1368–1644
	Qing	1644–1911
Republican China	—	1911–1949
Socialist China	—	1949–present

How can we explain China's extraordinary achievement of maintaining political unity over such a prolonged period of time? An equally compelling issue involves explaining the periods of disunity or fragmentation, totaling perhaps five hundred of those two thousand years. On the side of maintaining unity, the answers have to do with the creation of a centralizing state and a highly productive economy; on the side of fragmentation, with nomadic invasions from the outside and peasant rebellions from within.

Governing and defending the Chinese Empire demanded tremendous wealth to retain the professional bureaucrats required to implement the emperor's will and to maintain the soldiers needed to protect the frontiers and keep internal peace. Both had to be paid from taxes collected from an agrarian economy. Thus, unity depended on a state sufficiently organized and powerful to extract taxes from a subject population and an economy rich enough to support the huge imperial-state edifice of bureaucrats and soldiers. Perhaps most astonishing about the Chinese Empire is that these conditions were met more often than not for two thousand years.

Properly speaking, China's imperial history began in 221 B.C.E., when a powerful tyrant who took the name Qin Shi Huang Di (or First August Sovereign of the Qin Dynasty) unified China after centuries of warfare. Known to Chinese history as a ruthless unifier, Qin Shi Huang Di established both the expectation that China should be ruled by a single sovereign and some of the material bases for that unity: he standardized weights and measures, China's written script, and axle lengths; he linked several defensive ramparts into what became the Great Wall; and he established the first state system staffed by professionals appointed by the emperor for their ability, not hereditary aristocrats whose claim to rule was based on birthright.

Although the Qin Dynasty lasted a short fourteen years (221–207 B.C.E.), the next dynasty, the Han (202 B.C.E.–220 C.E.), put the imperial state on a firm philosophical-religious basis. In a struggle to replace aristocrats who had helped found the new dynasty with bureaucrats loyal to the emperor, Han emperors turned to scholars schooled in Confucian thought. These Confucian scholars equated the political and social order of the Han Dynasty with the universe itself, and explained the change of dynasties by referring to the old Chinese idea of the "mandate of heaven."

According to this idea, heaven—a vague, impersonal, supernatural force—gave the emperor a mandate to maintain order and harmony "everywhere under heaven." As long as a dynasty maintained order, it kept the mandate to rule. But heaven could also take away the mandate if the dynasty failed to maintain order, and then bestow it on a new emperor. According to the Confucian scholars, this is what explained the rise of the Han Dynasty. The Qin emperors were so ruthless that the people revolted, evidence that heaven had withdrawn the mandate from them; the victor in the civil war that followed then claimed to have received the mandate to rule "all under heaven" as the "son of heaven."

The body of thought surrounding the mandate-of-heaven idea derived from the ancient philosopher Confucius (551–479 B.C.E.), who saw social relationships in hierarchical terms and stressed the importance of each person finding his or her proper place in that hierarchy. To Confucius, five relationships were crucial to the social order: ruler and subject, father and son, husband and wife, older and younger brother, and friends. In all but the last relationship, the former member was the superior one and the latter the inferior. Subjects, for example, owed loyalty and obedience to the ruler, and the ruler was benevolent to his subjects. With each member of society acting according to his or her station in life, social order would be preserved and the dynasty would retain the mandate of heaven. This complex of social, ethical, moral, and political thought—originating with Confucius and developed over the centuries by others—is called *Confucianism.*

In Confucianism, hierarchy ensured order. Within society, the scholarly elite was superior to all commoners; in theory, peasants were considered superior to merchants because they produced wealth rather than merely trading goods; and Confucians considered warriors to be at the bottom of the hierarchy. The Confucian ideal was not often (or ever) realized, of course, because power arising from wealth or military prowess frequently raised the fortunes of merchants and warriors. And if the truth were told, peasant farmers were always at the bottom of the real social hierarchy.

Hierarchy was as evident in the family as it was in the political system. In fact, Confucius saw the maintenance of proper hierarchy within the family as essential to social and political stability. Elders ex-

Confucius (551–479 B.C.E.) articulated an outlook on government and society that has informed Chinese culture into the late twentieth century. *The Bettmann Archive*

pected respect from those younger; parents expected strict obedience from their children, as did husbands from their wives. Within the Confucian order, regardless of social class, men were considered superior and women inferior.

Over the centuries, Confucian thought led to two quite different patterns of life, one for men and the other for women. As in the Western tradition, public roles were reserved for men, as women allegedly lacked the intellectual ability to achieve high-status positions as scholars and bureaucrats. They were limited to the private or domestic sphere of life, where they were to exercise moral influence in the home. Whatever positive might be said about Confucianism's contributions to the continuity of the Chinese Empire and the stability of Chinese culture, most modern scholars view it as a disaster for women. One writer recently put it this way: "Few societies in history have prescribed for women a more lowly status or treated them in a more routinely brutal way than traditional Confucian China."[1]

Examinations and Bureaucracy: The Civil Service System

Although the Han emperors had tried to centralize political power by replacing a military aristocracy with Confucian-trained bureaucrats, they were not wholly successful. The final victory of scholars over aristocrats as the source of state functionaries had to await the invention and universal implementation of a remarkable system of civil service examinations. That process began with the establishment of the Sui Dynasty in 589 C.E. and reached its high point under the Song Dynasty (960–1279). The first Song emperors established a vast information system that reached into each county in the empire; they reorganized the central state administration so that a prime minister and his staff came to have greater power and influence than the emperor; and they supervised a wide range of economic activities. The reforms of the civil service system adopted in the Song Dynasty from the eleventh through the thirteenth centuries significantly increased the number and quality of candidates by establishing three levels of competition, by settling on an examination format that stressed solution of practical problems, and by devising a grading system that ensured the anonymity of the candidates.

The Song civil service system was so successful that a new culture of educational achievement overtook the values and ideals of a military aristocracy: it was said that "just as good iron is not used to make nails, good men are not used to make soldiers." The preferred path to advancement was to rise through the ranks of the civil service system by taking the higher-level examinations. By the time of the Song Dynasty, then, China had succeeded in eliminating the aristocracy as a competitor of the central state, creating instead a vast central government staffed by people recruited through civil service examinations. Although the system was nominally democratic (anyone could take and pass the examinations), in practice, preparation required schooling and long hours of study, which only the wealthy could afford. And since wealth was anchored in land ownership, scholars and bureaucrats generally derived from those with large landholdings.

Thus, by 1000 C.E., China had created a centralized state to rule over a vast empire, extracting sufficient wealth from the society to maintain a large state bureaucracy and a huge army. This contrasted markedly with Europe in 1000 C.E., where political authority was fragmented under a feudal system in which military aristrocrats extracted small amounts of surplus from an agrarian economy based on serfdom. In China, the aristocracy and the military had been removed as competitors for political power. China's economic growth likewise surged ahead of Europe's, so enlarging the economy that the centralized imperial state was able to grow even stronger—maintaining a large bureaucracy to extract taxes and sustaining a huge standing army—all the while taking progressively less from the economy.

China's Economic Revolution: 700s–1200s

After the founder of the Song Dynasty reunited the country in 960 C.E. following a half-century of civil war, China would never again experience centuries-long fragmentation between dynasties. According to historian Mark Elvin, "an economic and technological revolution reduced the burden of the imperial administrative superstructure, increased the efficiency of the Chinese war machine, and created enough economic integration to be a real obstacle to renewed political fragmentation."[2] The economic revolution occurred in many fields of activity, made China the major center of innovation in the world system, and contributed much of benefit to the other civilizations of Eurasia.

In agriculture, new seeds, techniques, tools, specialization, and organization of farming resulted in impressive increases in total output as well as in the efficiency of production. These advances occurred on the large estates of wealthy landowners, not by individual peasant families. Indeed, peasants on these estates had lost most of their personal freedom and were considered serfs. But as in Europe, manors alone had the resources to undertake massive land-reclamation projects and agricultural innovation. The result was that by the thirteenth century, China had the most advanced agriculture in the world.

The creation and maintenance of roads and the emergence of cheap water transport, which allowed bulk goods such as grain to be transported long distances, aided the development of regional markets and perhaps even a national market in which agricultural produce could be sold. At the same time, the invention of paper money and credit facilitated exchange. During Song times (from the tenth to the thirteenth century), the Chinese economy became commercialized, and new and large cities developed. The city of Hangzhou, located in the lower Yangzi River region, may have had as many as one million residents, and perhaps 6 percent or 7 percent of China's total population of 100 million lived in cities of over 100,000.

China's dramatic spurt of economic growth may be compared with a similar process occurring in Europe between 1000 and 1300 C.E. At both ends of the Eurasian landmass, rapidly improving agricultural productivity provided the basis for growing long-distance trade, urbanization, and technological innovation. In China, this economic revolution sputtered to a halt, whereas in a few dynamic European centers, economic growth became self-perpetuating and continuous, despite periodic setbacks. Herein lies one of the great contrasts of world history.

At the time, however, the medieval economic revolution allowed the Song to create and maintain a large state apparatus. The Song state subsidized all scholars who passed the civil service exams, even if they could not be placed in a position, and maintained the largest and most powerful army the world had ever seen: 1.25 million strong. Instead of going to war with the northern nomadic tribes, who had again begun pressing China in the tenth and eleventh centuries, the state bought them off with annual payments of silver and silk amounting to about 2 percent of the government budget. These large expenditures required increased revenues, which the expanding economy supported. In the early Song Dynasty, tax receipts doubled those of the preceding Tang Dynasty; by the eleventh century, they were twenty times as large. The medieval economic revolution also meant that the surplus produced by the peasantry had become so enlarged that under normal conditions both the state and large landowners were able to extract sufficient wealth without the competition for peasant surplus undermining their mutual cooperation and support.

By the thirteenth century, then, the elements necessary to maintain a unified Chinese Empire had been created. The Qin Dynasty had created the imperial state in the third century B.C.E., thus bolstering the Confucian ideas that rule by a single sovereign was normal and that disunity was distinctly abnormal. The Sui and Tang destroyed the military aristocracy, a process that culminated during the Song in the flourishing of a civil service system for the recruitment of people to govern the empire. Finally, the economic revolution of the middle empire allowed the maintenance of a large state bureaucracy and standing military, and it fostered China's economic integration.

Forces of Fragmentation

Despite China's success in maintaining imperial unity and stability over many centuries, powerful forces of conflict and instability periodically erupted. The two most important were nomadic invasion and peasant rebellion.

China's riches were so splendid that a thirteenth-century traveler from Europe, Marco Polo, wondered in awe at the wealth and power of the Chinese Empire. Thus, it is not surprising that China attracted the attention of the nomadic tribes who lived beyond its borders to the north and west, in areas unsuited for settled agriculture. Ethnically different from the Han Chinese, the nomads operated a pastoral economy, raising herds of sheep, goats, cows, horses, camels, and yaks, and, in normal times, trading them for Chinese agricultural products. The Chinese considered them barbarians because they had not adopted the ways of Chinese civilization. A primary objective of all imperial dynasties was to keep the barbarians pacified and north of the Great Wall, with careful regulation of the trade conducted with them.

Whenever the military power of the Chinese Empire declined, however, the nomads invaded and sometimes conquered China. Such invasions helped bring down the Han Dynasty in the third century C.E., for instance, and in 1126 C.E. invasion split the Song empire into a north ruled by non-Chinese and a south ruled by Chinese. Sometimes the nomads grew so strong that they were able to conquer and rule all of China, as happened in the thirteenth century when Mongols led by Genghis Khan subdued the Song, and in the mid-seventeenth-century conquest by the Manchus. For most of its history, a tension thus existed between "inner China," ruled by Chinese, and "outer China," the pastoral lands roamed by the nomadic tribes. Only in the eighteenth century was outer China successfully incorporated into the empire.

VOICES
A Peasant's Story

In 1739, a young peasant in Guangxi province refused to pay rent to his landlord. A scuffle ensued, and the peasant's stepfather was killed. In the deposition that follows, the peasant told the court what had happened, providing us with an intimate look at peasant life and class relations in eighteenth-century China.

Han Fuhan is my stepfather. He had no heirs, so I became his adopted son. Stepfather was an old man and couldn't farm. I was like his own son and planted the fields to support him and stepmother. Stepfather lived in the same village as [landlord] Luo Fuyuan and certainly bore him no malice.

We rented four *sheng* of Luo Fuyuan's rice fields. In the second year of the reign of the Qianlong emperor (1737), we ate the whole harvest ourselves, and thus were 275 *jin* of rice in arrears on the rent. Luo Fuyuan came several times to collect the rent, but our family was in dire straits and couldn't clear the debt. This year (1739) stepfather became ill, so in February we pawned Luo Fuyuan's land to Tan Fufu for four ounces of silver to buy food and daily necessities. We didn't think Luo Fuyuan would find out.

But on March 15, Luo Fuyuan came to plow those fields himself. We have tilled those fields for generations, and the custom is that the landlord could not evict the tenant. This was considered a permanent tenancy. And even if we pawned the land, it was still ours to till. If the landlord

tilled it himself, we wouldn't have anything to eat. Because of this, I blocked him from plowing the fields.

Luo Fuyuan turned on me and wanted to take me to the county town to file a complaint. I refused to go. Stepfather then came and told Luo Fuyuan not to file a complaint against me. If he had something to say, the two of them could go to the county town. Luo Fuyuan then let me go, saying we would go to the village headman to discuss the matter.

Luo Fuyuan went first; stepfather and I followed behind. On the way, Luo Fuyuan cursed us mercilessly. When we got to town, Luo Fuyuan stopped; stepfather and I were still following close behind. I was very angry and struck a blow to his shoulder. Luo Fuyuan turned with his fists clenched. I saw how fierce he looked, so I jumped to the side. He hit stepfather on the side of the head, knocking him to the ground. I jumped to help stepfather up, but already he had stopped breathing. From January until that time, he had been ill and had not recovered. On that day, when he feared Luo Fuyuan and I would come to blows, even with his illness he was brave enough to come to my aid. Who would have figured that Luo Fuyuan would knock him to the ground and he would die?

Source: Translated by Robert B. Marks, from *Qing dai zu boxiao xingtai* (Forms of land rent exploitation in Qing times) (Beijing: Zhonghua shuju, 1982), pp. 490–92.

The other major force threatening China's unity was peasant rebellion. Such upheavals had brought down the Qin, Han, Yuan, and Ming dynasties and prepared the way for various barbarian invasions. The causes of these revolts varied, but they usually involved the exploitation of the peasantry by large landowners and the imperial state, both of which extracted surplus from the peasant economy.

Although peasant rebellions invariably weakened and sometimes brought down dynasties, they did not in the end have revolutionary consequences, for the imperial system was reconstituted in a new dynasty. Peasant rebellions generally challenged only the abuses of the traditional order—such as excessive taxes, arrogant officials, or neglect of public works—not its structure. No matter how massive, disruptive, or destructive China's peasant rebellions were, then, they did not bring imperial China to an end; rather they reconstituted it in another round of what traditional Chinese historians have called the *dynastic cycle*.

The Dynastic Cycle

Just as change is constant in the universe, imperial Chinese historians reasoned, so too was change in human affairs. A new dynasty received the mandate of heaven to restore harmony in the universe, whereas in the natural course of its life, corruption and moral dissipation prompted heaven to withdraw its mandate and give it to someone else. Floods, famines, and peasant rebellions signaled heaven's disfavor and foreshadowed the advent of a new dynasty, which would begin the cycle anew. So influential was the idea of the dynastic cycle that it structured Chinese conceptions of time. Rather than thinking in terms of centuries, Chinese time is dated by the year of an emperor's reign; for example, "the fortieth year of the Qianlong emperor's reign" is 1775 C.E..

Modern historians do not need to accept the idea of the mandate of heaven to understand the dynastic cycle. When a new dynasty was first formed, it destroyed the landed upper class in order to tap the financial and human resources of the empire—to "enrich the state" and "strengthen the military," as the first Qin emperor put it. Over time, a new landed elite emerged, which competed with the imperial state for these resources, while the need to maintain large military forces to keep the nomadic tribes north of the Great Wall continued. These pressures on the peasants, from both the imperial state and the landowning class, resulted in peasant rebellions that brought the dynasty down, beginning a new cycle of property redistribution.

The maintenance of a unified empire thus depended on the ability of the imperial state to extract sufficient resources from society in order to staff a central bureaucracy, maintain a large standing army, and display the splendor of court and aristocratic life. Because China was an agrarian empire, this surplus could be extracted only from the peasant producers. And until the economic revolution that began in the tenth century, the amount of surplus that could be obtained without pushing the peasants below subsistence was pretty much fixed: only expanding the population and bringing new lands under production could enlarge the resources available to the state.

But the large landowners competed directly with the state for the surplus produced by peasants: the more the state took, the less was available for the large landowners, and vice versa. And the more both took, the less was left over for peasants. The peasants' willingness and ability to revolt when the extraction of surplus threatened their subsistence put a final check on the ability of both landlords and the state to exploit the rural economy.

The Late Empire

The late imperial period encompasses China's last two dynasties, the Ming (1368–1644) and the Qing (pronounced "ching") (1644–1911). The transition between them represents the last dynastic transition in imperial Chinese history. In many ways, the fall of the Ming Dynasty in 1644 followed the pattern of earlier dynastic cycles. The last Ming emperors were largely incompetent and corrupt. The later emperors' harems swelled to more than three thousand women, and the twenty thousand eunuchs hired to watch over them meddled in palace affairs to enrich themselves. They so pilfered the treasury that in 1643, when the last Ming emperor inspected the treasury room, he found nothing but a small red box and a few faded receipts.

Other troubles plagued the Ming rulers. Population had increased from 65 million to 150 million in the two centuries after 1400; then around 1600, cooler weather reduced the harvests, and plague produced death and starvation. Impoverished peasants lost their land and in many cases their freedom to large landowners, who hid their lands from the tax rolls. Roving bands of peasants soon linked up to form large peasant armies, which contested with the Ming armies for control of the empire. After more than a decade of warfare, in 1644, a peasant army under the command of Li Zicheng captured Beijing and brought down the Ming Dynasty.

At this point, however, the completion of the dynastic cycle took a new turn. For rather than the peasant rebels' establishing a new dynasty, Manchu armies—nomadic warriors from many tribes unified into a formidable military force—poured into China from north of the Great Wall, suppressed the rebels, and established the new Qing Dynasty. Receiving aid from Ming generals and others who wanted to restore order, the Manchu rulers reunified China by the early 1680s and then sent their armies to conquer border peoples, more than doubling the country's land area during the eighteenth century. Ethnically different from the Han Chinese, the Manchus remained sepa-

A provincial member of the scholar gentry with his family. *Library of Congress*

rate from their conquered subjects while using Chinese bureaucratic techniques to govern the empire. They ruled China until 1911.

Besides the intervention of the Manchus, the transition from Ming to Qing differed from earlier dynastic changes in one other significant way: China was becoming part of the emerging global system. As Europeans moved into Asia in the sixteenth century in search of new trade, silver flowed into China to pay for the silk, porcelain, and gold exported to Europe. Much of the silver came from Japan in trade conducted by the Dutch through the port of Nagasaki, but an equal amount came from the mines of the New World. One historian has estimated that in the first third of the seventeenth century, half of the precious metals extracted from the Americas wound up in China.[3]

The large import of silver accelerated the commercialization of agriculture in the Yangzi Delta region and fueled inflation. However, when European wars disrupted trade in the early 1640s, imports of silver into China dropped to almost nothing. This in turn brought on a contraction of the Chinese economy and contributed to economic collapse and the victory of the peasant rebels over the Ming Dynasty.[4]

By the mid-seventeenth century, China was very much a part of the emerging global order. But its fate turned out to be very different from that of Europe, where the processes of state formation and capitalist development continued to transform society. China's historical development during late imperial times was important because it shaped the society that had to encounter an increasingly aggressive and intrusive Europe.

State and Society in Late Imperial China

Historians disagree about whether the Chinese state in late imperial times was getting stronger and more absolutist, as was occurring in Europe, or becoming weaker vis-à-vis society and the economy. The creation of the civil service had eliminated the need of the emperor to rely on an aristocracy to govern. Thus, the central government strengthened itself at the expense of local interests. The founder and first emperor of the Ming Dynasty, Zhu Yuanzhang, continued this process by gathering even more authority in the hands of the emperor: he abolished the post of prime minister and made all of his officials subject to flogging with a bamboo stick. From the late 1300s to 1911, Chinese emperors assumed the duties of the prime minister, ruling through the state bureaucracy, which they personally headed, as well as reigning over the empire. While the Ming and Qing emperors gained more control over the central bureaucracy, however, there were indications that the state itself was loosening its grip on Chinese society.

In contrast to earlier times, the burden of the state and military on society lightened as the economy grew faster than the revenue needs of the government. At the beginning of the Ming, for instance, the land tax, the primary source of state revenue, took about 15 percent to 20 percent of total economic output. During Qing times (1644–1911), it dropped to about 5 percent. In short, the financial drain of the government on the economy was greatly reduced in late imperial China. This enabled the Chinese Empire to remain integrated and largely immune to the pressures of fragmentation that had plagued the country earlier.

Economic growth also laid the foundation for China's continuous population increase. Though punctuated by several periods of contraction, the number of people rose from about 100 million in 1200 to 400 million in 1800, reaching 584 million by 1953. But even with a growing population and the more complex economy, the actual size of the late imperial state did not increase. The number of administrative units, for instance, stayed basically the same. During Ming and Qing times, China was divided into eighteen provinces, each with a governor; each province had ten or so prefectures, each of which had six to eight counties. The official at each level was responsible to his superior, and all answered to the emperor and his staff in Beijing. To govern China in this manner required only about 20,000 officials and another 7,000 military officers. But whereas in 1400 a county had a population of perhaps 50,000 governed by a magistrate and a small staff, by 1800 that magistrate was responsible for 200,000 people.

Thus, many scholars now think that from the mid-sixteenth century on, the Chinese state lost power to other levels of society, in particular to a group known as the lower gentry. These were people who had passed to a certain level in the civil service examinations but were unable to be placed in official positions. Although it was a great honor to pass even the lowest-level exam, in practice only those who succeeded at the highest level became eligible for appointment to one of the twenty thousand posts in the state bureaucracy. Around 1800, China had about one million living degree holders, 47,500 of whom had degrees high enough to make them eligible for official appointment.[5]

Because the state bureaucracy extended only to the level of county magistrate, the state came to rely on the lower gentry to govern the villages and towns of rural China. Usually owning considerable amounts of land that they rented to peasant tenants, the lower gentry became increasingly powerful during the late imperial period. In the last years of the Ming Dynasty (early seventeenth century), gentry managers took over the many tasks of local administration such as firefighting, social welfare, water control, and public security.[6] This devolution continued slowly during the eighteenth and nineteenth centuries. It became particularly important in the middle of the nineteenth century, when the gentry acted to suppress a massive peasant rebellion, and it accelerated in the early twentieth century, after the Qing Dynasty collapsed in 1911.

The destruction of the aristocracy, the development of the civil service system, and the growth of both the economy and the population were the conditions that made a unified Chinese Empire possible. But they also set in motion a process that tugged at that unity by creating a local landowning-scholar-gentry elite whose interests lay in the preservation of the agrarian status quo, not in economic development.

Chinese Women in the Late Empire

All of the institutions of late imperial China described so far—the state with its bureaucracy and military forces; the farms, businesses, and markets that comprised the economy; and the Confucian family—were created and dominated by men. Imperial China was a patriarchy, and the history of China is the history of patriarchal institutions. Long neglected by scholars, the history of women's roles in China has only recently been the subject of serious research.

Women lived their lives in a gender hierarchy where men set the rules of conduct and constructed the stereotypes of proper behavior for women, conveniently summarized in the Confucian concept of the "Three Bonds of Obedience": to obey fathers when young and unmarried; to obey husbands when married; and to obey adult sons when widowed. The "three obediences" marked the stages of life for women; they were in many respects considered the property of men. Women were sold into marriage or prostitution, and from one marriage to another, as the story in the box on page 338 illustrates.

A woman's life chances in late imperial China were not good. Husbands preferred male children; the birth of a girl was considered bad luck; and the birth of two girls without a boy was considered a disaster. Girls were both a bother and an expense; they could bring neither economic benefit to the family nor produce male heirs, since they were married out of the family at the youngest possible age. Training and education thus were lost on girls. Female infanticide—the killing of unwanted girls at birth—thus was not unknown, resulting in skewed sex ratios with men greatly outnumbering women.

Most women were limited to marriage, childbearing, and then celibate widowhood. Education, jobs, and careers were unknown to the women of late im-

VOICES
A Woman's Story

The sharp subordination of women in nineteenth-century China is clearly illustrated in this first-hand account of a ten-year period in the life of a young woman, ending when she was but twenty-four years old.

My parents were always kind to me, and would gladly have kept me at home until I was older, but my father died, and when I was fourteen my mother was forced to marry me. I went into a family in another village, and she got two [ounces of silver] for me. I had never seen any of that family before I went to live in it. My husband, who was just my own age, hated me as soon as he saw me. There are a great many couples who hate at first sight. My mother-in-law was not unkind to me. I cooked the rice, fed the ducks and pigs, and helped her in the house all I could. But my husband was very cruel to me; he would not let me sleep beside him on the pine boards of the bedstead, but made me lie on the mud floor beside the bed; he had the coverlet, and I had nothing over me, and I used to lie and shiver all night. I did not tell anyone how he treated me, lest that should make him more cruel. But he got to hating me so that every night he took a knife to bed with him, and told me that he would keep it there ready to kill me if he felt the desire to do it in the night. My mother-in-law saw how much he hated me, and fearing the consequences of keeping me with him, she engaged a matchmaker to marry me to someone else, and when I was sixteen I was married, to a man at the village of Be Chia.

My mother-in-law received five [ounces of silver] for me. This second husband was twenty-seven years old, and a gambler. His father was dead; the ancestral property had been divided among the sons, and the mother lived with her children, going daily to the house of each by turn. . . . My husband could not stop [gambling], and continually lost money. There was nothing for his mother to eat, and she ceased to come to our house for any meals, but lived with her [other] sons. I had then three children—two boys and a girl. It seemed likely that we would starve. My husband had no money to gamble with either. He said to me: "You have a hard time with me; the children are thin, and you are miserable; it would be much better for you to be married to some kind man who would give you enough to eat. I will find such an [*sic*] one, and marry you to him. I myself am going away to foreign countries to seek my fortune, and I shall never come back." I assented to this, for I saw that the children would otherwise starve.

So my husband himself secretly took me and the children to Kam E, the village in which I was born, and to the house of the man to whom he had engaged me. He got five [ounces of silver] for me and the children. He did not let anyone know about my going, because if people had known it, all the poor in the village would have come out and intercepted us on the road, and made him pay a fine. . . . That is [what] people do when a man marries off a wife that ha[s] borne him children. I did not cry at all when he left me, for I thought I could be no more wretched [than when] I had been with him. He spent the money he got for me in gambling, and did not go to foreign parts, but died soon afterward. I was then twenty-four years old, my oldest son was five years old, and my daughter was ten months old.

Source: As told to Adele Fielde about 1880 in Guangdong province. Quoted in Margery Wolf, *Revolution Postponed: Women in Contemporary China* (Stanford: Stanford University Press, 1985), pp. 3–4.

perial China. In some rural areas women worked in the fields, but for many such work was impossible because they had had their feet bound in early childhood to produce small, deformed feet that Chinese men had come to fetishize. Mothers felt that bound feet would improve the marriage prospects for their daughters and the practice became a rite of passage—part of becoming a woman—in every social class. The bound feet immobilized women, keeping them in and close to the home, and suggested that

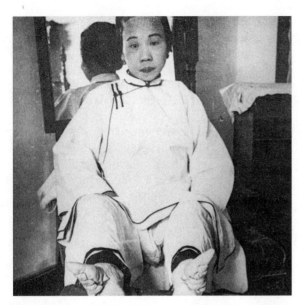

Footbinding was but one of the many restrictions endured by generations of Chinese women and girls. *Visual Studies Workshop*

their economic contribution was of little value. If a father, husband, or adult son mistreated a woman, she had but one option: suicide; divorce was unknown.

There was one way in which women could carve out a limited sphere of independent action—"by creating a family from her own body." As mother, she won the loyalty of her children—boys and girls alike—with her love, affection, and support; the Confucian family code had prescribed a remote role for the father. A skillful mother thus could influence family affairs through her male children as they grew older and more important in family and village life.[7]

Resistance to these restricted roles for women was rare indeed. Only in the nineteenth and twentieth centuries, when Chinese reformers began to criticize their society, did the oppressive structure of the family and the abuses of women begin to be discussed. But that occurred only after the Western intrusion into Chinese history posed a challenge to China's very survival.

Why Not Capitalism?

In comparing China's development with that of Europe, we are struck by a mystery: despite vigorous and continued economic activity, capitalism did not develop in China. By the eighteenth century, China's economy was sophisticated, complex, commercialized, and beginning to be involved in the capitalist world economy. The industrial sector, though small, included mining and smelting, textiles, ceramics, shipbuilding, and food processing, to mention just a few of the most important industries. Agriculture, accounting for the bulk of China's late imperial economy, was regionally specialized, with some areas growing industrial crops, such as cotton, sugarcane, mulberry trees (the leaves of which fed silkworms), tea, and tobacco, and oil-producing crops, such as sesame and rapeseed. New and better rice varieties, some of which allowed planting on drier land or double- and triple-cropping, also increased agricultural productivity. The trade flows of the capitalist world system brought to China not only silver but also New World crops such as peanuts, corn, sweet potatoes, and potatoes. Furthermore, a significant amount of agricultural production entered local and long-distance markets.

Also stimulating the agricultural economy was the emergence of a rural economy based on the peasant family farm. During the preceding Ming Dynasty, large estates owned by nobles or powerful commoners and worked by serfs and servile tenants dominated the Chinese countryside. The large peasant uprisings at the end of the Ming severely weakened this agrarian system, and the new Manchu rulers abolished it by acknowledging the economic and personal freedom of the peasants. This freedom then allowed peasants to specialize and produce for the market, further stimulating economic activity.

By the end of the eighteenth century, rural China had taken on the class structure that would remain into the twentieth century. It was a structure with five main groups: landlords (those who rented out their land), rich peasants (those who employed a few hired hands), middle peasants (those who tilled the family farm with their own labor), poor peasants (those who rented others' land and/or sometimes worked for rich peasants), and landless rural laborers. The rich peasants, who accounted for about 10 percent of the rural population, acted much like capitalist farmers, hiring labor and managing their farms to maximize profit. But managerial farming was never able to expand; as a result, the small peasant farm, worked by middle and poor peasants to meet their subsistence needs, rather than market demand, continued to dominate Chinese rural life.

During the first 150 years of the Qing dynasty (from 1650 to 1800), this economy was able to accommodate a significant growth in population (from about 150 million to 400 million people) without generally declining living standards and in the absence of technological breakthroughs that characterized the development of capitalism in Europe. This situation has given rise to a highly debated negative question about Chinese history: Given the economic revolution of the middle empire and the highly sophisticated and productive economy achieved in the eighteenth century, why did capitalism and industrialization not develop in China?

Historians have provided many different answers to this question. No longer do they put much stock in explanations proposed in the 1950s that China's traditional Confucian culture was ill-adapted to the requirements of the modern world. Confucianism, it was assumed, blocked China's modernization because it devalued mercantile activity and promoted orthodoxy and stability over experimentation and change. But so did the Christian culture of Europe. And the recent history of rapid economic growth in Taiwan, Singapore, and Korea—all of which maintained key elements of Confucian culture—demonstrates that Confucianism is no barrier to modern economic growth and may actually support it.

Culture, then, is not an adequate explanation for the pattern of China's economic history. Recently, the focus among historians seeking such an explanation has been on China's late imperial social and economic structure. Indeed, the very sophistication of China's economy, paradoxically, has become the basis of a compelling explanation as to why full-fledged capitalism did not develop there. In Europe, unlike in China, scarcity, bottlenecks, and labor shortages spurred technological inventiveness and the search for new means of profit making. However, as historian Mark Elvin has argued, it may be precisely because the Chinese economy functioned so efficiently and because labor was so plentiful that Chinese farmers, merchants, and artisans felt little need to tinker with new machinery to increase production and productivity. Still, this is surprising, for China had a long and impressive tradition of scientific and technological accomplishments that rivaled those of any other civilization and surpassed most of them. The list includes creating the decimal point and blank space for zero in the Han Dynasty; solving linear equations during Song times; building astronomic clocks; inventing movable-block printing; casting iron (fifteen centuries before its achievement in Europe); and concocting gunpowder and then using it in warfare as early as the eleventh century, just to mention a few world-significant inventions.

But just as China's medieval economic revolution did not continue beyond the thirteenth century, neither did its scientific and technological progress persist into the late imperial period. As Europe was taking off into its modern industrial development, China's science and technology stagnated. The explanation, according to historian Joseph Needham, lies in the "enormous difference in social and economic structure between traditional China and the traditional West," particularly the difference between an aristocratic, military-based feudalism in the West and a centralized empire run by bureaucrats in China.[8] Needham argues that the Chinese state defined some intellectual pursuits as orthodox and hence worthy of support, such as the calendar, mathematics, and engineering, and others as unorthodox, such as alchemy, which the state suppressed. He also argues that the imperial state attracted the most highly trained and sophisticated minds in the empire, rewarding them for state administrative service and drawing them away from independent scientific speculation and technological tinkering.

Needham's thesis that China's imperial state retarded science and technology has been used to explain the absence of capitalist development as well. Although late imperial China had a substantial class of wealthy merchants, the state limited entrepreneurial initiative in many ways. For example, the government monopolized the production and distribution of salt, iron, and other important goods and regulated merchant guilds. With ready access to ample revenues through its ability to tax an expanding economy, the state did not need the merchant community for financial support, as did the less securely established monarchies of Europe. In the face of the scholar-gentry's prestige, merchants had little social status and even less political power. The existing system of values and rewards led many to invest their wealth in land in an effort to acquire gentry status, rather than in industry to make more money.

Nor did international trade serve to stimulate the economy and provide for the accumulation of mercantile wealth. The Ming court in 1433 abruptly terminated a series of massive maritime expeditions that had taken Chinese ships into the Indian Ocean

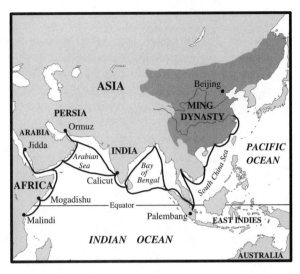

MAP 16.2 Ming Dynasty Voyages

and as far as the east African coast (see Map 16.2). Begun in 1405 shortly after the formation of the Ming dynasty and intended to extend the power and prestige of the Ming throughout Asia, the flotillas of more than twenty Chinese ships manned by twenty thousand sailors under the command of the Chinese Muslim admiral Zheng He established contact with lands and peoples in what is now Southeast Asia, India, the Persian Gulf (including Egypt), and east Africa. These early maritime expeditions demonstrated the technical and organizational lead of China over Portugal and Spain.

However, by the time those European maritime powers set sail to explore nearly a hundred years later, China had halted the maritime expeditions to concentrate on protecting its northern inner-Asian frontiers from Mongolian attacks and pressure. China's expansion thereafter was internal, especially to the south, where millions of tiny peasant holdings absorbed the population increase but without contributing to the accumulation of investable wealth or to economic growth. As long as the imperial state was committed to maintaining an agrarian economy of small producers, there was little chance that industrial capitalism would develop.[9]

By the nineteenth century, China's economy had entered a period of stagnation. The imperial state, the smooth market mechanism, the fragmentation of farms into tiny plots tilled by peasant families, and landlord-gentry use of surplus for unproductive purposes all contributed to it. For the Qing Dynasty, the timing of this economic stagnation could not have been worse. For it occurred just as Europe's economic development exploded with a capitalist dynamism that increasingly encompassed China. Furthermore, it coincided with the final stages of a dynastic cycle in which the forces of imperial dissolution became ever more apparent. Paradoxically, China's success in creating and maintaining a centralized empire left it unprepared to face European states whose military power and views of the world had been formed in their peculiar system of competitive, warring, independent states.

The Decline of the Qing Dynasty

Signs of dynastic decline appeared during the last years of the Qianlong emperor's reign (1736–1795). Corruption began to sap the central administration. Officials throughout the empire commanded graft from their underlings, while the emperor's bodyguard, a man named He Shen, rose to become the most powerful and feared man in China, amassing a fortune along the way. The fighting ability of the Manchu armies, known as "banners," which had conquered China in the mid-seventeenth century, deteriorated during the eighteenth century as salaries and training decreased.

Under these conditions, peasant dissatisfactions, never far beneath the surface, bubbled to the top in the activities of "secret societies," the Triads in south China and the White Lotus sect in north China. Government prosecution of White Lotus leaders prompted the Buddhist sect to revolt in 1793. The Manchu banners, corrupt and uninterested in fighting, proved unable to suppress the rebellion, which spread throughout central China. Only after landowning gentry raised their own militias was the revolt put down in 1804. By the turn of the nineteenth century, then, the Qing Dynasty had passed its golden age and was entering a period of decline.

I Conclusion

There is more than a touch of ethnocentrism in asking the question about the absence of capitalist and industrial development in China. It seems to assume European standards of measurement and to see history as a race to the finish line of industrial society and global domination. Europe got there first; therefore, China "failed." But the main thrust of China's imperial history revolved around the creation and maintenance of an empire, rather than capitalist economic development. And in the pursuit of a stable system, the Chinese were exceptionally successful: over the millennia, they created an imperial state legitimized by Confucian ideology; they removed the aristocracy; and they knit the country together economically. All of this provided for a stable imperial China. This was the China that encountered Europeans in the sixteenth and seventeenth centuries as they began exploring and remaking the world.

Notes

1. Kay Ann Johnson, *Women, the Family, and Peasant Revolution in China* (Chicago: University of Chicago Press, 1983), p. 1.

2. Mark Elvin, *The Pattern of the Chinese Past* (Stanford: Stanford University Press, 1973), p. 69. This section is based on Elvin's analysis.

3. This section is based on Frederic Wakeman, Jr., "China and the Seventeenth-Century Crisis," *Late Imperial China* 7 (June 1986): and Wakeman's *The Great Enterprise* (Berkeley: University of California Press, 1985).

4. William S. Atwell, "Notes on Silver, Foreign Trade, and the Late Ming Economy," *Ch'ing-shih wen-t'i* 8 (Dec. 1977): 22.

5. Albert Feuerwerker, *State and Society in Eighteenth-Century China* (Ann Arbor: University of Michigan Center for Chinese Studies, 1976), p. 39.

6. William T. Rowe, "Modern Chinese Social History," in *Reliving the Past: The Worlds of Social History,* ed. Olivier Zunz (Chapel Hill: University of North Carolina Press, 1985), p. 267.

7. Margery Wolf, *Revolution Postponed: Women in Contemporary China* (Stanford: Stanford University Press, 1985), p. 9.

8. Joseph Needham, *Science in Traditional China* (Hong Kong: Chinese University Press, 1981), p. 23.

9. Ramon Myers, *The Chinese Economy Past and Present* (Belmont, Calif.: Wadsworth, 1980), pp. 52–55.

Chapter **17**

"Foreign Devils": China and Western Imperialism, 1500–1900

The Chinese Empire, confident in its millennia-old imperial splendor, collided with the expansionist West. Beginning in the sixteenth century, contact along the edges of these two powerful worlds grew, until the nineteenth century, when the power born of European industrialization tipped the balance against China. Chinese society, which had developed to the rhythms of empire formation and dissolution, then became increasingly incorporated into the emerging capitalist world system as the pace of economic and technological development pushed Europe far ahead of China. Following a period of painful dislocation in the nineteenth century, new patterns of historical development emerged in the twentieth, woven from the warp of China's imperial past and the woof of its encounter with the modern world.

Three related themes chart this historic, abrupt, and painful transition. First, the shattering impact of the West, which placed this proud and ancient empire in the position of a semicolony by the end of the nineteenth century. Second, the beginning of China's modern revolution, with a peasant-based rebellion in the 1850s, a full century before the Communist party consolidated that revolution in 1949. And, third, the failure of China's traditional ruling group to carry out a conservative modernization that might have preserved the old order.

In the process, many of China's cultural values and assumptions were called sharply into question, and new social groups made their appearance as capitalist industry gained a toehold in the country. All of this occurred in the context of growing political, social, and economic tensions reflected in peasant uprisings, rampant official corruption, and a rapidly growing population. The combined effect of a quickening internal momentum for change and devastating external pressures produced in the twentieth century a massive social revolution that swept away the old order and imperialist influence alike.

Why did China's fortunes change so dramatically in the course of a single century? Why was it unable to follow Japan's example in successfully modernizing and maintaining its political independence? Why did China's encounter with the modern world foster a social upheaval far more profound and far-reaching than anything experienced in India or the Middle East? These are some of the larger issues this chapter and the next will explore.

From Trade to Imperialism: China and the West

The eighteenth-century Chinese empire was large, powerful, well governed, rich, and unchallenged. But during the nineteenth century, the powerful and aggressive capitalist nations of the West—Britain, France, Germany, and the United States—posed a terrible challenge to China. Could the country maintain its integrity as a political unit and avoid the colonial fate of Africa, India, and Indochina? Could it fashion a state sufficiently powerful to defend itself against these industrialized aggressors? The central dilemma confronting the Chinese ruling elite was how to meet the harsh demands of the modern world while preserving the traditional social, economic, and cultural world of the empire and Confucian society. Ultimately, that dilemma proved unsolvable, and China was forced to radically transform its society and culture in order to save its independence as a nation.

The dilemma facing China was a wholly new and perplexing situation. For well over a thousand years, China had faced military challenges only from the nomadic barbarians to the north and west; its other neighbors, far from challenging China's cultural superiority, adopted much that Chinese civilization had to offer. And for three hundred years, it had successfully applied its conception of the world to relations with European powers. Given this history, it is no wonder that China found it extremely difficult to deal with the European intrusions of the nineteenth century.

The World According to the Chinese

Until the early nineteenth century, China was an empire that conceived of itself as the Central Kingdom to which all other peoples were subordinate. Regarding the empire as wholly self-sufficient, imperial officials considered foreign trade a form of tribute that symbolized the emperor's benevolent attitude toward less cultured peoples. Trade was thus a privilege bestowed on foreigners. It was not a right they automatically enjoyed; nor was it considered central to the well-being of the Chinese Empire.

In this worldview, China alone represented civilization, and all others were barbarians to one degree or another, depending on the extent to which they participated in Chinese civilization and accepted its cultural hegemony. Thus, Japanese emperors and Korean kings, who recognized the suzerainty, or dominance, of the Chinese by sending tribute missions to the emperor, were more civilized than Mongolian chieftains or the Portuguese traders and English sailors who began to arrive at the end of the sixteenth century. But all were inferior to the Chinese, whose emperor, the Son of Heaven, acted to ensure peace and harmony in the entire universe. The notion that China was merely one of any number of equal civilizations or nations was utterly alien to the Chinese conception of the world.

Unlike the Egyptian, the Mesopotamian, or even the Roman Empire, China had never confronted another imperial power sufficiently strong to challenge these views. This was due in part to the natural barriers. The Gobi Desert to the north, the Himalayan Mountains to the west, and the Pacific Ocean to the east and south all served to isolate and protect China. Contacts with Indian and Roman civilizations were sparse and limited mostly to trade conducted by intermediaries. In East Asia, China *was* civilization, and its claims to that effect were never challenged.

Despite impressive natural barriers, the Chinese state maintained large and powerful military forces to keep at bay the various nomadic peoples of the central Asian steppe. Indeed, the Great Wall of China was designed to keep the nomads out, and the million-soldier armies maintained by the Song and Ming dynasties served the same purpose. Nonetheless, nomads periodically did invade from the north and sometimes succeeded in capturing and ruling China or parts of it. But even then, the empire remained distinctively Chinese. As Genghis Khan discovered, China could be conquered, but not ruled, from horseback. For the task of governing a large agrarian empire, barbarian rulers needed Chinese officials with their extensive experience in state management. Over time, the barbarian invaders became "Sinicized" and adopted Chinese culture, rather than China's becoming "barbarized." China simply absorbed its foreign rulers.

As a land-based empire, China's military expertise was not in naval defense and warfare but in protecting against nomadic invaders from the north. Significantly, the early Westerners who approached and then threatened China were maritime powers, first the Portuguese and Dutch and then the British.

Dealing with the West on China's Terms: 1500–1800

When European traders first ventured into East Asian waters in the sixteenth and seventeenth centuries in search of spices and other luxury items, they encountered a Chinese civilization that was already two millennia old and that had been unified since the thirteenth century. Although China represented the outermost edge of the emerging European capitalist world economy, for three centuries China was sufficiently strong and the Europeans sufficiently weak to ensure that China dictated the terms of the relationship. This is evident in their dealings with European missionaries and traders.

From the late Ming Dynasty until the early eighteenth century, about five hundred Christian missionaries came to China, initially Portuguese friars but increasingly members of the Society of Jesus, or Jesuits. The first to find real favor with China's rulers were the Jesuits, for they adopted Chinese dress, learned the Chinese language, and generally accommodated their religious ideas and rituals to those of China in ways similar to the middle kingdom's other tributary relationships. The most famous Jesuit was Matteo Ricci, who lived in China from 1583 until his death in 1610. Like many other missionaries, Ricci was well schooled in Western philosophy and science and was China's source of considerable knowledge about the West. From the missionaries the Chinese learned the art of making cannons and modern maps, the use of Western astronomy to construct accurate calendars, and the latest advances in mathematics.

Controversies within the Catholic church over whether Chinese converts could continue their Confucian ancestral rites contributed to the missionaries' loss of favor with the early Qing emperors. By the early eighteenth century, most missionaries had been forced to leave. Ironically, China thus lost its best contact with the world of Western science and technology just as the political and industrial revolutions would transform first Europe and then the world. But it was Europe's traders, far more than its missionaries, who made the deepest inroads into China.

Until 1685, European trade with China was meager and sporadic. But then the emperor Kangxi (reigned 1661–1722) lifted the restrictions and opened customs houses in four ports. In the ensuing decades, trade gravitated toward the large southern city of Guangzhou (Canton), a historic commercial center. Then, in 1759, the Qianlong emperor restricted Western trade to Guangzhou only, where it could be more easily controlled.

Although allowed to establish factories, or agency warehouses, on the waterfront in Guangzhou, Western merchants could not trade freely. Instead, they had to conduct business only with Chinese commercial firms, known as *cohongs,* which had received special monopolies from the emperor. The fees, gratuities, outright bribes, and other restrictions that marked this commerce generally bothered Western merchants, who pressed with increasing insistence the virtues of free trade. Attempts to revise the Guangzhou system, however, met with little success.

Nonetheless, the British were not about to withdraw from the China trade. It had become an integral economic ingredient in their emerging network of global commerce. Under the Guangzhou system, British trade, monopolized by the British East India

Company, fast outstripped that of all other Western nations, a situation that reflected Britain's rise to economic and political dominance in Europe. Its early trade with China had been primarily in luxury goods and medicinal herbs, for which the British tried unsuccessfully to exchange woolens and then simply paid for, mainly with silver bullion.

As this trade expanded and as tea became an everyday beverage in England, more and more silver flowed into China. This irritating inability to find Western products the Chinese would buy was aggravated when the American Revolution cut off British access to Latin American silver, which it had used to balance its China trade. The East India Company went in search of another commodity with which it could sustain a trade that had become so important in the workings of the capitalist world system. What it found was opium.

The Chinese had long used small amounts of opium for medicinal purposes, and as the East India Company came to depend on it to pay for its tea, the increased supplies and addictive nature of the drug created a ready market. Still, its importation was illegal; therefore, it had to be smuggled into the country, and in growing amounts. This illegal trade surged after 1815, when the East India Company lowered its price, and again in 1834, when the company lost its monopoly on trade with China and private merchants steamed into the lucrative exchange. At this point, American companies jumped into the trade, becoming the second-largest exporter of opium to China and greatly increasing its availability. In 1835 alone, 27,000 chests of opium, weighing about 133 pounds each and selling for 17 million ounces of silver, entered the country.

The opium trade was ugly, and its effects were as baneful as the financial stakes were high. It corrupted Chinese officials, who were bribed to turn their heads when boats laden with opium chests arrived. It vastly increased the number of addicts, whose numbers may have reached ten million by the mid-1830s. The trade stimulated a massive outflow of silver amounting to some thirty-four million ounces during the 1830s. And peasants, who paid taxes in copper cash, found their charges increased as the copper-silver exchange rate was altered, and they may well have faced increased rents as gentry landlords sought more money to cover an opium habit.

The Qing government knew it had a drug problem with far-reaching economic, social, and political repercussions, and by the late 1830s, it acted decisively. Strict enforcement of the regulations against opium use

VOICES
The Chinese Emperor and King George III

In 1793, the British sent a mission to Beijing under the leadership of Lord Macartney to open up all of China for British trade. In reply, the British received a stinging rebuke from China's Qianlong emperor in the form of a famous letter to King George III. The letter disclosed both the Chinese conception of the world and their continuing ability to enforce that view on Europeans, even at the dawn of the nineteenth century.

You, O King, from afar have yearned after the blessings of our civilization, and in your eagerness to come into touch with our converting influence have sent an embassy across the sea bearing a memorial. I have already taken note of your respectful spirit of submission, have treated your mission with extreme favor and loaded it with gifts, besides issuing a mandate to you, O King, and honoring you with the bestowal of valuable presents. Thus has my indulgence been manifested. Yesterday your Ambassador petitioned my Ministers to memorialize me regarding your trade with China, but his proposal is not consistent with our dynastic usage and cannot be entertained. Hitherto, all European nations, including your own country's barbarian merchants, have carried on their trade with Our Celestial Empire at Guangzhou. Such has been the procedure for years, although Our Celestial Empire possesses all things in prolific abundance and lacks no product within its borders. There was therefore no need to import the manufactures of outside barbarians in exchange for our own produce.... Nevertheless, I do not forget the lonely remoteness of your island, cut off from the world by intervening wastes of sea, nor do I overlook your excusable ignorance of the usages of Our Celestial Empire. I have consequently commanded my Ministers to enlighten your Ambassador on the subject, and have ordered the departure of your mission.... If, after the receipt of this explicit decree, you lightly give ear to the representations of your subordinates and allow your barbarian merchants to proceed to Zhejiang and Tianjin, with the object of landing and trading there, the ordinances of my Celestial Empire are strict in the extreme, and the local officials, both civil and military, are bound reverently to obey the law of the land. Should your vessels touch the shore, your merchants will assuredly never be permitted to land or to reside there, but will be subject to instant expulsion. In that event your barbarian merchants will have had a long journey for nothing. Do not say that you were not warned in due time! Tremblingly obey and show no negligence! A special mandate!

Source: Harley Farnsworth MacNair, *Modern Chinese History, Selected Readings* (Shanghai: Commercial Press, Ltd., 1923), pp. 2–9. The transliteration of place names has been changed to be consistent with current usage.

and smuggling began in 1838, and the British firms most involved in the trade began to lose money. Then, in the spring of 1839, the man newly appointed to suppress the trade, Commissioner Lin, seized and destroyed twenty thousand chests of opium.

Opium Wars and Unequal Treaties

British traders and commercial organizations in London immediately began pressing their government for military action to reopen the China trade, to obtain an indemnity for losses suffered, and to create new and freer conditions for commerce. The British government willingly complied with the wishes of the opium smugglers. Advances in British technology had changed the military balance of power as steam-powered gunboats, perfected in the British East India Company's conquest of Burma in the 1820s, became available for use in China. In early 1840, an expeditionary naval force arrived, and after two years of sporadic fighting, British warships sailed up the Yangzi River and trained their cannons on the city of Nanjing.

An opium den in nineteenth-century Guangzhou. *The Library of Congress*

The Qing court saw the futility of any further resistance and decided to negotiate an end to the hostilities in the Treaty of Nanjing, signed on 29 August 1842.

Besides agreeing to pay a $21 million indemnity to the British and ceding the island of Hong Kong, the treaty required opening five ports to trade, fixing the tariff on imported goods at a low 5 percent, granting "extraterritoriality" to foreigners, and accepting the "most-favored-nation" clause. Extraterritoriality meant that foreign nationals would be subject not to Chinese laws but to the laws of their own country; the most-favored-nation clause meant that the concessions China granted to any one foreign country would apply to all of them. As a result, other Western nations, in particular the United States and France, benefited from the First Opium War.

The Treaty of Nanjing was the first of several agreements collectively known as the *unequal treaties,* which turned China into a semicolony by the turn of the twentieth century. Unable and probably unwilling to rule the country directly, the West-

ern imperialist powers settled for a weakened Qing state to provide sufficient social order for the conduct of business. The Second Opium War, in 1856–1858, and the 1860 Convention of Beijing, which concluded it, furthered China's subordination to the West: it opened eleven more ports to foreign trade (see Map 17.1); allowed foreigners the right to travel around China and to buy land; opened the country to missionaries and required the Chinese government to protect them; granted Western vessels and gunboats access to certain of China's inland waterways; and, finally, legalized the opium trade. As a result, China's economy became open to the influences of the world market; its sovereignty was sharply curtailed; Western manufactured goods flowed into the country; and, increasingly, Chinese were forced to think of themselves not as the center of the civilized world but as just one of many nations in a world of nation-states, and an oppressed and beleaguered one at that. It would be hard to imagine a more profound humiliation for the ruling class of the middle kingdom.

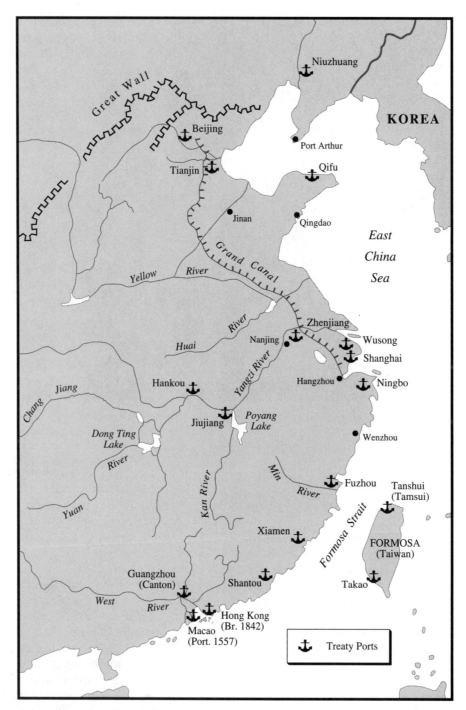

MAP 17.1 Treaty Ports in 1874

The Imperialist Penetration of China: 1860–1895

Following this painful opening, the Western presence in China grew gradually until the end of the nineteenth century. Then, strengthened by continued and rapid industrialization and driven by the competition among themselves, the imperialist powers rapidly expanded their influence and control. China was further defeated by the French in 1884–1885 and by Japan a decade later, opening the floodgates for further imperialist penetration and domination.

In both cases, war was sparked by conflicting claims to tributary states on China's border. Following the war with France, China was forced to conclude a treaty that turned all of Vietnam into a French protectorate and opened southwest China to French trade. In the Sino-Japanese War of 1894–1895, the issue was control of Korea, likewise a tributary state to China. In this case, the Japanese, who had been extraordinarily successful with their modernization program, handily defeated the numerically superior Chinese navy and sank half of it. In the 1895 Treaty of Shimonoseki, which ended the hostilities, China granted a whole new set of concessions. It ceded to Japan the island of Taiwan, recognized Japanese hegemony over Korea and the Pescadore Islands, paid an indemnity of two hundred million ounces of silver, and agreed to allow Japanese to open factories in all of the open ports.

The defeat also set off a scramble for concessions, in which China was carved up into spheres of influence dominated by the various imperialist powers. Once the Western nations—now including Russia, Germany, and Italy—saw China's weakness, they pressed for and received special privileges, including rights to establish military bases, extract raw materials, and build railroads. By 1899, Germany, France, Britain, Russia, and Japan had all carved out special spheres of influence.

The only country left out of this scramble was the United States, having just become a Pacific power as a result of the Spanish-American War of 1898, which gave it control of the Philippine Islands. Having participated in the opium trade early in the century and then expanding their commercial activities under the treaty system, American firms worried that the scramble for concessions would lead to the European colonization of China. Fearful that the United States

would thus be excluded, Secretary of State John Hay sent notes to the Western powers and Japan requesting that they respect equal opportunity for trade and refrain from giving their citizens preferential tariffs in their spheres of influence. Perhaps concerned that the partition of China might lead to tensions and war among European countries, the imperialist powers agreed to the American open-door policy. Preventing China's total dismemberment, this policy is often cited as evidence of American friendship for China. Actually, the Americans never questioned the unequal treaty system or the spheres of influence but were concerned about maintaining their access to the China market. In that, the open-door policy succeeded.

The Significance of Imperialism in Chinese History

The role of imperialism in Chinese history is highly controversial. On one level, it raises large questions about the relative importance of internal and external forces of change in China's modern history: Was China incapable of modern development on its own, or was it already changing prior to the arrival of the West, either toward capitalism or in other directions that imperialism arrested? For Chinese, such issues touch on matters of national identity and pride. For Western scholars, the issue highlights the different historical trajectories of China and Europe in modern times.

On another level, the issue of imperialism is important for understanding the failure of China to develop a modern industrial society in the century after the Opium Wars. Some scholars argue that even before the imperialist impact on China, the country's economy had so stagnated that it was the historic contribution of the West to provide the science and technology that China needed to break out of this trap. That China was not able to use Western science and technology effectively had little to do with imperialism, these scholars argue, and more to do with internal obstacles to their adoption, such as the conservatism of the landlord class. Others think that imperialist powers, far from providing the impetus toward capitalist modernization, actually prevented China from developing and kept it dependent on the West for manufactured goods while encouraging the export of raw materials and foodstuffs.

The Taiping Revolution came to an end as forces loyal to the government stormed the rebel capital of Nanjing in 1864.

The balance of this chapter explores this issue, but here, in brief, is our best judgment about the role of imperialism in China's nineteenth-century history: Western and Japanese imperialism first undermined China's traditional order and then sharply limited its ability to create the strong state, industrial economy, and modern military that was needed for its survival as an independent nation in a highly competitive world of aggressive nation-states.

Ideologically, imperialism challenged and then broke down China's traditional conception of the world order. The combination of overwhelming technological and military superiority, the humiliating arrangements of the unequal treaties, and the destruction of their tributary relations with Vietnam and Korea forced the Chinese to recognize that their country was no longer the center of civilization to which barbarian states paid homage. Nor could they any longer view trade as tribute. China was a state, and perhaps a nation, enmeshed in a world of other states and nations, some of which were demonstrably more powerful than China. It was a bitter recognition.

The imperialist powers also contributed to the political and military weakness of the central government. Western policy became one of pressuring the weak Qing government and keeping it weak to maintain trade concessions. Chinese sovereignty was further limited in the treaty ports, which increased in number from fifteen in 1870 to forty-five in 1899. In each treaty port, foreigners created special enclaves with their own courts and even their own postal service, which gave real substance to extraterritoriality. The imperialists thereby enfeebled the Chinese state at a point in history when China needed a strong government to manage its entrance into the modern world.

In economic terms, imperialism also stifled China's development. First, the tariff, limited by the various treaties to 5 percent *ad valorem,* both closed an important source of revenue to the central government and limited China's ability to protect its industries, as the capitalist countries themselves had done. Furthermore, the Imperial Maritime Customs was administered not by Chinese but by foreigners, most of them British. Although honest and efficient, the customs officers nonetheless ensured that first the various powers were paid their indemnities from the import duties, and that certain regional officials, not the central government, received the lion's share of what remained.

Western and Japanese manufactured goods, including everything from matches and textiles to locomotives, flooded the Chinese market. The ensuing unfavorable balance of trade inhibited the formation and accumulation of capital, much of which flowed out of China. Furthermore, foreigners controlled most modern sectors of Chinese industry, from textile firms in Shanghai and Guangzhou to the operation of railroads. Foreign involvement in manufacturing accelerated after the signing of the Treaty of Shimonoseki and the scramble for concessions, and increased throughout the early twentieth century. Under foreign control, modern economic development served not to unify and strengthen China but to integrate its economy into the capitalist world in ways that benefited foreign investors.

Socially, imperialist economic activity was primarily responsible for the weakness of China's two modern social groups—the working class and the bourgeoisie or capitalist class. China's own native bourgeoisie consisted mostly of compradores, the intermediaries who served as the link between China and the world market. By far the largest amount of domestic capital was invested in activities that served foreign enterprises; Chinese capitalists invested much less in independent ventures. Thus, although China experienced a significant amount of modern economic development, it was not accompanied by the emergence of an indigenous, independent bourgeoisie able to lead the country's economic modernization.

Like other colonial and semicolonial countries, China did not enter the modern world on terms of its own choosing. Rather, it was forced at gunpoint into that world on terms dictated by Europeans. That enormously humiliating fact has informed Chinese history from the early nineteenth century to the present.

The Taiping Revolution: 1850–1865

The Opium Wars and their aftermath were only part of the upheaval that shook China in the mid-nineteenth century, for it also experienced a series of peasant uprisings that began around 1850 and touched every one of its eighteen provinces. The largest and most important of these was the massive Taiping Revolution of 1850–1865, which in some respects anticipated and resembled the more successful Communist revolution of the twentieth century.

The Background of the Taipings

The Taiping Revolution unfolded against a background of internal tensions exacerbated by the new imperialist presence, whose effects were felt most acutely in the port city of Guangzhou, the surrounding province of Guangdong, and other coastal areas. For a set of complex economic reasons, the outflow of silver to pay for opium increased the peasants' taxes. Opening five ports also disrupted China's trade routes. Coolies who had packed silk and tea to Guangzhou lost work as trade routes shifted north toward Shanghai, which emerged as the center of foreign trade. And as European steamships continued to lower their freight rates, tens of thousands of Chinese sailors and coolies, the workers who dragged the boats along canals, also found themselves without work.

To complicate matters, the area of south China most affected by the social and economic consequences of the Opium Wars also was beset with a long-standing social conflict between the landowning natives of the region, known as *bendi,* and more recent arrivals, known as *hakka,* or "guests." Afflicted with population pressures, rising taxes, higher rents, and official corruption, south China was ripe for social unrest. The form it took was a millenarian peasant revolution inspired by the visions of a man who had been touched by Christian ideas.

Hong Xiuquan (1814–1864), son of a well-to-do *hakka* farming family, had repeatedly failed the imperial examinations. By itself, this was hardly unique, for China's rising population had produced a growing number of failed examination candidates, many of whom then turned away from Confucianism and toward Buddhism or Daoism. Hong too might have gone in this direction had it not been for a chance encounter with an American Baptist missionary on the streets of Guangzhou after his third failure, in 1836. The missionary gave Hong some religious tracts, which he took home and apparently did not think much about for the next seven years. In the meantime, he twice more failed the imperial examinations and suffered a severe nervous breakdown, with hallucinations and delirium. Shortly after his final failure, in 1843, Hong reread the missionary tracts and began to reinterpret his illness. He had not been ill, he decided, but had instead journeyed to heaven, where he had met God and learned that he was none other than the younger brother of Jesus

Christ, charged with the task of returning to earth to expel the demons and to prepare the way for the coming of the heavenly kingdom. Over the next few years, Hong and a cousin studied the missionary literature and proselytized their new understanding of Christianity. In the process, they gathered a small number of followers, who organized themselves into the Society of God Worshipers.

The Taiping Movement

Most extraordinary, however, was not Hong's personal vision, but that within a few years, tens of thousands and then millions of Chinese responded to his millenarian message of the imminent creation of a new world. In doing so, they fueled a massive revolutionary movement that nearly toppled the Qing Dynasty. Domestic and foreign social forces had prepared the ground in the areas of Guangdong and Guangxi provinces where Hong and his lieutenants preached: recently unemployed teamsters and charcoal burners, landless peasants, and hard-pressed *hakka* all responded to Hong's message of expelling the demons, increasingly understood as the Manchu rulers of China, and preparing for a new world.

As the Society of God Worshipers grew to thirty thousand by 1848, Hong Xiuquan added a political theme to his message. In early 1851, he proclaimed the establishment of a new order, the Heavenly Kingdom of the Great Peace *(Taiping Tianguo)*, from which the Taipings derived their name. He called himself Heavenly King and announced that the Manchu-run Qing Dynasty would be overthrown.

Organizing their followers into a unified military-communal society, the Taipings exploded north out of their base in Guangxi province toward the Yangzi River Valley, capturing and looting the large city of Wuhan in late 1852 and sweeping into Nanjing in early 1853. By this time, their army numbered a half million, mostly peasants from the rich agricultural province of Hunan who had given up their property and local ties to participate in the creation of a new and better world. Establishing Nanjing as their capital, in 1855–1856 the Taipings sent armies farther north to take Beijing. It looked as if the Qing Dynasty had come to an end.

A Revolution in the Making?

At similar points in the history of earlier peasant rebellions, the landowning Confucian gentry often sided with the rebels and helped establish a new dynasty, for the old one had lost the mandate of heaven. But in this case, the gentry did not defect to the Taipings but chose instead to side with the Manchu rulers of China and the Qing Dynasty. This difference had profound consequences for Chinese history in the nineteenth and twentieth centuries.

It was the alien and revolutionary character of the Taiping rebellion that persuaded the gentry to cast their lot with the Manchu Dynasty. The rebels rejected not only Confucianism but also Buddhism and Daoism, ideologies traditionally associated with peasant upheavals. They propounded their version of Christianity and promised the advent of the Kingdom of God on earth. Rejecting the notion of the mandate of heaven, Hong received his legitimacy from a transcendent and personal God who gave orders to change the world rather than accept the existing order. This represented a fundamental challenge to the Confucian view of the universe. So, too, did the implicit Taiping acceptance of the idea that China was simply a nation in a system of nation-states, for the rebels were willing to establish regular diplomatic relations with all other countries.

Finally, the Taipings proposed a program of radical social reform that would have completely overturned the existing order. Unlike other peasant rebels who called for land redistribution, the Taipings sought the abolition of private property altogether and the gathering of all wealth in a communal treasury from which the needs of everyone could be met. Men and women were considered equal, and the Taipings prohibited footbinding and concubinage. They initially segregated people into "men's camps" and "women's camps" for military purposes; thus, women participated in labor and formed their own military units led by women generals. After settling into the Nanjing area, the separate camps for men and women were replaced with communal units of twenty-five families working and living together in an egalitarian society.[1] Given the demands of the Taipings' war against the Manchu government, their communal, egalitarian vision was not realized in practice, but its implications were apparent to China's landlord gentry.

Thus, the Taiping movement was revolutionary rather than merely rebellious. Instead of seeking to change only the ruling dynasty, as had been the case in prior peasant rebellions, the Taipings envisioned an altogether different world in which the gentry would cease to exist, and male-dominated institutions would give way to a more egalitarian society of gender equality. Their vision of a new social order was accompanied by a conscious attempt to create new social values, such as asceticism and self-discipline, which in other societies fostered modern social and economic change. These values predisposed the Taipings to innovation, economic growth, and the adoption of modern Western technology. Indeed, the Taipings developed extensive plans for industrialization.

The plans were formulated in 1859 by Hong Rengan, a cousin of the Taiping leader, who had recently joined the movement and was appointed prime minister. Having received a thorough missionary education in Hong Kong, Hong Rengan knew a great deal about the West and put that knowledge to use in drawing up his plans. He saw China developing from an agrarian into an industrial nation and planned for railroads, highways, shipping lines, and postal services to serve a rapidly expanding economy under both private and state control. He wanted to offer all citizens life, health, and property insurance and to raise China's cultural level by expanding public education and establishing newspapers. In short, Hong Rengan proposed to make China into a modern industrial nation.

Might he have succeeded and thus pushed China's development in a far different path? Despite some internal opposition, the Taipings were not weighted down by the rural-landlord interests that have blocked attempts at reform in other countries: the Taiping Land Equalization Program would have removed China's gentry from the social scene. Furthermore, the Taipings had built a new state apparatus and had the military force needed to implement these plans. And they were free of ideological barriers to profit making, to urban industrial growth, and to the material rewards that were anathema to the Confucian elite. Thus, the Taipings might have begun the creation of a strong state, an industrial economy, and a powerful military that would have ensured China's survival in a world of hostile nation-states. And they might have done so just thirty years after the first railroads were built in Britain.

This picture of American sailors entering a pedicab in Shanghai in 1945 symbolizes the final stages of more than a century of Western dominance in China. *AP/Wide World*

However, the Taiping plans were never realized, in large part because their revolutionary implications pushed China's landlord-gentry class into strong support of the Qing Dynasty, in an attempt to preserve both the dynasty and the class's own many privileges. As the shaken imperial military forces proved incapable of defeating the Taipings, provincial gentry leaders came forward to mobilize their own local armies, which in the end destroyed the revolutionary rebels. With the creation of gentry-led armies, the defeat of the Taipings came swiftly. In June 1864, the Taipings' Heavenly King Hong Xiuquan committed suicide, and in July, one of the gentry-led armies broke into the rebels' capital city of Nanjing and slaughtered its remaining 100,000 supporters. By the end of 1864, the Taiping Revolution was crushed.

In addition to the opposition of the landlord-gentry class, the Taiping movement was weakened by internal divisions as a number of people began to claim direct contact with God. Furthermore, some of the leaders failed to follow their own strict codes of behavior, choosing instead a licentious and debauched life-style. Differences arose over military strategy and the social and economic program that the Taipings would implement upon their victory.

The Western powers contributed as well to the downfall of the Taipings. Initially, foreign governments followed a policy of neutrality, as the Taipings' professed Christianity evoked considerable sympathy from Western missionaries and diplomats. But in 1860, when Taiping troops appeared to threaten Shanghai, which had become the center for foreign commercial enterprise in China, the imperialist powers realized that protection of their privileges depended on the continued existence of a weakened Qing Dynasty. Neutrality then gave way to support for the beleaguered regime as the British and American governments contributed to the formation of foreign-supported armies, which intervened in minor ways on behalf of the Qing government.

The Historical Significance of the Taiping Revolution

In the short run, the devastation and destruction caused by both sides in this massive civil war seriously disrupted and weakened China's economy. Vast expanses of the Yangzi River Valley became virtual wastelands, as travelers reported walking for days in previously densely populated regions without seeing a living person. Indeed, the estimates of those killed both in battle and as a consequence of the ravages of war range from twenty million to thirty million. It took more than a decade for China to recover from the destruction of war.

The Taiping Revolution, and especially the way in which it was defeated, had long-term consequences for Chinese history. Most important, the failure of the revolution consolidated the political, social, and economic position of the landlord gentry and their male-oriented Confucian ideals. The Qing court lost power to regional gentry leaders, such as Zeng Guofan and Li Hongzhang, who commanded their own armies, collected their own revenues, and dispensed their own justice. The establishment of regional armies was the first step in the process of local militarization that culminated in the warlordism of the 1920s. Finally, the Taiping Revolution put the ques-

tions of social justice for China's peasants and women on the historical agenda, but the victory of the landlord gentry postponed resolutions of those very questions. The defeat of the Taipings, in short, strengthened the gentry class, which was most diametrically opposed to the radical changes necessary for China's survival as a nation. The failure of the Taiping Revolution, then, did not merely delay China's attempts to industrialize; it also created new obstacles to that process.

The Failure of Conservative Modernization: 1860–1895

The suppression of the Taiping Revolution and other rebel movements was but the first in a series of actions taken in the latter half of the nineteenth century to defend and then restore China's Confucian order after its battering by foreign imperialists and domestic rebels. Known broadly as the *self-strengthening movement*, these efforts represented an attempt to rejuvenate a sagging dynasty and a failing society by vigorous application of traditional Confucian principles combined with very limited and cautious borrowing from the West. In the end, it failed, but the self-strengthening movement was a kind of experiment to test the limits of conservative modernization. Could China survive while adhering fundamentally to its old ways?

The Self-Strengthening Movement

In its initial stages, the primary goal of self-strengthening was to re-create the stable agrarian society in which Confucian values and gentry rule had been so secure. Beyond suppressing the various rebellions, it was necessary to find and promote "people of talent." This search reflected the basic Confucian outlook that social order would be guaranteed not by laws or regulations but by the quality of people. Thus, the imperial examinations were reinstalled and revamped to find officials who could deal with the massive reconstruction that faced China in the 1860s and 1870s.

In addition, land had to be brought back into production and the peasants encouraged to take up agriculture after the dislocations of the Taiping Revolution. The key to this reconstruction was the gentry. The Qing state reaffirmed and supported the gentry's position in rural society, restored their claims to land, and granted them tax relief. To promote food production, the state also encouraged and supported the repair of irrigation and dikes. Under landlord-gentry supervision, the rural social and economic order recovered quickly.

The rural emphasis of self-strengthening was quite deliberate, for its conservative leaders among the gentry and the court quite rightly feared the social effects of urban, industrial, and commercial development. As one local official put it, "when the profits of commerce are small, those who plow and weave will be numerous."[2]

Although the main thrust of self-strengthening was traditional, the gentry leaders of the new regional armies recognized the superiority of Western military technology and decided that they needed to obtain and produce modern weapons. As the Chinese general Li Hongzhang wrote in 1863:

I have been aboard the warships of the British and French admirals and I saw that their cannons are ingenious and uniform, their ammunition is fine and cleverly made, their weapons are bright, and their troops have a martial appearance and are orderly. These things are actually superior to those of China. . . . I feel deeply ashamed that Chinese weapons are far inferior to those of foreign countries. Every day I warn and instruct my officers to be humble-minded, to bear the humiliation, to learn one or two secrets from the Westerners in the hope that we may increase our knowledge.[3]

Thus, China established a number of modern arsenals and shipyards, and supported foreign-language schools, translation services, and scientific personnel.

But even this very limited borrowing from the West aroused profound fears in the minds of many conservatives: How could they use non-Chinese means to preserve a Confucian China? Many thought that the slightest borrowing from the West would erode their world. Nonetheless, the self-strengtheners pushed on, resolving their dilemma with the slogan "Chinese learning as the base, Western learning for use." They believed it was possible to borrow selectively from the technology of the West, without adopting the scientific knowledge and social and economic institutions that had made that technology possible in the first place. This fallacy would have

tragic consequences for China in its military encounters with the French and then the Japanese.

To a few of China's elite, power was inseparable from wealth, and a strong military required at least some elements of modern industry. This line of thinking led to the establishment of a number of new firms, some designed to lessen China's dependence on foreign imports. The Hanyang Steelworks in Hubei province opened with blast furnaces, purchased from Britain, capable of producing one hundred tons of steel per day. To supply the steelworks, iron mines were established and coking coal was purchased from private suppliers. Additionally, prominent officials established textile mills to reduce foreign imports of cotton cloth. By 1894, there were 135,000 spindles for making cotton operating in Shanghai alone.

Choosing the Past: The Failure of Self-Strengthening

Despite its accomplishments, the self-strengthening movement turned out to be a rather superficial affair. To be sure, the new enterprises saw the very early beginnings of a new social class in China, the working class or proletariat, and even the emergence of a few Chinese capitalists. But the new industries remained largely dependent on foreigners for machinery, materials, and expertise. Furthermore, these enterprises were largely controlled, not by the central government, but by regional Chinese officials seeking to strengthen their own position rather than that of the nation as a whole. In both the Sino-French War of 1884–1885 and the Sino-Japanese War of 1894–1895, these regional leaders refused to coordinate their military efforts, preferring to see the forces of their rivals destroyed rather than come to the defense of China as a nation. The results were devastating. These humiliating defeats—two in a single decade—clearly revealed the failure of self-strengthening as a means of enabling China to withstand imperialist pressures.

The most fundamental flaw of the self-strengthening movement was its attempt to use the fruits of the emerging industrial world to preserve the Confucian gentry's stable agrarian empire. The gentry leaders of that movement, representing China's dominant class, had no interest in creating a modern industrial society and a strong centralized state. They were

This French cartoon shows the European powers and Japan carving up the "cake" of China in 1898. *Jean-Loup Charmet*

very much aware, according to historian Mary Wright, that a "stable agrarian society" that protected their power and privileges "could not survive the drastic changes that would follow in the wake of railroads, factories, and increased urbanization. . . . The requirements of a modern state proved to run counter to the requirements of Confucian order."[4] Thus, China's traditional ruling class failed to carry out the political and economic tasks demanded in a world of capitalism, imperialism, and nation-states. In the process, this class became a major obstacle to China's modernization and, in the twentieth century, was swept away in a torrent of revolutionary upheaval.

Although the self-strengthening movement could not solve China's nineteenth-century problems, its failure at least posed a decisive question: What was China trying to preserve—its traditional socioeconomic order and Confucian culture or its independence as a nation? To most members of the elite, the answer throughout the nineteenth century remained

the former. But after China's defeat by the Japanese in 1895, some began to wonder of what use that tradition was if it could not ensure China's survival into the twentieth century.

By the turn of the century, China's prospects were bleak indeed. The failure of conservative modernization under gentry auspices left the country open to the imperialist powers, which carved it up into spheres of influence. But for the American fear of losing access to the market, China might well have been politically partitioned, ceasing to exist as a state at all. The country had been incorporated into the world economy on terms that were distinctly neither of its own choosing nor to its advantage.

The choice was becoming clear: to cling to Confucian values and an agrarian society would lead to China's dismemberment at the hands of the imperialist powers, whereas to create a strong state to guide the modern economic development necessary to support a powerful military meant the destruction of the old order. The massive revolutionary upheavals of the twentieth century represented the consequences of traveling the second route.

Conclusion: Comparing China and the Ottoman Empire

China's encounter with the imperialist West bears comparison with that of the Islamic world. Both represented civilizations that had for a thousand years or more dominated their respective regions; both drew great self-confidence from their historical achievements and felt little need to learn from the infidels or barbarians of the West; neither was prepared for the humiliating change in the global balance of power occasioned by the rise of Europe. But the world of Islam had been a near neighbor to the West for many centuries, and in its most prominent state, the Ottoman Empire, internal decay and penetration by Europeans were well advanced by the early eighteenth century. China and the West, in contrast, had encountered one another directly only since the sixteenth century, and China dictated the terms of that relationship until the 1830s. Thus, the impact of the West on China was far more sudden and abrupt than it had been in the Middle East.

In neither area, however, did imperialist penetration lead to outright colonial rule, though the Ottoman Empire lost more of its territory to nationalist movements and imperialist aggression than did China, which remained largely intact. And in the face of European pressure, both China and the Ottoman Empire launched efforts at conservative modernization designed to strengthen the old regimes and preserve their independence. The Ottoman version of this reform program was, however, far more vigorous and far-reaching than the timid and half-hearted measures of self-strengthening in China. In the aftermath of the Taiping Revolution, the Qing Dynasty found itself dependent on the highly conservative gentry class, whereas the Ottoman Empire had experienced no such massive internal upheaval.

In the twentieth century, however, both the Chinese and Ottoman empires were swept away. In China, the collapse of the old regime was followed by a vast revolutionary upheaval that led to a Communist regime. The collapse of the Ottoman Empire led to the creation of a new nation-state in the Turkish heartland of the old empire and to "revolution from above" within that state. But China's revolutionaries rejected traditional Confucian culture more thoroughly than even the secularizing leaders of modern Turkey rejected Islam. And elsewhere in the Islamic world, traditional religion retained its hold on the loyalties of most people and became a basis for social renewal in many places. Islamic civilization, unlike its Chinese counterpart, had many independent centers and was never so closely associated with a single state. Furthermore it was embedded in a deeply religious tradition that was personally meaningful to millions of adherents, in contrast to the more elitist and secular outlook of Confucianism. All of this perhaps facilitated the survival and renewal of Islamic civilization in the twentieth century in a way that was not possible for traditional Chinese civilization.

Notes

1. Ono Kazuko, *Chinese Women in a Century of Revolution, 1850–1950,* ed. Joshua Fogel, trans. Kathryn Bernardt et al. (Stanford: Stanford University Press, 1989), chap. 1.

2. Quoted in Mary C. Wright, *The Last Stand of Chinese Conservatism* (New York: Atheneum, 1966), p. 156.

3. Quoted in Teng Ssu-yu and John K. Fairbank, eds. and trans., *China's Response to the West: A Documentary Survey, 1839–1923* (New York: Atheneum, 1963), p. 69.

4. Wright, *Chinese Conservatism,* pp. ix, 312.

Chapter 18
Nationalists and Communists:
The Chinese Revolution, 1900–1949

Nationalism has been among the most powerful forces of the modern world. It accompanied the formation and the destructive competition of national states in nineteenth-century Europe, and it has fueled efforts by developing countries in the twentieth century to throw off European domination and create modern societies. But unlike nationalism in India, the Middle East, and most of Africa, Chinese nationalism nurtured a massive revolutionary upheaval that swept away China's political institutions, its social structure, and much of its traditional culture as well as foreign domination. Why did the growth of nationalism in China provide an environment conducive to social (and Socialist) revolution? How was the Chinese Communist party, an organization with only a handful of members at its founding in 1921, able to come to power only twenty-eight years later, and to remain in power even after the collapse of communism in the Soviet Union and Eastern Europe?

The End of Imperial China: 1895–1912

China's humiliating defeat by Japan in 1895 marked the origin of modern Chinese nationalism. As intellectuals began to choose the preservation of China as a nation-state over the preservation of their Confucian heritage, they not only expressed a nationalist commitment but also defected from the defense of the old order. With China threatened by disintegration and subjugation, many Chinese concluded that anything in China's past that did not preserve the na-

tion was unworthy of protection. In that belief lay the seeds of revolution.

Reform and Reaction

At the end of the nineteenth century, even calls for modest reform in China proved threatening to defenders of the old order. Following the defeat by Japan, a short-lived reform movement supported by the young Guangxu emperor produced a violent conservative reaction that placed the most backward-looking Manchu princes and Chinese ministers in power. Led by the empress dowager Cixi (reigned 1875–1908), the widow of a previous emperor, the reactionaries precipitated another disaster for China, the Boxer Rebellion of 1900.

The context for the Boxer Rebellion was created by foreign penetration. Not only had missionaries with strange garb propagated strange ideas among the peasantry, but foreign merchants, sailors, soldiers, and diplomats dominated life in the treaty ports as well. When drought followed by hunger and epidemics coursed through north China at the turn of the century, peasants ascribed these inauspicious happenings to the pollution of their world by foreigners. Lurid rumors that Christian missionaries ran orphanages to eat the eyeballs of the children heightened hatred and fear of Europeans.

The rebels were members of antiforeign secret societies who were supported and encouraged by the empress dowager and reactionary court officials. Believing that magical preparations made them impervious to foreign bullets, the Boxers called for the elimination of foreigners and support for the Qing Dynasty. Invited to Beijing in June 1900, the Boxers

Captured members of the "Boxer" secret society. *Visual Studies Workshop*

fueled antiforeign riots in which some Europeans were killed, several churches burned, and foreign embassies besieged.

The Western powers and Japan, fearing the worst for their citizens, organized an expeditionary force that lifted the siege and sent the Qing court fleeing from Beijing. Once again, the foreign powers imposed onerous demands on China, including public apologies for the outrage and a huge indemnity of nearly $750 million. Like the Indian mutiny some forty years earlier, the Boxer Rebellion represented a futile attempt to restore an idealized version of a vanishing world. Following by just five years the disaster of the Sino-Japanese War, the occupation of Beijing by foreign troops finally shocked the Qing court into a program of reform designed to strengthen and preserve the dynasty.

Reform from Above

The New Policy Reforms, as they were known in China, covered education, recruitment of officials, the military, commerce, and the political system. Beginning in 1901, new schools offered Western subjects, including science, mathematics, geography, and foreign languages. The government encouraged students to study abroad, and within a few years

nearly ten thousand were attending schools in Japan alone.

In 1905, the ancient civil service examination system was abolished. Thus, the traditional route into the state bureaucracy disappeared, and gentry ties to the state weakened as new avenues to wealth, power, and status opened up. In the military, new officer training schools created a professional officer corps. To encourage the growth of commerce, merchants were guaranteed protection from irregular state impositions and allowed to form modern chambers of commerce.

Japan's astounding victory over Russia in 1905 suggested to many reformers that a constitutional monarchy, such as Japan had developed, was the secret to national power. As a step in that direction, local self-government associations formed in 1908, followed by provincial elections in 1909 and national elections in 1910. Property and educational qualifications limited the voting to a very few of the gentry and wealthy merchants, ensuring that only the elite of the elite were elected to the provincial and national assemblies. Nonetheless, when this group met in Beijing, thinking that they would create a new government, they discovered instead that they were merely to advise the Manchu rulers. Constitutionalism was stillborn.

Some of the gentry and merchants were likewise outraged when the government prevented them from buying out foreign interests in railroads and mines. This action sparked massive protests throughout China in June 1911, and led to an uprising in Sichuan province that drove out the imperial governor. The end of imperial China was in sight.

China's Political Revolution: 1911

Instead of shoring up the tottering Qing Dynasty, the New Policy Reforms had the unintended consequence of renewing and strengthening opposition to the dynasty. Designed to recoup the central government's lost power, the reforms had alienated the provincial gentry in the constitutionalist movement, angered gentry and merchants by its railroad policy, disturbed peasants with the increased taxes to pay for the reforms and for the huge Boxer indemnities, and alienated the intellectuals sent abroad to master

Western technology. Rather than extending the life of the old order, the reforms hastened the revolution that ended it.

Politically sensitive Chinese increasingly concluded that the Qing government was incapable of carrying out meaningful reform to save China and therefore had to be removed. Revolutionary ideas and organizations were most prevalent among radical intellectuals studying abroad, especially in Japan. Publications such as Liang Qichao's *New Citizen* introduced these students not merely to constitutionalism but also to a wide range of modern Western ideas.

In 1905, several groups came together to form the Revolutionary Alliance under the leadership of Dr. Sun Yat-sen. Educated in Hong Kong, Dr. Sun had long held revolutionary ideas, and his followers had made several unsuccessful attempts to seize power in the south China province of Guangdong. The revolutionary movement, however, was hopelessly divided and quite isolated from the masses, with only the crudest anti-Manchu racism tying it to secret societies.

The origins of the 1911 Revolution, which brought down the Qing Dynasty and the old order, lay in the suppression of the Taiping Revolution and in the effects of imperialism. By 1911, the Qing Dynasty had been seriously undermined by the growth of regional armies and provincial gentry power and by the potential dismemberment of China at the hands of the imperialist powers. And the results of the New Policy Reforms ensured that the dynasty had few bases of support left. Even the professional officer corps of the New Armies, which constituted the ultimate prop for the dynasty, were disenchanted with the regime.

Junior officers in the central and southern provinces had become interested in republican ideas and were open to revolutionary propaganda. Organizing on their own, some units stationed in Wuhan, a large metropolitan area on the Yangzi River, had planned an uprising in the fall of 1911. When an accidental bomb blast revealed their plans, they forced their commander, General Li Yuanhong, to lead the rising anyway. The Manchu governor fled, and General Li proclaimed Hunan an independent republic. Other provinces soon followed suit, and the Qing Dynasty melted away in all but name. And even the name went, on 12 February 1912, when the last Qing emperor abdicated, ending 268 years of Qing rule and two millennia of China's dynastic history. It was less

a revolutionary overthrow than the internal collapse of a failed regime. But for the next thirty-seven years, the Chinese fought bitterly over what would replace it.

Although it removed the Qing Dynasty, the 1911 Revolution failed to create a new state that could unify China and deal with its massive problems. Instead, the revolution furthered the disintegration of China's state power and put the country at the mercy of hundreds of warlords, or local strongmen with their own private armies. From 1916 to 1928, warlords fought one another for control of resources and for personal enrichment. Furthermore, the gentry, whose ideological claims to special privilege and status fell with the dynasty, became little more than landlords who extracted wealth from the countryside without providing anything in return. In the process, China dissolved into an era of political disorder.

The 1911 Revolution in Perspective

China's 1911 Revolution did little more than remove the tottering old regime from the historical stage. In terms of its own goals—establishing a republican and more democratic form of government—the revolution was a complete failure. Nor did the 1911 Revolution address China's fundamental social problem: a rural class structure in which innumerable peasant families eked out a living on tiny plots of land while landlords extracted surplus from the peasantry without investing any of it in industrial development. The failure to confront that social problem postponed its resolution for another forty years. In the meantime, it provided the fuel for China's Communist-led rural revolution.

It is sometimes argued that 1911 represents a failed "bourgeois-democratic" revolution similar in its goals to that of the French Revolution of 1789. Both movements, after all, overthrew despotic monarchies in the name of progressive ideas. But whereas the French Revolution, at least in part, acted in the interests of a growing middle class or bourgeoisie, the ideas of China's 1911 uprising were neither articulated nor supported by a Chinese bourgeoisie, for that class was weak and poorly developed.

At the turn of the twentieth century, then, there simply was no social-class base for the modern ideas of republicanism and middle-class democracy.

Rather, a radicalized intelligentsia, most of whose members had been educated abroad, articulated revolutionary ideas, and in the context of 1911 China, republican ideas were revolutionary. But without a firm social base, neither the ideas nor the institutions of republicanism could take hold. Some other form of state would have to be developed to transform the country.

Modern Chinese nationalism, therefore, did not originate with a bourgeoisie but with an intelligentsia. The very notion of nationalism derived from nineteenth-century Europe but took a far different form in China. For early Chinese nationalists did not celebrate their cultural traditions, as European, Indian, African, and most other nationalists did. Instead, they demanded the abandonment of those traditions and institutions that had prevented the establishment of a strong state and modern economy.

In China's historic setting, this meant that nationalism had revolutionary implications, whereas in many other places, it played a socially conservative role. For in China, most nationalists saw their own traditions as worse than useless, even harmful, for the preservation of the nation. The 1911 Revolution, then, is less important for what it accomplished than for what it promised: an anti-imperialist social revolution.

China's First Cultural Revolution: 1915–1923

While China fragmented politically during the warlord era, new forces that would ultimately transform its entire society gathered momentum. Among the most important of these was a dramatic change in outlook on the part of a new generation of young Chinese intellectuals. In the last years of the nineteenth century and the first decade of the twentieth, China's intellectuals, led by Liang Qichao and Kang Youwei, had tried to reform Confucianism in order to save it. But within just a few years of 1911, this numerically tiny but culturally important group had altogether rejected China's ancient traditions and embarked on a fervent quest for Western alternatives. The failures of the 1911 Revolution, they concluded, were rooted in those very traditions. Before

China could create a modern state, they reasoned, its traditional culture would have to be thrown out and a wholly new one created.

The New Culture Movement

The New Culture movement can be dated from the initial publication of *New Youth* magazine in 1915. Organized by a few professors and students at Beijing University, *New Youth* advocated the all-out Westernization of Chinese life and culture. Confucianism, classical education, arranged marriages, sexual inequality, reverence for age—all this and more had to go. China had to adopt Western ideas and ways not merely for physical survival, the young Chinese intellectuals believed, but also because Western civilization was far superior to the barbaric and fundamentally corrupt culture of old China. These reformers found in the West all those things lacking in China and expressed a particular passion for Western science and democracy. Their slogans were "Down with Confucius and Sons" (that is, Chinese tradition) and "Up with Mr. Science and Mr. Democracy."

The New Culture intellectuals distrusted overt expressions of nationalism, feeling that it inhibited individual freedom. Rather, they upheld internationalism and cosmopolitanism as their standards. Deeply appalled by the debacle of the 1911 Revolution and the sorry state of warlord politics, the New Culture generation initially refused to participate in politics, arguing that until the Chinese people had changed their way of thinking completely, any political change would be superficial. That was the lesson of 1911.

All of this produced a cult of youth, for the Chinese veneration of the old, they felt, had led to national impotence. Only the young had not been corrupted by the old and rotten culture. As Lu Xun, China's greatest modern writer, put it, "Save the children!" Thus, over the course of just a few years, the New Culture generation concluded that the old order was so corrupt and rotten that nothing less than a total cultural revolution could even begin to resolve China's modern crisis. "Destruction before Construction" had become their motto.

Among the most important of the traditional institutions to be destroyed, they argued, was the Confucian family system. These young intellectuals focused their attack on arranged marriages, calling instead for "free marriage" and, even more radically, "free divorce." While cosmopolitan young men advocated the idea of free marriage to express their rejection of traditional arranged marriages, for women the idea of divorce struck at the central mechanism of male domination in traditional China: with the right to divorce, men could no longer treat women as chattel to be disposed of as they pleased.

Not surprisingly, though, the radical attacks on the Confucian traditions of marriage and the family did not merely fall on deaf ears, but aroused considerable hostility from defenders of the status quo. Nonetheless, during the New Culture movement the ideas of family reform and gender equality were first articulated, and the young men and women who held those ideas tried over the subsequent decades to make substantive changes in the family, marriage, and the position of women in Chinese society. However, the ideas of gender equality and family reform more often than not were compromised in favor of other goals in the course of the Chinese revolution.[1]

The May Fourth Movement of 1919

Until the end of World War I, the New Culture intellectuals, preoccupied with learning from the West, did not focus heavily on imperialism as a source of China's problems. But their country's treatment at the Versailles Peace Conference of 1919 persuaded them otherwise.

Chinese delegates came to Versailles expecting the conference to reconstruct the world on the basis of the principles of democracy and self-determination as set forth in President Woodrow Wilson's Fourteen Points. Thus, they expected China would soon be free of the unequal treaties and would at least recover territories occupied by the defeated Germans in Shandong province. However, they received instead a lesson in imperialism. Honoring secret agreements made during the war, the Western powers awarded German territories not to China but to Japan. Thus, Shandong fell under Japanese control, and the unequal treaty system remained in force. To the New Culture intellectuals who had admired everything about the West, it was a great shock.

News of China's treatment at the hands of "Mr. Science and Mr. Democracy" reached Beijing on 1 May 1919. On May 4, parading to the various foreign embassies, five thousand Beijing students expressed their outrage over imperialist machinations and attacked the weakness and corruption of their own government for selling out Chinese interests. Passing the house of their prime minister, the students broke in and set it on fire. Even more massive protests on May 7 secured the release of arrested students. Demonstrations spread throughout the country, involving not only students but merchants and workers in other cities as well as Chinese student communities overseas, even in Tokyo. Soon an anti-Japanese commercial boycott took hold in China's cities, with people in all walks of life refusing to use Japanese passenger steamers, buy Japanese goods, or unload Japanese freighters.

The significance of the May Fourth movement can hardly be overestimated. It was the first mass protest of students, workers, and merchants against imperialism, and it prepared the way for the acceptance of Marxism by China's intellectual elite and for the formation of the Chinese Communist party.

Marxism in China

Mainstream European Marxism, with its emphasis on the urban proletariat as the agent of Socialist revolution, had seemed irrelevant to Chinese intellectuals: China was an agrarian society with a small working class and with little industrial development. But Lenin had just led a successful Socialist revolution in Russia, a similarly agrarian and backward country. Furthermore, he had made several innovations in Marxist theory that, after the experience of Versailles and the May Fourth incident, appealed to Chinese intellectuals.

First, Lenin introduced the idea of the vanguard party, which would give intellectuals a significant role to play in Socialist revolution. More important, though, Lenin had articulated a theory of imperialism that attributed the weakness and poverty of nations such as China to imperialist exploitation and domination. Such ideas justified China's emerging nationalism and its anti-imperialist movement.

After the lesson of Versailles, anti-imperialism was a powerful message. Young Chinese intellectu-

An impoverished peasantry fueled the Chinese communist revolution. *Visual Studies Workshop*

als who had rejected their own cultural past now found the Western culture they had championed equally distasteful. For those bothered by such contradictions, Marxism may have eased the emotional pain: by accepting Marxism, they could embrace the most progressive part of the Western tradition and at the same time find there a powerful tool for attacking the imperialist and capitalist aspects of that world. They could also continue to be Chinese nationalists, for that nationalism easily accommodated demands for social revolution.

From the numerous groups formed in late 1919 and early 1920 to study socialism and Marxism, eleven representatives gathered in Shanghai in July 1921 to found the Chinese Communist party. Initially composed mostly of intellectuals such as university professors and students, including the young Mao Zedong, the party soon set about organizing workers and miners into trade unions. By 1925, the Chinese Communist party had sixty thousand members, mostly urban workers.

Over the next quarter-century, that party rose to power in the world's most populous nation. It is a story of epic dimensions, and central to it was an enormous struggle with the party's major domestic rival over the direction of China's modern history.

The National Revolution: 1923–1927

Following the May Fourth movement, China's two modern political parties took shape. One was the Chinese Communist party (CCP). The other was the Guomindang (GMD), the Nationalist party, an outgrowth of Sun Yat-sen's earlier efforts to overthrow the Qing Dynasty. On several occasions, these two contenders for control of China found it convenient to join forces, first against the warlords and later against the Japanese. But for the most part, they were rivals whose conflicting visions of China's future dominated their country's history in the second quarter of the twentieth century, twice erupting into civil war. How the CCP won this historic struggle and the GMD lost it constitutes a central storyline in China's twentieth-century history.

The failure of the 1911 Revolution had left Sun Yat-sen with little political influence. Frustrated by the absence of Western support and eager to reorganize the Guomindang into a force that could unify all of China, Dr. Sun welcomed overtures from the Soviet Union in 1920–1921. The immense prestige and excitement generated by this successful revolution had been enhanced in China when the new Soviet government, alone among the Western powers, renounced the unequal treaties the tsarist regime had negotiated with China. Furthermore, Sun was impressed with Soviet organizational capacities and with the possibilities of a highly disciplined party organized along Leninist lines.

Sun's Soviet advisers, having concluded that China was not yet ripe for Socialist revolution, insisted that members of the Chinese Communist party join the GMD rather than organize on their own. Sun's objective, and the basis for GMD-CCP cooperation, was summed up in the notion of national revolution. The first goal was to unify China, driving out the warlords; then China could deal with the imperialists.

Before the GMD and its Communist allies could move decisively against the warlords, two events intervened. First, Sun Yat-sen died, on 12 March 1925, setting off a scramble for political power in the GMD. Emerging as the new leader of the Guomindang was a young military officer who controlled the army, Chiang Kai-shek. Second, the National Revolution acquired, quite unexpectedly, mass support and showed signs of turning into a social revolution.

In February 1925, Chinese workers at a Japanese-owned textile mill in Shanghai went on strike for higher wages, and violence soon broke out. These events set off a massive wave of anti-imperialist strikes and boycotts that rippled through the cities and towns of China. In Hong Kong, 100,000 workers walked off their jobs, bringing the trade of the colony to a halt and swelling the ranks of the GMD army.

The immediate result of these events was to increase greatly the power of the GMD and the CCP in areas outside their small enclave in south China. The wave of anti-imperialism that rolled through China prepared the way for GMD and CCP organizers, who were able to create labor unions and peasant unions throughout much of south and central China.

Moreover, the issues of family reform and gender equality became inextricably intertwined with the history of the Communist party during the first phase of the national revolution and the collaboration between the CCP and the Guomindang. Many of the radical May Fourth youth joined the CCP, bringing their commitments with them. Prevailing Communist ideology, though, subordinated women's liberation as secondary to broader revolutionary goals. In the words of Mao Zedong: "As for the clan system, superstition, and inequality between men and women, their abolition will follow as a natural consequence of victory in the political and economic struggles."[2] In this milieu, those interested in gender equality organized women workers and peasants into women's unions that operated parallel to the labor and peasant unions established by Communist cadre.

By 1926, a mass social movement was shaking China, with workers looking for higher wages and better working conditions, peasants pressing for rent reductions, and women pressing for equality, all of which prepared the way for the GMD army to move north against the various warlords. In the face of this northern expedition (see Map 18.1, p. 365), the opposition warlord forces melted away as the GMD was preceded by strikes, boycotts, and uprisings of peasants and workers organized by CCP advance teams. In only nine months, the GMD-CCP allies took the southern half of China and were on the verge of conquering the rest. But then the alliance split.

Tension between the GMD and the CCP had existed since the very beginning of their cooperation in 1922, and intensified after the death of Sun Yat-sen. As the army moved north, the split widened, particularly on the question of social revolution. With many of his army officers from landlord families, Chiang Kai-shek was not about to let social upheaval continue unchecked.

As the GMD army approached Shanghai, the workers there, in March of 1927, staged an armed uprising, seizing power from the police and soldiers of the local warlord. At this point, Chiang Kai-shek broke with the CCP, turning his army against his former Communist allies with a vengeance. All told, hundreds of thousands of Communists, labor leaders, and peasant organizers lost their lives in the White (or counterrevolutionary) Terror. Chiang then consolidated his power, negotiated settlements with the remaining northern warlords, and sent his army north to take Beijing. By 1928, he was titular master of China.

The split with the GMD and the ensuing counterrevolution were disastrous for the Chinese Communist party. Its urban presence was destroyed; the few Communists who managed to escape found refuge in the most inaccessible reaches of the countryside. The CCP, which had built its base among urban workers, found itself separated for two decades from the prole-

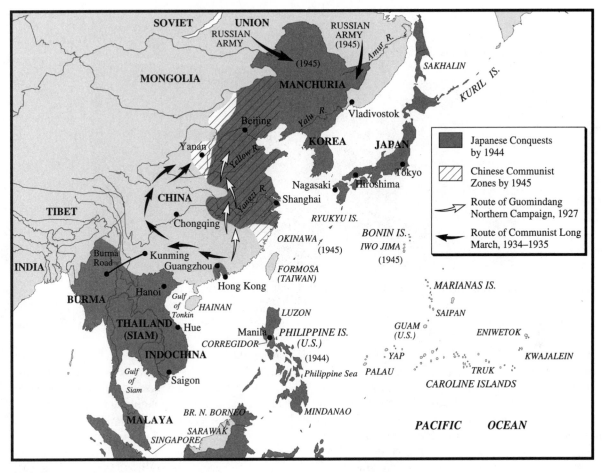

MAP 18.1 War and Revolution in China and Japan, 1911–1949

tariat. After 1927, the urban working class vanished from China's revolutionary scene, and the cities, which Karl Marx had characterized as the stage of modern revolution, became centers of political conservatism. Finding themselves hounded out of the cities and into the countryside, the CCP began to develop a strategy of rural revolution that within two decades would lead them to victory over Chiang Kai-shek and the GMD.

Revolutions often succeed less as a result of their own strength than as a consequence of the weakness of the existing state authority. With the defeat of the CCP and the unification of China, Chiang Kai-shek was in a position to create a strong state and an industrial economy. That he was unable to accomplish these tasks is often attributed to the Japanese invasion of 1937; but even so, he had a decade within

which to strengthen China's state and economy and to bring a modicum of social justice to its countryside, and still he failed. Why?

The Nanjing Decade (1927–1937): The Second Failure of Conservative Modernization

The "Great Revolution" of 1925–1927, as China's Marxist historians called it, revealed both the deep antagonism between landlord and peasant in the

Chiang Kai-shek and Madame Chiang in 1945, with high government and military officers of the Nationalist regime. *Visual Studies Workshop*

countryside and the revolutionary potential of the peasantry. Organized by the CCP into rural unions, peasants in many areas had pressed for rent and interest reductions. Landlord resistance often led to demands for thoroughgoing land reform. In Haifeng county, in Guangdong province, for example, peasants under Communist leadership even carried out a violent land revolution in late 1927, intending to redistribute land equitably to all peasants. Thus, when Chiang Kai-shek succeeded in unifying China, he inherited a rural time bomb waiting to explode. The Nanjing Decade, so named for the capital city of China under Chiang Kai-shek's rule, was a last chance to carry out those reforms that would have defused it, but Chiang's regime proved unable or unwilling to do so.

Chiang Kai-shek was a military man, not an intellectual or even a very deep thinker, and more than anything else he was committed to preserving his own power. He had made deals with several warlords. And like the leaders of the self-strengthening movement, whom he greatly admired, Chiang came to rely on the rural landlords to preserve order in a countryside he saw threatened by Communist subversion.

Under Sun Yat-sen, the GMD had urged a modest 25 percent rent reduction for all peasants, but even this Chiang Kai-shek was unwilling to risk, fearing that it would erode his base of support among the landlords. Under these conditions, Chiang had whatever successes could be claimed in creating an industrial economy and a modern state. Most progress was made in the fields of finance, communications, light industry, and education. Four modern banks were established to control China's currency; the railroad network was increased from five thousand to eight thousand miles; and highways, airlines, and telecommunications were improved. Little of this, however, directly touched the rural masses.

Because Chiang had allowed the land tax to stay in the hands of the provincial officials and did not touch the rents collected by landlords, the revenue for his government was limited to that collected as customs duty and taxes on commerce. With the landlord class intact, there was little enough tax revenue to pay for Chiang's military, let alone to embark on an ambitious industrialization program. Indeed, the historical experience of both the self-strengthening movement of 1860–1895 and the Nanjing Decade demonstrates that the landlord class constituted a serious impediment to any efforts to create a modern economy in China. Not until the Chinese Communists led a peasant revolution that destroyed that class was the door opened for modern economic development.

The Chinese Communists and Peasant Revolution: 1928–1949

To orthodox Marxists, it was the urban working class that was to be the agent of Socialist revolution in the modern world, and it was only with great difficulty that Chinese Communists broke out of that orthodoxy to lead a rural peasant revolution. After all, a working-class revolution had almost succeeded during the 1925–1927 period. Even the disaster of 1927 did not automatically lead the CCP to the peasantry, for into the early 1930s, the official leaders of the CCP clung to the hope of regaining an urban base from which to launch a revolutionary movement. It was not easy to break the Marxist habit of seeing peasants as conservative and urban workers as the sole agent of revolution.

Communists and Peasants

China's peasants had a long tradition of rebellion, but their movements had usually resulted only in the reconstitution of the imperial system under a new dynasty. It was the Taipings in the mid-nineteenth century who had shown that the peasantry could participate in a revolution designed to replace the Confucian state and overturn the rural socioeconomic system. But until some in the Communist party began to look to the peasantry, their revolutionary potential in the twentieth century remained untapped.

The first Communist to recognize the peasants' revolutionary potential was Peng Pai, a young man from Haifeng county in Guangdong province. After studying in Japan and participating in the May Fourth movement there, Peng returned to his native Haifeng and began organizing peasant unions. By 1926, he had helped set up unions in nearly all of the villages of Haifeng, and as peasants began demanding not merely rent reductions but also the land itself, he led them in the establishment of China's first "soviet," or Communist-led, government. Despite the crushing of the Haifeng Soviet in the White Terror of 1928 and Peng's execution, his successes demonstrated the revolutionary potential of China's peasants, and he pioneered the techniques that could be used to organize them. These lessons were not lost on Mao Zedong.[3]

As a young man from a well-to-do peasant family in Hunan, Mao Zedong (1893–1976) had participated in the 1911 Revolution as a student. He also worked as a library assistant at Beijing University for one of the founders of the Chinese Communist party. Mao was one of the first members of the party, and he played an important role during the period of GMD-CCP cooperation in the 1920s. Most striking about Mao during this early period, however, was that, like Peng Pai, he was intellectually predisposed to find a revolutionary message in the actions of the peasantry. Here is part of a famous report he wrote in 1926:

> The present upsurge of the peasant movement is a colossal event. In a very short time, in China's central, southern, and northern provinces, several hundred million peasants will rise like a mighty storm, like a hurricane, a force so swift and violent that no power, however great, will be able to hold it back. They will smash all the trammels that bind them and rush forward along the road to liberation. They will sweep away all the imperialists, warlords, corrupt officials, local tyrants and evil gentry into their graves. Every revolutionary party and every revolutionary comrade will be put to the test, to be accepted or rejected as they decide. There are three alternatives. To march at their head and lead them? To trail behind them, gesticulating and criticizing? Or to stand in their way and oppose them. Every Chinese is free to choose, but events will force you to make the choice quickly.[4]

The peasants had forced Chiang Kai-shek to choose, and that choice led to his break with the Communists and his decision to suppress the worker and peasant movements. Chiang's choice also meant that Communists had to flee into the countryside to save their lives. Mao thus found himself, in 1928, with a small army hiding on a remote Jiangxi mountaintop, surrounded not by workers and students but by bandits, peasants, and soldiers. And although organizing the peasantry and building a revolutionary base in the countryside was considered heretical by the more orthodox Communist party leaders, Mao and his small band of followers began doing precisely that.

The Jiangxi Soviet

In the hill country of the Hunan-Jiangxi border, far from the areas controlled by the GMD, Mao developed a number of policies and approaches that gave the peasants what they wanted—the land—and created the Red Army to protect them against the GMD forces and the return of the landlords. Under Mao's leadership, land was redistributed equally to all peasants, rich and poor alike. Younger peasants enrolled in the Red Army, commanded by General Zhu De. Mao established a separate party and government structure—a soviet—and as peasant support for the land revolution grew, so did the soviet areas. Soon a dozen soviets had been created, and at Mao's urging, in 1931, they established the Chinese Soviet Republic with a territory of about fifteen thousand square miles and three million to four million people.

Under the Jiangxi Soviet, the elements of Mao's revolutionary strategy began to emerge. Essentially, Mao's idea was to create rural base areas as part of a protracted struggle expected to last for decades. The key was to gain the wholehearted support of the peasantry. This would be accomplished through an egalitarian land revolution that redistributed land to all peasants; an economic policy ensuring self-sufficiency; creation of a politically motivated military subordinated to the control of the Communist party; and the establishment of an autonomous government under Communist leadership.

To mobilize women for the revolution, the Communist authorities of the Jiangxi Soviet also addressed the issue of family reform. Their 1934 Marriage Law extended to women the rights to vote, to own property, and to divorce. With peasant men enrolled in the Communist army, women were mobilized into production, assuming roles in handicraft industry, agriculture, weapons manufacture, and care of the wounded.

However, the Jiangxi experience also demonstrated the limits of communist support for family reform and gender equality. Paradoxically, successful land reform had addressed the most pressing economic issues facing peasants, with the result that peasants could once again form stable families. The right to immediate divorce nullified the patriarchal power of men to treat women as property, thereby threatening peasant men who had purchased wives and struggled to keep the family together. To maintain the support of peasant men for the revolution, the Communist party began backing away from a commitment to gender equality. Thereafter, the Communist-led revolution had the character of a coalition between the Communist party and peasant men.[5]

In Jiangxi, the revolutionary strategy combining land reform with an army recruited from peasants worked as long as peasants felt secure that landlords and Chiang Kai-shek's GMD would not return. But increasingly, that security was difficult to maintain. Using techniques of guerrilla warfare rather than fighting frontal battles, the Red Army was able to protect the Jiangxi Soviet from 1928 through 1934. Then, however, Chiang's numerically superior and better equipped forces finally drove the Communists out of Jiangxi and forced them into an enormous trek across virtually the entire country.

The Long March: 1935

The Long March of 1935 is one of the truly heroic chapters in military history (see Map 18.1). Over the course of a year, the Communist forces marched 6,000 miles from Jiangxi to a new base in the northwest province of Shaanxi. Of the 100,000 men and 35 women who began the march, only 8,000 survived to see the city of Yanan, where the new government was established. Crossing several major mountain ranges, forging scores of rivers, and fighting a full-dress battle on average every two days, the survivors, Mao Zedong included, emerged with an intense sense of mission, comradeship, and even invincibility.

By the time the Communists reached their new base in Yanan, they had become committed to a peasant-based revolution. Furthermore, they had built an army, developed effective guerrilla tactics, and established a working government that administered sizable areas. Finally, Mao Zedong had gained full control of the Chinese Communist party in defiance of Stalin's wishes. From then on, the CCP, under Mao's leadership, was independent of Moscow. And with a new base area in Yanan, Mao set out to re-create the successes of the Jiangxi Soviet in a new location. Before long, though, Japanese military aggression impinged once more on the course of the Chinese Revolution.

Japanese Imperialism and the Chinese Revolution

For those inclined to ponder the role of accidents in history, the Japanese invasion of China in 1937 is an interesting case. Without that invasion, some have argued, a Communist victory might never have occurred. And yet the Japanese invasion itself was no accident; it arose out of the imperialist system in Asia, the transformation of Japanese society, and the course of the Chinese Revolution.

Japanese imperialism had emerged in the course of its dramatic modernization efforts in the late nineteenth century (see Chapter 20). To Japan, China represented both a market for its industrial production and a source of raw materials for the heavy industry required to support its military needs. Until the Great Depression of the 1930s, the Western powers had set the rules of imperialism in Asia, and Japan had to play by those rules. Nor had Japan counted on the explosive growth of Chinese nationalism. Although Chiang was a conservative, he was committed to reclaiming China's sovereignty. Chiang thus threatened Japanese interests in Manchuria, which it had gained by defeating Russia in 1905.

In September 1931, Japanese troops poured into Manchuria, and shortly thereafter Japan created the puppet state of Manchukuo, complete with the last Chinese emperor on the throne. The direct military takeover of Manchuria was the first instance of Japan's refusing to conform to the West's definition of the imperialist game in Asia.

It was the Great Depression that finally caused Japan to go it alone in China. Japan's foreign trade dropped by almost 50 percent in the two years following the stock-market crash in 1929, and as it began to recover, Western powers acted to exclude it from foreign markets. Increasingly, Japanese came to believe that the most secure markets were those they could control politically. Since Britain already had its empire and the United States had its Latin American backyard protected by the Monroe Doctrine, Japan set out to create its own exclusive trading sphere and to resolve the contradictions of capitalism in the same way the leading capitalist nations were doing. Under these circumstances, it was only a matter of time before Japan used military means to accomplish what it could not get China to agree to at the negotiating table.

The Japanese Invasion of China

What finally sparked Japan's all-out invasion of China was the creation of a second united front between the CCP and the GMD. In the face of Japanese aggression in Manchuria, anti-Japanese feeling ran high in China, and calls for national unity became more insistent. Mao and the CCP were willing, but Chiang Kai-shek resisted working with his bitter enemies until one of his own warlord allies forced him at gunpoint into an alliance in late 1936. Confronted with the possibility that a united China would prove an even greater obstacle to their imperial plans in Asia, the Japanese soon acted:

The invasion began in July 1937, and by mid-1938, the Japanese controlled much of eastern China. Japan's military planners had expected a quick victory over what appeared to them to be the weaker and disorganized Chinese forces. But Chiang Kai-shek, following a strategy of trading territory for time, retreated to Chongqing and refused to surrender. And the Chinese Communists, from their base in Yanan, launched a guerrilla war against the invaders behind Japanese lines. For the Chinese, then, what Americans and Europeans call the "Second World War" started in 1937.

The Japanese invasion in 1937 was of decisive importance for the rise to power of the Chinese Communists. Not only did it allow the CCP to organize behind enemy lines, it also drove Chiang Kai-shek and his Nationalist government out of the cities, forcing them to spend the rest of the war holed up in Chongqing. The Chinese Communists, however, made a different choice: to resist the Japanese.

The CCP, under Mao Zedong's leadership, transformed itself from the ragtag army of eight thousand, which had arrived in Yanan at the end of the Long March, into a government with a million-soldier army administering a population of one hundred million over a territory of one million square miles by 1945. Their aggressive struggle against the Japanese won for the Communists a reputation as determined nationalists, and their popular appeal grew as they seemed to have answers for both of China's modern problems—imperialism and social injustice. During the Yanan Era of 1937–1945, the Chinese Communists developed the policies and created the institutions that led them to total victory by 1949.

The Yanan Way in Revolutionary China

Yanan was the capital of the Communists' new government in the northwest province of Shaanxi. The "Yanan Way"[6] refers to the distinctive strategies and institutions that led to success for the Chinese Communists. Through the practice of *People's War,* a mobilized peasantry led by the CCP defeated an industrialized power in a protracted war and in the process destroyed landlord political power. As a result, both Japanese imperialism and landlord domination were removed as obstacles to China's economic development.

The United Front and Its Breakdown

Upon arriving in Yanan at the end of 1935, Mao and his supporters found a small but organized Communist group that had been carrying out a radical land revolution in the surrounding area. But it was not enough to destroy the economic power of the landlords; it was also necessary to mobilize the peasants politically. For once the land was redistributed, peasants had a tendency to return to their farms rather than join the army to protect their new gains. Mao's solution was to insist that the land revolution not be carried out from above; rather, the peasants themselves had to rise up. In the process, peasants acted against landlords, smashed their political and economic power, and created new political institutions in which they had significant power. The land revolution, in short, was accompanied by a transformation of peasants from passive and oppressed subjects into political and historical actors. Seized by a vision of a better future, peasants, and especially the young ones, joined the Chinese Communist party and the army; the average age of the army rank and file, for

instance, was nineteen, and that of officers was twenty-four.

Upon forming the United Front with Chiang Kai-shek in 1937, the CCP agreed to moderate its revolutionary program and to cooperate with the GMD against Japan, all in the name of national unity. But the United Front was an uneasy truce that largely broke down by 1941. From then on, Chiang Kai-shek reassigned his troops in the north to blockade the Communists' Yanan base area, rather than fight the Japanese. In doing so, Chiang and the GMD lost whatever nationalist credentials they had, and the CCP emerged as the champions of Chinese nationalism.

Even though the United Front had broken down, the Communists maintained their moderate social policies and limited the land revolution to the strict enforcement of rent and interest reductions. To sustain peasant support, the CCP developed a novel technique of mass participation known as the *mass line.* As conceived by Mao, the Communists would listen carefully to the ideas and aspirations of the peasant masses, formulate those ideas into a political program in concert with the party objectives, and then return to explain the policy to the peasants. "From the masses, to the masses" was Mao's explanation of the mass-line technique. It represented a generally effective attempt to provide for popular participation in political life in an illiterate peasant society wholly unaccustomed to involvement in public affairs.

Women were among those who took on new roles in the public and political life of Yanan. Even though northern China was more conservative than the south, where the Communists had established the Jiangxi Soviet, People's War drew men to the front, rendering it necessary to mobilize women in production, politics, and land reform. Under land reform, all people—including women and children—were to receive land. Although this measure was not vigorously implemented (most land was deeded in the name of the family), women did speak out publicly against their oppression by landlords and other tyrants. For some it was the first time in their adult lives to be called by their own names rather than "so and-so's wife." By and large, though, gender issues were subordinated to the larger objectives of rural revolution, as they had been in the Jiangxi Soviet.

VOICES
Revolution in Long Bow Village

The Chinese Revolution occurred in thousands of separate villages as Communist party officials called cadres encouraged peasants to "speak the bitterness" of their personal experiences, to "struggle" with their landlords, and to "settle accounts" with them. In the process, men and women who had long been passive and inarticulate in the face of landlord oppression became politically conscious and active. Here is a brief account of one such struggle in Long Bow Village.

There was no holding back. . . . So vicious had been Ching-ho's practices and so widespread his influence that more than half of the families in the village had scores to settle with him. . . . Old women who had never spoken in public before stood up to accuse him. Even Li Mao's wife—a woman so pitiable she hardly dared look anyone in the face—shook her fist before his nose and cried out, "Once I went to glean wheat on your land. But you cursed me and drove me away. Why did you curse and beat me? And why did you seize the wheat I had gleaned?" Altogether over 180 opinions were raised. Ching-ho had no answer to any of them. He stood there with his head bowed. . . . When the committee of our [Peasant] Association met to figure up what he owed, it came to four hundred bags of milled grain, not coarse millet.

That evening all the people went to Ching-ho's courtyard to help take over his property. . . . We went in to register his grain and altogether found but two hundred bags of unmilled millet—only a quarter of what he owed us. Right then and there we decided to call another meeting. People said he must have a lot of silver dollars. . . .

We called him out of the house and asked him what he intended to do since the grain was not nearly enough. He said, "I have land and house."

"But all this is not enough," shouted the people. So then we began to beat him. Finally he said, "I have forty silver dollars under the *k'ang*." We went in and dug it up. The money stirred up every-

one. We beat him again. He told us where to find another hundred after that. But no one believed that this was the end of his hoarding. We beat him again and several militiamen began to heat an iron bar in one of the fires. . . .

Altogether we got $500 from Ching-ho that night. . . . We were all tired and hungry. . . . So we decided to eat all the things that Ching-ho had prepared to pass the New Year—a whole crock of dumplings stuffed with pork and peppers and other delicacies. He even had shrimp.

Another struggle became a part of the revolutionary process as well. As women formed a Women's Association, they encountered much hostility from their menfolk, who regarded public activity by women as "steps leading directly to adultery." Not a few were severely beaten by their husbands or fathers-in-law. Here is the story of one such woman in Long Bow Village.

Among those who were beaten was poor peasant Man-ts'ang's wife. When she came home from a Women's Association meeting, her husband beat her as a matter of course, shouting, "I'll teach you to stay home. I'll mend your rascal ways. . . ." She went the very next day to the secretary of the Women's Association and registered a complaint against her husband. After a discussion with the members of the executive committee, the secretary called a meeting of the women of the whole village. At least a third, perhaps even half of them, showed up. In front of this unprecedented gathering of determined women, a demand was made that Man-ts'ang explain his actions. Man-ts'ang, arrogant and unbowed, readily complied. He said that he beat his wife because she went to meetings and "the only reason women go to meetings is to gain a free hand for flirtation and seduction."

This remark aroused a furious protest from the women assembled before him. Words soon led to deeds. They rushed at him from all sides, knocked him down, kicked him, tore his clothes, scratched his face, pulled his hair and pummelled him until he could no longer breathe.

"Beat her, will you? Beat her and slander us all, will you? Well, rape your mother. Maybe this will teach you. . . ."

"Stop, I'll never beat her again," gasped the panic-stricken husband who was on the verge of fainting under their blows. . . .

From that day onward, Man-ts'ang never dared beat his wife and from that day onward his wife became known to the whole village by her maiden name, Ch'eng Ai-lien, instead of simply by the title of Man-ts'ang's wife, as had been the custom since time began.

Source: William Hinton, *Fanshen* (New York: Random House, 1966), pp. 137–38, 158. Reprinted by permission.

Ironically, the Communists did carry out a family revolution, though it was not the one talked about in party propaganda or promised in the various marriage laws. For over a century, the peasant family had been sinking deeper and deeper into crisis as increasing numbers lacked the economic means to form and then support a family. Successful land reform shored up the economic fortunes of peasants, enabling most to form families once again. According to historian Judith Stacey:

> Almost all peasant families could reasonably hope to maintain and reproduce themselves. They could rear infants born to them, arrange marriages for their sons and daughters, and bury their dead with honor. Families had been reunited; prospects for intergenerational geographic stability were better than they had been in decades. To many it seemed time to "set up a household and make one's fortune." Communism had played its ironic role as savior of peasant family life.[7]

To be sure, by destroying landlordism, land reform also destroyed the Confucian-based structure of elite families. But patriarchy and the dominant position of men was supported and reaffirmed in the peasant families, made possible by the Communist-led revolution.

People's War and Communist Victory

The institutions and policies described earlier supported the practice of People's War, in which the active support of the populace was considered essential to the Communist-led resistance to Japanese aggression. The Japanese themselves also did much to foster popular support for the CCP. Following a Chinese offensive in 1940–1941, the Japanese retaliated with their "three-all" policy: "burn all, kill all, destroy

all." In practice, this meant surrounding a given area, killing everyone in it, and making it uninhabitable. The result, however, was to stiffen the resistance of the Chinese peasants.

It is sometimes supposed that the viciousness of the Japanese invasion instilled in the peasants of north China a primitive nationalism that the Communists tapped and then rode into power in 1949. This view emphasizes the decisive impact of the Japanese invasion on the Chinese Revolution. But the Chinese Communists were nationalists long before the Japanese invasion, and they brought a modern sense of nationalism to the peasants, rather than vice versa. Furthermore, the peasants responded at least as much to the social and political programs of the Communists as to their anti-Japanese messages, for Mao and the Communists held out the promise of land and land reform.

And yet the Japanese invasion did prove crucial to the success of the Communists because it effectively destroyed Guomindang power in both the cities and the countryside over large parts of China. The landed gentry, upon whom GMD authority had rested, fled from the countryside or stayed to collaborate with the Japanese. In either case, they provided an easy target for Communist organizing. In the areas controlled by the Communists, landlord power was decisively broken. Furthermore, because Chiang Kai-shek and the GMD retreated to Chongqing, the popular mantle of Chinese nationalism fell to the Communists, who were perceived by the people as leading the anti-Japanese struggle, especially in north China. As corruption, decadence, and declining morale settled over the GMD in Chongqing, the Communists thrived.

Japan's surrender to American forces on 14 August 1945, precipitated a dash by GMD and Communist armies to occupy Japanese-held territory. Airlifted by American planes, Chiang's forces soon held all the major cities, while Mao's Communists controlled the north China countryside. With a four-to-one troop superiority over the Communists and an even greater advantage in modern military technology (thanks to American aid), Chiang Kai-shek was confident of a quick military victory. Negotiations mediated by the United States for the formation of a GMD-CCP coalition government soon collapsed, and civil war resumed.

Following the principles of People's War, the Communist armies had swollen to two million while corruption sapped GMD forces. The tide turned in mid-1947, and GMD armies quickly collapsed. Chiang and his GMD forces continually retreated, finally fleeing to the island of Taiwan at the end of 1949. In Beijing on 1 October 1949, Mao Zedong proclaimed the birth of the People's Republic of China. "Ours no longer will be a nation subject to insult and humiliation," he announced. "We have stood up."[8]

I Conclusion

If nationalism and nation-building swept Europe in the nineteenth century, they became elemental processes in China during the twentieth. But Chinese nationalism differed significantly from that of Europe, primarily in its revolutionary thrust. Nationalism in Europe largely coincided with the institutions and culture of a ruling elite as it tried to make the "nation" a viable economic, social, and cultural unit for the growth of capitalist enterprise and bourgeois culture.[9] Chinese nationalism, in contrast, burst on the scene following the Sino-Japanese War of 1894–

1895, and took the form of a revolutionary rejection of China's traditional culture in the New Culture and May Fourth movements of the early twentieth century. Nationalism also fueled the anti-imperialist movement, which drove the Western and Japanese imperialists out of China, and it supported the Communist programs of rural revolution. Nationalism and social revolution, then, reinforced each other in China in ways they did not in India or Africa. Thus, China's revolutionaries removed both imperialists and landlords, the two major obstacles to China's national development. After that was done, China's fate was in its own hands.

Notes

1. See, esp., Kay Ann Johnson, *Women, the Family and Peasant Revolution in China* (Chicago: University of Chicago Press, 1983); and Judith Stacey, *Patriarchy and Socialist Revolution in China* (Berkeley and Los Angeles: University of California Press, 1983).

2. *Selected Works of Mao Tse-tung,* vol. 1 (Beijing: Foreign Languages Press, 1975), p. 22.

3. Robert B. Marks, *Rural Revolution in South China: Peasants and the Making of History in Haifeng County* (Madison: University of Wisconsin Press, 1984).

4. *Selected Works of Mao Tse-tung,* pp. 23–24.

5. See Johnson, *Women;* and Stacey, *Patriarchy.*

6. The heading for this section and much of the analysis that follows are derived from Mark Selden, *The Yanan Way in Revolutionary China* (Cambridge: Harvard University Press, 1971).

7. Stacey, *Patriarchy,* p. 155.

8. *Selected Works of Mao Tse-tung,* vol. 4, pp. 16–17.

9. Eric J. Hobsbawm, *The Age of Capital, 1848–1875* (New York: New American Library, 1984), chap. 5.

Chapter 19
Socialism, Development, and Politics: The People's Republic of China

The Chinese Revolution is one of the three great social upheavals of the modern world. The French Revolution of 1789 destroyed feudalism throughout Europe with the imposition of the Napoleonic Code and articulated the values of a liberal society. The Russian Revolution of 1917 charted a noncapitalist path to rapid industrialization and claimed to create the world's first Socialist society. Both swept away old social classes and destroyed the previous ruling elite. China's revolution joins the French and the Russian not only in remaking society but also in changing the course of global history.

It represented a vast extension of communism, bringing an additional 20 percent of the world's population under the sway of Marxist ideology. But that very success soon led to a decisive split in the Communist world, as China and the Soviet Union became sharp rivals for political influence in the developing nations. China's revolutionary heritage and its unique approach to modern development fired enthusiasm among poor or oppressed peoples in many places, much as the Russian and French revolutions had done before it. After 1978, China's highly successful economic reforms provided a model for other Communist societies seeking to renew their stagnant economies. And China's huge population, nuclear capacity, and booming economy had made it by the 1990s a major player in the post–Cold War world.

With the establishment of the People's Republic of China in 1949, China entered a new stage in its history. Dominated by the towering presence of Mao Zedong, the history of the People's Republic was marked by radical swings from one developmental strategy to another as the Chinese tried to build a society that was both Socialist and modern. The only other major country in the twentieth century to face similar circumstances was the Soviet Union.

Starting Points: Comparing China and the Soviet Union

Compared with the Soviet Union on the morrow of the Bolshevik Revolution of 1917, China had both greater advantages and greater handicaps. First, in the Soviet Union, the Bolshevik seizure of power was followed by a debilitating three-year civil war that the revolutionaries nearly lost; the Chinese Communists, by contrast, had already won their civil war when they assumed power in 1949. Second, as the first successful Communist revolution, the Bolsheviks faced almost universal hostility and international intervention in their civil war. China, however, had a secure northern border with the Soviet Union and faced an international environment in which one of the great powers was an established Communist state. Third, unlike the Bolsheviks, who came to power literally overnight in an urban insurrection, the Chinese Communists had substantial administrative and governing experience; by the early 1940s, they already ruled an area with 100 million inhabitants. Finally, whereas the Bolsheviks had little support from the peasantry and lacked experience of any kind in the countryside, the Chinese Communists came to power as the champions of the rural masses, who constituted some 80 percent of China's population.

This last comparative advantage, however, had its roots in the single greatest problem China faced:

massive backwardness and grinding poverty in a land with a dense population and scant opportunity to open new agricultural land. Russia, too, had been backward, but the tsarist regime had invested in an industrial base, and in 1917, modern industry accounted for 16 percent of Russia's national income. In China of 1949, industrial income amounted to only 3.5 percent. Russia's urban working class claimed 5 percent of the population; China's minuscule proletariat barely made up 1 percent. Moreover, China's manufacturing sector was concentrated in light industry such as textiles, whereas Russia had a base of heavy industry. Finally, in 1917, Russia had a complete railroad system that integrated the economy and made possible Bolshevik rule from a single city, whereas China's railroad system had been developed by imperialists to export raw materials to the coast rather than to unify the country.

Backwardness, Development, and Socialism

The fundamental question confronting China following its 1949 revolution was rapid economic development, and particularly industrialization. There was no question or debate about that; it was in large part the *raison d'être* of the revolution. But where would a desperately backward and impoverished China find the funds for industrialization? It certainly did not have access to the kind of economic windfall that accompanied Europe's imperial expansion and assisted its industrial growth. Nor did China receive substantial loans and foreign investment, as so many other developing countries have in the twentieth century. The United States, which had emerged from World War II as the strongest nation on earth and the dominant economic power, had sided with Chiang Kaishek during China's civil war. After the Communist victory, it acted to isolate what Americans called "Red" or Communist China from the world community by imposing an economic boycott that shut it off from international trade and capital markets.

Thus, China's substantial industrial development from 1949 to the early 1980s was financed almost wholly on its own, a strategy that came to be known as "self-reliance." As its only ally at the time, the So-

viet Union did provide a small amount of financial assistance to China, but that was rapidly repaid after 1960 when the Soviets severed economic ties with China.

Revolutionary China shared with the rest of the developing world the belief that a strong state could usher in rapid economic growth. Creating wealth and power had been Chinese nationalist objectives since the mid-nineteenth century. But China also sought at the same time, to create a Socialist society—to eradicate old inequalities, to prevent the emergence of new ones, and to reshape Chinese values and culture in light of Communist ideals. How to combine these twin commitments—rapid development and socialism—has been the central dilemma in China's history since 1949. And since the demise of the Communist bloc in 1989 and the Soviet Union in 1991, China stands increasingly alone in proclaiming socialism as a goal.

In attempting to combine rapid economic growth with socialism, China has followed three different models of development (excluding the initial period of recovery). Though all accepted the political monopoly of the Chinese Communist party, each approach had assumptions, objectives, and consequences that were bitterly opposed by some in the party. These strategies can be identified as the Stalinist model, followed in the mid-1950s; the Maoist model, formulated first in the Great Leap Forward of the late 1950s and continued during the Cultural Revolution of the late 1960s; and the market socialism reform model, attempted briefly in the early 1960s, and, since 1979, the cornerstone of China's developmental strategy. The implementation of these various strategies has shaped much of Chinese life since 1949, and the conflict surrounding them has brought the country to the edge of civil war more than once.

The New Chinese State and Economic Recovery: 1949–1953

When Mao Zedong proclaimed the People's Republic of China in 1949, he did not anticipate the immediate creation of a Socialist society; rather, he was more concerned with building a strong new state and an industrial economy. These were prerequisites for sheer survival in a harsh world. Though the ultimate Marxist goal of a classless Communist society had been announced months before, the country's Communist leadership believed that a period of political stability and economic recovery was necessary before China could move toward socialism.

The new government of China was a party-state, in the sense that the Chinese Communist party (CCP) had both created the state and defined its agenda. By comparison with anything China had known for over 150 years, it provided strong and effective government. Penetrating more deeply into Chinese society than any previous state, it imposed and collected taxes from the populace, established and maintained order with a new police force, and protected the national boundaries and interests with its armed forces. Moreover, it mobilized the resources necessary for economic recovery from the devastation of war and laid plans for further development. And to organize and implement all of these activities, the Communist party created and staffed the necessary state bureaucracy.

The first task of the new state was to complete the unification of China and establish sovereignty over its territory, for in 1949 large parts of China remained under the control of others. The People's Liberation Army soon pushed Chiang Kai-shek's armies to the island of Taiwan and extended its control over China's vast border regions and non-Chinese inhabitants. These included Tibet, located between China and India; Xinjiang, bordering the Soviet Union in the northwest; and inner Mongolia, to the north of the Great Wall. By the end of 1950, the task of the reunification of China—with the notable exceptions of Taiwan and Hong Kong—had been completed.

The Land Revolution

Under Communist leadership, peasants had struggled for the land from 1946 through the end of 1952 as the land revolution spread from north to south China. In thousands of villages, Communist cadres organized peasants, invited them to "speak the bitterness" of their exploitation and oppression, and encouraged them to confront the landlords, often violently.

Mao Zedong, shown here proclaiming the People's Republic of China on October 1, 1949, was the central historical figure in China's twentieth-century upheavals. *AP/Wide World Photos*

Those classified as landlords had their land expropriated and redistributed to peasants. Frequently, the landlords also lost their animals, money, tools, and houses, and were granted only a small plot equivalent to what a poor peasant would receive. Many landlords were executed or imprisoned. It was a bloody process, but it ended the centuries-old problem of landlordism and eliminated the class that had dominated old China.

The historic significance of China's land reform can hardly be overstated. It consolidated the position of the Communist party in the countryside and facilitated the rise to power of young (and largely male) rural cadres. To that extent, it was a fundamental step along China's state-building road.

Land reform also had consequences for economic development. Under the old regime, the landlord class had blocked industrialization and the creation of a strong state and had consumed a substantial portion of China's economic surplus without investing in productive enterprises. By removing the landlord class, the new state expanded the portion of the GNP available for investment in industry from the 5 percent actually invested in 1933 to more than 25 percent in 1953.

Thus, the land revolution freed up substantial funds for China's industrialization, permitted immediate improvement in the livelihood of its poorer peasants, and substantially leveled a very unequal society. But there was nothing particularly Socialist about this, for peasants received the redistributed land as private property, and distinctions among rich, middle, and poor peasants continued to exist.

The 1950 Marriage Law and Family Reform

One of the first acts of the new government was the June 1950 promulgation of the new Marriage Law. The intent of the law was to end the "feudal marriage system" of forced, compulsory marriages and to lay the framework for "a new democratic marriage system . . . based on the free choice of partners, on monogamy, on equal rights for both sexes, and on the protection of the lawful interests of women and children." The law abolished "bigamy, concubinage, child betrothal, interference in the remarriage of widows, and the exaction of money or gifts in connection with marriages," and, among other things, extended the rights to own property and to divorce to women. The most immediate effect of the law was upon the tens of thousands of women who used divorce to end marriages that were at best unhappy.[1]

Initially, the CCP was reluctant to push the Marriage Law, fearing it would distract attention from the more fundamental task of land reform. But by 1953, as land reform was being successfully completed, the party undertook a mass education campaign to inform the entire population of the content of the Marriage Law and of the new rights of women. Unlike the land reform campaign that had mobilized the peasant population to struggle against landlords, the campaign to study the Marriage Law used educational, not confrontational, tactics. In the end, the Marriage Law and land reform did change

China's marriage patterns and did reform the family structure. They eliminated many of the abuses of the Confucian family system and permitted the formation of stable peasant families. But peasant male prerogatives within the family were left largely intact. Nor did the law touch the custom of "patrilocal marriage," wherein young women moved to their husbands' households, a practice that limited the independence of young brides and provided little incentive for the education of girls.

Urban Recovery

Like most orthodox Marxists, the Chinese leadership in the 1950s equated socialism with an urban industrial economy. Upon assuming power, the new state seized factories and banks belonging to the supporters of Chiang Kai-shek and imperialist firms. This amounted to two-thirds of China's industrial capacity. All other capitalist enterprises, owned by the so-called national capitalists, or those who supported the Chinese Communists in the civil war, remained in private hands. The new state also controlled all banking and foreign trade. But with a shortage of CCP-trained cadres to manage factories and industry, it was necessary to rely on politically untrustworthy managers and former capitalists.

The first few years of the People's Republic of China (PRC) was a period of economic recovery based on this mixed ownership system. China's cities, with a population of sixty million, faced problems of massive unemployment, rampant underworld crime, opium addiction, and prostitution, not to mention production levels that had fallen to less than half the pre–World War II standards. The establishment of internal peace helped, but political campaigns to clean up the cities and to bring the non-Communist managerial and technocratic elite under CCP control also created conditions under which the urban economy revived. By 1952, the economy had rebounded to its prewar levels of production.

The Korean War

China's initial recovery, land reform, and industrial development all occurred under conditions of war with the United States. The issue was Korea, which had been divided between a Communist North and an American-installed southern regime after World War II. When North Korean forces invaded the South in 1950, the United States, acting under the auspices of the United Nations, sent troops to South Korea. As U.S. forces advanced north toward the Chinese border, the new Communist leadership feared that the Americans were seeking to overthrow their revolution and so sent their army to assist the North Koreans. A cease-fire in 1953 left North and South Korea in roughly their prewar situation.

The costs of the Korean War were enormous for China: nearly one million Chinese were killed or wounded (including Mao Zedong's son); plans for industrialization were postponed; the "liberation" of Taiwan was put off; and China was excluded from the world economy for the next twenty years because of a U.S.-enforced economic boycott. But China had demonstrated to the world, and to itself, that it could fight the most powerful nation to a standstill. China had indeed stood up.

The Stalinist Model and the Transition to Socialism

China's Communist leaders did not merely want a strong, modern, and industrial China; they wanted a Socialist China. Capitalism may have vastly increased the world's productive power, Marxists argued, but it also oppressed workers and enslaved the peoples of Asia, Africa, and Latin America. Socialism would restore human dignity, create a more egalitarian society, and maintain peaceful relations among nations. By building socialism, China's leaders expected their country to play a significant role in creating this new world.

Concretely, China's transition to socialism in the mid-1950s took the form of creating a heavy industrial base for the economy, abolishing private ownership of industrial enterprises, and collectivizing the rural economy. Despite considerable consensus on these goals, as the consequences of China's initial developmental path became apparent, deep rifts emerged among leaders who had different visions of how China would build its Socialist society.

The First Five-Year Plan

To establish an economic basis for socialism, China adopted the Stalinist model of industrialization by emphasizing heavy industry such as steel, machine tools, electric power, and basic chemicals. The results of the First Five-Year Plan, which embodied these priorities, were stunning. The economy surged ahead at a rate of 18 percent per year, more than doubling industrial output by 1957. During the First Five-Year Plan, China's privately owned industrial enterprises also were nationalized, adding to the size of the state-owned industrial sector. By any measure, the First Five-Year Plan created an important heavy industry base for China's further economic development.

Financial aid from the Soviet Union played a very small role in China's early industrialization, amounting to a minuscule $300 million in short-term loans. What the Soviets did provide was expertise in designing, building, maintaining, and operating large-scale industrial enterprises. Between 1953 and 1960, Soviet advisers helped build 130 industrial sites in China, which represented a significant technology transfer. Nonetheless, China generated the investment funds to support these projects internally: the country's peasants paid for its industrial development through direct taxes, compulsory sales of grain to the state at low set prices, and high prices for manufactured goods.

Not surprisingly, the adoption of the Stalinist model of industrialization led to the emergence of Soviet forms of centralization and bureaucratization. The new State Planning Council set production goals and managed the economy through central planning; the Ministry of State Control checked for inefficiencies and corruption; and factory managers pushed the Communist party into the background in the operation of industrial plants.

New patterns of inequality also emerged. A bureaucratic elite of planners and managers was joined by a new technological elite of engineers and scientists, all of whom enjoyed the cultural, economic, and social comforts of urban life. As the gap between booming towns and rural areas widened, so too did the distance between workers, who played no role in the management of factories, and the new managers, as well as the gulf between the government and the people it ruled. To Mao and other Marxists who thought that Socialist development ought to narrow these gaps, the results of the First Five-Year Plan made it appear that industrialization had become an end in itself rather than a means to achieve socialism.

Agricultural Collectivization

The First Five-Year Plan did little to increase agricultural output, an economic reality that in turn threatened the drive to industrialization. Under the leadership of Communist party Chairman Mao Zedong, the solution that emerged was rapid collectivization of agriculture. It had begun slowly during land reform as poor peasant families formed "mutual-aid teams" to share scarce tools and draft animals. With the encouragement of rural Communist party members and state support, mutual-aid teams expanded in number and linked together in larger-scale cooperatives. In the cooperatives, peasants pooled their tools and land, receiving a portion of the harvest based on how much land and how many tools they had put into the co-op. From that stage, cooperatives merged into collectives, in which the peasants' income was based not on the amount of land they contributed but on the amount of labor they undertook, calculated in terms of "work points" assigned to various tasks.

Originally, the collectivization process was expected to take at least a decade, but it was largely completed by the end of 1956. China's 100 million peasant households had joined 485,000 collective farms. Despite brief resistance from richer peasants, collectivization was generally a peaceful process. This contrasted markedly with the experience of the Soviet Union, where peasants were forced into collective farms and violence was extensive. In the process, Russian peasants slaughtered and consumed hundreds of thousands of pigs and draft animals rather than lose them to the collective. The peaceful transition in China owed much to the close relationship established between the Communist party and the peasants during three decades of struggle.

The collectivization of agriculture gave the state much more direct control over China's peasants and allowed the government to transfer wealth directly out of the countryside and into industrialization. Although the Stalinist collectivization of agriculture

had been a more violent affair, the effect of the more peaceful process in China was much the same.

Consequences of the Stalinist Model

With agricultural collectivization, the nationalization of industrial enterprises, and the elimination of the market by 1956, China's leaders concluded that the institutional transition to socialism had been completed. If socialism meant the abolition of private property and the control of the state by the Communist party, China was then a Socialist society. To be sure, massive problems of economic backwardness still haunted China's leaders, but most thought that China was on the correct path to communism. Hence, a second Five-Year Plan that followed the Stalinist model was drawn up.

However, Mao had sharp reservations about this approach to China's development. The growth of bureaucratic management inherent in a planned economy seemed quite the opposite of the revolutionary "mass line" that the party had used so effectively in the Yanan period. Mao became concerned that the party was losing its revolutionary edge, becoming conservative and distant from the people.

Furthermore, the Stalinist strategy required both the creation of an intellectual elite and reliance on the Soviet Union for the mastery of modern science and technology. China invested heavily in urban higher education, paid intellectuals high wages for their contributions, and granted them privileges not generally available to China's workers and peasants. As far as Mao Zedong was concerned, this consolidated the inequities between town and countryside and between mental and manual labor that socialism was supposed to diminish. China's intellectuals then began to demand more political and artistic freedom and thus challenged the Communist party bureaucracy.

Believing that the transition to socialism had been completed and that the people of China, including the intellectuals, were solidly behind the party and its policies, Mao and other leaders loosened the ideological reins in the Hundred Flowers Movement of 1957. Given greater intellectual and artistic freedom, intellectuals flooded newspapers with a torrent of criticism that first surprised and then worried and

This woodcut celebrates and idealizes the economic successes of Chinese communism in the 1950s.

angered the party leadership. The leaders quickly crushed the movement, signaling the beginning of the suppression of intellectuals and artists that would last for another twenty years. It also marked the beginning of the end of the Stalinist model in China and the origins of a distinctively Maoist vision of Socialist development.

The Maoist Model of Socialist Development: 1958–1976

Following the completion of the First Five-Year Plan, a different set of policies came to guide China's Socialist development. Formulated and implemented under Mao's leadership, these policies attempted to revolutionize Chinese society on a perpetual basis, to speed up the economic development process, and to move rapidly toward communism—all at the same time. The Maoist approach found expression

first in the rapid collectivization of agriculture after 1955, then, and especially, in two broader movements known as the Great Leap Forward of 1958–1960 and the Great Proletarian Cultural Revolution of 1966–1976.

The Great Leap and People's Communes

The Great Leap Forward emerged during 1958, "the product of a vision rather than of a plan,"[2] and coalesced as a set of radical policies designed to address problems arising from the Stalinist model of development. Primary among these was centralization. As a result of the First Five-Year Plan and the collectivization of agriculture, the entire economy had come under the control of the state planning agencies. The central state was to determine not only what and how much was to be produced but also the price of each commodity and its allocation throughout the country. In a nation as large, populous, and diverse as China, these were daunting tasks. By 1957–1958, party leaders agreed on the need for decentralization but were deeply divided on how to achieve it.

Basically, China could decentralize control of the economy in one of two ways.[3] The first, supported by some economic planners, was to grant greater autonomy to enterprises and collectives, allowing prices and the market, not a central planning agency, to allocate resources. The other was administrative-political decentralization, redistributing party control of decisions from the central government to the provinces or municipalities. Because of Mao's deep distrust of the market, the only alternative was administrative decentralization.

But the issue of incentives remained unresolved: how to get workers, peasants, and managers to improve productivity and increase output. Without material incentives such as higher industrial wages or agricultural prices, Mao was to rely on the use of "nonmaterial incentives" promulgated during intense mass-mobilization campaigns, such as the Great Leap Forward, to encourage greater production.

The solution to these problems—decentralization with continued party control and incentives without markets—lay, Mao argued, in the creation of new and larger organizational units in the countryside, the People's Communes. Combining political and economic functions, integrating industry and agriculture, and tapping China's vast reservoir of seasonally underemployed labor, the People's Communes would provide the basis for a "great leap forward," propelling China past the industrialized West and into a Communist future.

Pushed by rural CCP cadres and supported by poorer peasants, the movement spread rapidly in late 1958 as China's 750,000 collectives combined into 24,000 People's Communes, each averaging 5,000 households (30,000 people). During the most radical phase, in the summer and autumn of 1958, private property disappeared and even families' cooking utensils became common property. Peasants received equal shares of the harvest, regardless of how much labor they contributed to the commune. Efforts to mobilize the labor of women produced experiments in communal dining and child care. Caught up with a vision of reaching communism within three years (or prodded by rural cadres), peasants across China joined massive construction projects—mostly dams and canals for irrigation—often far from home and with little or no pay. Working at a frenzied pace and exhausting themselves, China's peasants nonetheless

completed projects that continue to benefit the country's agriculture to this day.

The People's Communes also promised a means by which China could master science and technology without relying on the Soviet Union or developing a technocratic elite. As part of a policy of rural industrialization, communes throughout China built 7.5 million small-scale rural "factories." These were mostly workshops that built and repaired agricultural implements, but they included the infamous backyard steel furnaces that were intended to teach modern technology to the peasants but generally produced poor-quality steel. By spreading the mastery of science and technology to the countryside, Mao hoped to forestall the emergence of a privileged urban technocratic elite and to raise the cultural level of the rural areas.

In sum, Mao saw the People's Communes as the organizational form that would catapult China forward economically while at the same time realizing the Marxist goals of eliminating the inequalities between mental and manual labor, between town and countryside, and between political rulers and the people. In this respect, it was a Marxist heresy, for orthodox Marxist theory held that communism would come only *after* a modern industrial economy had been created. But the impatient and revolutionary Mao would not wait on history. The communes, he thought, would unleash China's most plentiful resource—human labor power—thus breaking the country out of its dependence on capital-intensive and bureaucratic strategies of development.

But what actually happened was quite different: China was swept into its greatest economic crisis. Harvests plunged and acute food shortages hit many rural areas. Furthermore, the state increased compulsory grain-sales quotas and raised the proportion of the GNP devoted to investment to an incredible 44 percent. When droughts, floods, and famine hit part of the country in 1959–1960, Mao and his policies came under fierce attack. By the time agriculture recovered in 1962, China had passed through what became known as the Three Bad Years—a famine in which about fifteen million people died.

The Sino-Soviet Split

Compounding the economic crisis of the Great Leap Forward, the Soviet Union, in the summer of 1960, withdrew its 1,400 specialists along with the blueprints for the various projects they were working on. Relations between China and the Soviet Union had been strained for several years and became worse when China abandoned the Stalinist model of development and embarked on the Great Leap Forward. Under Nikita Khrushchev, the Soviet Union had begun to back off from its military commitments to China, ultimately reneging on a promise to help China develop nuclear weapons. Sino-Soviet relations deteriorated quickly into an open rift, which led in 1969 to armed border clashes along the Amur River, in the northeast.

The withdrawal of Soviet advisers hastened the arrival of an explicit policy of self-reliance: China would develop solely on the basis of its own resources without relying on help from other Socialist countries or becoming dependent on the capitalist West. This was perhaps making a virtue of necessity, since after 1960 China was isolated from both the Soviet Union and the West. On its own, China would attempt simultaneously to industrialize, to feed and clothe its huge and growing population, and to develop a nuclear capability (which it did by 1964). This was a developmental strategy not attempted by any other nation, but in the 1960s it was put forward as a policy all developing countries could follow.

Retrenchment: The Origins of Market Socialism

By 1960, with the Chinese economy in a shambles, severe food shortages causing widespread hunger, and the break with the Soviet Union, Mao Zedong and his policies had been discredited. Since the Soviet model was also no longer creditable, alternatives were now possible. As Mao withdrew from the daily operation of the party, other high Communist party officials, in particular Liu Shaoqi and Deng Xiaoping, began fashioning *ad hoc* solutions that rescued China from the brink of disaster and that soon coalesced into an approach to economic development at sharp odds with Maoist perspectives.

Under the leadership of Liu and Deng, the first step was to revive the centralized planning that had been abandoned with the Great Leap Forward. Their agricultural policy reauthorized the private plots that had been eliminated in many villages during the Leap, allowed peasants to engage in private handi-craft production, and reopened free rural markets. Although only 12 percent of the arable land reverted to private plots, it produced one-third of the peasants' income and 25 percent of all produce sold in the forty thousand markets that had opened by 1961.

The People's Communes were not abolished, but they shrank in size and their political tasks reverted to the administrative hierarchy. Within the commune structure, the primary unit for managing agriculture returned to the "production team" (most often a traditional village), many of which in turn contracted basic farming chores to peasant households, thus establishing a clear link in peasant minds between personal effort and reward. To stimulate agricultural production further, the state lowered taxes by one-third (from 15 percent to 10 percent of the cereal harvest) and encouraged specialization by allocating chemical fertilizer to those areas with the highest rates of return. As a result, agricultural production revived, with output rising from 195 million tons of grain in 1961 to 240 million in 1965.

Investment in new projects was drastically curtailed. Instead, the state closed down the thousands of inefficient, small-scale rural enterprises established during the Great Leap Forward, reestablished central planning of industry, returned one-person management to factories, and reinstated material incentives for workers and managers. Under these policies, industry rebounded during the first half of the 1960s, growing at a rate of 11 percent per year.

Although these moderate economic policies got China out of the crises of the early 1960s, they had social and cultural dimensions that greatly alarmed Mao Zedong and some of his closest associates. In the countryside, allowing private plots and free markets meant that some peasants became rich while the fortunes of others declined. In the cities, a stratum of highly paid and skilled workers emerged. Most disconcerting to Mao was the cultural and material gap between the countryside and the cities. As he caustically complained in 1965 about health care:

Tell the Ministry of Public Health that it only works for fifteen percent of the total population of the country and that this fifteen percent is mainly composed of gentlemen, while the broad masses of the peasants do not get any medical treatment. First, they don't have any doctors; second they don't have any medicine. The Ministry of Public Health is not a Ministry of Public Health for the people, so why not change the name to the Ministry of Urban Health, the Ministry of Gentlemen's Health, or even to the Ministry of Urban Gentlemen's Health.[4]

From Mao's perspective, what was at issue was not merely China's path to socialism but also the very survival of socialism itself. Unlike many other Chinese Marxists, he had come to equate the use of markets with the restoration of capitalism, rather than as a viable alternative to centralized control of the economy. Thus, he believed that the class struggle still continued and that the victory of socialism was by no means ensured. In fact, Mao feared that the self-centered, materialistic values of capitalism as well as its social inequities were being restored. He increasingly came to see those who opposed his vision as representatives of the "capitalist road" and to conclude, incredible as it seems, that the Communist party was overseeing a capitalist restoration in China. By January 1965, Mao was organizing for a revolutionary attack on the very party he had spent his entire adult life constructing.

"To Rebel Is Justified": The Cultural Revolution

The Great Proletarian Cultural Revolution lasted from 1966 to 1969, and, in less dramatic ways, until Mao's death in 1976. During its first three years, Mao Zedong mounted a campaign that removed his political opponents and brought him and his followers again to the pinnacle of political power. When the Cultural Revolution was launched, it caught both China and the world by surprise, as political turmoil degenerated into violent factional conflict that threatened to plunge the country into civil war. At the same time, the United States was escalating its military involvement in Vietnam, on China's southern border.

Calling together young people throughout the country in huge mass rallies in Beijing, Chairman Mao blessed these Red Guards as "worthy successors" to the Socialist cause. Screaming their support for Mao, the Red Guards pledged their allegiance to his brand of communism before spreading out across the country to eliminate all hints of what seemed to them to be capitalism. They attacked local party and government officials, teachers, intellectuals, factory managers, and others who had connections to prerevolutionary China or were associated with the moderate wing of the CCP. To root out capitalist, Western, or traditional Chinese influences, Red Guard groups desecrated Buddhist temples, invaded the homes of professors, and often beat and abused those who offended them. In January 1967, the workers of Shanghai entered the movement, toppling the municipal government during the short-lived Shanghai Commune.

Rival revolutionary groups soon began fighting with each other, and violence erupted in every province of the country. Thousands were killed in an idealistic youth movement that soon turned to anarchy. The Cultural Revolution unleashed forces that surprised even Mao and that were so complex as still to evade succinct analysis or rational understanding.

With extensive support from the military and high school and college students, Mao regained political power and set the Cultural Revolution on a course designed to remove "those within the party taking the capitalist road." During 1968, the political struggle sharpened at the highest levels as the Maoist attack on Liu Shaoqi and Deng Xiaoping came to a climax: both fell from power in disgrace.

Building a Maoist Society

The Cultural Revolution caused serious socioeconomic problems and disruptions, though none approaching the scale of the Great Leap Forward disasters. Both industrial and agricultural production had been interrupted, resulting in a decline in national income in 1967–1969; the educational system was in turmoil; the Communist party had been decimated; and China's standing in the world suffered. From the disorder of the Cultural Revolution, Mao and his supporters hoped to construct a distinctly Maoist society.

Mao's basic concern was to fashion a developmental strategy that used Socialist means to achieve Socialist ends, a theme that had first emerged in the Great Leap Forward. Mao thus designed social and economic policies that stressed the development of a collective spirit: egalitarian values, moral rather than material incentives to work, mass participation, self-

A disgraced official is paraded through the streets by Red Guards during the Cultural Revolution. *AP/Wide World Photos*

sufficiency in grain and in China's overall development. To implement these policies, Mao held up models in agriculture and industry for other production units to emulate. "In agriculture, learn from Dazhai" was the slogan that drew throngs of visitors to a production brigade in north China. There peasants had raised agricultural output by bringing new land into production through a massive collective effort in the off-season, but they had also received funds secretly from Mao's supporters in the government. Nationally, the "learn from Dazhai" policy meant strengthening the collective rural economy, restricting private plots to 5 percent of the sown area, and encouraging all rural areas to become self-sufficient in grain.

In industry, the model was the Daqing oil field in Manchuria. There workers had created an industrial complex that integrated industry and agriculture, rendering Daqing self-sufficient in grain. Nationally, factories received quotas and operated regardless of whether they made a profit. Factory managers answered to a "revolutionary committee"; an egalitarian, eight-grade work scale replaced bonuses and

other material incentives formerly used to increase production.

Mao had long been critical of the elitist tendencies of China's educational system. Entrance to colleges and universities, based on admissions tests, naturally had favored children of the urban elite. To reverse this trend, Mao called for an educational system that trained students who were both "expert and red"; that is, both technologically proficient and committed to the revolution. As the universities reopened in 1969, after the three years of chaos, examinations as admissions criteria were replaced by class background and political recommendations, and a certain number of positions were reserved for peasants to ensure that they had access to higher education. Similar efforts were made to overcome the rural-urban gaps in health care. China mobilized well over a million "barefoot doctors," ordinary peasants who were trained in preventative health care and paramedical techniques, to bring the benefits of modern medicine to the rural masses.

As a developmental strategy, the Maoist vision trusted neither the central planning mechanism nor the market. It was left, therefore, with little more than ideological prescriptions such as self-reliance and the heavy hand of the party. Furthermore, the army gained prominence as Mao turned to it to restore order in the country. And to compound China's problems, armed clashes with Soviet troops in 1969 raised the threat of war.

With China in desperate need of funds and technology to modernize its military, Premier Zhou Enlai persuaded Mao to consider opening communications with the United States. For its part, the United States, under President Richard Nixon, was searching for ways to negotiate a settlement to the Vietnam War and to balance the growing power of the Soviet Union. These mutual interests finally led to Nixon's historic journey to China in February 1972, opening the way for rapprochement between the two countries and the establishment of full diplomatic relations in 1979.

Within China, however, factional political conflict heated up as it became clear that Mao was dying. By 1975, most of those who had led the revolution were in their seventies, and that generation's passing was imminent. The main contenders were the moderates, allied with Deng Xiaoping, and the radical defenders of Maoist ideology (later known as the Gang of Four), organized around Mao's wife, Jiang Qing. In January 1976, Zhou Enlai died, followed in September by Mao himself. In the political turmoil that followed, the moderates triumphed, setting the stage for yet another turn in China's continuing search for an effective strategy of development.

The Maoist Era in Retrospect

Mao Zedong was one of the towering figures of the twentieth century; his accomplishments were awesome. He led the Chinese Communist party to victory, reunifying China after a century of political disintegration, and placed his stamp on the history of the People's Republic. But he also presided over the disasters of the Great Leap Forward and the Cultural Revolution. Reconciling these two aspects of his career remains a troublesome issue for a party that seeks to claim his mantle as a "revolutionary" while decrying his mistakes as the leader of a great nation.

The Maoist era is filled with ironies, the greatest of which concerns China's peasants. Mao presented himself as the champion of the peasants and sought to avoid the urban bias that has characterized so much of modern development. Yet under his policies, the standard of living of the peasantry remained unchanged from 1957 to 1977. Even maintaining a stable standard of living in the face of massive population increases was no small feat, as the recent history of African nations attests, but under Mao's successors, per-capita rural income has increased dramatically.

That peasants fared so poorly under Mao points to another irony in the Maoist legacy: despite Mao's criticisms of the Stalinist model of development, his strategy also emphasized investment in heavy industry to fuel rapid economic growth, relying on the peasantry to pay for it. This accounts for the stagnant rural standard of living, for the Maoist strategy presupposed very high rates of investment, ranging from 30 percent to 44 percent of the total national income, nearly all of which was extracted from the peasantry by means of the communes. Yet under Mao's leadership, China constructed a powerful centralized state, an economy with a growing industrial base, and a powerful military, thereby becoming a major player in the modern world system.

Despite these accomplishments, neither the Stalinist nor the Maoist strategy of development allowed China to catch up with the industrialized, capitalist world. While Mao disliked the non-revolutionary consequences of bureaucratic, centrally planned economies, he likewise equated markets with capitalism. The result for China was continued economic backwardness.

The Market Socialism Model: 1978 to the Present

The most recent phase in China's development strategy began in December 1978 and represented the triumph of moderates in the political struggles following Mao's death. The Four Modernizations, as the strategy was first called, sought to turn China into a powerful Socialist country with modern agriculture, industry, armed forces, and science and technology by the year 2000. But unlike the doctrinaire Maoist approach, it has been a pragmatic reform strategy, willing to put immediate economic results ahead of Socialist values. It also represents a reaction against the disruptions caused by wild swings in policy over the previous two decades. Since the reform policies rely heavily on the market as a means to stimulate greater production, the entire approach can be briefly described as market socialism.

Dismantling the Communes

China's post-Mao leaders concluded that collectivized agriculture had failed. If agriculture was to remain a prime source of funds for investment in industry as well as provide a better living for the peasants, it simply had to become more productive. The answer was not more modern technology and certainly not calls for more mass mobilization, but a new organizational framework and a new system of incentives.

This meant dismantling collective agriculture and replacing it with what was called the "household-responsibility system." Under this policy, land is leased to individual peasant households to farm as they see fit. In return for long-term leases, which could be inherited, the households pay a small fixed tax and agree to sell a portion of their harvest to the state at fixed prices. Amounts over the contracted figure can be sold to the state at higher prices, or in rural free markets. Begun slowly in 1979, the household-responsibility system has become nearly universal throughout the Chinese countryside. By the early 1990s, China's agriculture was dominated by the peasant family farm.

This reform marked a significant departure from collective farming in which decisions on cropping patterns, irrigation, fertilizer use, and labor allocation were made by various official leaders. Now peasant households make many of these decisions independently. Furthermore, the state raised prices for agricultural products in 1979, 1981, and 1991 for a total increase of over 50 percent, resulting in a significant rise in rural income, and authorized rural free markets to operate once again. Departing from the Maoist goal of local self-sufficiency in grain, the agricultural reforms not only allow but also encourage agricultural specialization. The state has identified twelve rural areas with high productivity where further investments in machinery, irrigation, and

chemical fertilizers are encouraged because it is thought the returns will be high.

As the Chinese explain it, this is a policy of "allowing some to get rich first." Indeed, the economic results of the new agricultural policy have been very impressive. From 1978 to 1990, the value of grain output grew at an average rate of 6 percent a year and rural standards of living have improved dramatically.[5]

Markets, Industry, and Bureaucrats

Reforms in industry followed the logic of those in agriculture: moving the level of decision making down from the planning ministry to the factory and introducing market forces. Instead of having industrial production decided by planners in Beijing, enterprise managers were given the authority to decide on suppliers, output levels, and prices. Managers also could use bonuses to reward productive workers. But they made these decisions in the context of market forces, for each enterprise competed with others and remained in business only if it turned a profit. Inefficient plants were closed. Unlike the agricultural reforms, however, those in industry have been much less eagerly embraced; and since 1989, the state enterprises have been protected from market forces to keep the plants running and the workers employed.

By allowing some market forces and competition among producing units, the leadership hoped to raise industrial production and productivity. By all accounts they have done so. During the 1980s, China's industrial production grew at over 12 percent a year, and by the early 1990s, China's economy was the fastest growing in the world. Much of this growth occurred in the rural areas, where by 1991 there were some 19 million rural industrial firms with 96 million employees. And much also occurred in Special Economic Zones created in a number of coastal areas to attract foreign capital and to promote industries producing for the export market. This new eagerness for inclusion in the world economy represents a sharp departure from the self-reliance of the Maoist era.

China's leaders hoped the market would also counteract the stifling effects of the huge state bureaucracy on the economy. Unlike Mao, who sought to cure bureaucratism with the revolutionary mobilization of the masses, Deng Xiaoping and the leaders of the reform movement see the market as the alternative to bureaucracy. Hence, some observers think that a major source of opposition to the current reforms will come from an entrenched bureaucracy that sees its economic and political power eroding.

Thus China, which has retained its Communist party dominance, has moved further and faster toward a market economy than Russia or most of the states of Eastern Europe where communism has collapsed. But the market generates inequities and produces social values—profit-seeking, competition, and individualism—that are at variance with China's stated Socialist goals. With much diminished state control of the economy, a booming private sector, and substantial foreign investment, does it still make sense to consider China's economy Socialist? China's leadership downplayed these dangers. Deng Xiaoping said that the market in China "is like a bird in a cage." The bird can fly freely, but only within the confines of China's Socialist system.

Those confines extend to the political system dominated by the Chinese Communist party. Despite the significant differences between Mao Zedong and his reform-minded successors, both have insisted that the Communist party must maintain its monopoly on political power. Mao demonstrated this commitment in the 1957 suppression of the Hundred Flowers Movement and again during the Cultural Revolution of the late 1960s. Following Mao's death and announcement of the 1978 reforms, hope for greater intellectual, artistic, and political freedom flowered briefly. The Communist party permitted a "Democracy Wall" in Beijing, where citizens attached posters advocating various points of view. But with the arrest of the leader who had called for China's "fifth modernization, democracy," the demand for greater political freedom was quickly stilled, even though intellectual and artistic freedoms slowly expanded. In 1989, the demand for greater political and intellectual freedom burst forth again in the "Beijing spring," when hundreds of thousands demonstrated in the capital's Tiananmen Square— and some Communist party officials looked on sympathetically. But the promises of the Beijing spring soon turned to tragedy.

The 1989 Tiananmen Massacre

On the night of June 3–4, 1989, troops of the People's Liberation Army (PLA) rolled into Beijing's Tiananmen Square, bloodying and killing thousands of residents who tried to slow their advance. The youthful demonstrators who had occupied the square for two months protesting Communist party corruption and demanding political freedoms, had vacated the square just hours earlier, averting an even greater bloodbath. The Tiananmen Massacre halted China's nascent democracy movement and showed an astounded world watching on television the choice an embattled Communist party could make when confronted with popular demands for more reform than it was willing to grant.

The origins of China's democracy movement, leading to the Tiananmen events, can be found in the economic reforms undertaken during the preceding decade.[6] Freeing up certain sectors of the economy allowed some (peasants, entrepreneurs, even taxi drivers) to benefit from new market opportunities, while employees of state enterprises unable to prove themselves "profitable" were laid off or furloughed, and others on fixed incomes (teachers, bureaucrats, and clerks) saw their living standard deteriorate as deregulated prices rose.

These new inequalities of opportunity and income were exacerbated by rampant corruption among Communist party officials and their families. With an economy only partially marketized and political connections still important, high officials and their families used their positions and power to profit handsomely. The largest new private trading and export firms, for example, were established and owned by children of Communist party officials, the most famous being Deng Xiaoping's son. By the late 1980s, official corruption, inflation, unequal economic opportunity, and growing income disparities led to growing public unrest. In the spring of 1989, university and secondary school students in Beijing began leading protest marches into Tiananmen Square, ultimately setting up a tent city to occupy the square and to welcome marchers from all other walks of life.

The Chinese Communist party was deeply divided over what to do. One faction, led by a Gorbachev-like figure, CCP Chairman Zhao Ziyang, supported the demonstrators and wanted to extend the reforms further into the political arena, possibly even ending the Communist party's monopoly on power. Hardliners within the party supported the use of strong measures to suppress the demonstrations and keep the reforms restricted to the economy. The hardliners prevailed. They placed party chief Zhao Ziyang un-

VOICES
The Next Revolution

Chinese student leaders of the Tiananmen demonstrations who fled abroad following the June 3–4, 1989 massacre formed various organizations to continue the struggle for greater political and intellectual freedoms. One of those leaders, Shen Tong, fled to Boston and became chairman of the Democracy for China Fund. The Chinese government allowed Mr. Shen to return to China in July 1992, with promises for his safety. Those promises were not kept: he was arrested on August 31, 1992, having passed this article to a friend just hours before.

I am back in China—and I have found a China that the outside world does not know about. . . .

These past weeks I have found a country in confusion. China is at a crossroads. It seems there is little political activity, that parts of the economy are bounding ahead, and that the Old Men have triumphed. But the truth is far different.

In recent days, I have felt the scars of ex-political prisoners who have been tortured. I heard of a retired man who starved to death in custody. I went into homes where parents grieve for sons and daughters who are still in prison, or simply missing—and the terrible thing is that many are frightened even to talk about it.

In one village I said to a group of people that ten years of reform had apparently improved their standard of living. One person spoke up and said, "But the Government does only two things: it takes money and it takes lives." Far more than the world realizes, corruption, strikes, dissent, hunger, violence and unbalanced development are forming storm clouds over China. It needs to be modernized, everyone agrees. But to move toward that goal requires not just economic development, but also progress toward a real market economy, liberalization of society, the advent of cultural pluralism and steps toward democratic politics.

Many forces of change swim below the seemingly calm surface. People have gone beyond the stage of saying: "I don't give a damn; I'm just going to make money." True, they have yet to seize on issues that will build a new politics. But they are quietly building a civil society independent of the decaying corpse of Marxist rule. . . .

[S]ome forces for political change are moving independently. The vigor of south China exists in spite of the politicians in the north. Because of contacts with the outside world, a limited but impressive free society is coming into being. One day there will be a new politics to match it, one that is combined with economic development and relative social stability. . . .

I call upon the current authorities to recognize that China's future lies with pluralism. Dialogue between the current regime and the opposition is the first step toward evolutionary change. I call upon reformers in the party: create open opposition within the establishment, using the limited freedom provided by the existing system.

I call upon China's established political underground networks to surface in a limited, organized fashion to create a larger role for themselves.

I call upon prominent individuals who have profound social influence—liberal scholars, artists, entrepreneurs, religious leaders—to speak out within their spheres. By protecting specific rights, such as freedom of creative expression, freedom of religious worship, freedom of publishing, they can build a base for pluralism and civil society.

These potential forces for change can no longer be silent. They must accept responsibility for their own rights and the rights of others. Rights, like power, must be taken; they are never given.

I have returned to China to encourage others to step forward. China is not lacking the forces to transform its repressive, authoritarian society.

A free China will be ours one day.

Source: Shen Tong, "The Next Revolution," *New York Times,* 2 Sept. 1992. Copyright © 1992 by the New York Times Company. Reprinted by permission.

This famous picture from the Tiananmen Square events of 1989 shows a solitary young man confronting a row of government tanks. *Reuters/Bettmann*

der house arrest, and ordered the army to take Tiananmen Square. In the days and weeks that followed, thousands of students and other protest leaders were seized and imprisoned.

The use of deadly force shocked a watching, disbelieving world. Governments around the globe condemned the massacre and decried the flagrant human rights abuses. China's international reputation was severely tarnished. But the greatest consequences of the Tiananmen Massacre have been felt within China. In the eyes of most urban Chinese, the Communist party has lost its legitimacy, relying solely on brute force to remain in power. Indeed, in the aftermath of the massacre, the party increased urban police forces and mounted campaigns within the army to ensure its loyalty. To buy quiescence with a growing economy, the state abandoned an anti-inflationary policy and ordered state enterprises to call back all workers who had been furloughed or laid off and to produce even if they had no buyers for their products. Many people, however, and especially those in the rural areas, seemed less concerned with politics than with making the most of new economic opportunities.

China's political calm in the early 1990s thus masked many unresolved tensions.[7] Can economic reforms continue without parallel political reforms? Can a growing economy and rising standards of liv-

ing blunt the demands for political liberties? Can a Chinese Communist party, theoretically committed to socialism, remain in power even as it nourishes an increasingly capitalist economy? Can China remain a unified state as booming, but regionally uneven, economic development proceeds? And what will happen when China's aging leadership passes from the scene?

Population Policy

China's current and future leaders face a daunting demographic challenge.[8] China's 1990 census placed the population at 1.13 billion people, double the 1953 figure. If the current 1.4 percent annual rate of population increase continues, by the year 2000 China's population will likely grow to 1.4 billion, an increase, in just ten years, greater than the population of the entire United States. Such increases, of course, place an enormous burden on the Chinese economy to maintain living standards, let alone to raise them.

Amazingly, China began to consider uncontrolled population growth to be a problem only in the early 1970s. Prior to that, the Chinese Communists under Mao Zedong's leadership dismissed the issue in the

Marxist belief that more people meant greater human labor power to propel the country's modern economic growth. By the early 1970s, pragmatists in Mao's China realized the importance of gaining control over a burgeoning population if the standard of living was to improve. Since then, the Chinese government has been trying to control the rate of population growth.

Nearly all efforts have focused on limiting the birthrate. In the face of an ancient tradition that idealized the large extended family, China's leadership in the 1970s established a one-child family program. To encourage families to have just one child, the state paid 5 yuan (then about 5 percent of a family's monthly income) to families that agreed not to have more than one child, and by an equal amount fined those that had three or more children. In some areas, couples had to receive permission to attempt a pregnancy.

The one-child family policy succeeded in the cities but failed in the countryside. In urban areas the birthrate slowed appreciably, because housing was scarce, local neighborhood organizations provided strict enforcement, and most people received state-provided retirement benefits. In rural areas, though, the one-child policy was unpopular, unenforceable, and hence ineffective: during the decade of the 1980s, most rural women of child-bearing age gave birth to more than two children.

The reasons for this failure were numerous. The rural economic reforms of the early 1980s, which decollectivized agriculture and promoted family farms, were also accompanied by a resurgence of traditional attitudes toward gender and family size. In the new and increasingly prosperous rural economy, families with more children would both receive and till more land. Growing incomes both required and, it seemed, could support larger families. Simply put, larger families were better, and boys were preferable to girls. When in the early 1980s Communist cadres tried to enforce the one-child policy on rural families, female infanticide increased and many families eagerly paid the fines for having more than one child.

By the mid-1980s, a more pragmatic population policy was adopted for the countryside: one son, or two children. Even this policy has been difficult to enforce, and the evidence so far is that it has not been effective in lowering rural birthrates. Thus, China

likely will have 1.4 billion people by the year 2000, and all the challenges a population that large engenders. But reducing China's population growth rate to 1.4 percent per year represented quite a successful population control program in comparison to most of the rest of the developing world. India's annual rate of population growth during the 1980s was 2.1 percent, and sub-Saharan Africa's was 3.2 percent.

Did Socialism Liberate Women?

Besides complicating China's population policy, the reconstitution of the peasant family farm has had consequences for women in rural China. The age-old practice of purchasing a wife has reemerged, largely because income disparities among the rural populace have increased. Some peasant families get rich while others continue to suffer poverty because of poor location, poor land, poor skill, or poor luck. According to recent reports, thousands of poor rural women have been sold by their families to brokers who make a living off the business, or directly to their future husbands. Like days of old, these women are held virtual prisoners in the new husband's village, often hundreds of miles from their home. Despite the passage of laws and stiff penalties ranging from ten years in prison to death, the practice continues.

From the establishment of the Chinese Communist party in 1921 through the history of the People's Republic of China, gender equality and women's liberation have been proclaimed as goals of the Chinese Revolution. But each time the revolution reached a critical point requiring the participation of peasant men, or when economic modernization demanded sacrifice from the Chinese people, the goal of gender equality was postponed to the indefinite future. Nonetheless, the actual position of women now is much improved from prerevolutionary days. Men and women alike live better and longer, nearly all with families with whom they celebrate births and marriages and mourn deaths.

But how are we to account for this mixed record? Some believe the Communists never really intended to bring women full equality in Chinese life. Others conclude the postponement of gender equality has been the natural result of a revolution made and won by men. The government and party remain dominated by men who are unable, in the words of one analyst, "to perceive and be aware of their own sexist assumptions."[9]

Conclusion

Communist efforts to build a strong, prosperous, and independent China are but the latest in a long line of such attempts dating from the mid-nineteenth century, when Western intrusion put the task of creating a centralizing state and a modern industrial economy on China's historical agenda. That China would succeed was by no means certain: it took a century of anti-imperialist struggle and revolutionary upheaval to remove the obstacles that foreign imperialists and domestic landlords had placed in the way of unifying and industrializing China, and another four decades after the establishment of the People's Republic to get on with those tasks. As the reforms of the 1980s illustrate, the process is hardly finished.

To appreciate the concerted effort expended over many generations in pursuit of those goals is to stand in awe of the Chinese achievement in the twentieth century. That drive has been sustained by a powerful nationalist commitment, tempered by a cultural heritage stretching back four thousand years, inspired at times by a Utopian Socialist vision, and most recently nurtured by enthusiasm for the new economic freedoms. As China enters the 1990s, though, Socialist goals have been tarnished by the Tiananmen tragedy and called into question by the regime's own economic reforms. Many Chinese await the passing of the aging Communist leadership to resume their quest for greater economic, artistic, intellectual, and political freedom.

Notes

1. For the full text of the Marriage Law, see Kay Ann Johnson, *Women, the Family, and Peasant Revolution in China* (Chicago: University of Chicago Press, 1983), pp. 235–39.

2. Franz Schurmann, *Ideology and Organization in Communist China* (Berkeley: University of California Press, 1968), p. 74.

3. Carl Riskin, *China's Political Economy* (New York: Oxford University Press, 1987), chap. 5.

4. Quoted in Stuart Schram, ed., *Mao Tse-tung Unrehearsed* (Harmondsworth, Engl.: Penguin, 1974), p. 232.

5. Riskin, *China's Political Economy*, p. 290; Tyrene White, "Reforming the Countryside," *Current History* (Sept., 1992).

6. Richard Baum, ed., *Reform and Reaction in Post-Mao China: The Road to Tiananmen* (New York: Routledge, 1991), chap. 1.

7. Richard Baum, "The Paralysis of Power: Chinese Politics since Tiananmen," in *China Briefing, 1991,* ed. William A. Joseph (Boulder, Colo.: Westview, 1992), p. 7.

8. This section is based on Tyrene White, "The Population Factor: China's Family Planning Policy in the 1990s," in William Joseph, ed., *China Briefing, 1991* (Boulder, Colo.: Westview, 1992).

9. Margery Wolf, *Revolution Postponed: Women in Contemporary China* (Stanford: Stanford University Press, 1985), p. 26.

Chapter 20

Japan: An Authoritarian Road to Capitalism

Japan's history fits awkwardly with that of its Asian neighbors. Despite a common cultural heritage drawn from the continent, Japan has followed the European pattern of early efforts at centralized rule disintegrating into feudalism that, in turn, gave way to capitalism, rather than China's experience of bureaucratic rule under imperial dynasties. Yet the evolution of capitalism in Japan has differed substantially from that of Britain, France, or the United States, where capitalist institutions and a capitalist class emerged initially in the context of relatively weak states. In Japan, by contrast, capitalism and the capitalist class itself were nurtured by a strong state where power was concentrated in the hands of a small elite. It was similar in this respect to nineteenth-century Germany, the major example of state-led development in Europe. But the comparison with Germany is far from exact, for the hold of an authoritarian state and a small elite persisted well after World War II in Japan, whereas that pattern had been decisively broken in postwar West Germany. Japan's uniqueness—in terms of Asian or European experience—assumed global significance when its rise to industrial power in the twentieth century presented other countries with both the threat of domination and the promise of an alternate model of development.

The greatest contrast has been with China. Since the dramatic political revolution known as the Meiji Restoration of 1868, Japan has undergone a distinctive state-led and authoritarian version of capitalist development that rapidly transformed the country into a powerful industrialized state. Until well after World War II, it was the only case of thoroughgoing industrialization outside of the Western world. China, meanwhile, was carved up into spheres of influence by Western imperialist powers and disintegrated into warlord regimes before finally setting out on a troubled Socialist path to industrialization following a Communist-led revolution in 1949.

The justification for Japanese authoritarianism has been that only a strong state could overcome internal divisions and propel industrial development forward at maximum speed, thus permitting a later-modernizing country like Japan to catch up with its already established Western rivals. Japanese leaders have long argued that democracy and popular rights would undermine the national goals of economic strength and military power by inviting indecisiveness, self-indulgence, and weakness. Furthermore, they claimed that the idea of democratic rights was an alien, Western import at odds with Japanese culture and traditions and certainly not a universal value. The military and economic success of the Japanese approach has given these arguments considerable weight in many circles.

Yet a desire for freedom from exploitation and oppression has long been visible in the histories of Japan and China, no less than in Europe. Ordinary peasants, indebted tenants, household maids, miners, new brides, day laborers, prostitutes, and charcoal burners—all of these and many others had long experienced the arbitrary rule and stern exactions of the powerful. While obedience and cooperation normally prevailed in the face of massive inequalities of power and opportunity, pressure from below for securing more autonomy and control has been visible in Japan for centuries. It took a variety of forms, including peasant rebellion, petitions to overlords, tax evasion, satire, and flight to the frontier or the city. Thus, when Western democratic ideas and institutions were introduced into Japan in the latter half of the nineteenth century, there were groups of people willing to embrace them in various ways as yet another means for pursuing their own struggles. Furthermore, the social transformations of capitalism that produced new urban middle and working classes prompted a growing desire for popular rights and economic justice in Japan, as they had done in Europe. Thus, Japanese society did not lack democratic impulses; nor was Japanese culture uniformly hostile to notions of individual rights or social justice.

Preview: Japan's Modern History

The leaders who set Japan on its course of capitalist industrialization in the decades after 1868 had the example of China's humiliation constantly before them. They sought to create the unity of purpose China was then unable to achieve by using the state to repress dissent and to impose both an ideology and a structure for authoritarian rule. By these means, the Japanese leadership insulated itself from demands from below for a share in power and became self-perpetuating. This ruling group recruited new members and changed in composition in response to demands from the new power centers in Japanese society—the military, the state bureaucracy, and the modern corporation.

Politics, then, became a matter of balancing the interests of various elites. Given the threat of domination by the Western imperialist powers, the main object of elite politics from the Meiji period onward was the pursuit of great-power status for Japan through industrialization and acquisition of empire. The attempt at empire building led to a catastrophic fifteen-year war with China (1931–1945) that expanded until Japan was at war with the rest of Asia as well as the Western powers. Japan lost that war along with millions of its people and its east Asian empire. At the war's end in 1945, the United States occupied Japan and presided over a groundswell for democratization that swept away the props of authoritarian rule. But when Japan's industrial workers, tenant farmers, and other groups victimized by the old order moved toward a thorough democratization of the entire society, they soon outran the limited intentions

of the U.S. occupiers, who became alarmed and joined hands with Japanese conservatives to restore elite power and authority within the new democratic institutions. Once again the rationale was that democracy leads to inefficiencies that hold back economic growth, which, in turn, was seen as vital to keeping communism at bay in Japan and Asia. The Cold War permitted the reconstituted Japanese elite to concentrate on economic growth, protected by American military power, and Japan was able to outstrip both superpowers some forty years later. The Japanese model has strongly influenced other Asian countries—Korea, Taiwan, Singapore, and now China itself. And Europe and North America have been increasingly attentive to the Japanese experience as well.

Thus, Japan's history over the past several centuries poses any number of questions. Perhaps the most often discussed issue involves an explanation for Japan's remarkable economic success. Was it the product of certain traditional values, of particular government policies, or of unique international conditions? A related question deals with the social costs of Japan's industrial development. Compared with Europe or the Soviet Union, for example, did Japanese industrialization give rise to more or less human suffering, class conflict, and political oppression? Who benefited from Japan's economic success? Another set of issues focuses on the relationship of capitalism to democracy. Does a market economy necessarily lead to respect for human rights? Is rapid economic development in a highly competitive world compatible with democracy? Can individual freedom flourish when the state plays a major role in the economy? And, finally, there is the question of Japan's uniqueness. In what ways has its modern transformation differed from that of other societies? Does Japan's experience hold useful lessons for some or all of today's developing countries? These are some of the larger issues that this chapter raises as we follow Japan's path to the modern world.

The Historical Setting

Japan is a moderately large country by European standards. In area it is larger than Germany, and its 1993 population of 124 million is more than double

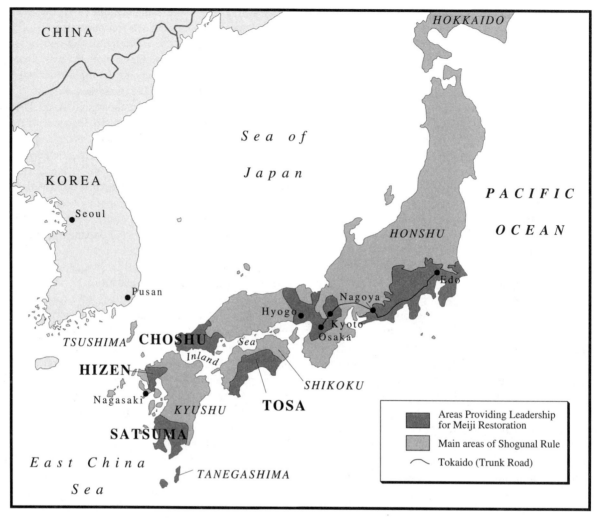

MAP 20.1 Tokugawa Japan

that of France. It is an island country like England, but rather remote from either the Asian continent or, until recently, from paths of world commerce. Although Japan was settled by disparate people from many parts of Asia and the Pacific, immigrants from the Korean peninsula seem to have provided the political and military techniques behind the emergence of an organized state in the Yamato plain in southwest Japan by the eighth century. Favored by distance, the warrior-rulers of Japan were able to resist even such a powerful neighbor as China. In contrast to its Asian neighbors and most European countries, Japan has not experienced repeated invasions, constant migration of peoples, or extensive cultural in-

termingling. Instead, the southwestern clans conquered the other peoples living on the archipelago and made their own language and culture predominant long before the arrival of the first Europeans. As a result of more than a thousand years of relative isolation, when the West arrived in force in the nineteenth century, the people of Japan found it easier to conceive of themselves as a distinct society or nation than did, for example, the Italians or Germans or, for that matter, the Chinese or Indians.

The four main islands describe an arc off the northeast coast of Asia (see Map 20.1). They are mostly mountainous, forested, and well watered, but provide little arable land except for riverine plains suitable for irrigation and wet-field rice culture. The two largest and most fertile areas are the Yamato and Kanto plains on the main island of Honshu, which have been centers of Japanese civilization for centuries.

Aside from rice and forest and marine resources, Japan has little natural wealth. Rugged and isolated, populated by a spartan society of peasants ruled by a warrior elite, Japan seemed to offer little in comparison to the spices and tropical products of Southeast Asia or the splendor of China. Accordingly, Japan received only fitful attention as an area for European exploitation or conquest until the mid-nineteenth century. Even then, the Western imperialist powers had their eyes on the bigger prize of China.

Samurai and Shogun: Japanese Political Life

By the time Europeans encountered Japan in the sixteenth and seventeenth centuries, its political life was quite different from that of the neighboring Chinese empire. Whereas the Chinese emperor was the head of state and directly responsible for its policies, the Japanese emperor had long ago lost direct governing authority to a series of feudal lords called *daimyo*. With the emperor a distant symbol of an earlier political unity, these aristocratic lords fought endlessly with one another, each employing their cadre of *samurai*, as this Japanese warrior elite was called. At the end of the seventeenth century, a trio of remarkable leaders achieved military supremacy and established an alliance of major daimyo capable of ending the recurrent civil wars and laying the foundations for a measure of national unity in Japan.

One of these military leaders, Ieyasu of the Tokugawa house, secured in 1603 the title *shogun,* which recognized his supreme authority to rule the country, ostensibly in the name of the emperor but largely by virtue of his own military and political skill. This began a period of more than 250 years, known in Japanese history as the *Tokugawa shogunate*. It was a regime of bureaucratic or centralized feudalism in which the Tokugawa military government established its hegemony over the competing feudal domains and in which the samurai warriors of old were transformed into a hereditary class of peacetime administrators and bureaucrats serving the shogunate

and the domains. The dominant role of the shogun distinguishes Japanese feudalism from its earlier counterpart in Europe, despite their similarity as highly decentralized political systems.

Tokugawa Ieyasu and the next two shoguns aimed above all at creating a stable political system after centuries of incessant civil conflict. They reorganized Japan into a complex structure, balancing the holdings of the Tokugawa overlords and their house retainers against the domains of semi-autonomous vassals, some loyal and others suspect. At the center was the Tokugawa shogunate or military government, ruling in the emperor's name from the Tokugawa administrative center in Edo (today's Tokyo). Through Tokugawa family members and retainers, the shogunate controlled the most fertile, productive, and populous regions of the main island.

The central political problem was how to control the feudal lords who, even after submitting to vassalage under Tokugawa rule, retained substantial autonomy, wealth, and military power in their own domains. Fearing that an attempt at outright conquest would trigger a general rebellion, the Tokugawa regime sought instead a balance of power that would favor themselves.

To achieve such a balance they parceled out the country among over 250 domains in addition to the centralized Tokugawa holdings. The least loyal lords were assigned domains in remote and poorer regions, while the most loyal were installed strategically in more prosperous regions. An essentially powerless imperial court lived in obscurity in distant Kyoto, providing a veneer of legitimacy to the Tokugawa regime. To keep the daimyo under control, the shogun strictly regulated internal travel and communications and required the daimyo to spend alternate years in his capital at Edo, leaving their families behind as hostages in times of absence.

While the Tokugawa regime was constructed to deal with Japan's internal conflicts, it also had to contend with European traders and missionaries. The Portuguese had arrived in the mid-sixteenth century, followed by the Spanish, Dutch, and English. European traders stimulated an already lively Japanese commerce with China and Southeast Asia and became a conduit for advanced military technology and Christianity to enter the country. All of this had an effect on daimyo power struggles. Trade enabled the daimyo controlling the southwestern ports to accumulate wealth and power independently from control of rice lands. Christianity, which had gained perhaps 300,000 converts (less than 2 percent of the population) by the early seventeenth century, potentially undermined loyalty to the shogun as secular representative of a sacred emperor that legitimized the Tokugawa rule. It also subverted the hereditary feudal status system through its premise of equality of all before God. Accurate muskets and cannon put a premium on firepower and massive castles that radically changed military strategy at the expense of smaller and less prosperous domains.

By 1612, Tokugawa leaders were aware of such implications and concluded that Christianity had to be rooted out as a political and social danger. The repression culminated in the Shimabara rebellion of twenty thousand Christian peasants in 1637–1638, which became the occasion for the final closure of the country to trade and other foreign contact. The shogunate had not been averse to foreign trade, but sought to monopolize it for themselves. The failure of this effort led to restrictions on all trade and foreign contact, including a ban in 1635 on Japanese leaving the country or returning on pain of death. Thus, by 1641, virtually the only contact with Europeans that remained was a small and strictly regulated trade with the Dutch at Nagasaki. For the next two centuries this provided glimpses of the world outside East Asia that fed the imagination of a small group of scholars who pursued what was called *Dutch learning*. Their limited and painfully gained knowledge of European science and medicine had almost no political or social impact, but it did at least leaven the Confucian orthodoxy that provided the general ethical framework for Tokugawa Japan. At the same time, Japanese relations with its near neighbors, China and Korea, were much more extensive and influential.

When the shogunate enforced the seclusion policy, Japan was roughly equal to Europe militarily, economically, and technologically; but when the European powers reappeared some two hundred years later, it was clear that isolation had bought political stability at the price of technological and scientific progress. Japan missed out on the great expansion of world trade that fed into the rise of capitalism and the Industrial Revolution in Europe. Thus, when the American Commodore Matthew Perry determined to end Japan's seclusion in 1854, he was able to sail his black ships into Tokyo Bay without resistance.

Daimyo revolt was but one of the dangers facing the Tokugawa shogunate. It had also to consider the aspirations of merchants and peasants for freedom from the political and economic exactions of the samurai class. The Tokugawa saw the task of bringing these people, more than 90 percent of the population, under their control largely as a moral and social problem.

The moral or ideological foundation of the Tokugawa order was neo-Confucianism, a doctrine borrowed from Korea and China and adapted to serve the purposes of the samurai. Knowing one's place in a natural social hierarchy and giving loyalty and obedience to superiors—subject to ruler, child to parent, female to male—were held to be the highest forms of ethical conduct. The family was similarly regarded as the natural building block of society. Such precepts were the basis for Tokugawa law and were enforced with great severity.

Japanese Society

The samurai ethic was embodied in an officially sanctioned social hierarchy of four functional classes—from top to bottom, the samurai, peasantry, artisans, and merchants. In fact, Tokugawa society was even more stratified since the highest officials and feudal lords constituted a samurai ruling elite at the top and a large group of outcastes were ostracized at the bottom. Crossing the official class lines was forbidden; and each class was required to observe restrictions on occupation, residence, marriage, clothing, and way of life.

The social hierarchy was based on sex as well as social class. According to official teachings, women were inferior to men and naturally suited to service in the narrow sphere of the household. Within the samurai class, women were considered subordinate to men in marriage, in property rights, and in passing on the family line. Such ideas weighed less heavily in the lower social ranks, with non-samurai women experiencing lives of much greater freedom and diversity. More egalitarian relations between men and women were especially evident in the village, where women's contribution of heavy labor in the fields and household was so crucial to family survival.

The samurai, who held a monopoly on political power and the bearing of arms, had the most at stake in imposing their moral and social order upon Toku-

The arrival of the Portuguese in the sixteenth century initiated Japan's encounter with Europe. *Giraudon/Art Resource, NY*

gawa society as a whole. Earlier in Japanese history, samurai dominance was imposed through force, and they had become a warrior elite, close to the peasants, dispersed in the countryside, and capable of leading troops in battle. But during the long Tokugawa peace, they were transformed into a body of government administrators and hangers-on clustered around their lord's castle or in the capitol at Edo. They lived on a rice tax squeezed out of the peasantry, and presumably earned their keep by enforcing public peace and order. In fact, many did nothing and lived parasitic lives at the peasants' expense. The sheer size of the samurai class—close to 6 percent of the population—was an oppressive weight on the peasant producers, far heavier than in Europe where the feudal elite was smaller.

Efforts to instill samurai values in the rest of the population met with mixed success. In the villages, frequently exploited peasants kept to their place but possessed their own code of fairness that was in constant tension with samurai precepts of obligation and duty to superiors. In the cities, the merchants accorded respect to the samurai and even aspired to rise to that status, but at the same time a pleasure-seeking merchant culture affronted the austere samurai morality of self-sacrifice. To some extent samurai values did permeate the rest of the population, but the borrowing was often quite selective and cultural influences went in both directions.

The peasantry—disarmed and fastened to their villages at the outset of the Tokugawa period—made up approximately 80 percent of the population. Although theoretically respected as the producing class, peasants were treated harshly and economically squeezed to extract as much revenue as possible. As the Tokugawa period wore on, peasant resistance began to take the form of riots that attacked landlords and rice merchants and destroyed certificates of debt. Many peasants also fled to the towns and cities to escape their rural misery.

Townspeople, encompassing both the artisan and merchant classes, accounted for something close to 15 percent of the population. Nearly half lived in the three largest cities. Edo, with about one million inhabitants in the late eighteenth century, was the largest city in the world.

The artisans in the cities lived under such wretched conditions that they were unable to reproduce themselves, but a steady flow of fleeing peasants replenished their ranks. These men and women provided the labor needed to produce the textiles, transport the goods, prepare the food, forge the swords, build the mansions, brew the *sake,* stock the pleasure quarters, and in general provide the trappings of samurai life. Possessing neither wealth nor power, fragmented by occupation, and lacking organization, the artisans posed no clear political threat to the samurai or the shogunate. Yet, by the late eighteenth century and early nineteenth century, urban rice riots, provoked by the indifference of the government and the extortions of rice merchants and moneylenders, greatly worried the authorities.

The merchants, at the bottom of the official class system, represented a greater danger. By the end of the Tokugawa period, they were in command of a countrywide network of commerce and banking that had developed in response to the samurai need to convert tax revenue in rice into coin and commodities. But Japanese merchants did not attempt to convert their wealth and organization into political power, as European merchants had done. The Osaka merchants, for example, might have controlled most of the country's wealth by the end of the Tokugawa era, but they had prospered in service to the samurai, not through independent trade between other classes or with other countries. Consequently, the merchant community became extraordinarily dependent on the Tokugawa regime.

Peasant villages increasingly felt the impact of these market relationships. Landlords, driven by considerations of profit and loss, used tenants and laborers to till their excess land and began to accumulate capital. Village society stratified along class lines. Ultimately, a distinct stratum of landlords, officials, and merchants—rice dealers, *sake* brewers, moneylenders—emerged as a local elite between the cultivating peasantry and the samurai overlords. Growing extremes of wealth and poverty in the countryside gave rise to recurrent peasant rebellions in the late eighteenth and early nineteenth centuries that shook the foundations of feudal rule.

In sum, the Tokugawa regime had effectively ended Japan's recurrent civil wars and the ensuing peace had fostered commercial capitalism, economic growth, and urbanization—all of which provided a strong foundation for Japan's remarkable industrial development in the late nineteenth century. But the Tokugawa feudal structure was showing signs of strain by the end of the eighteenth century. These became even more pronounced as the regime confronted a far more aggressive Europe in the nineteenth century. By 1850, it was far from clear that Japan would escape some form of domination by the Western imperialist powers.

The Meiji Revolution from Above

In 1853–1854, U.S. Commodore Matthew Perry sailed to Japan to "open" the country to Western trade, much as the British had done in China fourteen years earlier. For the previous two centuries, Japan's Tokugawa rulers had secluded the country from nearly all contact with the world beyond East Asia. But under the clear threat of American military action and seeing what Britain had done to China in the Opium Wars, Japan initially signed a series of "unequal treaties" with the Western powers. The humili-

ation that these treaties entailed undermined the shogunate and stimulated a number of samurai from clans opposed to the Tokugawa regime to overthrow it in 1868. Only limited military action had been required to establish the new government, which nominally restored the emperor to power but was run by a remarkable group of younger samurai leaders.

The entire process is known as the *Meiji Restoration,* after the reign name of the then-current emperor. Western military power had convinced these samurai reformers that defiant seclusion was futile and that the West had to be fought on its own terms—making use of superior Western techniques of state administration and of the science, technology, and industry that lay behind Western military prowess. The Meiji regime then proceeded with an enormous reform program—a "revolution from above"—that enabled Japan to avoid European domination, to become the first non-Western country to industrialize, and to join the ranks of the world's great powers. Why was Japan able to do what China had not?

Contrasting China and Japan

In some ways, China was perhaps better prepared than Japan to confront the Western threat. It had a large population, substantial resources, an earlier tradition of technological innovation, a highly developed state bureaucracy, and a ruling class composed of scholar-officials recruited through merit.

But China's ability to undertake radical reforms was limited by the power of a land-holding gentry. Furthermore, a moralistic Confucian ideology may have made it difficult to accommodate the materialistic and scientific foundations of industrial capitalism. Other factors may also have limited China's capacity for vigorous response to Western aggression, including Manchu fear of arousing Chinese nationalism, the absorption of China's energies in putting down the Taiping revolution, and an aversion to cultural borrowing rooted in the belief that China alone represented civilization. When confronted with British demands, China's instinct was to turn inward, minimize outside contact, and strengthen old ways.

In explaining Japan's contrasting "success," scholars have pointed to a number of internal factors. The existence of a military ruling class of samurai created a potential for national unity that China, with its locally oriented landed gentry, lacked. After 250 years of peace, this large class had become in its upper ranks an officialdom skilled in the practice of political power and not directly dependent on owning land, while the rest had declined into resentful impotence, anxious to regain their fortunes and their "rightful" place in society. An oligarchy of such people led the Meiji Restoration in 1868 and ruled the country until the early twentieth century.

Furthermore, Japan was a compact territory, without China's huge hinterland, and well knit together by commercial ties. Its population was under close political control; some 40 percent of its men and 15 percent of its women were literate; it possessed some of the largest cities in the world and a flourishing urban culture; and a productive agriculture generated a large surplus available for industrial and military development. Here were the economic foundations for Japan's remarkable transformation.

But more important than these internal differences was the fact that China excited Western interest far more than Japan. The powerful myth of the China market as well as the prospect of natural resources and exotic products lured European attention away from a less attractive Japan. Located on the periphery of Asia, apparently without important markets or resources, Japan was also defended by a troublesome warrior class. The country was "opened" to the West following Perry's voyages but was spared the intense pressure applied to China. And after coming to power in 1868, Japan's new oligarchy took advantage of the breathing space offered by the West's preoccupation with China to carry out an ambitious program of reforms aimed at increasing Japan's military and industrial strength.

The Meiji Restoration has provoked a lively debate about Japan's late nineteenth-century transformation. Those who celebrate its achievements praise the samurai elite for skillfully taking Japan through the early stages of capitalist modernization, for avoiding European domination, and for promoting rapid industrial development and growing military strength. Critics of that process point to the popular suffering and political oppression that also characterized the Meiji era and highlight the tragedy of democratic possibilities denied. Japan's authoritarian road to capitalism, the nation-state, and empire took a high toll on its own people. And China too paid dearly for Japanese accomplishments, from the Sino-Japanese War of 1894–1895 through the Second

World War. Thus, despite its remarkable achievements, Japan's modern transformation was hardly an unambiguous success story.

Consolidating Power and Building Industry

To the new rulers of Meiji Japan, creating a modern state and establishing industrial capitalism were inseparable tasks, for Japan had no ambitious bourgeoisie eager to limit state power and give the market free reign. Japan's merchant class had been nurtured from birth to accept subordination to the samurai. Merchant houses like Mitsui might have accumulated great wealth and, therefore, influence over their chronically debt-ridden samurai betters, but they did not take the lead in Japan's industrialization, nor did they challenge the samurai class for power. On the contrary, they looked to the state for leadership in establishing modern industry and accepted the Meiji strategy of state-led industrialization. The combination of a timid merchant class and a grave imperialist threat produced in Japan a reversal of the sequence of capitalist development seen in Europe. Japanese capitalism and Japanese capitalists were the creations of the authoritarian Meiji state in the hands of a small oligarchy of former samurai.

Upon claiming leadership in 1868 in the name of a restored emperor, the successful band of samurai had to solve a series of related problems: to centralize political authority in one national government; to secure a monopoly on military power; and to establish a nationwide system of taxation capable of supporting a much expanded central government and army. All three tasks required an attack upon the powers and autonomy of the feudal domains and of their own samurai class. It was a remarkable demonstration of a portion of a ruling class abolishing the political and social order that secured its class privileges.

A series of edicts in the first few years addressed these problems. By 1871, the new regime had abolished the feudal domains with their considerable political and economic powers, and had installed a system of prefectures headed by appointed governors responsible to the central government. That government now collected the domain's taxes and assumed its debts and obligations, especially payment of stipends to the samurai. After intense debate, a new

Despite its European appearance, the early Japanese parliament, shown here in 1890, had little power. Notice the Meiji emperor (far right) and the empress and her ladies in waiting (*upper left*). *Hulton Deutsch Collection Limited*

national army based on universal conscription was established in 1873, and the samurai lost their identity as a military caste. In that same year, land reform and a new system of taxation assigned individual ownership of land to peasant farmers and levied taxes payable in cash based on the assessed value of their land. This made government finance both secure and predictable.

Despite some samurai resistance, the legacy of Tokugawa feudalism was largely swept away. Class restrictions on occupation, residence, marriage, and clothing were abolished, and all Japanese became formally equal as commoners. Limitations on travel and trade likewise fell as a nationwide economy came to parallel the centralized state.

The fate of the former samurai was a major problem. In 1876, the new regime bought off with lavish settlements the daimyo and high-ranking samurai who posed the most danger to the new state. They commuted the stipends of the rest on ruinous terms. Many former samurai became officers in the new army, police officers, government bureaucrats, or school teachers, but most had to take up occupations like farming, small business, or manual labor, at which they did poorly. Their resentments fueled the emerging political opposition and provoked a rebel-

lion in 1877. The new peasant conscript army defeated the samurai forces and thus ended their resistance as a class, though many remained involved in politics as individuals.

The state played a major role in the industrialization program of the new regime. The government took over and modernized Tokugawa and daimyo enterprises such as iron foundries, munitions plants, and dockyards. It also established model factories to produce cement, chemicals, glass, sugar, and silk and cotton goods. And it opened mines, built railroads, and established postal, telegraph, and banking systems. By the turn of the century, Japan's economic transformation was well under way. Although the country was still overwhelmingly agrarian, Japan's factories were now producing not only textiles for export, but also munitions for the military and industrial goods for private industry.

The cost of this ambitious program was borne almost entirely by the peasantry through the land tax, which initially produced 90 percent of government revenue. In addition, the peasants had to provide conscripts to the army and students to a new system of compulsory education that was financed by additional local taxes. Soon taxes took 40 percent to 50 percent of peasant crop yields. Thus, more and more peasants slid into poverty. Well before the end of the Meiji period in 1912, approximately 70 percent of farm families were tenants or part-tenants paying rents that often left them little more than a third of the land's yield.

Popular Protest and State Power

The accumulated grievances of the samurai and the peasantry combined briefly in the early 1880s in protest against continued government favoritism to private business. This "people's rights movement" included a national leadership of ex-samurai, a local leadership of rural landlords and businesspeople, liberal intellectuals and journalists, and a popular base of peasant farmers. They united behind a program of lower taxes, higher rice prices, opposition to government favoritism to big business, and democratic political reform.

A growing demand for popular rights and a national representative assembly persuaded the government to issue an imperial rescript in 1881, promising to draft a constitution and establish an assembly by 1890. The government also permitted the open formation of opposition parties advocating a parliamentary form of government. But party unity soon fractured under the pressure of government repression and interference.

Peasant uprisings peaked in 1883–1884 with attacks on government offices and moneylenders' homes aimed at destroying records of debt. Yamagata Aritomo, then home minister, used military police and army troops to put them down, and the leaders were executed or imprisoned. The government did little to help long-term peasant distress, though hundreds of thousands of families were reduced to destitution. Despite substantial private relief efforts, infanticide, the sale of daughters, and starvation began to appear in the countryside.

Under the leadership of Ito Hirobumi and Yamagata Aritomo, the Meiji oligarchy began in the 1880s to fortify the state against future demands for a sharing of power. In doing so they gave shape to the two institutions that would loom over Japanese society for decades to come: the army and the bureaucracy.

During the early Meiji years, the army's most important task was to crush internal opposition, not to fight foreign enemies. Thus, it was crucial to ensure the loyalty of peasant conscripts who increasingly made up the army. To this end, the oligarchs obtained an imperial rescript in 1882, which demanded of soldiers and sailors unconditional obedience and loyalty to superiors, the emperor, and the state. The rescript reserved the right of supreme command to the emperor forever, thus blocking civilian control of the armed forces and establishing a long tradition of military autonomy. And the rescript established an antidemocratic ideology that was drummed into the recruits, who carried it back to the villages after military service.

Japan's new bureaucrats were nurtured as a meritocratic elite in a state-controlled education system capped by Tokyo Imperial University. Their training fostered pride as servants of the emperor and contempt for the abilities of common people. The bureaucracy was not subordinate to parliament nor was it open to partisan appointments. Bureaucrats were not public servants; they were defenders of authoritarian rule entrenched in the state administrative apparatus.

Education too was reorganized in the 1880s, as an elitist but efficient structure for tracking students into careers in teaching, in science and technology, and in law and administration. Compulsory universal elementary education provided basic skills in reading, writing, and mathematics; and it exposed children to ethics courses stressing individual self-sacrifice for parents, emperor, and nation and unquestioning obedience to higher authority.

The 1889 Constitution, the capstone of the Meiji state, was presented as a gift from a sacred and inviolable emperor in whom resided all rights and powers of sovereignty. The ministers of state in the cabinet and the Privy Council were to be directly responsible to the emperor, not to the parliament, which could advise but not control the government. The emperor's subjects had no absolute guarantee of their rights. The constitution used the fiction of imperial rule as a barricade against the establishment of representative government that had been the object of the popular rights movement. It fastened upon Japan an authoritarian structure of government that delivered the cabinet into the hands of an elite of Meiji oligarchs, high-level bureaucrats, and military officers, ultimately accountable only to themselves. But there was a parliament, there were political parties, and democratic ideals did spread among the public. Such ideals became central to the opposition, even if truly representative government remained elusive.

Joining the Imperialist Club

Japan's economic and industrial takeoff soon had military implications. Within the decade of 1895 to 1905, Japan decisively defeated both China and Russia, began to acquire an empire in Korea, Taiwan, and Manchuria, and in the process stunned the Western powers (see Map 20.2). By 1911, the unequal

treaties were gone, and the West had come to regard Japan as a competitor in Asia.

The Sino-Japanese War of 1894–1895 strengthened Japan's economy even as it drained China's. An indemnity in gold saddled China with debt, but enabled Japan to go on the gold standard and engage profitably in world trade. Japan got access to China's resources, especially iron ore, and markets for

MAP 20.2 The Japanese Empire, 1895–1933

Japan's exports, particularly textiles. Both were critical for the Japanese economy. Similarly, the Russo-Japanese War of 1904–1905 brought access to the minerals and other resources of Korea and southern Manchuria. Moreover, increases in military spending caused industry to leap ahead. By 1914, Japan was on the threshold of a modern industrial economy, though agriculture and small-scale business would be dominant for some time to come.

Japan had been able to defeat China and Russia despite its relatively small size and lack of resources primarily because the new regime had succeeded in erecting a modern, bureaucratic state capable of disciplined policy-making and of mobilizing the country economically and socially behind military goals. The contrast with the creaking administrative structures of Manchu China and tsarist Russia was sharp. Yet, bureaucratic rationality in government and business intertwined after the turn of the century with a nativist ideology exalting Japan's spiritual and cultural superiority over other nations and peoples. Such attitudes waxed and waned, but unquestionably fed into successive wars, fostered a climate of nationalist extremism, and served to divert popular attention from the many costs of pursuing industrial capitalism by authoritarian means. Finally, the expense of empire contributed to Japan's chronic shortage of capital and to its growing indebtedness.

The Social Cost of Industrialization

Industrial development required the accumulation of both domestic capital and of foreign exchange to pay for imports of equipment and technology. How would this money be raised? The land tax, which bore heavily on the peasantry, largely financed basic industries, while landlords, depending on tenant labor, also invested their profits in private enterprise. The export of textiles was the chief means of earning foreign exchange. They were produced in a modern but labor-intensive textile industry geared for export, using cheap female and child labor from poverty-stricken peasant households to become competitive in the world market. Thus, tenant farmers and young girls from the countryside carried the burden of Japan's industrialization on their backs.

When the Meiji emperor died in 1912, Japan was well on its way to capitalist industrialization. A business class had emerged, as had the beginnings of a factory-based working class and a class of mid-level employees in government and business bureaucracies. But the country was still overwhelmingly rural and agricultural. Only about 800,000 people worked in factories, of which 60 percent or more were female textile workers. Men primarily worked in enterprises producing metals, machinery, and chemicals, many of them in small shops.

As in Europe, brutal treatment was commonplace from the outset of modern Japanese industry, especially for the girls and young women in the silk and cotton mills. The majority of textile workers came from the countryside where life was hard. A desire to help the family created a large pool of young females available for work at a pittance. Most did not return to the village to stay, instead working in the mills until marriage and often beyond. They became part of Japan's rapidly growing working class. Pay was at or below subsistence, and a combination of bad food, overwork, inhuman working conditions, and jail-like dormitories left many cast-off employees in their twenties without mates but with terminal diseases like tuberculosis and dependent for survival on degrading occupations such as prostitution. Resistance to these conditions was reflected in a high turnover rate, strikes, and efforts to organize unions. Under the double burden of unrelenting employer supervision in dorms and factories and a patriarchal family system, female textile workers found it most difficult to unionize. Thus, the union movement, after its birth in the late 1890s, was dominated by male skilled workers who had greater freedom of action.

A series of repressive laws allowed the government and employers to treat unions and strikes as criminal activities. These laws were used so effectively that the budding labor movement had been crushed by the end of 1901. But the authorities also began to draw upon the familiar themes of service to state and emperor in support of a rudimentary ideology of the enterprise as family, which would emerge after World War I as a primary means of eliciting worker loyalty to the firm.

The very success of the Meiji elite in fastening an authoritarian order upon Japan and blocking impulses for democratic reform gave legitimacy to leftist ideas of a more radical kind that were entering Japan in the late nineteenth century. Anarchism, Marxism, and syndicalism all had their advocates within the intelligentsia before the end of the Meiji era. All met with the same kind of reception as the

Social Democratic party, which was disbanded by the government on the same day it was established. In the face of such suppression, some leftists continued to work and hope for peaceful reform, but others turned to radical solutions. The year before the Meiji emperor died in 1912, the Meiji era ended symbolically with the execution of twelve revolutionary Socialists and anarchists for their alleged involvement in a plot to assassinate the emperor.

Imperial Japan in the Era of the World Wars

During the decades spanning the two world wars, the contrasts between Japan and China grew ever sharper. Japan saw the growth of cities populated by new wage-earning classes with interests far different from the agrarian concerns of China's mostly rural population. Although social misery accumulated at the base of both societies, the movements to protest and rectify these wrongs differed greatly.

The Chinese Guomindang government somewhat resembled the Japanese ruling elite in that both involved coalitions of military, business, and landlord interests, seeking to create an authoritarian state capable of industrializing their countries. But in China's case, dependence on the landlords sharply limited the government's ability to create a strong state and an industrial society. Furthermore, China's landlord system and widespread peasant distress had prompted a broad-based peasant revolutionary movement under an unorthodox Communist leadership.

The situation in the Japanese countryside was similar in that the injustices of the landlordism provoked widespread tenant resistance. But no peasant-based revolutionary movement appeared. Although the Meiji regime subordinated agriculture to the state policy of industrialization, the government also underwrote the landlords' prosperity by protecting the institution of tenancy. Thus, the state secured the support of landlords who later helped to mobilize local village society behind Japan's imperialist aggression in the 1930s and 1940s.

In contrast to China's primarily rural society, Japan by the mid-1930s had become predominantly urban, and its working class, not the peasantry, was the specter haunting Japan's elite. During the 1920s,

many industrialists and officials feared that militant unionism, if left unchecked, would fuel a revolutionary political movement. Thus, the state elite dealt harshly with the radicals, using terror, surveillance, oppression, and jail for those who would not recant. But the Japanese elite, unlike their Chinese counterparts, tempered its oppression of radical movements with concessions. The Diet granted the right to vote to all males, and employers seeking labor harmony improved economic conditions for some workers in the largest and most advanced enterprises and even promoted conciliatory unions.

The greatest difference between Japan and China in this period was also the most obvious. Japan was an imperialist aggressor and China was its chief victim. It might have seemed that these two countries had a common interest in combatting the imperialist ambitions of the Western powers in Asia. After all, Japan had attracted large numbers of Chinese and other students who were eager to learn from the Japanese example in industrializing and standing up to the West. But once Japan committed itself to empire in the war with China in 1894–1895, its claim to lead an anti-imperialist and pan-Asian coalition became much less credible. And when Japan took advantage of World War I to claim further Chinese territory, the die was cast. Henceforth in Chinese eyes, Japan was just another imperialist aggressor and worse in many ways because it was so close.

Japan's Dual Economy

The authoritarian Meiji order looked unshakable in 1912 when the emperor died. Each attempt at democratic reform had been contained and stirrings among workers and leftist intellectuals had apparently been extinguished. Power rested securely with the bureaucratic and military elites. Heavy industry had progressed greatly in tandem with munitions, providing the sinews for military victories abroad.

The First World War was pivotal for Japan in many ways. In early 1915, Japan presented to China the infamous Twenty-one Demands, designed to open up economic opportunities for Japanese business and to allow Japan to compete more effectively with Western powers in exploiting Chinese markets and resources. These demands were largely accommodated and Japan soon became the dominant imperialist power in China.

The war also produced an economic boom, and a few state-favored enterprises soon occupied the commanding heights of the economy. By 1919, fewer than 2 percent of Japanese firms accounted for over half the country's industrial capital. The largest of these private, family-run corporations came to be known as the *zaibatsu* and included Mitsui, Mitsubishi, Sumitomo, and Yasuda.

After World War I, *zaibatsu* leaders were able to assert their interests forcefully in the inner circles of government. They joined the bureaucratic and military elites as a third wing of Japan's ruling class. The *zaibatsu* leaders, seeking to advance their economic interests, became so involved in party politics as members, candidates, and suppliers of funds that in the 1920s the two major parties were seen as creatures of Mitsui and Mitsubishi. But the *zaibatsu* acquisition of political power did not lead to parliamentary democracy and popular sovereignty. After all, most big-business owners and managers relied on hierarchical and authoritarian methods in managing their employees and fully shared the antidemocratic values of their conservative counterparts in the government.

If the *zaibatsu* represented one side of the Japanese economy, numerous small labor-intensive and low-technology businesses were the other. They supplied Japanese households with consumer goods and increasingly produced cheap products as subcontractors for *zaibatsu* firms, thus enabling big business to keep wages and costs down. So did the continuing migration of children and young women and men to the city in search of jobs. That migration partially reversed itself in bad times to place the burden of support for the unemployed on farm families at no cost to employers and the government. In short, Japan had developed a dual economy that subsidized modern industry at the expense of agriculture and small business. This worked well in producing arms, exports, and capital for economic and military expansion, but it failed badly in meeting the needs of the Japanese people and in creating a domestic base for economic growth.

Democracy Denied:
The Defection of the Parties

A 50 percent jump in the price of rice sparked rice riots in the summer of 1918 that involved a million people across Japan. The causes ran deep. Along with popular outrage over a rapidly declining standard of living, anger boiled over against the injustices of landlordism, the appalling treatment given to workers, and discrimination against the large outcaste population. After suppressing the uprisings with massive force, the government permitted Hara Kei to form Japan's first cabinet dominated by the majority party. Thus, the politicians of Japan's major parties joined the bureaucratic, military, and industrial elites of the country as a subordinate part of its ruling class. For a moment it seemed as if there might be some prospect of democratic reform.

The rice riots, the Russian Revolution, and the victory of the Allied democracies in World War I all stimulated an opposition movement concerned about popular rights and social justice. A labor movement, previously small and conciliatory, now began to grow in size and militance. In the countryside, tenant disputes with landlords led to the founding in 1922 of the All-Japan Farmers' Union. Japan's outcastes launched their own national organization in 1922 to protest discrimination in work, residence, and marriage. Agitation for women's rights gathered momentum in 1919, focusing on equal opportunity for women and universal suffrage. A student movement appeared in late 1918 and helped to spread Marxist thought. Socialist and Communist parties organized in the 1920s and sought to forge links with the labor movement.

Despite these many pressures, a postwar economic slump provided poor conditions for real reform. Instead, in an effort to gain worker cooperation, the *zaibatsu* began to offer permanent employment and other benefits to a select group of trained recruits. The effect was to establish a two-tiered labor force in which the privileges extended to a small, skilled, and entirely male elite were offset by poor conditions for the majority of low-paid and harshly disciplined female and male workers. The ideology of the enterprise as family, favored by more conservative employers and government bureaucrats, portrayed unions and demands for better treatment as undermining the natural harmony of Japanese society, where paternalistic employers and loyal employees pulled together for the sake of enterprise and nation. Others in business and government promoted a more liberal version of the enterprise family in which cooperative unions would be recognized as part of a conflict-resolution system designed to promote social harmony and higher productivity. In practice such ideas did little more than provide a cloak for a patriarchal and hierarchical system of management in which women were subordinated to men and workers had few if any rights, only a moral duty to work hard without complaint.

The 1920s began with a hopeful movement for universal suffrage and parliamentary democracy that seemed on the way to establishing permanently the right of the majority party in the Diet to form a government. Many people have seen these developments as evidence that Japan was then following a "normal" path to constitutional government. But ultimately no such transition occurred in the 1920s. When universal male suffrage was legislated in 1925, it was accompanied by the Peace Preservation Act, which made it a criminal offense punishable with up to ten years' imprisonment (later increased to death) to advocate alteration of Japan's political structure or the abolition of private property. Despite the pressure of labor and tenant unions, the intellectual prestige of democratic theories, and the liberal ferment among the growing white-collar middle class, the political parties proved all too willing to abandon their democratic ideals in the 1930s as they sought to preserve their power base through compromise with deeply conservative groups in the Japanese elite. The parties came to be seen as dominated by powerful interests such as Mitsui and Mitsubishi and thus discredited themselves, the Diet, and even the idea of democracy itself. This defection of the parties from popular democratic trends contributed much to the resurgence of the highly conservative and militaristic forces in the 1930s.

While there were groups of reform-minded liberals, parliamentary democracy did not find broad support among the elite during the interwar period. Landlords, well represented in both the Diet and the parties, wanted state support in keeping down unruly tenants and small farmers. Civil and military bureaucrats, entrenched in the state structure, opposed conceding any substantial powers to mass-based parties in the Diet. And business feared the rise of labor and the Left as a consequence of liberalization.

The tragedy of Japanese democracy, therefore, was not a failure of an entire people to understand the meaning of popular rights or to transcend the imperial myth. Rather, it was the tragedy of a repressed and splintered popular movement from below falling short in attempts to unite and achieve democratic change against an entrenched elite bent on securing its dominant position through economic, cultural, or more forceful means. When the world Depression and the foreign policy crises of the early 1930s sent the parties and the Diet off the track of constitutional development, the "transcendental" (nonparty) governments of the 1930s reverted to the authoritarian path to industrial capitalism that would lead the Japanese elite to its day of reckoning in 1945.

The Drift toward World War II

Foreign policy was the most contentious issue during the era of party politics. Japanese leaders regarded their special rights in China as essential to Japan's economic and strategic interests. But there were threats to these rights from the open-door policy intended to give Western nations access to Chinese resources and markets. An even greater threat was the growth of Chinese nationalism, reflected in both the Guomindong and the Chinese Communist party, and now directed increasingly against Japanese as well as Western imperialism. The groups that constituted the Japanese elite were often at odds over how to deal with these threats. Accordingly, government policies oscillated among pursuing diplomatic agreements with the Western powers to guarantee Japan's rights in China, seeking China's good will and compliance, and using military might to dominate China, thereby forcing the West to acknowledge Japan's hegemony on the continent.

What made the military option increasingly attractive was the accumulation of anticapitalist discontent in the country at large. The advent of the world Depression compounded the problem. During the early 1930s, food consumption and real wages at first declined and then stagnated as a result of mass unemployment in the cities and misery in the countryside. As the 1930s wore on, many in the elite saw advantages in redirecting this popular discontent outward in a nationalist reaction against supposed enemies on the continent and in the West. Military and right-wing forces were especially sensitive to the plight of the countryside. They promised that the military would rescue farmers from debt, hunger, and the sale of daughters into prostitution and open the way for Japan to realize its destiny abroad by removing corrupt and selfish politicians and *zaibatsu* figures from power. This identification of popular welfare at home with expansion abroad came to be commonly held by the Japanese elite and was integrated into an official state ideology demanding absolute loyalty and self-sacrifice for the state and exalting Japan's unique imperial mission. Accordingly, the calls from popular movements for economic justice and political rights within Japan were branded as selfish and subversive. In this atmosphere, military leaders gained the upper hand over the *zaibatsu* and bureaucratic members of the elite. Furthermore, a boom in manufacturing—stimulated by rapidly expanding exports, deficit spending, and a military buildup—meant that by the time full-scale war broke out in China in 1937, Japan was able to produce nearly all the machinery and tools needed to keep a modern industrial economy running and supplying the war effort.

After the Depression began, the Western powers resorted to trade blocs and tariff barriers to counter cheaply priced Japanese goods, but at the same time demanded that China be both united and open to all

for trade. In the eyes of the Japanese elite, the West wanted to deny Japan recourse to either trade or empire as a way out of its current difficulties. This left only a choice between accepting permanent economic dependence and political and military inferiority or attempting to break free from the Western-imposed international order that had a clear racial dimension. The temporary accommodation Japan and the West had worked out in the 1920s had been shattered by the Depression and by China's drive for unification, but in a larger sense Japan's imperial expansion in the 1930s and 1940s simply continued its late nineteenth-century efforts to acquire a colonial empire.

These were the circumstances in which Japan launched its renewed quest for an Asian empire in the early 1930s (see Map 20.3). The first conquest came in 1931–1932 in Manchuria, where the Japanese installed the puppet state of Manchukuo. By 1935, Japan ruled all of Manchuria as well as adja-

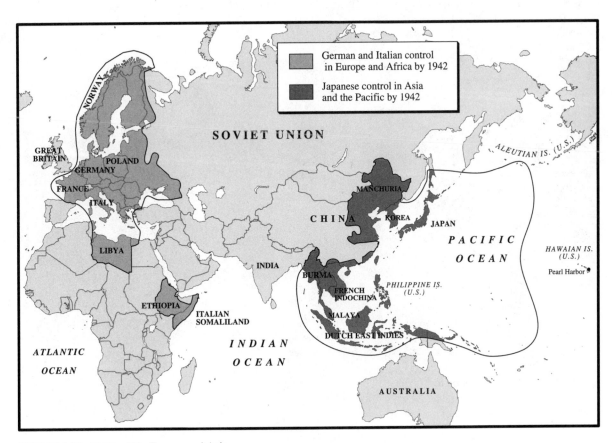

MAP 20.3 World War II in Europe and Asia

cent areas of north China. Japanese cabinets equivo-cated but ratified these military-initiated adventures. Chinese resistance prompted a full-scale attack in 1937, and Japan, while controlling the coast and the major cities of China, soon found itself bogged down in a punishing guerrilla war that it could not win.

Japan's aggression in China had aroused the hostility of the United States, which responded with a series of economic actions designed to force Japan to withdraw from China and Manchuria. At stake was supply of critical materials that Japan did not have at home or in its colonies—steel and oil from the United States, and oil, rubber, tin, and other resources from Southeast Asia. Japan's defiant move into southern Indochina in 1941 brought on an embargo on oil shipments to Japan that forced the issue. The Japanese government soon approved a military plan to attack Pearl Harbor in December 1941 to put the U.S. Pacific fleet out of action, as a prelude to the conquest of Southeast Asia. In a brilliant campaign, Japanese forces took the Philippines, Malaya, Burma, and the Dutch East Indies by storm. By the

end of March 1942, Japan had reduced the British, French, Dutch, and American colonial empires to ruins and was threatening Australia and India.

Since Japan had apparently beaten the Western imperialist powers at their own game, first by industrializing and then by defeating them on the battlefield, Japan's claim to leadership of a pan-Asian movement to break the hold of the white colonial powers at first gained a sympathetic hearing in South and Southeast Asia (though not from the Chinese and Koreans who had firsthand experience of Japanese imperialism). Despite propaganda about a Greater East Asia Co-Prosperity Sphere, Japanese actions were typically governed by a colonial policy of economic exploitation and political repression.

Although the Japanese empire was now vast, Japan was unable to secure its supply lines against U.S. naval attack. The destruction of the merchant fleet and almost total blockade brought Japan to the verge of catastrophic economic collapse before the shattering atomic bombings of Hiroshima and Nagasaki in 1945. Japan's leaders recognized from the

Two dazed residents of Hiroshima walk through the utter destruction of their city shortly after the dropping of the first atomic bomb. *UPI/Bettmann*

start that they could not hope to prevail in a protracted war, but they expected to gain recognition of Japan's dominance in Asia in a negotiated peace when its Western opponents tired of fighting. But within three years, destruction was raining down on the home islands, and on 15 August 1945, the emperor spoke to the people for the first time to announce Japan's surrender.

Postwar Japan: Peace, Managed Democracy, and the Economy

The situations in postwar Japan and China were very different. Japan had completed its industrialization along Western capitalist lines, though under an authoritarian state rather than a democratic one. China was still an agrarian society undergoing a peasant-based social revolution, and was far from developing an industrial base. Nonetheless, what both had in common was tremendous popular pressure for political rights and economic justice.

Clearly, Japanese workers and farmers had a different task before them: how to overthrow the authoritarian order that had for so long denied them most of the economic benefits of industrialization, deprived them of basic political and human rights, and sent them off to die for state and emperor. They had to accomplish as well the reconstruction of their war-shattered economy. Whether that would take a Socialist or a capitalist direction was very much on the agenda. The most pressing problems for China, in contrast, were landlordism and massive economic backwardness. China and Japan had gone their separate ways.

Japan's war against the Western imperialist powers shattered the myth of white supremacy and undermined European and American colonialism in Asia. As the only power unscathed by the fighting and strengthened economically by the war, the United States attempted the construction of a new world order that would include the decolonization of Asia and economic development along American lines. Anticommunism and free trade were the twin themes of this effort. The victory of the Maoist revolution in China and the outbreak of the Cold War soon gave Japan a pivotal role in this American

scheme as both anti-Communist bastion against social revolution and workshop for a capitalist revival in the region.

After 1945, Japan's elite was forcibly weaned from its imperial dreams by loss of its colonial empire and the dismantling of its military machine. The Americans wrote a democratic constitution for Japan that made parliament supreme, established popular sovereignty, prohibited rearmament, guaranteed civil rights, and enfranchised women. U.S. sponsorship helped Japanese capitalism to rise from the rubble of war and to become a world economic power by the 1970s. And this economic revival occurred without a parallel growth in military power, partly because the American-imposed constitution forbade it, but also because of a deep popular commitment to democracy and peace and a determination to protect the postwar constitutional order that guaranteed them both.

Japan's rise as an economic superpower in the 1960s and 1970s deeply impressed the whole world, especially given its lack of natural resources. And with rapid economic growth came a rise in living standards to European and American levels. Explaining this so-called Japanese miracle has been a major issue for scholars, business leaders, and politicians alike.

The basic infrastructure and technical know-how of an industrial society were already in place. And for four decades since the 1950s, a tightly interlocked coalition of big-business leaders, government bureaucrats, and conservative politicians effectively monopolized political power. They jointly used the state to plan and to manipulate the economy to put private business interests first. Furthermore, Japan was the key to U.S. foreign policy in Asia and benefited economically from preferential access to U.S. markets, from the immense stimulus of war procurements for Korea and Vietnam, and from small military budgets permitted in part by the *pax Americana*.

The absence of social welfare measures in the critical early decades allowed business to avoid heavy tax burdens and to shift those burdens to individuals and families. This contributed to a high rate of savings and a stress on education in order to get a job with a large corporation able to provide welfare benefits to employees. The reemergence of the dual economy and enterprise familism and the breaking of the militant unions in the 1950s greatly increased the ability of management in the large enterprises to incorporate the unions within the "family" at the enterprise level. In exchange for conceding to management almost total control in the workplace, the unions received unwritten assurances for the core unionized employees of lifetime employment and steadily increasing wages. Of course, only a minority of Japanese male workers, and almost no female workers, achieved the status of core employees. It was the subordination of labor to enterprise goals that allowed business to hold the average wage down even while raising productivity dramatically through automation and speed up. As in other advanced capitalist countries, the personal sacrifices and strenuous labors of the Japanese people have been accompanied by a significant decline in real participation in decision making in both national politics and the workplace.

In this respect, Japan became the very model of a modern capitalist society, where absence of control over most areas of life would be compensated for by symbolic participation in electoral politics and by leisure time spent in consuming a dazzling array of products. This is perhaps the most compelling evidence that there is, after all, a basic similarity between Japan and the other advanced capitalist countries. In the Japanese case, there is no doubt that rapid economic growth was instrumental in obscuring and defusing the social tensions that made the first fifteen years after World War II a period of bitter class conflict.

The Occupation: Democracy and Economic Efficiency

Japan narrowly avoided mass starvation and total disintegration in the first winter after surrender. The bombings and the blockade had brought severe economic dislocation and food shortages that were worsened by Japan's leadership. Seeking to escape the consequences of their actions, the Japanese civil bureaucracy and *zaibatsu* elites had plundered the treasury and looted government stockpiles just before American occupation forces arrived. They destroyed records, shut down enterprises, cornered scarce goods, and profiteered and speculated on the black market. The result was devastating. In the winter of 1945–1946 industrial production plummeted to 10 percent of what it had been in the mid-1930s, inflation destroyed the value of what little money people had, while unemployment reached an incredible thirteen million. The major cities were bombed out, and villages were bursting with urban refugees that they could scarcely accommodate.

Popular reaction to the moral bankruptcy of the elite began in late fall of 1945 with worker seizure of mines and other enterprises and the arraigning of company executives before workers' courts reminiscent of the Russian Revolution of 1917. Concurrently, the occupying forces, known as SCAP (Supreme Command for the Allied Powers), were dismantling the authoritarian police state that dated back as far as Meiji.

The disintegration of the authoritarian state produced a phenomenal burst of popular initiative that found expression in labor unions, tenant unions, and other movements, all seeking a fundamental reshaping of Japan's economic and social institutions. SCAP policies at first reinforced this drive for a democratic reconstruction by aiming at constitutional reform, breakup of *zaibatsu* firms, land reform, and encouragement of labor unions.

By spring 1946, the various popular movements were coalescing into a national mass movement for revolutionary change that was leaving behind the leftist parties and their policy of socialism through the ballot box. But just as power seemed to be shifting into the streets, SCAP stepped in with a threat to use military force to prevent these revolutionary groups from coming to power.

Not even the most optimistic revolutionary was ready to attempt a popular uprising if it meant risking confrontation with U.S. troops. When Yoshida Shigeru, an old-line conservative politician, formed a government with SCAP's blessing and turned to the attack, the movement in the streets and factories lost its momentum. But popular sentiment for root-and-branch democratization of Japanese society gathered force and now provided support for a social democratic strategy based on winning elections.

The movement for social democracy gained support especially in the labor and tenant unions, and found political expression in the parliamentary politics of the Japanese Socialist party (JSP) and the Japanese Communist party (JCP). Elections in April 1947 gave the Socialist party the most seats in the Diet and led to a coalition government headed by Socialist Premier Katayama Tetsu.

A faltering economic recovery and *zaibatsu* resistance undermined the ability of this coalition government to realize the social democratic policies on which so many hopes had been pegged. It ended in futility, bringing disillusionment with the Socialists for failing to overcome inflation and shortages. And as the Cold War loomed in both Europe and Asia, American authorities had little sympathy left for even a moderate social democratic government in Japan. Thus, occupation priorities shifted toward economic reconstruction and political stability. If the democratic reforms of the first two years got in the way, SCAP was ready to roll them back. By the end of the 1940s, Japanese figures purged for their complicity in military aggression and political oppression were being rehabilitated, while suppression of labor and the Left began in earnest.

This so-called reverse course was based on the notion that an excess of democracy was the cause of political and social instability and had blocked economic recovery by allowing workers to organize and win wage increases that priced Japanese goods out of international markets. In 1948, SCAP put forth a vision of economic reconstruction through austerity that targeted the labor movement, especially its more militant elements, as the root cause of the lagging economic recovery, not *zaibatsu* or bureaucratic footdragging.

By the end of 1948, a conservative counterattack on democratic reforms was well under way with SCAP's active cooperation. Yoshida was back in power and being prodded by SCAP to implement a U.S.-devised plan for rigid economic austerity. He worked closely with a big-business elite to reassert "the right to manage," which involved a program of union busting, mass dismissals, red purges in public and private enterprises, and a conservative revision of Japan's new labor laws. But the reverse course produced renewed confrontation with defenders of Japan's democratization and an economic slump so severe that in the spring of 1950 many thought Japan was on the brink of depression. The outbreak of the Korean War in June 1950 rescued the economy from collapse, but provided no resolution to Japan's political conflicts.

Political Compromise and Economic Growth

For much of the 1950s, the confrontation continued. On the one side was a reconstituted conservative elite of bureaucrats, businesspeople, and politicians

in the Liberal Democratic party (LDP) that governed Japan from 1955 to 1993; on the other was a popular movement focused on labor and leftist parties that favored Socialist and pacifist policies. The decade was marked by sometimes violent clashes over Japan's rearmament and Cold War role as anti-Communist ally of the United States, and over conservative attempts to rewrite the constitution, recentralize police, regiment education, and break the union movement. In 1960, these conflicts broke out in protests by hundreds of thousands of people, forcing the government to resign.

The next cabinet, under the leadership of Prime Minister Ikeda Hayato, sought to shore up the LDP's badly eroded position by initiating a historic compromise between the conservative elite and the popular movement that would shape Japanese politics for decades to come. Ikeda and the LDP backed away from direct attacks on the constitution and the postwar democratic legacy. The conservative elite feared the consequences of further political strife and shifted to a strategy of all-out economic growth and trickle-down prosperity as best suited to ensuring their continued hegemony under postwar democratic order. In 1960, Ikeda announced a plan to double Japan's national income in ten years, in effect enshrining high-speed economic growth as the supreme national goal in place of the pursuit of Japan's imperial glory as in the past. Japan's postwar ideology had become the formerly despised materialism. And most Japanese settled down to tend their personal lives.

Under conservative rule, elections became a matter of corrupt money politics where business supplied unlimited campaign funds in exchange for political favors. An electoral system that radically overvalued the conservative rural vote guaranteed LDP control of the Diet even when its popular vote fell substantially below 50 percent. Changes in the leadership occurred through backroom negotiations rather than through elections. As in the past, power came to reside in the corridors of the bureaucracy and big-business enterprises. The term *soft authoritarianism* captures this style of Japanese elite politics.

But high-speed economic growth did not ensure social harmony and political unity. A student-led popular movement in the late 1960s and early 1970s went into the streets to protest Japan's involvement as a staging area for the American war in Vietnam and to repudiate the pervasive materialism of postwar Japanese life, for the single-minded pursuit of economic growth had brought environmental destruction and not-so-benign neglect for many members of society. Movements for citizens' rights, environmental protection, women's rights, and better treatment for the aged challenged LDP policies at the local and national levels. At the same time, the economy was in trouble owing to U.S. retaliation against rising Japanese exports and to a quadrupling in oil prices in 1973–1974. Momentarily, the economy contracted, bringing unemployment and a sense of crisis.

In response to such pressures, the government aided business in pursuing an export strategy to restore relatively high growth rates. The LDP began to deal more decisively with long-standing issues like pollution, the aged, social security, and medical care. After a strong start toward dealing with environmental problems, the government's efforts soon slack-

ened; and Japan has since gained an international reputation as a major contributor to global environmental degradation, through the practices of Japanese enterprises abroad engaged in manufacturing, mining, logging, and fishing. In contrast, the social welfare network improved dramatically. Although not as comprehensive as in some European countries, it has in many respects outstripped that of the United States. In short, the welfare state came to Japan, as it had in varying degrees to Europe and North America.

Japan at the End of the Twentieth Century

In the 1980s, Japan became a world economic giant and a full-fledged consumer society at home. A ballooning balance of trade surplus generated funds that

These Japanese women demonstrated against the revision of the country's Peace Constitution in 1993. *Rodo Joho: The Japanese Labor Information Journal*

were increasingly invested abroad. Japan's big corporations steadily enlarged their share of world trade by concentrating on high-tech, knowledge-intensive goods and services. At the same time, its heavy industrial base in metals, chemicals, and shipbuilding contracted, often moving overseas.

The country's relatively high rate of economic growth produced full employment and a renewed emphasis on expanding the internal market, but the benefits of both were spread unevenly. The greater concentration on exports since the mid-1970s had put pressure on employers to cut labor costs, which they did by automation, by intensification of the pace of work, and by hiring women (especially middle-aged married women) to fill low-paying part-time jobs. There was a notable feminization of the nonpermanent work force that raised the issue of equal opportunity for women in the workplace, for they were still excluded from the highly desirable permanent jobs in big business. In search of cheap labor, businesses moved overseas where repressive governments kept workers and wages down to levels far below Japan's. Firms inside Japan also began hiring foreign workers who entered the country illegally and were willing to work for much less. Such developments have taken place because the competitiveness of large Japanese corporations relies heavily on a vast network of labor-intensive and low-paying small businesses to produce and transport the cheap components. In short, the inequalities of the economy have not only persisted; they have also taken on sexual and international dimensions.

Despite considerable economic success, the LDP did not fare particularly well in the 1980s and was voted out of office in 1993. Voting rates dropped and popular disillusionment with Japan's managed democracy spread. The conservative elite was wracked by recurring revelations about a network of big-business, underworld, and right-wing corruption and influence peddling that touched even prime ministers. It appeared that the advent of mass consumerism had depleted, if not exhausted, the LDP's most potent source of appeal to Japanese voters—that it alone knew best how to produce economic growth.

Prime Minister Nakasone Yasuhiro attempted in the early 1980s to revive the flagging political fortunes of the conservative elite by moving the national center of attention away from economics and toward the emperor-centered nationalism espoused by the right wing. He envisaged the rehabilitation of the military as an offensive fighting force, raising the emperor to transcendent mythological and political status, and enforcing through the education system the moral certainties of the prewar order—familism, respect for authority, consciousness of Japan's racial distinctiveness, and self-sacrifice for the nation.

Nakasone's evocation of imperial glory and cultural superiority did beckon to some, giving the LDP 49 percent of the popular vote in the 1986 parliamentary elections, up about 4 percent from 1983. It tapped a vague but spreading feeling of resentment over Japan's apparent subservience to U.S. foreign policy despite its reputation as the world's foremost economic success. More importantly, it spoke to the right-wing nationalist groups that gained unsettling prominence in conservative circles owing to their usefulness to businesspeople and politicians in areas going outside the bounds of legality. A case in point was the construction industry, where organized crime built an empire through domination of the labor gangs and through immense contributions to conservative politicians. But this conservative ideology sat uneasily with the materialism and individualism of the postwar era and did not gain widespread support.

The economic boom had created many "new people" bent on the pursuit of personal goals and self-realization, indifferent to calls for sacrifice for nation, business enterprise, and family. The citizens' movements of the 1970s had spawned a multitude of groups working for specific goals, such as opposition to nuclear power and promotion of organic farming. Women have gone to the university, traveled, and taken jobs in greater numbers than ever before, some achieving careers outside the home and others chafing against the many restrictions that remain. This social ferment suggests that prosperity itself may have legitimized the individual search for a meaningful life and blunted the appeal of the Right with its message of nationalism and self-sacrifice. The end of the Cold War further diminished the appeal of conservative ideology.

Nakasone and the conservatives have had some success in dismantling state regulations and welfare policies and in enhancing the emperor's political status, but the goal of constitutional revision has eluded them. One significant victory has been the strengthening of the Japanese military, which in the early 1990s expanded its mission to include operations abroad as a fighting force in peacekeeping operations. Nonetheless, the leftist parties have managed to survive, at least for the moment, by minimizing their Marxist roots and by capitalizing on public disillusionment with LDP money politics.

Conclusion

It is far easier to describe Japan's transformation from an isolated feudal society to world capitalist powerhouse than it is to assess the meaning of the Japanese accomplishment. While no final judgment can be offered, Japan's historical trajectory over the past century and a half does highlight certain questions about the processes and direction of global history.

Japan's transformation is commonly held to be the result of a unique amalgam of "Eastern" ethics and "Western" techniques. Certainly, Japan's leaders from the outset have shown great skill in mobilizing aspects of traditional culture behind capitalism—particularly a certain conception of the family. But that use of tradition has been highly selective, omitting aspects running counter to capitalist needs, such as traditional contempt for merchant-class materialism. Japan's capitalist elite has been able to control the process of redefining traditional values to fit the new order. Such a view suggests that many cultures can adapt to capitalism, rather than that only certain cultures can generate capitalism.

Above all, there is the question of democracy's survival in an age of capitalist efficiency, large-scale production, and mass consumption. It is abundantly clear from Japan's historical experience that capitalism and democracy need not automatically go together. Indeed, many Japan-watchers have recently drawn the "lesson" that the "failure" of the West to meet Japanese competition stems from an excess of democracy that has produced conflict and undermined business efficiency in extracting the utmost productive effort from its work force. Their prescription for those who would copy the Japanese economic miracle—from the United States to Russia to Thailand—is to forge an alliance between business and the state and to impose order on society and discipline on the work force. The more successful attempts to do this in Asia—Singapore, Korea, Taiwan—have followed an overtly authoritarian road to capitalist development much like Japan had done before 1945, rather than the soft authoritarian path of managed democracy and corporate familism.

But Japan's experience also shows that gains for human rights and democracy can emerge from the struggles of the oppressed. Although opportunities for bottom-up social change may have been sharply limited at times, the Japanese people have shown persistence in that struggle. The democratic structure of postwar Japan—qualified though it may be—owes its survival to tenacious popular movements unwilling to hand over their fate to elites, no matter how efficient in pursuing economic growth.

Japan's economic transformation lends urgency as well to the long-standing problem of what to do about the cumulative effects of open-ended growth at a time when environmental costs have become prohibitive. Here there are more questions than answers for countries like Japan, where political legitimacy depends on growth and consumerism. Will faltering growth bring political crisis and authoritarianism? Will a continuation of business as usual bring conflict abroad? Or will new grounds for social accommodation and wider sharing of power be found? These are some of the questions that the Japanese and many other peoples will confront in the twenty-first century.

Comparative Essay

COMPARING REVOLUTIONS AND COMMUNIST REGIMES: RUSSIA AND CHINA[1]

Massive social upheavals are rare in human history, with the French, Russian, and Chinese revolutions providing the major modern examples. At first glance, the two twentieth-century revolutions on this list appear to be quite similar. They both took place in countries subjected to heavy imperialist pressure and repeated military defeats by Europeans and Japanese, though without being formally colonized. In both cases, long-established monarchies collapsed under this pressure, China's in 1911 and Russia's in March 1917. Intellectuals in both societies had turned against the old regime, and widespread peasant revolts were part of the revolutionary process. Leadership for these revolutionary movements came from well-educated, modernist elites who found in European Marxist socialism an ideology to guide the revolution and to define its goals. Finally, in both societies, the revolutionaries destroyed the dominant class of landowners, expropriated foreign and domestic capitalists, and created Communist regimes.

Yet a closer look reveals striking differences in the way these revolutionary Socialist regimes came to power and in the strategies they developed for transforming their societies. And behind these differences lie further contrasts in the traditional social structure and modern historical experience of the two societies.

Lenin and the Bolsheviks came to power on the basis of an urban insurrection less than a year after the tsarist regime collapsed, whereas in China the Communist party was not even formed until a decade after the 1911 revolution and then struggled for another twenty-eight years before it came to power on the crest of a rural peasant movement. How can we account for these differences?

An important part of the answer lies in the prerevolutionary societies of Russia and China. The tsars of Russia had long ago subordinated the landowning nobility to the service of the state. By the mid-nineteenth century, most nobles were impoverished or in debt to the government, despite their legal privileges and social status. When the state collapsed in 1917, the nobility had little independent source of power, wealth, or prestige and was extremely vulnerable to peasant uprising.

The position of the landowning gentry in China was quite different. They were deeply rooted in their local areas and performed many of the functions of local government for the imperial bureaucracy. Furthermore, the gentry was periodically renewed as wealthy merchants purchased land as a means of increasing their status. Since the mid-nineteenth century, they had considerably increased their power relative to the imperial bureaucracy by helping to preserve the regime against the Taiping rebels. The fall of the imperial government in 1911, then, made little immediate difference at the local level except to increase the power of the more prominent gentry and warlords. While China disintegrated politically, it remained socially intact. Almost the reverse was the case in Russia.

The very different roles of the peasantry in the revolutionary process also had roots in their respective societies. In Russia, the peasants made a spontaneous revolution in the rural areas in 1917, largely without any prodding or leadership from urban elites or political parties. They seized landlords' estates and redistributed land according to traditional communal practices. What made this possible was a long tradition of autonomy and self-government in peasant villages, which included the practice of periodically redividing the land to ensure relative equality within the village. So long as peasant villages paid their rent and taxes and supplied recruits for the army, they had been allowed to manage their own affairs. Thus, they were able to move against the hated landlords once the tsar's government and army collapsed.

In China, however, peasant villages were part of larger market communities directly managed by local gentry. Peasants themselves controlled none of the institutions of these communities—temples, secret societies, militias, or water control projects. Combined with the continuing power of local gentry, this lack of peasant autonomy helps to explain the relative absence of spontaneous peasant uprisings. Not until the Communist party was able to provide military protection from the gentry forces was it possible to persuade Chinese peasants to move against their oppressors, and this was a slow process that took the better part of three decades.

The urban and working-class character of the Russian Revolution was a product of the country's more advanced industrial development. Since the late nineteenth century, the government had urgently pushed industrialization largely for military reasons, but without much concern for its impact on the role of the nobility, who were in any case altogether subservient to the state. But in China a conservative gentry, oriented toward the rural world of Confucian ideals, had actively prevented the reforms needed for developing a modern economy, fearing correctly that these would undermine its dominant social position. Thus, the working class played only a modest role in the Chinese revolutionary process, whereas it was central to events in the Soviet Union.

The role of war was also different in the two revolutions. In the Russian case, World War I displayed the gross incompetence of the tsarist regime and stimulated a widespread desire for peace to which the Bolsheviks responded. But the Communist party in China led the struggle against the Japanese invaders and in doing so gained greatly in mass support.

These differences in revolutionary process also decisively shaped postrevolutionary strategies for development in the Soviet Union and China. Building on Russia's substantial industrial base, the Soviets emphasized heavy industrial development above everything else and were willing to sacrifice and exploit the rural areas for that end. And lacking any real roots in the countryside, Soviet efforts to collectivize agriculture took the form of Stalin's brutal coercion. In China, however, the party's long history of intimate association with peasants made the process of collectivization in the 1950s far less traumatic than had been the case in the Soviet Union in the 1930s. Though China's industrialization strategy similarly exploited the countryside, the state articulated a more balanced development strategy that included a real concern for improving rural conditions.

Finally, the historical experiences of China and Russia have shaped their respective efforts to reform their Communist societies in the 1980s and contributed to the very different outcomes of those reforms. China's post-Mao reforms began and have had their greatest impact in the countryside, essentially returning the country to a system of family farms and raising rural standards of living dramatically. Gorbachev's economic reforms, on the contrary, focused on spurring industrial production and indefinitely postponed real change in the agricultural sector. The result has been continued stagnation in agriculture and falling production in industry.

The Soviet program combined modest economic reform with quite dramatic political and cultural changes that unleashed a torrent of popular protest leading to the disintegration of this huge and hugely diverse country in 1991. China not only lacked the powerful ethnic minorities whose secession undermined the Soviet Union, but it also carefully limited reform efforts to the economic sphere, maintaining clear Communist party control over culture and politics. Furthermore, China's rapidly growing economy has been able to buy off social discontent, while Russia's declining economy has been a major factor in promoting mass unrest.

The Russian and Chinese revolutions certainly marked a decisive break with their countries' respective pasts. But they did not "wipe the slate clean." Rather, those upheavals and the subsequent experience of the two countries reflected their earlier and quite different histories. The past lives on, even in revolutionary circumstances.

Note

1. This essay draws heavily on Theda Skocpol, *States and Social Revolution* (Cambridge: Cambridge University Press, 1979); and William Rosenberg and Marilyn Young, *Transforming Russia and China* (New York: Oxford University Press, 1982).

SUGGESTIONS FOR FURTHER READING: CHINA AND JAPAN

China

Chang, Hsin-pao. *Commissioner Lin and the Opium War.* 1964. (A detailed account of the war that began China's nineteenth-century subordination to the West.)

Chow, Tse-tsung. *The May Fourth Movement.* 1960. (The best single-volume summary of a definite moment in modern Chinese history.)

Elvin, Mark. *The Pattern of the Chinese Past.* 1971. (An influential history of imperial China focusing on the interaction of social, economic, and technological change.)

Fairbank, John K. *China: A New History.* 1992. (A readable one-volume synthesis by the acknowledged father of China studies in the United States; includes an excellent guide to the latest scholarship.)

————, and Denis Twitchett, eds. *The Cambridge History of China.* 15 vols. 1976. (An attempt to provide the definitive history of China in fifteen volumes.)

Hinton, William. *Fanshen: A Documentary of Revolution in a Chinese Village.* 1966. (A sympathetic account of the Chinese Revolution from the viewpoint of the peasants of Long Bow village.)

————. *Shenfan: The Continuing Revolution in a Chinese Village.* 1983. (The changes in Long Bow village from 1949 to 1979.)

Johnson, Kay Ann. *Women, the Family, and Peasant Revolution in China.* 1983. (The role of women in the Chinese Revolution and the limitations of that revolution for women.)

Meisner, Maurice. *Mao's China and After.* 1986. (The best single-volume history of the People's Republic.)

Rawski, Thomas. *Economic Growth in Pre-War China,* 1989. (A revisionist view of China's twentieth-century economic performance, arguing that it was much better than usually believed.)

Riskin, Carl. *China's Political Economy: The Quest for Development since 1949.* 1987. (The best one-volume analysis of China's economic development since 1949, including chapters on the post-Mao reforms.)

Sheridan, James E. *China in Disintegration: The Republican Era in Chinese History, 1912–1949.* 1975. (The best one-volume history of the republican period.)

Snow, Edgar. *Red Star over China.* 1938. (An American journalist's classic account of Mao and the Chinese Communists on the eve of the Japanese invasion.)

Spence, Jonathan. *The Death of Woman Wang.* 1978. (An innovative attempt to convey a sense of the world of late seventeenth-century village life in north China.)

Stacey, Judith. *Patriarchy and Socialist Revolution in China.* 1983. (Argues that the CCP never intended to make a revolution to liberate women but planned to construct a "Socialist patriarchy.")

Wakeman, Frederic Jr. *The Fall of Imperial China.* 1975. (Addresses the rise and fall of the Qing Dynasty.)

Wolf, Margery. *Revolution Postponed: Women in Contemporary China.* 1985. (An anthropologist's assessment of the position of women in the 1980s based on field research in China.)

Japan

Dower, John W. *War without Mercy: Race and Power in the Pacific War.* 1986. (A balanced analysis of perceptions and actions on both sides of the Pacific conflict.)

Field, Norma. *In the Realm of a Dying Emperor: A Portrait of Japan at Century's End.* 1991. (Reflections on Japanese life and its future on the occasion of the death of the emperor.)

Gordon, Andrew, ed. *Post-War Japan as History.* 1993. (A collection of essays by leading historians.)

Halliday, Jon. *A Political History of Japanese Capitalism.* 1975. (A Marxist account, especially strong on the 1945–1960 period.)

Hane, Mikiso. *Peasants, Rebels, and Outcasts: The Underside of Modern Japan.* 1982. (The lives of those who were forgotten, often in their own words.)

Kawanishi, Hirosuke. *Enterprise Unionism in Japan.* 1992. (Covers postwar trade unions.)

Morris-Suzuki, Tessa, and T. Seiyama, eds. *Japanese Capitalism since 1945: Critical Perspectives.* 1989. (A collection of essays by Marxist scholars.)

Nakamura, Masanori. *The Japanese Monarchy, 1931–1991.* 1992. (Explores the decision to maintain the emperor after World War II.)

Reischauer, E. O. *Japan: The Story of a Nation.* 1981. (A very readable account by a former American ambassador to Japan.)

Tsurumi, E. Patricia. *Factory Girls: Women in the Thread Mills of Meiji Japan.* 1990. (Addresses the lives of women in the textile industry.)

PART VII

COLONIALISM, NATIONALISM, AND DEVELOPMENT: AFRICA IN THE MODERN WORLD

Chapter 21: *Old Africa and New Pressures*

Chapter 22: *Modernization or Distorted Development? The Colonial Experience in Africa*

Chapter 23: *Toward Independence: Shaping New Societies in Africa*

Chapter 24: *Development or Deterioration? Beyond Independence in Africa*

Suggestions for Further Reading: *Africa*

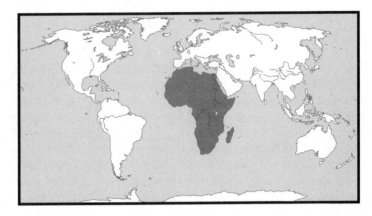

Like the Middle East, India, and China, Africa's modern history has included a fateful encounter with Europe's expanding empires and their corresponding economic networks. For several hundred years that encounter took the unique form of the Atlantic slave trade, which sent Africans by the millions to the Americas and created a permanent connection between the two regions. But not until the end of the nineteenth century, considerably later than elsewhere, was Africa fully incorporated into Europe's colonial empires. Its colonial experience was not only shorter than that of India and China, but its struggle for independence was, in most places, also briefer and more readily successful. In terms of Europe's major cultural or ideological exports, Africa proved far more receptive to Christianity, equally receptive to nationalism, and less receptive to Marxism and communism than its major Asian counterparts. In its struggle to incorporate changing and culturally diverse communities into modern state structures, Africa's experience bears comparison with a similarly diverse India. But, sadly, its efforts at modern economic development since independence compare unfavorably with most of its Asian neighbors. These are some of the features of Africa's modern history that the chapters of Part VII highlight.

Chapter 21 traces the broad patterns of Africa's precolonial development and its connection to the larger themes of world history. Chapter 22 examines the impact of colonial rule on African societies and asks whether that experience served to modernize Africa in an effective and balanced fashion or to limit and distort its development. Africans' efforts to reconstruct their own communities and to get out from under European control represent the main themes of Chapter 23, while Chapter 24 continues that story by exploring both the gains and the disappointments of the several decades since independence.

Chapter 21
Old Africa and New Pressures

Africa is a very large and a very diverse continent. With an area some three times that of the continental United States, it is the world's second-largest continent and accounts for about 20 percent of the earth's land. Human cultures of virtually every description have evolved within its boundaries. Although modern scholars have identified patterns of similarity and connection among its many societies, there was little if any consciousness of an "African" identity until the nineteenth century. As in Europe, India, and elsewhere, people thought of themselves in terms of their local communities even while their cultures took shape through encounters with their immediate neighbors and by assimilating changes originating in distant parts of the world.

Contributing to Africa's cultural diversity has been the variety of its physical environment (see Map 21.1). In the very center of the continent, a large area of rain forest occupies the Zaire River basin and the coastal area of west Africa. To the north and south of this forest lie broad expanses of rolling grasslands called the Tropical Savannah. Moving farther from the equator in both directions are the desert areas of Africa, the Sahara in the north and the Kalahari in the south. At the far ends of the continent lie narrow bands of temperate Mediterranean climate and vegetation. The rough parallels of these environmental zones are interrupted in eastern Africa, where an extensive area of highland plateau and mountains produces a cooler and more temperate climate despite its tropical latitude.

From a geological viewpoint, Africa is a vast plateau that drops off sharply near the oceans into a narrow coastal plain. Thus, many of the great river systems that drain the plateau—the Nile, Niger, Zaire, Volta, and Zambezi—plunge down the escarpment in great falls and rapids that prohibit navigation

inland from the sea. But once the plateau is mounted, few natural barriers forbid the movement of people.

A final environmental factor shaping Africa's history has been the quality of its soils. As the only continent straddling the equator, much of Africa experiences tropical conditions of constant high temperatures and torrential rains, which have produced thin and easily exhausted soils. Although African farmers have adapted to these conditions by practicing shifting cultivation, their agriculture has been less productive than in areas with naturally richer lands.

Economic Foundations of African History

In its broad patterns, the economic foundations of Africa's history have been similar to those of other parts of the world. Over long periods, a hunting-and-gathering way of life based on the use of stone tools yielded to agriculture, to the domestication of animals, and later to the knowledge of metalworking. But two important technological innovations prevalent in Eurasia—the plow and the wheel—did not spread south of the Sahara except in Ethiopia. The absence of the plow limited the area of land that could be cultivated, and the lack of wheel technology restricted the use of animal, wind, and water power as well as mechanical means of irrigation. How can we explain this difference in Africa's technological history?

Some scholars have pointed to the prevalence of animal diseases as limiting the use of the plow or

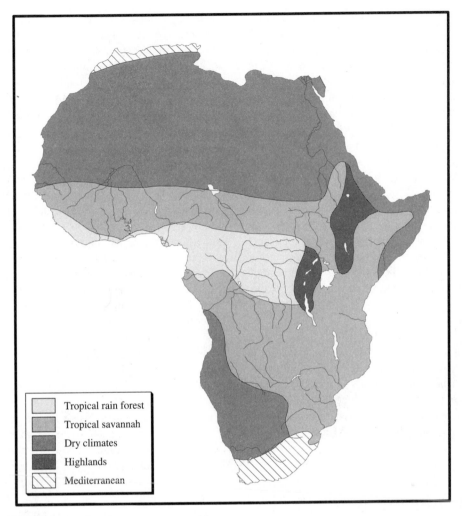

MAP 21.1 Environmental Zones of Africa

wheeled cart. Others have suggested that deep plowing would have been ineffective in the thin soils of much of Africa and that the camel in the desert, the donkey in the savannah, and human porters in the forests were each more efficient carriers than the ox cart in their respective environments. Still others have pointed to the relative isolation of sub-Saharan Africa from the major centers of technological innovation in Asia, the Middle East, and the Mediterranean basin, which had for centuries stimulated one another's development. Like northwestern Europe, Africa south of the Sahara was for much of its history on the margins of this intercommunicating zone. "The Alps created a small barrier compared to the Sahara,"[1] and although the new European civilization that emerged after 1000 C.E. was accessible enough to benefit from developments in the Islamic world, Byzantium, India, and China, much of Africa south of the Sahara, and especially south of the forest area, remained comparatively cut off from the stimulus of these contacts.

Africa's technological limitations, environmental conditions, huge size, and relatively sparse population combined to shape its social and economic development in ways that diverged to some extent from that of Eurasia.[2] Since land was seldom scarce, there was little incentive to define it as private property, and in most African societies, neither individuals nor kinship groups claimed large territories as their exclusive preserve. Africans generally regarded political authority, therefore, as the exercise of power over people rather than over a fixed territory, and though core areas might have been tightly held, boundaries between societies were often hazy and fluctuating.

Although land was plentiful, poor soil and limited technology frequently made it less productive than in much of Eurasia. Thus, less surplus was available to support classes of people (artisans, scholars, priests, merchants) who did not themselves work the land. Inequalities and class differences were apparent in many African societies, but social stratification and differences in wealth were normally less sharp than in the wealthier societies of Eurasia. Unlike India, China, and Europe, Africa produced few societies dominated by a landowning nobility. Various forms of slavery were practiced in Africa, as they were almost everywhere else, but most ordinary farmers were freer than their counterparts on the estates of European and Asian landlords. If conditions became oppressive, they could, and often did, simply leave. Such mobility was certainly a constraint on the power of African rulers.

An interesting exception to much of this occurred in the Ethiopian highlands, which did have plow agriculture in a fertile environment with ample rainfall. There a landowning nobility, a wealthy church, and a dependent peasantry produced a society with marked resemblances to that of feudal Europe. But it was the exception, not the rule, in Africa.

The Evolution of African Societies

What kind of societies developed on these environmental and economic foundations? How and why did they change over time? To what extent were they shaped by interactions with neighboring peoples and by participation in wider networks of trade, culture, and conquest? These are the sorts of questions historians of Africa have tried to answer.

Kinship and Political Order: Lineage-based Societies

The principle of kinship or descent has played an important role in shaping African communities, as it

has in all human societies. But more than many other peoples, Africans organized their societies at the local level in terms of kinship groups or lineages, which incorporated large numbers of people well beyond the immediate or extended family. These lineages were groups who traced their descent through either the male or female line to some common ancestor, real or mythical. Such kinship groups, united by the belief that their members were kin to one another, played a far more significant role in social life than was common in Europe or parts of Asia.

African lineage organizations were remarkable in that they frequently provided the political framework within which large numbers of people could make and enforce rules, maintain order, and settle disputes without going to war. In short, the lineage system performed the functions of government but without the formal apparatus of government; that is, without kings or queens, chiefs, or permanent officials associated with a state organization. The political system in such a society was the sum of its lineages; decisions were reached and disputes resolved by negotiation among the representatives of equivalent kinship groups. The Tiv of central Nigeria organized close to a million people in this fashion on the eve of colonial conquest. Theirs was a system in which power was dispersed throughout the society rather than being concentrated in particular people or institutions. In fact, the Tiv had no word for *politics* as a separate aspect of life, for there was no state that specialized in political matters.

Many lineage societies evolved other social organizations that cut across kinship groups and thus reinforced the unity of the society. Among the Igbo of southeastern Nigeria, village assemblies brought together all men for important decisions such as the declaration of war, whereas similar organizations for women dealt with farming, trading, and mistreatment by men. Nilotic-speaking peoples of east Africa as early as the first millennium C.E. created "age sets" in which adolescent boys from a variety of lineages were initiated together and then moved through a series of "age grades," or ranks, during their lives. This system made it possible to mobilize a large number of men for military purposes and provided a means of integrating aliens into the society. Thus, lineages operated within a framework of checks and balances in which organizations based on residence, age, or gender limited those that were based on kinship.

Despite their democratic qualities, at least among

This striking terracotta head reflects the ancient west African artistic traditions of the Nok culture, which dates to some 2000 years ago.
Art Resource

males, and the absence of centralized political authority, lineage societies often developed social and economic inequalities. Elders were able to exploit the labor of junior members of the community and sought particularly to control the reproductive powers of women, which were essential for the growth of the lineage. Among the Igbo, title societies enabled men and women of wealth and character to earn a series of increasingly prestigious titles that set them apart from other members of their community. Lineages also sought to expand their numbers, and thus their prestige and power, by incorporating war captives or migrants in subordinate positions, often as slaves.

The ideas that explained and justified these social arrangements were everywhere religious. Particularly important were the spirits of ancestors, especially those regarded as founders of the lineage. They were the closest links of the living with the world of the supernatural and were generally more approachable than the High God, who was seen as responsible for creation but not in direct or intimate contact with people. In addition, a pantheon of local deities was associated with particular functions, such as fertility or thunder and lightning. A final element of religious belief evident in many African societies was an effort to explain personal or social misfortune (illness, infertility, or drought, for example) by reference to witchcraft. Witches were commonly thought to be men or women who had some evil power that they used to cause harm to others. Elaborate techniques for identifying witches and counteracting their powers developed in many African societies, and anti-witchcraft movements were particularly evident in times of great social tension. Thus, Africans explained the world by reference to a variety of super-human forces or beings and sought to invoke or control their powers through a variety of means—ritual observances, sacrifices, spirit possession, divination, or prayer. Like Hinduism but unlike Christianity, most African religions were open to a wide variety of practices and beliefs, and changes in the religious sphere paralleled closely those in social, economic, and political life.

Lineage-based societies have frequently been referred to as "tribes." But at least in the West, that term has come to imply a simple, primitive, and changeless society occupying a fixed territory whose quaint or savage customs placed that society outside the mainstream of human historical development. Historians generally avoid the word *tribe* because its popular implications are so at odds with what their research has disclosed.

Certainly such societies have not been geographically static, for they undertook the great migrations that have peopled the African continent. The most carefully studied of these migrations is associated with the Bantu-speaking peoples who occupied Africa south of the equator. Careful analysis of the relationship among the many languages spoken in Africa's great southern bulge has shown that they probably had their origin somewhere in present-day Nigeria or Cameroon. Over many centuries, Bantu speakers spread around and through the forest to the savannah regions of the south and the highlands of eastern Africa. The actual process of migration owed much to the dynamics of lineage society, which easily split or segmented as local populations grew or conflicts created unresolved tensions.

Contrary to the tribal notion, historical studies show that Africa's lineage societies were far from homogeneous and changeless. Nor were they isolated from one another, for they absorbed people, borrowed ideas and techniques, and exchanged goods with neighboring peoples. Change sometimes occurred as the result of movement to a new environment. As the Kamba of present-day Kenya moved from a wetter and more fertile highland area to a drier lowland location, they came to rely less on agriculture and more

on cattle-raising. By the nineteenth century, they began to supplement their income by pioneering trade routes for the collection of ivory and selling it on the east African coast. Some individuals grew rich from this trade and used their new wealth to enlarge their lineages through multiple marriages and by adopting the victims of famine. To ensure a good supply of ivory, they often married into the lineages of those who actually hunted the elephants.

At other times and places, change was occasioned by the direct encounter of culturally different peoples. When the pastoral and Nilotic-speaking Masaai came into contact with the agricultural and Bantu-speaking Kikuyu in the highlands of central Kenya around 1750, they engaged in frequent military conflicts, which the Masaai most often won. As the military weakness of a purely lineage system became apparent, the Kikuyu adopted from the Masaai age-based military regiments and related customs, such as the use of ostrich-feather headdresses for warriors and the drinking of cow's milk before battle.

Some institutions or practices spread quite widely. The position of *elombe,* a medicine man specializing in war magic, was found in the northern savannah, the forest areas of equatorial Africa, and in the southern savannah, among peoples who were otherwise culturally very different. "They all apparently wanted more effective war magic," wrote historian Jan Vansina, "and so borrowed their neighbors' way of getting it."[3]

Many African societies, then, chose to conduct their affairs without the alleged benefits of formal centralized states and full-time rulers even though they were perfectly well aware of these institutions and practices from nearby peoples. The Igbo proudly proclaimed, "The Igbo have no kings." Given the frequent oppressiveness of the state in human history, African experiments with stateless forms of social organization represent a major contribution to world civilization. Such societies pioneered the human settlement of vast areas of Africa; created in the process numerous cultural, artistic, and religious traditions; adapted to a variety of environments; incorporated new crops, institutions, and people into their cultures; and interacted continuously with their neighbors. In other parts of Africa, however, lineage-based societies slowly gave rise to chiefdoms, kingdoms, and empires in which political rulers and the state played a larger role (see Map 21.2). Such societies more closely resembled the classical civilizations of Eurasia.

Gold, Empire, and Islam in West Africa

Although the earliest African states arose in the northeast, probably the best known and most studied developed in west Africa in an area known to the Arabs as the *bilad al-Sudan* ("land of the blacks"). Archaeological evidence suggests the existence of a powerful chiefdom in what is now southern Maureta-

nia as early as 1000 B.C.E., but the classical states of the Sudan—Ghana, Mali, Songhai, Kanem and Bornu, and the Hausa kingdoms—flourished between 400 and 1600 C.E. They arose, therefore, at about the same time as the modern states of Europe and during the expansion of Islamic civilization.

Their geographical setting, astride the frontier between the desert and the savannah, played an important role in the development of these states, for the perennial conflict between nomadic pastoralists and settled farmers provided opportunities for herders to dominate agriculturalists and the need for farmers to organize defenses against pastoral incursions. Furthermore, the introduction of the

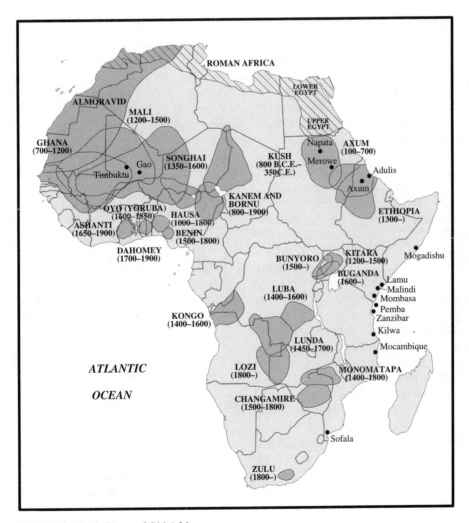

MAP 21.2 Major States of Old Africa

camel at about the time of Christ fostered a lucrative trade across the Sahara in which the products of the savannah and forest—pepper, kola nuts, cloth, leather goods, slaves, and, above all, gold—were exchanged for products of the Sahara and north Africa. Salt, scarce in the savannah, was the chief import, but the list included horses for the cavalries of Sudanic states, fine cloth and jewelry, as well as dates, grapes, and nuts for the wealthy of west Africa. The desire to control this profitable trade clearly stimulated and sustained the process of state formation in the western Sudan.

Ghana, Mali, and Songhai are properly called empires, for they incorporated many local communities, chiefdoms, and kingdoms in very large territorial states. At the center sat the monarch, enthroned in great splendor, regarded as sacred, and elevated far above commoners or even those of his own lineage. In Mali, the king always ate alone, and those who came into his presence fell prostrate and scattered dust and ashes on their heads. A substantial bureaucracy and a large standing army, including powerful cavalry forces, projected the king's authority into the provinces. The fourteenth-century Arab traveler Ibn-Battuta commented about Mali:

> Amongst their good qualities is the small amount of injustice amongst them, for of all people they are the furthest from it. Their sultan does not forgive anyone in any matter to do with injustice.... There is also the prevalence of peace in their country, the traveller is not afraid in it nor is he who lives there in fear of the thief or of the robber by violence.[4]

But as in many premodern empires, the central government did not really penetrate the society very deeply, and local communities were generally left undisturbed as long as they remained loyal and rendered occasional tribute to the capital. Furthermore, these empires were politically fragile and subject to recurrent internal conflict over succession to the throne. And both Ghana in 1076 and Songhai in 1591 were subject to crushing military defeats from north Africa that effectively destroyed their centralized power.

The economic basis of these imperial systems was a hoe agriculture sufficiently productive to support elaborate and extensive trading networks; specialized craft production of iron, goldwork, leather, and cotton cloth; and a very wealthy court. On a visit to Egypt in 1324, the Malian monarch Mansa

Musa spent so much gold that the price of the metal was depressed on the Egyptian market for some time. The surplus that this wealth represented was not extracted directly from the peasants through rent or labor obligations, as in those Eurasian societies that had a powerful landowning nobility. It was rather the king's ability to control and tax trade, especially long-distance trade across the Sahara, that supported the state and the luxury of the elite. Mali's kings, for example, monopolized the import of strategic goods such as horses and metals, levied duties on the import of salt, copper, and other merchandise, and reserved for themselves the larger nuggets of gold while permitting the free export of gold dust. Slave villages, devoted to producing for the royal granaries, further enriched the king and his dependents.

It was in the cities of these Sudanic empires that the social and cultural consequences of their economic and political development were most apparent. The great trading city of Timbuktu contained perhaps 25,000 people in the fifteenth century, and the Songhai capital of Gao and the Hausa city of Kano numbered about 75,000 each a century later. Court officials, artisans, scholars and students, and local and foreign merchants crowded these cosmopolitan centers. A visitor from the city of Fez in north Africa described Timbuktu in 1510:

> Here are many shops of artificers and merchants, and especially of such as weave linen and cotton cloth. And hither do the Barbary [north African] merchants bring the cloth of Europe. All the women of this region except maid-servants go with their faces covered, and sell all necessary victuals.... Corn, cattle, milk, and butter this region yieldeth in great abundance.... Here are great stores of doctors, judges, priests and other learned men, that are bountifully maintained at the king's cost and charges. And here are brought divers manuscripts or written books out of Barbary which are sold for more than any other merchandise.[5]

Across the routes of the trans-Saharan trade came not only the goods of north Africa but also the religion of Islam. Introduced by Muslim merchants, the new faith was accepted primarily in the urban centers of the Sudanic empires. For African merchant communities, this provided an important link to Muslim trading partners in north Africa. For the monarchs and their courts, it provided a source of literate officials to assist in state administration and a further religious legitimation of their rule, particularly for those who gained the prestige conferred by a pilgrimage to Mecca. Islam was a world religion with a single creator-god able to protect and comfort people whose political and economic horizons had expanded well beyond the local realm, where ancestral spirits and traditional deities might be effective. Islam thus had a religious appeal for societies undergoing rapid change.

By the sixteenth century, a number of Sudanic cities had become major centers of Islamic religious and intellectual life and attracted scholars from throughout the Muslim world. Timbuktu boasted some 180 Quranic schools and thousands of students from all over the Sudan. Monarchs subsidized the construction of mosques in many of these towns. West Africa thus became an integral part of the Islamicate world system.

But Islam remained the culture of an urban elite and spread very little into the rural areas of Sudanic empires. Its incomplete introduction, in fact, created major tensions within the culture of the western Sudan that were not resolved until the nineteenth century. Although many Sudanic kings adopted Islam, they governed people who steadfastly practiced African religions and whose cultural sensibilities had to be respected if social harmony were to prevail. Thus, they made few efforts to impose the new religion on their rural subjects or to govern in strict accordance with Islamic law.

Furthermore, the practice of Islam was thoroughly mixed with local religious customs and was frequently far removed from the "authentic" religious traditions of the Islamic heartland in the Middle East. Sonni Ali, king of Songhai in the fifteenth century, observed the fast of Ramadan and contributed to the construction of mosques in his realm, but he also

These worshippers, at prayer in front of the Great Mosque at Kano in northern Nigeria, are participating in Islamic religious traditions long established in many African cultures. *The Granger Collection*

consulted diviners and performed customary sacrifices. This sort of blending eased the spread of the new religion in west Africa but deeply offended those converts who adhered to a strict or orthodox version of their faith.

In the eighteenth and nineteenth centuries, the spread of such a strict or purified Islam created a revolutionary situation in much of the western Sudan. Part of a more general movement of revival and religious reform in the Muslim world, this new form of Islamic teaching was sharply critical of the religious blending of the past, called for a strict adherence to the belief in one God, and was tinged with the notion that the end times had arrived and that an Islamic messiah, or *mahdi,* might be expected. To oppressed or excluded groups in society, this was a potentially revolutionary message, for it provided religious justification for their opposition to the existing order and, in the notion of *jihad,* supplied a means to struggle for a new society.

One such group were the Fulani, a pastoral society whose members were spread out across much of the west African savannah and who frequently found themselves at odds with their agricultural neighbors. A number of Fulani had settled in the cities, became ardent reformist Muslims, and supplied much of the leadership for a series of *jihads* that profoundly shaped west African societies between 1680 and 1880. In these violent assaults on the old order, the Fulani were joined in various places by slaves seeking their freedom, by peasants resentful of the corruption and privileges of the local aristocracy, and by others who felt dispossessed or exploited.

The consequences were far-reaching. New rulers replaced old ones and, in the process, sometimes created very large political units. In what is today northern Nigeria, a Fulani empire, called the Sokoto caliphate, was established over a series of small Hausa city-states. These religious revolutions also immensely strengthened and extended the hold of Islam on west African societies, with results that continue to be felt. The spread of Islamic literacy in northern Nigeria fostered resistance to Western education during the colonial era and thus contributed to northern "backwardness," in comparison to the previously illiterate southern Nigerian societies that rapidly adopted Christianity, education,

and modern ways in general. The tension between the north and the south of Africa's most populous country persists into the late twentieth century but had its roots in processes of change in the distant past.

Variations on a Theme

The evolution of west African savannah societies illustrates with particular clarity the larger historical processes of state formation, long-distance trade, encounters among very different peoples, and cultural change. Similar, though not identical, processes operated in other regions of Africa. Even a quick survey illustrates the variety of societies and cultures that evolved on the African continent.

In the highlands of present-day Ethiopia, the ancient monarchy of Axum emerged around 500 B.C.E., and from its contacts with the Mediterranean world of the Roman Empire, Christianity was introduced about 350 C.E. Both the Christian religion and the monarchy persisted over many centuries into modern times and served to support a feudal society dominated by landowning aristocrats. It was only the revolution of the 1970s that fundamentally changed that ancient society.

Since the early C.E. centuries, the peoples of the east African coast had traded with Mediterranean and Middle Eastern societies. Out of this encounter, Swahili civilization emerged sometime after 1000 C.E. It was centered in more than forty frequently quarreling city-states and expressed in a written Bantu language with many words borrowed from Arabic. The economic basis of Swahili society was its trading connections with the world of Indian Ocean commerce, which included Persia, India, and China. The absorbing of Arab settlers into an essentially African population was accompanied by the introduction of Islam, though neither the religion nor Swahili culture generally penetrated into the coastal hinterland until the nineteenth century. Then, as inland trade routes developed, the knowledge of Swahili spread rapidly, and the language is now spoken widely from Kenya to Mozambique.

A further belt of state formation lay across the savannah region south of the equator. With the combining of small chiefdoms into larger political units, often on the basis of magical-religious authority and kinship ties, a number of substantial kingdoms had emerged by the sixteenth century or earlier, including those of the Kongo, Luba, Lunda, and Monomutapa.

In most of Africa, state formation seems to have been a long and gradual process. But in the far-southeast corner of the continent, it occurred very rapidly and with great violence in the early nineteenth century. By 1800, the Bantu-speaking peoples of the area were running out of land to accommodate their growing population; their outlets for expansion were limited by the deserts to the west and the expanding frontier of European settlement to the south. As a consequence, competition among the many small chiefdoms of the region became far more intense, and traditional cattle raids, which produced few casualties, turned into deadly conflict over land, water, pasture, and hunting grounds. Since the advantage lay with those who could command the largest and most effective military forces, a number of societies began to abandon their traditional initiation rites for adolescent boys and to recruit them directly into "age regiments" whose purpose was entirely military.

The most successful innovators were the Zulu, under the leadership of the famous Shaka (died 1828). He introduced new tactics in the form of highly disciplined military formations and new technology in the form of a short stabbing spear for effective hand-to-hand combat. In addition, he established continuous military service for young men and housed the aged regiments in barracks at the royal households scattered throughout the kingdom. No one could marry until his unit was formally dissolved.

In this new Zulu kingdom, southern Africa saw a much larger and wholly different kind of political unit: highly centralized, militaristic, very aggressive, and multiethnic. Shaka's conquests were extensive and very destructive, but they gave rise not only to an enlarged Zulu state that incorporated many conquered peoples but also to a massive series of population movements that extended as far north as southern Tanzania. Many peoples displaced by Zulu expansion—the Swazi, Ngoni, and Ndebele, for example—established their own conquest states more or less on the Zulu model.

This entire sequence of events is known in southern Africa as the *mfecane,* or the "crushing." It killed or uprooted innumerable people and depopulated large areas; it created new, larger, and more powerful states; and, by forcibly mixing south Africa's many small-scale societies, it gave rise to new ethnic identities. In short, the *mfecane* produced the social and political structures that would soon have to confront the even more powerful forces of European expansion.

History and Myth in Africa

Historical study of African societies, both those structured largely in lineage terms and those that developed states, provides a powerful corrective to the pervasive misunderstandings of the continent that have emerged from centuries of the slave trade, racism, and colonial rule. By the late nineteenth century, Europeans generally saw Africa as an exotic continent, a "world apart," altogether different from other societies and largely isolated from them. Its achievements were generally credited to outsiders, usually with white skins. Africa, in their view, had no history of its own. In the mid-twentieth century, a British colonial governor summed up a widely accepted view: "For countless centuries, while all the pageant of history swept by, the African remained unmoved in primitive savagery."[6]

It is clear, however, that African societies had changed substantially over time and that they interacted continuously with one another, and, in some places, with peoples outside the continent. Although the shape of African history naturally reflected its unique conditions, its broad outlines and major themes are similar to those of Europe and Asia.

Furthermore, the trajectories of African history did not end when Europeans appeared on the scene. The slave trade tapped into existing patterns of commerce in west Africa, whereas the invading Portuguese became but one of many players in the highly competitive politics of the east African coast. Islam continued to spread in west Africa under colonial rule, as did the use of Swahili in the eastern part of the continent. Colonial rulers found

The stone churches of Lalibela, constructed around 1200 C.E.., reflect the incorporation of Christianity into the culture of Ethiopia. *Robert W. Strayer*

themselves baffled by the complexities of lineage-based societies and had to accommodate their administrative systems to these continuing realities. African religious beliefs and institutions provided the basis for many of the early revolts against European rule, influenced African understandings of Christianity, and frequently expressed the hopes and frustrations of people undergoing rapid social change and colonial domination. In these and other ways, long-established patterns of African development persisted and served to shape African encounters with the new pressures of European expansion.

Africa and the West

As Europe's nearest neighbor, Africa was the first part of the world touched by the West's voyages of overseas expansion, which began in the early fifteenth century. Although gold, gum, pepper, and other products figured in the Afro-European commerce that ensued, by 1650, and in some places much earlier, these trading patterns came to focus primarily on the purchase of slaves and continued to do so for the next two hundred years.

The Slave Trade: Patterns and Consequences

The origins of the slave trade, briefly described in Chapter 6, lay in Europe's seafaring technology, in the movement of plantation economies from the Mediterranean to the New World, and in the relative immunity of Africans to both tropical and European diseases. Here we are concerned with the impact of the slave trade within Africa and the ways in which African societies participated in, adapted to, and sometimes resisted this tragic traffic in human beings.

The area involved in the trans-Atlantic trade lay primarily along the west coast of Africa, from Senegal in the north to Angola in the south. Although the societies of this region were generally not as highly developed as those of the Sudanic region, there were by 1500 several large kingdoms, such as Benin and Kongo, many "microstates" or chiefdoms, and a large number of lineage-based societies. Local and regional trade was well established by the time the Europeans arrived, and parts of the area also had commercial links with the Sudanic kingdoms of the savannah. Although the slave trade was important, and in some cases decisive, for the societies of this area, their histories were shaped by other forces as well. New states developed and older ones declined or disintegrated; armed conflict punctuated the relationship among west African societies; substantial trade to the north continued as new opportunities along the coast appeared; and even the trade with Europe was never exclusively in slaves.

Still, the impact of the slave trade was profound, though highly uneven both over time and among the many societies that it affected. During the early centuries of the trade, the price of slaves was relatively low. Thus, there was little incentive for African rulers to mount expensive expeditions for the specific purpose of acquiring slaves for export. Most of the slaves, therefore, came from the immediate coastal area, where they were already war captives, criminals, or people "pawned" by their families in times of debt or famine. They had lost the protection of their own lineages and were clearly subordinate members of society. Some had been put to work on the estates of kings or other wealthy people, but most had become dependent members of their masters' lineages, where they or their descendants could be absorbed into that society and even rise to positions of power and influence as soldiers, traders, or court officials. It was a different kind of servitude from the permanent chattel slavery that developed on New World plantations. But as owned persons, slaves in African societies had an economic value, and as marginal persons, they were vulnerable to sale if the price was right.

Increasingly, it was. Between 1680 and 1840, the real price paid for slaves rose by 500 percent. At the same time, the price of European firearms fell, and thus the numbers of this favored import item increased. By 1730, some 180,000 guns per year were being imported into the area known as the Gold and Slave Coasts. After 1750, the figure rose to somewhere between 280,000 and 390,000 per year. The rising price of slaves and the declining price of guns combined to increase the slave trade vastly in the eighteenth century. Slaves were now drawn from the distant interior as well as the coastlands, and large, militarized coastal states mounted expeditions for the express purpose of capturing slaves for sale to America. Over the roughly four centuries of the slave trade, almost twelve million people were forcibly removed to the New World.

The participation of various African societies in the slave trade and its impact on them varied greatly depending on their social and economic organization, proximity to inland trade routes, the local political condition, population density, and other factors. Some small societies, targeted for extensive slave raiding, were virtually destroyed. Large kingdoms such as the Kongo were torn apart as outlying provinces and ambitious individuals established their own trading connections with European merchants. Other states such as Asante and Dahomey arose in reaction to the slave trade and tried to take advantage of its economic possibilities while protecting their own people from its ravages.

In some cases, participation was brief. Along the coast of Sierra Leone, for example, a series of wars in the mid-sixteenth century produced a large number of slaves for sale, but when political stability returned, trade focused much more heavily on local products such as beeswax, camwood, ivory, and gold. Elsewhere, extensive and prolonged involvement produced major social changes. Along the delta of the Niger River, societies of fishing villages organized on lineage principles were transformed into small monarchies in which extended family groups assimilated large numbers of slaves and became powerful "houses" with extensive commercial networks. Drawing on sources of slaves among the Igbo in the immediate interior, these transformed societies of the Niger Delta became the largest slave exporters in eighteenth-century west Africa.

The contrasting experience of Benin and Dahomey illustrates very different reactions to the European demand for slaves. The kingdom of Benin, in the forest area of present-day Nigeria, was one of the oldest and most highly developed states in the coastal hinterland of west Africa, dating perhaps to the eleventh century C.E. Its capital was a large, walled city with wide avenues, a lavish court, a wealthy elite, and a powerful monarch, or *oba,* who strictly controlled the country's trade. Benin's uniqueness lay in its relatively successful efforts to

VOICES
Inside the Slave Trade

Born about 1745 in what is now southeastern Nigeria, Olaudah Equiano was captured in a slave raid at the age of ten and during his teenage years worked for a variety of masters in the West Indies. He traveled widely with them, became fluent in English, and after his release from slavery in 1766, played a role in the anti-slavery movement. He also wrote an autobiography that contains the following account of his initial encounter with the west African slave trade.

The first object which saluted my eyes when I arrived on the coast was the sea, and a slave ship which was then riding at anchor and waiting for its cargo. These filled me with astonishment, which was soon converted into terror when I was carried on board. I was immediately handled and tossed up to see if I were sound by some of the crew, and I was now persuaded that I had gotten into a world of bad spirits and that they were going to kill me. Their complexions too differing so much from ours, their long hair, and the language they spoke united to confirm me in this belief. . . . I asked [some of the other slaves] if we were not to be eaten by those white men with horrible looks, red faces, and loose hair. They told me I was not. . . .

I was soon put down under the decks, and there I received such a salutation to my nostrils as I had never experienced in my life; so that with the loathsomeness of the stench and crying together, I became so sick and low that I was not able to eat nor had I the least desire to taste anything. I now wished for that last friend, death, to relieve me. . . . [O]n my refusing to eat, one of the [white men] held me fast by the hands and laid me across I think the windlass and tied my feet while the other flogged me severely. . . . I feared I should be put to death, the white people looked and acted, as I thought, in so savage a manner; for I had never seen among my people such instances of brutal cruelty and this shown not only to us blacks but also to some of the whites themselves. . . . I asked [other slaves] if these people had no country but lived in this hollow place (the ship); they told me that they did not but came from a distant one.

One day . . . two of my countrymen who were chained together (I was near them at the time), preferring death to such a lot of misery, somehow made through the nettings and jumped into the sea. . . .

At last we came in sight of the island of Barbados at which the whites on board gave a great shout. . . . We thought by this we should be eaten by these ugly men, and when soon after we were all put down under the deck again, there was much dread and trembling among us, and nothing but bitter cries to be heard all night from these apprehensions insomuch that at last the white people got some old slaves from the land to pacify us. They told us we were not to be eaten but to work. . . . We were conducted immediately to the merchant's yard where we were all pent up together like so many sheep in a fold without regard to sex or age.

Source: Paul Edwards, ed., *Equiano's Travels: His Autobiography— The Interesting Narrative of the Life of Olaudah Equiano or Gustavus Vassa the African Written by Himself* (London: Heinemann, 1967), pp. 25–31.

avoid a deep involvement in the slave trade and to diversify the exports with which it purchased European firearms and other goods. As early as 1516, the *oba* began to restrict the slave trade and soon forbade the export of male slaves altogether, a ban that lasted until the early eighteenth century. By then, the *oba*'s authority over outlying areas had declined, and the country's major exports of pepper and cotton cloth had lost out to Asian and then European competition. In these circumstances, Benin felt compelled to resume limited participation in the slave trade. But even at the height of the trade in the late eighteenth century, Benin exported fewer than one thousand slaves a year.

Among the Aja-speaking peoples to the west of Benin, the situation was very different. There the slave trade had thoroughly disrupted a series of small and weak states along the coast. Some distance inland, the kingdom of Dahomey arose in the early eighteenth century, at least in part as an effort to contain the constant raiding and havoc occasioned by the coastal trade. It was a unique and highly authoritarian state in which commoners and chiefs alike were responsible directly to the king and in which the power of lineages and secret societies was considerably weakened. For a time, Dahomey apparently tried to limit the external slave trade, to import European craftspeople, and to develop plantation agriculture within the kingdom. But all this failed, and in view of hostile relations with the neighboring kingdom of Oyo and others, Dahomey turned to a vigorous involvement in the slave trade under strict royal control. The army conducted annual slave raids, and the government soon came to depend on the trade for its essential revenues. Unlike Benin, Dahomey turned the slave trade into the chief business of the state until well into the nineteenth century.

In a strange way, the story of African participation in the slave trade further discredits common European images of stagnant African societies that could at best respond to the actions of others. Here is the conclusion to a recent study of the central Zaire River basin during the era of the slave trade:

> The European traders could do no more than come to the coast; it was African initiative that forged trade routes seventeen hundred kilometers into the interior and developed the marketplaces and diplomatic machinery for long-distance trade [in slaves and ivory]. . . . Trade had existed for a long time, and so had the practices of renting out capital goods and paying wages in kind. The international economy provided opportunities for expanding and strengthening the mercantile and capitalistic elements that already existed in riverine society; it did not create them.[7]

The overall impact of the slave trade on west Africa is difficult to assess. It certainly limited population growth, though it does not seem to have caused any general decline. It surely fostered social and moral corruption, particularly as judicial proceedings were manipulated to produce victims for the slave trade. It expanded local and regional commerce in general alongside the traffic in slaves. And it initiated Africa's integration into the global network of economic and political relationships gradually spreading out from Europe. "The total impact of the trade," writes a leading historian of the era, "has to be measured not by what actually happened but against the might-have-been if Africa's creative energy had been turned instead to some other end than that of building a commercial system capable of capturing and exporting some eighty thousand people a year."[8]

Creeping Imperialism in the Nineteenth Century

During the nineteenth century, the slave trade gradually came to an end under the pressure of liberal and humanitarian opinion in Europe, the rise of industrial capitalism dependent on free wage labor, and British naval patrols in the south Atlantic. In the process, a variety of new European interests began to operate in Africa. The most important of these was the so-called legitimate trade, as the needs of an industrializing Europe stimulated increased demand for a variety of African products—gum, hides, ivory, and vegetable oils, among others. In the north and south of the continent, Africa also became a place to invest at considerable profit some of Europe's surplus capital. Particularly in southern Africa, where Dutch settlement had been established since the seventeenth century, a new wave of British settlers added to the permanent white population and gave rise to a long conflict between the two immigrant groups. Finally, Christian missionaries and European explorers fanned out all over the continent in a vast effort to open Africa to the alleged benefits of Christian civilization and capitalist commerce.

These were largely private efforts. With the exception of Algeria, southern Africa, and scattered bases along the west African coast, European governments showed little interest in acquiring large chunks of territory until the 1880s. Thus, there was a "window" of perhaps sixty or seventy years during which independent African societies were in contact with a rapidly modernizing Europe before colonial conquest dramatically altered the framework of Afro-European encounter. How did African societies respond to these new possibilities?

In answering this question, it is important to keep clearly in mind that the stimulus of an expanding Europe was not the only force for change in nineteenth-century Africa. The Islamic revolutions in the west African savannah and the *mfecane* in southern Africa were the product of internal tensions and were largely unrelated to the European presence. Older patterns of commerce, such as the trade in kola nuts between the forest and savannah regions of west Africa, grew as rapidly as the new trading opportunities with Europe.

Nonetheless, many African societies, groups, and individuals sought to take advantage of the growing European presence to further their own interests. One aspect of Western culture attractive to many ruling groups was military technology. A number of African states acquired substantial quantities of firearms during the nineteenth century and on this basis set out to enlarge their own domains. Egypt broke away from the Ottoman Empire and carved out a large territory to its south in which its major interest was slave-raiding. Likewise in east Africa, Arab rulers on the island of Zanzibar used Western-style naval power to consolidate their control over the Swahili cities along the coast. The development of extensive clove plantations on Zanzibar stimulated a growing slave trade into the interior of East Africa, made possible in part by the latest European guns. Thus, one of the ironic consequences of African military modernization was the expansion of ancient slave-trading patterns in northern and eastern Africa while the Atlantic trade in west Africa was on the decline.

Another new opportunity involved the vast expansion of cash-crop production, especially in west African societies already connected to the European market. In the area of Senegal and Gambia, the production of peanuts by African peasants grew rapidly after 1840, and by 1890, this region was exporting some forty thousand tons a year. In the Niger Delta and elsewhere, the export of palm oil, used in Europe for soap, candles, and industrial lubricants, replaced that of slaves as production rose from a thousand tons per year in 1820 to thirty thousand tons in the 1850s. By the 1890s, the Yoruba people of Nigeria alone had some fifteen million palm trees in production for the export market. An unexpected side-effect of this growth in legitimate commerce was to increase slaveholding in west Africa, for much of the

labor used in the production of these export crops came from slaves who were put to work domestically when they could no longer be exported. Imports, likewise, grew rapidly. West Africans bought some 2.4 million yards of British cloth in 1830, and almost 17 million yards in 1850.

This great expansion of Afro-European trade has been called a *commercial revolution*. It substituted legitimate products for commerce in people; it greatly enlarged the quantity of trade between Africa and Europe; and it involved parts of Africa ever more deeply in the emerging world economy. In the process, it changed the entire focus of west African commerce from the north to the south. By the end of the nineteenth century, the trans-Saharan trade had largely dried up, and the products of both the savannah and forest regions were shipped to the coast, where they were exchanged for European goods. But there was no revolution in the structure of west African economies, which continued to operate largely in a traditional lineage framework. A number of wealthy African merchants emerged, but they were largely dependent on European firms for credit and marketing opportunities. The tremendous growth in trade, however, showed that African economies could considerably increase their production in response to external demand once freed of the slave trade.

Accompanying the commercial revolution in west Africa was the growth of a class of Africans, closely associated with European enterprises, who had adopted aspects of European culture. Many were traders, and some quite wealthy, who acted as intermediaries between the large European commercial firms and African producers and consumers in the interior. Freed or returned slaves represented an important section of this new, Westernized class. Freed blacks from the United States established settlements in what became Liberia, and a number of former slaves in Brazil returned to Dahomey and elsewhere. In Sierra Leone, the British established a colony for slaves, freed after their recapture on the high seas.

Most of these people acquired a Western-style education in mission schools, looked to British or French culture as a point of reference, and adopted Christianity as their religion. Many held important positions in European commercial firms, in missionary churches, and in the administration of small European outposts scattered along the west African

The construction of forts with African labor was part of the process of European conquest in the late nineteenth century.

coast. Under their influence, several small coastal societies experimented with European-style political systems. They generally accepted the superiority of European culture and looked forward to leading Africa in the direction of "commerce, Christianity, and civilization." Few would have suspected in 1850 that colonial conquest lay only a few decades away.

Africa in the nineteenth century was a dynamic and rapidly changing place. New states, new economic relationships, the assimilation of new cultures—all this raises fascinating but unanswerable questions about the directions African history might have taken had the continent not been enclosed by European colonial rule at century's end.

Conquest and Resistance

Historians have long debated precisely why European governments decided, quite abruptly, to undertake the conquest of Africa, between roughly 1880 and 1900, after many decades of relative indifference to the acquisition of African territory. Part of the answer lies in the larger momentum of Europe's global expansion, made possible in part by its medical and military technology. By the end of the nineteenth century, for example, Europeans could survive in a tropical-disease environment far better than had been possible at the beginning of the century. Given Europe's dynamic economy and powerful military forces, there was a certain inevitability to Africa's incorporation into its empires, in one form or another.

By the 1870s, growing pressure for government intervention was coming from already existing European interests in Africa. Traders in west Africa who sought direct access to the interior found their way blocked by African merchants determined to preserve their intermediary role. Investors with money in Egypt felt increasingly nervous as that society became highly nationalistic by 1880, and British capitalists in South Africa strenuously objected to obstacles created by the original Dutch settlers, now known as Boers. Some missionaries felt that ending the slave trade and converting the "heathen" could be more readily accomplished if Africa were under Europe's political control. Local European officials were increasingly concerned about competition from European rivals.

And no wonder, for relations among Europe's great powers were becoming more competitive, fueled by the recent unification of Germany and of Italy, by the growth of a popular and emotional nationalism, and by a long recession (1874–1896) in world trade. In this setting, governments became far more sensitive to African issues and far more inclined to intervene on behalf of their citizens' interests. The result was an orgy of competitive annexations in which Britain took the largest number of colonies, followed by France, with Germany, Italy, Portugal, and Belgium each getting a smaller share.

The diplomatic wrangling that determined who got what in Africa was accomplished, surprisingly enough, without war between the European powers. But making those claims effective in Africa involved a tremendous amount of violence. Many African societies attempted some accommodation with encroaching European powers but then turned to military resistance when it became apparent that compromise was impossible. A few large-scale battles occurred, and in some places, skirmishes or "bush wars" lasted five to ten years. But most of the colonial conquest took place in small, brutal engagements such as that described, obviously from his own viewpoint, by a young British officer on a campaign in Kenya in 1902:

> I have performed a most unpleasant duty today. I made a night march to the village at the edge of the forest where the white settler had been so brutally murdered the day before yesterday. Though the war drums were sounding throughout the night, we reached the village without incident and surrounded it. . . . I gave orders that every living thing except children should be killed without mercy. I hated the work and was anxious to get through with it. So soon as we could see to shoot we closed in. Several of the men tried to break out but were immediately shot. I then assaulted the place before any defense could be prepared. Every soul was either shot or bayoneted, and I am happy to say that there were no children in the village. They, together with the younger women, had already been removed by the villagers to the forest. We burned all the huts and razed the banana plantations to the ground.[9]

By about 1900, Europeans had crushed most such resistance by taking advantage of their overwhelming military force. The colonial era had begun.

Notes

1. Paul Bohannan and Philip Curtin, *Africa and Africans* (Garden City, N.Y.: Natural History Press, 1971), p. 227.

2. This and the following two paragraphs draw heavily on Jack Goody, *Technology, Tradition and the State in Africa* (London: Oxford University Press, 1971), chap. 2.

3. Philip Curtin et al., *African History* (Boston: Little, Brown, 1978), p. 274.

4. Said Hamdun and Noel King, *Ibn Battuta in Black Africa* (London: Collins, 1975), p. 47.

5. Leo Africanus, *History and Description of Africa* (London: Hakluyt Society, 1896), pp. 824–25.

6. Quoted in Thomas Hodgkin, *Nationalism in Colonial Africa* (New York: New York University Press, 1956), p. 173.

7. Robert W. Harms, *River of Wealth, River of Sorrow* (New Haven: Yale University Press, 1981), p. 234.

8. Curtin et al., *African History,* p. 248.

9. R. Meinertzhagen, *Kenya Diary* (London: Oliver and Boyd, 1957), pp. 51–52.

Chapter 22

Modernization or Distorted Development?
The Colonial Experience in Africa

Compared to India's more than 150 years of British rule, colonialism in Africa had a relatively short life, amounting to 60 to 75 years in most places. But since Africa caught Europe at the high point of its military and industrial development and at the peak of its racial and cultural arrogance, colonialism was a powerful and transforming experience. From the perspective of global history, colonial rule served primarily to link Africa to a European-dominated world economy and to transmit to Africa the ideas and technologies of modern life first developed in Europe. But did these colonial connections stimulate Africa's modern development or retard and distort it? And what kind of new social and cultural patterns did the economic changes generate? These are among the central issues in Africa's modern history as well as in current political debate.

States, Governors, and Chiefs: The Political Framework of Colonial Rule

The most immediate and apparent effect of colonial conquest was the creation of new political units—Senegal, Nigeria, the Belgian Congo, Mozambique, and many others. (See Map 22.1.) Unlike India, Burma, Vietnam, and Korea, where colonial states coincided with some earlier political unit, the vast majority of African colonies were wholly new creations whose boundaries bore little relationship to any traditional community. Most of these new colo-

nial states incorporated many different peoples or societies that had never before regarded themselves as members of a single political system. By itself, this was hardly a unique situation, for African kingdoms and empires had often encompassed many societies. But the great differences in culture, values, and technology between the new rulers and their diverse subjects was a new factor in African history, as were the dramatic social changes that colonial rule brought in its wake.

Within these new states, Europeans exercised power through political systems described by one writer as "various kinds of dictatorship, sometimes mild and at other times harsh."[1] The colonies were generally headed by governors and administered by a very small number of Europeans. The British, for example, ruled the whole of Nigeria—which had a population of some 40 million in 1938—with a staff of 386 political officers and 1,663 specialists in such fields as education, public works, and health. This meant that Europeans had to recruit and rely on a very large cadre of African officials—police, clerks, servants, and above all "chiefs"—to govern the colonies.

Such collaboration generally worked most smoothly in those centralized states where African ruling classes benefited from close cooperation with the Europeans. In northern Nigeria, for example, the British found a well-organized aristocracy of Fulani-speaking people entrenched in power over a Hausa-speaking peasantry. Organized in a number of city-states headed by *emirs* (an Arabic term for Muslim rulers), this political system had many features the British found useful and attractive, including a centralized administration, a specialized court system, Muslim law codes, regular taxation, and a dominant aristocracy. By us-

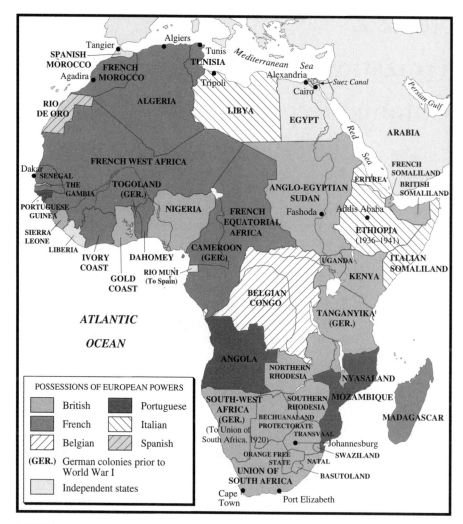

MAP 22.1 Colonial Africa

ing the *emirs* to govern northern Nigeria through their traditional institutions, the British acted here, as they had with the "princes" in India, to strengthen a very conservative ruling elite and thus to retard the modern development of the area. Because the British wanted to protect the *emirs* from potential threats to their positions, they strictly limited missionary activity and thus the development of schools and churches in northern Nigeria. By the time of independence in 1960, the north was far less educationally developed than the south, where mission education had spread rapidly. This difference contributed much to the Nigerian civil war in the late 1960s and to continu-

ing tensions between the northern and southern parts of the country.

Where the British had to govern complex and unfamiliar lineage-based societies, they experienced greater difficulty. Wrongly assuming that all African societies had chiefs, the British frequently appointed to official positions any locally prominent man who was willing to work with the new colonial rulers. Such was the case among the highly democratic and decentralized Igbo people of southeastern Nigeria, who had previously governed themselves through councils of elders and mass meetings of village men. The appointment of official "warrant chiefs" among the Igbo provoked a great deal of resentment, particularly among women, and contributed to a violent uprising in 1929 that forced the British to rethink their entire system.

Thus, the colonial state was never a wholly European enterprise; rather, it was an unequal alliance between a small but dominant group of white administrators and a much larger but clearly subordinate group of African chiefs. In French West Africa, an area eight times the size of France itself and with a population of about 15 million in the late 1930s, the colonial state consisted of 385 French administrators and over 50,000 African chiefs.

Among the immediate losers in these arrangements were African women, who had often exercised considerable power in their precolonial societies. Although nowhere politically equal to men, they frequently controlled certain activities such as farming or trading and had councils or other organizations through which to influence male decision making. Some societies had a "dual-sex" system in which "each sex [managed] its own affairs, and women's interests [were] represented at all levels."[2] Colonial officials generally brought with them common Western notions of the proper role of women and were ignorant of these more flexible political systems. Thus, women were deprived of official political positions that they had earlier enjoyed.

For the male chiefs themselves, the results of their appointments were paradoxical. In the short run, many of them gained considerably in both wealth and power, partly because they were now largely free of traditional restraints and answerable only to colonial officials, who were seldom able to keep very close track of them. Their official position provided them with substantial government salaries, frequently supplemented by approved rebates from the taxes they collected. Opportunities to extort even further taxes coupled with customary rights to land, labor, and tribute often enabled chiefs to become quite wealthy and to turn this wealth to such modern uses as cash-crop farming, marketing, and Western education for their children.

In the longer run, however, African chiefs were unable to retain the exclusively dominant position they had held earlier in the colonial era. In the increasingly nationalistic mood of African politics after World War II, chiefs often found themselves tainted by their role as willing collaborators with the colonial regime. They were also widely resented for their wealth, gained, many believed, at the expense of their own people. But perhaps most important, the chiefs were increasingly challenged by a new elite, consisting usually of younger men, who had mastered Western education, were more modern in outlook, and were increasingly critical of the colonial system. It was this new elite that would lead African colonies to independence and assume the major role in shaping Africa's development.

The Economics of Colonialism

Occurring beneath the surface of colonial rule, the transformation of African economic life was even more significant than that of conquest and political reorganization. Although relatively few Africans came into regular contact with colonial administrators, the opportunities and demands of the colonial economy touched almost everyone. Forced labor on roads and railroads; planting and selling cash crops; migrating long distances to work at European-owned farms or mines; buying bicycles, radios, and sewing machines; losing land to European settlers; paying taxes and school fees; working as clerks for the government or as teachers for the mission—these were among the ways that ordinary Africans experienced the economic changes of the colonial era.

But the economic issue is also important because it is at the center of a major controversy about the effects of colonial rule, a debate that has profound political and moral implications. Did the colonial experience, as its defenders insist, bring advances in technology, stimulate Africans to produce more wealth than ever before, provide access to modern education, and create rich opportunities for beneficial trade with other parts of the world? Or, as its critics argue, did colonial rulers steal African land, exploit African labor, gain easy and profitable access to raw materials, transfer large corporate profits back to Europe, and in general limit and distort Africa's economic development?

Capitalism and the Colonial State

Precolonial economies in Africa were never as backward and stagnant as European colonizers liked to believe. These economies produced sufficient surpluses to support elaborate royal courts and aristocracies in centralized states and distinct differences in wealth even within some lineage-based societies. But both agriculture and handicraft manufacturing were everywhere organized on a small scale, largely within kinship or extended-family groups. And most production was for local and immediate use rather than for sale on some distant market. Africans were, of course, not ignorant of market principles of supply and demand, for there had long been extensive networks of both local and long-distance trade. But relatively few goods entered the market, and items such as land and labor were seldom offered for sale. African economies, in short, were inner directed, and nowhere did market principles dominate economic life.

These features of African economic life changed substantially during the colonial era. As African economies became more heavily linked to those of Europe, land and labor were increasingly devoted to outer-directed production for a world market. The colonial experience extended Africa's integration with the world economy to almost all parts of the continent and deepened it to include a far greater range of products and number of people than before. In doing so, colonialism also expanded the modern market economy within Africa so that more and more products and services were bought and sold for money, including in some places even land and labor. Thus, Africans were being involved ever more deeply in capitalist relationships, both internationally and within their own societies.

Colonial governments themselves played an important but limited role in this transformation. Their most important function was to establish a regular system of taxation, one that would raise enough money locally to pay the costs of administration without requiring subsidies from the ruling country. The purpose of colonial taxation, however, was not simply to raise revenue but also to produce labor. Africans, after all, had to find some way to get the cash to pay their taxes, and this often involved working on farms or in mines owned by Europeans. In addition, colonial governments built roads, railroads, ports, and telegraph lines. Although these elements of infrastructure were a valuable and necessary contribution to Africa's economic development, they also served to orient African economies primarily toward the needs and interests of Europe.

Whatever their particular policies, colonial governments had neither the desire nor the ability to direct the economic development of Africa in a vigorous, planned, and systematic fashion. They were, after all, the products of capitalist societies in Europe that believed governments should largely stay out of economic matters. Furthermore, the colonizers' first loyalties were to Belgium, Germany, or France, rather than to their African subjects. But even when the Europeans were well intentioned, they had very little money with which to operate. They assumed that by opening up Africa to world trade and by encouraging private investment from Europe, they would automatically promote Africa's economic development. Much of the debate about colonial modernization turns on whether they were correct in this assumption.

Forced Labor and Crude Exploitation

In assessing the Europeans' claims, it is useful to distinguish several types of colonial economic systems, for they varied considerably both over time and from place to place. Early in the colonial era, for example, many African peoples found themselves subject to a very crude and direct form of exploitation, sometimes amounting to little more than plunder. In one form or another, forced labor was practiced in almost all of the colonies and was used for building roads, railroads, and government buildings. Portuguese authorities in Mozambique actively recruited thousands of Africans for work in the mines of South Africa, on the assumption that those who were not employed for wages were idle. In French west Africa, all "natives" were legally obligated for "statute labor" of ten to twelve days a year, a practice that lasted through 1946.

The worst abuses occurred in the Congo Free State, personally controlled by Leopold II, king of Belgium. Here private companies were granted huge concessions of forest land rich in rubber, which was much in demand for bicycle and automobile tires in the early twentieth century. With political and administrative authority over their concessions, these companies compelled local Africans to collect the rubber and enforced their demands through hostage-taking, torture, and murder. A reign of mass terror lasted a decade, until the Belgian government took direct control of the colony in 1908.

In the long run, however, direct exploitation and the extensive use of force were neither acceptable to public opinion in Europe nor effective in raising revenue, securing labor, or promoting trade. Thus, colonial economies began to evolve in a variety of other directions.

Peasant Agriculture and the World Economy

In many places, particularly west Africa, colonial governments came to rely on African farmers to produce the export products that would generate a taxable trade. Somewhat to their surprise, they found many African peoples both willing and able to respond to new market opportunities. Peanuts in Senegal and Gambia, cocoa in the Gold Coast, cotton in Uganda, coffee in Tanganyika—these were among the cash crops African farmers began to produce for the world market, and in considerable quantities.

What did this new pattern of economic life mean to those people and societies caught up in it? One outcome was an enormous expansion of overseas trade; in west Africa by 1960, such trade amounted to ten times the volume of 1910. This meant that many African farmers gained substantial cash incomes with which they could pay their taxes and school fees and buy a variety of imported goods. These were people who clearly benefited from the growth of cash-crop agriculture.

But in linking their economic lives so heavily to a world market over which they had little control, Africans also came to experience the fluctuations of the capitalist world economy. The Great Depression of the 1930s dramatically revealed this new dependence on the outside world, for although it originated in the United States and Europe, it touched Africa with painful consequences. In many colonies, the volume of trade fell by half, and prices even more.

By 1932, cotton producers in the Congo were receiving only one-third of the pre-Depression price, and palm oil prices by 1934 had fallen to one-fifth of the 1929 value. However, African farmers benefited when the world economy boomed after World War II. The uncertain rhythms of the international marketplace were now added to those of the seasons and weather.

In addition, most colonies came to specialize very heavily in one or a few crops and had the bulk of their trade with the country governing them. This very narrow base for economic development proved a serious obstacle to balanced growth after independence. Furthermore, some African colonies devoted so much land and labor to producing luxury crops for export that they had to rely on imported food to feed their own people. This happened first in Senegal and Gambia, where peanut production was so intensive that rice had to be imported from Asia. By the 1970s, such deficiencies had become common throughout the continent, caused in part by an overemphasis on export agriculture and a corresponding neglect of domestic food production. Here was one source of the terrible vulnerability to famine that afflicted so much of Africa in the 1970s and 1980s.

Land, Labor, and Settlers

If the expansion of cash-crop farming represented a mixed blessing for Africans, those who lived in areas with a large and permanent European-settler population had a decidedly more difficult experience. In Algeria, Kenya, Rhodesia (now Zimbabwe), Angola, and especially South Africa, production for export was undertaken primarily by resident white settlers. The South African situation was unique, for there the history of settlement dates back to 1652 and includes more than a century of conflict between Dutch and British settlers. By the early twentieth century, the settlers were so numerous and politically powerful that Britain granted the country its independence in 1910 with a government controlled entirely by whites. Elsewhere in Africa, the settlers were more recent immigrants, most having arrived in the twentieth century, and although they were influential in local affairs, they did not generally have the formal political power achieved in South Africa.

The impact on Africans of living in a settler colony can be summarized briefly: land and labor. Colonial governments intervened decisively on behalf of European settlers, took large areas of African land, and reserved it for exclusive white ownership. In Kenya's "white highlands," some four thousand white farmers owned 7.3 million acres of the colony's richest land. Even more extreme was the situation in South Africa, where the Land Act of 1913 legally reserved 88 percent of the land for whites, who constituted less than 20 percent of the population.

Apart from the emotionally wrenching experience of losing land to foreign invaders, Africans experienced the economic side-effects of settler-dominated agriculture in a number of ways. It was often difficult for African farmers to compete effectively with settlers in growing lucrative cash crops because Europeans had the support of the colonial government and therefore much better access to good land, credit, and scientific and technical information. In Kenya, Africans were for a time actually forbidden by law to grow certain kinds of coffee, and Kenya's four thousand settlers produced 95 percent of agricultural exports. But where settlers were less politically powerful and had to compete with African producers on more nearly equal terms (in the Ivory Coast, Tanganyika, and Uganda, for example), Africans were often more efficient and successful than their white counterparts.

An even more serious consequence of settler domination was the creation of vastly overcrowded and impoverished "native reserves," as areas limited to Africans were known in British territories. The Bantustans of South Africa, the official "homelands" of the country's African population, have been described as "rural slums," undeveloped, overgrazed, and seriously eroded. This was not entirely accidental, for limiting the size of African reserves was one means of forcing Africans to work on European-owned farms. The experience of rural wage labor for white settlers became a familiar one for hundreds of thousands of Africans who lived in or near settler territories. By the early 1950s, about 30 percent of the African male population of South Africa worked, and usually lived, on European-owned farms.

Mines and Profits

If cash-crop farming and settler agriculture were two ways in which Africa became integrated into a global economy, a third involved the mining industry. Although there was relatively little private investment in Africa during the colonial era, most of it involved the extraction of minerals in central and southern Africa. Copper in the Congo and Zambia and gold and diamonds in South Africa represented several of the major products of the mining industry. Such enterprises created a vast pattern of labor migration all over the southern part of Africa, as men by the thousands left their homes in the rural areas for work in the mines. This was a "natural" product of economic development, comparable to patterns of urbanization in many parts of the world.

In South Africa, however, government policy served to alter this normal pattern of change in ways quite detrimental to Africans. Attempting to prevent the growth of a stable and permanent black urban population, the government enforced a pattern of circulating labor migration. Without their wives and children, men would come to the mines on contract, for a fixed term, and then be required to return to the overcrowded reserves, only to repeat the whole process sometime later. Such a pattern, involving by

These African miners and their European supervisor reflect a longstanding racial hierarchy in the South African labor force. *Visual Studies Workshop*

the early 1950s over two million men, undermined rural society, for it meant the absence of large numbers of men and it prevented the development of a normal urban society because settled family life was forbidden. African laborers were caught in the middle.

Furthermore, although these mining enterprises frequently earned quite substantial profits, based in part on the very low wages paid to African workers, the profits were not, for the most part, reinvested in Africa and certainly did not contribute much to the modern industrialization of the colonies. This was largely because the people who invested the capital, and therefore who reaped the profits and bore the losses, were Europeans, who had little real interest in developing local industries aimed at a poor African market. In this respect, South Africa was an exception to the rule, for a local market of well-to-do whites and local capital gained from the mining industry combined to produce an advanced industrial society by the mid-twentieth century. It was, however, a society whose benefits were skewed massively in favor of the country's white minority.

Women and the Colonial Economy

If colonial economies varied greatly from place to place, they also offered a different combination of opportunities and hardships to women than they did to men.[3] In precolonial times, African women were almost everywhere active farmers with responsibility for planting, weeding, and harvesting in addition to food preparation and child care. Men cleared the land, built houses, herded the cattle, and in some cases assisted with field work. Within this traditional division of labor, women were expected to feed their own families and were usually allocated their own fields for that purpose. Many were also involved in local trading activity. Although clearly subordinate to men, African women nevertheless had a measure of economic autonomy.

As the demands of the colonial economy grew, women's lives more and more diverged from those of men. In colonies where cash-crop agriculture was dominant, the need to produce for export often altered the traditional division of labor as men withdrew from subsistence production in favor of more lucrative cash crops. Among the Ewe people of southern Ghana, men almost completely dominated the highly profitable cocoa farming, whereas women assumed almost total responsibility for domestic food production. In neighboring Ivory Coast, women had traditionally grown cotton for their families' clothing, but when that crop acquired a cash value, men insisted that cotton grown for export be produced on their own personal fields. Thus, men acted to control the most profitable aspects of cash-crop agriculture and in doing so greatly increased the subsistence workload of women. One study of the Beti people of Cameroon estimated that women's working hours increased from forty-six per week in precolonial times to over seventy by 1934.

Another factor increasing women's workload and differentiating their lives from those of men was labor migration. As more and more men sought employment in the cities, on settler farms, or in the mines, their wives were left to manage the domestic economy almost alone. In many cases, they also had to supply food to men in the cities to compensate for very low urban wages. Among the Gusii of western Kenya, women took over such traditionally male tasks as breaking the ground for planting, milking the cows, and supervising the herds, in addition to their usual responsibilities. In South Africa, where the demands of the white economy were particularly heavy, some 40 percent to 50 percent of ablebodied adult males were absent from the rural areas, and women headed 60 percent of households. In Botswana, which supplied much male labor to South Africa, married couples by the 1930s rarely lived together for more than two months at a time. In such situations, the lives and the cultures of men and women increasingly diverged—one focused on the cities and working for wages, the other on village life and subsistence agriculture.

Women coped with these difficult circumstances in any number of ways. Where labor migration was widespread, many sought closer relations with their families of birth rather than with their absent husbands' families, as would otherwise have been expected. Among the Luo of Kenya, women introduced labor-saving crops, adopted new farm implements, and earned some money as traders. In the cities, they established a variety of self-help associations, including those for prostitutes and for brewers of beer.

In addition, the colonial economy sometimes provided a measure of opportunity for enterprising women, particularly in small-scale trade and marketing. In some parts of west Africa, women came to dominate this sector of the economy by selling foodstuffs, cloth, and inexpensive imported goods, whereas men or foreign firms controlled the more profitable wholesale and import-export trade.

Such opportunities sometimes gave women considerable economic autonomy. By the 1930s, for example, Nupe women in northern Nigeria had gained sufficient wealth as itinerant traders that they were contributing more to the family income than were their husbands and frequently lent money to them. Among some Igbo groups in southern Nigeria, men were responsible for the prestigious yams, but women's crops—especially cassava—came to have a cash value during the colonial era, and women were entitled to keep the profits from selling them. "What is man? I have my own money"[4] expressed the growing economic independence of such women. At the other end of the scale, women of impoverished rural families often became virtually independent heads of household, by necessity, in the absence of their husbands. Such challenges to patriarchal values elicited various responses from men—increased accusations of witchcraft against women, fears of impotence, and feelings of hostility. One writer suggested that Christianity in general and Catholicism in particular were popular among the Igbo in part because they reinforced the values of male dominance that new economic opportunities for women tended to undermine.[5]

Race, Class, and Tribe: Cultural Identity and Social Structure in Colonial Africa

Conquest, taxation, mission education, production of cash crops, labor migration, new trading opportunities, growth of large cities—all of this and more eroded the older communities of African societies.

Thus, colonial rule changed not only the ways in which people worked and earned their livelihood but also the ways they defined themselves and their communities. Although older ties based on kinship and village life certainly did not disappear, many Africans found themselves in situations that made it useful to think, organize, and act as members of new racial, national, class, religious, or ethnic groups. As in India, new forms of community and new patterns of social identity emerged from the experience of colonial rule.

Colonial Racism

The central division of all African colonial societies was racial. Europeans consistently refused to permit Africans to advance in accordance with their educational qualifications. They could be clerks or chiefs, but few were allowed to enter the higher ranks of the colonial civil service. Within the missions, highly qualified African priests found it extremely difficult to become bishops, a position in which they might exercise authority over white missionaries.

Race also played a major role in the distribution of material benefits and opportunities within colonial societies. A two-tiered labor system in South Africa legally reserved highly paid positions of skilled labor for whites, so that by 1935, the average wage paid to European miners was eleven times what African miners earned. At about this time, the per-capita public expenditure for education in Kenya was a half-shilling per year for each African student and 852 shillings for each European student.

In daily social life as well, race frequently intruded. Adult male Africans called white men in east Africa *bwana* (Swahili for "master"), whereas Europeans regularly called African men "boy." British missionaries often opposed their African converts' wearing trousers, hats, and shoes, and were quite reluctant to teach English because of "the danger of [Africans'] organizing against the government" and "the danger in which such a course would place . . . white women and girls."[6] Here was the fear that African familiarity with European culture might breach the ultimate taboos of colonial society—political rebellion and sexual relations.

A young African boy looks across one of South Africa's beaches, where a sign informs him that it is reserved "for the sole use of members of the white race group." *Reuters/Bettmann*

There were, of course, variations within the African experience of colonial racism. Well-educated Africans, who had frequent contact with Europeans, were far more likely to encounter outright discrimination than Africans living in rural areas. And in those colonies that had a large European settler population, the pattern of racial separation was much more pronounced than in places like Nigeria, which had few permanently settled whites.

South Africa was the most extreme case. There a long history of racial conflict culminated by 1948 in the *apartheid system,* which established race as a legal, not just a customary, feature of South African society and provided for separate "homelands," educational systems, residential areas, public facilities, and much more. South African whites sought to maintain an advanced industrial country by incorporating Africans into the economy as cheap labor while attempting to limit their social and political integration into South African society in every conceivable fashion.

More than military conquest or economic exploitation, racial discrimination was responsible for

the bitterness of educated Africans, who on other grounds found much to admire in modern Western culture. What they found so offensive was European hypocrisy—the contradiction between the "civilizing" and "modernizing" rhetoric and the reality of racial exclusiveness—together with a frequent disparagement of African culture for being backward, primitive, or savage. Thus, colonial racism provoked well-educated Africans into a spirited defense of their own cultures and an equally vigorous attack on elements of Western culture. In the process, widening circles of people came to find meaning in the notion of being "African." For most, it was a new idea.

The New Elite

If a continental or racial identity represented a new cultural reality in Africa, class identity was not, for many African societies had developed complex social organizations with several strata or groups that differed sharply in wealth, privilege, power, and

Mission-sponsored education was an important element of the colonial experience for many Africans. Here is a class of schoolgirls from an Anglican mission in central Kenya in the 1920s. *Robert W. Strayer*

prestige. The colonial experience did serve to reshape African social structures, though in ways that were very different from modernizing societies in Europe and the United States.

The most characteristic class to emerge almost everywhere in colonial Africa was a group that historians have come to call simply the *new elite,* people whose status was defined by modern criteria, such as education and employment, rather than by traditional criteria, such as kinship, political role, or age group. At its upper levels, the new elite contained lawyers, doctors, writers, intellectuals, high-ranking civil servants, and others who had been educated at European or sometimes American universities. Such people had been active in west Africa from the mid-nineteenth century, though elsewhere they emerged much later. Far more numerous were the interpreters, clerks, and teachers who had a primary or sometimes secondary school education. Wealthy African entrepreneurs, mostly traders and merchants, can likewise be counted as part of the new elite. Compared to the population as a whole, this group was extremely small. Ghana, one of the most highly developed British colonies, had a population of about 7 million by 1960 but only about 40,000 persons employed in elite positions, 25,000 secondary school graduates, and 3,760 university graduates.

These were people with social horizons that extended beyond the lineage and village to include some identification with the new states colonial rule had established. Living for the most part in towns and cities, they held jobs in the modern sector of the colonial economy, with the government as the major employer. Others worked for Christian missions or European commercial firms, whereas some were self-employed as lawyers, doctors, or traders. What set them apart from other Africans most clearly and gave them status in the new order was their Western education. They had mastered the world of the whites, learned the language of their conquerors, and gained access to the highest-paying positions in the colonial economy. And since mission schools provided most of the educated employees demanded by the colonial system, the great majority of the new elite were Christians who adopted at least the outward elements of a Western style of life—speaking European languages, taking European names, wearing European-style clothes, building houses in the English or French tradition. Thus, a new social and cultural division was born. Much of modern African literature explores the struggles of these educated Africans to balance their modern ambitions (money, jobs, school, cars) with their traditional loyalties and obligations to family, clan, and village.

Although the new elite ultimately provided the political leadership of the nationalist movements that ousted the colonial regimes, its members did not become a capitalist entrepreneurial class that could spur the economic development of African societies, as the bourgeoisie had done in Europe. In part this was because the new elite, though containing many members from traditionally high-status families, was not primarily a property-owning class. Its members were employees of one or another colonial bureaucracy far more often than they were employers. Their economic base lay in holding particular jobs rather than in owning land or capital. In this respect, the African middle class was very different from its European counterpart.

Even the merchant group within the new elite was limited in its economic impact. The vast expansion of trade during the colonial era had created opportunities for thousands of African traders, merchants, and small businesses. In Ghana by 1960, for example, there were over 320,000 traders, of whom 250,000 were women. But it was huge European firms that dominated the highly profitable import-export business, particularly in west Africa, leaving for Africans the much more competitive and less profitable small-scale retail trade in little shops or market stalls. Thus, few African businesspeople were able to accumulate the kind of capital that would permit large-scale reinvestment in industrial enterprises. The absence of a substantial African capitalist class meant that the new states of post-colonial Africa had to rely on foreign investment or government initiative for undertaking large-scale economic development.

The Urban Poor

The cities of colonial Africa contained not only a small educated elite but also a much larger urban lower class. In Africa, as elsewhere, this was associated with the rapid growth of cities. Some of these colonial cities had enjoyed a long history before the coming of the Europeans, but others were altogether new. Still, growth was their primary characteristic, particularly after World War II. Lagos, a city in southern Nigeria, is a case in point. A major political and commercial center in west Africa, it grew from about 40,000 people in 1870 to 230,000 in 1951 and reached an estimated 500,000 by the time of Nigeria's independence in 1960.

The male lower-class inhabitants of these cities worked as unskilled daily laborers, domestic servants, petty traders, miners, and, in a few places, in factories. Many others were unemployed. In the towns of colonial Africa, there was very little demand for female labor, and, particularly in southern Africa, governments actively discouraged urban migration by women. Those who did migrate to urban areas, either to be with their husbands or to seek new opportunities on their own, found their economic prospects very limited. Prostitution, the sale of cooked food, brewing illegal beer, and small-scale trading represented the major occupations open to women in colonial cities.

The dominant feature of urban lower-class life was poverty. The appeal of urban life to many Africans, and the economic necessity of urban employment, far exceeded the ability of the colonial economy to generate enough jobs, thus producing substantial unemployment or underemployment. One scholar concluded, shortly after independence, "Well over half, and perhaps three quarters, of west Africa's urban workers are living in conditions of extreme poverty."[7]

In settler colonies, the general pattern was to pay a male worker as if he were single, on the assumption that the extended family in the countryside could support his wife and children. Here is what a British investigating commission wrote about Nairobi, Kenya's largest city, in 1955: "The wages of the majority of African workers are too low to enable them to obtain accommodation which is adequate to any standard. . . . This, with the high cost of food in towns, makes family life impossible for the majority."[8] Thus, after a half-century of British rule, the British themselves admitted that the colonial economy could not support normal family life in the capital city of one of their richest colonies.

Despite their poverty, the urban lower classes in colonial cities were considerably different from the working class of industrial Europe and certainly did not become revolutionary in the way that many Russian urban workers had just a few decades earlier. Whereas most urban workers in nineteenth-century Europe had come to depend wholly on their wages, most African urban residents retained a close connection with the rural areas from which they had come. They regarded their stay in the city as temporary and, given the insecurity of urban life, had a strong incentive to maintain a place in rural society. So they sent money to family members back home, returned to their villages on holidays or weekends, and in general retained their cultural and religious roots in the countryside. Furthermore, since very little industrialization took place in colonial Africa, there was little factory labor, and the vast majority of workers were unskilled, paid on a daily basis, and barely literate, if at all.

It is not surprising, therefore, that trade unions were relatively weak during colonial times. Only 10 percent to 20 percent of employed west African workers were members of unions, and in South Africa, the only really industrialized part of the continent, African workers were forbidden by law from striking and from collective bargaining. Unions did on occasion organize strikes and protests, but only in Guinea did the trade union movement become a really important part of the struggle for independence. The urban lower classes, in short, had not become conscious of themselves as a group during the colonial era.

Classes in the Countryside

In the rural areas of colonial Africa, it is even more difficult to speak of modern classes, for people still regarded themselves overwhelmingly in terms of kinship ties, villages, and ethnic groups. Even here, however, the processes of economic change had created several new social strata that might on occasion become the focus of new loyalties and actions. One such group involved cash-crop farmers, who gained most or all of their income from the sale of agricultural products. At least occasionally such farmers acted together in their own interests. In 1937, for example, cocoa farmers in Ghana organized to withhold their produce from the market in a largely successful attempt to break a price-fixing arrangement by nine European companies.

People who worked for wages on someone else's land were another new social group in colonial Africa. In west Africa, cash-crop farming set in motion a vast pattern of labor migration in which men from more remote and undeveloped interior areas moved toward the coastal and forest regions to work on African cocoa or peanut farms. In settler territories, of course, large numbers of Africans worked and frequently lived on white farms. Like their wage-earning counterparts in the cities, farm workers retained close contacts with their village homes and thus seldom became conscious of their common interests as a class. In Kenya, however, landless laborers on settler farms provided the backbone of the Mau Mau revolt against British rule in the 1950s.

Despite the appearance of new and important social groups in colonial Africa, class consciousness was not strong. The colonial situation in which whites ruled over blacks made race, not class, appear as the primary social division. The leadership of nationalist movements, largely from the new elite, made every effort to downplay class divisions in an attempt to promote unity on the African side. Foreign ownership of mines, major businesses, and modern industry meant that the emerging African middle class was economically weak, and continuing ties to the countryside ensured that urban workers sought

support more from their compatriots in the rural areas than from unions or political parties in the cities.

Colonial "Tribalism"

The most important new identity to evolve from the colonial experience was neither race nor class; rather, it was the idea of *tribe*. It may seem strange to think of African tribes as new social units or a recent pattern of identity, for most Westerners are accustomed to thinking of tribes as an old or traditional feature of African society and to seeing "tribalism," in recent years, as an unfortunate hangover from the past. But this is not at all the case. At the local or village level, most precolonial African societies consisted of small-scale communities in which people saw their relationships with one another in terms of kinship, whether real or imagined. Even where such communities were part of larger language groupings, culture areas, states, kingdoms, or empires, the local unit commanded the emotional loyalty of most people. Only when these societies were incorporated into new colonial states and thrust into unprecedented contact with other such peoples did the exclusive, competitive, and sharply defined political loyalties of modern ethnic nationalism emerge. Furthermore, this was a process of global dimensions and by no means uniquely African.

The idea of Africa as divided into distinct tribes, each with its own clearly defined territory, language, customs, and chief, was in fact a European colonial notion that expressed the Western view that African societies were primitive or backward, representing an early stage of human development. It was also a convenient idea, for it reduced the enormous complexity of African societies to a more manageable state and thus made colonial administration easier.

In some places, a precolonial state provided the basis for modern cultural and political loyalties. Asante in west Africa and Buganda in east Africa were well-established kingdoms that were incorporated into Ghana and Uganda, respectively, and that became the basis of modern ethnic identities. Elsewhere the "tribes" of twentieth-century Africa were built on more slender foundations. When the British, for example, began to govern the peoples living along the northern side of Lake Tanganyika (in present-day Tanzania), they found a series of communities that were similar to one another in language and customs but that governed themselves separately and certainly had never regarded themselves as a tribal unit. It was British attempts to rule them as a single people—first through a "paramount chief" and later through a council of chiefs and elders—that resulted in their being called, collectively, the Nyakyusa. In the Congo, the Belgians applied the tribal label of Bangala to men from a number of small and separate communities along the Congo River who worked in colonial enterprises. The Belgians adopted one of the river dialects as their means of communicating with these African workers, and thus it became Lingala, or the language of the Bangala. Prior to the coming of the Belgians, the notion of a Bangala identity had simply not existed; it was a creation of the colonial state. By requiring people to identify their tribe on applications for jobs, schools, and identity cards, colonial governments spread the idea of tribe widely within their colonies.

But tribalism and new ethnic identities were not simply imposed by Europeans, for Africans, also confronted by the changing circumstances of the colonial era, needed to identify themselves in new ways and found ethnic, or tribal, labels useful. This was especially true in the growing urban areas of colonial Africa. Although Europeans often expected, and feared, that Africans coming to the cities would become "de-tribalized," quite the opposite happened, for the cities became in many cases the spawning ground of new ethnic identities. Surrounded by a bewildering variety of people and in a setting where competition for jobs, housing, and education was very intense, migrants to the city found it useful to categorize themselves and others in larger ethnic terms. Thus, in many colonial cities people who spoke similar languages, shared a common culture, or came from the same general part of the country began to think of themselves as a single people—a new tribe. They organized a rich variety of ethnic associations to provide mutual assistance while in the cities and to send money back home to build schools or clinics.

Educated Africans—teachers and priests, for example—played an important role in creating these new ethnic identities, as did European intellectuals such as missionaries and anthropologists. Such peo-

Europeans relied on African security forces and often recruited from members of ethnic groups regarded as particularly "martial." *Visual Studies Workshop*

ple wrote about the unique customs, languages, and histories of particular peoples and so provided them with a pedigree in much the same way that intellectuals contributed to the ethnic nationalisms of central and eastern Europe in the nineteenth century. Furthermore, many of the new chiefs of colonial Africa found it useful to present themselves as representatives of some long-established tribe. And migrant mine workers in southern Africa, far from home and wishing to protect their rights to land and to their wives and families, found a sense of security in being part of a recognized tribe with its chiefs, courts, and established authority. Thus, a growing circle of Africans found meaning in these new definitions of community. One historian has summarized the process in this way: "Europeans believed Africans belonged to tribes: Africans built tribes to belong to."[9]

The Igbo people of southeastern Nigeria are a case in point. Prior to the twentieth century, they were organized in a series of independently governed village groups. Although speaking a series of related languages, they had no unifying political system and no myth of common ancestry. Occupying a region of unusually dense population, many of these people seized eagerly on Western education and moved out in large numbers to the cities and towns of colonial Nigeria. There they gradually discovered what they had in common and how they differed from the Yoruba, Hausa, Tiv, and other peoples of Nigeria. By the 1940s, they were organizing on a national level and calling on Igbo everywhere to "sink all differences" and to "unite under the banner" of their "great objective": the "tribal unity, cooperation, and progress of all the Igbos." Yet, fifty years earlier, no one had regarded himself or herself as an Igbo.

The unevenness of colonial development also fostered this new sense of ethnicity. For a variety of reasons, some groups or areas gained advantages in terms of education, jobs, cash-crop opportunities, or other signs of modern progress. Less favored groups could easily perceive their neighbors' advantage as a threat and could express their fear in ethnic terms. As the educational advantages for the Igbo in Nigeria became increasingly apparent, other groups such as the Yoruba and Hausa came to fear that the Igbo would be in a position to dominate once the country became independent. Such fears contributed much to Nigeria's bloody civil war in the 1960s.

Occasions for this kind of fear became more frequent as the colonial era drew to a close. During the 1950s, colonial governments began to Africanize their civil service bureaucracies, a process that considerably heightened ethnic rivalry as members of one group came to fear and resent the prospect of being ordered around by members of another. Governments also sponsored elections designed to determine who would run the new independent states. The political parties that competed in these elections often championed the interests of one or another ethnic group or were at least perceived by their rivals as doing so. Thus, although the colonial state had in some ways fostered a new tribalism, the departure of the colonial "referee" seemed to stimulate ethnic identity even further.

Conclusion: The Limits of Colonial Development

What can we conclude about the relationship between colonial rule and modern development in Africa? Clearly, colonial regimes did introduce into Africa a variety of modern ideas and techniques that otherwise would have occurred much more slowly, if at all. Those who focus on the positive elements of colonial rule argue that there was essentially no other way for Africa to modernize, unfortunate though that may have been. There were few indications that African societies at the beginning of the twentieth century would have been able to raise the capital or develop the skills for modernization wholly from within. The price of attracting foreign capital and foreign skills was to provide Europeans an opportunity to make a profit, and this involved allowing them to shape African economies largely in their own interests. Colonial rule provided a framework within which they could do so. But in the process, African societies themselves received a solid start on the road to modern development. This is the argument of those who see the colonial experience as a positive, modernizing force in Africa. It assumes, of course, that modernization was something to be desired.

Certainly, colonial governments recognized that it was in their interest to promote at least enough development to generate trade, to encourage foreign investment, and to produce the trained work force the economy demanded. Particularly after World War II, the British, the French, and Belgians substantially increased investment in the colonies, largely in the form of funds to build hydroelectric facilities, construct better roads and harbors, and expand their educational systems.

The clearest evidence of success was the obvious growth of African economies—that is, their ability to produce more goods than ever before. Some, though by no means all, of this new wealth enriched particular African individuals and groups, especially cash-crop farmers, members of the new elite, official African chiefs, and the better-paid urban workers.

These were among the beneficiaries of the colonial experience.

An additional indication of colonial modernization lay in the field of health care and was reflected in substantial increases in population. Although the early decades of the colonial era saw numerous epidemics and in many places population decline, a process of natural recovery coupled with colonial public health measures, including better sanitation and vaccination campaigns, led to a rapidly increasing population. By 1960, the African population as a whole was growing at an extremely rapid 2.5 percent per year, owing largely to a sharp decrease in the death rate. Those individuals who were spared an early death were surely among the beneficiaries of colonial modernization. The growth of basic literacy and the provision of a more advanced education for a few were also among the benefits of colonial rule.

The question of colonial modernization, however, is not only whether particular individuals or groups benefited but also whether the colonial system was able to construct new societies, using the great possibilities of modern science and technology to meet Africans' needs and goals. It is at this point that critics of colonial rule make their most persuasive case. Many historians, economists, and others have come to see the colonial era as one of "growth without development." This phrase suggests that although colonial African economies grew (that is, produced more cocoa, tea, copper, or diamonds than before), they did not develop in terms of their capacity to meet the needs of their increasing populations.

Colonial economic growth, these critics note, was limited largely to the export sector of minerals and cash crops. It resulted in countries becoming highly dependent on one or very few export products, such as cocoa in Ghana, rubber in Liberia, copper in Zambia, and peanuts in Senegal. As a consequence, local food production received little attention. In Algeria, where population tripled during the colonial era, it has been estimated that the average person in 1940 had only half the grain supply that had been available in 1871. Not until after World War II did colonial governments make even modest efforts to introduce scientific agriculture to those farmers—mostly women—producing basic food crops. As a result, most African farmers greeted independence with the same set of tools and techniques that they had when the colonial era began.

Export-oriented economies were unbalanced in yet another way, for both public and private investment favored those limited areas that were close to a major city, rail terminal, seaport, or cash-crop area. Thus, African colonies came to independence with very unevenly developed economies. Since foreigners controlled both private investment and government policy, it is not surprising they made decisions that reflected the needs of Europe more than those of Africa.

The limits of colonial modernization, therefore, were not so much that it altered traditional patterns of African life, for that was inevitable, nor even that it involved suffering and exploitation, for modern development has never been smooth or easy. It was rather that the colonial system seemed unable or unwilling to build a sound basis for new societies. In Europe and America, industrialization had been at the very heart of the modernizing process, but in colonial Africa, very little progress had been made toward developing modern manufacturing industries, even where it might have been profitable to do so. The profits from foreign investment were mostly remitted abroad rather than invested locally, and few African capitalists had sufficient wealth to make a real difference. Thus, rapid population growth occurred without an agricultural revolution to provide adequate local food supplies, and massive urbanization took place in the absence of an industrial revolution to meet basic material needs or to provide employment opportunities.

In the view of its critics, colonial development had produced by the 1950s nothing less than a social crisis. Labor migration had impoverished many rural areas, and the growth of cities gave rise to huge urban slums. Despite pockets of prosperity, the lot of ordinary Africans was one of deepening poverty and social disruption. The rapid growth of nationalist movements after World War II reflected the belief of many that colonial rule had run its course and now posed an obstacle to the further development of African societies.

Notes

1. Basil Davidson, *Modern Africa* (London: Longmans, 1983), p. 10.

2. Kamene Okonjo, "The Dual-Sex Political System in Operation," in *Women in Africa,* ed. Nancy J. Hafkin

and Edna G. Bay (Stanford: Stanford University Press, 1976), p. 45.

3. This section draws heavily on Margaret Jean Hay and Sharon Stichter, eds., *African Women South of the Sahara* (London: Longmans, 1984), esp. chaps. 1–5.

4. Quoted in Robert A. Levine, "Sex Roles and Economic Change in Africa," in *Black Africa,* ed. John Middleton, (London: Macmillan, 1970), p. 178.

5. Frank Salamone, "Continuity of Igbo Values after Conversion," *Missiology* 3 (Jan. 1975): 33–44.

6. Quoted in Robert W. Strayer, *The Making of Mission Communities in East Africa* (London: Heinemann, 1978), p. 89.

7. P. C. Lloyd, *Africa in Social Change* (Baltimore: Penguin, 1967), p. 122.

8. Quoted in Davidson, *Modern Africa,* pp. 79, 81.

9. John Iliffe, *A Modern History of Tanganyika* (Cambridge: Cambridge University Press, 1979), p. 324.

Chapter 23
Toward Independence:
Shaping New Societies in Africa

We often understand the history of colonial societies, in Africa or elsewhere, as something that happened to them. Conquest, new political-administrative systems, growing connections to the world economy, the missionary presence—all of these and more were imposed from the outside. Supporters of colonial rule may praise it, critics damn it, and others draw up balance sheets of pros and cons. All, however, portray Africans themselves as largely passive, the beneficiaries or the victims of European actions.

But there is another side to the colonial coin. In recent decades, historians have discovered how African and other subordinated peoples took action to shape their own lives and cultures even within the difficult and oppressive conditions of colonial rule. At times, Africans sought to preserve existing ways of life against the pressures of European culture and modern alternatives. Among the Chewa people of Malawi, for example, masked-dancing societies called *Nyau* defended Chewa cultural identity and the independence of Chewa villages against Europeans as they had done earlier against African invaders. They created masks and songs designed to ridicule major Christian figures, such as Mary and Joseph, and campaigned to enroll children in *Nyau* societies before they could be recruited into mission schools. This conservative reaction remained for decades a major obstacle to the spread of Christianity in Malawi.

However, such actions by no means implied an overall unwillingness to change. Many Africans were quite willing to take advantage of opportunities for cash-crop farming, urban jobs, and Western education. Likewise, large numbers of people became active proponents of such European ideas as Christianity, nationalism, and socialism. Traditional insti-

tutions were used for modern purposes, as in the case of west African descent groups or lineages that sometimes came to function as modern business enterprises. By the 1940s, and in many places much earlier, there was widespread and eager acceptance of much that was new, European, and modern—far more so than in many parts of Asia.

Accepting what was new, however, often involved adapting it to African needs and circumstances. In the late nineteenth century, the leadership of the kingdom of Buganda in east Africa treated the coming of the British as an opportunity to expand its own territory at the expense of traditional rivals, and they did so quite successfully. The Ganda used the British, even as they were incorporated into the British Empire. Furthermore, Africans who accepted Christianity frequently did so very much on their own terms. Thus, they may have treated baptism as a healing rite, the saints as "rain givers," and Christian rituals as a means of dealing with witchcraft. More recently, Africans who espoused socialism often presented it as a modern version of traditional African communal life. In such ways was the new cloaked in the garb of the old.

Whatever Africans thought of European culture, they frequently rejected European control. By the 1950s, most Africans who had occasion to think about the matter had concluded they could neither preserve valuable elements of traditional life nor gain wider access to modern opportunities so long as European political control was intact. Reforming the colonial system seemed no longer enough, and political independence for the colonial states became the shining goal to which so many hopes were pegged.

The African quest for independence was largely successful, and occurred quickly. As a part of the larger global contraction of European empires following World War II, some forty-six former African colonial units achieved independence between 1955 and 1975. Zimbabwe joined their ranks in 1980 and Namibia in 1989, while South Africa finally ended apartheid and achieved African majority rule in early 1994.

The achievement of African independence poses a number of interesting questions and suggests comparisons with similar processes in other parts of the world. Why, for example, did most African countries achieve independence so quickly, whereas India had a much more prolonged period of struggle and negotiation? Was African independence gained by the active struggle of mass movements or, as some have argued, granted rather easily by European governments eager to be rid of colonial responsibilities? Were nationalist movements in Africa associated with revolutionary social change, as in China, or did they seek to preserve the existing social structure, as in India? How did nationalist movements in Africa cope with other emerging patterns of identity, expressed in ethnic rivalries and class conflicts, as they sought independence?

In the process of accommodating, resisting, or adapting to colonial rule and the changes associated with it, Africans were also redefining and reshaping the communities in which they lived. New ethnic, class, and racial identities, new religious communities, new national loyalties—all of these emerged from the caldron of the colonial experience to shape African encounters with foreign rulers and to lay the foundation for independent societies.

Before Nationalism: Rebellions, Churches, and Intellectuals

Not until after World War II did African efforts to throw off European authority come to focus primarily on achieving political independence for the new states created by colonial rulers. Nationalism in this sense was a recent phenomenon. But well before this, many Africans had been involved in movements to resist as much colonial dominance as possible and to preserve old forms of community or create new ones in the process.

Rural Rebellion: The Case of Maji Maji

One expression of this effort lay in a wave of rural rebellions that punctuated the "colonial peace" during the first several decades of the twentieth century. In South Africa, southwest Africa, Sierra Leone, Kenya, and elsewhere, Africans made use of traditional beliefs and institutions to unite in vigorous opposition to colonial rule and to the particular economic and social changes it introduced. In doing so, they created, briefly, movements that were often far more radical and sought far more fundamental changes than many of the later nationalist movements of the 1950s.

A particularly interesting example is the Maji Maji Rebellion, which took place in the southern part of German east Africa (now Tanzania) between 1905 and 1907. Twenty years earlier, the Germans had established a protectorate over the numerous, separate, and small-scale chiefdoms of the area and had subsequently imposed the forced cultivation of cotton, which seriously interfered with production of local food crops. Here is how one man remembered the experience: "The cultivation of cotton was done by turns. Every village was allotted days on which to cultivate.... After arriving you all suffered very greatly. Your back and your buttocks were whipped and there was no rising up once you stooped to dig.... And yet he [the German] wanted us to pay him tax. Were we not human beings?"[1]

In response to such conditions, a major rebellion began in 1905, with groups of angry peasants uprooting cotton fields and attacking both Europeans and those Africans associated with the colonial regime. Most remarkable was the way the many different African societies of the area cooperated and coordinated their actions. It was not a common political organization that bound them together, for nothing of the sort existed; rather, a set of religious traditions were shared by the diverse people of the region. A cult of a great spirit called Kolelo, associated with fertility, had shrines and ministers throughout the area, and in 1904, a man named Kinjikitile, claiming to be a prophet of Kolelo, called on all African people in the region to rebel against German rule. Here was an effort to overcome traditional political and cultural divisions in the name of a shared religious tradition. The leadership of the movement began to dispense a medicine which, they claimed, protected those who received it by turning German bullets to water (maji). Such medicines had been used frequently to confer prosperity, to end famine and sickness, and otherwise to provide religious power for dealing with the problems of life.

As the movement spread, it linked up with still another local religious tradition—antiwitchcraft movements. Efforts to identify and destroy witches, who were thought to be the source of evil and misfortune, had occurred in times of great difficulty in the past, and now, in the desperate circumstances of severe German oppression, Maji Maji rebels proclaimed again that a new world was coming. It would be a world without Europeans and without witches— which is to say, without evil. It was a revolutionary, millenarian message that united very diverse peoples and swept aside, at least temporarily, traditional chiefs who tried to oppose the movement.

By 1907, German military technology had triumphed over the religious technology of the Maji Maji rebels, and the repression and famine that followed were terrible indeed. Some 75,000 people died as a result of the rebellion. But it showed how rural Africans could adapt their traditional religious beliefs to the needs of an anticolonial movement. In doing so, they were dealing with the same problem that the nationalists would face some forty years later— how to create among Africans a wider set of loyalties with which to confront the colonial system. Although Maji Maji clearly failed to achieve its goals, it made the Germans far more cautious about their methods of ruling and induced them to give up forced cotton growing. It also became an inspiring part of the nationalist mythology of later generations.

There were other rebellions and other answers to the problems of creating wider loyalties. But in all of them, African people pushed to the point of open rebellion tried to find in their own traditions a basis for dealing with the colonial intruders.

The Africanization of Christianity

Violent rebellion was not the only way that Africans in the early colonial era expressed their rejection of European domination, nor were traditional religious and social institutions the only basis for establishing new communities and new loyalties. Christianity and Christian churches provided another means of accommodating the changed circumstances of the twentieth century. But in the process of making the immigrant religion their own—that is, of Africanizing it—Africans sometimes found themselves in conflict with white missionaries and with colonial states.

Far more than in India or China, Africans adopted the religion of their colonial rulers. In the mid-nineteenth century, missionaries from Europe and America had introduced Christianity, and by 1950, many millions had affiliated in some fashion with the new religion, which has continued to grow ever since. This was a remarkable cultural change, due in part to opportunities for education, employment, and status available to people identified as Christians.

However, many Africans also saw in Christian rituals, symbols, and practices a powerful religious resource for dealing with the practical problems of life: illness, infertility, the need for rainfall, protection from witchcraft, to say nothing of the many upheavals and disruptions of the colonial era. These had been among the concerns of traditional African religions, so it was not surprising that Africans would think that people so obviously powerful as Europeans should have access to supernatural power that might be applied to such problems. In addition, some historians have suggested that Christianity, a world religion focused primarily on an all-powerful creator, was becoming more relevant than local divinities and ancestral spirits in explaining and controlling the new and wider world of the twentieth century. To people who interpreted the world in religious terms, a universal religion might well seem more appropriate than a local one in the new circumstances of the colonial era. Christianity, in short, could provide both secular opportunities and religious resources for dealing with societies in the process of rapid change. Thus, the new religion spread in the early twentieth century "like other African religious movements—through rumors of prophecy and healing, by seizure of those Christian rites and symbols which resonated most in a particular society, often accompanied by an enthusiastic surrender of charms and medicines."[2]

But the high hopes that Africans held for mission Christianity were often disappointed, and from that disappointment emerged thousands of separate, inde-

Mission schools, such as this teacher training class in Kenya in the 1930s, helped to spread Christianity in Africa and generated a politically active elite. *Robert W. Strayer*

pendent African churches. Organized and run by Africans, they represented at once a clear rejection of European authority; a willingness to make use of Christian symbols, ideas, and techniques; and an insistence on adapting these new forms to local conditions and needs.

Some of the disappointment and hostility that stimulated independent churches was political and racial. Missionaries were often closely associated with the colonial government, were frequently no less racist than other Europeans, and were reluctant to promote Africans into positions of authority in the church. Furthermore, many Africans were critical of the amount and type of education offered by mission schools, feeling that the schools were holding back their progress toward achieving educational equality with whites. Missionary opposition to polygamy or to initiation rites, for example, was also a source of tension.

Many Africans were disappointed with mission Christianity on a religious level as well. Whereas white missionaries emphasized the issues of sin, salvation, and the afterlife, Africans were frequently more concerned about faith healing, prophecy, ecstat-

ic forms of worship, and protection from witchcraft. In many independent churches, these matters received great attention. Nor were such adaptations limited to independent churches, for in many mission churches, particularly those not directly supervised by European missionaries, Africans blended new Christian concepts and rituals with those of their own religious heritage.

These were attempts to create, in the words of one writer, "a place to feel at home."[3] In doing so, independent Christians often linked up with older values and traditions such as spirit possession and anti-witchcraft practices. But they also reached out to establish a spiritual connection to the new and powerful world of their European rulers. Usually the independents were not directly anti-European and often refused to participate in politics at all, seeking rather to create a new culture and new communities amid the upheavals and oppression of the modern era.

Nevertheless, colonial governments frequently sensed that these churches had political implications and acted to suppress them. Such was the case in the Belgian Congo, where a young educated Baptist named Simon Kimbangu had a series of visions and, in 1921, began a ministry of healing and preaching in very Christian terms. In just a few months, he had attracted an amazing following and so frightened the Belgian government that he was imprisoned for the rest of his life. But the movement spread, largely underground, and Kimbangu came to be regarded as an African prophet with a status equivalent to that of Moses, Jesus, Muhammad, or Buddha.

The Protest of the Intellectuals

Whereas rebellions and independent churches involved large numbers of ordinary Africans in communities of resistance and adaptation, members of the new elite—literate, often well educated, and employed in the modern sector of the economy—found themselves dealing with similar issues, though in very different ways. These were the people most closely in touch with European culture and most sharply affected by the racism of much European thinking and behavior. From the mid-nineteenth century through the colonial era, the new elite attempted through their books, articles, and speeches to revive the cultural self-confidence of African peoples, to challenge the European assumption of white superiority, and to lay the foundation for greater unity among Africa's very diverse peoples.

The central problem faced by these African intellectuals was how to defend their culture, society, and history against denigration by Europeans while accepting much that they found good and useful in Western civilization. One line of argument held that African culture and history possessed the very characteristics that Europeans exalted. If Europeans valued large empires and complex political systems, African intellectuals pointed with pride to the ancient kingdoms of Ethiopia, Mali, Songhai, and others. C. A. Diop, a French-educated scholar from Senegal, argued that Egyptian civilization, which Europeans had generally claimed as a Western achievement, was actually the work of black Africans. Turning European assumptions on their head, Diop argued that Western civilization owed much to Egyptian influence and was therefore derived from Africa. Black people, in short, had a history of achievement fully comparable to that of Europe and deserved, therefore, just as much respect and admiration.

A second, and quite different, approach to defending African cultures lay in admitting fundamental differences between African and European cultures but insisting that African ways of life were at least as worthy as those of the West, and perhaps more so. The most influential proponent of such views was Edward Blyden, a west African born in the West Indies and educated in the United States, who became a Presbyterian minister in 1860 and a professor of Greek and Latin at Liberia College, and who briefly served as an official in the Liberian government. Until his death in 1912, he was the major voice for the first generation of west African intellectual leaders.

Blyden accepted the assumption that the world's various races were different but argued that each had its own distinctive contribution to make to world civilization. The uniqueness of African culture, Blyden wrote, lay in its communal, cooperative, and egalitarian societies, which contrasted sharply with Europe's highly individualistic, competitive, and class-ridden societies; in its harmonious relationship to nature as opposed to Europe's efforts to dominate and exploit the natural order; and particularly in its profound religious sensibility, which Europeans had lost in centuries of attention to material gains. Here is Blyden's vision of Africa's mission in the world:

> Africa may yet prove to be the spiritual conservatory of the world.... When the civilized nations, in consequence of their wonderful material development, shall have had their spiritual sensibilities darkened and their spiritual susceptibilities blunted through the agency of a captivating and absorbing materialism, it may be, that they may have to resort to Africa to recover some of the simple elements of faith; for the promise of that land is that she shall stretch forth her hands unto God.[4]

Yet these new ideologies of Africanness did not look to a fixed or static past, for there was much hopeful talk of regeneration and progress after a long night of the slave trade, conquest, and colonial humiliation. The brighter future, however, was conceived largely in terms of nation-states, based on European models. While African intellectuals might take pride in earlier African achievements, few among them actually contemplated a future role for traditional political systems or existing African rulers. They generally regarded such traditional authorities and institutions as backward, primitive, and inappropriate to the needs of modern Africa. "[W]e must emerge from the savage backwoods," wrote the west African clergyman Attoh Ahuma in 1911, "and come into the open where nations are made."[5] This general rejection of African political experience as relevant to Africa's future meant that the new nations of independent Africa would have only the most shallow of roots in the soil of their own cultures.

Discussions of Africa's past and future soon came to embrace not only the colonized people of the continent but also the peoples of African descent scattered to the New World by the slave trade. American and West Indian blacks, such as W. E. B. Du Bois and Marcus Garvey, actively identified with their ancestral continent, and their writings and their movements served to inspire and embolden African intellectual and political figures. At a series of pan-African conferences between 1897 and 1945, African and New World black leaders met to exchange ideas, pass resolutions, and press for greater world recognition of the rights of Africans. Although such meetings had little direct political effect, they gave expression to the new ideas of Africanness now being discussed on four continents.

These new ideas began the process of liberation from the mentality and assumptions of colonialism, particularly among educated and politically active Africans. They represented an effort to identify some of those qualities shared by Africa's many peoples. It is important to realize that only in the past hundred years have people on the African continent regarded themselves as Africans. Though there were similarities and connections among separate African societies, there was little consciousness of a common cultural tradition, nor was there any unified political system to embody these similarities. In this regard, the African situation was quite different from that of India, China, and the Middle East, where intellectuals could refer back to the long-standing and well-recognized traditions, or "high cultures," of Hinduism, Confucianism, or Islam. African intellectuals of the nineteenth and twentieth centuries, in contrast, had the task of creating such an awareness from the common experience of colonial oppression and of articulating a "new tradition" of Africanness for the first time. It was an important achievement, for it provided a foundation of cultural self-confidence that made it possible to challenge European supremacy and, at the same time, adopt many of the techniques and ideas of a modernizing Europe.

Politics and the New Elite

In addition to their intellectual work, members of the new elite began to organize politically in the early years of colonial rule. But if their writings sometimes had revolutionary implications, their political activity was usually limited to requesting modest reforms of the colonial system, and by the most moderate of means. Elite politics, therefore, reflected the emergence of an elite class that felt oppressed by the colonial system but had benefited greatly from it.

A particularly telling example of early elite politics can be found in the activities of the National Congress of British West Africa. Established in 1920, it was an organization consisting primarily of lawyers and merchants, with a sprinkling of journalists, teachers, doctors, members of the clergy, and chiefs from the four west African colonies of Great Britain: Nigeria, Gold Coast, Sierra Leone, and Gambia. They sought increased African representation in the colonial governments, greater opportunities for Africans in commerce and industry, more schools, and an end to racial discrimination. In short, they were willing to operate within colonial structures if they could find there an enhanced and more nearly equal role. They felt their mastery of European culture and modern ways had entitled them to recognition and status as the primary representatives of African interests within the councils of colonial government.

If the issues that animated the Congress were those of primary concern to the elite, its members' tactics were moderate and strictly constitutional, such as sending petitions and delegations to colonial authorities. They failed almost completely to link up with the demands and grievances of the rural masses and the urban poor despite numerous opportunities to do so in the 1920s and 1930s. There were peasant outbursts against the abuses of colonial chiefs, anti-tax riots by small-scale traders and groups of women, attempts by cocoa farmers to boycott European buyers, strikes by urban workers, and the anti-European feelings expressed by independent churches. To all of these "mass" concerns the new elite was largely oblivious. Nor was it much affected by the revolutionary ideas stemming from the Russian Revolution, though nervous and insecure colonial officials often saw any protest activity as "Bolshevist." The timidity of elite politics was partly due to the overwhelming strength of the colonial regimes but also to the class privileges and narrow political vision of the leadership. Not until after World War II would elite political organizations begin to seek wider support and to transform their goals from reform to independence.

In French territories, the educated elite was even less inclined to offer vigorous opposition to the colonial regime, for French colonial theory offered the privileges of French citizenship to a very small group of highly educated and "assimilated" Africans. The deliberate prevention of a well-educated elite in the Belgian Congo and the poverty, corruption, and authoritarianism of Portuguese colonies meant that there was little early opposition from the elite in those areas as well.

The Nationalisms of Colonial Africa

The movements that swept colonial Africa after World War II were quite different from those discussed so far. They combined elite leadership with various degrees of mass support; they sought not merely to reform colonial rule but to end it; and the struggle for independence was waged not on behalf of traditional communities but for the new and largely artificial states that Europeans had created at the end of the nineteenth century. Such movements are generally termed *nationalist* and reflect the widespread, though historically inaccurate, modern belief that the world is divided into "nations," each of which deserves to be ruled by its own people.

Such ideas became powerful and popular in the 1940s and 1950s throughout Africa and many of the developing nations. But they were a double-edged sword, for nationalism divided as well as united groups of people. There was, after all, no clearly defined answer to the basic question: What people constitute the "nation" whose independence and self-government should be secured?

In Africa, that question elicited at least three answers, and they were not always entirely compatible.

Sometimes it was all Africans, or even all black people, who seemed to be the nation of Africa. The pan-African movement and various attempts to join several countries together are examples of this definition. It is still alive in the activities of the Organization of African Unity, a body in which all the independent states of Africa attempt to coordinate their activities and work out common problems.

But the movements that gained political independence operated at a second level—that of the colonial territory, such as Algeria, Mozambique, or Tanzania. Here the problem was not simply to gain independence for the state but also to create a sense of loyalty and commitment to these new units. Modern nations in Africa did not exist; they had to be built in the process of acquiring independence. This was quite the reverse of the way nationalism developed in much of Europe. There the idea of being German or Italian or Hungarian preceded the formation of a state that could give expression to that nationality.

The process of nation-building, however, was made more difficult by the simultaneous emergence of nationalism at still a third level—that of the ethnic group. Nearly every African colony encompassed a large number of culturally different peoples, many of whom came to feel they had as much claim to nationhood as did the larger state. Thus, the struggle for independence involved not only an effort to oust the Europeans but also a confrontation with rival ethnic nationalisms.

Nationalist Origins

The nationalist movements that finally ended European colonial rule in Africa had their origins in the years following World War II. In many ways they were stimulated by that war and by the changed international environment that followed from it.

The war had weakened and humiliated the major colonial powers. Furthermore, Franklin Roosevelt and Winston Churchill had solemnly declared in 1941, "We respect the right of all peoples to choose the form of government under which they will live." Many Africans came to feel that such lofty rhetoric applied to their situations as well. Finally, tens of thousands of African men had fought for the British or French, had seen white people die, had enjoyed the company of white women, and had returned

Elections in late colonial Africa, such as this one in Britain's Gold Coast colony (now Ghana) in 1951, came in response to the pressures of growing nationalist movements. *AP/Wide World Photos*

home with very different ideas about white superiority and the permanence of colonial rule.

For different reasons, the new superpowers—the United States and the Soviet Union—opposed formal colonial empires of the European type, though they came to exercise enormous power over other peoples in various ways. Important in the 1940s, however, was that the newly dominant powers of the world were apparently on the side of colonized peoples. So too was the United Nations Organization. Founded in 1945 to promote international cooperation, it soon became a prestigious forum for the denunciation of colonialism. And in Asia, the Philippines had achieved independence in 1946 and India and Indonesia in 1947. Moreover, the Chinese Communists

came to power via revolution in 1949, and unceremoniously expelled Europeans from that huge and troubled country. All of this undermined the moral legitimacy of colonialism and suggested to Africans that their freedom movements were on the side of history.

In Europe, these new international circumstances of the 1940s put the colonial powers on the defensive and forced them to think more seriously about the need to reform their colonial empires—and, in the British case, even to contemplate withdrawal. What made this rethinking less painful than it might have been was the increasingly solid economic links that were being forged between the African colonies and Europe. During the war, a greatly increased demand for African raw materials and food products fueled a general economic upsurge in many parts of the continent, and the postwar recovery of Europe and America expanded the demand for African products even further. Exports from the Belgian Congo, for example, increased by 1953 to fourteen times their 1939 value. As part of their postwar reform programs, the British and French especially sought to foster these economic links by providing money for building schools, highways, railroads, ports, and other projects that would strengthen the integration of Africa into the world economy.

All of this made it easier for Europeans to consider political withdrawal, particularly if it were possible to turn over control to groups of middle-class Africans solidly committed to continuing trade and investment relations with Europe. This suggests that independence was not so much gained by strenuous African effort as it was granted by European powers, confident now that they could protect their essential economic interests without the expense and trouble of colonial administration.

But if the colonial powers were increasingly ready to leave, nowhere did they do so without a considerable push from nationalist movements. The degree of "push" necessary to achieve independence varied considerably from place to place, but almost everywhere it involved a struggle.

The primary vehicles for that struggle were political parties, and in the decade following the war, they were established or reinvigorated almost everywhere in Africa. The leadership of the parties was drawn from the well-educated elite, but from a new generation of the elite—younger, more impatient and demanding, more prepared to use direct-action tactics, and increasingly insistent on independence rather than modest reforms. Their greatest difference from the moderate associations of the 1920s and 1930s lay in their desire to reach out to a broader constituency and to articulate the concerns of the masses. The processes of economic and social change in the colonies, many of which were speeded up by the postwar economic boom, created a number of groups who were increasingly receptive to the nationalist message and who felt that their fortunes would improve if the Europeans were expelled.

Thousands of World War II veterans made up one such group. Returning home with new military skills, political ideas, and a wider perception of the world,

they stimulated nationalist activity in many French and British colonies. Another group included what the British called "unemployed school leavers," products of the postwar educational expansion who were unable to find "modern" jobs commensurate with their expectations. It was natural, though perhaps unrealistic, for them to feel that if the colonizers departed, many more opportunities would be available to them. In a number of colonies, the very small urban working class erupted in a series of major strikes in the 1940s, and thousands of small-scale African traders felt restricted and harassed by colonial governments that favored European, Indian, or Lebanese business interests. The urban poor in the rapidly growing cities had organized a rich variety of ethnic associations, social clubs, and cultural groups, which were fertile recruiting grounds for the new nationalist parties.

In the rural areas as well, there were identifiable groups with acute grievances against the colonial system. In settler territories such as Kenya and Rhodesia, those who had lost land to whites and those who found themselves restricted to impoverished rural reserves were increasingly receptive to the call for independence. Furthermore, postwar colonial efforts to "improve" African agricultural practices (through compulsory destocking of cattle on overgrazed lands or enforced destruction of diseased cocoa trees) represented a sharp new intrusion of the colonial state into the lives of peasant farmers that was much resented. Likewise, the inability to market their cash crops except through foreign brokers was a source of antagonism to numerous farmers now caught up in widespread commercial networks. Sporadic riots in opposition to the abuses of rural chiefs and to colonial taxation were additional signs of a growing "rural radicalism."

The widening support for national independence in postwar Africa was thoroughly modernist. It was not primarily motivated by a desire to preserve traditional societies from the pressures of modernizing change. Rather, it was fueled by the perception of many diverse groups and individuals that their ability to make it in the modern world was being frustrated by colonial rule. The task of nationalist leadership in the various colonies was to bring together a sufficiently large coalition of frustrated people to persuade the colonial governments that independence was a cheaper and less difficult course than maintaining European dominance against growing opposition. How this was accomplished varied considerably from place to place.

Achieving the Political Kingdom: The Way of Negotiated Settlements

The primary road to independence followed by most of the French and British colonies involved a relatively brief struggle conducted largely through legal means such as demonstrations, elections, and political organization. Although sporadic violence occurred, there was no sustained military confrontation with the colonial regimes and consequently only limited mass participation in the nationalist movements. Agreements to end colonial rule were negotiated between major political parties in Africa and the British or French governments. This kind of political transition generally saw the transfer of power to quite moderate pro-Western elites who had little intention of implementing dramatic social change.

Such a breakthrough to decolonization occurred first in Britain's colony of the Gold Coast, the most highly developed west African territory. There the growth of a cash-crop economy, considerable postwar urbanization, rising prices, and growing numbers of literate people combined to produce a fertile environment for nationalist politics. Kwame Nkrumah, an American-educated politician and a skilled organizer, was able to capitalize on these conditions when he founded the Convention People's Party (CPP) in 1949. With the slogan "Self-Government Now," the CPP soon gained considerable support throughout the colony, but particularly in the urban areas. A series of boycotts, strikes, and urban rioting between 1948 and 1950 persuaded the British to make substantial concessions to prevent the further radicalization of the nationalist movement, and full independence was granted in 1957. Most of the rest of British Africa followed soon after. Compared to India's extended independence movement, Ghana's was very much shorter and required far less agitation to persuade the British to leave. The Second World War and all that followed from it had made the world far less hospitable to old-style colonialism than it had been thirty years before.

French colonies in western Africa received their independence at about the same time as the British colonies (in roughly 1960) but in a somewhat different way. Not until the mid-1950s did the French even admit the possibility of independence. Before that, all African agitation and political reform was directed to permitting more Africans to have more representation in the French Parliament and in local territorial assemblies. It was the pressure of external events—Ghana's independence, the French defeat in Vietnam, the war in Algeria—that created the momentum leading to complete independence by 1960. Owing to the French policy of assimilating its African elites, much of the leadership of nationalist movements in French Africa had close cultural and political ties with France and sought to maintain this relationship even after formal independence was granted. With some exceptions, these leaders could be seen as reluctant nationalists.

There were still other variations on the theme of negotiated independence. In the huge Belgian colony of the Congo, a period of intense economic growth after World War II was accompanied by an almost total absence of modern African political activity. The Belgian policy of widespread primary school education but very little higher education had prevented the growth of a politically active elite, and not until 1956 did a small group of moderately well-educated Congolese call for "gradual, but total, emancipation" within thirty years. This statement broke the African political silence, and within a few months, far more radical demands for immediate independence were being heard. When serious urban rioting broke out in late 1958, Belgian authority in the colony began to collapse rapidly. With little support in Belgium for a policy of forcible suppression, colonial authorities had little choice but to agree to grant independence quickly. By mid-1960, this had been accomplished amid great confusion, spreading violence, and the rivalries of numerous political parties. Independence had come to the Congo almost overnight.

How should we understand these movements that won independence for their respective countries? Few if any of them were solidly united African efforts to expel the European intruders. On the contrary, most were quite fragile alliances or coalitions of groups that might unite temporarily to oust a common enemy but often had quite different interests in the long run.

Such was the case in Nigeria, Britain's large west African colony, which gained independence in 1960. No single or dominant party ever developed to express Nigerian opposition to British rule. Rather, there were three major parties, each of which was prominent among one of the major ethnic groups: the Igbo, Yoruba, and Hausa. The negotiations of the 1950s were not so much between Africans and the British as among the various African groups. The Muslim Hausa, who inhabited the northern part of the country, feared that independence would mean domination by the largely Christian Yoruba and Igbo of the south, since the latter had a considerable lead in modern education. Thus, the Hausa sought to delay independence and argued for a weak central government in which they might preserve their way of life. Ethnic nationalism proved an obstacle to Nigerian unity.

This was even more the case in the Congo, where over twenty-five parties, most of them based in a particular ethnic group, competed for power in the final chaotic years of Belgian rule. It was not surprising that within six months of independence, the southern part of that wealthy country sought to secede. The coming of independence heightened the sense of ethnic rivalry, for it was apparent that various opportunities—government jobs, roads, schools, development projects—would soon be distributed by an African government and that it mattered very much which Africans controlled that government. Many nationalist movements, therefore, consisted of fragile and shifting alliances among ethnically based parties.

The movements also contained class alliances. The elite members did not always see independence in the same way as their impoverished or aspiring supporters among the peasants or the urban poor. To better educated and more prosperous Africans, nationalism was primarily a political struggle, an effort to win the power of the colonial state for an African bourgeoisie and in doing so to eliminate the racial limitations that had been such an insulting part of their experience with Europeans. They sought, in short, to inherit the colonial system, not to dismantle it. Their mass supporters, however, saw the promise of independence more in economic and social terms—higher wages for workers, land for those who

had lost it, lower prices for consumers, an end to the interference of an oppressive and foreign government, and, above all, a higher standard of living. Such aspirations might require substantial changes in the colonial system and limits on the power and privileges of the elite.

Achieving the Political Kingdom: Wars of National Liberation

Not all African colonies were able to achieve independence so quickly or with such relative ease as those described thus far. In particular, where large settler communities existed, the struggle was far more difficult and prolonged. In Algeria, a French territory in north Africa with about a million settlers, a bitter seven-year war and over 150,000 deaths were required before the French were willing to relinquish their grip in 1962. Far to the south, an even more extended armed struggle took place in Zimbabwe (then Rhodesia) and in the Portuguese territories of Angola, Mozambique, and Guinea-Bissau. In such places, independence was achieved only through extended wars of national liberation. The difference between these struggles and those culminating in an early negotiated settlement is illustrated by the experience of the former Portuguese colonies.

Modern nationalist movements came later to Portuguese colonies than elsewhere in Africa due largely to the backward and highly repressive nature of Portuguese colonial rule. As the poorest, by far, of Europe's colonial powers, Portugal fostered little economic growth of benefit to Africans, relied on various forms of forced labor until the 1960s, and recruited hundreds of thousands of Africans to work in the mines of South Africa. Very little educational development took place, so that as late as 1950, there were only 737 primary school students in all of Angola and an illiteracy rate of 99 percent. Thus, there was only a tiny educated elite in the colonies, though it was members of this group that established the first modern political parties in the late 1950s and early 1960s.

It became apparent very quickly that Portugal would be unable or unwilling to promote reform and conduct negotiations with the nationalists, as the British and French had done. Portugal relied on the

Samora Machel, a leader of the liberation struggle in the Portuguese colony of Mozambique and later president of the country, instructs a group of both male and female fighters in a forest camp. *Sygma*

colonies both economically and for whatever pretensions it had to great power status. By the early 1970s, over 160,000 Portuguese troops were engaged in the colonies, and over half of the government's revenues went to military spending. In these circumstances, Portugal turned to the other Western powers for assistance. It offered foreign firms generous incentives to invest in the colonies, and it received massive military assistance from the United States and NATO. It was, therefore, against an internationalized Portuguese empire that the nationalist movement had to contend.

The first task was one of political preparation for what would obviously be a long, difficult, and violent struggle. Party cadres visited villages, explained the goals of the movement, recruited trustworthy people, and studied local conditions. This was a far different matter from persuading people to demonstrate or vote in elections. In doing so, the leadership confronted apathy, fear, witchcraft accusations, and

ethnic rivalries. At a critical meeting in the forests of Guinea-Bissau in 1964, Amilcar Cabral, leader of the African Party for the Independence of Guinea and Cape Verde (PAIGC), dealt directly with these issues. Here is a report of what he told the assembled leaders of his party:

> [Cabral] said that he had not created the party to give any tribe or group an advantage over others, but for the liberation of our whole people. He said that the party had to be the instrument of a national unity. He said that this unity must be forged in our struggle against the colonialists. He spoke of the old resistances that had all failed—and why? Because then each people had fought for itself and so the Portuguese could always win. Now was the time to resist with all our people fighting together against the same enemy. About witchcraft, he said this was indeed a reality in African belief, but that we must go beyond it.[6]

Guerrilla warfare soon began with attacks on Portuguese military and administrative posts and occasionally on African collaborators. Despite massive bombing and forced removal of thousands of people, the nationalist parties slowly began to carve out liberated areas and to create within them the institutions of a new society. They sponsored the election of village committees with representation of women and young people. They established schools and clinics, often for the first time. They set up cooperatives, collective farms, and "people's stores." Women assumed new roles in agriculture, politics, and combat, and early marriage and polygamy were actively discouraged. In the course of the struggle against the Portuguese, the elements of a new society were being created. Nothing of this sort occurred in those places where a negotiated end to colonial rule took place.

The movements, furthermore, developed and began to practice a Socialist ideology that was much more radical and far-reaching than the nationalist ideas common in British and French colonies. Because they had to resort to armed struggle, it was necessary to mobilize the masses far more extensively than in places where the struggle was only political. Serious inequalities and class privileges are difficult to sustain in the midst of a revolutionary struggle that depends on mass participation. In such a setting, socialism was both practical and relevant. Furthermore, Marxism provided a helpful framework for analyzing these societies and their history in preparation for the struggle, and support from the established Socialist countries reinforced these convictions.

A military coup in Portugal in 1974 brought to power a government willing to end quickly the exhausting wars in Africa. Thus, by 1975, all three territories had achieved independence, though in a far different way from the British, French, and Belgian colonies.

Achieving the Political Kingdom: South Africa

With the independence of the Portuguese colonies in 1975 and Zimbabwe in 1980, South Africa remained the major outpost of white domination in Africa, or indeed in the developing world as a whole. Given the general withdrawal of Europeans from political control over non-European peoples, why did South Africa prove so resistant to the forces of nationalism?

Certainly it had not been for lack of effort, for there was a long and vigorous tradition of African resistance to white control in South Africa. The African National Congress (ANC), founded in 1912, provided the modern focus for many of these efforts. For years, it was primarily an elite organization, but after World War II, like similar movements elsewhere in Africa, it began to broaden its base of support and launched a series of passive-resistance campaigns, including boycotts, strikes, demonstrations, and burning of identification passes. The failure of such efforts to produce changes in the apartheid system led to the beginning of limited violence and sabotage by the early 1960s. To all of this, the government of South Africa responded with tremendous repression, including the shooting of sixty-nine unarmed demonstrators at Sharpeville in 1960, the banning of the ANC, and the imprisonment of its leadership.

When active opposition resurfaced in the mid-1970s, it focused on young student groups that were part of the Black Consciousness movement, an effort to foster pride, unity, and political awareness among the country's African majority. Such young people were at the center of an explosion of African protest in 1976, in a large black township called Soweto, outside Johannesburg, where hundreds were killed. The momentum of the Soweto rebellion persisted, especially among the young, and by the mid-1980s, spreading urban violence and the radicalization of urban young people had forced the government to declare a state of emergency. Furthermore, South Africa's black labor movement, legalized only in 1979, became increasingly active and political. In June 1986, the Congress of South African Trade Unions (COSATU) orchestrated a general strike, involving some two million workers, to commemorate the tenth anniversary of the Soweto uprising.

But the conditions under which the South African struggle was conducted were far different from those elsewhere on the continent. First, that struggle was against an internal enemy, not a distant colonial power. South Africa, in fact, had been independent of Great Britain since 1910. The problem was to overcome the intransigence of a white minority of

Enormous lines of voters wait to cast their ballots in South Africa's 1994 elections, which marked the end of more than three centuries of white rule in that country.
AP/Wide World

over four million people, many of whom had been in South Africa for generations, had nowhere else to go, and felt that their way of life and standard of living were in mortal danger.

Unlike anywhere else in Africa, the whites controlled a mature industrial economy, based in mining of gold, diamonds, and other minerals but including also such secondary industries as steel, chemicals, automobiles, rubber processing, and heavy engineering. Particularly since the 1960s, the economy benefited from extensive foreign investment and loans. Almost all Africans were involved in this complex modern economy, working in urban industries or mines, providing labor for white farms, or receiving payments from relatives who do. The extreme dependence of most Africans on the white-controlled economy together with widespread urbanization, made it much more difficult to mount prolonged and disruptive guerrilla warfare.

A third unique feature of the South African situation was the enormous apparatus of repression at the disposal of the whites. The military and police power of the government far exceeded that anywhere on the African continent, and included the possession of nuclear weapons. An elaborate system of "pass laws" served until 1986 to monitor and control the movement of Africans, whereas the establishment of impoverished ethnic homelands, or Bantustans, for various "tribal" groups further hindered the development of a united African movement.

Despite these obstacles, the internal pressure of growing African resistance and rebellion and the external pressures of international economic sanctions brought major changes to South Africa by the early 1990s. The government repealed much of the major apartheid legislation, legalized African political parties, and released Nelson Mandela, leader of the ANC, from decades of imprisonment. It also entered into formal negotiations with the ANC and other groups about power sharing and a transition to majority rule. Those negotiations eventually produced a new constitution that eliminated the hated Bantustans, affirmed the equality of all citizens, and enfranchised everyone. In April 1994 the country's first inclusive elections brought Nelson Mandela to the presidency, marking the formal end of white rule in the long and painful history of South Africa.

Conclusion: "All These Other Things . . ."

Africa's first modern nationalist hero, Kwame Nkrumah of Ghana, paraphrased the biblical commandment as he urged his followers: "Seek ye first the political kingdom and all these other things will be added unto you." In obtaining independence from colonial control and white domination, nationalist movements had succeeded in winning the political kingdom, even in South Africa. But what of "all these other things"—industrial growth, more employment opportunities, expanded education, an end to oppression, the abolition of poverty? Whether they would follow was the key issue of the years that lay beyond independence.

Notes

1. Quoted in G. C. K. Gwassa and John Iliffe, *Records of the Maji Maji Rising,* part 1 (Nairobi: East African Publishing House, 1967), pp. 4–5.

2. Terrence O. Ranger, "Religious Movements and Politics in Sub-Saharan Africa," *African Studies Review,* 29 2 (June 1986): 33.

3. F. B. Welbourne and B. A. Ogot, *A Place to Feel at Home* (London: Oxford University Press, 1966).

4. Edward Blyden, *Christianity, Islam and the Negro Race* (Edinburgh: Edinburgh University Press, 1967), p. 124.

5. Attoh Ahuma, *Gold Coast Nation and National Consciousness* (Liverpool, 1911; reprint London: Frank Cass, 1971), p. 11.

6. Basil Davidson, *Let Freedom Come* (Boston: Little, Brown, 1978), p. 348.

Chapter 24

Development or Deterioration? Beyond Independence in Africa

Independence in Africa inevitably fostered great expectations. The old colonial powers of the world, considered invincible only a generation earlier, had been defeated. After such a triumph, surely anything was possible. Furthermore, a booming postwar world economy held the promise of rapid development. After all, the shattered economies of Western Europe were recovering quickly; the Soviet Union had created a modern industrial society in record time; the "miracle" of Japan's economic growth was under way; and China was striking out in bold new directions. Why should Africa not join their ranks? With its people mobilized by the struggle for independence and given an apparently hospitable climate in the world, "there came a vivid consciousness of having grasped destiny by the hand," wrote historian Basil Davidson, "so that Africa's history could begin again."[1]

The experience of the first several decades of independence has sharply eroded this early optimism. More than fifty military coups, civil war in a number of countries and the virtual political collapse of several, and widespread and recurrent famines have led some observers to speak about decay and deterioration rather than development as the primary historical trend since independence. At the heart of these disappointments has been a pattern of economic performance in Africa that compares unfavorably to every other area of the developing world, as Table 24.1 illustrates.

Such observations raise a number of questions. How have African states attempted to cope with the common problems of developing countries—creating political order in culturally diverse societies and directing economic growth to overcome massive poverty? Why has Africa experienced so much po-

litical upheaval, instability, and military intervention compared to the relatively more peaceful politics of an equally diverse India? Why has Africa been unable to match the economic performance of most Asian countries?

TABLE 24.1 Average Annual Growth of Per-Capita GNP: 1965–1990

Developing Area	Percent of Growth
Sub-Saharan Africa	0.2%
East Asia and Pacific	5.3
South Asia	1.9
Middle East and north Africa	1.8
Latin America	1.8

Source: World Bank, *World Development Report, 1992* (New York: Oxford University Press, 1992), p. 219.

Changing the Political Framework

At independence, Africans inherited both political borders and systems of government from their colonial rulers. In general, they kept the first, and dismantled the second. In retrospect, it is a little surprising that African political leaders have almost unanimously chosen not to alter the artificial boundaries imposed by colonial conquest. (See Map 24.1.) Partly this is because a whole set of political and economic relationships and vested interests had developed within these states. But national leaders also feared that tinkering with African

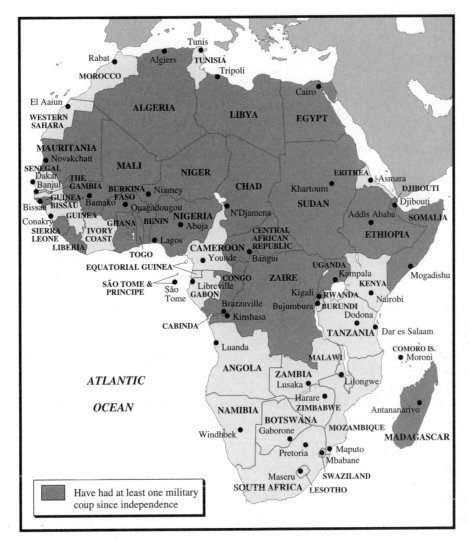

MAP 24.1 Independent Africa

boundaries could trigger a growing set of demands for ethnic states that could not be easily controlled. Keeping colonial borders of some fifty states intact, however, has meant that modern development often has been pursued within small and economically shaky states rather than in the larger areas similar to India and China. The experience of Korea and Taiwan, however, suggests that small size is not an automatic barrier to economic success. Efforts to merge or federate several of these African states into larger and more viable units, as well as attempts at economic cooperation, have been generally disappointing.

The Decline of Imported Democracy

The acceptance of colonial borders, however, did not imply a similar adoption of the system of government that Europeans had established within them. Although colonial rule had been for the most part highly authoritarian and bureaucratic, with little interest in African participation, during the 1950s the British, French, and Belgians attempted, rather belatedly, to transplant democratic institutions to their colonies. They established legislatures, permitted elections, allowed political parties to operate, and in general anticipated the development of constitutional, parliamentary, multiparty democracies similar to their own. It was with such institutions that most African states greeted independence.

By the early 1970s, however, there were few such regimes to be found among the new states of Africa. Many of the apparently popular political parties that had led the struggle for independence lost mass support and were swept away by military coups. When the army in Ghana took power in 1966 and abolished the Convention People's party, no one lifted a finger to defend the party, which had led the country to independence only nine years earlier. In Nigeria, Ethiopia, Sudan, Zaire, and elsewhere, military officers took power from civilian regimes, often to great popular acclaim. Other states, such as Kenya, the Ivory Coast, Senegal, and Tanzania, evolved into one-party systems, some highly authoritarian and bureaucratic and others more open and democratic. Still others, such as the Central African Republic and Idi Amin's Uganda, degenerated into personal tyrannies or dictatorships.

The contrast between Africa's initial post-independence political evolution and that of India is particularly striking (see Chapter 15). There a Western-style democracy, including regular elections, multiple parties, civil liberties, and peaceful changes in government, has been practiced for some forty-five years since independence. But the struggle for independence in India was a far more prolonged affair, thus providing time for an Indian political leadership to sort itself out. Furthermore, the British began to hand over power in a gradual way well before India's complete independence was granted in 1947. Thus, a far larger number of Indians had useful administrative or technical skills than was the case in Africa, where the coming of independence was a much more abrupt process. And in sharp contrast to the highly fragmented independence movements of Nigeria and Zaire, for example, the nationalist movement in India was embodied in a single national party (the Congress), which encompassed a wide variety of other parties and interest groups and had enormous prestige. Even the tragic and painful partition of colonial India into two countries

eliminated a major source of internal discord as independent India was born. Ethnic- and religious-based conflict in Africa was, by contrast, just beginning. Finally, Indian statehood could be built on cultural and political traditions rooted in the experience of the Mughal Empire and other all-India political experiments. African states, by contrast, were almost wholly artificial creations with almost no connection to earlier patterns of African historical development.

Other explanations for the initial abandonment of Western-style democracy in Africa have focused on cultural factors. Some have suggested that African political traditions, based on communal rather than individualistic values and concerned with achieving local consensus rather than majority rule across a large country, were not compatible with the competitiveness of large-scale party politics.

Many Africans have claimed that Western political institutions were simply inadequate for the tasks of development confronting the new states. Creating national unity, they argued, was certainly more difficult when competing political parties identified primarily with particular ethnic or "tribal" groups, as has frequently been the case in Africa. And the immense problems that inevitably accompanied the early stages of economic development may have been compounded by the heavy demands of a political system based on universal suffrage. Certainly Europe did not begin its modernizing process with such a system. Why, many Africans have asked, should they be expected to do so?

These have been some of the larger explanations for the initial decline of Western-style democracy in independent Africa. Whatever the merits of these ideas, three immediate conditions undermined the popular support of many post-independence governments in Africa, made political stability difficult to achieve, and stimulated a search for new directions in Africa's political development. These included widespread economic failure, growing social inequality, and frequent ethnic conflict.

Economic Failure and Political Legitimacy

By almost any measure, Africa's economic performance since independence has been poor. The overall growth rate of sub-Saharan African economies on a per-person basis has been only 0.2 percent per year between 1965 and 1990, far lower than any other developing area. The agricultural picture has been especially disappointing. Whereas per-capita food production has grown in much of Asia and Latin America, Africa has been the only part of the world in which these figures have shown a decline. By 1980, the average person had only 80 percent of the homegrown food that had been available in 1961. This has meant massive food imports, widespread malnutrition, and vulnerability to famine, which broke out in epidemic proportions in 1972–1974, in 1983–1985, and again in the early 1990s. By 1985, the United Nations estimated that some ten million Africans had left their homes to look for food, often in relief camps. In 1983, only Zimbabwe among the sub-Saharan countries produced enough food to feed its own people, but a decade later it too was importing food. The urban-industrial picture has not been any more encouraging. Rapid urban growth, together with very modest industrial growth, has produced massive unemployment and poverty in the cities. During the 1970s, some thirty-three million people were added to the work force in Africa, but only about 60 percent of them were able to find regular paid employment.

Students denied the white-collar careers they expected; urban migrants with little opportunity for work; farmers paid low prices for their cash crops; consumers resentful about shortages and inflation; and millions of impoverished and malnourished peasants pushed to the brink of starvation—these were people for whom independence was unable to fulfill even the most minimal of expectations, let alone the grandiose visions of a better life that so many had embraced in the early 1960s. Because modern governments everywhere staked their popularity on economic performance, it is little wonder that many Africans became disaffected and withdrew their support from governments they had enthusiastically endorsed only a few years earlier. Political parties that had acted to foster discontent and express popular grievances during the colonial era now found themselves suppressing dissent and counseling patience. It was a difficult adjustment, and many regimes, unable to make it, were swept away and replaced by others eager to try. Political stability in such circumstances was a rare commodity, and democracy was a casualty of that instability.

Social Inequality and Class Resentment

Economic failure did not affect everyone to the same extent, and for some, independence offered great opportunities for acquiring status, position, and wealth. Thus, the resentments born of social inequality have compounded the frustrations of poverty and contributed to political instability in Africa. Nigeria's great novelist Chinua Achebe described the situation in this way:

> The trouble with our new nation . . . was that none of us had been indoors long enough. . . . We had all been in the rain together until yesterday. Then a handful of us— the smart and the lucky and hardly ever the best—had scrambled for the one shelter our former rulers had left, and had taken it over and barricaded themselves in. And from within they sought to persuade the rest through numerous loudspeakers, that . . . all argument should cease and the whole people speak with one voice.[2]

Who were "the smart and the lucky"? Unlike in Latin America and parts of Asia, those who benefited most from independence were not large landowners, for most African societies simply did not have an established class whose wealth was based in land. Rather, they were members of the relatively well-educated elite who had found high-paying jobs in the growing bureaucracies of the newly independent states. This was "the one shelter" left by colonial rulers, and it grew very rapidly in the years following independence. In the Congo, for example, government spending on salaries almost doubled in the four years after independence, while in Zaire, the government consumed an amazing 59 percent of the country's production in 1974. This enormous growth in state spending generated thousands of jobs in party and government bureaucracies and, in the process, gave rise to a "state bourgeoisie," which some have identified as Africa's ruling class.

The privileges of this dominant class have been widely resented. In Kenya, such people were called *waBenzi* because of the Mercedes-Benz cars in which they were chauffeured about. Government ministers in many countries earned the title "Mr. Ten Percent," a reference to the bribes or "gifts" they received from private contractors working for the state. The enormous gap between this dominant class, which controlled the political apparatus, and the rest of society contributed a great deal to the weakness of the state in Africa. Despite independence, the state remained "foreign" to many Africans.

Resentment broke out in Zaire between 1964 and 1968 in the form of a widespread peasant rebellion calling for a "second independence" against the "new whites" of the elite class. At least briefly, the rebellion swept the government's authority from half of this immense country. Urban unrest and riots in Congo-Brazzaville, Ghana, Liberia, Ethiopia, and elsewhere paved the way for military takeovers and expressed the resentments of the poor against the extravagance of the rich. But with the possible exception of Ethiopia, nowhere in post-independence Africa has class conflict produced a popular revolutionary movement such as that in China (1949), Cuba (1959), or Nicaragua (1979). The absence of well-established classes or strong social organizations, independent of state control, has enabled many governments to maintain repressive and tyrannical regimes. Inequality in Africa has been more often felt and expressed in ethnic terms than in class terms. Dissatisfied and frustrated Africans have been far more likely to think of themselves as a deprived "tribe" than as a deprived "class."

Tribes and Politics

Ethnic or regional hostilities have been at the heart of most political conflict and instability in African societies since independence. Extended civil wars in Chad, Sudan, Ethiopia, Rwanda, Angola, Mozambique, Nigeria, and Zaire, and in the early 1990s in Liberia and Somalia, represent its most violent expression, but almost everywhere, ethnic conflict has been a central element of political life. Chapter 22 outlines the process by which modern ethnic identities developed out of the uneven social changes taking place within the artificial and culturally diverse colonial states. That sense of ethnicity has remained strong after independence, according to sociologists David Wiley and Marylee Crofts, "because it is a means of identifying people, of categorizing strangers, of obtaining favors, and of acquiring help in times of insecurity."[3] Far more than national identity, ethnic loyalties at the subnational level came to define the meaningful social groups within which most Africans operated.

But this pattern of cultural identity has become increasingly politicized since independence, as the common enemy of colonial rule was removed and as Africans had to sort out, often very quickly, the fundamental question of politics everywhere: Who gets what? The location of a new road, school, or factory; the taking of a census; the appointment of ministers, school principals, or university officials; and, above all, the holding of national elections—all of these occasions served to activate ethnic fears and heighten ethnic tensions.

Many in the West have called these rivalries "tribalism" and have regarded them as reflecting ancient and backward-looking loyalties, unique to Africa. On the contrary, they are similar to patterns of ethnic nationalism found in many parts of the world. While these forms of community may draw selectively on early cultural or historical patterns, they are most often of fairly recent origin and reflect the competition for scarce modern resources (jobs, school places, seats in parliament, and so on), rather than ancient feuds. What makes the expression of ethnic hostility in Africa different from India's culturally based conflicts is that it has occurred in deteriorating economic circumstances and in far weaker state structures, commanding much less popular support or legitimacy. Thus, ethnic conflict in Africa has been more destructive and destabilizing, resulting in the early 1990s in the total collapse of state authority in Liberia and Somalia.

Nigeria's first decade of independence provides a useful case study in the dynamics of ethnic conflict. The country achieved its freedom from British rule in 1960 as a federal state and a parliamentary democracy; it had three major political parties, each closely identified with one of three regions. The Northern People's Congress (NPC) represented that half of the country, and particularly its primary ethnic group, the Hausa, a conservative and highly stratified Muslim society whose leaders feared the domination of the more aggressive and highly educated southerners. But the southerners were sharply divided between the Igbo of the eastern region, represented by the National Council of Nigeria and the Cameroons (NCNC), and the Yoruba, located in the western region, whose major political party was the Action Group (AG). Within each region, smaller parties spoke for minority ethnic groups. Unlike in India, where the Congress party provided a national framework for political accommodation, bargaining, and compromise, Nigeria had parties that were primarily regional.

From the beginning, therefore, politics was a matter of ethnic alliances. The stakes were high, and both federal and regional elections were marked by violence and fraud. In 1964, a national census raised ethnic tensions even higher, for it found that over half of Nigeria's fifty-five million people lived in the north. This meant that the north could dominate the Federal House of Assembly without southern assistance, and it provoked the two southern parties to join in a Grand Alliance with several smaller parties from the north. It was in the context of growing ethnic violence and widespread resentment at the blatant corruption of the political elite that Nigeria's first military coup occurred, in January 1966. At first, it was widely welcomed, and its stated aim—"to establish a strong, united, and prosperous nation free from corruption and internal strife"—was generally acclaimed.

Within a few months, however, the ethnic prism through which almost all political action was perceived seriously changed this initial perception. By May 1966, northerners in particular had come to view the coup as an attempt at Igbo domination. Many of the military leaders of the coup were Igbo, and although a number of Hausa and Yoruba politicians had been killed in the takeover, no Igbo politicians had lost their lives. In late July, a second military coup took place, led this time by junior officers from the north, thus returning political power in Nigeria to northern hands. All of this had inflamed ethnic feeling to the breaking point, and in a number of northern cities, enraged mobs attacked Igbo traders, officials, and settlers, killing thousands and forcing the evacuation of some two million Igbo to their homeland in the southeastern part of the country.

Despite efforts at conciliation, the Igbo felt threatened with nothing less than genocide in their own country and so declared their independence from Nigeria in the separate state of Biafra in May 1967. A bloody civil war lasted until 1970, when a Nigerian victory ended Biafra's attempted secession and a generous peace settlement eased its reintegration into a united country.

Many African states avoided outright civil war and coped with ethnic conflict through political means. In Zambia, Kenneth Kaunda governed the

Refugees by the hundreds of thousands flee Rwanda's 1994 civil war between the Tutsi and Hutu peoples. *Reuters/Bettmann*

country almost single-handedly from 1964 to 1991 and was regarded for a time as the "father" of his country, standing above the rivalries of its many ethnic groups. But Kaunda carefully balanced appointments to the cabinet, civil service, military, and the country's sole political party, ensuring that each major ethnic group was represented.

New Directions

Under the pressures of economic failure, social inequality, and sharp ethnic conflict, the transplanted democracies of the early independence era failed to take root, and Africans found themselves required to develop alternative political structures and practices. From the mid-1960s on, there has been much experimentation, some of which has led to frustration, dead ends, and even disaster, but other attempts have produced hopeful new beginnings.

The most common new direction involved government by soldiers. An established pattern of political life in Latin America, by the early 1980s the military had intervened in at least thirty of Africa's forty-six independent states and actively governed more than half of them (see Map 24.1). Usually, the military took power in a crisis, after the civilian government had lost most of its popular support. The soldiers often claimed that the nation was in grave danger, that corrupt civilian politicians had led the country to the brink of chaos, and that only the military had the discipline and strength to put things right. Thus, they swept aside the old political parties and constitutions and vowed to begin anew. But in most cases, military government continued in another form the rule of the Westernized elite. Most army officers were themselves part of this elite, and they had to depend on educated civil service officials to govern the country. Few military regimes acted to curtail elite privileges in a serious way. In the Congo, for example, a new military government in 1968 awarded 20 percent to 40 percent pay increases to members of the army and the civil service. This was not an exception.

Although most military regimes have provided little real opportunity for popular participation in the political process, several African countries—Tanzania, Kenya, and the Ivory Coast among them—have conducted interesting experiments in one-party democracy. These have been very different from the one-party systems of the Soviet Union and East European states, where little real choice has been permitted. In Tanzania since the mid-1960s, for example, local committees of citizens have selected several candidates for the national parliament in each of the country's election districts, all of them members of the country's ruling party. During the campaigns preceding elections, candidates have been forbidden to discuss ethnic, religious, or racial issues and required to speak in Swahili, the national language, rather than in one of Tanzania's many local languages. Despite these restrictions, the elections, held every five years, have resulted in a large turnover in members of parliament as voters expressed their dissatisfaction with incumbents. Innovative arrangements such as this represent an attempt to provide opportunities for participation and renewal, while sharply limiting the divisive effects of political competition in new and fragile states.

The most recent new direction in African political life has been a quite remarkable resurgence of democracy, as parties, elections, popular movements, and new constitutions reappeared in the 1980s and early 1990s in many countries. Free and competitive elections have been held in Benin, Gabon, the Ivory Coast, Malawi, and Zambia. Nigeria's military government initiated a carefully managed return to civilian democracy, but then abruptly canceled it following disputed elections in 1993. Grass-roots movements have put great pressure on long-time dictators in Zaire and Kenya. Authoritarian Marxist regimes have been transformed or ousted in Ethiopia, Angola, and Mozambique, while many other countries have held national conferences to legalize opposition parties and a free press and to initiate a dialogue among competing groups.

How can we explain this rather sudden, though still fragile, revival of democracy in Africa? Perhaps the most important internal factor is the evident failure of authoritarian governments to remedy the disastrous economic situation. Disaffected students, religious leaders, urban workers, and women's groups have joined in a variety of grass-roots movements to demand democratic change as a means to a better life. This pressure from below for political change has reflected the growing strength of civil society in many African countries. In Kenya, for example, there were some 25,000 local women's groups operating in 1988. Churches have become involved in environmental and agricultural issues and have in certain places taken the lead in opposing oppressive governments. These and other organizations independent of the state have provided a social foundation for the renewal of democracy in Africa.

Such movements found encouragement in the establishment of a democratic state in newly independent Namibia in 1990, while the demands for democracy as part of the South African struggle against apartheid prompted opposition leaders in other African countries to ask for nothing less. Furthermore, the revival of democracy in Eastern Europe provided a stimulus and international legitimacy for African demands, while the end of the Cold War reduced the willingness of the superpowers to underwrite their authoritarian client states. Democracy, in short, was no longer seen primarily as an imposed Western system, but as a universal political principle to which Africans could also aspire.

The variety of Africa's political forms—one-party or multiparty democracy, military rule or personal tyranny—suggests that the search for an appropriate political structure is far from over. But the test of all political systems in independent Africa has been that of development. Can a way be found to lift the burden of a crushing poverty from the backs of Africa's peoples?

The Dilemma of Development: Identifying the Obstacles

For individuals living in the highly developed countries of the late twentieth century, it requires imagination even to begin to grasp the kind of poverty and underdevelopment characteristic of many African societies. Even the images of starving children and emaciated adults that appear occasionally in the mass media present only the most extreme cases. "The everyday reality of malnutrition," writes journalist Paul Harrison, "is less dramatic. It is adults scraping through, physically and mentally fatigued and vulnerable to illness. It is children—often dying, not so frequently of hunger alone as of hunger working hand in hand with sickness; but more often surviving

impaired for life."[4] It is 50 percent of Kenya's young people who cannot find work after leaving school. It is rapid population growth but without the corresponding economic growth to provide for minimum needs. And it is all of this occurring in societies where advertising billboards, radios, sometimes television, and the extravagant life-style of both foreign and local elites loudly proclaim that such conditions are not the fate of all. This is "modern poverty," the product of partial and unbalanced development, and quite distinct from the "original poverty" of traditional African societies.

What factors produce and maintain this kind of underdevelopment? Does it derive from the physical limits of the African environment, from the continuing legacy of colonial rule, from the constraints of the world economy, or from weak societies and misguided policies that Africans have shaped themselves? Responsible people do not always agree about the answers, but few would dispute that these are the central questions about Africa in the late twentieth century.

Nature, Tradition, and Famine: The Environment and African Development

The starting point for any analysis of African underdevelopment lies in its natural conditions and economic history. A combination of technological and environmental limitations (see Chapter 21) meant that Africa began the process of modern development with less accumulated wealth and fewer commercialized economies than many other areas of the developing world. Part of the low productivity of African agriculture was due to the quality of its tropical soils, for they are generally thin, poor in nutrients, and vulnerable to erosion by heavy tropical storms. And rainfall in many places is variable and unpredictable. Precolonial agricultural societies adapted to these conditions by using a simple technology: by maintaining the groundcover of forest, grass, and shrubs; by keeping population low; and by practicing shifting cultivation, which allowed long recovery periods for fields. But these practices did not allow the same degree of wealth to be accumulated in Africa as in the major civilizations of Eura-

VOICES
Left Behind in Morocco

One of the major features of unequal development in Africa, both within and between countries, has been the migration of men to distant sites in search of work. The following poem, written by an anonymous Moroccan woman in the 1970s, poignantly captures the feelings of a young wife whose husband left for work in Europe.

Germany, Belgium, France
and Netherlands
Where are you situated?
Where are you?
Where can I find you?
I have never seen your countries, I do not
speak your language.
I have heard it said that you are beautiful,
I have heard it said that you are clean.
I am afraid, afraid that my love forgets
me in your paradise.
I ask you to save him for me.
One day after our wedding he left,
with his suitcase in his hand, his eyes looking
ahead.

You must not say that he is bad or aggressive;
I have seen his tears, deep in his heart, when he
went away.
He looked at me with the eyes of a child;
He gave me his small empty hand and asked me:
"What should I do?"
I could not utter a word; my heart bled
for him. . . .
With you he stays one year, with me just one
month,
to you he gives his health and sweat,
to me he only comes to recuperate.
Then he leaves again to work for you, to beautify
you as a bride, each day anew.
And I, I wait; I am like a flower that
withers, more each day. . . .
I ask you: give him back to me.

Source: *Bulletin of the Committee of Moroccan Workers in Holland,* 1978, quoted in Hazel Johnson and Henry Bernstein, eds., *Third World Lives of Struggle* (London: Heinemann, 1982), pp. 173–74. Translated by Gavin Hudson.

---

sia. Those who emphasize these natural and traditional obstacles to Africa's modern economic growth see its current underdevelopment as rooted in its original poverty.

However, the colonial intrusion dramatically altered these traditional adaptations to the environment, as a rapidly growing African population increasingly responded to the demands of the world economy. Intensive cultivation and annual harvesting of such cash crops as peanuts, tobacco, and cotton permanently removed the groundcover from large areas and prevented the natural renewal of the soil. By the 1950s, population growth and widespread cash-crop agriculture made shifting cultivation impossible in many areas and required peasant farmers to work the same land repeatedly. The export of timber products and the increased demand for firewood and charcoal produced extensive deforestation, with serious effects not only on the soil but also, in

some places, on rainfall patterns and the underground water table. "Exhaustion of the soil is now so widespread," writes one scholar, "that it makes a good deal of sense to attribute some of the decline in Africa's per-capita food production to the deterioration of the land base brought about by overuse."[5]

Such pressures have pushed more and more people onto marginal lands, poorly suited for agriculture in the best of circumstances and extremely vulnerable to crop failures when the unpredictable rains fail to come. In 1992, for example, a devastating drought in southern Africa destroyed 80 percent of Namibia's maize crop and forced the country to spend precious foreign currency on imported food rather than development projects. The frequent result of such conditions has been famine and all that accompanies it— mass starvation, extensive migration in search of food, political crisis, and international attention. In Ethiopia, Sudan, Mozambique, and Somalia, bitter civil wars have exacerbated famine and hindered international efforts to relieve it. Triggered rather than caused by drought, famine is the end product of a long historical process of impoverishment and social conflict, not simply the product of natural or traditional conditions. Indeed, the Sahel region, which has borne the worst of recent famines, had supported the richest and most sophisticated African societies and kingdoms in precolonial times. Extensive famine conditions in 1972–1974, again in 1983–1985, and yet again in the early 1990s suggest that Africa has become more rather than less vulnerable to famine in recent decades.

Africa and the World Economy: External Obstacles to Development

One of the central requirements for modern economic development is capital, particularly in the form of international currency with which to buy imports needed for development—fertilizer, trucks, lathes, typewriters, hydroelectric equipment, medicine, and the many other things that Africa does not produce for itself. Participation in the world economy has been the major means by which independent African states have sought to generate this capital and acquire these goods. But many feel that the world economy has operated to Africa's disadvantage. In this view, independence has done little to alter the continent's weak and dependent position in the global economic system, and its poor economic performance therefore may be the result of factors largely beyond its control.

Foreign trade has been by far the major source of capital for African countries seeking modern development. However, most countries came to independence with economies that relied heavily on the export of one or two products. In 1967, for example, Gabon depended on oil, manganese, and timber for 82 percent of its exports; Senegal on peanuts for 66 percent; Zambia on copper for 93 percent; Chad on cotton for 83 percent; and Ghana on cocoa for 69 percent. Such heavy dependence on a very small number of products meant that these economies were extremely vulnerable to changes in the demand for and price of their few exports. Frequently, these prices fluctuated widely. In 1954, shortly before Ghana's independence, its major export crop of co-

coa fetched $1,575 per ton. Eleven years later, just before the military coup that ousted the Nkrumah regime, the price for cocoa had fallen to $256 per ton. During the 1970s, the purchasing power of mineral exports declined on average 7.7 percent a year. This unfavorable relationship between the price of African imports and the price of African exports is what economists mean by "deteriorating terms of trade." It has represented a heavy burden on many African economies, one over which they have almost no control. President Julius Nyerere of Tanzania provided a concrete example of this situation when he estimated that his country had to export 38 tons of sisal to buy a 7-ton truck in 1972, but in 1982 the same truck required the sale of 134 tons of sisal.

The dramatic rise in oil prices during the 1970s further eroded the purchasing power of African agricultural exports. The World Bank calculated that whereas in 1970 oil imports absorbed 4.4 percent of African export earnings, by 1980 African states had to spend 23 percent of their export earnings to pay their oil bill. It is not surprising that many Africans have seen their international trading relations as a matter of running hard just to stay even.

This situation has stimulated many countries to increase export production, particularly of agricultural crops, even if this meant that less good land was available for the growing of food crops. Although experts disagree as to whether cash-crop farming limits local food production, the experience of five countries of the Sahel hardest hit by the famines of the early 1980s (Burkina-Fasso, Mali, Niger, Senegal, and Chad) strongly suggests this possibility. In 1983–1984, a year of severe drought and famine, these countries produced a record 154 million tons of cotton (compared to 22.7 million tons in 1961–1962) and imported a record 1.77 million tons of grain to feed their people (up from 200,000 tons in the early 1960s). That farmers could grow cotton but not food suggests that economic policies and relationships, rather than natural disaster alone, were at the core of Africa's agricultural crisis.

The general poverty of African states together with their desperate need for development drove most of them to borrow heavily from Western banks, governments, and international agencies. Debts that piled up in the 1960s and 1970s came home to roost in the 1980s. In 1984, for example, Nigeria spent 44 percent of its foreign-exchange earnings from the sale of oil to pay the interest on its $22 billion foreign debt. And as the market for oil contracted in the early 1980s, so too did its ability to import goods necessary for its development. These dry statistics translated into deepened poverty for millions of ordinary Africans.

Closer to Home: Internal Obstacles to Development

Clearly not all of Africa's problems derived directly from the world economy. The economic weakness and Westernized values of African middle-class elites represented an important internal obstacle to their countries' development. Unlike the middle class of nineteenth-century Europe, which was based on the ownership of industrial capital, Africa's dominant class gained its wealth from holding office and from the opportunities for corruption and private advantage that such positions provided. With the possible exceptions of Nigeria and Kenya, there has been little sign of a local African capitalist class with the resources to undertake major industrialization. Nonetheless, this elite, reflecting its colonial origins, has assimilated Western tastes and consumer values. Much of its wealth, therefore, is not invested productively in the local economy but is spent for cars, televisions, tape recorders, and other foreign-produced luxuries that have to be imported at great expense.

With Western models of development in mind, many African governments have invested in prestigious projects such as national airlines, elaborate foreign embassies, and the most modern of medical facilities, usually available only to wealthy urban dwellers. President Nyerere of Tanzania wrote about the results of such efforts:

> Judging by our actions, our national objective seems to be to "catch up with the North," and development seems to mean buying the most elaborate building and the latest invention in every field, regardless of our capacity to pay for it—even to maintain it. Thus we have created a continuing dependency on the importation of technology and spare parts, which then requires us to produce for export regardless of our people's present hunger and present needs.[6]

Women's groups affiliated with the African National Congress demand a role in the negotiations leading to elections and the end of apartheid in South Africa.
Reuters/Bettmann

Such efforts to put the industrial cart before the agricultural horse are now widely viewed as a major policy error in many African countries.

With a weak capitalist class, it has fallen to African states to assume major responsibility for development and to undertake far more extensive activities than European governments had to deal with at an early stage of their development process. Since independence, African states have become directly involved in marketing, banking, transportation, mining, manufacturing, and in some cases, agriculture.

Despite their frequently authoritarian character, however, many of these states have been weak, inefficient, corrupt, and possessed of very limited administrative ability. Some of them—particularly former Portuguese and Belgian colonies—came to independence with very few trained or experienced people. In Zaire, for example, there were only three Africans, but some 4,600 Europeans, in top civil service positions when independence came. The need to Africanize the bureaucracy as rapidly as possible often led to ill-prepared persons in top positions. And many heads of state have remarked that government officials are all too often incompetent, indifferent to their public responsibilities, and inclined to treat their positions as private fiefdoms. The mismatch between the many development functions that governments are expected to perform and their limited capacity to do so effectively remains a serious internal constraint on African development.

Weak or shaky governments naturally cater to their most powerful and vocal constituents. Since these are primarily urban dwellers—salaried officials, industrial workers, and the city poor—it is not surprising that the development policies of many African states have reflected an urban bias, which has neglected the rural areas and been partly responsible for the deterioration of African agriculture.

Almost everywhere, cities have better schools, health facilities, freshwater supplies, and public amenities than in the rural areas. Government policies to ensure cheap food for the cities have meant low prices for farmers, and in many places peasants have withdrawn into subsistence or black-market agriculture, thus making the country even more dependent on food imports. Highly trained people—teachers, doctors, and administrators—vigorously resist appointment to the rural areas where they are needed most, for their career interests are better served in an urban setting, to say nothing of their nat-

ural desire for the comforts and pleasures of city life. Such practices, which amount to an exploitation of the countryside by the cities, are rooted in internal political realities. "We must establish a better balance between the city and the countryside," said President Abdou Diouf of Senegal in 1983. "But I cannot do it, because I do not have the organized political power in the rural areas to counter the organized political power in the urban areas."[7]

The development process has been characterized by male bias as well as urban bias. Women represent close to half of the agricultural labor force in Africa, but they are responsible for the vast majority of food production. Increased private ownership of land by men and their control of the more lucrative cash and export crops have frequently pushed women onto plots that are "smaller, located on the less desirable land in the village, overtilled and left fallow for shorter periods, and furthest from home."[8] Furthermore, government services for farmers, such as credit and extension, have focused on cash and export crops, which men control, rather than on food crops, which are largely the domain of women. Agricultural extension agents usually have been male and often not very sensitive to women's role in the food system. When women were targeted for assistance, it was usually as homemakers rather than as food producers. Thus, the economic resource that women farmers represent has frequently been neglected, and the lives of women themselves often deteriorated in the process of development.

Rapid population growth has been another factor affecting African development. With over five hundred million people by the mid-1980s, Africa represents about 11 percent of the world's population. But it is growing faster than any other major region of the world. At over 3 percent a year, its growth rate is more than double that of China. Many fear that the output of food, schools, jobs, and government services simply cannot keep up with that rate of population growth. Indeed, during the 1970s and early 1980s, food production did not keep up, and by 1985, an estimated 170 million Africans were being fed with imported grains.

But are these high rates of population growth the cause or the result of continuing poverty in Africa? With 10 percent to 15 percent of African babies dying before their first birthday, there is a strong incentive to have many children, to ensure that several survive. And in conditions of low wages and economic insecurity, children represent potential contributors to family income, a sign of male potency, and in some cases, a link to their parents' spirits after death. The absence of much economic security and opportunity outside the family reinforces traditional values that put a premium on fertility. And not until the 1980s did African governments even begin to develop serious population control programs.

A tragic counterpoint to Africa's rapid population growth, and a further obstacle to its economic development, lies in the massive spread of AIDS, especially in the central and southern parts of the continent. By the end of the 1980s, some 2.5 million people were infected and there was little sign that the disease, spread largely by heterosexual contact in Africa, was waning. In some urban areas of central Africa, up to 30 percent of the population was infected. Because most of the victims are urban dwellers in their twenties and thirties, the disease is killing the most highly trained and economically active section of the population. It is also putting an added strain on already limited resources available for health care.

There is a danger in thinking about African development only in terms of "obstacles," because we may come to view Africa as a helpless victim of its physical environment, of its position in the world economy, or of its domestic structures and policies. But history moves through human efforts to cope with obstacles. Africans have been performers as well as audience in the drama of development, as their search for more effective strategies clearly demonstrates.

The Dilemma of Development: Searching for Strategies

Most of the newly independent African states initially accepted the capitalist framework inherited from their colonial rulers and confidently expected that capitalism would transform and modernize their societies as it had done in Europe a century earlier. But during the 1960s and 1970s, faced with the enormous obstacles to development, many African states became highly critical of capitalism and adopted in its place an African version of socialism, while oth-

ers claimed some variation of Marxism as their guide to development.[9] By the end of the 1980s, however, such solutions to the development problem, which relied on heavy state involvement, were widely seen as failures. Country after country returned to the market as a means of promoting growth, stimulated in part by the failure of communism in Eastern Europe and the Soviet Union. In the economic sphere, as in the political, Africa's history since independence has been one of experimentation and adaptation.

Capitalism in an African Setting

Capitalism in independent Africa has been far more widely practiced than celebrated. Because of its historical association with colonial conquest and foreign exploitation, capitalism has often been a bad word in African political rhetoric, in much the same way that socialism has been taboo in American politics. Nonetheless, over half the states of Africa in the early 1980s still followed an essentially capitalist approach to development, and by the end of the decade most of the rest had begun to reform their economies to favor the free market. Basically, this involved relying on private enterprise and the market forces of supply and demand to stimulate economic growth, on an openness to foreign investment and trade with the West, and on a willingness to accept and even encourage the growth of a wealthy elite, especially if that wealth was derived from successful ventures in trade, commercial agriculture, or manufacturing.

However, African capitalism of the late twentieth century was different in several important ways from its counterpart in the early stages of European development. The state has played a far more active role in modern African economies than it did in those of nineteenth-century Europe. This is partly due to the weakness of the private sector in most African states, but it also reflects global expectations that governments will assume responsibility for the welfare of their people, expectations not widely held before the twentieth century. Whereas liberal democracy developed in tandem with capitalism in Europe, until the late 1980s there was little indication of a similar relationship in Africa, where democracy has been a fragile transplant in a harsh environment. Finally, African capitalist states face a problem the early European capitalist societies did not: how to protect their new and fragile economies from total domination by the already developed and enormously powerful Western economies, while also remaining open to trade and investment opportunities in the international marketplace.

The example of the Ivory Coast, clearly among the most successful of African capitalist states, illustrates the dilemmas of this approach to development. The country's economic growth rates were remarkable by any comparison, averaging 7 percent to 8 percent a year during the 1960s and 1970s, and including an industrial growth rate as high as 15 percent per year. Despite rapid population growth, per-capita income in the mid-1980s was about double the African average of non-oil-producing states. For the most part, this growth was based on export crops—especially cocoa and coffee—produced by over 500,000 small-scale capitalist farmers and an important logging and timber industry financed largely by foreign investment. Finally, the Ivory Coast has enjoyed remarkable political stability as a one-party state under the leadership of Felix Houphouet-Boigny.

The other side of the Ivory Coast miracle has been a substantial and continuing dependence on France, its former colonial ruler. The number of French living in the country grew from 10,000 at independence to about 50,000 in the early 1980s; 75 percent of its trade was still in foreign hands in 1981; and its indebtedness to foreign lenders grew from $267 million in 1970 to over $6 billion in 1984. Furthermore, there is a real question as to whether an Ivorian capitalist class is developing outside of the rural areas. In 1978, about 46 percent of investment in the modern sector of the economy came from foreigners, 47 percent from the government of the Ivory Coast, and only 7 percent from private investors in the country.

Critics also have pointed to great inequalities in Ivorian society. In 1971, Europeans represented 6.8 percent of the salaried urban work force but received 32 percent of total wages. During the 1970s, while industry was growing at a very impressive 11 percent per year, the share of national income available to the poorest 60 percent of the population dropped from 30 percent to 22 percent. Probably most exploited have been the thousands of immigrant laborers from surrounding countries, who make up a very poorly paid agricultural work force. President Houphouet-Boigny was clear about the priorities of capitalist development: "We do not believe in giving priority to the distribution of wealth but wish to encourage the

Celebrations of socialism, such as this rally in Zimbabwe, diminished sharply in Africa during the 1980s as free market economic policies were implemented across the continent. *Robert K. Wheeler/Sygma*

creation and multiplication of wealth first of all. . . . We are following a policy of state capitalism."[10]

During the 1980s, that policy fell on hard times as indebtedness and declining prices for coffee and cocoa slowed economic growth and fueled pressures for political change. Multiparty elections in 1990, widely regarded as flawed, returned Houphouet-Boigny and his party to power but raised questions about the prospects for continuing stability in the country, particularly following the "old man's" death in 1993.

African-Style Socialism

Not everyone agreed to the tradeoffs of a capitalist strategy—high growth rates in return for greater dependence and inequality—and many were skeptical that capitalism could do the job at any price. During the 1960s, therefore, a number of African states—Ghana, Mali, Guinea, Algeria, and Tanzania among them—began to express their development strategies in terms of socialism. But it was not a socialism that Karl Marx or his nineteenth-century European followers would have recognized. Rather, it was an effort to find a form of socialism that would be compatible with African culture and historical conditions.

To its major philosophers, such as L. S. Senghor of Senegal and Julius Nyerere of Tanzania, African socialism was rooted in traditional African society and values, which, they argued, had been cooperative, communal, egalitarian, and without conflicting classes and individual greed. Whereas Marx and his followers had believed that modern socialism could be achieved only by going through a capitalist stage and enduring severe class conflict in the process, African Socialists sought to avoid these developments at all costs. It was both possible and desirable, they felt, to move directly from traditional communal life to one of modern socialism and to apply the old values of mutual sharing and equality to a new national economy. All of this meant a greater willingness than the capitalist states showed to nationalize major segments of the economy, to promote radical reform in the rural areas, to limit the privileges of the elite, and to mobilize the population through an active single party.

More than any other African state, Tanzania shaped its development strategy to realize these goals. Under the leadership of Julius Nyerere, one of modern Africa's most respected figures, the country remained a "mixed economy" with an important private sector. But by the mid-1970s, the state controlled about 80 percent of medium- and large-scale economic activity. Without trained and experienced managers, however, there was much inefficiency, corruption, and many unprofitable enterprises, some of which were later returned to private hands. Tanzania's commitment to equality was reflected in a strict leadership code that forbade top party and government employees from holding directorships or shares in private firms or from owning rental property. Furthermore, sharp restrictions on the import of luxury goods such as private cars made it difficult for the political elite to maintain the kind of extravagant life-style common in capitalist states.

But the most important and controversial feature of Tanzania's Socialist program lay in the rural areas, where the government sought to relocate a scattered peasantry into compact villages, to which modern services could be more readily provided, and to promote communal agriculture within them. A mixture of persuasion and outright coercion resulted in the creation of some seven thousand *ujaama,* or Socialist villages, accommodating over thirteen million people by the end of the 1970s. The provision of educational and health services to these villages has been impressive. The country made substantial strides in promoting literacy and was moving toward universal primary education. But the economic and social consequences of this experiment in rural socialism were less successful. The speed and sometimes the force with which *ujaama* villages were established resulted in sharp declines in agricultural production. And peasants have greatly resisted government pressures for communal farming, much preferring to work their own family farms. In the decade of 1974–1984, the country suffered a negative rate of per-capita GNP growth.

When President Nyerere stepped down in late 1985, Tanzania began to modify, if not dismantle, its Socialist program. In 1986, it dissolved the largest state-run marketing organization and came to an agreement with the International Monetary Fund about revamping its economic policies to favor free enterprise. Various state-run manufacturing enterprises have also been privatized. A reasonable assessment of Tanzania's experiment, and of African socialism generally, comes from historian John

Iliffe: "African governments have shown that they can prevent capitalism; they have not yet shown that they can replace it with anything else that will release their people's energies."[11]

Conclusion: Time and Perspective

Most contemporary discussion about Africa has been guarded, somber, and often pessimistic. But after fewer than three decades of independence, is this attitude fair? Is the judgment premature?

There have, after all, been successes. Massive investment in education has raised continental literacy rates from about 5 percent of the population in 1960 to 50 percent in 1990. Life expectancy at birth has increased from 39 to 51 years, during the same period. Goods regarded as luxuries in the 1950s—toilet soap, canned milk, transistor radios, bicycles—became necessities by the 1980s and were widely owned. Nor should the cultural gains of independence be minimized. Literature, arts, theater, and the study of history benefited from the creative energies stimulated by independence and the removal of colonial racism, as did the emergence of popular music, dance, and cultural festivals.

Furthermore, independence has produced a greater clarity and realism about what is possible, about what works and what doesn't in terms of development. There was a greater willingness among African officials and intellectuals to take responsibility for their own mistakes, rather than simply bemoaning the injustices of colonialism or the world economy. By the early 1990s, for example, almost all shades of opinion agreed that greater attention to rural needs and food production was necessary. Moreover, a general consensus has emerged that the key to African agricultural recovery lies in assisting the small family farmer, and especially women farmers, who produce, after all, the vast majority of the continent's homegrown food. And a widespread skepticism has grown about the usefulness of Western, high-technology models of development, as well as about those that rely heavily on centralized government control of economic enterprises. Many African countries have become more democratic and supportive of private enterprise. Finally, more governments are emphasizing the importance of active population-control measures.

None of this diminishes in the least the policy failures, endemic poverty, and suffering that millions of Africans continue to endure. It poses, rather, the question of perspective: Should we view the first three decades of independence as a prelude to permanent backwardness or as the difficult initial stage in a long journey toward more effective development?

Notes

1. Basil Davidson, *Let Freedom Come: Africa in Modern History* (Boston: Little, Brown, 1978), p. 284.

2. Chinua Achebe, *A Man of the People* (Garden City, N.Y.: Doubleday, 1967), pp. 34–35.

3. David Wiley and Marylee Crofts, *Africa* (Guilford, Conn.: Dushkin Publishing Group, 1984), p. 71.

4. Paul Harrison, *Inside the Third World* (New York: Penguin, 1981), p. 261.

5. Michael F. Lofchie, "Africa's Agrarian Malaise," in *African Independence: The First Twenty-Five Years,* ed. Gwendolyn Carter and Patrick O'Meara (Bloomington: Indiana University Press, 1985), p. 165.

6. Quoted in Wiley and Crofts, *Africa,* p. 49.

7. Quoted in *World Development Forum* 3 (30 Nov. 1985).

8. Barbara Lewis, "The Impact of Development Policies on Women," in *African Women South of the Sahara,* ed. Margaret Jean Hay and Sharon Stichter (London: Longmans, 1984), p. 176.

9. This approach to African strategies of development is derived from Crawford Young, *Ideology and Development in Africa* (New Haven: Yale University Press, 1982).

10. Quoted in Alexander G. Rondos, "Ivory Coast: The Price of Development," *Africa Report* 24 (Mar.–Apr. 1979): 4.

11. John Iliffe, *The Emergence of African Capitalism* (Minneapolis: University of Minnesota Press, 1983), p. 79.

SUGGESTIONS FOR FURTHER READING: AFRICA

Ayittey, George B. N. *Africa Betrayed,* 1992. (A critical account of post-independence politics.)

Boahen, A. Adu. *African Perspectives on Colonialism,* 1987.

Bohannan, Paul, and Philip Curtin. *Africa and Africans.* 1988. (An overview of African culture and history.)

Carter, Gwendolyn, and Patrick O'Meara. *African Independence: The First Twenty-Five Years.* 1985. (A survey of accomplishments and disappointments by well-respected scholars.)

Collins, Robert O., ed. *Historical Problems of Imperial Africa.* 1994. (Readings in colonial history.)

Curtin, Philip, et al. *African History.* 1978. (A synthesis of much recent scholarship by four highly respected historians.)

Davidson, Basil. *The Black Man's Burden: Africa and the Curse of the Nation State.* 1992. (A review of recent African history with an emphasis on the shortcomings of nationalism and the nation-state.)

Omer-Cooper, J. D. *History of Southern Africa,* 1994. (Examines historical background to apartheid and the upheavals of the 1980s.)

Freund, Bill. *The Making of Contemporary Africa.* 1984. (An interpretation of nineteenth- and twentieth-century African history stressing the evolution of class differences within African society.)

Gann, L. H., and Peter Duignan, eds. *Colonialism in Africa, 1870–1960.* 3 vols. 1969–1971. (A favorable summary of colonial achievements.)

Harrison, Paul. *The Greening of Africa.* 1987. (Addresses the development projects that have worked in Africa.)

Hay, Margaret Jean, and Sharon Stichter. *African Women South of the Sahara.* 1984. (Discusses how social and economic changes have affected African women in the twentieth century.)

July. Robert. *Pre-Colonial Africa: An Economic and Social History.* 1975.

Khapoya, Vincent. *The African Experience,* 1994. (A wide-ranging overview.)

Mallaby, Sebastian. *After Apartheid.* 1993. (A discussion of the issues confronting South Africa as apartheid collapsed.)

Manning, Patrick. *Slavery and African Life.* 1990. (Covers the impact of three distinct slave trades on African societies.)

Mazrui, Ali. *The Africans.* 1986. (A provocative and lavishly illustrated interpretation of the African experience by a well-known African scholar.)

Ramsay, F. Jeffress. *Africa.* 5th ed. 1993. (An annual collection of articles and country summaries focusing on contemporary developments.)

Rodney, Walter. *How Europe Underdeveloped Africa.* 1972. (A highly critical account of Europe's role in African history by a West Indian scholar.)

Sandbrooke, Richard. *The Politics of Africa's Economic Stagnation.* 1985. (Finds the source of Africa's economic crisis in the weakness of its states and social classes.)

Whitaker, Jennifer S. *How Can Africa Survive?* 1988. (An explanation of Africa's contemporary crisis.)

Conclusion
East and West, North and South:
Problems and Prospects
in the Global Village

In 1974, economist Robert Heilbroner opened his book *An Inquiry into the Human Prospect* with this searching question: "Is there hope for man?" He was asking not about the prospects for this or that country, but about the permanence of modern industrial society in the face of rapidly growing population, resource depletion, and environmental decay. A decade later, the American writer Jonathan Schell published *The Fate of the Earth,* a bestselling book about nuclear war that explores the possibility and meaning of human extinction. Studies such as these, which frame important questions in global terms, have become so common in recent decades as to no longer provoke much notice. Our "problems," if nothing else, have made us global citizens.

Yet only a century ago, there was little popular consciousness anywhere of what we would call "world problems," and certainly not of those that might call into question the very existence of life on earth. Widespread awareness of such issues, which threaten the well-being of people all across the planet, is a quite recent product of the modern world, dating from the end of World War II. However, current global problems have their roots in the major themes of modern history—in the unprecedented mastery of nature represented by science and technology; in the proliferation of independent, competitive, but highly unequal nation-states; in the ideological antagonisms of the Cold War; and in the multiple global connections forged in the wake of Europe's world expansion.

To bring this account of the world's modern history into the present, this final chapter highlights three of our most recent and serious global dilemmas. We will place them in a historical context, outline their current dimensions, and speculate briefly about possible futures.

The East and the West:
The Cold War
in World History

The latter half of the twentieth century has been shaped decisively by the global conflict between the Western world, led by the United States, and the Communist world, led by the former Soviet Union. With its origins in the struggle for control of Eastern Europe following World War II (see Chapter 5), that conflict soon came to be seen as an ideological clash between incompatible ways of life. It found expression in competition for political influence around the world and in an enormous and competitive buildup of military forces, including nuclear weapons, wholly unprecedented in human history. Between 1945 and the mid-1980s, the world moved from a mere handful of nuclear weapons to a global arsenal of close to sixty thousand warheads, and to delivery systems that included bomber aircraft and missiles, some launched from submarines, that could propel numerous warheads across whole continents and oceans with accuracies measured in hundreds of feet.

Hot Wars, the Cold War, and the Long Peace

Among the consequences of the East-West conflict has been a vast expansion of the role of war and of preparation for war in many human societies, especially in those of the great powers. The proportion of total world output devoted to military purposes grew from about 1 percent in the 1930s to approximately 6 percent in the mid-1980s. From 1960 to 1985, global military expenditures rose from $400 billion to $940 billion. The latter figure represented more than the combined income of the poorest half of the world's population. By 1980, about 23 percent of all investment in science and technology supported the military and employed 22 percent of the world's scientists and research workers.

Yet the process of militarization was not limited to the rival Cold War powers. In the 1980s, developing countries spent about $22 billion annually to import weapons. Since World War II, 130 separate wars (civil and international), almost all of them in developing nations, have killed nearly 25 million people. Civil war in Nigeria in the late 1960s, the carnage in Cambodia in the 1970s, the Iran-Iraq conflict of the 1980s, the almost complete breakdown of civil order in Somalia, Rwanda, and Liberia in the early 1990s—these are but a few of the conflicts fought largely with imported weapons.

Military matters came to assume such prominence in the affairs of nations that the line between war and peace became blurred. Even in peacetime, military budgets grew, and "national security" was defined in almost exclusively military terms. The term *Cold War,* used to characterize relations between the United States and the Soviet Union after 1945, captured this sense of pervasive threat and anxious military preparation short of violent conflict.

What accounts for this unprecedented global militarization?[1] Perhaps the most important factor was the acceleration of technology applied to military purposes. For much of the nineteenth century and earlier, nations had time to mobilize their resources for conflict after war broke out or just shortly before.

But with the advent of the railroad, telegraph, radio, and the airplane, it became necessary for hostile states to be constantly ready for war because there would be little time to prepare once conflict erupted. The addition of long-range bombers in the 1950s and intercontinental ballistic missiles in the 1960s reduced the warning time of an enemy attack to a matter of minutes.

Furthermore, since the 1930s, the dominant global conflicts of the twentieth century have been ideological rather than merely national or dynastic. Like the threat of Nazi Germany, the Cold War struggle between Western capitalist democracies and the Communist states raised questions about the entire social order and fundamental values. To both sides, the stakes appeared total and seemed to require a sustained military buildup. Finally, the dissolution of colonial empires, which had imposed a kind of global peace within the areas they controlled, and the ready availability of all sorts of military hardware meant that ancient hostilities and modern conflicts in the developing nations could be fought with contemporary weapons, happily supplied by the competing superpowers. The Middle East, awash in oil revenues and politically volatile, absorbed 42 percent of the world's arms imports in 1982. And a number of developing nations had either already acquired nuclear weapons capability (India and China) or were apparently in the process of doing so (Pakistan, North Korea, Iraq, South Africa, Israel).

Global militarization has clearly had economic consequences, for resources devoted to military spending were unavailable for other more productive purposes. The cost of a single modern tank could provide storage facilities for 100,000 tons of rice or build 1,000 classrooms for 30,000 children. It is surely no accident that Japan, which spends less than 1 percent of its GNP for military purposes, has had a far higher economic growth rate than the United States, which has typically invested between 5 percent and 8 percent of its GNP for defense. And at least some of the long-term stagnation of the Soviet economy surely was due to the diversion of resources—over 20 percent of GNP—to military purposes.

The psychological dimension of militarization has been the fear of nuclear war, a threat with which several generations of people, particularly in the Northern Hemisphere, have grown up. Since 1945, people have lived in the shadow of nuclear weapons, whose destructive power is scarcely within the bounds of human imagination. A single bomb in a single instant can obliterate any major city in the world. The detonation of even a small fraction of those weapons currently in the arsenals of the former Soviet Union and the United States could reduce the target countries to radioactive rubble and social chaos. Warnings about "nuclear winter" suggest that the effects of such a war may not be limited to the immediate participants. Responsible scientists have seriously discussed the possible extinction of the human species under such conditions.

While contributing to global militarization, the Cold War also decisively structured international political relations after 1945. In Korea and Vietnam, El Salvador and Nicaragua, Angola and Ethiopia, Afghanistan and the Middle East, local conflicts within or between nations were caught up in the Soviet-American rivalry and were thereby exacerbated. Both sides funneled assistance to their respective client states on the basis of political advantage, rather than economic or humanitarian need. Both sides supported corrupt and highly authoritarian regimes in the developing nations and tried to undermine established governments in the opposing camp. Both sides got bogged down in protracted and unpopular wars—the United States in Vietnam and the Soviet Union in Afghanistan. And it was conflict over Cuba in 1962 that brought the world to the very brink of nuclear war.

Back at home, the domestic institutions and internal politics of both superpowers were greatly influenced by the demands of the Cold War. In the United States, the need for quick and often secret decision making gave rise to a strong or "imperial" presidency and a "national security state," in which defense and intelligence agencies acquired great power within the government and were often unaccountable to Congress. Thus power was focused in the executive branch, and in the view of many observers, this undermined the democratic process. Fear of internal subversion produced the intense anticommunism of the 1950s and narrowed the range of political debate in the country as both parties competed to appear "tough" on communism. All of this served to strengthen the influence of

what President Eisenhower called the "military-industrial complex"—a coalition of the armed services, military research laboratories, and private defense industries that both stimulated and benefited from increased military spending and Cold War tensions.

In the Soviet Union, the Cold War justified, after World War II, a continuing emphasis on military and defense industries and gave rise to a Soviet version of the military-industrial complex. Sometimes called a "metal-eater's alliance," it joined the armed forces with certain heavy industries to press for a weapons buildup that benefited both. As in the United States, such a concentrated bloc of political power acted to constrain political leaders, such as Khrushchev who sought to redirect government spending to other purposes. Soviet citizens, even more than Americans, were subject to incessant government propaganda that glorified the Soviet system and vilified that of their ideological opponents.

Given the duration and intensity of the Cold War, it is more than a little surprising that it never once led to a "hot" or shooting war between the two superpowers. How can we explain this "long peace" of the Cold War?[2] Fundamentally, it derived from the possession of nuclear weapons. Unlike the First and Second World Wars, in which the participants were greatly surprised by the destructiveness of modern weapons, the leaders of the two superpowers knew beyond any doubt that a nuclear war would produce only losers and utter catastrophe. Furthermore, the deployment of reconnaissance satellites made it possible to know with some clarity the extent of the other side's arsenals. Particularly after the frightening Cuban Missile Crisis of 1962, in which the United States forced the Soviet Union to remove its recently installed missiles from Cuba, both sides carefully avoided further nuclear provocation, even while continuing the buildup of their own nuclear arsenals. And since they feared that a conventional war would escalate to the nuclear level, they implicitly agreed to sidestep any direct military confrontation. Thus, the Soviet Union invaded Czechoslovakia (1968) and Afghanistan (1979) and supported Cuban troops in Africa, while the United States took on the Dominican Republic (1965), Vietnam (late 1960s), and Grenada (1982). But Soviet and American troops never faced one another directly in a military encounter.

The End of the Cold War

Between 1985 and 1991 Cold War rivalries first eased and then ended. When Russia joined the International Monetary Fund in 1992 and entered a partnership with NATO in 1994, the East-West division, which had been such an important element in the world of the twentieth century, seemed to have been overcome. This was both an unexpected and surprisingly rapid development. It was the Gorbachev reform program in the Soviet Union that broke the logjam of Cold War hostilities. That program of economic revival required resources that were being spent on the military. And it required Western economic cooperation that could not be gained without radical changes in Soviet foreign policy. This logic gave rise to Gorbachev's "new thinking": that economic reform at home must drive Soviet foreign policy; that interdependence of nations rather than conflict between socialism and capitalism was the order of the day; that national security was not primarily military but had to be mutual as well; that capitalism

was not about to collapse any time soon; that developing nations were a drain on Soviet resources. All of this represented a dramatic change in Soviet thinking about the world. The actions that grew out of this "new thinking," together with the American response to them, soon resulted in an extraordinary transformation of international politics. It raised both expectations and fears about the future.

The division of Europe, which had been the cockpit of the Cold War, was overcome as Communist governments in Eastern Europe collapsed, the Berlin Wall fell, and Germany was reunified—all with Soviet approval. A series of arms-control agreements began the process of either destroying or withdrawing a substantial number of both conventional and nuclear weapons, thereby easing the intense fears of nuclear annihilation. The combined arsenals of the United States and Russia are scheduled to drop from a high of 57,000 nuclear warheads in 1988 to about 12,000 by early in the twenty-first century.

Superpower conflicts likewise diminished in developing nations. Gorbachev withdrew Soviet forces from Afghanistan and sharply cut Soviet assistance to client states. The United States and Soviet Union cooperated in resolving civil wars in Angola, Cambodia, and El Salvador and jointly sponsored Arab-

The partial dismantling of their nuclear arsenals by Russia and the United States represents one of the most dramatic and significant outcomes of the end of the Cold War. *Reuters/Bettmann*

Israeli peace talks in the Middle East. And the Soviet Union consistently supported the American-led war against Saddam Hussein's Iraq in 1991, though it did not contribute forces to that effort.

As Cold War hostilities dissolved, democratic forces within a number of developing countries were able to emerge as the great powers found it less necessary to support unsavory dictators. In the Philippines, El Salvador, Chile, Zaire, Ethiopia, Kenya, and elsewhere, highly authoritarian regimes were replaced or severely challenged as superpower support for them waned. In this environment, the United Nations greatly expanded its original peacekeeping role in such diverse places as Cambodia, Yugoslavia, Somalia, and Iraq. Its peacekeeping expenditures rose from under $300 million in the mid-1980s to $2.7 billion in 1992.

The end of the Cold War has likewise raised new possibilities within the United States and the former Soviet Union. Both sides began to cut their military budgets and to think seriously about the "conversion" of defense industries to civilian production. And both began to debate the potential uses to which a so-called "peace dividend" might be put.

But there have also been less positive outcomes to the end of the Cold War. Ethnic conflicts held in check by strong Communist governments tore Yugoslavia apart in the early 1990s, brought Czechoslovakia to a peaceful breakup, and erupted in or between most of the component states of the former Soviet Union. Thus, eastern Europe joined India, much of Southeast Asia, most of Africa, and many other states in confronting perhaps the most explosive political issue of the late twentieth century: how to accommodate within a single state the conflicting demands of various culturally different, highly politicized, and economically unequal peoples.

It is not, of course, a new problem, but one that had arisen from the modern transformation itself. The disintegration of old empires; the spread of nationalist rhetoric and ideas around the world; the mixing of diverse peoples through massive urbanization, wage employment, and migration; the unevenness of modern economic development; mass participation in political life—these have been the ingredients from which modern ethnic nationalism has been brewed. The end of the Cold War seems to have encouraged political separatism by minimizing its connection to great power rivalries, while an open world economy makes it possible for even small nations to find a trad-

ing niche. Thus Canada, Spain, Belgium, and China face separatist pressures as well as the more obvious cases of Yugoslavia, Somalia, Russia, and India. Ethnic nationalism will clearly rank high on the historical agenda of the twenty-first century.

The end of the Cold War poses starkly the question of global priorities. As late as 1988, the world was spending roughly $1 trillion per year (about $200 per person) on preparing for war. To what extent would it be possible to turn those material resources and human energies to dealing with the planet's other major difficulties—the gap between its richest and poorest societies and the looming environmental crisis arising from its modern transformation?

The North and The South: Global Inequality and the Search for a New Order

The declining significance of the East-West conflict has served to highlight the other profound rift in the contemporary world—that between rich and poor nations. As the world has grown "smaller" or more interdependent over the past several centuries, its various societies have also grown far more unequal. Certainly, there have always been great disparities of wealth in the world, and the conflicts of the rich and poor have since ancient times provided a central thread to the human story. But the curse of massive economic inequality has until modern times occurred primarily *within* particular societies rather than among them.

In the roughly two centuries since England's Industrial Revolution began, the economic divergence of the world's societies has been remarkable and rapid. "The richest country was only about twice as well off as the poorest at the beginning of the nineteenth century," writes political scientist Stephen Krasner. "Now [1981] the richest countries are eighty to one hundred times better off than the poorest,"[3] at least as measured in terms of per-capita income. This divide between the relatively few rich societies and the many impoverished ones is often referred to as the North-South issue, because most of the wealthy areas (the United States, Canada, Europe, and Japan) lie to the north of most of the poor societies (Asia, Africa, and Latin America).

Measuring Global Inequality (1984)

Military and Social Expenditures	Developed	Developing
GNP, per capita	$9,795	$752
Public expenditures, per capita, for education	$497	$28
School-age population per teacher	25	53
Literacy rates	99%	62%
Population per physician	398	2,043
Infant mortality rate (deaths per 1,000 live births under age 1)	16	88
Life expectancy	73	59
Calories (as a percent of requirement)	132%	106%
Protein supply, per capita (in grams, 1982)	100g	58g
Percent of population with safe water	97%	53%

Source: Ruth Sivard, *World Military and Social Expenditures, 1987–88* (Washington, D.C.: World Priorities, 1987), pp. 36–37.

The dimensions of the gap between the North and the South are startling by any measure, particularly since they are so recent in the history of the world. Although the North contains only about 25 percent of the world's population, it accounts for 80 percent of its production of goods and services. The South, in contrast, has 75 percent of the world's people but produces only 20 percent of the world's output each year. The disparity in consumption is equally striking: the United States, with only 6 percent of the world's population, consumes between 25 percent and 40 percent of world resources. Other indicators of global inequality are shown in the accompanying table.

Many have found such conditions morally offensive and an affront to any conception of a human community. But global inequality also has become a problem in very practical ways as the wealthy nations became increasingly connected to the poor. Major American banks in the 1980s became nervous about the consequences of default by southern borrowers. With 35 percent of American exports going to developing nations by 1980, many U.S. exporters stood to benefit directly from a growing purchasing power in the South. And the Soviet-American rivalry for influence among developing countries gave political and military significance to the facts of international inequality. However, it was the actions of developing countries themselves that brought the North-South issue into sharp focus during the 1970s.

The Demands of the South

By the 1970s, a great many leaders of developing countries believed that an unfair world economy, the historical product of Europe's head start in the modernizing process, made it extremely difficult for more than a few southern societies to move rapidly toward industrialization. If the South were to develop, they argued, the international economic system would have to change substantially. During the 1970s, developing countries forcefully articulated a set of demands to effect such a change, calling for nothing less than a New International Economic Order (NIEO).

On one level, the demand for an NIEO was a continuation of the struggle against European dominance that had occupied so much of the world's history in the twentieth century. It was an effort to use political independence to gain greater economic advantage on a global level, much as the lower classes in Europe and America had used political pressure and the vote to demand economic improvements on the domestic level. The creation of the United Nations and other international bodies provided a forum in which these demands could be expressed and negotiated. In 1964, at a U.N. Conference on Trade and Development (UNCTAD), a number of developing states joined together in the Group of 77 to demand concessions from the wealthy countries. This was the real beginning of organized class struggle at the international level.

But more than anything else, the success of the Organization of Petroleum Exporting Countries (OPEC) in quadrupling the world price of oil in 1973 stimulated the movement for international economic reform. Here was a dramatic breakthrough in the struggle of the poor against the rich, for OPEC presided over the greatest and most rapid transfer of wealth the world had ever seen. Whereas a barrel of oil could be exchanged for a single bushel of wheat in 1972, eight years later Americans and Europeans had to pay the equivalent of six bushels of wheat for that same barrel of oil. It was a kind of historical revenge for centuries of Western imperialism. While others were talking about a new international economic order, OPEC had created one, at least temporarily. Capitalizing on this remarkable success, virtually every country in the developing world coalesced around the demands for an NIEO at the Sixth Special Session of the U.N. General Assembly in 1974. What they sought was a revolutionary overhaul of the existing international economic system.

Since export earnings provided about 80 percent of the money flowing into developing countries from abroad, they were particularly eager to reform the international trading system. Thus, they sought to raise and stabilize the prices of their exports. To do so, they proposed to negotiate with the wealthy countries a price range for their major export products and to "index" these prices to those of their imports. Thus, if imports rose in price, so too would their exports.

Meeting in Lima, Peru, in 1975, representatives of the developing nations also called for an increase in their share of world industrial production from an existing 7 percent to 25 percent by the year 2000. To foster this growth, they asked the already developed countries to reduce or eliminate tariffs on manufactured goods from the South without requiring developing countries to reciprocate. They also sought northern cooperation in regulating the activities of large multinational corporations and in facilitating the transfer of technology to the developing countries.

Furthermore, developing countries sought larger and more automatic flows of foreign aid. Only five Western countries (the Netherlands, Sweden, Norway, Denmark, and France) and six OPEC nations (Iraq, Saudi Arabia, Kuwait, Qatar, the United Arab Emirates, and Libya) had met the widely accepted U.N. standard of 0.7 percent of GNP as a target for their official development assistance. American aid, for example, declined from 0.58 percent of GNP in 1965 to 0.15 percent in 1989, putting it at the bottom of Western industrialized nations as an aid donor.

Finally, developing states sought greater power for themselves in international agencies, such as the World Bank and the International Monetary Fund, where important economic decisions were made. In the mid-1970s, for example, the developing countries (excluding OPEC) had only 31 percent of the total voting power in the World Bank, since its voting system was weighted in favor of countries whose financial contributions to it were greatest.

The Response of the North

Taken together, the demands for an NIEO would have meant a very substantial transfer of wealth from the North to the South. The NIEO also would have created a new method of economic decision making in the world, one that would have moved away from market criteria, where economic strength counted, to negotiated agreements within international bodies, where each country's vote would carry the same weight. It is hardly surprising that the Western industrialized countries, led by the United States, were decidedly unenthusiastic about most of these proposals. Despite frequent conferences and much negotiation, little real headway was made in substantially reforming the international economic system in favor of the developing nations.

The Western industrialized countries resented the implication of the NIEO demands that poverty in developing nations was the result of a capitalist world economy rather than the mismanagement, corruption, and inefficiency of developing nations' governments themselves. In addition, there was a tone to much of the NIEO rhetoric that suggested the West owed developing countries some compensation for centuries of imperialist exploitation. This was not a notion that appealed to many Western leaders or to their voting publics. Furthermore, the NIEO demands sought to interfere with the free working of the market economy, a principle many in the West found offensive. "The best model for economic prosperity," wrote U.S. Secretary of the Treasury William Simon in 1976, "is a system which unites freedom of commerce with freedom of the individual."[4]

During the 1980s, much of the original steam went out of developing countries' demands for an NIEO. Their massive investments in the West gave the OPEC countries a major stake in the existing international system, leading some to speak of an Arab "betrayal" of the developing nations. Moreover, the world oil glut of the 1980s seriously reduced developing nations' bargaining power. And the global recession of the early 1980s forced many southern countries to turn their attention away from the re-

Food aid to a number of developing countries represents one indication of the continuing North/South gap in the contemporary world. Here Tuareg people from west Africa receive UN relief supplies. *UN/F.A.O.*

structuring of the world economy to the more immediate problem of economic survival.

For many countries the central problem was an enormous and growing indebtedness, amounting to about $1 trillion for the developing world as a whole by 1987. That debt had mounted very rapidly in the 1970s and 1980s, as massive OPEC oil revenues were recycled through Western banks and granted as loans to increasingly desperate developing countries. Paying only the interest on their foreign debts in 1984 took 80 percent of Sudan's export earnings, 56 percent of Argentina's, 48 percent of Bolivia's, and 38 percent of Brazil's. To qualify for additional credit, some forty-six countries had to adopt severe austerity programs supervised by the International Monetary Fund. In these circumstances, long-term

struggles for a more equal world had to be put on hold.

Prospects for Catching Up

If substantial reform of the international economy favorable to developing countries seems unlikely, what are the prospects for overcoming the North-South divide or at least of easing the worst aspects of human poverty and misery in the poor countries of the world? On this question, as on most other important issues, there is conflicting evidence, and the judgments of experts and laypeople alike vary greatly.

It is important to see the efforts of developing countries in a historical perspective. Most have been on the road to self-conscious development for less than fifty years, and during that time there has been substantial economic progress, demonstrating that rapid and sustained development is by no means impossible. Progress has been most evident in the fields of education and health. The World Bank estimated that between 1950 and 1980, the proportion of literate adults in developing countries increased from 30 percent to 50 percent of the population. Even in the poorest developing countries, infant mortality has declined and average life expectancy has increased by 15 years since the early 1950s. By 1985, people in the developed world could expect to live on average 73 years, and those in poorer developing countries 60 years.

Furthermore, some developing countries have begun to industrialize in major ways. These newly industrialized countries (NICs), including Taiwan, South Korea, India, Mexico, Argentina, and Brazil, have become important exporters of manufactured goods. Some of the oil-producing countries of the Middle East have achieved high standards of living, though without massive industrialization. Asia clearly has been the most successful part of the developing world. Its four "mini-dragons"—Taiwan, South Korea, Singapore, and Hong Kong—produce half of the manufactured exports of the developing countries. China's revolutionary redistribution of land in the 1940s and 1950s, coupled with its booming economy in the 1980s, has lifted millions of Chinese out of wretched poverty. In India, grain production has at least kept up with rapid population growth, and the country has produced a substantial middle class of over 100 million people. None of these are small accomplishments.

In addition, some scholars profess to see signs of real hope, for even the poorest of countries, in a changing development strategy that seems to be sweeping the world. With the success of the East Asian NICs, the collapse of communism in the former Soviet Union, and the dramatic economic reforms in China, the model of highly centralized, state-controlled development, adopted in various forms by many developing countries, has been greatly discredited, much like purely laissez-faire capitalism had been earlier. Everyone, it seems, has rediscovered the virtues of the free market as an engine of economic growth. And most experts today would encourage the state to play an important but limited role—investing in education, health, family planning; building an efficient administrative, legal, and physical infrastructure; and providing overall economic stability. In places as far apart as India, Ghana, Chile, and China, this approach of blending the market and the state has been applied with at least some initial success in revitalizing stagnant economies.

However, other indicators and other examples point in a different direction. Africa and Latin America have had the slowest rates of growth among the developing areas, averaging, respectively, 0.8 percent and 1.2 percent per year since 1950. In the 1980s, per-capita income in Africa, Latin America, and the Middle East actually contracted, and living standards dropped sharply for many people in these areas. Surging population growth in many places pushed the number of severely impoverished and often malnourished people to 1.1 billion (close to 20 percent of the world's population) in 1990, according to the World Bank. Interest payments, capital flight, and other mechanisms have led to a net *outflow* of capital from the South to the North, conservatively estimated at $43 billion per year since 1986. This massive transfer of wealth from the poor to the rich clearly has contributed to the ongoing poverty of many developing countries. In addition, civil war and ethnic hostilities pushed the number of refugees to a record forty-four million people by 1993, most of them in the poorest countries. All of this cautions against optimistic expectations about closing the North-South gap. It also reminds us that the concepts of the "Third World" or the "South" hide a growing differentiation among developing countries. Thus,

the short answer to the question about whether the poor countries are catching up is that some are and some are not.

There is, of course, a final and ultimate constraint on the possibilities of overcoming global economic inequalities. It lies in the ecological and environmental relationships that sustain and support us all.

All of Us: Sustainability and the Limits to Modernity

Beneath the inequalities of the international order, there has emerged an even more fundamental and compelling global issue. It is the problem of *sustainability*.[5] Can the world's resource base and its natural life-support systems sustain on a permanent basis an improving standard of living for our rapidly growing population? Does the "modern way of life," particularly as reflected in the most developed industrial societies of Europe, Japan, and the United States, represent a viable future for the rest of the world's people or even for the minority who currently enjoys its material benefits? If not, can we muddle or manage our way to more sustainable societies without facing catastrophe on a global scale?

"Borrowing from Our Children": The Environmental Dilemma

Human activity has altered the environment since the days of the first hunters and early farmers, sometimes with disastrous results. The collapse of early civilizations in places as far apart as early Mesopotamia, the Indus River Valley, and Central America owed something to the pressures of overpopulation, deforestation, erosion, and other environmental stresses. But modern industrial civilization has encroached more heavily on the natural setting than any other human culture. The global implications of this encroachment became increasingly apparent during the third quarter of the twentieth century, a period of unprecedented growth in population (which rose at a world rate of 1.9 percent per year) and in overall production (which increased about 5 percent per year).

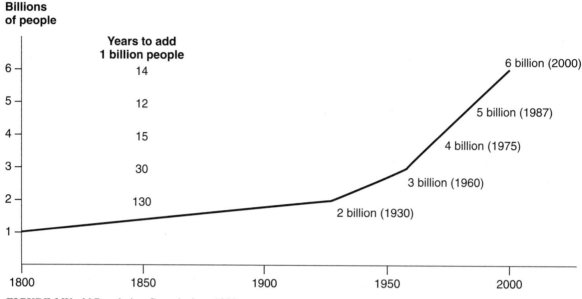

FIGURE 1 World Population Growth since 1800

Whether such patterns of growth can be sustained indefinitely is an increasingly open-ended question.

The sheer weight of rapidly growing numbers has put increasing pressures on the environment. The accompanying figure illustrates global population growth since 1800, when the world's population reached the 1 billion mark. U.N. projections suggest that world population will approach about 12 billion before stabilizing in the late twenty-first century. The bulk of this enormous growth is expected to occur in South Asia, the Middle East, Africa, and Latin America. Their current rates of population growth are far higher than were Europe's during the early industrial era at the start of the nineteenth century. And Europeans had opportunities for emigration to the Americas and elsewhere. It is difficult to imagine population growth of this magnitude apart from enormous environmental damage, sharply lowered standards of living, and widespread social disaster.

To the basic needs of the poor must be added the growing demands of the rich as a threat to the world's environment. Commercial logging and ranching in the tropics, for example, are primarily oriented toward the consumption needs of the industrialized countries. And dangerous pesticides in developing countries are applied far more often to export crops than to staples grown for the poor. Clearly, a child born in North America will consume during

his or her lifetime far more of the earth's resources and contribute far more to its pollution than a child born in west Africa. Together, the needs of the poor majority and the appetites of the rich minority produced, by the 1970s, clear signs of ecological deterioration on a global scale.

One of these signs has been massive soil erosion. Between 1950 and 1973, world demand for grains doubled as a result of population growth and rising incomes. Farmers thus began to work previously marginal lands that were dry, steep, and especially vulnerable to erosion. Time-tested agricultural methods such as careful terracing, crop rotation, and fallowing broke down under the pressure of rising demand. By 1985, a total of 35 percent of the world's croplands were losing topsoil faster than it was being created, producing a net loss of 25 billion tons of topsoil per year. Since erosion can seriously reduce the productivity of the soil, "in effect," writes Lester Brown, "the world is mining much of its cropland, treating it as a depletable resource."[6]

Closely related to soil erosion is deforestation. The growing demand for forest products such as lumber and paper, the clearing of forests for agricultural use, and the increasing need for firewood in much of the developing world has reduced the forested proportion of the world from about 25 percent in 1950 to 20 percent in 1980. The growing threat to Brazil's rain forests in the Amazon basin illustrates the process. The government has granted huge concessions to wealthy individuals and firms, who have transformed these forest lands into pasture for cattle. The beef, however, does not go to feed Brazil's poor but is exported to North America, western Europe, and the Middle East. Some of the Amazon forest area has been opened to impoverished and landless farmers, not because other and better land is unavailable but because it is held by a small and powerful elite who have successfully resisted efforts at land reform. In both cases, the trees continue to fall.

Although most deforestation has occurred in tropical areas, acid rain and other industrial pollutants have seriously damaged large forest areas in parts of Europe and North America. A recent survey showed serious damage to 54 percent of Germany's forests. The global loss of forest cover has contributed to soil erosion and the enlargement of desert areas, has damaged hydroelectric and irrigation projects, and has forced millions of people to travel long distances or pay high prices for firewood. For millions in the developing world, the growing scarcity of wood, not oil, is the real energy crisis.

A similar pattern of overuse—"borrowing from tomorrow"—has become evident in the fisheries and grazing lands of the world. Between 1950 and 1970, the world fish catch more than tripled, and by the early 1980s, many oceanic fisheries were threatened. In 1992, Canada forbade for two years all cod fishing off the coast of Labrador and Newfoundland. Likewise, a vast increase in demand for livestock products led to a doubling of world beef consumption between 1950 and 1975, and corresponding pressure on the world's pasture lands. By the early 1980s, for example, Syrian grasslands were carrying three times the number of animals they could realistically support. In Africa, the Middle East, India, Latin America, and the United States, grasslands were turning into deserts under the pressure of overgrazing.

If properly managed, the soil, forests, fisheries, and grasslands are renewable resources. They can sustain human life indefinitely. Not so with oil. But until the oil-producing nations of OPEC sharply raised prices in the 1970s, the world—and especially its industrialized states—acted as if oil supplies were infinite or renewable. The rapid growth of food supplies and industrial production from 1950 to 1973 all depended very heavily on plentiful supplies of cheap oil. Particularly in the wealthy capitalist countries, petroleum led the way to an automobile-centered culture and a throw-away society. If consumption had continued at that rate—increasing at 7 percent a year—the world's known oil reserves would have been exhausted by early in the twenty-first century.

The steep oil price increases of 1973 and again in 1979 have forced far more efficient and careful use of petroleum, such that total world consumption of oil in 1991 was only 12 percent higher than it had been in 1973, while population had grown by 40 percent. OPEC's action, therefore, has bought time— perhaps a generation or two—for the world to find ways of tapping more abundant or renewable sources of energy or, should that prove impossible, to adjust to a sharply lowered standard of living. In either case, the end of the age of petroleum is in sight.

Beyond even the depletion of the world's resource base, there is growing evidence that human activity and intervention in the ecosystem may be changing both local and global climates. By sharply reducing the amount of water returned to the atmosphere, deforestation may reduce rainfall and thus contribute to a "drying out" of local environments and the growth of desert areas. The Amazon basin and large areas of Africa, the Middle East, and northern India may be involved in this kind of vicious cycle. The release of chlorofluorocarbons (CFCs) into the atmosphere has been shown to cause a thinning of the ozone layer, which protects us from the harmful effects of ultraviolet radiation.

Furthermore, the tremendous increase in the burning of fossil fuels and the shrinking of the earth's forests have produced a significant increase in the amount of heat-trapping carbon dioxide in the atmosphere. China, for example, has attempted to fuel its economic growth almost entirely with coal, but in the process increased its carbon emissions by 60 percent during the 1980s. One study has predicted an average temperature rise of 5 degrees Fahrenheit by 2030, if present growth rates of fossil fuel use continue. In the long term of a century or two, this pattern of global warming would alter rainfall patterns, raise the average sea level, inundate agricultural lowlands, make many species of plant life vulnerable, and require enormous capital investment in dikes, drainage, and irrigation systems. Some coastal cities in the United States have begun to plan already for rising water levels and erosion of coastal lands.

A final signal of the impact of human activity on the earth's environment involves the question of biological diversity. Degradation of the world's forests, wetlands, prairies, mangroves, and reefs has meant the extinction of thousands of plant and animal species every year. Fully 75 percent of the world's bird species are declining or are threatened with extinction. One expert has estimated that 25 percent of all tropical plants will likely disappear over the next three decades. Such an enormous loss of life forms nurtured over millions of years of evolution represents to many people an unimaginable scientific or aesthetic tragedy. But it also risks upsetting delicate and poorly understood ecological relationships on which human welfare depends. Mangroves cut for firewood offer no more protection from coastal erosion; predators made extinct can no longer keep rodents or insects in check.

The cumulative impact of these processes points in a single direction: the patterns of the present are not sustainable over the long run. Whatever the foreseeable future of the world may be, it is unlikely to hold a universal extension of the wasteful, energy-intensive, affluent, and industrial societies pioneered in Europe and North America. Indeed, there already are clear signs of a slowdown in the rapid economic growth of the post–World War II era. Whereas the annual per-capita increase in overall world production was 3.1 percent between 1950 and 1973, it dropped to 1.1 percent in the 1980s. This meant that output was just barely keeping pace with population growth on a global level.

Although some aspects of this recent slowdown may be explained as part of a "normal" cycle in the capitalist world economy, it may also represent the early indications of overpopulation, resource depletion, and environmental stress. If so, it signals the transition to an era of slower growth, declining standards of living, and increased social tension in many parts of the world.

Toward Sustainable Societies

It is not difficult to identify the requirements of a more sustainable society. "They include," writes Lester Brown, "reestablishing climate stability, pro-

Automobile pollution in Mexico City has killed the trees along this boulevard and obscured the view of the mountains that are visible on a clear day. *UPI/Bettmann Newsphotos*

tecting the stratospheric ozone layer, restoring the earth's tree cover, stabilizing soils, safeguarding the earth's remaining biological diversity, and restoring the traditional balance between births and deaths."[7] However, moving decisively in these directions on an adequate global scale represents a profound challenge to human adaptability.

Efforts to control population growth provide a good example. There are essentially three major routes to a more stable global population, and all of them have been evident in recent decades. The first is stability through disaster, an idea associated with Thomas Malthus, an eighteenth-century English clergyman who argued that food production could not forever keep up with population growth and that a balance would be restored through "periodical misery" in the form of famine, war, and disease. A Malthusian process has operated in parts of Africa, where between 1970 and 1984 per-capita food production fell 11 percent, mortality rates rose, and famine became widespread.

At the other extreme lies population control as an indirect product of industrial development. In all industrialized countries, birthrates declined sharply as average income rose, education and employment opportunities for women increased, and raising a large number of children became a serious economic burden. Thus, by the 1980s, many European countries had achieved zero population growth, and several other developed nations (the United States, Soviet Union, and Japan) had growth rates of under 1 percent per year. Clearly, this is the preferred route to population stability.

But in many developing countries, rapid industrial development is out of sight and Malthusian "misery" on the horizon. In these societies, the only realistic alternative is population control via policy—deliberate and planned efforts to reduce the number of births even without substantial economic development. China's "one-child family" program has been the most impressive of these efforts. By combining massive public education, easy availability of birth-control devices, a system of economic incentives and punishments, and political intrusion into the most personal areas of life, China had reduced its population growth rate to about 1.4 percent per year by the 1980s. But China's success involved more than birth control. It rested more fundamentally on a broad-based program to provide economic security to the masses, thus reducing the incentive to have large families. Thailand, Sri Lanka, Mexico, Costa Rica, Indonesia, and parts of India have also had some success in limiting births through active family-planning programs coupled with social and economic reforms.

In other efforts at creating more sustainable economies, there have been impressive models in several countries but an altogether inadequate response on a global level. Perhaps the most encouraging sign in terms of soil conservation has been occurring in the United States, where farm legislation in 1985 moved sharply in the direction of conservation, including restrictions on the plowing of land vulnerable to erosion. During the 1970s, South Korea mounted a major and successful program to reforest huge areas of its almost bare hills and mountains, and China increased its tree coverage from 8 percent of its territory in 1960 to 12.7 percent in 1986. Denmark has banned throw-away beverage containers, the Netherlands has actively pushed the bicycle as personal transportation, while Brazil has come to rely on ethanol, derived from sugarcane, for a substantial amount of its automotive fuel.

Perhaps the greatest success on the road to sustainability has been the sharp reduction of oil consumption, which fell by 9 percent between 1979 and 1985 and has grown modestly since then. But what will substitute for petroleum? Nuclear power, touted in the 1970s as the wave of the energy future, has experienced severe financial problems and, in the wake of accidents at Three Mile Island in the United States and Chernobyl in the Ukraine, seems in most places a declining alternative. Coal usage has increased sharply as oil-fired electric generating plants have switched to coal. But coal's potential for producing acid rain and raising carbon dioxide levels in the atmosphere seems to limit its future use.

The most promising and rapidly growing energy alternatives have been those deriving from renewable sources, such as wood, wind, falling water, the sun, and heat from the earth's crust. In 1987, such sources provided 21 percent of the world's energy, a figure projected to rise slowly for the rest of the twentieth century.

But sustainability will require not only producing more energy from different sources but also using less of it. "Conservation possibilities are so great," writes one expert in the field, "that economic growth could resume without large increases in total energy use."[8] The United States could save up to one-third of its coal-fired electric energy simply by using the most efficient lights.

Environmental problems clearly transcend national boundaries and this recognition has encouraged cooperation at the international level, reflected in the signing of some 150 environmental treaties. A Law of the Sea treaty negotiated during the 1970s sought to regulate access to resources of the world's oceans, to protect them from pollution, and to share the wealth derived from them. Between 1985 and 1990, over 90 nations agreed to phase out ozone-depleting CFCs altogether by the year 2000. In 1992, some 10,000 delegates representing 178 countries met in Rio de Janeiro for the world's largest environmental gathering, dubbed the "Earth Summit." The subject was sustainable development—how to combine the economic growth necessary to reduce poverty and the ecological sensitivity essential for preserving the earth's environment. The participants emerged with treaties requiring countries to control the emission of those gases that produce global warming and to protect the plant and animal species within their borders.

Such attempts to work out broad international agreements have inevitably come up against sharp North-South differences. Developing countries have sometimes felt that environmental protection measures advocated by the industrialized nations would limit their own prospects for growth. Thus, they have resented efforts to protect tropical rain forests, when the United States was proceeding with the cutting of its own ancient forests in the Pacific Northwest. They have also felt that the cost of expensive environmental protection measures should be borne disproportionately by the rich countries. The ozone depletion treaty was successful in part because the richer states agreed to establish a fund of $240 million to assist developing countries to make the transition away from harmful CFCs. In the aftermath of the Earth Summit, the United States was sharply criticized for its role in watering down the global warming treaty and for its initial refusal to sign the biodiversity pact, owing to pressure from American business interests.

Thus, the claims of the environment have been assuming an ever-greater role in public and private life alike. "Green" political parties, focusing on environmental issues, have sprung up in many European countries, and such concerns have become a staple of political debate around the world. Ecological issues have been prominent among the grievances of nationalist groups in the former Soviet Union. Some corporations have sought to capitalize on the environmental concerns of consumers in their packaging, labeling, advertising, and sometimes in their production processes—often pushed by governments in this direction. Numerous civic and religious groups of ordinary people have embraced environmentalism as an overriding moral and practical concern. And millions of individuals have begun to think about their private life-style choices in light of environmental perspectives. This growing global consciousness about the fragility of our common home is surely a prerequisite to any effective action.

Conclusion: Rethinking Basic Assumptions of the Modern Era

Clearly, the transition to sustainability raises the most profound and far-reaching questions about the capacity of human societies to manage and assimilate changes of enormous proportions. It also raises questions about some fundamental assumptions that have governed much of the modern era. For the already-developed countries, the challenge of the twenty-first century may require adaptation to a far less affluent life than that to which we have become accustomed. For the developing world, the transition may very well involve giving up hope of ever matching Western development. And for both, it may require a painful change in those modern values that have equated a good society with a rapidly growing GNP and personal success with expanding consumption.

The environmental crisis likewise raises questions about the adequacy of modern institutions for handling the transition to sustainable economies. While market economics and democratic politics have recently triumphed in the long struggle with Communist alternatives, these institutions also have drawbacks for the tasks ahead. The capitalist societies of

The devastating civil war in the former Yugoslavia has raised questions about the future of many multiethnic states in the contemporary world. *Reuters/Bettmann*

the West, predicated for centuries on the assumptions of competition and constant growth, will surely be severely tested if the future brings slower growth, declining incomes, and the need for cooperative action. Furthermore, market economics finds it difficult to factor environmental costs into the balance sheets of its corporations. The manufacturing enterprises that produce the massive pollution in Mexico City, for example, need not take account in their planning for paying the medical bills of those who come down with respiratory illnesses.

Will the democratic political systems that have been recently sweeping away authoritarian regimes all over the world provide an effective means of forging necessary compromises and resolving social tensions, particularly under conditions of scarcity? Or will they dissolve into paralysis as the competing demands of various social groups exceed the limits of consensus and peaceful accommodation? Many have wondered if electoral politics with competing parties is an adequate mechanism for dealing with long-term problems requiring sacrifice on the part of voters.

And what about the nation-state itself, that political unit which has become almost universal in the course of modern history? Its assumption of absolute sovereignty has been challenged by a variety of global processes and problems, and the nations of the world have already accepted some limits on their independence. The recent global-warming treaty wrote into international law the requirement that nations take global environmental consequences into account when making their internal economic decisions. More such limitations on national independence will surely be necessary in dealing with issues that so clearly call for a cooperative response. Yet such cooperation may be difficult to achieve in light of deeply rooted assumptions about the independence of sovereign states.

Furthermore, the traditional definition of national security as a largely military problem seems increasingly outdated in view of the collapse of the Soviet empire and in light of common environmental threats to human welfare. If the ingenuity and resources so often devoted to preparing for war were mobilized in support of sustainable development, our shared future would no doubt be considerably more secure.

A final challenge to the nation-state derives from the surging ethnic consciousness that animates so many peoples in the late twentieth century. If the environmental crisis suggests that the nation-state is too small to deal effectively with global issues, ethnic nationalism argues that it is too large to provide a sense of meaningful community in a technological and impersonal world. Thus, the nation-state finds itself challenged at the end of the twentieth century both by larger and more inclusive institutions, such as multinational corporations and various international bodies, and by smaller and more intimate communities of culturally similar people.

Notes

1. This paragraph follows the analysis of Richard Smoke, *National Security and the Nuclear Dilemma* (Reading, Mass.: Addison-Wesley, 1984), pp. 15–17.

2. John Lewis Gaddis, "The Long Peace," *International Security* 10 (Spring 1986).

3. Stephen D. Krasner, "Transforming International Regimes: What the Third World Wants and Why," *International Studies Quarterly* 25 (March 1981): 126.

4. Quoted in Karl P. Sauvant and Hajo Hasenpflug, eds., *The New International Economic Order* (Boulder, Colo.: Westview Press, 1977), p. 67.

5. The concept of "sustainability" and much of the data in this section derive from the work of Lester Brown and the Worldwatch Institute. See Brown, ed., *Building a Sustainable Society* (New York: Norton, 1981) and the volumes entitled *State of the World,* ed. Lester Brown, published annually since 1984 by W. W. Norton.

6. Brown, *State of the World, 1984,* p. 62.

7. Brown, *State of the World, 1993,* p. 17.

8. William U. Chandler, "Increasing Energy Efficiency," in *State of the World, 1985,* ed. Lester Brown (New York: Norton, 1985), p. 149.

SUGGESTIONS FOR FURTHER READING: THE GLOBAL VILLAGE

Barash, David. *The Arms Race and Nuclear War.* 1987. (A comprehensive survey of the problems associated with the possession of nuclear weapons.)

Brown, Lester, ed. *The State of the World.* 1984–present. (An annual survey of global economic and ecological conditions.)

Elliot, Jeffrey M., ed. *Third World 94/95.* 1994. (Includes selected readings on development issues. An annual publication.)

Erlich, P. R., and E. A. Erlich. *The Population Explosion.* 1990.

Gore, Albert. *Earth in the Balance.* 1992. (A comprehensive survey that illustrates the growing role of environmental issues in political life.)

Kennedy, Paul. *Preparing for the Twenty-First Century.* 1993. (A survey of global problems and the relative ability of various regions to cope with them.)

Lappe, Francis Moore. *World Hunger: Twelve Myths.* 1986. (An argument that finds the source of hunger in economic inequality rather than in insufficient supply or growing population.)

Lynch, Allen. *The Cold War Is Over—Again.* 1992. (Reviews the history of the Cold War and its ending.)

Russett, Bruce, and Harvey Starr. *World Politics: The Menu for Choice.* 1989. (A discussion of global problems from the viewpoint of political science.)

INDEX

Abbasids, 213, 216
Abbas the Great, 226
Abd al-Hamid II, 232
Abd al-Qadir, 238, 239
Abd al-Wahhab, 230
Achebe, Chinua, 473
Action Francaise, 88
al-Afghani, 237
Afghanistan, 197, 489
Africa
    classes in colonial, 447–450
    colonial chiefs in, 441
    colonial economic change in, 441–446,
        452–53
    colonial government in, 439–441
    commercial revolution in, 436
    compared to Eurasia, 423
    compared to India (post-independence), 472
    debt crisis in, 479
    democracy in, 472, 476
    economic evolution of, 422–24
    economic problems of, 472–73, 477–82
    ethnic politics in, 474–76
    ethnicity in colonial, 450–52
    European conquest of, 437
    European expansion in, 435
    famine in, 478
    geography of, 422
    Great Depression in, 443
    independent churches in, 458
    Islamic revolution in, 430
    Islam in, 428
    lineage-based societies in, 424–26
    military government in, 476
    nationalism in colonial, 461–68
    population growth in, 481
    racism in colonial, 446
    religious traditions in, 425
    settler colonies in, 443
    slave trade in, 432
    weakness of states in, 481
    West Africa kingdoms, 427–30
    women and agriculture in, 481
    and world economy, 479
African National Congress, 467
Akali Party, 318
Akbar, 279–81
Alaska, 182
Alexander II, 183, 185
Algeria, 238, 443, 465
Ali (Muhammad's son-in-law), 212
Allende, Salvador, 176
All India Women's Conference, 314
Ambedkar, B .R., 308, 316
American Revolution, 142–144
Americas
    conquest of, 118–120
    depopulation of, 118
Amin, Idi, 472
Amritsar Massacre, 301
Angola, 117, 443, 465
Anselm, 31
Anti-colonial movements
    American and Afro-Asian compared, 132
Anti-Semitism, 88, 95, 98
Apartheid, 447
Arab empire, 2, 212–14
Arab nationalism, 242–44
Arab socialism, 241, 247–50
Arabs, 209
Arafat, Yasser, 250
Argentina, 166, 176
Aristotle, 39
Arya Samaj, 294, 297
Asante, 433, 450
Ashoka, 270

Ataturk, Mustafa Kemal, 244–45
Aurangzeb, 283, 319
Auschwitz, 98
Avicenna, 215
Axum, 430
Ayodhya, 319
Aztec civilization, 159

Babur, 279
Bacon, Francis, 42
Bacon, Roger, 30
Balfour Declaration, 243
Bangala, 451
al-Banna, Hassan, 255
Bano, Shah, 313
Bantu-speaking peoples, 426
Beard, Charles and Mary, 146
Belgian Congo, 463
Benet, Stephen Vincent, 147
Bengal, 287
Bengal partition, 299, 300
Benin, 433
Bernard of Clairvaux, 32
Beveridge, Albert J., 149
Bhakti, 277
Bharatiya Janata Party, 318
Bhindranwale, Sant, 318
Biodiversity, 498
al-Biruni, 215
Bismarck, Otto von, 79, 83
Black Consciousness movement, 467
Black Death, 35, 56, 220
Blum, Leon, 98
Blyden, Edward, 459
Bolivar, Simon, 168
Bolivia, 171
Bolsheviks, 185–88
Bonaparte, Napoleon, 168
Botswana, 445
Boxer Rebellion, 358
Brahe, Tycho, 40, 226
Brahmans, 270, 271
Brahmo Samaj, 294
Brazil, 161, 169, 170, 173, 176
Brezhnev, Leonid, 196
British East India Company, 286, 287–88
Bruno, Giordano, 42
Buchenwald, 98
Buddhism, 2, 270
Buganda, 450, 455
Bukharin, Nikolai, 190
Burke, Edmund, 80
Bush, George, 157
Byzantine Empire, 21, 213

Cabral, Amilcar, 466
Cambodia, 128
Canada, 497
Capitalism, 91
    in Africa, 482–84
    in China, 53, 339–41
    in eastern Europe, 57
    in England, 61–62
    European, 9, 34, 53–54
    and family life in Europe, 66
    in France, 63–65
    in Germany, 61
    in the Islamic world, 53
    in Italy, 60
    in the Netherlands, 61
    opposition of the Catholic church, 55
    origins of European, 55
    in Portugal, 60
    and Protestantism, 61
    in Spain, 60
    and voyages of discovery, 56
Cardenas, Lazaro, 172
Cartwright, Edmund, 75
Castro, Fidel, 170, 174
Catherine the Great, 182
Chartist movement, 76
Chaudhuri, Nirad, 300
Chelebi, Kateb, 227
Cheng Ho, 220
Chernobyl, 499
Chewa, 455
Chiang Kai-shek, 364, 366, 372
Chile, 170, 171, 176
China
    and capitalism, 339–42
    carbon emissions from, 497
    Christian missionaries in, 344
    civil service examinations, 332
    collectivization of agriculture, 379
    compared to Europe, 328
    compared to Ottoman Empire, 356
    compared to Soviet Union, 374
    decollectivization of agriculture, 386
    democracy movement, 387
    early trade with Europe, 345
    in East Asia, 328
    economic achievements of ancient, 20, 332
    European conceptions of, 45
    European concessions in, 349
    Four Modernizations, 385
    geography of, 328
    Great Leap Forward, 380–81
    Great Proletarian Cultural Revolution, 383–85
    Hundred Flowers Movement, 379

industrialization after 1949, 375, 378
informal empire in, 124
Japanese invasion of, 369
Jiangxi Soviet, 368
land revolution in, 376
liberation of women in, 377, 390
Long March, 368
Marriage Law of 1950, 377
Marxism in, 362–63
Ming voyages, 20, 110–111, 220, 340–41
New Culture movement, 361
"New Policy" reforms, 359
nomadic invasions of, 333
northern expedition, 364
opium usage in, 345
Opium Wars, 346
population control efforts, 389–390, 499
revolution of 1911, 360
significance of imperialism in, 349–51
split with Soviet Union, 381
strategy of "self-reliance", 375
Tiananmen Massacre, 1989, 387–89
traditional view of foreign relations, 344
unequal treaties, 347
war with France, 349
withdrawal from world system, 128
women in ancient, 331
Chinese Communist party
   founding of, 363
   role after 1949, 376
   split with Guomindang, 364
   women and, 364, 368
   and Yanan Way, 370
Chinese Empire
   compared to Roman Empire, 22
Chingiz Khan, 218
Chlorofluorocarbons, 497
Christianity, 2
   in Africa, 457
   in Japan, 395
   and the rise of science, 30, 42–43, 48
   in the Roman Empire, 21
Chulalongkorn, 131
Cistercians, 22
Cixi (empress dowager of China), 358
Clinton, Bill, 157
Clive, Robert, 287
Cold War, 102, 153, 188, 197, 487–491
Columbus, Christopher, 6, 35, 118, 119
Columbian exchange, 121
Commissioner Lin (China), 346
Confucianism, 330, 340
Confucius, 330, 331
Congo, 444

Congo Free State, 442
Congress Party (India), 307, 310, 316–318
Conservatism, 80
Conservative modernization, 131, 231,
   354, 356–57
Containment, 154, 156
Copernicus, 40
Corn Laws, 76
Cornwallis, Lord, 287
Cortes, Hernan, 118, 160
Costa Rica, 499
Council for Mutual Economic
   Assistance (COMECON), 105
Creoles, 164
Crimean War, 183
Cromer, Lord, 236
Cromwell, Oliver, 62
Crusades, 112
Cuba, 128, 174–75
Cuban missile crisis, 154, 489
Cuban Revolution, 174
Czechoslovakia, 101, 105

Dachau, 98
Da Gama, Vasco, 6, 56
Dahomey, 433, 435
Dante, 40
Da Vinci, Leonardo, 30, 34
Darwin, Charles, 47, 123
Debt crisis, 494
Declaration of Independence, 138
Declaration of the Rights of
   Man and the Citizen, 64
Deforestation, 496
De Gouges, Olympe, 88
De Las Casas, Bartolome, 119
De Maistre, Joseph, 80
Democracy
   in Africa, 472
   in Britain, 77
   in Europe, 14, 88
   in Germany, 79
   in Japan, 405
   in Latin America, 171
Deng Xiaoping, 382, 385, 386
De San Martin, Jose, 168
Descartes, Rene, 42
De Tocqueville, Alexis, 144
Dias, Bartholomew, 56
Diop, C.A., 459
Dominican Republic, 125, 489
Du Bois, W.E.B., 460
Duma, 186
Dutch empire, 114

Earth Summit (1992), 500
Eastern Europe
    anti-Soviet revolts, 105
    liberation from Soviet control, 105
    serfdom in, 113–14
Economic development
    measures of, 201–02
Edib, Halide, 245
Egypt, 124, 209, 246
    Arab socialism in, 247–48
    British occupation of, 236
    compared with Japan, 235
    conquest of the Sudan, 436
    European influence in, 235
    French occupation of, 233
    nationalism of, 237
Einstein, Albert, 50
Eisenhower, Dwight D., 155
El Salvador, 176
Enclosure movement, 57, 62
Encomienda, 163, 166
Engels, Friedrich, 81
English Revolution, 61–62
Enlightenment, 43–47, 80
Environmental problems (global), 495–500
Ethiopia, 128, 424, 474
Ethnic nationalism, 322, 491
    in Africa, 450–52, 474–476
    in India, 315–317
Europe
    changing perceptions of others, 122
    crisis of the fourteenth century, 35
    emergence of competitive state system, 32
    emergence of national states, 23
    emigration from, 118
    empires of, 8
    geography of, 25
    population growth in nineteenth century, 87
    re-emergence after 1000 A.D., 22
    technological development of, 28
    voyages of discovery, 6
European Economic Community, 103
Extraterritoriality (China), 347

Fascism, 94–98
Feminism, 88
Feudalism, 22, 23, 34
Final Solution, 98
Ford, Henry, 153
Fourteen Points, 150, 243
France
    foreign policy and World War I, 91
    industrialization in, 77
Franklin, Benjamin, 46, 142

French Revolution, 64–66
Freud, Sigmund, 49
Fulani, 430

Galileo, 40, 42
Gandhi, Indira, 310, 317
Gandhi, Mahatma, 301, 303, 307, 310
Garvey, Marcus, 460
Genghis Khan, 333
Genoa, 112
Germany, 90, 122
    conservative modernization in, 131
    fascism in, 96–98
    foreign policy and World War I, 90
    industrialization in, 79
    unification of, 79
Ghana, 448
Ghana (ancient), 428
al-Ghazzali, 216, 219
Gilbert, William, 40
Glasnost, 197
Global warming, 497
Goa, 114, 308
Gokalp, Ziya, 233
Gold Coast, 464
Gompers, Samuel, 149
Gorbachev, Mikhail, 105, 197, 490
Goulart, Joao, 173
Government of India Act (1935), 303
Great Britain
    capitalism in, 61–63
    foreign policy and World War I, 90
    industrialization in, 74–77
Great Calcutta Killing, 305
Great Depression, 96, 150
    in Africa, 443
    in Japan, 406
Great Society, 155
Greek civilization, 21
Green Revolution, 310
Grenada, 489
Grosseteste, Robert, 31
Guatemala, 154, 171, 176
Guomindang, 363
Gupta Empire, 273

Hacienda, 163
Hadith, 212
al-Hallaj, 216
Han Dynasty, 331
Harvey, William, 41
Hausa, 465, 474
Herzl, Theodor, 243
Hidalgo, Miguel, 168

Hijra, 211
Hindu Marriage Code, 313
Hindu nationalism, 317–19
Hinduism, 271
Hitler, Adolf, 96–98
Ho Chi Min, 154
Hobbes, Thomas, 44
Holocaust, 98
Holy Roman Empire, 23
Hong Rengan, 353
Hong Xiuquan, 351
Hormuz, 114
Houphouet-Boigny, Felix, 483
Hulegu, 218
Human rights, 202
Hungary, 101, 105
Husayn (Sharif of Mecca), 243
Hussein, Saddam, 260
Hyderabad, 307

Ibn Battuta, 3, 220, 233
Ibn Saud, Abd al-Aziz, 255
Igbo, 425, 426, 433, 440, 446, 452
Ijtihad, 215, 219
Ikeda Hayato, 411
Ilbert Bil, 295
Inca civilization, 160
India
    ancient civilization of, 270–73
    British economic impact, 297–99
    British expansion in, 286
    British takeover, 287
    British understanding of, 291
    Buddhism in, 270
    caste system in, 271
    compared with China, 270, 273, 306
    cultural diversity of, 271
    economic policies after independence, 308
    emergence of "Hindu" and "Muslim"
        communities, 293, 300
    geography of, 268
    Green Revolution in, 310
    Hindu nationalism in, 317–19
    independence movement, 299–305
    Islamic penetration of, 213, 217, 273
    language and politics in, 315–16
    partition of, 304
    secularism in, 307, 319
    Tamil identity in, 316
    in world history, 267
Indian Councils Act (1909), 293
Indian Mutiny, 290
Indian National Congress, 294, 300, 304
Indonesia, 499

Industrialization
    in Brazil, 263
    in British India, 299
    consequences in Europe, 12
    East Asian, 13, 263–64, 494
    European and Third World
        compared, 262
    and imperialism, 72–73, 121
    and invention, 72
    Japanese, 400
    Latin American, 262
    and population growth in Europe, 71
    social consequences of in Britain, 76
Industrial revolution, 9, 14
    in France, 77–79
    in Germany, 79
    in Great Britain, 74–77
    impact on European women, 84
    in Russia, 183
    significance of in world history, 70
    in Soviet Union, 191
Informal empire, 123
Intercommunicating Zone, 23
Interdependence, 1
Intifadah, 252
Iqbal, Muhammad, 256
Iran, 154, 156, 246, 252
    Islamic revolution in, 256
Iran-Iraq War, 260
Iraq, 246
Islam, 2
    in Africa, 428–30
    expansion of, 20, 213, 217
    five pillars of, 212
    origins of, 210
    revivalist movements within, 230
    Sunni/Shi'ite division, 212
Islamic civilization
    agricultural revolution in, 214
    compared to China and India, 207
    expansion of, 213
    extent of, 209
    flowering of, 213
    interaction with West, 208
    as a world system, 214, 218
Islamic revivalism, 241, 254, 255
Islamic Salvation Front, 255
Ismail (Egyptian ruler), 236
Ismail, Shah, 225
Israel, 208, 249–52
Italy, 93, 122
    fascism in, 96
Iturbide, Agustín, 168
Ivory Coast, 483

al-Jabarti, 233
Jackson, Andrew, 145
Janissaries, 222, 223, 230
Japan, 156
    American occupation of, 410–11
    Christianity in, 396
    colonial rule in Korea and Taiwan, 263
    compared with China, 392, 398, 404
    compared with Europe, 392
    constitution of 1889, 401
    democracy in 1920s, 406
    Dutch learning in, 396
    early political history, 395
    economic success after 1945, 409
    education in, 401
    geography of, 394
    Greater East Asia Co-Prosperity Sphere, 408
    imperialism in China, 406
    industrialization of, 400, 403
    Marxism in, 403
    seclusion policy of, 396
    Shimbara rebellion, 396
    "soft authoritarianism" in, 411
    World War I and, 404
    World War II and, 408
Jayamma, 314
Jefferson, Thomas, 144
Jiang Qing, 385
Johnson, Lyndon B, 154, 155
Jones, Sir William, 291
Jordan, 250
Junkers, 79

Karlowitz, Treaty of, 227
Kashmir, 307
Kaunda, Kenneth, 475
Kay, John, 75
Kellogg-Briand pact, 94
Kennedy, John F., 154
Kenya, 443, 444, 450
Kepler, Johannes, 40
Keynes, John Maynard, 94
Khadijah, 210
Khalifat movement, 302
Khomeini, Ayatollah, 256, 258
Khrushchev, Nikita, 154, 195
Kikuyu, 426
Kimbangu, Simon, 459
Kinjikitile, 456
Kipling, Rudyard, 123
Kongo, 433
Korea, 125, 263, 471
Korean War, 154, 377
Kuchuk Kaynarja, Treaty of, 227

Kulaks, 190
Kumar, Roop, 314
Kuwait, 254, 260

Laos, 128
Lateran accords, 96
Latin America
    class structure in colonial, 164–65
    colonial experience of, 161–68
    demographic disaster in, 161
    English economic penetration of, 169
    European conquest of, 160
    exploitation of labor in, 163
    indebtedness, 170
    literacy and education in, 167
    race relations in, 163–65
    social conditions in, 176
    United States influence in, 170
    wars of independence, 168
    and the world economy, 170
Lausanne Treaty, 244
Law of the Sea Treaty, 500
League of Nations, 93, 150, 243
Lebanon, 157
Lenin, 185–88
Lepanto, Battle of, 226
Liang Qichao, 360
Liberalism, 67, 80
    in Germany, 79
Liberia, 436
"Limits to Growth" debate, 15
Lincoln, Abraham, 146
Liu Shaoqi, 382
Locke, John, 44
Louisiana Purchase, 145
Luba, 431
Luce, Henry, 152
Lucknow Pact, 300
Lunda, 431
Luther, Martin, 35

Macaulay, Thomas Babington, 292
Machiavelli, Niccolo, 43
Magellan, Ferdinand, 6
Mahabharata, 271
Mahanavami Festival, 276
Mahdism, 239
Mahmud II, 231
Maji Maji rebellion, 456
Mali, 428
Malpighi, Marcello, 41
Malthus, Thomas, 499
Mamluks, 217
Manchukuo, 407

Manchuria, 407
Mandela, Nelson, 468
Manifest Destiny, 146, 149
Mansa Musa, 428
Mao Zedong, 363, 367–68
  development strategy of, 383
  historical assessment of, 385
  origins of Cultural Revolution, 382
Marco Polo, 3, 333
Marshall Plan, 101
Marx, Karl, 48, 81
Marxism
  in China, 362–63
  in Japan, 403
  in Russia, 185
Maryland, 140
Masaai, 426
Massachusetts, 140, 141
Mayan civilization, 159
May Fourth Movement
    (China), 362
Mecca, 209
Medina, 211
Mehmed II, 224
Meiji Restoration, 392, 398, 399
Mensheviks, 185
Mercantilism, 166
Mestizos, 120, 163, 164, 165
Methodism, 46
Mexican Revolution, 171
Mexico, 118, 171–173, 176, 499
Mfecane, 431
Michelangelo, 34
Middle East
  geography of, 209
  negative images of, 208
  oil in, 252
  origins of term, 209
Militarization (global), 488
Ming voyages, 20, 110, 220
Moctezuma, 161
Modernization
  concept of, 11
Mongol Empire, 110
Mongolia, 376
Mongols, 3, 180, 218
Monomutapa, 431
Monroe Doctrine, 150
Morocco, 239
Mountbatten, Viceroy, 305
Mozambique, 465
Mughal Empire, 220, 228, 274
  administrative system of, 279
  cultural expression in, 280

decline of, 283
economic development in, 281
establishment of, 279
European trade with, 285–86
patronage in, 279
religious festivals in, 284
Muhammad, 209, 210, 212
Muhammad Abduh, 237
Muhammad Ahmad, 239
Muhammad Ali, 228, 235
Muhammad Ibn Saud, 230
Muhammad Reza Shah (Shah of Iran), 256
Muharram, 284
Mulattos, 120, 163, 164, 165
Murad III, 226
Muslim Brotherhood, 248, 255
Muslim League, 295, 300, 303, 304
Mussolini, Benito, 93, 96
Mustafa Kamil, 237

Nakasone Yasuhiro, 413
Namibia, 477, 478
Napoleon Bonaparte, 65
Nasser, Gamal Abd al-, 247
National Congress of British West Africa, 460
Nationalism, 82, 93, 133
  African, 461
  anti-colonial, 126, 322
  Arab, 242
  Chinese, 322
  cultural, 322
  Egyptian, 237
  in Europe, 10, 321
  "Hindu", 319
  Indian, 29
  in Middle East, 241, 242
  Palestinian, 250
  in Portuguese Africa, 465
  Serbian, 323
  Sikh, 318
  Turkish, 233
National Socialist (Nazi) Party, 94, 96
Nehru, Jawaharlal, 303, 307
New Economic Policy, 189
New imperialism, 124
New International Economic Order, 492–94
Newly Industrialized Countries (NICs), 263, 494
Newton, Sir Isaac, 43, 50
Nicaragua, 171, 176
Nicholas II, 186
Nigeria, 439, 465, 474
Nixon, Richard, 385
Nkrumah, Kwame, 464, 469
Non-alignment movement, 308

Non-Brahman movement, 295
North Atlantic Treaty Organization
       (NATO), 101–02, 154
North/South issues, 491–95
Nuremburg laws, 98
Nyakyusa, 451
Nyerere, Julius, 479, 484

O'Higgins, Bernardo, 168
Oil crisis, 497
Open-door policy, 349
Organization of Petroleum Exporting
       Countries (OPEC), 252
Ottoman Empire, 218, 220,
    decline of, 226–27
    end of, 244
    and European expansion, 227–29
    expansion of, 208, 222–25
    Greek independence from, 228
    internal weaknesses of, 226
    reforms in, 231–33
    rivalry with Safavid Empire, 225

Pakistan, 303
Palestine, 208
Palestine Liberation Organization (PLO), 250
Palestinian-Israeli conflict, 249–52
Pan-Africanism, 460, 461
Panama, 157
Panama Canal, 170
Pan-Islamism, 242
Pearl Harbor, 408
Peng Pai, 367
Pennsylvania, 140
Perestroika, 197
Permanent Settlement in Bengal, 288
Perry, Commodore Matthew, 396, 398
Persian Gulf War, 252
Peter I (the Great), 182
Philosophes, 45, 47, 49
Phrenology, 123
Physiocrats, 45
Pietism, 46
Pizarro, Francisco, 160
Plantation economy, 117, 119
Poland, 105, 113
Polo, Marco, 11
Pope, Alexander, 45
Population growth (global), 496, 499
Portugal, 112
    voyages of discovery, 114
Portuguese empire, 114
Prince Henry the Navigator, 56
Printing press, 43

Provisional Government (Russia), 187
Ptolemy, 39
Puritans, 139, 140

Qaddafi, Muammar, 254
Quran, 210, 211, 213, 219

Rabi'ah, 216
Rabin, Yitzhak, 252
Racism, 123, 446–47
Railroad industry, 75
Ramakrishna, Sri, 296
Ramasami, E.V., 316
Ramayana, 271, 277
Raphael, 34
Rashid al-Din, 225
al-Razi, 215
Reagan, Ronald, 157
Reformation, Protestant, 35
Renaissance, 34
Revolutions compared
    American, 144
    French, Russian, and Chinese, 131
    Russian and Chinese, 415–16
Rhodes, Cecil, 122
Rhodesia, 443
Ricci, Matteo, 345
Robespierre, Maximilien, 65
Roman Catholic Church
    in Latin America, 166
    liberation theology in, 171
    and modern science, 42
    opposition to capitalism, 55
Roman Empire, 21
Romania, 105
Romanov dynasty, 322
Roosevelt, Franklin Delano, 151
Roosevelt, Theodore, 149
Round Table Conferences, 303
Rousseau, Jean-Jacques, 44
Roy, Ram Mohan, 294
Russia
    abolition of serfdom in, 183
    Constituent Assembly in, 186
    enserfment of peasants in, 181
    geography of, 180
    imperial expansion of, 181
    industrialization of, 183
    Marxism in, 185
    Mongol impact on, 180
    Provisional Government of, 186
    role of intellegentsia, 184
Russian Orthodox Church, 180
Russian Revolution, 186–88, 461

Russian Social-Democratic Labor Party, 185
Russo-Japanese War of 1905, 185, 403
Ryotwari system, 290

Sadat, Anwar, 248, 255, 259
Safavid Empire, 220, 225–26
Salinas de Gortari, Carlos, 173
Samurai, 396, 400, 401
Sanatan Dharm Sabha, 297
Saraswati, Dayanand, 294
Sasanian empire, 213
Sati, 294, 314
Satyagraha, 301, 303
Saudi Arabia, 254–55
Schlieffen Plan, 90
Science
    in ancient China, 38
    and concept of progress, 47
    in the Islamic world, 38
    origins of modern, 38
    and religion in Europe, 42, 46, 48
Self-Strengthening Movement
    (China), 354–56
Selim III, 231
Seljuks, 217
Senegal, 117
Senghor, L.S., 484
Serbia, 90, 323
Shah Jahan, 281
Shaka, 431
Shariah, 212, 216, 224, 230
Shi Huang Di, 330
Shi'ism, 212
Shivaji, 283
Siberia, 181
Sierra Leone, 436
Sikhism, 316
Sikhs, 284
Sino-Japanese War, 349, 359, 402
Sino-Soviet split, 156
Slave trade, 116, 118, 432–35
Slavery (American), 140, 144, 147, 163
Smith, Adam, 45, 67, 103
Social Darwinism, 48, 148
Socialism, 81, 83
    in Africa, 484
    in China, 378
    and feminism, 89
    Indian, 306
    in Soviet Union, 194
Sokoto caliphate, 430
Solidarity, 105
Songhai Empire, 220, 428
Sonni Ali, 430

South Africa, 443, 444, 447
Southeast Asia Treaty Organization
    (SEATO), 154
Soviet Union, 99, 157
    challenge to world system, 125
    civil war in, 189
    collapse of, 199
    collectivization of agriculture, 190
    coup of August 1991, 198
    decline of Communist Party, 197
    de-Stalinization of, 195
    Five-year plans in, 191
    Great Purges in, 192
    historical significance of, 188
    industrialization in, 191, 194
    interpretations of, 179
    nationalist consciousness in, 195
    New Economic Policy in, 189
    origins of Glasnost, 196
    social inequalities in, 194
    takeover of eastern Europe, 101
    World War II in, 194
Soviets, 185, 187
Soweto, 467
Spain, 161, 166
    colonial role in Latin America, 161
Spanish-American War, 149, 170
Spanish Empire, 118
Stalin, Joseph, 101, 190
Stalinism, 190–195
Stolypin, Peter, 186
Sudan, 239
Suez Canal, 235, 247
Sufism, 216, 219
    in India, 274
Suleyman, 223, 226
Sun Yat-sen, 360, 363
Sustainable development, 202, 498–500
Swahili civilization, 430
Sykes-Picot Agreement, 243
Syria, 246

Tagore, Rabindranath, 296, 301
Taiping Revolution, 351–54, 367
Taiwan, 263, 376, 471
Tanzania, 484
Teotihuacan, 159
Thags, 289
Thailand, 131, 499
Tibet, 376
Tijaniyya, 229
Timbuktu, 428
Tiv, 424
Tobacco, 140

Tokugawa Ieyasu, 395
Tokugawa shogunate, 395
Trading post empires, 114
Treaties of Rome, 103
Treaty of Nanjing, 347
Treaty of Shimonoseki, 349
Treaty of Versailles, 93
Treblinka, 98
Triangular trade, 7
Triple Alliance, 90
Triple Entente, 90
Truman Doctrine, 154
Turkey, 244–45
Turks, 112, 222, 242
Turner, Frederick Jackson, 138
Twain, Mark, 149
Twenty-one Demands, 404

Ukraine, 182
Ulama, 212, 218, 224, 232
Umayyad dynasty, 213
United Nations, 153, 462, 492
United Nations Conference on Trade
    and Development, 492
United States
    Civil War, 146
    Cold War, 154
    colonial origins, 139
    colonial self-government in, 142
    compared to Europe, 141
    debate on "decline", 156
    declining economic role, 128
    "deferential society" in, 142
    dominant role in world system, 125
    "exceptionalism" of, 144
    global role after 1945, 153
    Great Depression in, 150
    hegemony over western Europe, 102
    immigration, 148
    imperialism, 149
    industrial expansion, 147
    informal empire, 124
    native Americans in, 139, 146
    New Deal, 151
    origins of slavery in, 140
    populism, 148
    progressivism, 148
    religious tolerance in, 167
    slavery and Civil War, 147
    socialism in, 148
    territorial expansion of, 145
    Vietnam War, 154
    World War I, 91, 150
    World War II, 152–53

Untouchables, 293, 302
Upanishads, 270
Urabi, Ahmed, 236, 242

Vargas, Getulio, 173
Vedas, 270
Venezuela, 171
Vesalius, Andreas, 41
Vietnam, 125, 128
Vietnam War, 154, 156
Vijayanagara, 276–79, 283
Vikings, 22, 112
Virginia, 140, 141
Vivekananda, Swami, 301
Voltaire, 45

Wahhabi movement, 230, 254
Wallerstein, Immanuel, 14
War communism, 189
Warsaw Pact, 102
Watt, James, 75
Weber, Max, 61
Weimar Republic, 96
Welfare states, 103, 412
Wellesley, Lord, 287
White Man's Burden, 123
Wilson, Woodrow, 149, 150
Winthrop, John, 140
Witte, Sergei, 183
Wollstonecraft, Mary, 88
Women
    African, 481
    and the American Revolution, 143
    and capitalism in Europe, 66
    in colonial Africa, 441, 445–446
    in communist China, 377, 390
    in early twentieth century China, 364
    in India, 294, 313–15
    and industrialization in
        Europe, 83–86
    and Islam, 211
    in Japan, 413
    in Latin America, 176
    in medieval Europe, 27
    in Mughal Empire, 281
    in pre-modern China, 331,
        337–39
    in Turkey, 245
    struggle for the vote in Europe, 89
    and South Asian religion, 277
    in World War I, 92
World system, 2, 7, 121
    African integration into, 118
    contraction of pre-modern, 110

incorporaion of the Americas into, 118
nature of European, 112
theory of, 14
World War I, 83, 92–94
consequences, 92
and Japan, 404–05
in the Middle East, 243
origins of, 89–91
and Russia, 186
World War II, 98–100, 152, 194
impact on Africa, 461
and China, 369, 372
and India, 304
and Japan, 406–409
in the Middle East, 246

Xinjiang, 376

Yoruba, 474
Young Ottomans, 232
Young Turks, 233, 242
Yugoslavia, 101, 105

Zaibatsu, 405, 406
Zaire, 473
Zambia, 444, 475
Zamindars, 282, 288
Zanzibar, 436
Zetkin, Clara, 89
Zhao Ziyang, 387
Zheng He, 341
Zhou Enlai, 385
Zimbabwe, 443, 465
Zionism, 243, 246, 249
Zulu, 431